SIXTH EDITION

MANAGEMENT

STEPHEN P ROBBINS
San Diego State University

MARY COULTER
Southwest Missouri State University

ROBIN STUART-KOTZE
Oxford University

Prentice Hall Canada Inc.,
Scarborough, Ontario

Canadian Cataloguing in Publication Data

Robbins, Stephen P., 1943–
Management

Canadian 6th ed.
Canadian 2nd ed. published under title: Management: concepts and applications.
Includes index.
ISBN 0-13-011782-X

1. Management. 2. Management—Canada—Case studies.
I. Coulter, Mary. II. Stuart-Kotze, Robin. III. Title.

HD31.R5647 2000 658.4 C98-932976-3

Prentice-Hall, Inc., Upper Saddle River, New Jersey
Prentice-Hall International (UK) Limited, London
Prentice-Hall of Australia, Pty. Limited, Sydney
Prentice-Hall Hispanoamericana, S.A., Mexico City
Prentice-Hall of India Private Limited, New Delhi
Prentice-Hall of Japan, Inc., Tokyo
Simon & Schuster Southeast Asia Private Limited, Singapore
Editora Prentice-Hall do Brasil, Ltda., Rio de Janeiro

ISBN 0-13-011782-X

Acquisitions Editor: Mike Ryan
Developmental Editor: Amber Wallace
Production Editor: Kelly Dickson
Copy Editor: Cathy Zerbst
Production Coordinator: Jane Schell
Permissions/Photo Research: Susan Wallace-Cox
Cover Design: Lisa LaPointe
Art Direction: Julia M. Hall
Cover Image: John Bleck
Page Layout: Bookman Typesetting Co.

Original English Language Edition published by
Prentice-Hall, Inc., Upper Saddle River, New Jersey, 07458
© 1999

3 4 5 04 03 02 01 00

Printed and bound in the USA.

Visit the Prentice Hall Canada Web site! Send us your comments, browse our catalogues, and more at **www.phcanada.com**. Or reach us through e-mail at **phcinfo_pubcanada@prenhall.com**.

To Dana & Jim Murray and
Jennifer Robbins

— S P R

To My Brothers — Duane, Rich,
Ron, Jim, and Mike

— M C

To my son Gavin, who made it
all happen

— R S-K

Brief Contents

Contents

CHAPTER 16

Leadership 397

PART 6 • CONTROLLING 426

CHAPTER 17

Foundations of Control 427

Preface

Our publisher recently informed us that in its last edition this book was the world's number one selling management textbook. We have no intentions of resting on our laurels, however. Being the market leader also means that we have an ongoing responsibility to you, the reader, to continue the types of innovative presentations of management topics that we have in the past.

Management is a dynamic discipline, and a textbook on the subject must constantly undergo significant changes to stay current. With this in mind, we've carefully revised this Canadian Sixth Edition of *Management*. We've retained the basic paradigm, content, and features that have proven successful in previous editions. And we've added new topics and features that better reflect the field of management, and capture its excitement in the twenty-first century.

New to This Edition

There are several new features and content topics that have been included in this revision. New topics to this edition include information technology, learning organizations, the "greening" of management, core competencies, project management, autonomous internal units, broadbanding compensation, skill-based pay plans, visionary leadership, team leadership, trust, customer-driven operations, ISO 9000, and numerous others. The research base for this revision has been updated as well. Additionally, there are several new features you'll find in this revision.

- *Testing ... Testing ...* This exciting innovation features questions that are interspersed throughout each chapter, reviewing key topics that have just been covered. These questions are designed to continually reinforce the material as it is presented, and to assess whether what has just been read has in fact been understood.

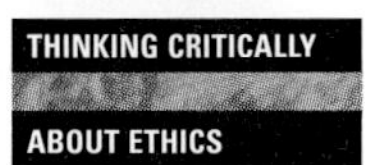

- *Thinking Critically About Ethics.* In each chapter, these boxes cover ethical matters, presenting situations and asking questions about how to handle them.

- *Take It to the Net.* At the end of each chapter we provide a reminder about the online study materials and research resources available in the text's Companion Website.

- *Management CD-ROM.* Each copy of *Management,* C/6/e, includes a ***free*** **CD-ROM** containing material to help you better study and understand managers and management. Some of the features include:
  - Question and answer format videos featuring real managers.
  - Self-Assessment exercises that can be completed and scored for immediate feedback.
  - Accompanying video material for the Showtime Networks Inc. cases included in the Instructor's Manual and Study Guide.
  - "Testing ... Testing ..." questions and answers.

Retained from the Previous Edition

The fifth edition contained a number of topics and features that adopters considered unique, useful, or particularly popular with the students. Obviously, these have been retained, and they include the following:

- *A Manager's Challenge.* Each chapter opens with a challenge that a real-life manager has recently had to face. The managers in these dilemmas come from a variety of organizations. From Isabel Hoffman of the young but dynamic and fast-growing Toronto company, H+a, to Pierre Lacombe of Quebec's vegetarian food producer Le

Commensal, to Ronald Oberlander of Canada's giant newsprint producer, Abitibi-Consolidated, these managers reflect a broad and varied cross-section of management situations.

- *Managers Who Make a Difference.* Throughout the text, these boxes feature managers whose actions have had a significant impact on their organization's performance. All of these examples are new to this edition, and feature male and female managers working in organizations of different sizes and types.
- *Managers Speak Out.* Profiles of real managers talking about issues covered in the chapter are featured in these boxes. The information gathered in these interviews provides a diverse perspective of managers and managerial philosophies.
- *Self-Assessment Exercises.* Readers will find that we've improved the focus and relevance of these exercises. You'll also find that several of the self-assessment exercises have been made more user-friendly; that is, we've included them on the accompanying CD-ROM where you can complete and score them.
- *For Your Immediate Action.* Each chapter has one of these assignments included in the end-of-chapter learning material. They attempt to capture the problem-solving dimensions of the manager's job by providing realistic problems related to specific chapter content. Many of these FYIA sections are new for this edition.
- *Case Applications.* Again, every chapter includes a case application to test some of the subjects discussed. Real companies and situations are used. These are predominately Canadian, but an international perspective is often provided from cases on companies around the world, from Denmark to Japan, to Hungary, to the US, to Finland. All of these case applications are new to this edition.
- *Video Cases.* The CBC programs *The National* and *Venture* are used to further test topics in the various sections of this book. All of these cases are new to this edition. Written cases accompany each of the video cases.
- *Emphasis on Workforce Diversity, Career, and Entrepreneurial Topics.* These topics are important in the study of management today. We have chosen to continue to highlight these topics in boxed themes throughout the chapters.
- *Writing Style.* This revision continues the authors' commitment to presenting management concepts in a lively and conversational style. We carefully blend theories and examples. Our goal is to present chapter material in an interesting and relevant manner without oversimplifying the discussion. Of course, writing style is subject to opinion, and only you can judge whether we've successfully achieved our goal.

In-Text Learning Aids

A good textbook should teach as well as present ideas. Toward that end, we've tried to make this book an effective learning tool. We'd like to point out some specific pedagogical features that are designed to help readers better assimilate the material presented.

- *Chapter Learning Objectives.* Before you start a trip, it's valuable to know where you're headed. That way, you can minimize possible problems or detours. The same holds true in reading a text. To make your learning more efficient, each chapter opens with a list of learning objectives that describe what you should be able to do after reading the chapter. These objectives are designed to focus your attention on the major issues within each chapter.
- *Chapter Summaries.* Just as objectives clarify where you're going, chapter summaries remind you of where you've been. Each chapter concludes with a concise summary organized around the opening learning objectives.
- *Key Terms.* Every chapter highlights a number of key terms that you'll need to know. These terms are highlighted in bold print when they first appear and are defined at that time in the adjoining margin.

- *Weblinks.* Useful Internet Websites related to the topics and organizations discussed in the chapter can be found in the margins throughout the text.
- *Testing ...Testing ... boxes.* Key factual material is highlighted by way of ongoing questions included in boxes throughout the chapters.
- *Thinking about Management Issues questions.* Every chapter in the book has questions that are designed to get you to think about management issues. These questions require you to integrate, synthesize, or apply management concepts. They allow you to demonstrate that you not only know the facts in the chapter but can also apply those facts in dealing with more complex issues.
- *Case Applications and Questions.* Each chapter includes a case application and questions for analysis. A case is simply a description of a real-life managerial situation. By reading and analyzing the case and answering the questions at the end of the case, you can see if you understand and can apply the management concepts discussed in the chapter.

Supplements

Management, Canadian Sixth edition, is accompanied by a complete supplements package.

Companion Website with Online Study Guide Our exciting new Website offers students a comprehensive online study guide with 20 multiple choice and 15 true/false review questions per chapter, experiential exercises, essay questions, Internet exercises, updated Internet destinations and search tools, CBC video case updates, and more. Instructors will be interested in our on-line syllabus builder and the password-protected Instructors area containing electronic versions of key supplements and updates to the text. (To obtain your password, please contact your Prentice Hall sales representative.) See **www.prenticehall.ca/robbins** and explore!

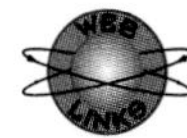

Prentice Hall Canada
www.prenticehall.ca/robbins

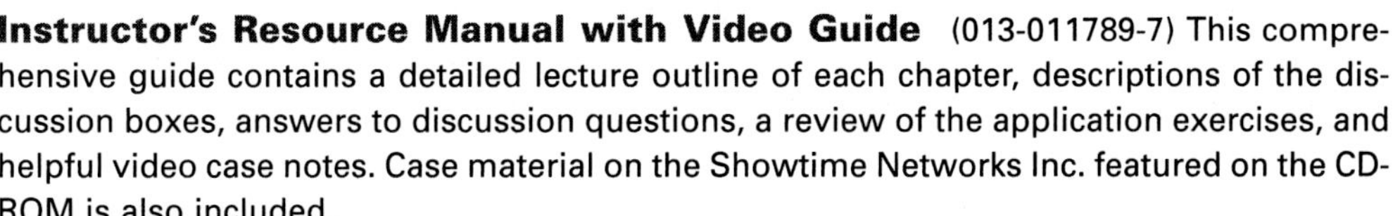

Instructor's Resource Manual with Video Guide (013-011789-7) This comprehensive guide contains a detailed lecture outline of each chapter, descriptions of the discussion boxes, answers to discussion questions, a review of the application exercises, and helpful video case notes. Case material on the Showtime Networks Inc. featured on the CD-ROM is also included.

The Test Item File (013-011783-8) The test item file contains over 2500 multiple choice, true/false, and short essay questions. Answers, with page references, are given for all objective questions and suggested answers are provided for essay questions. All questions are rated by level of difficulty (easy, moderate, challenging). The file is available in both printed and electronic formats.

PH Test Manager (013-011786-2) Utilizing our new Test Manager program, the computerized test bank for *Management* offers a comprehensive suite of tools for testing and assessment. Test Manager allows educators to easily create and distribute tests for their courses, either by printing and distributing them through traditional methods or by online delivery via a Local Area Network (LAN) server. Once you have opened Test Manager, you'll advance effortlessly through a series of folders allowing you to quickly access all available areas of the program. Test Manager has removed the guesswork from your next move by incorporating Screen Wizards that assist you with such tasks as managing question content, managing a portfolio of tests, testing students, and analyzing test results. In addition, this all-new testing package is backed with full technical support, telephone "request a test" service, comprehensive online help files, a guided tour, and complete written documentation. Available as a CD-ROM for Windows 95.

Transparency Resource Package (013-011791-9) Over 100 transparencies in PowerPoint 7.0 have been created for the text, reproducing figures and illustrating important concepts. Detailed teaching notes with page references accompany each slide. This package is available in printed and electronic format.

Management CD Each copy of *Management,* C/6/e, includes a ***free*** **CD-ROM** containing question-and-answer format videos featuring real managers; Self-Assessment exercises that can be completed and scored for immediate feedback; accompanying video material for the Showtime Networks Inc. cases included in the Instructor's Manual and Study Guide; and "Testing ...Testing ..." questions and answers.

Prentice Hall Canada/CBC Video Library Prentice Hall Canada and the CBC have worked together to bring you ten segments from the CBC series *Venture* and *The National.* Designed specifically to complement the text, this case collection is an excellent tool for bringing students in contact with the world outside the classroom. These programs have extremely high production quality and have been chosen to relate directly to chapter content. Teaching notes are provided in the *Instructor's Resource Manual with Video Guide.* Please contact your Prentice Hall Canada sales representative for details.

Study Guide (013-011793-5) The Study Guide lists chapter objectives, outlines chapter contents and sets out key terms and their definitions. Three sections of exercises, Multiple Choice, True/False, and Matching Definitions, help students understand the concepts of management more effectively. And, in order to encourage students to make full use of the Self-Assessment exercises from the text, we've reproduced them at the end of each chapter in the Study Guide, where students should feel free to mark up pages and jot down comments. Case material on the Showtime Networks Inc. featured on the CD-ROM is also included.

Acknowledgements

The authors would like to thank the following reviewers for their feedback: Kirk Bailey, Ryerson Polytechnic University; Elisabeth Carter, Douglas College; Denny Dombrower, Centennial College; Gerry Rice, SAIT; Shirley A. Rose, Mount Royal College.

We would also like to thank the staff at Prentice Hall who helped with the Canadian sixth edition: Mike Ryan, Acquisitions Editor; Amber Wallace, Developmental Editor; Kelly Dickson, Production Editor; Cathy Zerbst, Copy Editor; and Jane Schell, Production Coordinator.

About the Authors

Stephen P Robbins received his Ph.D. from the University of Arizona. He previously worked for the Shell Oil Company and Reynolds Metals Company. Since completing his graduate studies, Dr. Robbins has taught at the University of Nebraska at Omaha, Concordia University in Montreal, the University of Baltimore, Southern Illinois University at Edwardsville, and San Diego State University. Dr. Robbins' research interests have focused on conflict, power, and politics in organizations, as well as the development of effective interpersonal skills. His articles on these and other topics have appeared in such journals as *Business Horizons*, the *California Management Review*, *Business and Economic Perspectives*, *International Management*, *Management Review*, *Canadian Personnel and Industrial Relations*, and the *Journal of Management Education*.

In Dr. Robbins' "other life," he participates in masters' track competition. Since turning 50 in 1993, he has set numerous indoor and outdoor world sprint records. He's also won gold medals in World Veteran Games in 100m, 200m, and 400m. In 1995, Robbins was named the year's outstanding age-40-and-over male track and field athlete by the Masters Track and Field Committee of USA Track & Field, the national governing body for athletes in the United States.

Mary Coulter received her Ph.D. in Management from the University of Arkansas in Fayetteville. Before completing her graduate work, she held different jobs including high school teacher, legal assistant, and government program planner. She has taught at Drury College, the University of Arkansas, Trinity University, and Southwest Missouri State University. Dr. Coulter's research interests have focused on competitive strategies for not-for-profit arts organizations and the use of new media in the educational process. Her research on these and other topics has appeared in such journals as *Journal of Business Strategies*, *Case Research Journal*, and *Journal of Business Research*. In addition to *Management*, Dr. Coulter has published another book with Prentice Hall, *Strategic Management in Action*, which is designed for the Capstone business course in strategy. When she's not busy teaching or writing, she enjoys puttering around in her flower gardens, playing the piano, reading all different types of books, and enjoying many different activities with daughters Sarah and Katie.

Robin Stuart-Kotze has a Ph.D from the University of Warwick, England. He did his undergraduate work and MBA in Canada at Bishop's and Queen's universities respectively and his doctoral coursework at Penn State. He was most recently a Visiting Fellow at Oxford University in England, and is Chairman of Behavioural Science Systems Ltd., an international consulting firm with operations in Europe, North America, and the Far East. He has had a career in the financial services business and was a vice president of a major Canadian financial institution. He has held a number of visiting professorships in Canada and the United Kingdom, and has written a number of textbooks and several professional managerial books. He travels extensively, sharing his time largely between Europe and the Far East, working with major multinational companies. His hobbies, which he determinedly makes time for, are golf and National Hunt racing (steeplechasing). Robin is pictured here with his son, Gavin.

The Prentice Hall Canada companion Website...

Your Internet companion to the most exciting, state-of-the-art educational tools on the Web!

The Prentice Hall Canada Companion Website is easy to navigate and is organized to correspond to the chapters in this textbook. The Companion Website is comprised of four distinct, functional features:

1) **Customized Online Resources**

2) **Online Study Guide**

3) **Reference Material**

4) **Communication**

Explore the four areas in this Companion Website. Students and distance learners will discover resources for indepth study, research and communication, empowering them in their quest for greater knowledge and maximizing their potential for success in the course.

A NEW WAY TO DELIVER EDUCATIONAL CONTENT

1) Customized Online Resources

Our Companion Websites provide instructors and students with a range of options to access, view, and exchange content.

- **Syllabus Builder** provides *instructors* with the option to create online classes and construct an online syllabus linked to specific modules in the Companion Website.
- **Mailing lists** enable *instructors* and *students* to receive customized promotional literature.
- **Preferences** enable *students* to customize the sending of results to various recipients, and also to customize how the material is sent, e.g., as html, text, or as an attachment.
- **Help** includes an evaluation of the user's system and a tune-up area that makes updating browsers and plug-ins easier. This new feature will enhance the user's experience with Companion Websites.

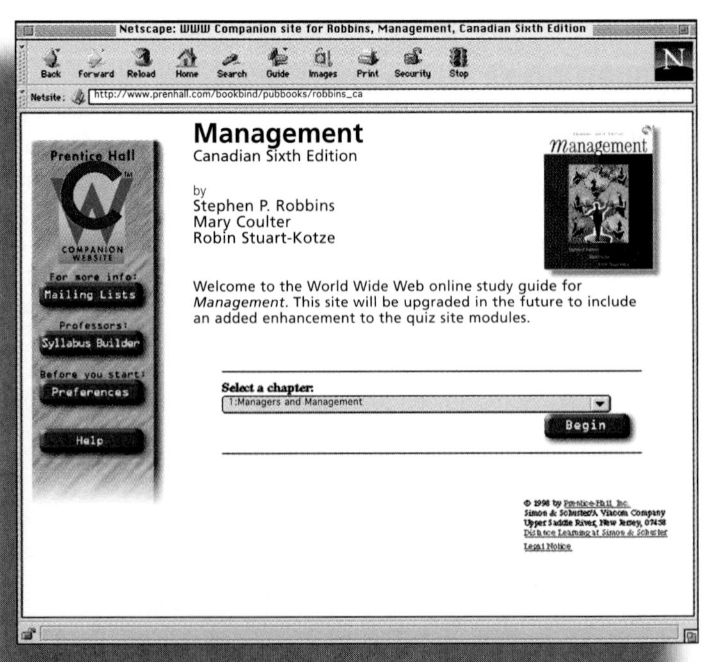

www.prenticehall.ca/robbins

2) Online Study Guide

Interactive Study Guide modules form the core of the student learning experience in the Companion Website. These modules are categorized according to their functionality:

- True-False
- Multiple Choice

The True-False and Multiple Choice modules provide students with the ability to send answers to our grader and receive instant feedback on their progress through our Results Reporter. Coaching comments and references back to the textbook ensure that students take advantage of all resources available to enhance their learning experience.

3) Reference Material

Reference material broadens text coverage with up-to-date resources for learning. **Web Destinations** provides a directory of Web sites relevant to the subject matter in each chapter. **NetNews (Internet Newsgroups)** are a fundamental source of information about a discipline, containing a wealth of brief, opinionated postings. **NetSearch** simplifies key term search using Internet search engines.

4) Communication

Companion Websites contain the communication tools necessary to deliver courses in a **Distance Learning** environment. **Message Board** allows users to post messages and check back periodically for responses. **Live Chat** allows users to discuss course topics in real time, and enables professors to host online classes.

Communication facilities of Companion Websites provide a key element for distributed learning environments. There are two types of communication facilities currently in use in Companion Websites:

- **Message Board** – this module takes advantage of browser technology providing the users of each Companion Website with a national newsgroup to post and reply to relevant course topics.
- **Live Chat** – enables instructor-led group activities in real time. Using our chat client, instructors can display Website content while students participate in the discussion.

Companion Websites are currently available for:

- Starke: Contemporary Management in Canada
- Kotler: Principles of Marketing
- Evans: Marketing Essentials
- Horngren: Cost Accounting
- Horngren: Introduction to Financial Accounting

Note: CW '99 content will vary slightly from site to site depending on discipline requirements.

The Companion Websites can be found at:

www.prenticehall.ca/robbins

PRENTICE HALL CANADA

1870 Birchmount Road
Scarborough, Ontario M1P 2J7

To order:
Call: 1-800-567-3800
Fax: 1-800-263-7733

For samples:
Call: 1-800-850-5813
Fax: (416) 299-2539
E-mail: phcinfo_pubcanada@prenhall.com

Canadian Introduction

The Context of Management in Canada

Management, as we will discuss in this text, is influenced by a number of factors, one of which is culture. Because management involves getting people to do things, certain types of behaviour and approaches work better in some cultures than others. While the essence of management is similar in all western industrialized countries, we also need to look at what John Redston refers to as the "unique context of Canadian business".[1] Global markets and, indeed, the North American Free Trade Agreement will continue to blur the differences between management in Canada and in the United States, as well as management in Mexico, in European nations, and elsewhere. But differences will still remain. Canada is a unique country—culturally, politically, geographically and structurally.

Peter C Newman has remarked that "we are a people with little talent for excess. Most of us would rather be Clark Kent than Superman. Our cities remain oases of relative civility on a continent where most urban areas are armed camps".[2] Newman's view is that Canadians are understated, self-deprecating, and short on heroes (we have heroes but we don't tend to make too much of them). He observes that a Canadian passport is a prized possession because it identifies the bearer as harmless. Olaf Rankis, executive vice president for security and intelligence at Gordon Liddy & Associates, has been quoted as saying, "I always travel wearing a red maple-leaf pin in my lapel. Nobody hates Canadians".[3]

Canada admits more immigrants per capita than any other country. While prejudices exist in every society, they seem to be less evident in Canada. The great American football Hall-of-Famer, Jim Brown, remarked that when he visited Canada, it was the first time in his life that he found that people didn't notice the colour of his skin. We tend to see people as people, and performance as more important than birth or genealogy. We are generally a modest culture, slightly shy, somewhat unsure of ourselves, and caring and peace-loving. Canada has had a record as a peacekeeper around the world for more than 40 years. But, while General Lewis

Mackenzie received a fair amount of media attention for his work in Bosnia, it was nothing compared to Stormin' Norman Schwartzkopf's Gulf War hype. We admire achievement but don't idolize it. Becoming a hero in Canada is not easy. While Washington's birthday is a national holiday in the United States, we don't celebrate the birthday of Sir John A Macdonald. We don't make much of John Cabot's landing in Canada, but Columbus Day is a US holiday. And we celebrate Canada Day as a day of togetherness and oneness while our neighbours to the south celebrate Independence Day. So in spite of US media influence, cross-border shopping sprees and winter holidays, we retain a Canadian difference.

But what about management in Canada? It's one thing to have cultural values of modesty, openness and non-conflict, but how about having to operate in the cut-and-thrust world of harsh competitive business? How do Canadian managers behave when they are faced with having to make cuts in staff or cost reductions? Or when they have to outbid, outsmart, outnegotiate and outperform competitors on the world stage? Canadians can stand with the world's best. Conrad Black is as much a force in British newspaper publishing as he is in the Canadian publishing scene. Sir Graham Day was knighted for turning around British shipbuilding and Rover Cars. The current president and CEO of Young & Rubicam Advertising's New York operation is a Canadian, Frank Anfield. But rather than steal the thunder from the rest of the book, we'll stop with these three people as examples for now. However, we mention many other outstanding managers throughout the next 19 chapters. Canadian managers are everywhere in the world. And they're good because they have learned to manage in a tough environment.

Peter Georgescu, president of Young & Rubicam Inc.—the parent company of the advertising company's operations worldwide—has summed up what this book tries to point out when he says, "People such as Frank Anfield have been chosen (as New York operations CEO) because they are brilliant managers. Yet there's no question that these individuals have benefited from working in the very challenging Canadian market. It's harder to succeed in Canada. And managers who do well, by definition, have honed business skills".[4]

Managerial styles differ according to culture. Japan is the most commonly illustrated "different" management culture. The Japanese spend a great deal of time trying to reach a consensus among managers and employees; they operate in groups and teams more than North Americans do; and they maintain a formal deference for seniority and age. As we shall see in this text, Canadian firms are moving towards a Japanese model in terms of teamwork, but there is still a wide gulf between the two cultural styles. Managers in China, France and Finland also have their own peculiar managerial styles, and Canadians may or may not adopt some of them. Certainly, Canadian managers cannot assume that Canadian techniques and approaches will be effective in other countries. But they can rest assured that there are a number of universal management activities—planning, organizing, control, leadership and communication—among them. Every manager has to do these things; some just do them differently from others.

What's Different About Managing in Canada?

Our culture is not vastly different from that of the United States. We watch many of the same television programs, see many of the same news stories, read a number of US magazines, go on vacation to the United States, see the same movies, eat the same food, drive the same cars, play the same sports, listen to a lot of the same music, and wear the same clothes. But our political systems are different, our geography is different, our climate is certainly different, and our view of the world is different. We have unique problems to deal with, and experience unique factors that affect how our organizations operate and how the people in them behave. There are certain cultural differences—we are, as mentioned previously, certainly more conservative and self-effacing than Americans—but US managers operate successfully in Canada. Diane McGarry, CEO of Xerox Canada, is one example. And Canadian managers are equally able to adapt to conditions in the US. Kevin O'Leary and Michael Perik of The Learning Co. are two of the examples found in this book.

More important than cultural differences, however, are some of this country's structural dimensions which make Canadian management distinctive and, as Peter Georgescu commented, more difficult. These structural dimensions force this country's managers to operate in a "Canadian" manner.

The Canadian Difference

The *Globe and Mail's Report on Business* magazine ran a cover article entitled "Canada Inc.", in which they asked a panel of 11 distinguished business people, economists and professors, including Michael Porter of Harvard, John Kenneth Galbraith, Tom Kierans (president and CEO of the C D Howe Institute), Norbert Walter of the Deutsche Bank in Frankfurt, and Kenichi Ohmae (consultant and business writer), to analyze Canada as if it were a stock they were considering for a long-term investment. They were also asked to comment on whether they considered it a "buy", a "sell", or a "hold". Among the facts they found different about Canada were that:

- Government is pervasive in Canadian business and in Canada as a whole.
- Economic factors that affect one part of the country may have no effect on other areas.
- Much of what happens in Canada depends on the United States and other global economies (outside influence is not unique to Canada, but is a major fact of life here).
- Canada carries a debt load higher than any other OECD country, except for Belgium and Italy, which limits its ability to mount major initiatives.
- Canada is still struggling with the issue of Quebec (which Kenichi Ohmae terms "a typical nineteenth-century issue").
- Canada may be in a cost-competitive position because of its already developed health care system, which lowers employers' costs.
- Canada has a higher proportion of people who are capable of competing in the world economy (on the basis of education and training) than the United States.[5]

The Geography

While the *Report on Business* panel didn't specifically comment on it, one of the major problems that Canadian managers have to deal with is the geography of the country. Ours is the world's largest country in area, covering 6 198 687 square kilometres. While it may not be the world's emptiest country, it contains less than 1 percent of the world's population. And 85 percent of Canada's population is huddled within 200 kilometres of the US border, concentrated in cities. The expanse of the country is immense. Halifax is closer to South America than to Vancouver, and Alert—on northern Ellesmere Island—is closer to Moscow than to Ottawa. It's cheaper to fly from the east coast of Canada to Europe than to the west coast of Canada. Southern Ontario has a disproportionate concentration of both the population and wealth of the country and, along with southwestern Quebec, is closest to the major markets of the United States.

Canada, many observers have remarked, is more a compilation of separate countries than one single nation. British Columbia's "separateness" is reinforced by the immense divide of the

Rocky Mountains. They form a huge physical as well as psychological barrier between British Columbia and the rest of the country. The Prairies, bounded by the Rockies on one side and the great expanse of the Canadian Shield on the other, embody a uniqueness that separates them from their eastern neighbour, Ontario. Quebec's language and culture sets it apart from its neighbours on either side, while the Maritimes maintain an aloofness from "Upper and Lower Canada" that dates back to the days of Confederation. Newfoundland is isolated from the Canadian mainland by the Strait of Belle Isle and by its distinction as the last province to join the Confederation. We all know how difficult it is for politicians to manage Canada. These same physical and psychological barriers affect business management. In order to operate on a national scale in Canada, an east-west flow of goods and services is required. But larger and more easily accessible markets usually lie on a north-south axis.

One of the consequences of the country's geographic constraints has been the development of extensive transportation systems: the Canadian National and Canadian Pacific railways, the Trans-Canada Highway, the two major airlines—Air Canada and Canadian Airlines—and the St. Lawrence Seaway system. Government has played a major role in establishing and maintaining many of these services—often at a financial loss—in order to resist the pull from large US centres. Our national transportation systems are political forces as well as commercial endeavours, acting as bonds to hold the country together. The federal government is active in the funding and operation of railways, airlines, trucking services, ferry systems, telecommunications and shipping, while provincial and municipal governments operate buses, port facilities, airports and pipelines.

It is difficult to cover a national market in Canada when one has to ship goods and services over great empty distances to get from one relatively small market to another. The cable television industry is a good example of this problem. The cost of running the cable is fixed per kilometre. If it runs through areas which are densely populated, the costs are distributed among many customers, and are minimal for each. However, if that same cable must then run across 100 kilometres of unpopulated land, a huge expense is incurred, with no associated revenue. To cover this cost, there must be many customers willing to buy the service when the cable reaches the next market.

The same principle applies to any product produced in one part of Canada and shipped to another. Salmon caught in British Columbia or New Brunswick and shipped to Ontario must command a price sufficient to cover transportation costs and still generate a profit. Canadian management has had to devise some ingenious plans to overcome these sorts of disadvantages. Often, of course, technology helps. For example, the *Globe and Mail* is delivered and sold daily in Atlantic Canada and British Columbia at almost the same price as it is in Toronto, because it is relayed by satellite to local printing plants.

There are climatic problems associated with our geography as well. The manufacturing of everything from housing and automobiles to clothing and food is affected by the changing seasons and harsh winters of our northern climate. Managers in the retail business know how important it is to be able to gauge the amount of stock for each season, so as not to be left with too little or too much as the seasons change. Producers of such things as housing or automobiles have to deal with the problem of increasing the costs of their products so that these may withstand winter cold and summer heat. It has been said that a major economic problem in Canada is the large percentage of our gross national product allocated to simply keeping warm.

Managing over long distances entails certain problems. There is a four-and-a-half-hour time difference between St. John's, Newfoundland and Vancouver, BC. If a significant event were to occur on the east coast at 9:00 a.m., those westerners who might need to react to it would still be asleep. If something were to break on the west coast at the close of business, east coast managers would need to be contacted at home. Even though the telephone companies promote teleconferencing and videoconferencing as an easy way to get people together, the number of mutually available hours for managers across the country is limited. Businesspeople also travel a great deal within Canada due to the expanse of the country. The airlines estimate that 40 percent of their total passenger business is made up of this class of travellers.

Canada's geographic constraints do not make the job of managing an impossibility, but they do make it challenging. Technology may begin to help solve the problem with information networks that link not only computers but also telecommunications (both audio and video) in order to connect suppliers and customers directly, and to control manufacturing.

Government Participation in Canadian Business

Canada's ten largest Crown corporations, as of 1998, are listed below in Table I-1. At that point, only one Crown corporation, Ontario Hydro, made it into *Canadian Business's* rankings of the top 25 companies in the country by sales. In 1993, three Crown corporations were in the top 25. In 1988, six made the list. The presence of government in business is decreasing as Crown corporations are being downsized and privatized.[6]

The Canadian government has traditionally played a role in most of the country's major industries—airlines, railways, trucking, petrochemicals, pharmaceuticals, fishing, steelmaking, the financial industry, agriculture, pulp and paper, mining, gas and oil, textiles, building materials, telephones and energy. In the last decade, this role has been decreased significantly as privatization has gradually spread. The government has sold Air Canada, as well as its interest in Dome Petroleum, Fishery Products, Polysar, and other companies. Several airports across the country, from small ones like Moncton to large ones like Vancouver, have been semiprivatized—in effect, their operations have been contracted out to independent groups. Governmental influence in business is on the decline in Canada, as both federal and provincial governments strive to cut back expenditures. The federal government announced, during the summer of 1995, that it was preparing Canadian National Railways for privatization. Still, Crown corporations remain major players in the economy: one estimate has placed the number of Crown corporations in Canada at over 800.[7]

What effect does this far-reaching government involvement have on management in Canada? Apart from the traditional civil service jobs that we usually associate with Crown corporations, there are thousands of other managerial jobs that have a governmental flavour to them. Critics of government management argue that without a profit motive there is less emphasis on excellence, output and performance.[8] But, in fact, as in any other set of organizations, the quality of management varies from one government corporation to another. This extended governmental presence also means that even managers in private business need to operate in two spheres concurrently: the private competitive world and the world of governmental control, regulation and influence. Government does not run Canadian business, but it does have an important influence, and managers must know how to deal with this. It is no accident that the number and importance of professional lobbyists has increased dramatically in Canada over the last 10 years.

Canadian business is tightly interwoven with Canadian government. Although this relationship is a longstanding one, it underwent significant change after World War II, through the efforts of C D Howe, a minister in the Liberal governments of Mackenzie King and Louis St. Laurent. Howe took a group of businessmen who had come to Ottawa to help in the war effort, introduced them to the corridors of political power, and transformed them into a group who knew how to get things done in government—where to go, who to see. When they dispersed

TABLE I-1 Canada's 10 Largest Crown Corporations as of 1998

Rank	Crown Corp.	Revenues $'000s	Assets $'000s	Net Income $'000s	Employees
1	Ontario Hydro	8 925 000	39 181 000	(–6 326 000)	21 130
2	Hydro-Quebec	8 287 000	55 194 000	786 000	17 164
3	The Canadian Wheat Board	6 110 000	8 424 948	na	574
4	Canada Post Corp.	5 085 092	2 725 782	112 523	63 529
5	Loto-Quebec	2 619 000	558 000	982 049	5 000
6	BC Hydro	2 403 000	11 456 000	339 000	5 819
7	Ontario Lottery Corp.	2 066 723	237 448	651 757	750
8	LCBO	1 996 791	388 246	701 030	2 828
9	Workers Comp. Board of Quebec	1 722 263	6 318 033	215 413	3 042
10	Société des alcools du Québec	1 076 500	246 681	371 596	1 974

after the war, either to return to industry or to head important government departments, they set the pattern for future government–business partnerships in Canada. As Peter Newman remarks, "It was the network of connections and interconnections between business and government, fathered by Clarence Decatur Howe, that became the Canadian Establishment—its great dynasties spreading into every form of commercial enterprise across the country".[9]

The two factions of Canadian business have produced managers who are adept at operating both within governmental bodies and in the private sector. As a result, senior bureaucrats in Ottawa often have business backgrounds, while senior managers in business have often worked in the government area. Ronald Osborne was appointed CEO of Ontario Hydro in 1998, after a career with Bell Canada. Apart from a change from private to public sector, this also meant a change from a profitable company to one that posted a $6 billion loss for the previous year (see Table I-1).

Living Next to the United States

Canadians have probably never been so acutely aware of the United States as a neighbour as they were during the 1988 federal election, when the Free Trade Agreement was the major issue. Now, with NAFTA being a fact of life, US influence on Canada is felt even more strongly. Over time, both the advantages and the disadvantages of letting down the trade barriers with the United States (and, of course, Mexico) have been seen. There have been a number of large corporate relocations south of the border, and mergers have become more prevalent among Canadian companies as they try to build in size and strength in order to compete. It remains to be seen exactly what the effects of NAFTA will be for Canada.

The Free Trade Agreement hastened a major economic restructuring in Canada. Michael Porter, in the study he conducted for the government of Canada, commented that "Canadians have lived in a relatively insulated environment brought about by paternalistic government policies, [and] a history of market protection". And he concurs with Peter Newman's view of Canadians when he adds, "Canadian demand conditions have not put strong pressure on firms to innovate, upgrade or anticipate international needs ... Canadian industries have not typically been driven by demanding domestic customers to seek higher order competitive advantages. Canadian buyers are rarely at the leading edge in demanding innovative consumer goods. They are also reluctant ... to voice complaints or to utilize consumer advocacy agencies to pressure providers of goods and services to enhance their products."[10]

But the reality now is that we have to compete not only in the American market, but in the North American market, which includes Mexico. This leaves Canada with little choice—it has to become more productive and more competitive in order to survive and prosper.

While the Free Trade Agreement with the US and Mexico is a high-profile issue in the Canadian business world, it is important to recognize that a significant proportion of companies operating in Canada are foreign-controlled. As of 1998, 25 percent of the 300 biggest companies in Canada were foreign-owned. Most of these are controlled by US interests, but there are many other countries represented, such as Japan (Honda Motor Co.), Hong Kong (Highburn Investments Ltd.), Holland (Trelleborg Intl. BV), Scotland (General Accidents plc), New Zealand (Fletcher Challenge Ltd.), Germany (Bayer AG), Singapore (Western Star Intnl. Pte.), and Switzerland (Zurich Insurance Co.). The list goes on, of course, but the point is that management in Canada often has a high degree of international flavour.

All countries have some foreign-owned companies but few as high a proportion as in Canada. Management's job is made more difficult in many cases because it serves two masters, one in Canada, and one elsewhere. There is often a conflict between how the parent company would like things done, and how things can be done in a host country. For obvious reasons, head office would like to see such matters as advertising campaigns, packaging, production processes, and financial reporting to be standardized in all of its international divisions. But in some cases this is simply not possible.

Nor do foreign subsidiaries in Canada necessarily have to take a backseat approach. Among US subsidiaries in Canada that have consistently achieved better results than their parents are Firestone Tire and Rubber Co. and A&P. The main reasons given for this superior performance are the autonomy granted Canadian operations, and the greater flexibility allowed by their smaller size.

Multinational companies have often been accused of having no loyalties to the countries in which they operate. They are said to manipulate prices, move funds, transfer costs, and otherwise operate their businesses in order to maximize their profits and minimize their taxes. For example, the process of transfer pricing (setting special prices when one part of a company sells its products to another part of the same company) has been used to benefit multinationals at the expense of their host country customers. Large oil companies have been known to "sell" oil being shipped into Canada from one subsidiary to another, increasing the price each time so that the final price, landed in Canada, was significantly higher than it had been when the oil was loaded onto the tankers. In one case, the oil company sold "cheap" oil to a Bermudan company, which then sold it as "expensive" oil to another company, which in turn sold the oil to a Canadian company. The big profit was taken, nominally, in Bermuda, where no tax had to be paid. In fact, the oil never left the tanker, and the tanker kept steaming right on course for Canada; all the "transfers" were on paper. The oil company therefore paid little tax, made huge profits, and Canadian customers paid more than they might have paid otherwise.

Of course, not all multinational companies operate in this manner (nor do all oil companies). But there is a strong feeling in many quarters that multinational companies are able to escape the controls of a single host country, and can therefore operate somewhat outside the law.

When there is a conflict between managing for the good of the multinational company or for the good of their own country, Canadian managers face dilemmas. The choice is not always clear, but a manager's actions can be strongly influenced by practices imposed from outside the Canadian subsidiary company.

The Importance of International Trade

Business activity is becoming increasingly global in scope. The North American Free Trade Agreement represents a major move towards breaking down trade barriers. Although it continually faces obstacles, the European Union is still moving towards its goal of dropping all of its internal trade barriers. Pacific nations have also been considering the possibility of an economic union. There is clearly an increasing trend towards global competition, with organizations becoming larger and positioning themselves to dominate world markets.

Marie Josée Drouin, executive director of the Hudson Institute in Montreal, has pointed out the pressures that Canada is experiencing. "In the economic sphere, we have just begun to feel how fiercely competitive economic life has become. Technological change is occurring so rapidly, it's beyond the ability of any single firm, province or country to manage. There's no patent so valuable, no production system so advanced and no market share so dominant that it prevents competitors from challenging an entrenched position."[11]

The ongoing challenge for Canadian management is to compete in global markets. As the executives interviewed by *Canadian Business* indicated, there is a high degree of optimism that we can compete successfully.[12] But this success depends on our ability to increase productivity, among other things. As companies in Pacific nations continue to emphasize productivity, it becomes increasingly difficult for Canadians to secure key markets, such as the consumer electronics and the computer chip markets. Productivity is an integral element in reducing costs and increasing quality—two key factors in securing markets. Canadian managers must become much more oriented towards productivity in order to make our goods and services competitive in the global market. We don't have a large enough market of our own to survive; our focus must be outward, and when we look out there, we see some tough competition. Canadian executives are confident that they can compete and succeed, but it takes increasing levels of skill to do so.

The Influence of French Canada

The 1995 Referendum made it irrevocably clear just how much influence the province of Quebec has on Canada. It was the major news story of the year in Canada—probably of the decade. The idea of Quebec leaving Confederation immediately focused attention on the possible consequences such an action would have on Canada as a whole. Inevitably, much of the talk about separation centred around economics—could Quebec survive on its own, and to what extent would its leaving affect the national economy? Obviously, the economic importance of Quebec was a subject of much interest for the news media, as it is inextricably wound up in the welfare of the nation.

If it was not clear before, it quickly became apparent to the rest of Canada just how much weight Quebec carries in the national economy. In the past, there has been a great void in Canadian business texts with regard to Quebec. Perhaps the scrutiny that the Referendum caused will serve to correct this failure in the future. It would be foolish to overlook Quebec as a major part of the Canadian business world. Quebec represents about 25 percent of the Canadian market for goods and services, and is the base of what may be the most active, vibrant, and growing entrepreneurial sector in the country.

This book has examples throughout its chapters showing the influence of French Canada in modern business. Quebec companies range from giant, internationally powerful corporations such as Bombardier, Seagram and Alcan Aluminium, to technology leaders such as Softimage and Corona Technologies, to small businesses thriving on entrepreneurial spirit such as furniture maker, Lacasse, and the advertising firm of Watt Burt. In this text, we have tried to reflect the major role played in Canada by Quebec businesses. Taking a quick browse through The *Globe and Mail*'s list of Canada's 25 most powerful corporate leaders for 1998, one can find many Quebec-born CEOs in the ranks. Jean Monty of BCE Inc., John Cleghorn of the Royal Bank, Jacques Bougie of Alcan, Brian Levitt of Imasco, and David O'Brien of CP are all amongst the top CEOs in the country. Many Quebec-born managers head up companies across the country, and conversely, many managers from English-speaking Canada lead Quebec companies—for instance, Paul Desmarais Jr. of Power Corp was born in Sudbury, Ontario, and John MacDonald of Bell is originally from Sydney, Nova Scotia.

In today's world, companies are being forced to look at their business in more global terms. This book deals with the changing face of management practice, the benefits of a global perspective, and the perils of parochialism. Businesses can no longer thrive without paying attention to their external environment. And within Canada, it would be a monumental error to allow provincial parochialism to blind us to the importance of Quebec.

Clearly, there are cultural differences between French and English Canada, but management principles transcend these disparities. The message for Canadian business people is clear: If you want to operate nationally, you must speak both official languages. The Canadian market is so small that it would be nonsensical to ignore a large segment because of a different language or cultural base. Life would, perhaps, be easier if everyone spoke the same language and acted and thought alike, but it would also be duller and lacking in challenges.

Small Domestic Markets

The Canadian market structure and its proximity to the United States may not affect our management style, but they do affect the way in which we must do business. Market size influences the decision of whether to buy or make a product. For instance, the Canadian computer industry must consider that the market here is less than one-tenth the size of the US market. Manufacturing costs based on the much smaller sales volumes for a purely domestic product make price competition against high-volume manufacturers like IBM, Apple and Compaq exceedingly difficult. Although the US market is on our doorstep, there are various barriers to entry that make it harder to compete there against indigenous companies than it is to compete at home.

This book is a good example of the effect of market size on business decisions. A US edition competes for a total market in excess of a quarter of a million management books sold per year. A number of US universities have more than 100 000 students, and have introductory management courses of between 5 000 and 10 000 students per year. The Canadian university scene is quite different in size and scope, and the total number of students taking an introductory management course nationwide is somewhere in the range of 25–35 000 per year. On the basis of these figures, the publisher must decide how many books to print, what potential sales may be, and how to price the book. The Canadian publishing industry has traditionally had a very difficult time because of the limited market for purely "Canadian" material.

The demands of small markets that are geographically separated and strongly influenced by a large neighbour have put flexibility, agility, sensitivity to moves and changes, and careful calculation of risk and opportunity at the heart of Canadian management. As a nation, we are reputed to be conservative (with a small c)! We rank among the highest buyers of life insurance in the world; we don't engage in many gigantic high-risk projects; we struggle to maintain our identity, individuality and independence from our powerful friends; and we choose the role of peacekeeper and mediator, rather than principal, in the armed and political struggles of the world. But our situation is not unique. The Swiss face many similar problems (they have three official languages, are surrounded by powerful neighbours and have a small domestic market). And other nations like Belgium and the Scandinavian countries are not too dissimilar. They survive, in an economic sense, as we do—on our wits, skill and flexibility.

The old boxing adage is that a good big man will always beat a good small man. But remember the lesson of David and Goliath. You can win if you are small—you just have to be good. This book attempts to get you launched in the right direction. We hope it will stimulate your interest and skill in management. It might even make you a Canadian David.

Kathleen Muller
Humber College
Etobicoke, Ontario

Brian Harrocks
Algonquin College
Nepean, Ontario

PART ONE

Introduction

LEARNING OBJECTIVES

After Reading This Chapter, You Should Be Able To:

1. Differentiate managers from non-managerial employees
2. Define management
3. Distinguish between effectiveness and efficiency
4. Describe the four basic management functions
5. Identify the roles performed by managers
6. Describe the skills managers need
7. Explain whether or not the manager's job is generic
8. Explain the value of studying management

A MANAGER'S CHALLENGE

Bobbie Gaunt, CEO, Ford Canada

The auto industry in the 1980s and early 1990s was generally defined by the Big Three auto makers trying to reclaim the market share they had lost to Japanese manufacturers. Decades of seemingly unstoppable growth allowed the North American companies to become complacent, increasingly taking the marketplace for granted. The past decade has seen Ford, Chrysler, and General Motors (GM) bringing the quality of their products up to the standards set by their Japanese competitors. Now, however, a new challenge is just beginning in the industry. Improved quality and the high cost of vehicles have led to consumers driving their cars longer, and have also led to significant growth in the used car market.[1]

So, how is this battle going to be fought? Ford Canada made its strategy fairly explicit when it appointed Bobbie Gaunt as chief executive officer (CEO) in April of '97. Gaunt comes from a marketing background, and has a very specific view of how to handle the new trends emerging in the industry. As she has stated:

"Ford has been a mass marketer for years, and it worked wonderfully. But when your industry becomes saturated and doesn't have a lot of natural growth, the only way you're going to find a way to grow in a profitable way is being smarter about the customer than anybody else".

Gaunt has been with Ford since 1972, when she joined the company with plans to enroll in its management training program (Chrysler and GM at the time refused to allow women into their executive ranks—their loss). In 1979, Gaunt helped form a women's marketing committee (unheard of amongst the Big Three at the time) to address the needs of female drivers. Management at Ford eventually took notice, and had the good sense to encourage the development of marketing directed towards women. By 1990, women accounted for 42 percent of car purchases—a giant leap from a decade earlier when men were the overwhelming consumer force. Today, women purchase at least half of the cars bought in North America. Gaunt, the first woman to head-up Ford Canada, came to her new position after handling sales and marketing for Ford in the US. Her predecessor at Ford Canada, Mark Hutchins, also concentrated on marketing through the company's dealerships. Hutchins left Ford Canada in good shape, with vehicle sales up by 22 percent from 1995. Gaunt has continued this success, as well as continuing the trend of making increases in both lease market share and customer satisfaction every year for the past six years.

Bobbie Gaunt's appointment as CEO is a watershed for Ford Canada. She will be steering the company through a time of major changes in the industry. The plans that are put in place now will determine how Ford Canada copes with these changes. The car-buyer in Canada is far more demanding than ever before, and the changes in consumer demographics will force companies to focus on the specific needs of their customers. As Gaunt has said, "... it's about how this product fits the customer, not how the customer fits the product". The new car market will become increasingly competitive, and executives such as Bobbie Gaunt will have to be prepared for shifts in consumer tastes.

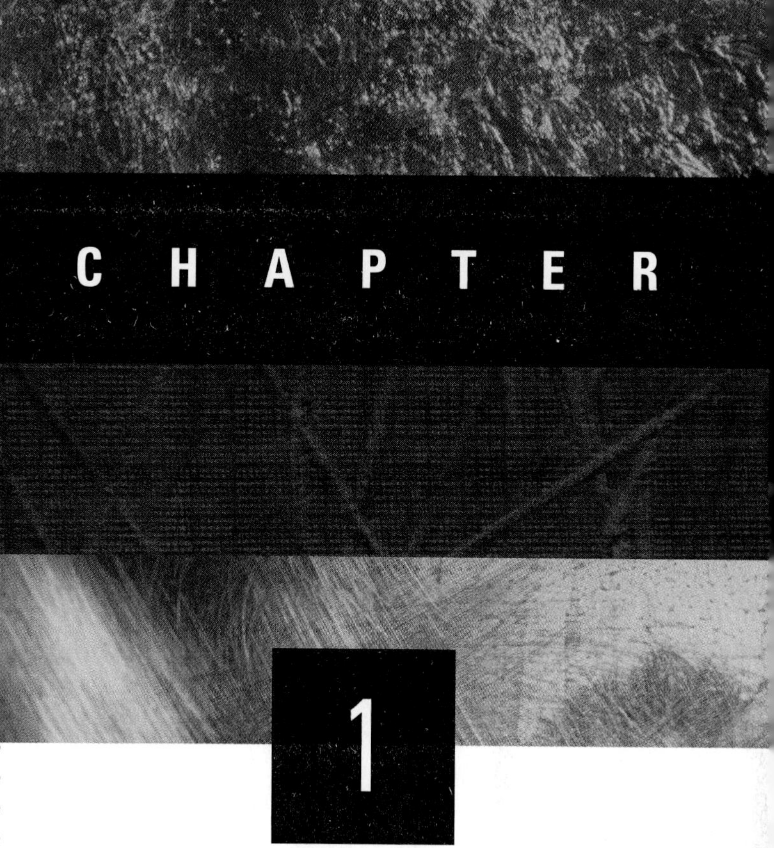

Managers and Management

Bobbie Gaunt is an excellent example of what today's successful managers are like. Successful managers may not be what you would expect! They can be anyone from under 18 to over 80 years of age. And managers run not only large corporations, but also small businesses, government agencies, hospitals, museums, schools, and such non-traditional organizations as co-operatives. Some hold positions at the top of their organizations, while others hold positions near the bottom. Managers can also be found doing their managerial work in every country on the globe.

Today they are just as likely to be women as they are to be men. The picture of the corporate world being controlled by the "old boys club" has largely disappeared, but the days of male dominance in the boardroom are not as far behind us as we may like to think. Management has certainly gone through vast changes. Today, 61 percent of major Canadian companies have at least one female director. However, there is still much further to go—in the US, this figure is 98 percent. While women make up 45 percent of the labour force and 57 percent of graduate degree holders, only 2 percent of CEOs among Canada's top 500 companies are female.[2] Comparatively, in the US, the figure is 10 percent. Still, it does not come as a surprise when a woman is chosen to head-up a major Canadian company. Some of our top producers are run by women, as is evidenced by Bobbie Gaunt. Our other major car manufacturer, General Motors Canada, also happens to be run by a woman—Maureen Kempston Darkes. In England, on the other hand, the appointment of Marjorie Scardino as CEO of the media company, Pearson, back in 1997, was the first appointment of a woman to head a top-100 firm.

This book is about the work that Bobbie Gaunt does, and the work that tens of millions of other managers like her do as well. Although you may not find yourself in a position similar to that of Gaunt, the fact remains that the work managers do is of essential importance in all types and sizes of organizations. In this chapter, we introduce you to managers and management by answering—or at least beginning to answer—the following questions: *What* is an organization and *how* is the concept of an organization changing? *Who* are managers? *What* is management and *what* do managers do? Finally, we'll conclude the chapter by discussing *why* you should spend your time studying management.

Maureen Kempston Darkes is Canada's most powerful corporate leader (as of 1999). As CEO of General Motors Canada, she represents the changing face of the boardroom.

WHAT IS AN ORGANIZATION?

organization
A group of people, systematically arranged, working to accomplish some specific purpose.

Managers work in organizations. Therefore, before we can identify who managers are, it is important to clarify what we mean by the term *organization*.

An **organization** is a group of people, systematically arranged, working to accomplish some specific purpose. Your college or university is an organization. So are fraternities, government agencies, churches, the Maritime Brewing Company in Halifax, your neighbourhood gas station, Mountain Equipment Co-op, the Calgary Flames hockey team, and the Salvation Army. These are all organizations because they all share three common characteristics, as shown in Figure 1-1.

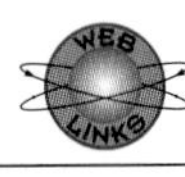

Mountain Equipment Co-op
www.mec.ca

First, each organization has a distinct purpose. This purpose is typically expressed in terms of a goal or set of goals. Second, each organization is composed of people. Third, all orga-

FIGURE 1-1 **Characteristics of Organizations**

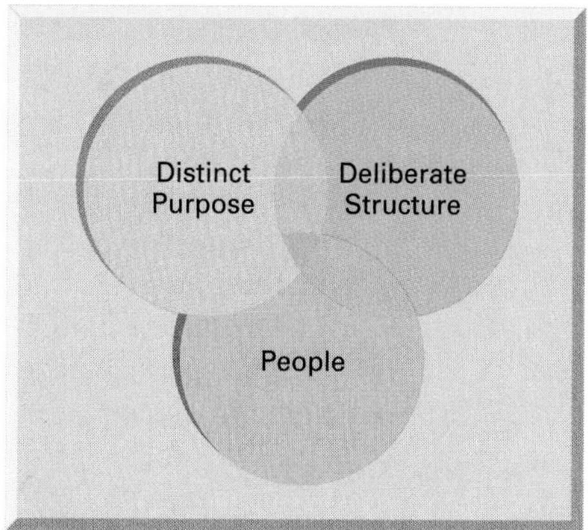

nizations develop a systematic structure that defines and limits the behaviour of its members. This includes, for example, creating rules and regulations; identifying some members as "bosses" and giving them authority over other members; or writing up job descriptions so that members know what they are supposed to do. The term *organization* refers to an entity that has a distinct purpose, includes people or members, and has a systematic structure.

Although these three characteristics are important to our definition of *what* an organization is, the concept of an organization is going through considerable change. It is no longer appropriate to assume that all organizations are going to be structured, for example, like Petro Canada, BCE or Canadian Pacific, with clearly identifiable divisions, departments and work units. Just how is the concept of an organization changing? Table 1-1 lists some differences between a traditional view and a contemporary view of an organization. Today's organizations are becoming more open, flexible, and responsive to changes.

Why are organizations changing? Because the world around them is changing. Societal, economic and technological changes have created an environment in which successful organizations (those that consistently meet their goals) must embrace new ways of getting their work done. Examples include the "information explosion", increasing globalization, and changing employee expectations. But the more the concept of organizations changes, the more important the roles of managers and management become.

WHO ARE MANAGERS?

It used to be fairly simple to define who managers were. They were the organizational members who oversaw and directed the work of other members. It was easy to differentiate *man-*

In his role as manager—integrating and co-ordinating the work of others—Bruce Poon Tip has been exceptionally successful. Founder of GAP Adventures Inc., he has built the company into an $8 million a year operation.

TABLE 1-1 The Changing Organization

Traditional Organization	New Organization
• Stable	• Dynamic
• Inflexible	• Flexible
• Job-focused	• Skills-focused
• Work is defined by job positions	• Work is defined in terms of tasks to be done
• Individual-oriented	• Team-oriented
• Permanent jobs	• Temporary jobs
• Command-oriented	• Involvement-oriented
• Managers always make decisions	• Employees participate in decision making
• Rule-oriented	• Customer-oriented
• Relatively homogeneous workforce	• Diverse workforce
• Workdays defined as 9 to 5	• Workdays have no time boundaries
• Hierarchical relationships	• Lateral and networked relationships
• Work at organizational facility during specific hours	• Work anywhere, anytime

agers from *operatives*; the latter term described those organizational members who worked directly on a job or task and had no subordinates. But it isn't quite so simple any more. The changing nature of organizations and work has, in many cases, blurred the lines of distinction between managers and operatives. Many traditional workers' jobs now include managerial activities, especially in work teams. For instance, team members often develop plans, make decisions and monitor their own performance. And as these operative employees assume responsibilities that traditionally belonged to management, definitions we've used in the past no longer apply.

manager
An organizational member who integrates and co-ordinates the work of others.

How *do* we define managers? A **manager** is an organizational member who integrates and co-ordinates the work of others. This may mean direct responsibility for a group of people in one department, or it may mean supervising a single person. It could also involve co-ordinating the work activities of a team composed of people from several different departments or even people from other organizations. Keep in mind, however, that managers probably have other work duties not related to integrating the work of others.

Is there some way to classify managers in organizations? There is, particularly for traditionally structured organizations (that is, those with deliberate work arrangements, or structures shaped like a pyramid which reflects the fact that the number of employees is greater at the bottom than at the top). As shown in Figure 1-2, we typically describe managers as either first-line, middle, or top managers, in this type of organization.

first-line managers
Supervisors; the lowest level of management.

middle managers
All levels of management between the supervisory level and the top level of the organization.

top managers
Managers at or near the pinnacle of the organization who are responsible for making the decisions and setting the policies that affect all aspects of the organization.

First-line managers are usually called *supervisors*. In a manufacturing plant, the first-line (or lowest level) manager may be called a *foreperson*. On an athletic team, for instance, the coach would be considered the first-line manager. **Middle managers** include all levels of management between the supervisory level and the top level of the organization. They may have titles such as department or agency head, project leader, plant manager, unit chief, dean, bishop, or division manager. At or near the pinnacle of the organization are the **top managers,** who are responsible for making organizational decisions and setting the policies and strategies that affect all aspects of the organization. These individuals typically have titles such as vice president, president, chancellor, managing director, chief operating officer, chief executive officer, or chairperson.

Bobbie Gaunt, as CEO of Ford Canada, is a prime example of a top-level manager, responsible for implementing broad changes that have a major effect on the entire organization.

Throughout this book, we'll be discussing organizations and managers from the perspective of this more traditional pyramid structure even though, today, many organizations do not operate under this structure. Organizations that have more flexible and loosely configured structures still need individuals to fulfill the role of manager—that is, someone who integrates and co-ordinates the work of others.

FIGURE 1-2 Organizational Levels

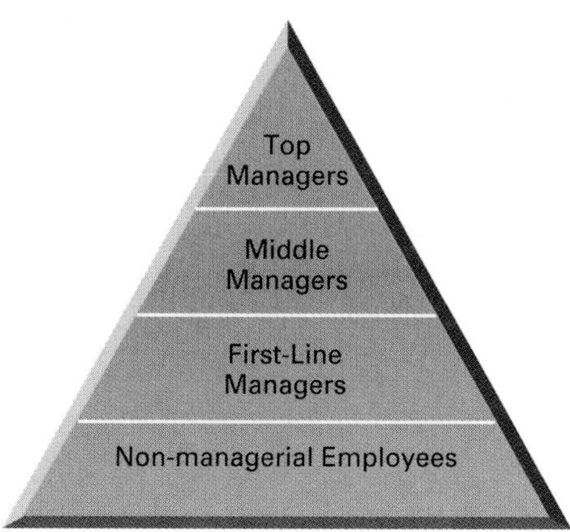

If you choose a managerial career, you'll likely have a variety of titles and job responsibilities. And, over the course of your career, these managerial jobs may take you to a number of organizations. If you decide on a career in management, you'll find yourself in an exciting and challenging profession!

WHAT IS MANAGEMENT?

Just as organizations have common characteristics, so do managers. Although their titles vary widely, there are common characteristics to their jobs—whether the manager owns and operates a small silviculture company on Vancouver Island, supervises a production line in a fish plant in Nova Scotia, or is CEO of Montreal's Power Financial Corp. These positions are all inherently different (obviously income is one difference—Robert Gratton earned over $27 million heading Power Financial in 1997), but they also involve some similar functions.

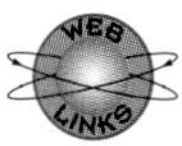

Power Financial Corp.
www.powercorp.ca

The term **management** refers to the process of co-ordinating and integrating work activities so that they are completed efficiently and effectively with and through other people. Let's look at some of the specific parts of this definition.

management
The process of co-ordinating and integrating work activities so that they're completed efficiently and effectively with and through other people.

The *process* represents the functions or primary activities engaged in by managers. These functions are typically labelled planning, organizing, leading and controlling. We elaborate on these functions in the next section.

Efficiency is a vital part of management. It refers to the relationship between inputs and outputs. If you can get more output from the given inputs, you have increased efficiency. Similarly, if you can get the same output from less input, you also have increased efficiency. Since managers deal with input resources that are scarce—mainly people, money and equipment—they are concerned with the efficient use of these resources. Management, therefore, is concerned with minimizing resource costs. Efficiency is often referred to as "doing things right".

efficiency
The relationship between inputs and outputs that minimizes resource costs.

However, it's not enough simply to be efficient. Management is also concerned with getting activities completed; that is, it seeks **effectiveness**. When managers achieve their organization's goals, we say they are effective. Effectiveness can be described as "doing the right things". So efficiency is concerned with means, and effectiveness with ends. (See Figure 1-3.)

effectiveness
Goal attainment.

Efficiency and effectiveness are interrelated. For instance, it is easier to be effective if one ignores efficiency. Timex could produce more accurate and attractive watches if it disregarded labour and material input costs. Some federal government agencies have been criticized regularly on the grounds that they are reasonably effective but extremely inefficient; that is, they get their jobs done, but at a very high cost. Management is concerned, then, not only with getting activities completed (effectiveness), but also with doing so as efficiently as possible.

Can organizations be efficient but not effective? Yes, by doing the wrong things well! Many universities have become highly efficient at processing students. By using computer-assisted learning, large lecture classes, and heavy reliance on part-time faculties, administrators have significantly cut the cost of educating each student. Yet students, alumni, and accrediting

FIGURE 1-3 Efficiency and Effectiveness in Management

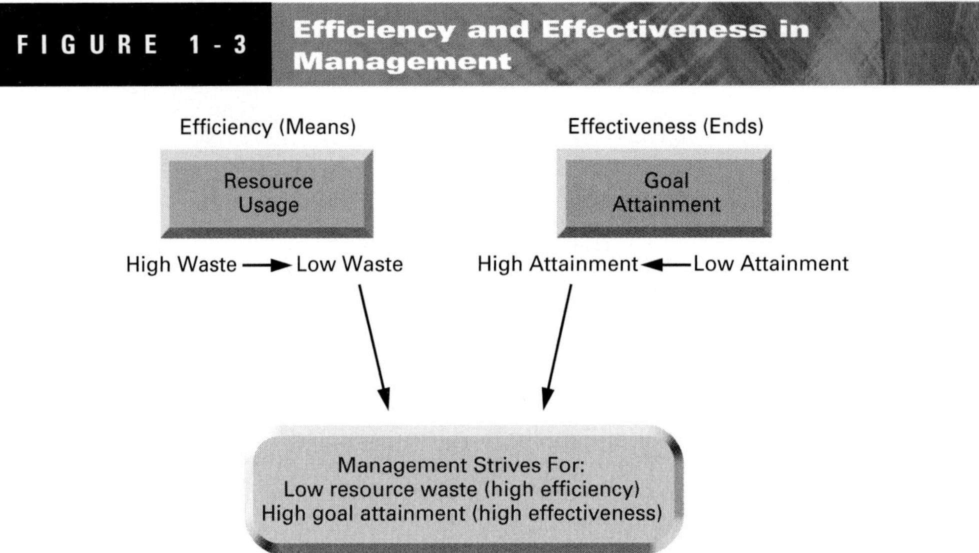

agencies have criticized some of these universities for failing to educate their students properly. Of course, high efficiency is associated more typically with high effectiveness. And poor management is most often due to both inefficiency and ineffectiveness or to effectiveness achieved through inefficiency.

WHAT DO MANAGERS DO?

Describing what managers do isn't a simple task. Just as no two organizations are exactly alike, so are no two managers' jobs exactly alike. But even given these constraints, we have well over 100 years of formal management study to draw from, and some specific categorization schemes that have been developed to describe what managers do. We're going to look at what managers do in terms of functions and processes, roles, skills, managing systems, and managing different and changing situations.

Management Functions and Processes

management functions Planning, organizing, leading and controlling.

planning Includes defining goals, establishing strategy, and developing plans to co-ordinate activities.

organizing Determining what tasks to do, who is to do them, how to group the tasks, who reports to whom, and where to make decisions.

In the early part of this century, a French industrialist named Henri Fayol wrote that all managers perform five management functions: they plan, organize, command, co-ordinate and control.[3] In the mid-1950s, two professors at UCLA used the functions of planning, organizing, staffing, directing and controlling as the framework for a textbook on management that, for twenty years, was the most widely sold text on the subject.[4] The most popular textbooks (and this one is no exception) still continue to be organized around **management functions**, although these have been condensed generally to the basic four: planning, organizing, leading and controlling. (See Figure 1-4.) Let's briefly define what each of these functions encompasses.

Since organizations exist in order to achieve some purpose, someone must define that purpose and the means for its achievement. That someone is management. The **planning** function involves defining an organization's goals, establishing an overall strategy for achieving these goals, and developing a comprehensive hierarchy of plans to integrate and co-ordinate activities.

Managers are also responsible for designing an organization's structure. We call this function **organizing**. It includes determining what tasks are to be done, who is to do them, how the tasks are to be grouped, who reports to whom, and at what level decisions are made.

TESTING... TESTING...

1 What is an organization? Why are managers important to an organization's success?

2 Are all effective organizations also efficient? Why or why not?

FIGURE 1-4 Management Functions

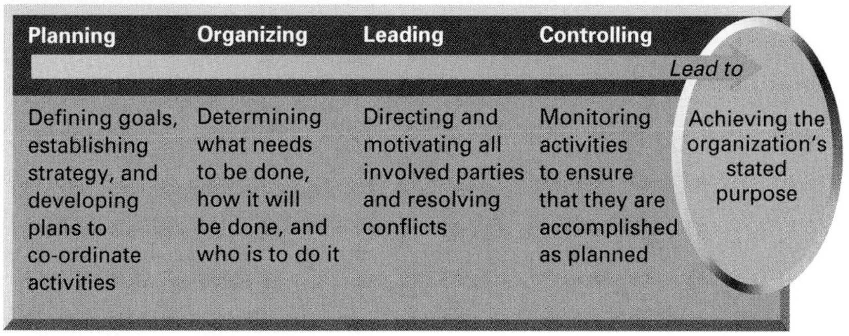

Planning	Organizing	Leading	Controlling	
			Lead to	
Defining goals, establishing strategy, and developing plans to co-ordinate activities	Determining what needs to be done, how it will be done, and who is to do it	Directing and motivating all involved parties and resolving conflicts	Monitoring activities to ensure that they are accomplished as planned	Achieving the organization's stated purpose

Every organization includes people, and management's job is to direct and co-ordinate these people. This is the function of **leading**. When managers motivate subordinates, direct the activities of others, select the most effective communication channel, or resolve conflicts among members, they are engaged in leading.

leading
Includes motivating subordinates, directing others, selecting the most effective communication channels, and resolving conflicts.

The final function which managers perform is **controlling**. After the goals are set (planning function), the plans formulated (planning function), the structural arrangements delineated (organizing function), and the people hired, trained, and motivated (leading function), something may still go wrong. To ensure that things are working as they should, management must monitor the organization's performance. Actual performance must be compared with the previously set goals. If there are any significant deviations, it's management's job to get the organization back on track. This process of monitoring, comparing and correcting is what we mean by the controlling function.

controlling
Monitoring activities to ensure that they are being accomplished as planned, and correcting any significant deviations.

The reality of managing isn't quite as simplistic as these descriptions of the management functions might lead you to believe. In fact, it's probably more realistic to describe the functions which managers perform from the perspective of a process. The **management process** is the set of ongoing decisions and work activities in which managers engage as they plan, organize, lead and control. What this means is that as managers do their work (as they "perform" the management functions), their work activities are often done in an ongoing and continuous manner—as part of a process. There is no simple, cut-and-dried beginning or ending point. As managers "manage", they often find themselves engaging in activities that involve some planning, some organizing, some leading, and some controlling, and not necessarily in any specific order.

management process
The set of ongoing decisions and actions in which managers engage as they plan, organize, lead and control.

The continued popularity of the functional and process approaches to describe what managers do is a tribute to their clarity and simplicity. But *do* they accurately describe what managers actually do? Following the functional and process approach, it's easy to answer the question, "What do managers do?" They plan, organize, lead and control through a series of ongoing decisions and work activities. But does that really describe what *all* managers do? One prominent management researcher, Henry Mintzberg, would say no, arguing that what managers do can best be described by looking at the roles they play at work.

Management Roles

In the late 1960s, Henry Mintzberg did a careful study of five chief executives at work.[5] What he discovered challenged several long-held notions about the manager's job. For instance, in contrast to the predominant views at the time that managers were reflective thinkers who carefully and systematically processed information before making decisions, Mintzberg found that his managers engaged in a large number of varied, unpatterned, and short-duration activities. There was little time for reflective thinking because the managers encountered constant interruptions. Half of these managers' activities lasted less than nine minutes each. But, in addition to these insights, Mintzberg provided a categorization scheme for defining what managers do, based on actual managers on the job.

Mintzberg concluded that managers perform 10 different but highly interrelated roles. The term **management roles** refers to specific categories of managerial behaviour. As shown in Table 1-2, these 10 roles can be grouped into those primarily concerned with interpersonal relationships, the transfer of information, and decision making.

management roles
Specific categories of managerial behaviour.

Andrew Badia (shown receiving an Entrepreneur of The Year award) performs interpersonal, informational, and decisional roles as CEO of Iris Hosiery Inc. in Quebec.

interpersonal roles Roles that include figurehead, leader and liaison activities.

Interpersonal Roles. All managers are required to perform duties that are ceremonial and symbolic in nature—**interpersonal roles**. When the president of a college hands out diplomas at commencement or a factory supervisor gives a group of high school students a tour of the plant, he or she is acting in a figurehead role. All managers have a role as a leader. This role includes hiring, training, motivating and disciplining employees. The other role within the interpersonal grouping is the liaison role. Mintzberg described this activity as contacting external sources who provide the manager with information. These sources are individuals or groups outside the manager's unit, and may be inside or outside the organization. The sales manager who obtains information from the company's human resources manager has an internal liaison relationship. When that sales manager confers with other sales executives through a marketing trade association, he or she has an outside liaison relationship.

informational roles Roles that include monitoring, disseminating and spokesperson activities.

Informational Roles. All managers, to some degree, fulfill **informational roles**—receiving and collecting information from organizations and institutions outside their own. Typically, they do so by reading magazines and talking with others to learn of changes in the public's tastes, what competitors may be planning, and the like. Mintzberg called this the *monitor* role. Managers also act as conduits, to transmit information to organizational members. This is the *disseminator* role. When managers represent the organization to outsiders, they also perform a *spokesperson* role, such as when the president of Bell Canada, John McLennan, represented the company in television commercials.

decisional roles Roles that include those of entrepreneur, disturbance handler, resource allocator and negotiator.

Decisional Roles. Finally, Mintzberg identified four **decisional roles**, which revolve around making choices. As *entrepreneurs*, managers initiate and oversee new projects that will improve their organization's performance. As *disturbance handlers*, managers take corrective action in response to previously unforeseen problems. As *resource allocators*, managers are responsible for allocating human, physical and monetary resources. Managers also perform as *negotiators* when they discuss and bargain with other groups to gain advantages for their own units.

Bell Canada
www.bell.ca/

An Evaluation. A number of follow-up studies have tested the validity of Mintzberg's role categories across different types of organizations and at different levels within given organizations.[6] The evidence generally supports the idea that managers—regardless of the type of

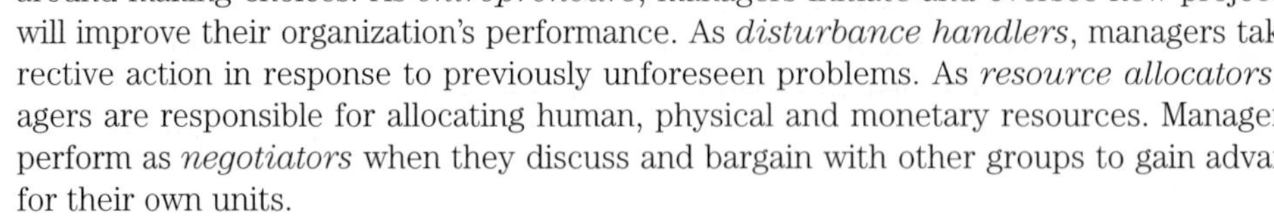

THINKING CRITICALLY ABOUT ETHICS

Suppose you're in a management position and you're asked to lie about information you have. Is lying always wrong, or might it be acceptable under certain circumstances? What, if any, would those circumstances be? What about simply distorting information that you have? Is that always wrong, or might it be acceptable under certain circumstances?

TABLE 1-2 Mintzberg's Managerial Roles

Role	Description	Identifiable Activities
INTERPERSONAL		
Figurehead	Symbolic head; obliged to perform a number of routine duties of a legal or social nature	Greeting visitors; signing legal documents
Leader	Responsible for the motivation and activation of subordinates; responsible for staffing, training, and associated duties	Performing virtually all activities that involve subordinates
Liaison	Maintains self-developed network of outside contacts and informers who provide favours and information	Acknowledging mail; doing external board work; performing other activities that involve outsiders
INFORMATIONAL		
Monitor	Seeks and receives wide variety of special information (much of it current) to develop thorough understanding of organization and environment; emerges as nerve center of internal and external information about the organization	Reading periodicals and reports; maintaining personal contacts
Disseminator	Transmits information received from outsiders or from other subordinates to members of the organization—some information is factual, some involves interpretation and integration of diverse value positions of organizational influencers	Holding informational meetings; making phone calls to relay information
Spokesperson	Transmits information to outsiders on organization's plans, policies, actions, results, etc.; serves as expert on organization's industry	Holding board meetings; giving information to the media
DECISIONAL		
Entrepreneur	Searches organization and its environment for opportunities and initiates "improvement projects" to bring about change; supervises design of certain projects as well	Organizing strategy and review sessions to develop new programs
Disturbance handler	Responsible for corrective action when organization faces important, unexpected disturbances	Organizing strategy and review sessions that involve disturbances and crises
Resource allocator	Responsible for the allocation of organizational resources of all kinds—in effect, the making or approval of all significant organizational decisions	Scheduling; requesting authorization; performing any activity that involves budgeting and the programming of subordinates' work
Negotiator	Responsible for representing the organization at major negotiations	Participating in union contract negotiations

Source: Henry Mintzberg, *The Nature of Managerial Work* (New York: Harper & Row, 1973), pp. 93–94. Copyright © 1973 by Henry Mintzberg. Reprinted by permission of Harper & Row, Publishers, Inc.

organization or level in the organization—perform similar roles. However, the emphasis that managers give to the various roles seems to change with hierarchical levels.[7] Specifically, the roles of disseminator, figurehead, negotiator, liaison officer, and spokesperson are more important at the higher levels of the organization than at the lower ones. Conversely, the leader role is more important for lower level managers than it is for middle- or top-level managers.

Have these 10 roles, which are derived from actual observations of managerial work, invalidated the more traditional functions of planning, organizing, leading and controlling? Definitely not!

First, the functional approach still represents the most useful way of conceptualizing the manager's job. "The classical functions provide clear and discrete methods of classifying the thousands of activities that managers carry out and the techniques they use in terms of the functions they perform for the achievement of goals."[8] Second, although Mintzberg may offer a more detailed and elaborate classification scheme of what managers do, these roles are substantially reconcilable with the four functions.[9] Many of Mintzberg's roles align smoothly with one or more of the functions. Resource allocation is part of planning, as is the entrepreneurial role. All three of the interpersonal roles are part of the leading function. Most of the other roles fit into one or more of the four functions, but not all of them do. The difference is substantially explained by Mintzberg's mixing the activities of managers with pure managerial work.[10]

All managers do *some* work that isn't purely managerial. The fact that Mintzberg's executives spent time in public relations or raising money attests to the precision of Mintzberg's observation methods, but shows that not everything a manager does is necessarily an essential part of the manager's job. This may have resulted in some activities being included in Mintzberg's classifications that shouldn't have been.

Do these comments mean that Mintzberg's role categories are invalid? Not at all! Mintzberg has clearly offered new insights into what managers do. The attention his work has received is evidence of the importance attributed to defining management roles. But, as we'll point out in the next chapter, management is a young discipline that is still evolving. Future research comparing and integrating Mintzberg's roles with the four functions will continue to expand our understanding of the manager's job.

Management Skills

As you can see from the preceding discussion, a manager's job is varied and complex. Managers need certain skills in order to perform the duties and activities associated with being a manager. During the early 1970s, research by Robert L. Katz found that managers need three essential skills or competencies: *technical*, *people* and *conceptual*.[11] He also found that the relative importance of these skills varied according to the manager's level within the organization. Figure 1-5 shows the relative importance of the different skills at the three management levels.

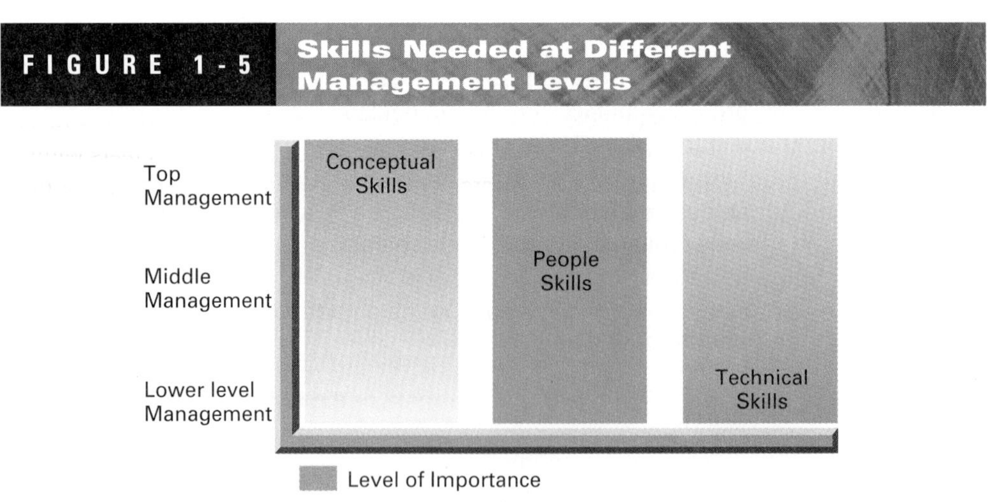

3 Describe the four common functions that all managers perform.

4 Contrast the four management functions with Mintzberg's ten roles.

Technical Skills. First-line managers, as well as many middle managers, are heavily involved in technical aspects of the organization's operations. **Technical skills** include knowledge of, and proficiency in, a certain specialized field such as engineering, computers, finance or manufacturing. For example, an accounts payable manager must be proficient in accounting rules and standardized forms so that she can resolve problems and answer questions that her accounts payable clerks might encounter. Although technical skills become less important as a manager moves into higher levels of management, even top managers need some proficiency in the organization's specialized field. Laval, Quebec's BioChem Pharma Inc. is a company that is perennially in *Profit* magazine's list of Canada's fastest growing companies and, in 1998, was the highest profit-earner in the rankings. As CEO, Dr. Francesco Bellini is responsible for the operations of the organization as a whole, but his background as a research chemist is certainly beneficial.

technical skills
Skills that include knowledge of, and proficiency in, a certain specialized field.

BioChem Pharma Inc.
www.biochempharma.com

people skills
The ability to work well with other people both individually and in a group.

People Skills. The ability to work well with other people both individually and in a group is referred to as **people skills**, or human skill. Since managers deal directly with people, this

MANAGERS WHO MAKE A DIFFERENCE

Marlene Conway, Envirolutions

A decade ago, Marlene Conway was climbing the ranks at CIBC, enjoying her work and living a very settled life in Toronto, when suddenly everything changed. Conway found herself having to raise two children and shoulder the burden of debts on her own. Faced with this situation, she decided to completely change her life—a challenge which most of us probably wouldn't be able to undertake. And the way in which Marlene Conway did this made the feat all the more impressive: she decided to enter a world that was wholly unfamiliar to her.[12]

For some time, Conway had been thinking about the vast amount of disposable diapers her children were going through. She had been thinking about the possibility of recycling, and had been researching the problem in her spare time while working at the bank. Suddenly, it became more than an idea in the back of her mind—it became her future. Conway quit her job at the bank and devoted herself to the company she formed, called Knowaste. Familiarizing herself with the scientific understanding involved was Conway's first task; her second was raising $1 million for research and development. Conway managed to achieve both feats within a year and a half. Soon, Knowaste formed strategic partnerships with some major companies, such as Procter & Gamble and DuPont. Eventually, Knowaste developed a process—which they patented—that allows wood pulp to be separated from the diaper's super-absorbent polymer. This allows the two substances to be recycled. This is cutting-edge technology and the potential for its use is enormous. Five million tonnes of diapers are disposed of each year in North America alone.

Conway today is the second-largest shareholder in Knowaste, but the company is controlled by Caithness Resources Inc., which owns most of the shares. Caithness has major plans for Knowaste, including constructing 21 plants worldwide over the next decade. Conway stands to make significant amounts of money from Knowaste, but she has moved on to form another company—Envirolutions—which is dedicated to environmental concerns. Some of the projects she and her team are working on include turning zebra mussels into fertilizer; producing bricks from materials culled from carpeting; developing an industrial waste water treatment process; and creating another process for recycling medical waste. Not bad for someone who began all of this without much in the way of scientific or managerial experience! ■

skill is crucial! In fact, it remains just as important at the top levels of management as it is at the lower levels. Managers with good people skills can get the best out of their employees. They know how to communicate, motivate, lead, and inspire enthusiasm and trust. In later chapters, we will cover many of the important behavioural topics that are part of this skill area.

Conceptual Skills. Managers must also have the ability to think and to conceptualize about abstract situations. They must be able to see the organization as a whole, as well as the relationships among its various sub-units, and they must be able to visualize how the organization fits into its broader environment. Why? These abilities are essential for effective decision making, and all managers are involved in making decisions. These types of **conceptual skills** are needed by all managers at all levels, but become more important as they move up the organizational hierarchy.

conceptual skills
The ability to think and conceptualize about abstract situations, to see the organization as a whole and the relationships among its various sub-units, and to visualize how the organization fits into its broader environment.

How relevant are these three management skills to today's managers? Katz's study served to highlight the importance of management skills in defining what managers do. More recent studies have expanded our view of skills by looking at those skills needed by effective managers.[13] Most of these skills are more specific and descriptive than Katz's broad categorization. In addition, employers continue to emphasize the importance of skills as they look at hiring university graduates.

Is the Manager's Job Universal?

We have previously mentioned the universal application of management. Up to this point, we have discussed management as if it were generic; that is, a manager is a manager regardless of where he or she manages. If management is truly a generic discipline, then what a manager does should be essentially the same, regardless of whether he or she is a top-level executive or low-level supervisor; is in a firm or a non-profit arts organization; is in a large corporation or a small business; or is located in London, England or London, Ontario. Let's take a closer look at the generic issue.

Weyerhaeuser Canada Ltd.
www.saic.com/fed/uscompanies/labor/n_z/Weyerhaeuser_Company.html

Organizational Level. We have already said that the importance of managerial roles varies depending on the manager's level in the organization. But the fact that a supervisor in a research laboratory at Saskatoon Chemicals Ltd. doesn't do exactly the same things as the CEO of its parent company, Weyerhaeuser Canada Ltd., should not be interpreted to mean that their jobs are inherently different. The differences are of degree and emphasis, not of function.

In functional terms, as managers move up the organization, they do more planning and less direct supervising. All managers, regardless of their level, make decisions. They plan, organize, lead and control. But the amount of time they give to each function is not necessarily constant. In addition, the content of the managerial functions changes with the manager's level. For example, as we'll show in Chapter 10, top managers are concerned with designing the overall organization, while lower-level managers focus on designing the jobs of individuals and work groups.

Save the Children Canada
www.savethechildren.ca

Organizational Type. Does Karen Dunnett from Moncton, New Brunswick—vice-president of Save the Children Canada—do the same things that Kevin Cuthbertson does in his capacity as quality leader for Joey Tomatoes restaurants across western Canada? Put another way, is the manager's job the same in both for-profit and non-profit organizations? The answer: For the most part, yes.[14]

First, let's dispense with a few myths which people accept about the manager's job in public organizations.

Myth 1: Decisions in public organizations emphasize political priorities, while decisions in business organizations are rational and apolitical.

Truth: Decisions in all organizations are influenced by political considerations. We'll discuss this fact in Chapter 6.

Myth 2: Public decision makers, in contrast to their business counterparts, are constrained by administrative procedures that limit managerial authority and autonomy.

Truth: As we'll show in Chapter 3, almost all managers find that significant constraints have been placed on their managerial discretion.

Myth 3: It's hard to get high performance out of government employees because, compared to their business counterparts, they're lazy, more security-oriented, and less motivated.

Truth: The evidence indicates that there is no significant difference in the motivational needs of public and business employees.[15]

Regardless of the types of organizations managers work in, there are commonalities to their jobs. All make decisions, set objectives, create workable organizational structures, hire and motivate employees, secure legitimacy for their organization's existence, and develop internal political support in order to implement programs.

Of course, there are some noteworthy differences. The most important is measuring performance. Profit, or "the bottom line", acts as an unambiguous measure of the effectiveness of a business organization. There is no such universal measure in non-profit organizations. Measuring the performance of charitable organizations, museums, schools or government agencies is therefore made considerably more difficult. Managers in these organizations don't generally face the market test for performance although they, too, must be efficient and effective in order to help their organizations survive.

Our conclusion is that, while there are distinctions between the management of for-profit and non-profit organizations, the two are far more alike than they are different. Both are similarly concerned with having managers who can effectively and efficiently plan, organize, lead and control.

FIGURE 1-6 Importance of Managerial Roles in Small and Large Firms

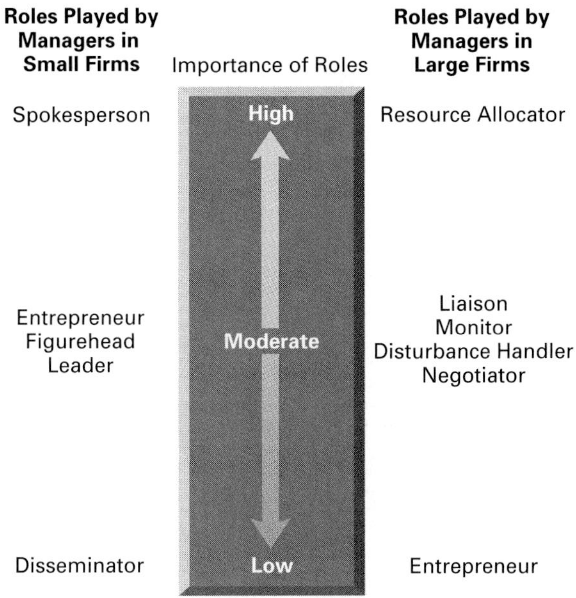

Source: Adapted from Joseph GP Paolilo, "The Manager's Self-Assessments of Managerial Roles: Small vs. Large Firms," *American Journal of Small Business,* January–March 1984 pp. 61–62.

TESTING... TESTING...

5 What management skills does a manager need? How does the importance of these skills change depending on management level?

6 What are the similarities and differences between managers at different organizational levels?

Organizational Size. Is the manager's job any different in a small organization than in a large one? This question is best answered by looking at the job of managers in small firms and comparing them to our previous discussion of managerial roles. First, however, let's define **small business** and the part it plays in our economic system.

small business
An independently owned and operated profit-seeking enterprise having fewer than 500 employees.

There is no commonly agreed upon definition of a small business because there are different criteria used to define "small"—for example, number of employees, annual sales or total assets. For our purposes, we'll call a small business any independently owned and operated, profit-seeking enterprise that has fewer than 500 employees.

Small businesses may be little, but they have a very large effect on our society. In Canada, virtually all of the job creation is found in small business. A similar scenario exists in the

ENTREPRENEURSHIP

entrepreneurship
A process by which people pursue opportunities, fulfilling needs and wants through innovation, without regard to the resources they currently control.

Beamscope
www.beamscope.com/

Throughout the text, we will have selected boxes on entrepreneurship issues that we feel are of particular importance to your study of management.[16] The first thing we need to do, however, is define what we mean by an entrepreneur. There are about as many definitions of an entrepreneur as there are authors who write about entrepreneurship. We'll define **entrepreneurship** as a process by which people pursue opportunities, fulfilling needs and wants through innovation, without regard to the resources they currently control.

It is also important to recognize that managing a small business is not necessarily the same as entrepreneurship. Not all small business managers are entrepreneurs. Many small business managers don't innovate. They merely operate their businesses like large, bureaucratic organizations. Why do we make such a distinction? Because there are some key differences in the managerial styles of entrepreneurs and traditional bureaucratic managers of small or large organizations. What are some of these differences?

Entrepreneurs actively seek change by exploiting opportunities while traditional managers tend to be more custodial. While searching for these opportunities, entrepreneurs often put their own personal financial security at risk. The hierarchical levels in bureaucratic organizations typically insulate managers from these financial wagers and reward them for minimizing risks and avoiding failures. In fact, traditional managers tend to avoid risk while entrepreneurs accept risk as part of the process of being an entrepreneur. In return, entrepreneurs are motivated by independence and the opportunity to create financial gain. Traditional managers tend to be motivated by career promotions and other traditional corporate rewards such as office, staff and power. Traditional managers are more oriented towards the achievement of short-term goals, whereas entrepreneurs are looking at the achievement of their business's growth over a five- to ten-year period. The managerial activities that the two engage in are also different. Entrepreneurs tend to be more directly involved in their organization's operational activities, while traditional managers tend to delegate tasks and supervise those workers performing the tasks. Finally, traditional managers and entrepreneurs have different views towards failures and mistakes. Entrepreneurs tend to accept mistakes as a normal part of doing business, while traditional managers tend to avoid putting themselves into situations where they could possibly fail or make a mistake.

Take, for example, Larry Wasser and Morey Chaplick, founders of Beamscope, a distribution company in Richmond Hill, Ontario. Beamscope began as a distributor of a single product: a Plexiglas sheet that would magnify the image from a television to twice its size. The product was a flop, but the two were not daunted by failure. They managed to get a contract deal in the home-video-game system, Nintendo, back in 1986 when it had just started to come into the marketplace. If you looked in the *Financial Post 500* for 1998, you would find Beamscope nestled snugly in at 350, with revenues of $327 million, and 300 employees—up from the original 2. In a large company, a manager responsible for a division or product line might not take the risks taken by Wasser and Chaplick and other entrepreneurs like them, and might be less firmly committed to seeing the venture succeed.[17]

So, even though managers in small businesses essentially perform the same managerial activities as managers in large organizations, we do find some clear distinctions between entrepreneurs and traditional business managers. ■

United States. In our neighbour to the south, small businesses constitute about 97 percent of all non-farming businesses. And statistics show that small businesses will generate more than half of all new US jobs created during the next generation.[18] The importance of small businesses is also increasing around the world in places like Japan, China and the United Kingdom.[19]

Now to the question at hand: Is the job of managing a small business different from that of managing a large one? A study comparing the two found that the importance of roles differed significantly.[20] As illustrated in Figure 1-6, the small business manager's most important role is that of spokesperson. The small business manager spends a large amount of time doing such outwardly directed activities as meeting with customers, arranging financing with bankers, searching for new opportunities, and stimulating change. In contrast, the most important concerns of a manager in a large organization are directed internally—towards deciding which organizational units get which available resources and how much of them. According to this study, the entrepreneurial role—looking for business opportunities and planning activities for performance improvement—is least important to managers in large firms.

Compared to a manager in a large organization, a small business manager is more likely to be a generalist. His or her job combines the activities of a large corporation's chief executive with many of the day-to-day activities done by a first-line supervisor. Moreover, the structure and formality that characterize a manager's job in a large organization tend to give way to informality in small firms. Planning is less likely to be a carefully orchestrated ritual. The organization's design is less complex and structured. And control in the small business relies more on direct observation than on sophisticated computerized monitoring systems.[21]

Again, as with organizational level, when we compare small and large organizations we see differences in degree and emphasis, but not in function. Managers in both small and large organizations essentially perform the same activities; only how they go about them and the proportion of time they spend on each are different.

Cross-National Transferability. The last generic management issue concerns whether management concepts are transferable across national borders. If managerial concepts were completely generic, they would apply universally, regardless of social, economic, political or cultural differences. Studies that have compared preferred managerial practices between countries have not generally supported the idea that management concepts are universal. In Chapter 4, we'll examine some specific differences between countries. At this point, it's enough to say that most of the concepts we'll be discussing in future chapters apply to Canada, the United States, Great Britain, Australia, and other English-speaking democracies. However, we may have to modify these concepts if we want to apply them in India, Korea, or any other country whose economic, political, social or cultural environment differs greatly from that of the so-called free-market democracies.[22]

Throughout this text you will read about companies that have cut management positions which were viewed as deadweight. And if you have been reading the newspapers over the past few years, you will have noticed constant stories about organizations downsizing. So, as a student of management, you may be asking yourself, "What are the odds of me securing a management position when they are being cut so frequently?" Well, as it turns out, although several large companies are indeed cutting many management positions, the opportunities in the field of management have perhaps never been better.

Recent estimates have speculated that there will be a 17 percent growth in executive, administrative and managerial jobs over the next 10 years.[23] But these jobs may not be in the organizations or fields that you might expect. Although there may be fewer jobs for managers in the traditional, large companies, there are increasingly good prospects for managers in small and medium-sized organizations. Several growing fields also hold excellent opportunities for managers, such as new media development; telecommunications; employee assistance and training; non-profit agencies; and any information technology area including computer software, organizational intranets, and Internet World Wide Web content development. ■

WHY STUDY MANAGEMENT?

The reality is that for most of you, once you graduate and begin a career, you will either *manage* or *be managed*. Of course, it would be naïve to assume that everyone who studies management is planning a career in management. A course in management may simply be a requirement for a degree you want, but that shouldn't make studying management irrelevant. Assuming that you will have to work for a living and recognizing that you will almost certainly work in an organization, you will probably be a manager and/or work for a manager. You can gain a great deal of insight into the way your boss behaves and the internal workings of your organization by studying management. And in today's business environment, with an increased stress on empowerment and team-based work structures, even people who are not managers technically will most likely be called upon to perform some management functions. The point is that you don't have to aspire to be a manager to gain something valuable from a course in management.

7 **In what ways would the mayor's job in a large city and the CEO's job in a large corporation be similar? How would they differ?**

8 **How might the job of owner-manager of a small business compare with the job of CEO of a large corporation?**

9 **How might the study of management benefit a computer programming major who plans on (a) working for a large software development firm, or (b) starting his or her own software development firm?**

SUMMARY

This summary is organized by the learning objectives found at the beginning of the chapter.

1. Managers are individuals in an organization who direct the activities of others. They have titles such as supervisor, department head, dean, division manager, vice president, president, and chief operating officer.
2. The term management refers to the process of getting activities completed efficiently and effectively with and through other people. The process represents the functions or primary activities of planning, organizing, leading, and controlling.
3. Effectiveness is concerned with getting activities completed—that is, goal attainment. Efficiency is concerned with minimizing resource costs in the completion of those activities.
4. Planning involves defining an organization's goals and establishing strategies and plans to achieve these goals. Organizing includes designing a structure to carry out the plans. Leading involves directing and co-ordinating the organization's people. Finally, controlling includes monitoring, comparing, and correcting the organization's performance.
5. Henry Mintzberg concluded from his study of five chief executives that managers perform ten different roles or behaviours. He classified the roles into three sets. One set is concerned with interpersonal relationships (figurehead, leader, liaison). The second set relates to the transfer of information (monitor, disseminator, spokesperson). The third set deals with decision making (entrepreneur, disturbance handler, resource allocator, negotiator).
6. Robert Katz identified three skills managers need: technical, people, and conceptual. The relative importance of these skills varies according to the management level within the organization.
7. Management has several generic properties. Regardless of level in an organization, all managers perform the same four functions; however, the emphasis given to each function varies with the manager's position in the hierarchy. Similarly, for the most part, the manager's job is the same regardless of the type or size of organization he or she is in. These generic properties of management are found mainly in the world's English-speaking democracies, and it is therefore unwise to assume that they are universally transferable outside so-called free-market democracies.

THINKING ABOUT MANAGEMENT ISSUES

1. Would you describe management as a profession in the same way that law or accounting is a profession? Support your position.
2. Is your college instructor a manager? Discuss in terms of Fayol's managerial functions, Mintzberg's managerial roles, and Katz's skills.
3. Of the three skills Katz said managers need, in which are you the strongest? In which are you the weakest? What are the implications of your assessment?
4. Some so-called managers oversee only assembly-line robots or a roomful of computers. Can they really be managers if they have no subordinates?
5. Is there one best "style" of management? Why or why not?

SELF-ASSESSMENT EXERCISE

EXERCISE IN SELF-PERCEPTION

One of the most important things you can do in preparing yourself for a successful career is to get to know your own personal strengths and weaknesses. At the end of each chapter throughout this text, we have included a Self-Assessment Exercise for you to complete and score. These exercises can assist you in your own self-awareness journey.

Even though behavioural experts say we should "know ourselves", most research shows that the majority of people are very poor self-evaluators. Yet, how we perceive ourselves is crucial to how we perceive and deal with others. As a manager, your approach or style to managing will reflect you, and your personal characteristics. This chapter's Self-Assessment Exercise is designed to help you to begin to understand your own characteristics.

Self-Perception Rating Scale

Instructions: Each of the following paragraphs gives a description of personal characteristics that might or might not be true of you. For each statement, try to determine the degree to which the statement is typical of you. Try to be as objective as you can. Rate each statement according to the following scale:

7 The statement is very characteristic of me.
6 The statement is somewhat characteristic of me.
5 The statement is slightly characteristic of me.
4 The statement is neither characteristic nor uncharacteristic of me.
3 The statement is slightly uncharacteristic of me.
2 The statement is somewhat uncharacteristic of me.
1 The statement is very uncharacteristic of me.

_____ **1.** I resent suggestions, keep to my present ways, and tend to resist pressures to change.

_____ **2.** I am orderly, and tend to systematize things and people.

_____ **3.** I am disorganized, and live in a state of "clutter".

_____ **4.** I do each day's work well but resist and resent evaluation. I am inclined to get involved in busy work and avoid tasks that call for a lot of future planning and preparation.

_____ **5.** I tend to do a lot of dreaming, and have sometimes been referred to as an "idea" person, but have been accused of having lost a sense of proportion or perspective.

_____ **6.** I spend much of my time and energy in criticizing political parties, school, work, other people, and so on.

_____ **7.** I am a "worrier". Often I worry about things that have not happened or about things that are already over.

_____ **8.** I am sarcastic, sometimes towards others in my presence and sometimes towards others who are not present.

_____ **9.** I am likely to "nag" if things aren't going well.

_____ **10.** I am a procrastinator, putting off decisions until I have sought out and questioned others; often it is then too late to take the best action.

_____ **11.** I am what people could call "decisive". I am efficient, size things up quickly, and act so as to get results right away.

_____ **12.** I avoid becoming entangled in other people's emotional problems and usually find some excuse to get away from people who are about to "unload" on me.

_____ **13.** I consider myself an honest person. I am often quite frank even if the truth is painful to others.

_____ **14.** I am quite sensitive and often take things said very personally. I am likely to "fly off the handle" with little provocation.

_____ **15.** I find it very difficult to "step down in responsibility" to make room for others. Once I have gained a position with status, I find it difficult to give it up.

When you have finished completing the scale, transfer your rating for each paragraph to the feedback chart shown in the scoring section.

See scoring key beginning on page SK-1.

for your IMMEDIATE action

Heartland's Traditional Quality Scents & Fragrances

TO: Curt Johnson, Vice President
FROM: Chris Henson, President
SUBJECT: Management Development

As you know, our sales numbers just keep going up and up—a 15 percent increase during the first quarter of 1999, a 12 percent increase during the second quarter and then, of course, our strong holiday season sales increase of 33 percent. However, there is a downside. These continual sales increases are putting a strain on our current manufacturing supervisors, who must keep line employees motivated. I'm afraid that if we don't take some action soon to help train our managers in dealing with this demanding pace, our manufacturing employees are likely to get stressed out, and product quality may decline.

I think it's important for Heartland to develop a training program that would focus on skills that these supervisors are going to need to be more effective under these conditions. As a first step in the development of this program, I'd like you to put together a list of the skills that you think would be most important for our supervisors to have, together with a justification of why you think these skills are important. Please keep the information under two typed pages in length, and get it to me as soon as possible. Once we've had a chance to discuss what you come up with, we'll be ready to proceed with actually designing some skills training sessions.

This fictionalized memorandum was created for educational purposes only. It is not meant to reflect positively or negatively on management practices at Heartland Fragrance Company.

TAKE IT TO THE NET

We invite you to visit the Robbins/Coulter/Stuart-Kotze Companion Website at www.prenticehall.ca/robbins for this chapter's Internet resources.

CASE APPLICATION

Square Peg, Round Hole Syndrome—Why Some Management Positions Are Not For Everyone

Matt Scott, armed with a graduate degree in computer science, took a job in 1994 with Fore Systems Inc. Fore is a rapidly growing computer technology company that specializes in a computer networking system—known as asynchronous transfer mode (ATM)—that allows for vast amounts of information. For example, ATM allows real-time video and audio to be delivered at a far faster rate than most existing systems. When Matt joined Fore, the company had 200 employees. As at 1998, it had 1400, and annual revenues had reached $400 million. With this rapid growth, there has been the need for more managers and, increasingly, the need for formal management systems.

When Matt Scott joined Fore it was similar to many computer software companies, in that it offered a free-wheeling, often unstructured environment wherein employees could take on extra tasks if they chose to. Matt was up for it, and he reorganized the computer lab, took over the ordering of equipment, and organized seminars in which the company's disparate teams could share and compare notes. His energy and enthusiasm impressed management at the company—especially the director of software engineering. At the end of 1995, Matt was put into the leadership position of a new team project. As the four-person team's leader, Matt didn't expect much more than a greater role in the project's codewriting. But he quickly found himself facing his first management challenge. One team member strongly disagreed with Matt about what features should be included in the computer network design the team was working on. Team meetings became heated arguments between Matt and this team member, while the other two uncomfortably sat by. Eventually Matt managed to overcome this unproductive environment, and forced himself to listen objectively to the disagreements of the second team member. The team finally came together and was able to focus on the work.

In 1996—while the project continued—Matt was offered an official management position. The new job combined project team leadership with increased management responsibilities. Matt was uncertain about accepting the promotion, due to his fear of losing touch with the actual work which he enjoyed so much but, after talking it over with his wife, he decided to accept. The promotion meant a raise, a larger cubicle office, stock options, and a laptop to take home. But it also meant a large shift in the type of work Matt was doing. The project that his team was working on was given a strict deadline—to be ready for an upcoming trade show. The work pace for the team members became intense, but Matt's time was taken up preparing and distributing employee performance reviews—as he saw it, he was no longer part of the team. The growth of the company also brought with it increasing paperwork.

At the trade show, the team discovered that what they had created was far ahead of anything produced by the competition. Their final product was produced and began distribution in 1997. Matt, however, was dissatisfied. He did not feel part of the final accomplishment and, as a result, he gave up his promotion. He is now working in a hands-on role within a team, on a new project.

QUESTIONS

1. Analyze Matt's job as team leader and as a manager using Mintzberg's roles framework.
2. Which management skills do you think would be important in both the team leader position and the management position that Matt held? Did you identify similar or different skills for the two? Why?
3. Use both the systems and contingency perspectives to describe Matt's team leader and management positions.
4. Why do you think some individuals might find little job satisfaction in a manager's job? What do you think are the implications for both organizations and individuals?
5. What characteristics do you think might differentiate people who would find satisfaction in a management position from those who would not?

Source: M. Murray, "Who's the Boss?" *Wall Street Journal*, May 14, 1997, p. A1.

LEARNING OBJECTIVES

After Reading This Chapter, You Should Be Able To:

1. Explain the value of studying management history
2. Identify some major pre-twentieth-century contributions to management
3. Define Frederick Taylor's principles of scientific management
4. Summarize scientific management's contribution to management
5. Identify Henri Fayol's contributions to management
6. Describe Max Weber's ideal bureaucracy
7. Explain the contributions of the Hawthorne studies to management
8. Compare the approaches taken by human relations advocates and the behavioural science theorists
9. Distinguish between the process, systems, and contingency approaches
10. Describe how the following trends are affecting management practices: globalization; workforce diversity; information technology; continually learning and adapting organizations; total quality management; dismantling of the organizational hierarchy; and ethics and trust

A MANAGER'S CHALLENGE

Isabel Hoffman, CEO, I Hoffman + Associates Inc. (H+a), Toronto

Perhaps you've heard of Isabel Hoffman. She has been featured in many media stories over the past several years as an example of the new technologically savvy entrepreneur.

Her reputation on the lecture circuit is well established in Canada. Hoffman is still under 40, but her status as a technology guru has left people impatient to see her achieve phenomenal business success. H+a is still a young company—formed in 1992—but a lot is expected of Hoffman. It is simply assumed that her technical expertise, combined with her charisma and entrepreneurial drive, will bring her modern-day success of the sort pioneered by Bill Gates.

H+a began as a consultancy, providing expertise in the development of CD-ROMs, and eventually became a CD-ROM producer itself. H+A's products were manufactured and distributed by the giant of the Canadian software industry, Corel. But Corel had more pressing considerations to deal with—the purchase of WordPerfect had brought Corel into direct competition with a far, far greater giant—

Microsoft. Corel had little time to spend developing its CD-ROM line. Seeing her products going down the drain, Hoffman began negotiations to buy back the rights to her products. Corel was more than willing to agree and, in fact, was moreover willing to part with its CD-ROM division altogether. H+a bought Corel's CD-ROM line in 1997. Since then, H+a has had to divest itself of some of the unpromising products acquired from Corel, but has succeeded in turning many into good sellers—mainly through Hoffman's distribution abilities. Hoffman has marketed many of the CD-ROMs directly to target areas such as toy stores, bypassing the traditional computer store route. She has developed the company quickly, and her distribution skills have impressed the likes of Bill Gates's private company, Corbis Corp., which has a deal with H+a to distribute Corbis CD-ROMs. H+a has also landed a deal with Mitsubishi, allowing H+a access to the Asian market through Mitsubishi's on-line distribution network.

These moves have assured H+a greater presence in the marketplace. But Hoffman isn't resting on her laurels; she has major growth plans for H+a. Aware of the opportunities for the Internet to replace CD-ROMs as the medium for H+a's products, Hoffman is ready to switch as soon as technology allows the Internet the kind of rapid access that would rival the simplicity of downloading a CD-ROM. H+a is working with Mitsubishi as well as other companies, such as Bell Canada, on developing games for high-speed networks. Rather than resisting such a major change to the way her company does business, Hoffman is looking forward to it, due to the increased profitability that will accompany it. With the new technology, H+a will no longer have the burden of product inventory and the costs that go along with it. Moreover, H+a can market its products directly to consumers, "cutting out the middleperson" of retail.

Whatever direction the technology takes, Isabel Hoffman and H+a will surely be willing to move with it and use it to the company's best advantage.[1]

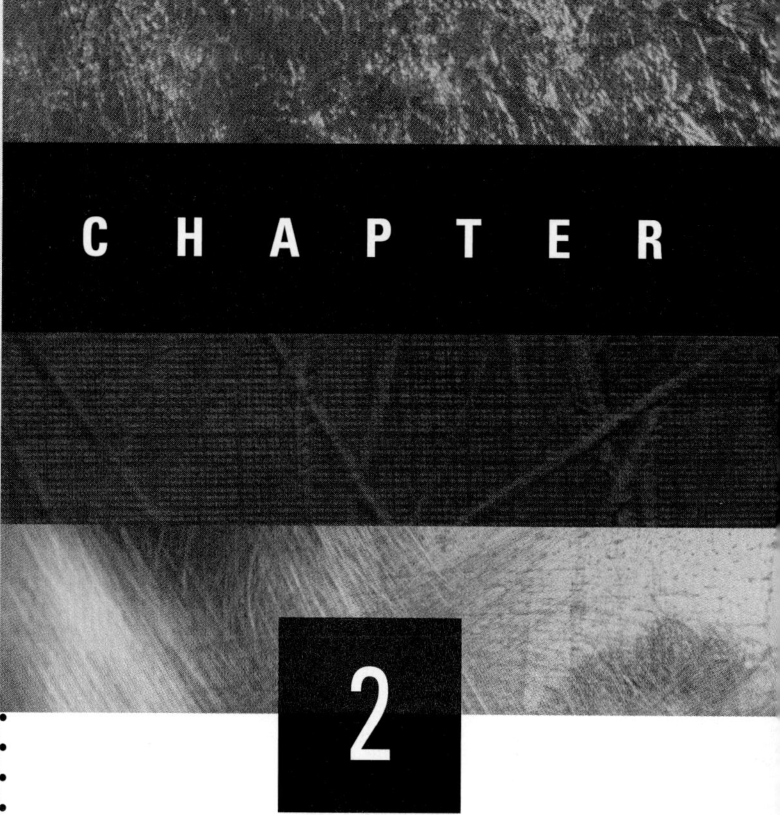

CHAPTER 2

The Evolution of Management

The purpose of this chapter is to demonstrate that a knowledge of management history can help you to understand theory and practice as they are today. We'll introduce you to the origins of many contemporary management concepts and show how they have evolved to reflect the changing needs of organizations, as well as society as a whole. We'll also introduce a number of important trends and issues which managers currently face, in order to link the past with the future and demonstrate that the field of management is still evolving—and how managers such as Isabel Hoffman are evolving with it.

HISTORICAL BACKGROUND

Organized endeavours directed by people responsible for planning, organizing, leading, and controlling activities have existed for thousands of years. The Egyptian pyramids and the Great Wall of China are tangible evidence that projects of tremendous scope, employing tens of thousands of people, were undertaken well before modern times. The pyramids are a particularly interesting example. The construction of a single pyramid occupied over 100 000 people for 20 years.[2] Who told each worker what to do? Who ensured that there would be enough stones at the site to keep workers busy? The answer to such questions is management. Regardless of what managers were called at the time, someone had to plan what was to be done, organize people and materials to do it, lead and direct the workers, and impose some controls to ensure that everything was done as planned.

These examples from the past demonstrate that organizations have been with us for thousands of years and that management has been practised for an equivalent period. However, it has only been in the past several hundred years, particularly in the last century, that management has undergone systematic investigation, acquired a common body of knowledge, and become a formal discipline for study. Two significant historical events also played a role in promoting the study of management.

division of labour
The breakdown of jobs into specific, repetitive tasks.

In 1776, Adam Smith published a classical economic doctrine, *The Wealth of Nations*, in which he argued the economic advantages that organizations and society would gain from the **division of labour**. By using the pin-manufacturing industry as an example, Smith claimed that 10 individuals, each doing a specialized task, could produce about 48 000 pins a day among them. However, if each person was working separately and had to draw wire, straighten it, cut it, pound heads for each pin, sharpen the point, and solder the head and pin shaft, it would be quite an accomplishment to produce a meagre 10 pins a day!

The largest of the pyramids contained more than 2 million blocks, each weighing several tons. The quarries the blocks came from were many miles from the sites where the pyramids were constructed. Someone had to design the structure, find a stone quarry, and arrange for the stones to be cut and moved—possibly over land and by water—to the construction site.

Smith concluded that division of labour increased productivity by increasing each worker's skill and dexterity, by saving time that is commonly lost in changing tasks, and by creating labour-saving inventions and machinery. The continued popularity of job specialization—in service jobs such as teaching and medicine, as well as on assembly lines—is undoubtedly due to the economic advantages cited over 200 years ago by Adam Smith.

Possibly the most important pre-twentieth-century influence on management was the **Industrial Revolution**. Starting in the eighteenth century in Great Britain, this revolution eventually made its way across the Atlantic to North America, and machine power rapidly began to take the place of human power. This, in turn, made it more economical to manufacture goods in factories. For instance, large numbers of blankets could be manufactured at a fraction of the previous cost in a factory where people did specialized tasks. Instead of one person working at home shearing the wool, twisting the wool into yarn, dying the yarn, weaving the blanket on a loom, and then selling the product to travelling merchants, machine power—combined with the division of labour—made it possible to have large, efficient factories using power-driven equipment. But these factories required managerial skills. Managers were needed to forecast demand, ensure that enough wool was on hand to make the yarn, assign tasks to people, direct daily activities, co-ordinate the various tasks, ensure that the machines were kept in good working condition and that output standards were maintained, find markets for the finished blankets, and so forth. When blankets were made individually at home, there was little concern with efficiency. Suddenly, however, when the factory owner had 100 people working and a regular payroll to meet, it became important to keep workers busy. Planning, organizing, leading and controlling became necessary.

Industrial Revolution
The advent of machine power, mass production, and efficient transportation.

The advent of machine power, mass production, the reduced transportation costs that followed the rapid expansion of the railroads, and the almost total absence of governmental regulation also supported the development of big corporations. John D Rockefeller (oil industry), Andrew Carnegie (steel industry), and other similar entrepreneurs were creating large businesses that would require formalized management practices. The need for a formal theory to guide managers in running their organizations had arrived. However, not until the early 1900s did the first major step towards developing such a theory occur.

THE EARLY YEARS

The first half of this century was a period of contrasts in management thinking. Scientific management looked at management from the perspective of how to improve the productivity of operative personnel. The general administrative theorists were concerned with the overall organization and how to make it more effective. One group of writers and researchers emphasized organizational behaviour—the human resource or "people side" of management, while another group focused on developing and applying quantitative models.

In this section we present the contributions of these four approaches (scientific management, general administrative, human resources, and quantitative). Keep in mind that each is concerned with the same "animal"; the differences reflect the backgrounds and interests of the writers.

Scientific Management

If you had to pinpoint the year in which modern management theory was born, 1911 would be a logical choice. That was the year in which Frederick Winslow Taylor's *Principles of Scientific Management* was published. Its contents would become widely accepted by managers throughout the world. The book described the theory of **scientific management**—the use of scientific methods to define the "one best way" for a job to be done. The studies conducted before and after the book's publication established Taylor as the "father" of scientific management.

scientific management
The use of the scientific method to define the "one best way" for a job to be done.

1 **What are the advantages of using division of labour in an organization?**

2 **How did the Industrial Revolution increase the need for a formal theory of management?**

FIGURE 2-1 **Development of Major Management Theories**

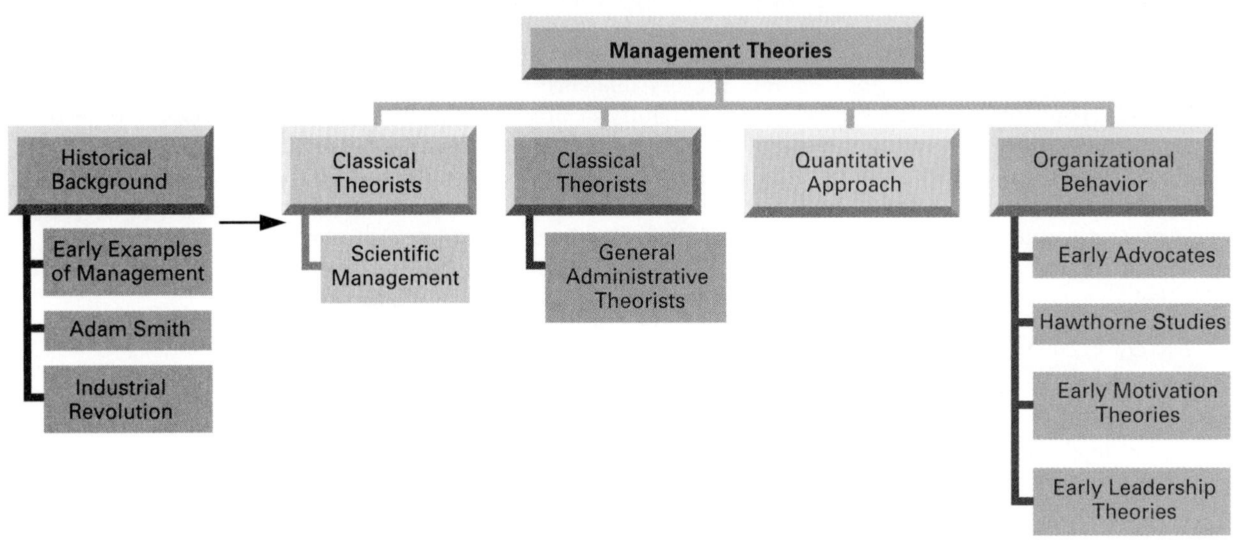

Frederick Taylor. Frederick Taylor did most of his work at the Midvale and Bethlehem steel companies in Pennsylvania. As a mechanical engineer with a Quaker and Puritan background, he was continually appalled by workers' inefficiencies. Employees used vastly different techniques to do the same job. They were inclined to "take it easy" on the job, and Taylor believed that worker output was only about a third of what was possible. Therefore, he set out to correct the situation by applying the scientific method to jobs on the shop floor. He spent more than two decades passionately pursuing the "one best way" for each job to be done.

It's important for you to understand what Taylor saw at Midvale that aroused his determination to improve the way in which things were done in the plant. At the time, there were no clear concepts of worker and management responsibilities. Virtually no effective work standards existed. Workers purposely worked at a slow pace. Management decisions were "seat of the pants", based on hunch and intuition. Workers were placed on jobs with little or no concern for matching their abilities and aptitudes to the tasks they were required to do. Most importantly, management and workers considered themselves to be in continual conflict.

Frederick Taylor (1856–1915) was the father of scientific management.

Rather than co-operating to their mutual benefit, they perceived their relationship as a zero-sum game—any gain by one would be at the expense of the other.

Taylor sought to create a mental revolution among both the workers and managers by defining clear guidelines for improving production efficiency. He defined four principles of management (see Table 2-1) and argued that following these principles would result in the prosperity of both managers and workers. Workers would earn more pay and managers would earn more profits.[3]

Probably the most widely cited example of scientific management was Taylor's pig iron experiment. Workers loaded "pigs" of iron weighing 92 pounds onto rail cars. Their daily average output was 12.5 tons. However, Taylor believed that by scientifically analyzing the job to determine the one best way to load pig iron, the output could be increased to between 47 and 48 tons per day. After a long period of scientifically trying various combinations of procedures, techniques and tools, Taylor succeeded in getting the level of productivity he thought possible. By putting the right person on the job with the correct tools and equipment, having the worker follow his instructions exactly, and motivating the worker with an economic incentive of a significantly higher daily wage, the 48-ton objective was reached.

Using similar approaches to other jobs, Taylor was able to define the "one best way" for doing each job. He could then, after selecting the right people for the job, train them to do it precisely in this one best way. To motivate workers, he favoured incentive wage plans. Overall, Taylor achieved consistent improvements in productivity in the range of 200 percent or more. He re-affirmed that the role of managers was to plan and control and that that of workers was to perform as they were instructed. Taylor's ideas spread to the United States and also to France, Germany, Russia and Japan. The early acceptance of scientific management techniques by US manufacturing companies gave them a comparative advantage over foreign firms, which made US manufacturing efficiency the envy of the world—at least for 50 years or so.

Frank and Lillian Gilbreth. Taylor's ideas inspired others to study and develop methods of scientific management. His most prominent followers were Frank and Lillian Gilbreth.

A construction contractor by trade, Frank Gilbreth gave up his contracting career in 1912 to study scientific management after hearing Taylor speak at a professional meeting. Frank and his wife Lillian, a psychologist, studied work arrangements to eliminate wasteful hand and body motions. The Gilbreths also experimented in the design and use of the proper tools and equipment for optimizing work performance.[4]

Frank Gilbreth is probably best known for his experiments in reducing the number of motions in bricklaying. By carefully analyzing the bricklayer's job, he reduced the number of motions in the laying of exterior brick from 18 to 4.5. On interior brick, the 18 motions were reduced to 2. Using Gilbreth's techniques, the bricklayer could be more productive and less fatigued at the end of the day.

The Gilbreths were among the first researchers to use motion pictures to study hand and body motions. They devised a microchronometer that recorded time to 1/2000 of a second, placed it in the field of study being photographed, and thus determined how long a worker

TABLE 2-1 Taylor's Four Principles of Management

1. Develop a science for each element of an individual's work, which replaces the old rule of thumb method.
2. Scientifically select and then train, teach and develop the worker. (Previously, workers chose their own work and trained themselves as best they could.)
3. Heartily co-operate with the workers so as to ensure that all work is done in accordance with the principles of the science that has been developed.
4. Divide work and responsibility almost equally between management and workers. Management takes over all work for which it is better fitted than the workers. (Previously, almost all the work and the greater part of the responsibility were thrown on the workers.)

Frank & Lillian Gilbreth, parents of 12 children, ran a super-efficient household. Two of their children wrote a book, *Cheaper by the Dozen,* that described life with the two masters of efficiency.

spent doing each motion. Wasted motions missed by the naked eye could be identified and eliminated. The Gilbreths also devised a classification scheme to label 17 basic hand motions—such as "search", "select", "grasp", "hold"—which they called **therbligs** (Gilbreth spelled backward with the "th" transposed). This allowed the Gilbreths a more precise way of analyzing the exact elements of any worker's hand movements.

therbligs
A classification scheme for labelling 17 basic hand motions.

Henry L Gantt. A close associate of Taylor at Midvale and Bethlehem Steel was a young engineer named Henry L Gantt.

However, Gantt is probably most noted for creating a graphic chart that could be used by managers as a scheduling device for planning and controlling work. The **Gantt chart** showed the relationship between work planned and completed on one axis, and time elapsed on the other. Innovative for its day, the Gantt chart allowed management to see how plans were progressing and allowed them to take the necessary action to keep projects on time. The Gantt chart and modern variations of it are still widely used in organizations today as a method of scheduling work.

Gantt chart
A graphic bar chart that shows the relationship between work planned and completed on one axis, and time elapsed, on the other.

General Administrative Theorists

Another group of writers looked at the subject of management but focused on the entire organization. We call them the **general administrative theorists**. They are important for developing more general theories of what managers do and what constitutes good management practice. Because their writings set the framework for many of our contemporary ideas on management and organization, this group and the scientific management group are frequently referred to as the **classical theorists**. The most prominent of the general administrative theorists were Henri Fayol and Max Weber.

general administrative theorists
Writers who developed general theories of what managers do and what constitutes good management practice.

classical theorists
The term used to describe the scientific management theorists and general administrative theorists.

Henri Fayol. We mentioned Henri Fayol in the previous chapter for having designated management as a universal set of functions that included planning, organizing, commanding, coordinating, and controlling.

Fayol wrote during the same time period as Taylor. However, whereas Taylor was concerned with management at the shop level (what we today would call the job of a supervisor) and used the scientific method, Fayol's attention was directed at the activities of all managers, and he wrote from personal experience. Taylor was a scientist. Fayol, the managing director of a large French coal-mining firm, was a practitioner.

Fayol described the practice of management as something distinct from accounting, finance, production, distribution, and other typical business functions. He argued that management was an activity common to all human endeavours in business, government, and even in the home. He then proceeded to state 14 **principles of management**—fundamental or

principles of management
Universal truths of management that can be taught in school.

universal truths—that could be taught in schools and universities. These principles are shown in Table 2-2.

Max Weber. Max Weber (pronounced Vay-ber) was a German sociologist. Writing in the early 1900s, Weber developed a theory of authority structures and described organizational activity based on authority relations.[5] He described an ideal type of organization that he called a **bureaucracy**. It was a system characterized by division of labour, a clearly defined hierarchy, detailed rules and regulations, and impersonal relationships. Weber recognized that this "ideal bureaucracy" didn't exist in reality but, rather, represented a selective reconstruction of the real world. He meant it as a basis for theorizing about work and how work could be done in large groups. His theory became the model for many of today's large organizations. The features of Weber's ideal bureaucratic structure are outlined in Table 2-3.

bureaucracy
A form of organization marked by division of labour, hierarchy, rules and regulations, and impersonal relationships.

Bureaucracy, as described by Weber, is a lot like scientific management in its ideology. Both emphasize rationality, predictability, impersonality, technical competence, and authoritarianism. Although Weber's writings were less operational than Taylor's, the fact that his "ideal type" still describes many contemporary organizations attests to the importance of his work.

TABLE 2-2 Fayol's 14 Principles of Management

1. *Division of Work.* This principle is the same as Adam Smith's "division of labour". Specialization increases output by making employees more efficient.
2. *Authority.* Managers must be able to give orders. Authority gives them this right. Along with authority, however, goes responsibility. Wherever authority is exercised, responsibility arises.
3. *Discipline.* Employees must obey and respect the rules that govern the organization. Good discipline is the result of effective leadership, a clear understanding between management and workers regarding the organization's rules, and the judicious use of penalties for infractions of the rules.
4. *Unity of Command.* Every employee should receive orders from only one superior.
5. *Unity of Direction.* Each group of organizational activities that have the same objective should be directed by one manager using one plan.
6. *Subordination of Individual Interests to the General Interest.* The interests of any one employee or group of employees should not take precedence over the interests of the organization as a whole.
7. *Remuneration.* Workers must be paid a fair wage for their services.
8. *Centralization.* This term refers to the degree to which subordinates are involved in decision making. Whether decision making is centralized (to management) or decentralized (to subordinates) is a question of proper proportion. The task is to find the optimum degree of centralization for each situation.
9. *Scalar Chain.* The line of authority from top management to the lowest ranks represents the scalar chain. Communications should follow this chain. However, if following the chain creates delays, cross-communications can be allowed if agreed to by all parties and if superiors are kept informed.
10. *Order.* People and materials should be in the right place at the right time.
11. *Equity.* Managers should be kind and fair to their subordinates.
12. *Stability of Tenure of Personnel.* High employee turnover is inefficient. Management should provide orderly personnel planning and ensure that replacements are available to fill vacancies.
13. *Initiative.* Employees who are allowed to originate and carry out plans will exert high levels of effort.
14. *Esprit de Corps.* Promoting team spirit will build harmony and unity within the organization.

3 Explain what relevance, if any, scientific management has to current management practice.

4 How do Fayol's principles of management compare with Taylor's?

TESTING...
TESTING...

TABLE 2-3 Weber's Ideal Bureaucracy

1. *Division of Labour.* Jobs are broken down into simple, routine, and well-defined tasks.
2. *Authority Hierarchy.* Offices or positions are organized in a hierarchy, each lower one being controlled and supervised by a higher one.
3. *Formal Selection.* All organizational members are to be selected on the basis of technical qualifications demonstrated by training, education, or formal examination.
4. *Formal Rules and Regulations.* To ensure uniformity and to regulate the actions of employees, managers must depend heavily on formal organizational rules.
5. *Impersonality.* Rules and controls are applied uniformly, avoiding involvement with personalities and personal preferences of employees.
6. *Career Orientation.* Managers are professional officials rather than owners of the units they manage. They work for fixed salaries and pursue their careers within the organization.

Putting the General Administrative Theorists into Perspective. A number of our current management ideas and practices can be directly traced to the contributions of the general administrative theorists. For instance, the functional view of a manager's job can be attributed to Henri Fayol. Also, although many of his management principles may not be universally applicable to today's wide variety of organizations, they become a frame of reference against which many current concepts and theories have evolved.

Weber's bureaucracy was an attempt to formulate an ideal prototype for designing organizations. This was a response to the abuses that Weber saw going on within organizations of that time. Weber believed that his model could remove the ambiguity, inefficiencies and patronage that characterized many organizations. Although many of bureaucracy's characteristics are still evident in large organizations today, it's not as popular as it was a decade ago. Many of today's managers feel that bureaucracy's emphasis on strict division of labour, adherence to formal rules and regulations, and impersonal application of rules and controls, takes away the individual employee's creativity and flexibility to respond to the dynamic and complex changes taking place in the global market.

Towards Understanding Organizational Behaviour

Managers get things done by working with people. This explains why some writers and researchers have chosen to look at management by focusing on the organization's human resources. The field of study concerned with the actions (behaviour) of people at work is called **organizational behaviour (OB)**. Much of what currently makes up the field of human resources (personnel) management, as well as contemporary views on motivation, leadership, teamwork, and conflict management, have come out of organizational behaviour research.

organizational behaviour (OB) The field of study concerned with the actions (behaviour) of people at work.

Early Advocates. While there were undoubtedly a number of people in the late 1800s and early 1900s who recognized the importance of the human factor to an organization's success, four individuals stand out as early advocates of the human resources approach. They include Robert Owen, Hugo Munsterberg, Mary Parker Follett and Chester Barnard.

Robert Owen was a successful Scottish businessman who bought his first factory in 1789 when he was just 18. Repulsed by the harsh practices he saw in factories across Scotland—such as the employment of young children (many under the age of 10), 13-hour workdays, and miserable working conditions—Owen became a social reformer. He chided factory owners for treating their equipment better than they did their workers. He argued that money spent on improving labour was one of the best investments that business executives could make. He claimed that showing concern for employees was highly profitable for management and would relieve human misery.

Owen proposed an idealistic workplace in which work hours would be regulated, child labour would be outlawed, public education would be provided, meals at work would be supplied, and businesses would be involved in community projects.[6] As one author noted, Owen is remembered more in management theory for his courage and commitment to reducing the suffering of the working class, than he is for his management successes.[7]

Hugo Munsterberg created the field of industrial psychology—the scientific study of individuals at work to maximize their productivity and adjustment. In his text, *Psychology and Industrial Efficiency*, published in 1913, he argued for the scientific study of human behaviour to identify general patterns and to explain individual differences.[8] He suggested the use of psychological tests to improve employee selection, the value of learning theory in the development of training methods, and the study of human behaviour in order to understand what techniques are most effective for motivating workers. Interestingly, he saw a connection between scientific management and industrial psychology. Both sought increased efficiency through scientific work analyses and through better alignment of individual skills and abilities with the demands of various jobs. Much of our current knowledge of selection techniques, employee training, job design, and motivation is built on the work of Munsterberg.

One of the earliest writers to recognize that organizations could be viewed from the perspective of individual and group behaviour was *Mary Parker Follett*.[9] Follett was a social philosopher in the early 1900s who proposed more people-oriented ideas, a radical change from the scientific management theories being promoted. Follett thought that organizations should be based rather on a group ethic than on individualism. She argued that individual potential remained only potential until it was released through group association. Her concepts had clear implications for management practice. The implication was that managers and workers should view themselves as partners—as part of a common group. As such, managers should rely more on their expertise and knowledge to lead subordinates, than the formal authority of their position. Her humanistic ideas influenced the way we look at motivation, leadership, teamwork, power and authority.

Chester Barnard was another person whose ideas bridged the classical and human resources viewpoints. Like Fayol, Barnard was a practitioner—he was president of New Jersey Bell Telephone Company. He had read Weber and was influenced by his writings. But unlike Weber, who had a mechanistic and impersonal view of organizations, Barnard saw organizations as social systems requiring human co-operation. He expressed his views in his book, *The Functions of the Executive*, published in 1938.[10]

Barnard believed that organizations were made up of people who had interacting social relationships. The manager's roles were to communicate and stimulate subordinates to high levels of effort. A major part of an organization's success, as Barnard saw it, depended on obtaining co-operation from its people. Barnard also argued that success depended on maintaining good relations with external groups and institutions with whom the organization regularly interacted. By recognizing the organization's dependence on investors, suppliers, customers and other external constituencies, Barnard introduced the idea that managers had to

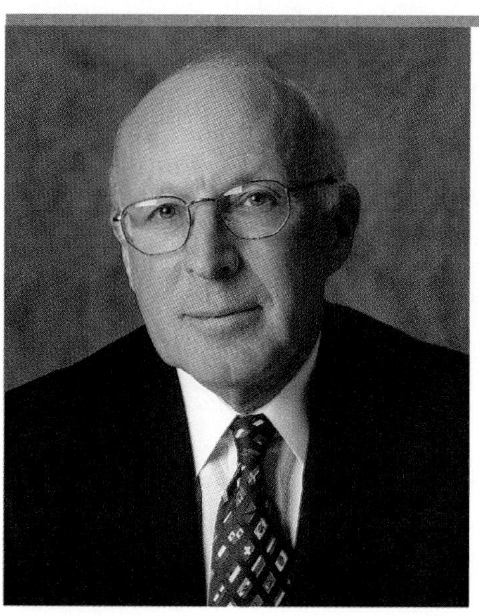

The measure of a company's *transnationality* is based on the percentage of that company's foreign business as compared to its domestic business. In the United Nations' rankings of companies with at least (U.S.) $4.5 billion in foreign assets, Canadian-owned Thomson Corp. (deputy chairman Michael Brown pictured here) was the *most* transnational company in the world.

examine the environment and then adjust the organization, in order to maintain a state of equilibrium. Regardless of how efficient an organization's production might be, if management failed to ensure a continuous input of materials and supplies or find markets for its outputs, then the organization's survival would be threatened.

Hawthorne studies
A series of studies during the 1920s and 1930s that provided new insights in group norms and behaviour.

The Hawthorne Studies. Without question, the most important contribution to the organizational behaviour approach to management came out of the **Hawthorne studies**, performed at the Western Electric Company's Hawthorne Works in Cicero, Illinois. These studies, originally started in 1924 but eventually expanded and carried on through the early 1930s, were initially devised by Western Electric industrial engineers to examine the effect of various illumination levels on worker productivity. Control and experimental groups were established. The experimental group was exposed to various lighting intensities while the control group worked under a constant intensity. The engineers had expected individual output to be directly related to the intensity of the light. However, they found that as the level of light was increased in the experimental group, output for both groups increased. To the surprise of the engineers, as the light level was decreased in the experimental group, productivity continued to increase in both groups. In fact, a productivity decrease was observed in the experimental group only when the level of light was reduced to that of a moonlit night. The engineers concluded that illumination intensity was not directly related to group productivity, but they could not explain the results they had witnessed.

In 1927, the Western Electric engineers asked Harvard professor Elton Mayo and his associates to join the study as consultants. Thus began a relationship that would last through 1932 and encompass numerous experiments in the redesigning of jobs, changes in workday and workweek length, introduction of rest periods, and individual versus group wage plans.[11] For example, one experiment was designed to evaluate the effect of a group piecework incentive pay system on group productivity. The results indicated that the incentive plan had less effect on a worker's output than did group pressure and acceptance, and the accompanying security. Social norms or standards of the group, therefore, were concluded to be the key determinants of individual work behaviour.

Emad Rizkalla, 30 years old, is president of Newfoundland information technology company Zeddcomm, which specializes in health care software. Zeddcomm produces software packages that allow medical professionals to create databases with fast access to information.

TESTING... TESTING...

5 Does Weber's view consider the needs of individual employees?

6 Why weren't human and social concerns given as much attention by early management theorists?

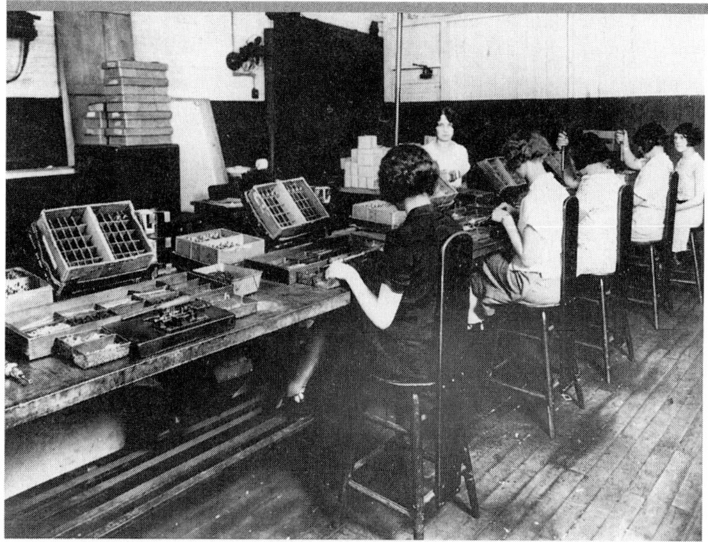

These women were part of the experiments at the Hawthorne plant of Western Electric. The Hawthorne Studies emphasized that a worker was not a machine, and scientific management's "one best way" approach had to be modified to recognize the effects of group behaviour.

Scholars generally agree that the Hawthorne studies had a dramatic impact on the direction of management thought. Mayo concluded that behaviour and sentiments were closely related, that group influences significantly affected individual behaviour, that group standards established individual worker output, and that money was less a factor in determining output than were group standards, group sentiments, and security. These conclusions led to a new emphasis on the human factor in the functioning of organizations and the attainment of their goals. They also led to increased paternalism by management.

However, the Hawthorne studies have not been without critics. Attacks have been made on procedures, analyses of findings, and the conclusions reached.[12] However, from an historical standpoint, it is of little importance whether the studies were academically sound or their conclusions justified. What is important is that they stimulated an interest in human factors in organizations. The Hawthorne studies played a significant role in changing the dominant view at the time that employees were no different from any other machines that the organization used—that is, they were there only to help the organization to efficiently reach its goals.

human relations movement The belief, for the most part unsubstantiated by research, that a satisfied worker will be productive.

The Human Relations Movement. Another group within the human resources approach is important to management history for its persistent commitment to making management practices more humane. Members of the **human relations movement** uniformly believed in the importance of employee satisfaction—a satisfied worker was believed to be a productive

Abraham Maslow (1908–1970), a humanistic psychologist, gave us one of our most widely recognized theories of motivation. Maslow believed that people possess an innate inclination to develop their potential and seek self-actualization.

worker. For the most part, names associated with this perspective—Dale Carnegie, Abraham Maslow and Douglas McGregor—were people whose views were shaped more by their personal philosophies than by substantive research evidence.

Dale Carnegie is often overlooked by management scholars, but his ideas and teachings have had an enormous impact on management practice. His book, *How to Win Friends and Influence People,*[13] was read by millions during the 1930s, 1940s and 1950s. In addition, during this same time period, numerous managers and aspiring managers attended his speeches and seminars.

What was the theme of Carnegie's book and lectures? Basically, he said that the way to success was through winning the co-operation of others. He advised that being a success meant (1) making others feel important through a sincere appreciation of their efforts; (2) making a good first impression; (3) winning people to your way of thinking by letting others do the talking, being sympathetic, and "never telling a man he is wrong"; and (4) changing people by praising good traits and giving the offender the opportunity to save face.[14]

Abraham Maslow was a humanistic psychologist who proposed a theoretical hierarchy of human needs: physiological, safety, social, esteem, and self-actualization.[15] In terms of motivation, Maslow argued that each level in the hierarchy must be satisfied before the next could be activated, and that once a need was substantially satisfied it no longer motivated behaviour. Managers who accepted Maslow's hierarchy attempted to change their organizations and management practices so that employees' needs could be satisfied. In Chapter 15, we'll discuss and evaluate Maslow's need hierarchy in more detail.

Douglas McGregor is best known for his formulation of two sets of assumptions about human nature—Theory X and Theory Y.[16] Very simply, Theory X presents an essentially negative view of people. It assumes that they have little ambition, dislike work, want to avoid responsibility, and need to be closely directed in order to work effectively. Theory Y offers a positive view. It assumes that people can exercise self-direction, accept responsibility, and consider work to be as natural as rest or play. McGregor believed that Theory Y assumptions best captured the true nature of workers and should guide management practice. These assumptions will also be discussed more fully in Chapter 15.

The common thread that united human relations supporters was an unshakeable optimism about people's capabilities. They believed strongly in their cause and were steadfast in their beliefs, even when faced with contradictory evidence. Of course, despite this lack of objectivity, advocates of the human relations movement had a definite influence on management theory and practice.

Behavioural Science Theorists. One final category within the human resources approach encompasses a group of psychologists and sociologists who relied on the scientific method for the study of organizational behaviour. Unlike the theorists of the human relations movement, the **behavioural science theorists** engaged in objective research of human behaviour in organizations. They carefully attempted to keep their personal beliefs out of their work. They sought to develop rigorous research designs that could be replicated by other behavioural researchers. In so doing, they hoped to build a science of organizational behaviour.

behavioural science theorists
Psychologists and sociologists who relied on the scientific method for the study of organizational behavior.

Psychologists such as Fred Fiedler, Victor Vroom, Frederick Herzberg, Edwin Locke, David McClelland and Richard Hackman have made important contributions to our current understanding of leadership, employee motivation and job design. Researchers with a sociological perspective have also made significant contributions to our understanding of organizational behaviour. For instance, Jeffrey Pfeffer, Kenneth Thomas and Charles Perrow have added important insights to our understanding of power, conflict and organizational design. The contributions of these behavioural scientists are covered in later chapters.

Putting the Human Resources Contributors into Perspective. Both the scientific management and the general administrative theorists viewed organizational employees as machines. Managers were the engineers. They ensured that the inputs were available and that the machine was properly maintained. Any failure by employees to generate the desired output was viewed as an engineering problem. Contributors to the human resources approach forced managers in many organizations to re-assess this simplistic machine model view.

The Quantitative Approach

We close our discussion of the early years of management with a review of quantitative contributions. This approach has also been labelled as *operations research* or *management science*. It evolved out of the development of mathematical and statistical solutions to military problems during World War II.

After World War II, many quantitative techniques that had been applied to military problems were moved into the business sector. One group of military officers—nicknamed the "Whiz Kids"—joined Ford Motor Company in the mid-1940s, and immediately began using statistical methods and quantitative models to improve decision making at Ford. Two of these individuals whose names are most recognizable are Robert McNamara, who went on to become president of Ford, US Secretary of Defence, and head of the World Bank; and Charles "Tex" Thornton, who founded the billion-dollar conglomerate, Litton Industries. What are the quantitative techniques that people such as McNamara and Thornton helped to develop and apply?

The **quantitative approach** to management includes applications of statistics, optimization models, information models and computer simulations. Linear programming, for instance, is a technique that managers can use to improve resource allocation decisions. Work scheduling can be more efficient as a result of critical path scheduling analysis. Decisions on determining the optimum inventory levels a company should maintain have been significantly influenced by the economic order quantity model.

quantitative approach
The use of quantitative techniques to improve decision making.

The quantitative approach has contributed most directly to management decision making in planning and control. However, the quantitative approach has never gained the influence on management practice that the human resources approach has, for a number of reasons: many managers are unfamiliar with the quantitative tools; behavioural problems are more widespread and visible; and most students and managers can relate more easily to real, day-to-day people problems than to the more abstract activity of constructing quantitative models. Yet the quantitative approach and the widespread availability of sophisticated computer software programs to aid in the development of models, equations, and formulas have added another dimension to the evolution of management practice and thinking. We cover many of these techniques in Chapters 9 and 20.

RECENT YEARS: TOWARDS INTEGRATION

We have covered four perspectives on management: the view of the foreperson or supervisor, the whole organization, the manager as guiding and directing human resources, and the manager as developing quantitative models to make optimizing decisions. Each perspective has validity but no single approach provides all the answers. Occasional efforts were made during the early years to synthesize the major writings of the time. For instance, in the early 1940s, Lyndall Urwick published *The Elements of Administration,* in which he noted numerous similarities in thought and terminology between scientific management and the general administrative theorists.[17] But these were exceptions. Concern with developing a unifying framework for management began in earnest only in the early 1960s. Like most fields of study, management, in its maturity, has moved towards integration.

The Process Approach

In December 1961, Professor Harold Koontz published an article in which he carefully detailed the different approaches to the study of management and concluded that there existed a "management theory jungle".[18] Koontz conceded that each of the approaches had something to offer management theory, but then proceeded to argue that (1) the human resources and quantitative approaches were not equivalent to the field of management, but rather were tools to be used by managers; and (2) a process approach could encompass and synthesize the various viewpoints. The **process approach**, originally introduced by Henri Fayol, is based on the management functions we discussed in the last chapter. The performance of these functions—planning, organizing, leading and controlling—is seen as circular and continuous. (Refer back to Figure 1-4.)

process approach
Management performs the functions of planning, organizing, leading and controlling.

Although Koontz's commentary stimulated considerable debate, most management teachers and practitioners held fast to their own individual perspectives.[19] But Koontz had made his mark. The fact that most current management textbooks follow the process approach is evidence that it continues to be a viable integrative framework. Look back at A Manager's Challenge and see if you can identify how Isabel Hoffman engages in the management process.

The Systems Approach

systems approach
A theory that sees an organization as a set of interrelated and interdependent parts.

closed systems
Systems that are not influenced by, and do not interact with, their environment.

open systems
Dynamic systems that interact with, and respond to, their environment.

During the 1960s, researchers began to analyze organizations from a systems perspective. The **systems approach** defines a system as a set of interrelated and interdependent parts arranged in a manner that produces a unified whole. Societies are systems and so, too, are automobiles, animals and human bodies. The systems perspective, for instance, has been used by physiologists to explain how animals maintain an equilibrium state by taking in inputs and generating outputs.

The two basic types of systems are closed and open. **Closed systems** are not influenced by, and do not interact with, their environment. Frederick Taylor's machine-like view of people and organizations was essentially a closed-systems perspective. In contrast, an **open-systems** approach recognizes the dynamic interaction of the system with its environment. Although Barnard proposed the idea of organizations as open systems in the 1930s, widespread acceptance of the notion took another 30 years. Today, when we talk of organizations as systems, we mean open systems; that is, we accept the organization's constant interaction with its environment.

Figure 2-2 shows a diagram of an organization from an open-systems perspective. For a business firm, inputs include raw materials, human resources, capital, technology and information. The transformation process turns these inputs into finished products or services through employees' work activities, management activities, and the organization's technology and operations methods. Outputs include products and services, financial results (profits, breaking even, or losses), information, and human results such as employees' levels of job satisfaction and productivity. In addition, the system's ultimate success depends on effective interactions with its environment (those groups or institutions on which it depends). These might include suppliers, labour unions, financial institutions, government agencies, and customers. For a business organization, the sale of products and services generates revenue that

FIGURE 2-2 The Systems Approach

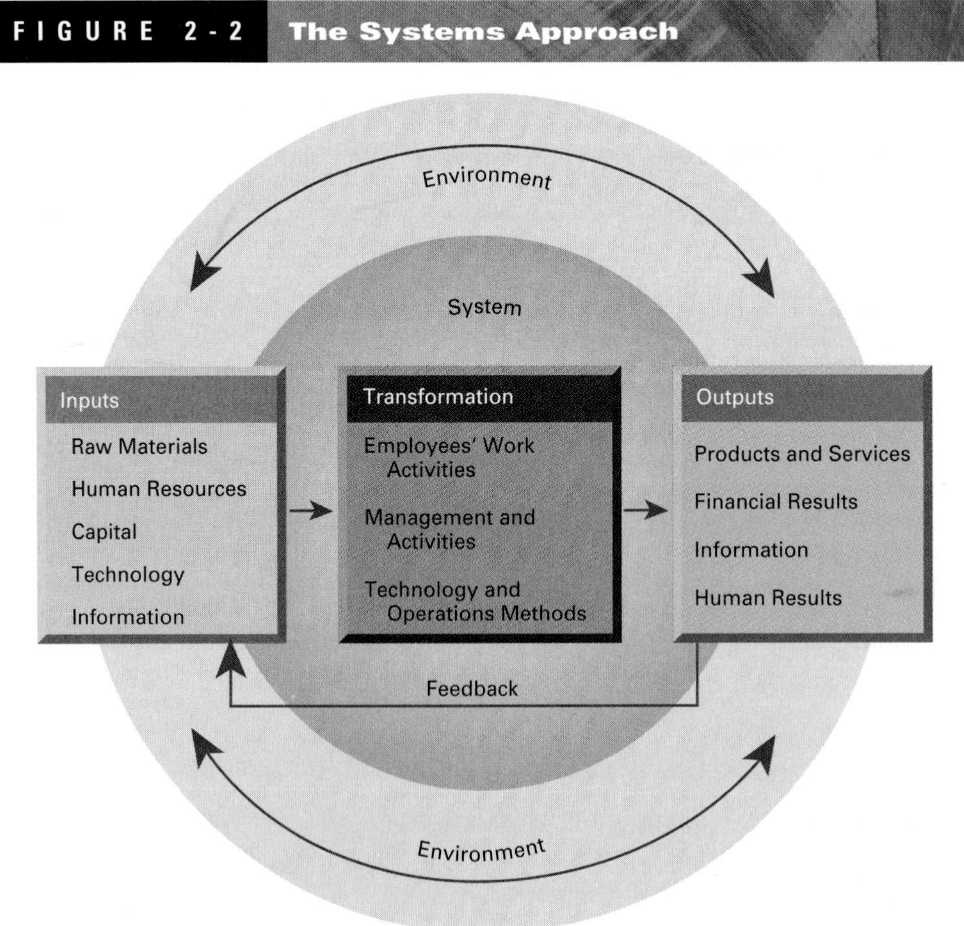

can be used to pay wages and taxes, buy more inputs, repay loans and generate profits for the owners. If revenues aren't enough to satisfy environmental demands, the organization downsizes or dies. We use the concept of an organization as an open system as we discuss in detail, in Chapter 3, how management must understand its environment and the constraints it imposes.

How can the systems perspective be used to integrate the various approaches to management? How could Isabel Hoffman (from A Manager's Challenge) use the concept of an open system to help her to change the way she manages her organization? Systems advocates envision the organization as being made up of "interdependent factors, including individuals, groups, attitudes, motives, formal structure, interactions, goals, status, and authority".[20] The job of a manager is to ensure that all parts of the organization are co-ordinated internally so that the organization's goals can be achieved. For example, a systems view of management would recognize that, regardless of how efficient the production department might be, if the marketing department doesn't anticipate changes in consumer tastes and work with the product development department in creating products consumers want, the organization's overall performance will suffer. Likewise, if the purchasing department fails to acquire the right quantity and quality of inputs, the production department will not be able to do its job effectively. So the systems approach recognizes the interdependence of the various activities within the organization.

In addition, the open-systems approach recognizes that organizations are not self-contained. They rely on their environment for essential inputs, and as sources to absorb their outputs. No organization can survive for long if it ignores government regulations, supplier relations, or the varied external constituencies on which it depends.

The Contingency Approach

Management, like life itself, is not based on simplistic principles. Insurance companies know that everyone doesn't have the same probability of being in an auto accident. Factors such as age, gender, past driving record, and number of miles driven per year are *contingencies* which influence accident rates. Similarly, you can't say that students always learn more in small classes than in large ones. Research tells us that contingency factors such as course content and the teaching style of the instructor influence the relationship between class size and learning effectiveness. The **contingency approach** (sometimes called the situational approach) has been used in recent years to replace simplistic principles of management and to integrate much of management theory.[21]

contingency approach Recognizing and responding to situational variables as they arise.

Early management contributors such as Taylor, Fayol and Weber gave us principles of management and organization that they generally assumed to be universally applicable. Later research, however, found exceptions to many of their principles. Division of labour, for example, is undoubtedly valuable in many situations, but jobs can also become too specialized. Bureaucracy as a structural form is desirable in many situations but, in other places, other structural designs are *more* effective. Allowing employees to participate in decision making is sometimes a preferred leadership style, but not all the time.

A contingency approach to management is intuitively logical. Since organizations are diverse—in size, objectives, tasks being done, and the like—it would be surprising to find universally applicable principles that would work in *all* situations. But, of course, it is one thing to say, *"It all depends"*, and another to say *what* it depends on. Management researchers have been trying to identify these "what" variables. Table 2-4 describes four popular contingency variables. This list is not comprehensive—at least 100 different variables have been identified—but it represents those most widely in use and gives you an idea of what we mean by the term *contingency variables*.

7 Describe the Hawthorne studies and their contribution to management practice.

8 Explain how practising managers can benefit by using the contingency approach.

TABLE 2-4 Popular Contingency Variables

Organization Size. The number of people in an organization is a major influence on what managers do. As size increases, so do the problems of co-ordination. For instance, the type of organizational structure appropriate for an organization of 50 000 employees is likely to be inefficient for an organization of 50 employees.

Routineness of Task Technology. In order for an organization to achieve its purpose, it uses technology; that is, it engages in the process of transforming inputs into outputs. Routine technologies require organizational structures, leadership styles, and control systems that differ from those required by customized or non-routine technologies.

Environmental Uncertainty. The degree of uncertainty caused by political, technological, sociocultural, and economic changes influences the management process. What works best in a stable and predictable environment may be totally inappropriate in a rapidly changing and unpredictable environment.

Individual Differences. Individuals differ in terms of their desire for growth, autonomy, tolerance for ambiguity, and expectations. These and other individual differences are particularly important when managers select motivation techniques, leadership styles and job designs.

CURRENT TRENDS AND ISSUES

Where are we today? What current management concepts and practices are shaping "tomorrow's history"? In this section, we'll attempt to answer these questions by introducing a number of trends and issues that are changing the way in which managers do their jobs. These include workforce diversity, ethics, innovation and change, total quality management, re-engineering, empowerment and teams, downsizing, and contingent workers. Throughout the text, we focus more closely on many of these themes in the various boxes, examples, and exercises included in the chapters.

Globalization

McCain Foods
www.mccain.com

Organizational operations no longer stop at national borders. A great many Canadian companies may be based here, but operate worldwide. Macmillan Bloedel has sadly been a prime example of a Canadian company which receives over 70 percent of its sales through exports. New Brunswick's McCain Foods—the world's largest french-fry producer—does business in places like Argentina, Brazil and India. Many people in eastern Canada would be surprised to hear that Tim Horton Donuts is in fact owned by the American fast-food corporation, Wendy's. Similarly, many Americans would be shocked to learn that Burger King is in fact owned by the Irish brewing company, Guinness. The world has undoubtedly become a global village and statistics showing that over 60 percent of Canadian manufactured goods are exported make it clear that we are indeed a part of this phenomenon.

Managers in organizations of all sizes and types around the world are faced with the opportunities and challenges of operating in a global market. Globalization is such a significant topic that we have devoted all of Chapter 4 to it, and we have also integrated the discussion of its impact on various management functions mentioned throughout the text. In fact, you will find that many of the opening managers' challenges sections, end-of-chapter cases, and manager profiles feature managers and organizations operating on the global stage.

workforce diversity
Employees in organizations are heterogeneous in terms of gender, race, ethnicity or other characteristics.

Workforce Diversity

Today's organizations are characterized by **workforce diversity**: that is, workers are more heterogeneous in terms of gender, race and ethnicity. But diversity includes anyone who is different—the physically disabled, the elderly, and even those who are significantly overweight.

Until very recently, organizations took a "melting pot" approach to differences. It was assumed that people who were different would somehow automatically want to assimilate. But we now recognize that employees don't set aside their cultural values and lifestyle preferences when they come to work. The challenge for management, therefore, is to make their organizations more accommodating to diverse groups of people by addressing different lifestyles, family needs and work styles. The "melting pot" assumption is being replaced by the recognition and celebration of differences.[22]

There is a new consciousness too. People are less willing to be assimilated, even if only at work. As diversity expert Roosevelt Thomas Jr. puts it, prospective employees are saying: "I'm different and proud of what makes me so. I can help your team and would like to join you, but only if I can do so without compromising my uniqueness".

Some managers perceive multiculturalism as a threat. However, Canada's diversity, making it in some sense a microcosm of the globe, is one of the greatest competitive advantages we could have and could be the key to our success in the global economy. Without diversity of thought and without workers feeling valued for their individuality and uniqueness, firms can spend millions on quality efforts to little or no avail. We will highlight many diversity-related issues and how companies are responding to these issues, throughout the text, using Managing Workforce Diversity boxes.

Information Technology

Information technology (IT) has had (and continues to have) a significant impact on the way in which organizations are managed. IT has created the ability to circumvent the physical confines of doing work only in a specified organizational location. With notebook and desktop computers, fax capabilities, high-speed modems, organizational intranets, and other forms of IT, organizational members can do their work anywhere, and at flexible times.

What are the implications of this vast spread of IT? One important implication is that employees' job skill requirements will increase. Workers will need the ability to read and comprehend software and hardware manuals, technical journals and detailed reports. This shift has already occurred to a large degree. A poll published in 1998 by *Maclean's* magazine found that the majority of Canadians are comfortable in the computer-dominated work environment—10 years previously the statistic would probably have swung heavily the other way.

Another implication of the spread of IT is that it tends to level the competitive playing field. IT provides organizations (no matter what their size or market power) with the ability to innovate, bring products to market rapidly, and respond quickly to customer requests. One company that supplies organizations with IT software is Descartes Systems Group Inc. of Waterloo, Ontario. Descartes has a 6 percent market share of the estimated $1 billion industry—providing industries such as the courier business or baked goods companies with supply-chain management software which allows total control of inventory, and reductions in the lag time between orders and delivery.

Of course, we can't have a discussion about IT without mentioning the impact of the Internet and the World Wide Web. Most of the organizations mentioned in this textbook, regardless of size, have Websites. And indeed this textbook itself has one: <www.prenhall.com./robbinsmgt>. The role of IT and its effect on the design of organizational structure will be discussed more fully in Chapter 10.

Ethics and Trust

Many observers believe that we are currently suffering an ethics crisis. Behaviours that were once thought unacceptable in organizations—lying, cheating, misrepresenting, covering up mistakes—have become, in many people's eyes, acceptable or necessary practices. Figure 2-3 shows the results of another survey of ethical issues administered to managers and students. What would your responses have been?

Concern over this perceived decline in ethical standards is being addressed at two levels. First, ethics education is being widely expanded in college curricula. For instance, the main accrediting agency for business schools now requires all its members to integrate ethical issues throughout their business curricula. Second, organizations themselves are creating codes of ethics, introducing ethics training programs and hiring ethics officers.

In Chapter 5, we'll discuss fundamental concepts relating to managerial ethics. In addition, we have included Thinking Critically About Ethics sections in each chapter.

Elvie Paryano has helped the Montreal Children's Hospital re-engineer its operations for greater efficiency.

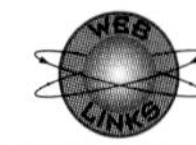

MacMillan Bloedel
www.mbltd.com

psychological contracts
The unwritten commitments and perceived obligations between workers and employers.

There seems to be a feeling, particularly given the seemingly callous nature with which some organizations lay off employees or re-engineer work processes, that organizations cannot be trusted. Vancouver forestry giant MacMillan Bloedel is sadly a prime example of this distrust between employees and management. Many observers feel that the **psychological contracts**, the unwritten commitments and perceived obligations between workers and their employers, have been violated.[23] In the past, employers essentially guaranteed workers long-term job security. In return, employees responded with hard work, commitment and loyalty. When employers broke this covenant through actions such as downsizing or re-engineering, employees responded in kind. Employees often no longer feel obligated to stay with one organization. In addition, employees have lost trust in their employers as a result of such practices as failing to confront poor performers, under-rewarding high performers, ignoring charges of workplace harassment, turning promotion decisions into political contests, and simply ignoring the grievances and suggestions of employees.

There's no doubt that the workplace has changed. The old loyalty bonds between employers and employees have loosened significantly. Yet, given the dynamic global competitive environment that organizations face today, the old employment relationships (that is, the old psychological contracts that were appropriate for a more stable time) are probably no longer realistic. The paradox is that the new technology-based organizational structures, the structural design options, and the practice of empowerment, all require *increased* trust within organizations. The issue of rebuilding trust is one that managers will have to address in order to provide a work environment in which all organizational members are encouraged and allowed to contribute their best. Employees have to trust management to treat them fairly, and management has to trust workers to conscientiously fulfill their work responsibilities.

Some organizations are taking steps to create this type of environment. For example, Kodak has developed a "social contract" in which workers pledge to better understand the business and the customers, to adapt to change, and to give 100 percent effort. In return, the company pledges to provide extensive employee training, career development and appraisal of managers' performance.[24] Although Kodak's actions are a good example of what organizations might do to rebuild employee trust, managers everywhere have the same challenge—to understand how current trends and issues, such as ethics and trust, affect the way in which they manage.

Continually Learning and Adaptive Organizations

The organizational world that existed when Taylor, Fayol, Weber or even Koontz were writing no longer exists. Managers now confront an environment in which change is taking place at an unprecedented rate; new competitors spring up overnight and old ones disappear through mergers and acquisitions, or by failing to keep up with the changing marketplace. Constant innovations in computer and telecommunications technologies, combined with the globalization of product and financial markets, have created a chaotic world. As a result, many of the

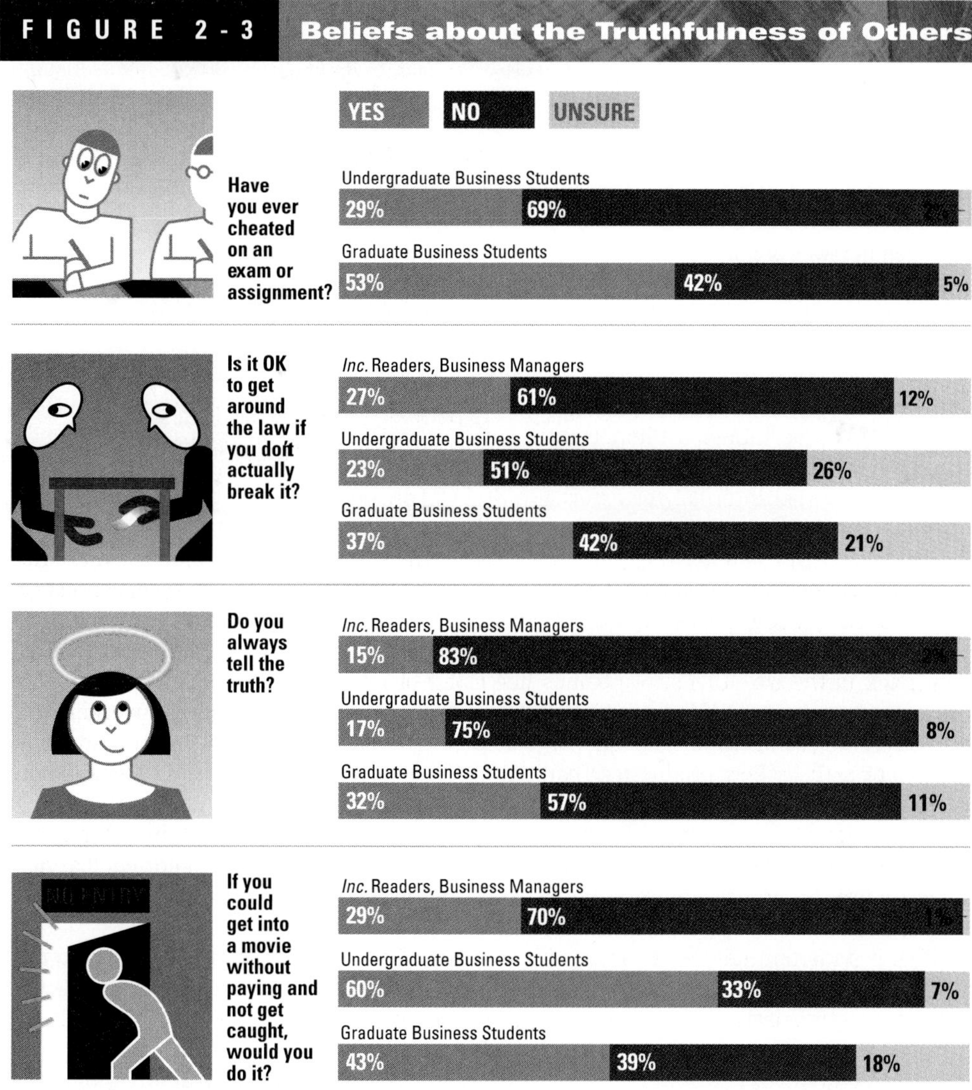

FIGURE 2-3 Beliefs about the Truthfulness of Others

past management guidelines and principles—created for a world that was far more stable and predictable—no longer apply. The successful organizations of the twenty-first century will be flexible, able to respond quickly, and will be led by managers who can challenge conventional wisdom and effectively enact massive and revolutionary changes.

As you will see throughout the rest of this book, organizations will need the capability to continually learn and adapt in order to achieve long-term success in this type of dynamic environment. A **learning organization** is one which has developed the capacity to continuously adapt and change. The need for continual change and innovation requires many organizations to re-invent themselves. Managers may be faced with restructuring their organizations by reducing vertical levels, redesigning jobs around teams, or re-engineering work processes. **Re-engineering** refers to a radical redesign of all or part of a company's work processes, to improve productivity and financial performance. Examples of this process will be shown throughout this text.

learning organization
An organization that has developed the capacity to continuously adapt and change.

re-engineering
A radical redesign of all or part of a company's work processes to improve productivity and financial performance.

Continually learning and adapting organizations are faced with a constant need for stimulating innovation and change. Managers play an important role in planning, organizing and leading any attempts at change and, in order to be effective, they are having to change their styles. Managers are transforming themselves from bosses into team leaders. Instead of simply telling people what to do and how to do it, an increasing number of managers are finding that they become more effective when they focus on listening, motivating, and coaching.

Total Quality Management

total quality management (TQM)
A philosophy of management that is driven by customer needs and expectations.

A quality revolution is taking place both in business and in the public sector.[25] The generic term used to describe this revolution is **total quality management**, or **TQM**. It was inspired by a small group of quality experts, the most prominent being an American named W Edwards Deming.

In 1950, Deming went to Japan and advised many top Japanese managers on how to improve their production effectiveness. Central to his management methods was the use of statistics to analyze variability in production processes. A well-managed organization, according to Deming, was one in which statistical control reduced variability and resulted in uniform quality and predictable quantity of output. Deming developed a 14-point program for transforming organizations. (We'll review this program in detail in Chapter 19 when we discuss operations management.)

Today, Deming's original program has been expanded into TQM—a philosophy of management that is driven by continual improvement and by responding to customer needs and expectations.[26] (See Table 2-5.) Importantly, however, the term *customer* in TQM is expanded beyond the traditional definition to include anyone who interacts with the organization's product or service, either internally or externally. So TQM encompasses employees and suppliers, as well as the people who purchase the organization's goods or services. The objective is to create an organization committed to continuous improvement.

TQM represents a counterpoint to earlier management theorists who believed that low costs were the only way to increase productivity. The American auto industry is often used as a classic example of what can go wrong when attention is focused solely on trying to keep costs down. Back in the late 1970s, companies like GM, Ford and Chrysler built products which many consumers rejected. Moreover, when the costs of rejects, repairing shoddy work, recalls, and expensive controls to identify quality problems were factored in, the American manufacturers were actually less productive than many foreign competitors. The Japanese demonstrated that it was possible for the highest-quality manufacturers also to be among the lowest-cost producers. American manufacturers in the auto industry and other industries soon realized the importance of TQM and implemented many of its basic components, such as quality control groups, process improvement, teamwork, improved supplier relations, and listening to consumers' needs and wants.

TQM is important, and we'll discuss it throughout the book. For example, we'll show the ways in which management can use TQM as a strategic weapon (Chapter 8) and for bench-

TABLE 2-5 What Is Total Quality Management?

1. Intense focus on the *customer*. The customer includes not only outsiders who buy the organization's products or services, but also internal customers (such as shipping or accounts payable personnel) who interact with, and serve others in the organization.
2. Concern for *continual improvement*. TQM is a commitment to never being satisfied. "Very good" is not good enough. Quality can always be improved.
3. Improvement in the *quality of everything* the organization does. TQM uses a very broad definition of quality. It relates not only to the final product, but also to how the organization handles deliveries, how rapidly it responds to complaints, how politely the phones are answered, and the like.
4. Accurate *measurement*. TQM uses statistical techniques to measure every critical variable in the organization's operations. These are compared against standards or benchmarks to identify problems, trace them to their roots and eliminate their causes.
5. *Empowerment of employees.* TQM involves the people on the line in the improvement process. Teams are widely used in TQM programs as empowerment vehicles for finding and solving problems.

marking competition (Chapter 9), as well as discussing methods for implementing TQM (Chapters 12 and 19), and the role of teams in TQM (Chapter 14).

Dismantling the Hierarchy

The large corporations of the 1960s, 1970s and 1980s sought to directly control as much of their operating activities as possible. Giant organizations such as IBM and General Motors were largely self-sufficient. They owned the manufacturing plants that built their products. They created powerful centralized departments at corporate headquarters to carefully monitor the decisions of lower-level managers throughout their company's numerous and widespread facilities. They also often acquired or merged with the organizations that supplied them with raw materials. And all support activities, such as accounting and maintenance, were done by people employed by the corporation.

This description no longer fits today's organizations. Most have aggressively dismantled their hierarchies in order to cut costs, improve efficiency and competitiveness, increase employee participation, increase flexibility, and concentrate on the activities they do best. These dismantling efforts have been executed through organizational actions such as downsizing, using contingent workers, and empowering individual employees and teams.

Empowerment and Teams

If you'll remember our discussion of scientific management, Frederick Taylor argued for division of work and separating management and worker responsibilities. He wanted managers to do the planning and thinking. Workers were only to do what they were told. This approach might have been effective at that time, but today's workers are far better educated and trained than they were in Taylor's day. In fact, because of the complexity of many jobs, today's workers are often considerably more knowledgeable than their managers about how best to do their jobs. This fact has not been ignored by management. Managers recognize that they can often improve quality, productivity, and employee commitment by redesigning jobs and letting individual workers and work teams make job-related decisions. We call this process *empowering employees*.[27]

empowerment
Increasing the decision-making discretion of workers.

The concept of **empowerment** builds on ideas originally advanced by human resources theorists. For many years, a lot of organizations stifled the capabilities of their workforce. They overspecialized jobs and demotivated employees by treating them like unthinking machines. Successful employee empowerment experiments have occurred across Canada in operations such as Syncrude Canada's oil-sands operation in Fort McMurray, Alberta; Saskatoon Chemicals; Algoma Steel in Sault Ste. Marie, Ontario; Circo Craft Co. in Kirkland, Quebec; and Imperial Oil's Dartmouth, Nova Scotia refinery, to name a few. The success of such forays into empowerment suggests that managers are considering expanding the worker's role in performing job activities rather than practising Taylor's segmentation of responsibilities. We will explore the concept of empowerment and teams in more detail in Chapter 14.

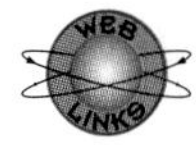

Algoma Steel
www.algoma.com/

Circo Technology Corp.
circotech.com/

FIGURE 2-4 Wages for Low-Skilled and High-Skilled Labour

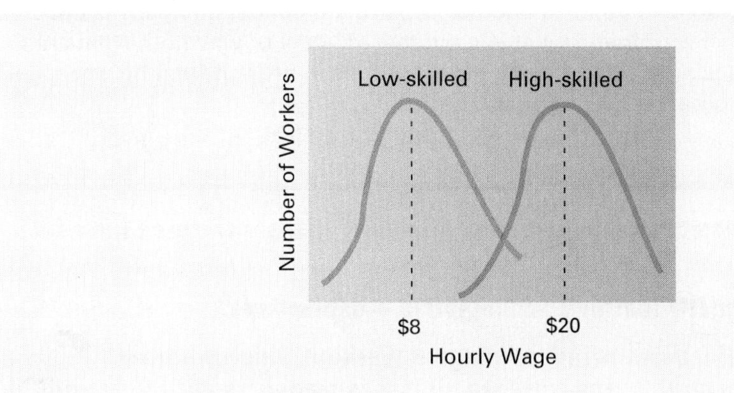

Downsizing

downsizing
An activity in an organization designed to create a more efficient operation through extensive layoffs.

Downsizing is an organizational action that reduces the size of the workforce through extensive layoffs. During the last few years, thousands of executives, managers and professionals have been laid off from their jobs as companies have streamlined, restructured and downsized. We have seen company after company—including major firms such as Air Canada, the major Canadian banks, Southam Inc., Sears Canada, Cape Breton Development Corp., and Canadian National Railways—downsizing in the late 1990s. This phenomenon is by no means limited to Canada; jobs are being eliminated in almost all industrialized nations. For example, Peugeot (France) has cut nearly 10 percent of its workforce in the past 5 years; AT&T (US) has cut 80 000 positions; and Volkswagen (Germany) began eliminating 30 000 jobs in 1997.

The benefits of downsizing are largely contentious. Organizational downsizing can have both a positive and a negative impact. On the positive side, a US study of the track records of the 10 largest downsizers during 1990-1995 showed that even though these companies shed a little over 29 percent of their workers, productivity *per worker* rose by nearly 28 percent.[28] But the downside has been the toll that downsizing can take on workers, as well as on financial gains. The human costs involved in downsizing can also be high. For instance, a survey of 62 companies that had downsized, reported that more than 70 percent of employees were grappling with serious problems of low morale and mistrust of senior management.[29] Another study of 52 corporate restructurings found that downsizing had little, if any, positive impact on corporate earnings or stock market performance.

Big isn't necessarily inefficient. Companies such as Corel, Bombardier and Northern Telecom have managed to blend size with agility. But they have typically divided their organizations into smaller, more flexible units. Moreover, not every large corporation is laying people off. Many are, in fact, increasing their workforces. Canadian Tire, for instance, saw its workforce grow by roughly 30 percent between 1993 and 1997. If adding staff in certain departments adds to the value of the organization as a whole, then this is obviously the route to pursue. The objective is to link staffing levels to organizational goals—a process called **rightsizing**.

rightsizing
Linking staffing levels to organizational goals.

Contingent Workers

contingent workers
Part-time, temporary or freelance employees.

Another workplace trend is the use of **contingent workers**, who are non-permanent workers including temporary staff, part-timers, consultants, freelancers and contract workers. Of course, the downsizing process has led to an increase in the contingent workforce, as employees who have been laid off from their full-time positions have then taken temporary jobs. Estimates of the numbers of contingent workers vary greatly, but there is no doubt that the number has been growing steadily over the past decade. Some experts have suggested that within the next decade contingent workers may account for 50 percent of the workforce.

Managing a contingent workforce has its own special set of challenges. Companies with experience in successfully managing large numbers of contingent workers say that treating these individuals fairly and flexibly is the key. Also, managers must work especially hard to make sure that contingent workers aren't treated as second-class citizens in the workplace. In fact, keeping the entire workforce motivated, creatively involved and committed to doing a good job, is the real work of today's and future managers.

THINKING CRITICALLY ABOUT ETHICS

Coming up in the elevator after lunch, you overhear, in a conversation between two managers, that a good friend of yours in another department of your company is about to be laid off. Would you tell your friend what you overheard? Why or why not? What are the ethical implications of telling your friend the news before she hears it from her manager? What are the ethical implications of not telling her? ■

9 **What implications does the increasing diversity of the workforce have for managers?**

10 **Describe continually learning and adaptive organizations.**

11 **Explain how TQM, downsizing, contingent workers, empowerment, psychological contracts, and trust are all issues managers must deal with.**

SUMMARY

This summary is organized by the learning objectives found at the beginning of the chapter.

1. Studying management history helps you to understand theory and practice as they are today. It also helps you to see how current management concepts have evolved over time. Current management concepts result from continual development, testing, modification, retesting, and so on.
2. Important pre-twentieth-century contributions to management included the building of the Egyptian pyramids, Adam Smith's writings on division of labour, and the Industrial Revolution. The building of the pyramids was an immense project requiring the co-ordination of tens of thousands of workers. Clearly, this demanded management skills. Smith's writings on the manufacturing of pins vividly illustrated the dramatic economies that could be achieved through division of labour. The Industrial Revolution made it more economical to manufacture goods in factories which, in turn, significantly increased the need for applying management techniques to production processes.
3. Frederick Taylor proposed four principles of management: (a) developing a science for each element of an individual's work, (b) scientifically selecting and training workers, (c) co-operating with workers, and (d) allocating responsibility to both management and workers.
4. Scientific management made possible dramatic increases—200 percent and more—in productivity. Applying its principles moved management from being a "seat-of-the-pants" practice to a serious, scientific discipline.
5. Henri Fayol was the first to define management as a universal set of functions: planning, organizing, commanding, co-ordinating, and controlling. He argued that management was an activity common to all human undertakings, and he identified 14 principles of management that could be taught.
6. Max Weber defined the ideal bureaucracy as having division of labour, a clearly defined hierarchy, detailed rules and regulations, and impersonal relationships.
7. The Hawthorne studies led to a new emphasis on the human factor in the functioning of organizations, and provided new insights into group norms and behaviour. Management began to actively seek increased employee job satisfaction and higher morale.
8. Human relations advocates held strong personal convictions about people at work. They believed in the capability of people and argued for management practices that would increase employee satisfaction. In contrast, the behavioural science theorists engaged in objective research on human behaviour in organizations. They carefully attempted to keep their personal beliefs out of their scientific research.
9. A unifying framework for management began in the early 1960s. The process approach was proposed as a way to synthesize the differences in the approaches of scientific management theorists, general administrative theorists, human resources theorists, and quantitative theorists. The systems approach recognizes the interdependency of internal activities in the organization and between the organization and its external environment. The contingency approach isolates situational variables that affect managerial actions and organizational performance.
10. Globalization affects all sizes and types of organizations. Workforce diversity requires managers to recognize and acknowledge employee differences. Information technology has an impact on many different aspects of managing organizations. Continually learning and adaptive organizations are faced with changing and improving the way in which work is done. Managers who emphasize the use of total quality management processes are committed to continuous improvement of work activities. Managers are dismantling organizational hierarchies in order to cut costs, improve efficiency and competitiveness, increase employee participation, increase flexibility, and concentrate on those work activities they do best. Finally, successful managers and organizations have to face the issue of a perceived decline in organizational ethics and trust.

THINKING ABOUT MANAGEMENT ISSUES

1. "The development of management thought has been determined by times and conditions." Do you agree or disagree with this statement? Discuss.
2. If Taylor's scientific principles are still found in many work settings today, does this mean that management really hasn't changed in the last 80 years? Explain.
3. What kind of workplace would Henri Fayol create? How about Mary Parket Follett? How about W Edwards Deming?
4. Can a mathematical technique help a manager to solve a "people" problem such as how to motivate employees or how to distribute work equitably? Explain.
5. In what ways do you currently use contingency theory? Explain.

SELF-ASSESSMENT EXERCISE

IS A BUREAUCRACY FOR YOU?

Many organizations still exhibit the characteristics of a bureaucracy as described by Weber. Some people would fit in well with highly bureaucratic organizations while others would feel stifled and cramped by a bureaucratic organization. What is your preference? To determine your level of comfort with bureaucratic organizations, take the following Self-Assessment Exercise.

Instructions: For each statement, check the response (either mostly agree or mostly disagree) that best represents your feelings.

	Mostly Agree	Mostly Disagree
1. I value stability in my job.	____	____
2. I like a predictable organization.	____	____
3. The best job for me would be one in which the future is uncertain.	____	____
4. The federal government would be a nice place to work.	____	____
5. Rules, policies and procedures tend to frustrate me.	____	____
6. I would enjoy working for a company that employed 85 000 people worldwide.	____	____
7. Being self-employed would involve more risk than I'm willing to take.	____	____
8. Before accepting a job, I would like to see an exact job description.	____	____
9. I would prefer a job as a freelance house painter to one as a clerk for the Ministry of Transport.	____	____
10. Seniority should be as important as performance in determining pay increases and promotion.	____	____
11. It would give me a feeling of pride to work for the largest and most successful company in its field.	____	____
12. Given a choice, I would prefer to make $40 000 per year as a vice president in a small company to $45 000 as a staff specialist in a large company.	____	____
13. I would regard wearing an employee badge with a number on it as a degrading experience.	____	____
14. Parking spaces in a company lot should be assigned on the basis of job level.	____	____
15. If an accountant works for a large organization, he or she cannot be a true professional.	____	____
16. Before accepting a job (given a choice), I would want to make sure that the company had a very fine program of employee benefits.	____	____
17. A company will probably not be successful unless it establishes a clear set of rules and procedures.	____	____
18. Regular working hours and vacations are more important to me than finding thrills on the job.	____	____
19. You should respect people according to their rank.	____	____
20. Rules are meant to be broken.	____	____

See Scoring Key beginning on page SK-1.

Source: A J DuBrin, *Human Relations: A Job Oriented Approach* © 1978, pp. 687–88. Adapted with permission of Reston Publishing Co., a Prentice Hall Co., 11480 Sunset Hills Road, Reston, VA 22090.

for your IMMEDIATE action

YOUR ADVERTISING PARTNERS · CHARLOTTETOWN, PEI

TO: Rebecca Stewart
FROM: Stephanie Green
RE: Contingent Employees

First of all, I'd like to welcome you to Creative Solutions as our summer intern. Creative Solutions has served the advertising and marketing communications needs of organizations in the southern Ontario area for over a decade. We like to think that a big part of our success is due to our ability to "sniff out" trends for our clients. This brings me to the first assignment that I'd like you to complete. We've been asked by a client of ours in the home health care industry to determine what impact the continuing trend of contingent workers is likely to have. I'd like you to do some research (please make use of our library or feel free to search the Internet) on this topic. Write up a brief (no more than one page, single-spaced) summary that answers the following questions:

- What is meant by the term *contingent employee*?
- What overall trends are forecasted for the health care industry as far as the numbers of contingent workers are concerned?
- What conclusions or implications could you draw from these data?

Thanks for all your help! I'm looking forward to seeing what you come up with on this topic.

This is a fictionalized account of a potentially real problem, written for academic purposes only.

TAKE IT TO THE NET

We invite you to visit the Robbins/Coulter/Stuart-Kotze Companion Website at www.prenticehall.ca/robbins for this chapter's Internet resources.

CASE APPLICATION

Philip Services Corp., Hamilton, Ontario

Now and then in the business world, there emerges an example of how the mighty can fall. Philip Services was a darling of the Canadian media, as well as a stock-market success for eight years, before the glory ended in 1998. This Hamilton, Ontario-based company was started by brothers Allen and Philip Fracassi. Philip Services began as a waste management firm, moved into metals recovery in 1993, and then by 1997, was billing itself as "the premier industrial services company", offering a broad range of services. It grew as a result of major acquisitions covering many sectors. The idea was that Philip Services could cross-sell its services, securing a large array of contracts from each client, cleaning up many different types of manufacturing waste. The stock market agreed that this was potentially a highly lucrative business, but the reality was that only 5 percent of the company's clients were using more than one of the offered services.

Then, in 1998, the bottom fell out. Early in the year, the company reported that $90 million in copper inventory was "missing" (an amount that would roughly fill 2500 dump trucks). Later, it transpired that rogue trading and overstated inventory had in fact accounted for $184 million (US) in trading losses over a three-year period. Analysts were obviously concerned about how it could have taken the company so long to uncover the huge losses. By June of 1998, 23 class action law suits had been filed against Philip Services by groups of shareholders claiming securities fraud. Philip Services refused to disclose who had been responsible for the accounting irregularities.

A portrait of a company without any specific direction began to emerge—one with too many divisions and no overall control. One former company insider stated: "We never got any mission statements, we never had any goals, there wasn't even an adequate employee training policy in place". A customer said that dealing with Philip Services could be "like dealing with 39 different companies," and that, "integrating those operations [I dealt with] into one central management theme evidently wasn't happening".

In early May, the company announced that its founders, the Fracassi brothers, were stepping down from their positions to assume different roles and that they were making Felix Pardo the new CEO. Allen Fracassi, however, was apparently still in charge of shaping Philip Services' strategies and future plans. The company began issuing statements concerning its turnaround efforts. Plans were announced to sell or spin-off five divisions, in order to use the proceeds in an effort to pay off $200 million in debt. Pardo vowed to cut $40 million from expenses. But confidence in the company had been severely shaken, and analysts did not expect the stock value to re-emerge too soon from the depths to which it had sunk.

QUESTIONS

1. How much trust would you think exists between top management and employees at Philip Services?
2. Using the description of TQM found in Table 2-5, explain how you think these ideas might be used at Philip Services.
3. In view of the customer's statement that dealing with Philip Services was "like dealing with 39 different companies", how could a systems view of management be used to improve operations at Philip Services?

Sources: Sean Silcoff, "Something's Missing", *Canadian Business,* March 13, 1998, pp. 72–80; Richard Blackwell, "Management Shakeup at Philip Services", *Financial Post,* January 6, 1998, p. 3; Janet McFarland and Paul Waldie, "A Breach in the House of Philip", *Globe and Mail,* February 14, 1998, p. B1; John Nicol and Stephanie Nolen, "Dark Days at Philip", *Maclean's,* March 2, 1998, p. 52–56; Janet McFarland, "Philip Shares Plunge Amid Controversy", *Globe and Mail,* January 7, 1998, p. B1; and Sean Silcoff, "New Face, Same Mess", *Canadian Business,* June 12, 1998, pp. 41–43.

P A R T   T W O

Defining the Manager's Terrain

LEARNING OBJECTIVES

After Reading This Chapter, You Should Be Able To:

1 Differentiate the symbolic from the omnipotent view of management

2 Define organizational culture

3 Identify the seven dimensions that make up an organization's culture

4 Explain how cultures can be strong or weak, and how an organization's culture reflects a certain personality

5 Describe the various ways in which employees learn culture

6 Explain how culture constrains managers

7 Distinguish between the general and specific environments

8 Contrast certain and uncertain environments

9 Describe the various components in the specific environment

10 Identify the factors in the general environment

11 Explain how the environment constrains managers

A MANAGER'S CHALLENGE

Stephen Bachand, CEO, Canadian Tire Corp.

When Stephen Bachand agreed to take over as CEO of Canadian Tire back in 1993, the 71-year-old institution was facing some hard times and its prospects were looking grim. Many of the smaller stores in the chain were losing money, service was often poor, and inventory was not always being kept up—resulting in customers going to stores only to find their desired product out of stock. Moreover, the marketplace was on the verge of being invaded on a large scale by major American chains such as Home Depot and Wal-Mart.

However, Canadian Tire was still a powerful force in Canadian retailing, accounting for roughly a third of the nation's retail sales in both sporting goods and hardware, and nearly half of all auto-parts. The challenge was to hold on to market share in the face of heavy new competition, while simultaneously bringing Canadian Tire's stores into the customer-oriented '90s. In order to achieve these goals,

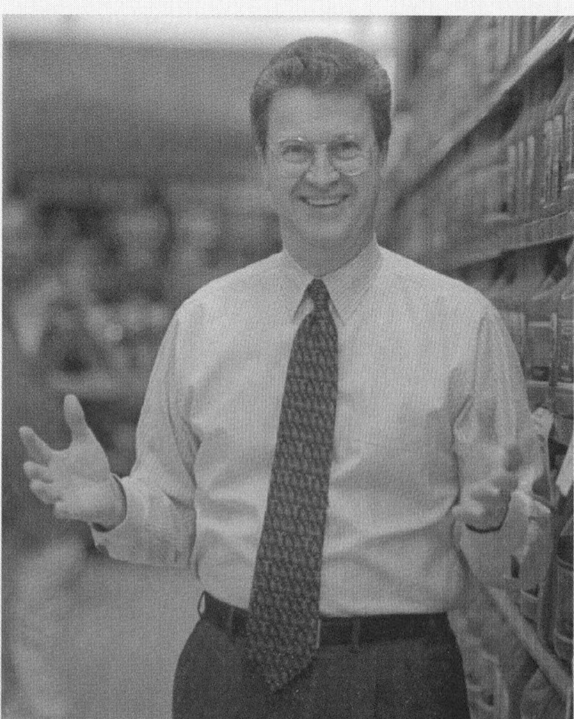

Bachand had to have the co-operation of the individual store owners as these owners collectively hold a significant amount of shares in the corporation itself. This is a fairly uncommon relationship between a head office and its store owners, and Bachand was forced to gain the approval of these dealers before he could institute any changes. This he did, and together they developed a strategy to bring Canadian Tire back to previous levels of profitability.

The company instituted a $1 billion renovation program, making stores more shopper-friendly—with more space, more competitive prices, a wider selection of products, and more stock. By 1997, 100 new stores had replaced the old, out-of-date versions. And the company made plans to overhaul another 140 by the year 2000. The objective was to meet the new competition head-on, and so far it has been working successfully. In every year since Bachand's appointment as CEO, Canadian Tire has reported increased revenue. By 1998, Canadian Tire was making sales worth $4 billion—continuing to break company records. Profits are steadily climbing as a result of increased sales coupled with cost-cutting measures in shipping, distribution and marketing.

Since Bachand took the helm at Canadian Tire, the company has reached the milestone of turning three-quarters of a century old, and has done so in a very profitable fashion. The challenge remains of staying profitable amid the changing nature of retailing in Canada, in the face of serious new competition (such as Eaton's, for example).[1]

Stephen Bachand is a manager who recognizes the challenges facing organizations today—challenges from both the external environment and internal culture. Like managers everywhere, Bachand wants to see his organization continue to succeed in the next century. But how much actual effect do managers have on an organization's performance? We need to explore more closely the question of whether an organization's successes or failures are always directly attributable to management.

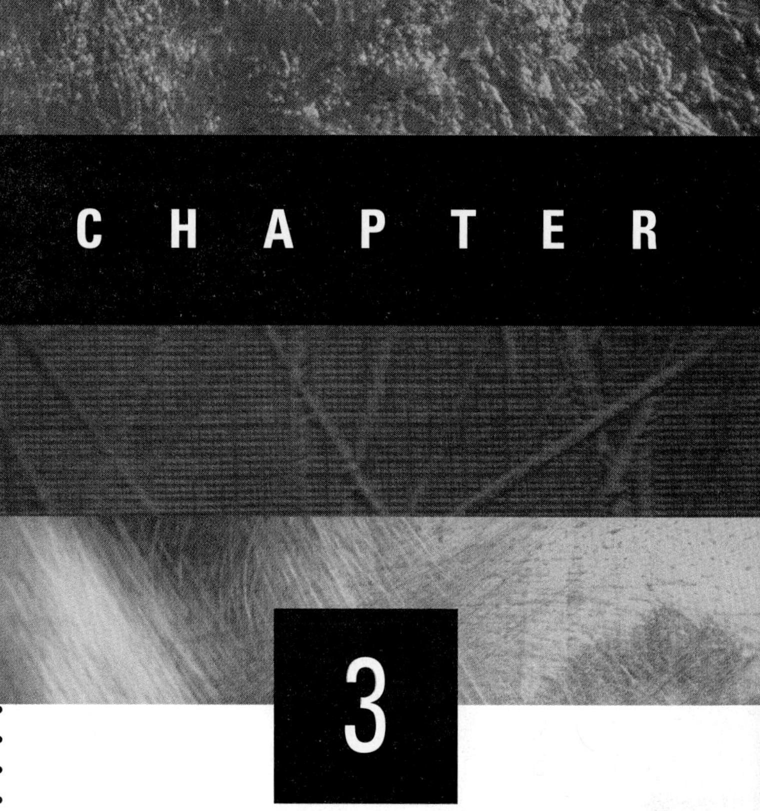

Chapter 3 Organizational Culture and Environment: The Constraints

THE MANAGER: OMNIPOTENT OR SYMBOLIC?

omnipotent view of management
The view that managers are directly responsible for an organization's success or failure.

symbolic view of management
The view that management has only a limited effect on substantive organizational outcomes because of the large number of factors outside of management's control.

The dominant view in management theory and society in general is that managers are directly responsible for an organization's success or failure. We call this perspective the **omnipotent view of management**. In contrast, some observers have argued that managers have little influence on organizational outcomes. They propose that much of an organization's success or failure is due to forces outside management's control. This perspective has been labelled the **symbolic view of management**.[2]

In this section, we want to review both of these positions. Our reason should be obvious. The analysis will help to clarify just how much credit or blame managers should receive for their organization's performance.

The Omnipotent View

A dominant assumption in management theory is that the quality of an organization's managers determines the quality of the organization itself. It's assumed that differences in an organization's effectiveness or efficiency are due to the decisions and actions of its managers. Good managers anticipate change, exploit opportunities, correct poor performance and lead their organizations towards their objectives (and even change those objectives when necessary). When profits are up, management takes the credit and rewards itself with bonuses, stock options, and the like. When profits are down, the board of directors replaces top management in the belief that new management will bring improved results.

Gulf Canada Resources
www.gulf.ca

One high-profile example of this type of scenario shook the Canadian business world in early 1998. JP Bryan left Gulf Canada Resources, where he had been CEO for three years, after prolonged conflict with the twelve-person board of directors.[3] Bryan's relatively short tenure at the helm of Gulf brought him a huge amount of media attention and, indeed, much praise from shareholders during his massive restructuring efforts. When he was appointed CEO, Gulf was in serious trouble with an unmanageable debt-load, and hadn't recorded a profit in the past six years. Bryan cut staff by 40 percent, significantly reduced costs, and increased capital investment by 275 percent. Gulf began to record a profit and shares were on a steady, rapid upswing. It was one of the quickest turnarounds in Canadian business history and Bryan was being hailed as a corporate saviour. However, Bryan's strategy involved a constant acquisitions binge and the long-term debt-load grew as a result. When Bryan left, the debt was an estimated $2.7 billion—four times Gulf's cash flow. The company immediately sold $850 million in assets to pay off some of the debt. Gulf's future seemed somewhat tentative once again, with rumours of a possible takeover abounding. Gulf's stock took a precipitous plunge, upon Bryan's resignation. However, many people on the board of directors obviously believed that Bryan was driving the company into ruin with his acquisition strategy. So, three tempestuous years later, Bryan was no longer with the Calgary oil company. At the time of his exit, he was either hailed as a master turnaround artist, or derided as a power-mad autocrat whose policies were bringing Gulf to ruin, depending on whom you asked! Either way, one point is very clear—the fortunes of Gulf were seen to have rested in the hands of this one man.

This omnipotent view, of course, is not limited to business organizations. We can also use it to help explain the high turnover among university sports coaches. These coaches manage their teams. They decide which players to recruit and which players start the game. They select assistant coaches, teach play strategies to their teams, and select every play strategy during games. Coaches who lose more games than they win are seen as being ineffective. They are fired and replaced by new coaches who, it is assumed, will correct the team's inadequate performance.

Regardless of extenuating circumstances, when organizations perform poorly, someone has to be held accountable. In our society, that role is played by management. Of course, when things go well, management gets the credit—even if it had little to do with causing the positive outcome.

The Symbolic View

Canadian mining giant, Inco Ltd., faced tough times in 1998 when it suffered from slumping world nickel and copper prices. If you took the position that senior management—including CEO Michael Sopko—were victims of factors beyond their control, then you would be taking the symbolic view of management.

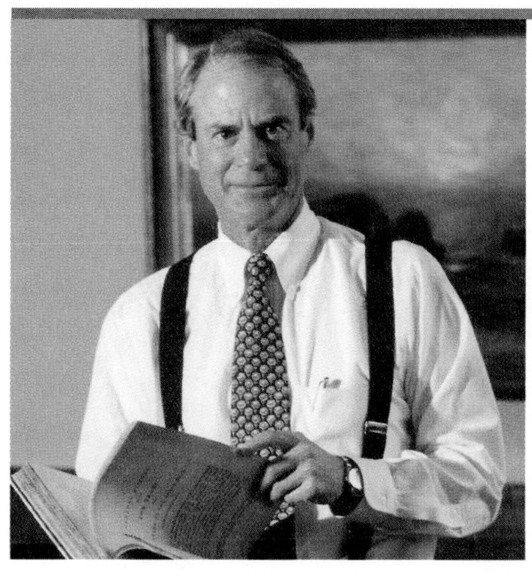

J P Bryan represents the ominipotent view of management: lauded with praise in good times, heaped with scorn in bad.

The symbolic view assumes that a manager's ability to affect outcomes is highly constrained by external factors. In this view, it is unreasonable to expect managers to have much effect on an organization's performance.

According to the symbolic view, an organization's results are influenced by a number of factors outside management's control. These include the economy, government policies, competitors' actions, the state of the particular industry, the control of proprietary technology, and decisions made by previous managers in the organization.

Following the symbolic view, management has, at best, only a limited effect on *substantive organizational outcomes*. What management does affect greatly are *symbolic* outcomes.[4] Management's role is seen as creating meaning out of randomness, confusion and ambiguity. Management creates the illusion of control for the benefit of shareholders, customers, employees and the public. When things go right, we need someone to praise. Management plays that role. Similarly, when things go wrong, we need someone to blame. Management plays that role, too. However, according to the symbolic view, the *actual* part management plays in success or failure is minimal.

Reality Suggests a Synthesis

In reality, managers are neither helpless nor all-powerful. Internal constraints which restrict a manager's decision options exist within every organization. These internal constraints are derived from the organization's culture. In addition, external constraints impinge on the organization and restrict managerial freedom. The external constraints come from the organization's environment.

Figure 3-1 shows the manager as operating within constraints. The organization's culture and environment press against the manager, restricting his or her options. Yet, in spite of these constraints, managers are not powerless. There still remains an area in which managers can exert a significant amount of influence on an organization's performance—an area in which

FIGURE 3-1 Parameters of Managerial Discretion

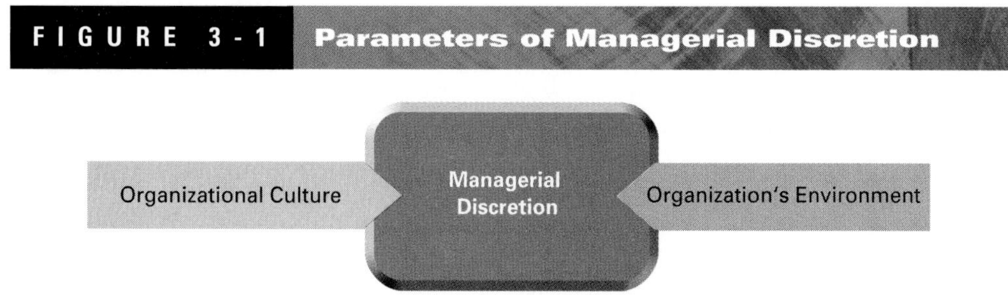

good managers differentiate themselves from poor ones. In the remainder of this chapter, we'll discuss organizational culture and environment as constraints. But, as we'll also point out later in this book, these constraints need not be regarded as being fixed in all situations. Managers may be able to change and influence their culture and environment and thus expand their area of discretion.

THE ORGANIZATION'S CULTURE

We know that every individual has something that psychologists call "personality". An individual's personality is made up of a set of relatively permanent and stable traits. When we describe someone as warm, innovative, relaxed or conservative, we are describing personality traits. An organization, too, has a personality, which we call its *culture*.

What Is Organizational Culture?

organizational culture
A system of shared meaning within an organization that determines, to a large degree, how employees act.

What do we specifically mean by the term **organizational culture**? We use the term to refer to a system of *shared meaning*. Just as tribal cultures have rules and taboos that dictate how members will act towards each other and outsiders, organizations have cultures that govern how their members should behave. In every organization, there are systems or patterns of values, symbols, rituals, myths and practices that have evolved over time.[5] These shared values determine, to a large degree, what employees see and how they respond to their world.[6] When confronted with a problem, the organizational culture restricts what employees can do by suggesting the correct way—"the way we do things here"—to conceptualize, define, analyze and solve the problem.

Our definition of culture implies several things. First, culture is a perception. Individuals perceive the culture of the organization based on what they see or hear within the organization. And even though individuals may have different backgrounds or may work at different levels in the organization, they tend to describe the organization's culture in similar terms. That is the *shared* aspect of culture. Second, "organizational culture" is a descriptive term. It is concerned with how members perceive the organization, not with whether or not they like it. It describes rather than evaluates.

Research suggests that there are seven dimensions which, in total, capture the essence of an organization's culture.[7] These dimensions have been described as follows:

1. *Innovation and risk taking.* The degree to which employees are encouraged to be innovative and to take risks.
2. *Attention to detail.* The degree to which employees are expected to exhibit precision, analysis, and attention to detail.
3. *Outcome orientation.* The degree to which managers focus on results or outcomes rather than on the techniques and processes used to achieve these outcomes.
4. *People orientation.* The degree to which management decisions take into consideration the effect of outcomes on people within the organization.
5. *Team orientation.* The degree to which work activities are organized around teams rather than individuals.
6. *Aggressiveness.* The degree to which people are aggressive and competitive rather than easygoing and co-operative.
7. *Stability.* The degree to which organizational activities emphasize maintaining the status quo in contrast to growth or change.

1 Why does the omnipotent view of management dominate management theory?

2 According to the symbolic view, what is management's role in organizations?

As illustrated in Figure 3-2, each of these characteristics exists on a continuum from low to high. Appraising the organization on these seven dimensions, then, gives a composite picture of the organization's culture. Table 3-1 demonstrates how these dimensions can be mixed to create significantly different organizations. Organizations also differ on the strength of their cultures.

Strong Versus Weak Cultures

Although all organizations have cultures, not all cultures have an equal impact on employees. **Strong cultures**—organizations in which the key values are intensely held and widely shared—have a greater influence on employees than do weak cultures. The more employees accept the organization's key values and the greater their commitment to those values, the stronger the culture is.

strong cultures
Organizations in which the key values are intensely held and widely shared.

Whether an organization's culture is strong, weak, or somewhere in between depends on factors such as the size of the organization, the length of its history, the turnover among its employees, and the intensity with which the culture was originated. In some organizations, it's unclear what's important and what's not, which is a characteristic of weak cultures. In such organizations, culture is less likely to affect managers. However, most organizations have moderate to strong cultures. There is relatively high agreement on what's important, what defines "good" employee behaviour, what it takes to get ahead, and so forth. In fact, one study of organizational culture found that employees in firms with strong cultures were more committed to their firms than were employees in firms with weak cultures. The firms with strong cultures also used their recruitment efforts and socialization practices to build employee commitment.[8] And an increasing body of evidence suggests that strong cultures are associated with high organizational performance.[9] What are the implications for the way in which managers manage? We might expect that an organization's culture will have an increasing impact on what managers do as it becomes stronger.

Culture as the Organization's Personality

In many organizations, especially those with strong cultures, one cultural dimension often rises above the others and essentially shapes the organization and the way organizational members do their work. For instance, at Corel Corp., new product development is of paramount importance, and employees' work decisions and actions support that goal (research and development at Corel as a percentage of revenue was 34.35 percent for 1997). Let's look at

FIGURE 3-2 Dimensions of Organizational Culture

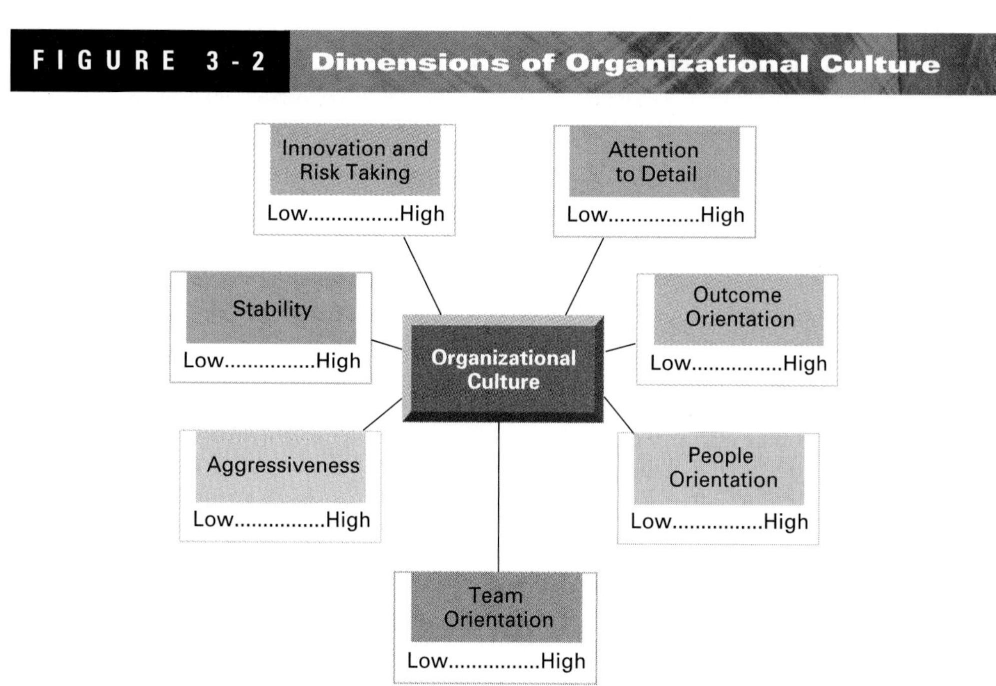

TABLE 3-1 Two Highly Diverse Organizational Cultures

Organization A

This organization is a manufacturing firm. Employees' loyalty is to the organization. There are extensive rules and regulations that employees are required to follow. Managers supervise employees closely to ensure that there are no deviations. Management is concerned with high productivity regardless of the impact on employee morale or turnover.

Work activities are designed around individuals. There are distinct departments and lines of authority, and employees are expected to minimize formal contact with other employees outside their functional area or line of command. Effort, loyalty, co-operation, and avoidance of errors are highly valued and rewarded. The company promotes only from within and believes that the best products are those developed inside the firm.

Organization B

This organization is also a manufacturing firm. Here, however, employees pride themselves on their technical skills, current expertise and professional contacts outside the company. There are few rules and regulations, and supervision is loose because management believes that its employees are hardworking and trustworthy. Management is concerned with high productivity but believes that this comes from treating its people right. The company is proud of its reputation as being a good place to work.

Job activities are designed around work teams and team members are encouraged to interact with people across functions and authority levels. Managers are evaluated not only on their department's performance but also on how well their department co-ordinates its activities with other departments in the organization. Promotions and other valuable rewards go to employees who make the greatest contributions to the organization, even when those employees have strange ideas, unusual personal mannerisms, or unconventional work habits. The company fills upper-level positions with the best people available, which sometimes includes hiring people away from competitors. The company prides itself on being market-driven and on rapidly responding to the changing needs of its customers.

how different organizations have chosen different cultural themes—or to put it another way, let's look at various organizational "personalities".

Strong Risk-Taking Personalities. The culture of some organizations encourage employees to take risks. For instance, employees at Hamilton-based Envirolutions Inc., an environmental waste solutions company, know that they will be supported in taking risks and trying new approaches.

Standard Aero
www.standardaero.com

Strong Attention-to-Detail Personalities. In this type of culture, the organization focuses intently on the nuts and bolts—the details—of the business. Organizations that have made quality their driving theme have attention-to-detail personalities. Standard Aero of Winnipeg is a good example of a company with a very strong attention-to-detail personality. The company spends millions on TQM efforts.

Strong Outcome-Orientation Personalities. Some organizations succeed by focusing on results or outcomes such as customer service. This type of culture is evidenced in the Quebec department stores, Les Ailes de la Mode, where customer service is all-important. A recent article on the stores gushed: "Staff are trained to provide the best customer service possible, and to prove it, they'll buy customers a coffee or dessert from the store's upscale food concessions or give them a free facial at one of its spa services. If an item isn't in stock, an employee will find a way to come back with the merchandise in hand, even if it means running to a competitor to buy it".[10] Employees at Les Ailes de la Mode know in no uncertain terms what is expected of them, and those expectations go a long way towards shaping behaviour.

The cultural dimension that shapes Toronto-based Hollinger is its strong aggressiveness, personified by Conrad Black.

Strong People-Orientation Personalities. Some organizations have made their employees a central part of their cultures. Husky Injection Molding Systems in Bolton, Ontario, is one such company. At Husky, workers are encouraged to set their own goals and are offered incentives; physical fitness is promoted with a state-of-the-art gym, a doctor, a nurse, a naturopath, a chiropractor and a massage therapist all on-site; all employees are part of a profit-sharing plan; salaries are above industry average; and employees have a say in management decisions through a rotating employee council.

Strong Team-Orientation Personalities. An increasing number of small organizations and divisions of large organizations are shaping their cultures around the team concept. At Algoma Steel Inc. of Sault Ste. Marie, Ontario, work teams are empowered to deal with everything from determining their own vacation schedules to redesigning their workplaces.

Strong Aggressiveness Personalities. Some organizations value aggressiveness above all else. The Toronto-based international newspaper group, Hollinger, is a perfect example of aggressiveness. Headed by Conrad Black, the perception that Hollinger gives off is a cutthroat, take-no-prisoners corporation—ruthlessly devouring competitors. Another good example of this type of organizational personality is Microsoft, which have been so successful in their aggressive growth that the US government has begun the biggest anti-trust case in history against them.

Tucows Interactive Ltd.
www.tucows.ca

Strong Non-stability Personalities. Finally, there are organizations that define their cultures by their overwhelming emphasis on growth. One such company is Toronto-based Tucows Interactive Ltd. Tucows is an Internet service provider (through its Internet Direct division) and shareware distributor (through its other division, The Ultimate Collection of Winstock Software, "TUCOWS"). Sales growth from 1992 to 1997 was a whopping 5306 percent—good for seventh place in *Profit* magazine's 1998 listing of Canada's fastest-growing companies. Tucows President, John Nemanic, has stated: "We want world domination through superior software delivery".[11] Another example of an organization dedicated to growth is Montreal's Power Corp., which went on a $7 *billion* spending spree in 1998, looking for acquisitions in Europe and North America in industrial sectors and in the audio-visual industry.

The Source of Culture

An organization's current customs, traditions and general way of doing things are largely due to what it has done before and the degree of success it has had with those endeavours. The original source of an organization's culture usually reflects the vision or mission of the organization's founders. Because the founders have the original idea, they may also have biases on how to carry it out. They're not constrained by previous customs or approaches. The founders establish the early culture by projecting an image of what the organization should be. The small size of most new organizations also helps the founders instill their vision in all organizational members.

Patagonia Inc.
www.patagonia.com

Yvon Chouinard is a good example of an individual who has had immeasurable influence on shaping his organization's culture. An avid "extreme adventurer", Chouinard founded the outdoor gear company, Patagonia Inc., a company which reflected his laid-back, casual manner. For instance, he hired employees not on the basis of any specific business skills, but because he had climbed, fished, or gone surfing with them. Employees were friends, and work was treated as something fun to do. In a speech Chouinard gave a few years ago, he uttered the classic line: "Let my people go surfing!" Although Patagonia is now a $125 million-a-year company with more than 500 employees, its culture still reflects Chouinard's values and philosophy.

The corporate culture of Calgary software developer, Merak Projects Ltd., bears the stamp of its director and co-founder, Adrian Zissos. Merak realizes that its employees are its lifeblood, and that they have lives outside of the office. The company goes out of its way to provide flexibility to its employees. Whether it's allowing one employee to follow his wife to her new career in China, and working via e-mail; letting a single father bring his young children to work with him; bringing a new mother back part-time; or allowing time off beyond paid vacation time for employees for some reason, Merak stresses an understanding culture.[12]

Influence on Management Practice

Because it establishes constraints on what they can and cannot do, an organization's culture is particularly relevant to managers. These constraints are rarely explicit. They are not written down. It is unlikely that they'll even be spoken. But they're there, and all managers quickly learn "what to do and not to do" in their organizations. To illustrate, you won't find the following values written down anywhere, but each comes from a real organization:

- Look busy even if you're not.
- If you take risks and fail around here, you'll pay dearly for it.
- Before you make a decision, run it by your boss so that he or she is never surprised.
- We make our product only as good as the competition forces us to.

Richard Branson, founder of the Virgin empire—which started with Virgin Records and now includes the highly successful Virgin Airlines—has stamped his flamboyant personality on the culture of his company.

- What made us successful in the past will make us successful in the future.
- If you want to get to the top here, you have to be a team player.

The link between values such as these and managerial behaviour is fairly straightforward. If an organization's culture supports the belief that profits can be increased by cost cutting and that the company's best interests are served by achieving slow but steady increases in quarterly earnings, managers throughout the organization are unlikely to pursue programs that are innovative, risky, long-term or expansionary. In organizations whose culture conveys a basic distrust of employees, managers are more likely to use an authoritarian leadership style than a democratic one. Why? The culture establishes what is appropriate behaviour for managers. Therefore a management style that works effectively at Edmonton's BioWare Corp.—where office attire is casual except for "formal fifteenths", when employees dress up for the day "to see how the other half lives"—would not be compatible with corporate culture at, say, IBM Canada.[13]

The challenge to overcome obstacles caused by corporate culture is one of the most difficult that managers face. Take, for instance, a merger situation. When Abitibi-Price and Stone Consolidated merged in 1997, thereby forming Canada's largest newsprint producer, two distinct corporate cultures came together. The operating chairman of the newly formed Abitibi-Consolidated, Ronald Oberlander, had to deal with the clash of cultures. His main task, as he put it, was to improve "lateral communications between equals from different plants and different departments". Not such an easy goal to achieve, considering the size of the company (13 000 employees in 7 sawmills and 18 papermills) and the fact that these disparate divisions had always been accustomed to their own ways of getting things done. For Oberlander, open communication was the main factor in attempting to create a new culture for the merged company: "The purpose of the merger was to get $200 million in synergies back. It won't happen if we hide in our separate corners".[14]

An organization's culture, especially a strong one, constrains a manager's decision-making options in all management functions. As shown in Table 3-2, the major areas of a manager's job are influenced by the culture in which he or she operates.

THE ENVIRONMENT

The recognition that no organization operates independently was a major contribution of the systems approach to management. Anyone who questions the impact of the external environment on managing should consider the following:

- The bankruptcy of Eaton's meant heavy losses for many suppliers. Adorable Junior Garment of Montreal was owed roughly $1 million for a shipment of spring clothes. Luckily, a US vulture fund purchased the debt at 80 percent—but the nearly 15 percent of Adorable's business that Eaton's accounted for was suddenly up in the air. The company was forced to refocus its efforts, concentrating on new US markets.
- Peerless Clothing of Montreal was faced with a major new development in its business environment when the Free Trade Agreement was implemented. One would assume that new competition from the US would pose a major threat for a small company such as Peerless but, in fact, a lower tariff on European wool in Canada meant that the company could produce its suits more cheaply than its American competitors. Peerless took advantage of this vast newly-opened US market, and today is the largest producer of men's wool suits in North America, with annual sales of over $140 million.
- When rebels deposed Zairian dictator, Mobutu Sese Seko, in the spring of 1997, rebel leader Laurent Kabila assumed power. Suddenly, Canadian mining company, Tenke, did

3 Contrast strong and weak cultures. Which has the greater effect on managers? Why?

4 How does culture affect a manager's execution of the four management functions?

TABLE 3-2 Examples of Managerial Decisions Affected by Culture

Planning
The degree of risk that plans should contain
Whether plans should be developed by individuals or teams
The degree of environmental scanning in which management will engage

Organizing
How much autonomy should be designed into employees' jobs
Whether tasks should be done by individuals or in teams
The degree to which department managers interact with each other

Leading
The degree to which managers are concerned with increasing employee job satisfaction
What leadership styles are appropriate
Whether all disagreements—even constructive ones—should be eliminated

Controlling
Whether to allow employees to control their own actions or to impose external controls
What criteria should be emphasized in employee performance evaluations
What repercussions will occur from exceeding one's budget

not know whether its agreement to develop a copper-cobalt mine would remain valid, as it had been made with the former dictator. Little was known about Kabila, and the future of what was now the Republic of Congo. The whole project, including a $60 million down payment made by Tenke, was no longer secure. As it turned out, Tenke's investment was honoured by the new government and, by the summer of 1998, the company was courting investors to begin the first stage of the project. However, by August, another coup was being staged, once again casting doubt over the political situation in the Congo.

As these examples show, forces in the environment play a major role in shaping managers' actions. In this section, we'll identify some of the crucial environmental forces that affect management and show how they constrain managerial discretion.

Defining the Environment

environment
Outside institutions or forces that potentially affect an organization's performance.

The term **environment** refers to institutions or forces that are outside the organization and that potentially affect the organization's performance. As one writer described it: "Just take the universe, subtract from it the subset that represents the organization, and the remainder is environment".[15] But it's really not that simple.

general environment
Everything outside the organization.

specific environment
The part of the environment that is directly relevant to the achievement of an organization's goals.

General Versus Specific Environment. The **general environment** includes *everything* outside the organization, such as economic factors, political conditions, sociocultural influences, globalization issues and technological factors. It encompasses conditions that *may* affect the organization but whose relevance is not clear. The development of the technology to place the contents of an entire bookshelf on one small computer disk is an example of a factor in the general environment of publisher McClelland & Stewart. Its long-term impact on the book industry is unclear, yet it could be very great. Similarly, the strength of the Canadian dollar against the pound and yen is an environmental force for Canadian companies that operate in Great Britain and Japan, but its effect is best described as being only *potentially* relevant.

The bulk of management's attention is usually given to the organization's specific environment. The **specific environment** is the part of the environment that is directly relevant

MANAGING WORKFORCE DIVERSITY

Creating a Supportive Culture for Diversity

We know from our discussion in Chapter 2 that managing a diverse workforce is a key challenge facing today's executives. As the composition of the workforce changes, managers must take a long, hard look at their organizational culture to see if the shared values and meanings that were appropriate for a more homogeneous employee base will support diverse views. How can managers create a culture that advocates and encourages diversity?[16]

The old approach to managing diversity was to expect people who were different to hide or adapt their cultural differences so that they would fit into the organization's dominant culture. Now, managers who accept diversity as a corporate asset recognize that it benefits the organization by bringing in a broad range of viewpoints and problem-solving skills. An organizational culture that nourishes and celebrates diversity allows employees to be themselves and encourages them to develop their own unique strengths and present innovative ideas from their diverse perspectives. No longer do diverse employees feel like they have to "play it safe" by hiding their differences.

Creating a culture that supports and encourages diversity is a major organizational effort. Managers throughout the organization at *every* level must fundamentally accept that diversity is valued and reflect this by what they say and do. An organization that truly wants to promote diversity must shape its culture to allow diversity to flourish. One way to do this is for managers to assimilate diverse perspectives while performing their managerial functions. The giant Canadian utility corporation, Union Gas Ltd., has made workforce diversity a priority. The company spent nearly two years and more than $200 000 to put each and every one of its 2600 employees (25 at a time) through a training program to familiarize them with diversity issues. According to Maureen Geddes, who is in charge of workplace diversity at Union Gas, the benefits of this program are not solely ethical. "Of course it's the right thing to do," Geddes states, "but diversity training is a priority here today because it makes us more productive and competitive as an organization."[17] ■

to the achievement of an organization's goals. It consists of the crucial constituencies or stakeholders that can positively or negatively influence an organization's effectiveness. Each organization's specific environment is unique and changes with conditions. Typically, it will include suppliers of inputs, clients or customers, competitors, government agencies, and public pressure groups. For example, as a result of the Helms-Burton law put into effect in the US, a Canadian company doing business in Cuba may suddenly have found that the US government was very much a part of its specific environment. Under the law, companies found to be profiting from property seized from US interests during Castro's revolution can be punished in the US. These companies can have their executives barred from entering the US (as happened to Toronto-based Sherritt International, Canada's biggest investor in Cuba) and can face heavy fines. In March of 1998, the Calgary-based petroleum company, Genoil Inc., suddenly found itself under investigation for possible Helms-Burton violations. Even a small company such as Ontario's Pizza Nova, which has a franchise in Cuba, finds the US government in its specific environment. However, Pizza Nova president, Sam Primucci, can afford to be amused by Senator Helms's mention of the tiny pizza chain, as the law's only effect on his company is in fact beneficial—helping to keep competition at bay. As Primucci says, "If the market was open, little guys like me wouldn't have a chance".[18]

An organization's specific environment varies depending on the "niche" that the organization has carved out for itself, with respect to the range of products or services it offers and the markets it serves. Tim Horton Donuts and The Second Cup both serve coffee, but their specific environments differ because they operate in distinctly different market niches. Fanshawe College and the University of Western Ontario are both institutions of higher education located in London, Ontario, but they do substantially different things and appeal to different segments of the higher-education market. The managers or administrators in these organizations face different constituencies in their specific environments.

The importance of our point should be clear: The environmental factors that one organization is dependent on and that critically influence performance may not be relevant

University of Western Ontario
www.uwo.ca/

Fanshawe College
www.fanshawec.on.ca/

to another organization at all, even though they may appear at first to be in the same type of business.

environmental uncertainty
The degree of change and complexity in an organization's environment.

Assessing Environmental Uncertainty. The environment is important to managers because not all environments are the same. They differ by what we call their degree of **environmental uncertainty**. Environmental uncertainty, in turn, can be divided into two dimensions: degree of change and degree of complexity.

If the components in an organization's environment change frequently, we call it a *dynamic* environment. If change is minimal, we call it a *stable* one. A stable environment might be one in which there are no new competitors, no new technological breakthroughs by current competitors, little activity by public pressure groups to influence the organization, and so forth. For example, the Société des alcools du Quebec, and New Brunswick Power Corp. are all examples of organizations which operate in very stable environments. In contrast, Research In Motion Ltd. (RIM) of Waterloo, Ontario, operates in a dynamic environment. RIM develops and markets radio-modem technology, and the wireless communications market is still in a state of technological infancy. There is great competition among companies to develop superior systems to take advantage of a rapidly growing worldwide market. RIM was ranked fourth in *Canadian Business*'s list of the fastest-growing technology companies for 1998, but it operates in an uncertain and unpredictable environment, and will have to handle constant change in order to stay at the forefront of its industry.[19]

What about rapid change that is predictable? Retail department stores are a good example. They typically make a quarter to a third of their sales in December. The drop-off from December to January is significant. Does this predictable change in consumer demand make department stores' environment dynamic? No. When we talk about degree of change, we mean change that is unpredictable. If change can be accurately anticipated, it is not an uncertainty which managers must confront.

environmental complexity
The number of components in an organization's environment and the extent of an organization's knowledge about its environmental components.

The other dimension of uncertainty describes the degree of **environmental complexity**. The degree of complexity refers to the number of components in an organization's environment and the extent of the knowledge that the organization has about those components. Furniture-maker, Lacasse Inc. of St-Pie-de-Bagot, Quebec, came up with a unique idea to keep its environmental complexity low, while outsourcing work to keep its fast-growing company manageable and focused. The company provides loans to entrepreneurs with sound business plans, and sells them land, as well as a factory developed by Lacasse. Through this process, Lacasse has fostered the start-up of 30 independent companies which provide the furniture-maker with various products. Lacasse thereby has its suppliers practically next door, so they can deliver on a just-in-time basis. Rather than always looking for new suppliers, Lacasse has a permanent system of suppliers with whose workings it is thoroughly familiar.[20] The fewer competitors, customers, suppliers and government agencies that an organization must interact with, the less uncertainty there is in its environment.

CAE Inc.
www.cae.ca/

Complexity is also measured in terms of the knowledge an organization needs to have about its environment. For instance, managers at CAE Inc. of Toronto, a designer and producer of aircraft flight simulators, must know a great deal about the operations of the companies they supply. Whether they are designing simulators for commercial or military pilots or space ventures for Russian cosmonauts, CAE must have a great deal of information concerning their customers' operations in order to ensure that the programs perform flawlessly.[21] Managers of retail grocery stores, in contrast, have a minimal need for sophisticated knowledge about their suppliers.

Environmental uncertainty can be described as shown in the matrix in Figure 3-3. There are four cells, with cell 1 being lowest in environmental uncertainty and cell 4 being highest. Management's influence on organizational outcomes is greatest in cell 1 and least in cell 4.

Since uncertainty is a threat to an organization's effectiveness, managers try to minimize it. Given a choice, managers would prefer to operate in environments like those in cell 1. But managers rarely have full control over that choice. For example, managers of firms that produced and marketed computers and information systems in the mid-1990s, found themselves in cell 4. Because they chose this particular niche to operate in, they faced a highly dynamic and complex environment. Had they chosen to manufacture standard wire coat hangers, they would probably have found themselves in cell 1.

FIGURE 3-3 Environmental Uncertainty Matrix

Degree of Complexity		Degree of Change: Stable	Degree of Change: Dynamic
Simple		**Cell 1** Stable and predictable environment Few components in environment Components are somewhat similar and remain basically the same Minimal need for sophisticated knowledge of components	**Cell 2** Dynamic and unpredictable environment Few components in environment Components are somewhat similar but are in continual process of change Minimal need for sophisticated knowledge of components
Complex		**Cell 3** Stable and predictable environment Many components in environment Components are not similar to one another and remain basically the same High need for sophisticated knowledge of components	**Cell 4** Dynamic and unpredictable environment Many components in environment Components are not similar to one another and are in continual process of change High need for sophisticated knowledge of components

The Organization and Its Environment. Figure 3-4 summarizes our position that an organization is an open system that interacts with, and depends on, its specific environment while remaining ever aware of the potential influences of its general environment.

In the following sections we elaborate on the components in both the specific and general environments and show how environments can constrain the choices available to managers.

FIGURE 3-4 The Organization and Its Environment

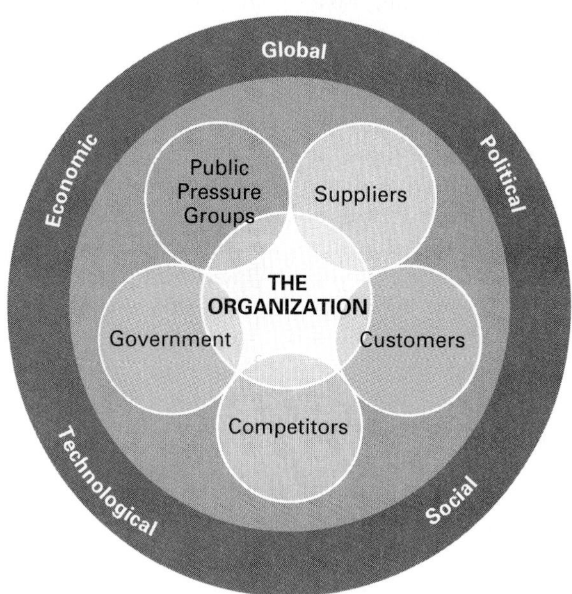

The Specific Environment

As previously noted, different organizations face different specific environments. Most organizations, though, are influenced by the following external factors that impose uncertainty: suppliers, customers, competitors, governmental agencies and special-interest pressure groups.

Suppliers. When you think of an organization's suppliers, you typically think of firms that provide materials and equipment. For Canada's Wonderland, this includes firms that sell soft drink syrups, computers, food, flowers and other nursery stock, concrete, and paper products. But the term *suppliers* also includes providers of financial and labour inputs. Shareholders, banks, insurance companies, pension funds and other similar institutions are needed to ensure a continuous supply of capital. Exxon can have drilling rights to an oil field that can generate billions of dollars in profits, but the profits will remain only potential profits unless management can obtain the funds necessary to drill the wells. Labour unions, occupational associations and local labour markets are sources of employees. A lack of qualified nurses, for instance, can make it difficult for a hospital to fulfill demand and achieve its objectives.

Management seeks to ensure a steady flow of needed inputs at the lowest possible price. Because these inputs represent uncertainties—that is, their unavailability or delay can significantly reduce the organization's effectiveness—management typically goes to great efforts to ensure a steady reliable flow. As you'll see later in this book, the reason most large organizations have purchasing, finance and human resources departments is to supply the machinery, equipment, capital, and labour inputs they need to operate.

Identifying Environmental Opportunities

In an uncertain environment the risks associated with starting a new business venture are high. Yet this doesn't stop individuals from pursuing their dreams of being an entrepreneur. How do entrepreneurs get their ideas?[22]

A survey of 100 entrepreneurs who created some of the fastest-growing private companies, showed that the overwhelming majority (71 percent) replicated or modified an idea gained through previous employment. As an example, take Jason Hanley and his company, Soccer Plus International Group Ltd. Hanley worked at a sporting goods store before deciding to go out on his own with a specialized outlet. At the age of 22, he is co-owner of a successful Peterborough, Ontario, store and won a Student Entrepreneur of the Year award in 1998.[23]

The next largest percentage of survey respondents (20 percent) said they got their ideas for an entrepreneurial venture from a serendipitous discovery. Included in this group were comments such as: "built temporary or casual job into a business", "happened to read about the industry", "wanted product and service as an individual consumer", and "thought up idea during honeymoon in Italy"! Three brothers from PEI have brought to market a product developed in response to their mother's admonitions to keep their hockey gear off the floor. Nicholas (19), Mitchell (15), and Chad (11) MacLean are marketing a multi-level metal hanger system for hockey pads, pants and helmets.[24]

Finally, a small percentage of respondents indicated that they got their ideas from the personal computer revolution (5 percent) and through systematic research for opportunities (4 percent). Scanning the environment to take advantage of trends can be a good approach for entrepreneurs to develop successful and profitable ideas. Greg Thompson was visiting England looking into a virtual-reality operation called Legend Quest, but upon asking directions to the site, local kids told him he must have been thinking of "Laser Quest". He was misdirected to a laser-tag game complex and immediately recognized that this was a great opportunity. Now Thompson's company, Versent Corp., in Mississauga, Ontario, runs over 50 Laser Quest centres in Canada and the US. In 1998 the company was ranked fourth in Canada on *Profit* magazine's list of the country's fastest growing companies. Versent's five-year revenue gains were up by 9804 percent.[25]

Although entrepreneurs get their ideas in different ways, it's obvious that they are particularly alert to environmental factors that can prove to be the beginning of a new business venture. ■

Customers. Organizations exist to meet the needs of customers. It is the customer or client who absorbs the organization's output. This is true even for governmental organizations. They exist to provide services and we are reminded, especially at election time, that we indicate how satisfied we actually are as customers, by the way we vote.

Customers obviously represent potential uncertainty to an organization. Customers' tastes can change. They can become dissatisfied with the organization's product or service. Of course, some organizations face considerably more uncertainty as a result of their customers than do others. Companies selling Canadian beef have been facing declining sales in recent years due to the changing tastes of many Canadians, who have become more health-conscious and who associate red meat with such things as clogged arteries and heart problems. No amount of marketing seems to have been able to change the way people perceive beef in this country. Beef is still seen as unhealthy, despite television advertising showing well-known athletes eating it. This change in customers' tastes has had a great impact on Canadian beef producers. But they may well have found a solution to their waning customer base. Instead of focusing on Canadian customers, as the industry has done traditionally, it is now paying more attention to Asian markets. Places such as Japan, Korea and Hong Kong have major markets hungry for Canadian beef—including cuts such as the tongue and feet, that are virtually worthless in the Canadian market.[26]

Competitors. All organizations—even monopolies—have one or more competitors. Canada Post has a monopoly on mail service (but it competes against Federal Express), as well as other forms of communication such as the telephone, e-mail, and fax machines. York University has to compete against the University of Toronto, McMaster, Queen's, Western, Guelph and a host of other universities, as well as colleges. Even non-profit organizations such as the Nova Scotia Youth Orchestra and Girl Guides of Canada compete for dollars, volunteers and customers.

No managers can afford to ignore the competition. When they do, they pay dearly! Many problems incurred by the railroads from the 1940s through the 1970s have been attributed to their failure to recognize who their competitors were. They believed they were in the railroad business when, in fact, they were in the transportation business. Trucking, shipping, aviation, and bus and private automobile transportation are all competitors of railroads. Twenty-five years ago, a handful of networks controlled what North Americans could watch on television. Today, with cable networks, VCRs and satellite dishes, viewers have a much broader choice of what to watch. In fact, as technological capabilities expand with the development of the information superhighway, the number of viewing options will explode, providing even more competition.

These examples illustrate that competitors—in terms of pricing, services offered, new products developed, and the like—represent an important environmental force that management must monitor and to which it must be prepared to respond.

Government. Federal, provincial and local governments influence what organizations can and cannot do. Legislation dictates business practices in that businesses must operate according to laws and regulations. Certain organizations, by virtue of their business, are scrutinized by specific government agencies. Organizations in the telecommunications industry—including telephone companies, and radio and television stations—are regulated by the Canadian Radio and Telecommunications Commission. The Bank of Canada establishes guidelines for the chartered banks.

CBC
www.cbc.ca/

Provincial and local government regulations extend and modify many federal standards. For instance, the government of British Columbia will be imposing increasingly strict pollution laws on companies in the next decade.

Organizations spend a great deal of time and money to meet government regulations.[27] But the effects of these regulations go beyond time and money. They also reduce managerial discretion. They limit the choices available to managers.

Consider the decision to dismiss an employee.[28] Historically, employees were free to quit an organization at any time and employers had the right to fire an employee at any time with or without cause. Recent laws and court decisions, however, have put increasing limits on what employers may do. Employers are increasingly expected to deal with employees by following

MANAGERS WHO MAKE A DIFFERENCE

Robert Stollery and Ross Grieve, PCL Construction Group Inc

As CEO of Edmonton's PCL, Ross Grieve's job of keeping employees motivated is made much easier by the company's strong organizational culture.

One of the strongest corporate cultures in Canada is evidenced in Edmonton-based PCL Construction Group. As CEO of PCL, Ross Grieve has the pleasure of heading up one of the country's most successful companies. PCL is among the 10 largest construction contractors in all of North America. The company did $1.7 billion worth of business in 1997, putting it in the top 200 Canadian companies for 1998. But what truly makes PCL stand out is the strength of its culture.

PCL's shares are owned by its employees. Around 750 employees out of 1300 working for the company have shares in PCL, while no one employee is allowed more than 10 percent of the company's stock. The idea for employee ownership was devised by Robert Stollery back in 1977, as part of the financing package he put together to buy the company from the existing owners. Stollery's stamp is firmly imprinted on PCL's corporate culture. He remained CEO of PCL until 1993, by which time the company was completely owned by its employees.

The ownership structure makes it very easy for employees to remain motivated. All salaried employees benefit from a profit-sharing plan (10 to 20 percent of pre-tax profits are distributed among employees) and also receive dividends on their shares. PCL's ownership structure mandates that employees at all levels of management must divest themselves of all shares when they reach age 64. This allows shares to constantly recycle through to younger employees, keeping PCL continually rejuvenated. The ownership structure not only motivates employees, it also keeps upper management on its toes. As Ross Grieve has said: "There are 750 sets of eyes watching that we're doing a good job". ■

the principles of good faith and fair dealing. Employees who feel that they have been wrongfully discharged can take their case to court. Juries are increasingly deciding what is or isn't "fair". This has made it more difficult for managers to fire poor performers or dismiss employees for bad off-duty conduct, or, in fact, for bad on-duty conduct. For an example of the legal limits placed on employers, take Imperial Oil Ltd.'s alcohol and drug-testing policies. In early 1998, an Ontario court unanimously decided against Imperial Oil's appeal to be allowed to keep its drug-testing policy.[29] Imperial's policy regarding drugs and alcohol subjected employees to random testing, and gave the company the right to question all employees concerning any history of substance abuse. Canadian law protects individuals' rights to privacy, as well as preventing employers from discriminating against individuals with drug or alcohol problems. Meanwhile, companies such as Imperial Oil and the Toronto Dominion Bank continue to appeal to higher courts to protect drug and alcohol policies, even though they have been found to be discriminatory.

Pressure Groups. Managers must recognize the special-interest groups that attempt to influence the actions of organizations. One of the best examples of pressure groups influencing corporate policy is that of MacMillan Bloedel. The largest forestry company in Canada had been fighting a public-relations war with environmental groups—and principally with Greenpeace—for years. Then suddenly, in the summer of 1998, it seemed as though MacBlo was surrendering. Environmentalists had convinced some major European timber retailers to boycott wood

The influence of pressure groups such as Greenpeace contributed to the gradual erosion of MacMillan Bloedel's profitability. Eventually MacBlo was forced to completely restructure its operations.

from British Columbia, and MacBlo could no longer afford to ignore the ever-growing public disapproval of its operations. MacBlo announced it was ending its clear-cutting practices—the environmentally-unfriendly method that accounted for 95 percent of BC logging.[30]

The General Environment

In this section, we discuss economic, political, social, global, and technological conditions that can affect the management of organizations. Although these factors usually do not have as strong an effect on an organization's operations as the specific environment, management must also take them into account.

Economic Conditions. Interest rates, inflation rates, changes in disposable income, stock market indexes, and the stage of the general business cycle are some of the economic factors in the general environment that can affect management practices in an organization.

When the Canadian dollar hit an all-time low in 1998, it was a great boon to Canadian companies who are major exporters. However, companies who have to rely on imported supplies found their costs rising dramatically. As another example of economic conditions affecting a company's operations, Seagram Co. Ltd. took a major loss as a result of the Asian economic crisis; when currency values plummeted, Seagram's spirits division in Asia was hit hard.

Political Conditions. Political conditions include the general stability of the countries in which an organization operates and the specific attitudes which elected government officials hold towards business.

THINKING CRITICALLY ABOUT ETHICS

You're the program director of an FM radio rock station in Calgary. One afternoon you receive a call from a well-respected businessman who is a spokesman for the Chinese community in Calgary. He says a popular song you are playing is degrading to women—particularly Chinese women—and he asks that you stop playing it. What do you do? What guidelines might you suggest for dealing with the demands of special-interest groups that would be both ethical and good for business? ■

TESTING... TESTING...

5 Describe an effective culture for (a) a relatively stable environment and (b) a dynamic environment.

6 How can pressure groups constrain managerial decisions?

7 How can federal government regulations constrain managerial discretion?

In Canada, organizations have generally operated in a stable political environment. But management is a global activity. Moreover, many Canadian firms have operations in countries whose record for stability is quite erratic—for example, Libya, China and Iran. The internal aspects of management require that organizations attempt to forecast major political changes in countries in which they operate. In this way, management can better anticipate political conditions, from the devaluation of a country's monetary unit to a dictator's decision to nationalize certain industries and expropriate their assets.

Social Conditions. Management must adapt its practices to the changing expectations of the society in which it operates. As values, customs and tastes change, so too must management. This applies to both their product and service offerings, as well as their internal operating policies. Examples of social conditions that have had a significant impact on the management of certain organizations include the changing career expectations of women and the aging of the workforce.

Inflation, the women's movement and an increased divorce rate have all contributed to a dramatic increase in female labour participation rates. Today, more than half of all adult women are employed outside the home. This change has profoundly changed the way that organizations such as Tupperware and Avon Products traditionally operated. Instead of purchasing cosmetics and housewares from a sales representative who comes to the home, today's working woman tends to buy these products during her lunch hour or at the grocery store on the way home after work. Banks, automobile manufacturers and makers of women's clothing have also found their markets changing because of women's career expectations. Women want higher credit lines; they look for cars that are consistent with their new lifestyles; and their wardrobe purchases tend to be more professional than casual. Management has also had to adjust its internal organizational policies because of the increase in the number of working women. Organizations that fail to offer child care facilities or family leave policies may find it increasingly difficult to hire competent, committed female employees.

The baby-boom generation, born between 1947 and 1965 in Canada (American statistics use the boundaries of 1946 and 1964), is the largest generation in the population. It is 70 percent larger than its parents' generation and 21 percent larger than the youth of today (aged 6 to 22). Now, in 1999, many of the first baby-boomers are turning 50. The peak birth rates occurred from 1954 to 1964, making the largest group of baby-boomers somewhere between

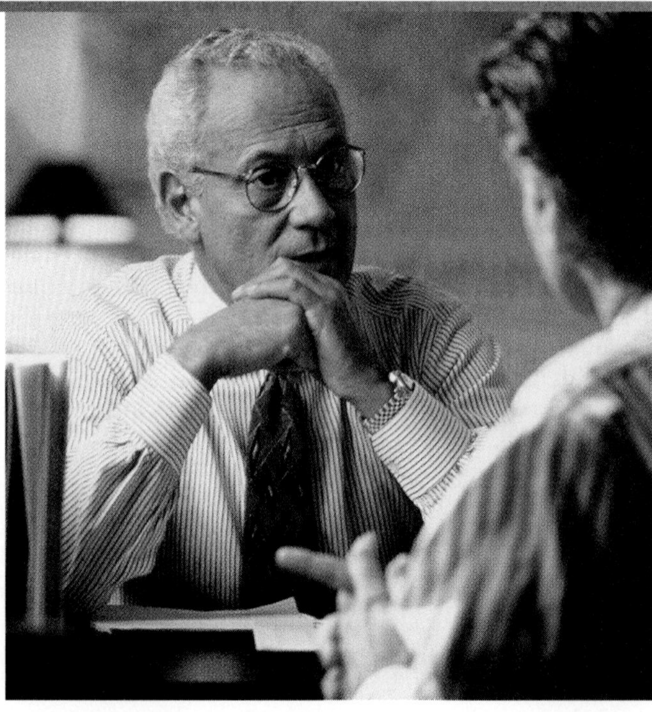

The aging of the workforce is having a significant impact on managerial practices both inside and outside the organization.

35 and 45 years old in 1999. All of this means that the next few decades will see a great rise in the need for health care services and retirement facilities.[31] It also means that organizations will have to redesign products and services for an aging market. Levi Strauss, for example, now produces fuller-cut jeans designed to fit the middle-aged person's body. Inside organizations, management can expect to have more employees in their fifties, sixties and even seventies! This is likely to translate into more experienced workers with needs that differ from those of their younger co-workers. For instance, older workers tend to place greater value on such employee benefits as health insurance and pension plans, and less value on college tuition reimbursement programs and generous moving allowances.

Global. Globalization has been identified as one of the major revolutions affecting management and organizations.[32] As part of the external environment, managers of both large and small international organizations are challenged by an increasing number of global competitors and consumer markets. In fact, we think this component of the external environment is so important that we devote the next chapter to discussing it.

Technological Conditions. Our final consideration in the external environment is technology. We live in a time of technological change. In terms of the four components in the general environment, the most rapid changes during the past quarter-century have probably occurred in technology. We now have automated offices, electronic meetings, robotic manufacturing, lasers, integrated circuits, microprocessors and synthetic fuels. Companies that take advantage of technology prosper, such as Syncrude Canada Ltd., with its synthetic oil, and Calgary-based Environmental Technologies, Inc., a company that extracts methane gas from landfills and converts it to energy.[33] Many retailers, such as the Bay, use sophisticated inventory information systems to keep on top of current sales trends. Other organizations, like Dofasco Inc. of Hamilton, Ontario, consider information a competitive advantage and have adopted technologically advanced information services to stay ahead of their competition. Similarly, hospitals, universities, airports, police departments and even military organizations that adapt to major technological advances have a competitive edge over those that do not.

Dofasco Inc.
www.dofasco.ca

Another example of how the technological environment affects management is in the design of offices. Offices have become virtual communication centres. Management can now link its computers, telephones, word processors, photocopiers, fax machines, filing storage and other office activities into an integrated system. Many organizations are using **intranets** (internal organizational communication systems that use Internet technology and are accessible only by organizational employees) to help employees do their work effectively and efficiently. For managers of all organizations, these technological advancements mean faster and better decision-making capabilities.

intranets
Internal organizational communication systems that use Internet technology and are accessible only by employees.

Influence on Management Practice

As we have seen, organizations are not self-contained or self-sufficient. They interact with, and are influenced by, their environment. Organizations depend on their environment as a source of inputs and as a recipient of its outputs. Organizations must also abide by the laws and regulations and respond to groups that challenge the organization's actions. As such, suppliers, customers, government agencies, public pressure groups and similar constituencies can exert power over an organization. This power, for instance, is unusually evident among publicly held companies whose stock is controlled by such institutional investors as insurance companies, mutual funds and pension plans. When these institutions hold a controlling amount of stock in an organization, their interests can dictate management's interests. They have the power to control boards of directors and, indirectly, to fire management. The result is that management's options are constrained to reflect the desires of these institutional investors. Even when an organization's managers do not face constraints from such groups, they must cope with other changes in the environment.

A survey of 400 chief executives indicates that they see the environment changing even faster than it is now.[34] As shown in Table 3-3, a large majority of those executives surveyed felt that change in their companies was rapid and that this pace of change would continue to accelerate. Even more surprising was the fact that fewer than half of these CEOs felt that their companies were extremely capable of coping with changing environmental forces.

TABLE 3-3 Executives' Views on External Environmental Changes (survey of 400 executives)

Change in their companies is rapid or extremely rapid	79%
They have a conservative or reluctant approach to change	62%
The pace of change will accelerate	61%
Their companies are very capable of coping with change	47%
Their companies have formal structures to handle change	44%
Large corporations are best equipped to manage change	32%
They could not name a company good at managing change	25%

Source: Keith H. Hammonds, "In Business This Week," *Business Week*, September 20, 1993, p. 44.

As we have stated throughout this chapter, many of the environmental forces are dynamic and create considerable uncertainty for management. Customers' tastes and preferences change. New laws are enacted. Suppliers can't meet contractual delivery dates. Competitors introduce new technologies, products and services. Because these environmental uncertainties cannot be anticipated, they often force management to respond in ways that it might not prefer. The greater the environmental uncertainty an organization faces, the more the environment limits management's options and its freedom to determine its own destiny.

TESTING... TESTING...

8 What can managers do to minimize environmental uncertainty?

9 Why do managers try to minimize environmental uncertainty?

10 What effect, if any, does the general environment have on managerial practice?

SUMMARY

This summary is organized by the learning objectives found at the beginning of the chapter.

1. The omnipotent view is dominant in management theory and in society. It argues that managers are directly responsible for the success or failure of an organization. In contrast, the symbolic view argues that management has only a limited effect on substantive organizational outcomes because of the large number of factors outside management's control; however, management greatly influences symbolic outcomes.
2. Organizational culture is a system of shared meaning within an organization that determines, to a large degree, how employees act.
3. An organization's culture is composed of seven characteristics: innovation and risk taking; attention to detail; outcome orientation; people orientation; team orientation; aggressiveness; and stability.
4. Culture constrains managers because it acts as an automatic filter that biases the manager's perceptions, thoughts and feelings. Strong cultures particularly constrain a manager's decision-making options by conveying which alternatives are acceptable and which are not.
5. The general environment encompasses forces that have the potential to affect the organization but whose relevance is not clear. The specific environment is that part of the environment that is directly relevant to the achievement of the organization's goals.
6. Environmental uncertainty is determined by the degree of *change* and *complexity* in the environment. Stable and simple environments are relatively certain. The more dynamic and complex the environment, the higher the uncertainty.
7. The components of the specific environment include suppliers, customers, competitors, government agencies and public pressure groups.
8. Factors in the general environment include economic, political, social, global and technological factors.
9. High environmental uncertainty limits management's options and its freedom to determine its own destiny.

THINKING ABOUT MANAGEMENT ISSUES

1. Classrooms have cultures. Describe your class culture. Does it constrain your instructor? If so, how?
2. Define a local hardware store's specific environment. How does it constrain the store manager?
3. Refer to Table 3-1. How would a first-line supervisor's job differ in these two organizations?
4. When a large corporation loses money for several years in a row, the board of directors almost always replaces the CEO. Why?
5. Managers are often characterized as being "boundary spanners". What do you think this term refers to, and why do you think it might be an important description of what a manager does in relation to external environmental factors?

SELF-ASSESSMENT EXERCISE

WHAT KIND OF ORGANIZATIONAL CULTURE FITS YOU BEST?

For each of the following statements, circle the level of agreement or disagreement that you personally feel:

SA = Strongly agree
A = Agree
U = Uncertain
D = Disagree
SD = Strongly disagree

	Strongly Agree				Strongly Disagree
1. I like being part of a team and having my performance assessed in terms of my contribution to the team.	SA	A	U	D	SD
2. No person's needs should be compromised in order for a department to achieve its goals.	SA	A	U	D	SD
3. I prefer a job where my boss leaves me alone.	SA	A	U	D	SD
4. I like the thrill and excitement of taking risks.	SA	A	U	D	SD
5. People shouldn't break rules.	SA	A	U	D	SD
6. Seniority in an organization should be highly rewarded.	SA	A	U	D	SD
7. I respect authority.	SA	A	U	D	SD
8. If a person's job performance is inadequate, it's irrelevant how much effort he or she made.	SA	A	U	D	SD
9. I like things to be predictable.	SA	A	U	D	SD
10. I'd prefer my identity and status to come from my professional expertise than from the organization that employs me.	SA	A	U	D	SD

See scoring key beginning on page SK-1.

Source: Stephen P. Robbins, *Organizational Behavior*, 6th ed. (Englewood Cliffs, NJ: Prentice Hall, 1993), p. 626.

for your IMMEDIATE action

To: Rick Katzfey, Director of Research
From: Freda Rowe, VP of Operations
Subject: Competitive Intelligence

First off, I'd like to say "welcome aboard!" The other members of the management team and I are looking forward to working with you as we develop and grow our chain of restaurants. As you're well aware, themed "eatertainment" restaurants (like our competitors, Planet Hollywood, Hard Rock Café, etc.) have been extremely popular. We think our idea for a Wild Wild West theme should mirror this success.

However, before we proceed further with our final business plan, we're going to need some information about our competition. We'd like to know the following: (1) Who are our major competitors? (2) What are their "themes"? (3) What unique activities are they doing? and (4) What are their sales and profits figures (if available)? Could you provide me with this information in a two-page report by the end of the week?

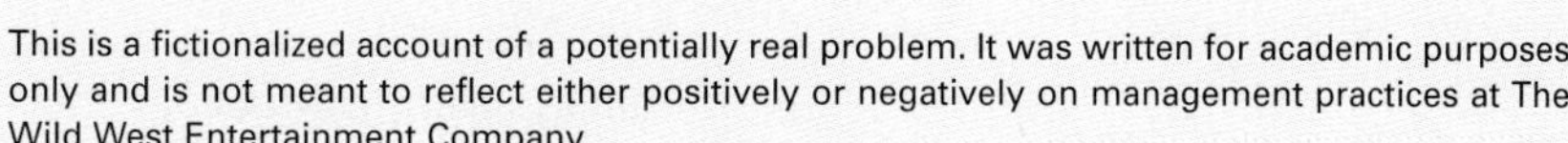

This is a fictionalized account of a potentially real problem. It was written for academic purposes only and is not meant to reflect either positively or negatively on management practices at The Wild West Entertainment Company.

TAKE IT TO THE NET

We invite you to visit the Robbins/Coulter/Stuart-Kotze Companion Website at www.prenticehall.ca/robbins for this chapter's Internet resources.

CASE APPLICATION

SOL Cleaning Services, Helsinki, Finland

In Helsinki, Finland, a cleaning company has created an organizational culture unlike any other in its industry. The headquarters of SOL Cleaning Service is awash with bright colours; work areas ("neighbourhoods") each have a distinct style, such as a treehouse motif, or tables made as a jigsaw puzzle; and the employee training room is a high-tech multimedia centre. Such bright and energetic surroundings might seem better-suited to creativity-driven companies like software firms of advertising agencies, than to a company like SOL, which is an industrial cleaner—scrubbing hospital floors, making hotel beds and sweeping grocery store aisles.

SOL began as a spin-off of a family-owned business. In its first five years (to 1997) its employees grew from 2000 to 3500, its customers from 1500 to 3000, and its revenues from $40 million to $70 million. And it has continued to grow successfully. What does SOL do differently in order to succeed in an industry notorious for high turnover, low wages and terrible service? The company is characterized by five values.

First, hard work has to be fun. Liisa Joronen, CEO, believes that since being a cleaner is not exactly most people's dream career, the job must be fun and individuals must have freedom, to ensure their job satisfaction. Cleaners wear bright jumpsuits. The company's logo—a yellow happy face—is plastered on everything from the company stationery to the most important financial statements. Employees enjoy the freedom of minimal rules and regulations; there are no titles; and, in the interests of promoting a less hierarchical workplace, the company has eliminated all upper management perks and status symbols.

The second corporate value characterizing SOL is that there are no low-skill jobs. The company invests significant amounts of time and money in training employees. There are only so many ways to polish a table or shampoo a carpet, so SOL employees also study topics such as time management, people skills and budgeting. Training is focused on turning cleaners into customer service specialists.

Another corporate value at SOL is allowing employees to set their own targets, and giving them significant amounts of responsibility and authority. The company's supervisors, each of whom leads a team of up to 50 cleaners, work with the teams to create their own budgets, do their own hiring and negotiate their own deals with customers. Joronen's philosophy is that people will set higher targets for themselves than those which anyone else would set for them. These self-managed teams can even build their own offices.

The fourth value is that loose organizations need tight measures. Although Joronen believes in employee autonomy, she is a fanatic about performance measurement and accountability. The company measures performance frequently, and most of these measures focus on customer satisfaction. As Joronen says, "The more we free our people from rules, the more we need good measurements."

Finally, SOL believes that great service demands cutting-edge technology. SOL may be in a "low-end" business, but that doesn't mean it has to be low-tech. In fact, laptop computers and cellular phones are standard equipment for all supervisors at SOL. Why? This investment in technology frees them to work where and how they want to work. The company also stores all of its critical budget documents and performance reports on its intranet and uses it for scheduling training, relaying company news, and informing employees about upcoming company events.

QUESTIONS

1. Using Figure 3-2, describe SOL's organizational culture.
2. Would the five values that characterize SOL's culture be as effective in other types of organizations? Why or why not?
3. Describe how you think new employees at SOL might "learn" culture?
4. Which of the seven types of organizational personality would you characterize SOL as having? Support your choice.
5. How might SOL's culture constrain the behaviour of a newly hired executive?

Source: G. Imperato, "Dirty Business, Bright Ideas". *Fast Company Web Page* <http://www.fastcompany.com>, April 16, 1997.

LEARNING OBJECTIVES

After Reading This Chapter, You Should Be Able To:

1. Explain the importance of viewing management from a global perspective
2. Describe problems created by national parochialism
3. Contrast multinational and transnational corporations
4. Explain why many countries have become part of regional trading alliances
5. Describe the typical stages by which organizations go international
6. Explain the four dimensions of national culture
7. Describe Canadian culture according to the four dimensions
8. Describe the challenges of being a manager on global assignment

A MANAGER'S CHALLENGE

Walter Kuskowski, CEO, Wentworth Technologies, Hamilton, Ontario.

Wentworth Technologies Co. Ltd. is a manufacturer of blow-moulds which are used to produce plastic containers for the food and beverage industry. It is a specialized market, and CEO Walter Kuskowski believes that this provides a definite competitive edge: "When you're focused like this, hopefully you can become number one or two in your chosen field. That means you'll have better market reach and more economies of scale". Wentworth has customers all over the world, since companies like soft-drink bottlers operate on a global scale. With plants in various markets such as the US, UK, Poland and Asia, Wentworth can service some customers with a relatively local presence but, when dealing with clients as far-flung as Fiji, it helps to be able to take advantage of information technology capabilities such as the Internet. "With the progress in communications, we can talk to anyone in the world—or even send our designs to anyone in the world—on a moment's notice," Kuskowski has said.[1]

The challenge for Wentworth in its quest for global domination of the marketplace is providing its customers with excellent service. Being able to respond quickly to its customers' needs can give Wentworth a competitive edge, and the company does everything in its power to provide rapid service. For instance, when a company in the Philippines had taken its moulds apart for maintenance but lacked the expertise to put them back together, operations had to be shut down. When Wentworth was contacted, they immediately put a technician on a plane to Manila. This sort of customer response is the kind that can ensure Wentworth's place in the global market. Another good example of Wentworth's commitment is the story of how a shipment of moulds was sent to the Crimea from Toronto, but was held up in Berlin when the plane destined for the Berlin-Crimea leg of the trip was found to be too small. The customer began calling for the shipment so Wentworth immediately hired a trucking firm to drive the shipment, rather than wasting time having the Crimean company try to secure another plane.

The demands of being a global competitor can be complex, but Wentworth is staying on top of its diverse markets by focusing great attention on fast response and customer satisfaction. Better understanding of customers' needs has allowed Wentworth to refine its own operations, and taking full advantage of improvements in technology has made the company far more efficient and responsive.

With the entire world as a marketplace and national borders becoming irrelevant, the potential for organizations to expand is reaching vast new proportions. However, the elimination of global borders and trade barriers works both ways—new competitors can appear at any time. Managers who don't closely monitor and respond quickly to changes in their global environment will find new competitors taking advantage.

Chapter 4 Managing in a Global Environment

WHO OWNS WHAT?

One way to grasp the changing nature of the global environment is to consider the country of ownership origin for some familiar products and companies. You might be surprised to find that many name brand products you thought were made by Canadian or American companies, aren't! Take the following quiz, then check your answers at the end of the chapter.

1. Labatt Brewing company is owned by a __________ company
   a. British b. Canadian c. Belgian d. American
2. The owners of Tim Horton Donuts are:
   a. American b. Japanese c. French d. Canadian
3. Tropicana orange juice is owned by a company with headquarters in:
   a. Canada b. the US c. Spain d. Japan
4. BC Tel is owned by a __________ company
   a. German b. American c. Canadian d. Dutch
5. The largest shareholders of DuMaurier cigarettes are:
   a. British b. Dutch c. American d. Canadian
6. The owner of England's leading "quality" newspaper is:
   a. American b. Canadian c. British d. Australian
7. The producers of Bic pens and lighters are:
   a. Canadian b. American c. French d. Japanese
8. The owners of Universal Studios—the movie, TV and theme-park giant—are:
   a. Japanese b. American c. German d. Canadian
9. The Hong Kong Bank of Canada is 100 percent owned by a company based in:
   a. The US b. The UK c. China d. Canada
10. Yogen Fruz World-Wide Inc. has its headquarters in which country?
    a. Canada b. France c. the US d. Switzerland

To further emphasize our point about the international aspects of business today, take a look at Table 4-1. This is a partial list of Canadian companies which derive half or more of their sales revenues from exports.

WHAT IS YOUR GLOBAL PERSPECTIVE?

It's not unusual for Germans and Italians to speak three or four languages. Most Japanese schoolchildren begin studying English in the early elementary grades. Canada is officially a bilingual country, although many Canadians do not speak both languages. On the other hand, most Americans study only English in school.

parochialism
A selfish, narrow view of the world; an inability to recognize differences between people.

Monolingualism is just one sign of **parochialism**.[2] People with a parochial perspective do not recognize that other people have different ways of living and working. Parochialism is a major obstacle to managers attempting to work and compete abroad, and is becoming more so with the increasingly prevalent "global marketplace". Managers can be guilty of rigidly applying their values and customs to foreign cultures, often with adverse results. Consider the following example:

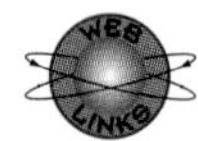

AT&T
www.att.com/

When Northern Telecom was trying to win a contract with China in order to form a joint venture to produce central office telephone switches, the Canadian telecommunications giant hosted China's vice-premier for a week in Canada. The Chinese official visited Niagara Falls, toured NorTel's facilities, and was treated to authentic cooking customary to his home province. NorTel believed that, after a week of lavish treatment, the deal would be secure. But a single day in the US under the hospitality of American Telephone and Telegraph was more impressive to the vice-premier. AT&T organized a police motorcade escort for the visiting dignitary, who drove through the streets in an armour-plated limousine, along with Secret Service protection. This sort of military-style treatment was taken as being a great compliment to the stature of Chinese leaders. Northern Telecom eventually won back the favour of the Chinese government, but not without enormous effort and at great cost.[3]

TABLE 4-1 Selected Canadian Companies Deriving More than Half of Sales Revenues from Exports

Company	Exports as Percentage of Sales
McDonnell Douglas Canada	100
Canadian Wheat Board	89
Chrysler Canada	85
XCAN Grain Pool	85
Pratt & Whitney Canada	83
Avenor Inc.	81
Donahue Inc.	79
Domtar Inc.	79
Weldwood of Canada	76
Canfor Corp.	76

Source: "50 Top Exporters", *Report on Business Magazine*, July, 1998.

Successful global management requires enhanced sensitivity to differences in national customs and practices. Management practices that work in Winnipeg might not be appropriate in Shanghai or Berlin. Later in this chapter and throughout the rest of the book, you will see how a global perspective on managing requires eliminating parochial attitudes and carefully developing an understanding of cultural differences between countries.

THE CHANGING GLOBAL ENVIRONMENT

A number of forces are reshaping the global environment. In this section, we'll discuss a few of the most important of these forces.

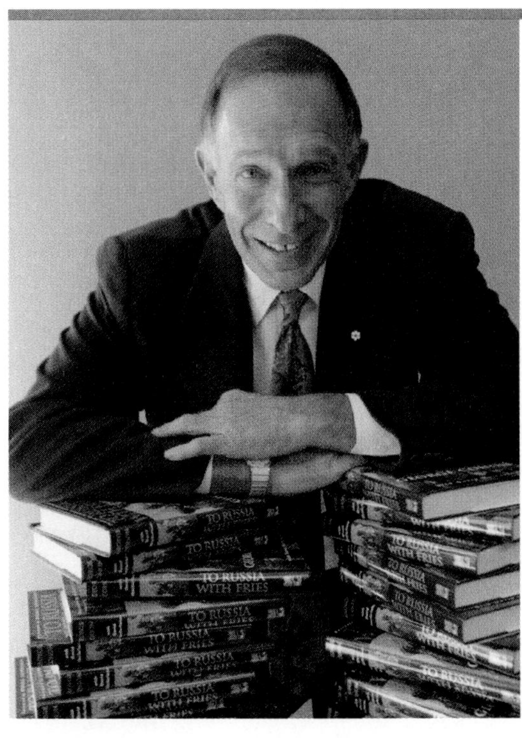

While he was CEO of McDonald's Canada, George Cohon undertook a massive challenge: taking the chain to Moscow, when it was still under Soviet rule. Training Soviet managers in Toronto helped, but overcoming such a vast cultural divide was no easy task. Language barriers, totalitarian bureaucracy, and setting up reliable supply chains in a country whose agricultural industry was on the verge of collapse were only a few of the obstacles Cohon faced.

From Multinationals to Transnationals to Borderless Organizations

International businesses have been around for a long time. Siemens, Remington and Singer, for instance, were already selling their products in many countries in the nineteenth century. Ford Motor Company set up its first overseas sales branch in France in 1908. By the 1920s, other companies, including Fiat, Unilever and Royal Dutch/Shell had gone multinational. But it wasn't until the mid-1960s that **multinational corporations (MNCs)** became commonplace. These corporations—which maintain significant operations in two or more countries simultaneously, but are based in one home country—initiated the rapid growth in international trade.

multinational corporation (MNC)
A company that maintains significant operations in more than one country simultaneously but manages them all from one base in a home country.

The expanding global environment is extending the reach and goals of MNCs to create an even more generic organization called the **transnational corporation (TNC)**. This type of organization doesn't seek to replicate its domestic successes by managing foreign operations from its home country. Rather, decision making in TNCs takes place at the local level. Nationals typically are hired to run operations in each country, and the product and marketing strategies for each country are uniquely tailored to that country's culture. Nestlé, for example, is a transnational corporation. With operations in almost every country on the globe, it is the world's largest food company, yet its managers match their products to their consumers. Thus, Nestlé sells products in parts of Europe that aren't available in Canada or the United States. Another example is Frito-Lay, a division of Pepsi Co., which markets a Dorito chip in the British market that differs both in taste and texture from the US and Canadian versions.

transnational corporation (TNC)
A company that maintains significant operations in more than one country simultaneously and decentralizes decision making in each operation to the local country.

Many large, well-known companies are moving to globalize their management structure more effectively by breaking down internal arrangements that impose artificial geographic barriers. This global type of organization is called a **borderless organization**. Dropping its organizational structure based on country, IBM, for instance, has re-organized into 14 industry groups. Ford merged its culturally distinct European and North American auto operations, with plans to add the Latin American and Asia-Pacific divisions in the future. Bristol-Meyers Squibb changed its consumer business to become more aggressive in international sales, and installed a new executive in charge of worldwide consumer medicines such as Bufferin and Excedrin. The move to borderless management is an attempt by organizations to increase efficiency and effectiveness in a competitive global marketplace.[4]

borderless organization
A global type of organization in which artificial geographical barriers are eliminated so that the management structure can be more effectively globalized.

We should point out that, while managers of multinational and transnational organizations have become increasingly global in their perspectives and accept the reality that national borders no longer define corporations, politicians and the public have been slower to accept this fact.

Free trade has also been blamed for taking Canadian jobs south to the United States. Now, with the North American Free Trade Agreement negotiations, the fear is that Mexico, with its

Many Canadian companies, such as Maple Leaf Foods, have been widely successful in the global marketplace, while still maintaining a distinctly Canadian identity.

low labour rates, will take even more Canadian jobs. There is, however, a weak spot in campaigns to "buy Canadian". Many of the so-called foreign products that critics attack are made in Canada. Toyota Canada has a plant in Cambridge, Ontario.

What about Xerox or McDonald's? When we buy a car, a copier or a burger, are we buying Japanese or American? Who made these products? The answer, of course, is Canadians. The message should be obvious: A company's national origin is no longer a very good gauge of where it does business or of the national origin of its employees. Companies such as General Motors, IBM and Husky Oil employ thousands of people in Canada. At the same time, such Canadian firms as Alcan and Northern Telecom employ thousands in places like Asia, Latin America, the United States and Europe. So, phrases like "Buy Canadian" represent old stereotypes that fail to reflect the changing global environment.

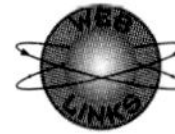

Alcan Aluminum Limited
www.alcan.com

Regional Trading Alliances

Just a few years ago, international competition could be described in terms of country against country—the United States versus Japan, France versus Germany, or Canada versus Australia or Mexico. During the 1990s, global competition is being reshaped by the creation of regional co-operation agreements. The most notable of these include the 15-nation European Union and the North American Free Trade Agreement.

FIGURE 4-1 European Union Countries

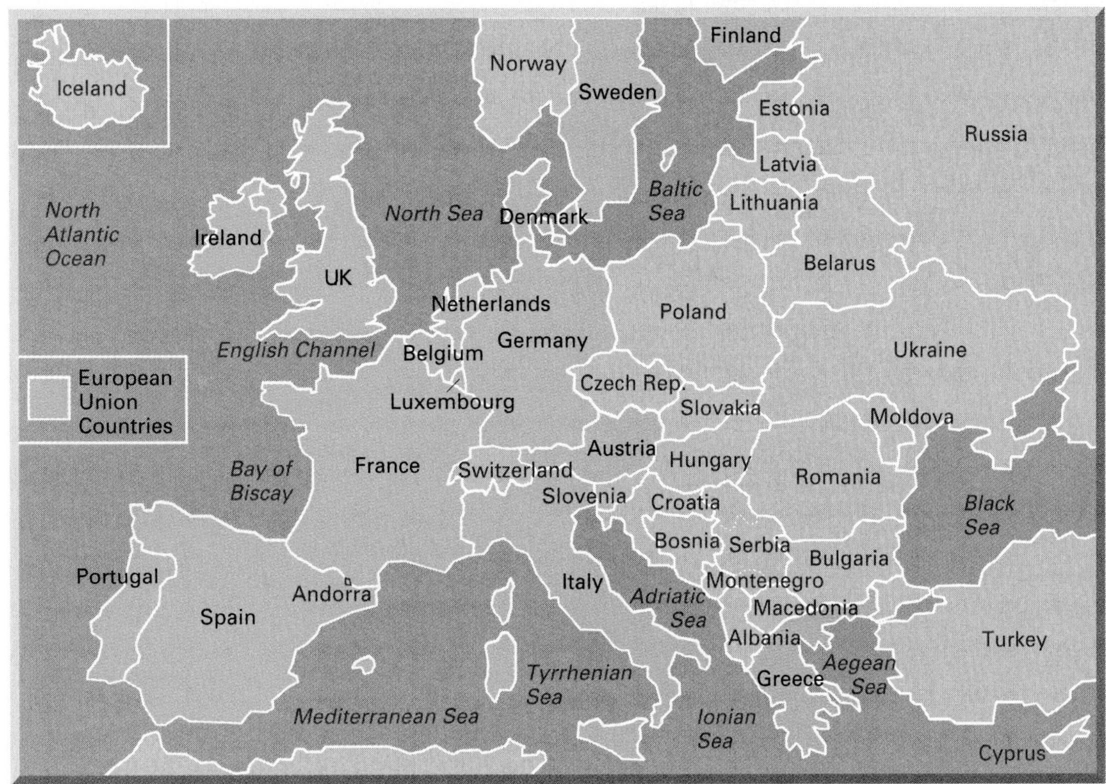

1 What is parochialism, and how does it create problems for managers?

2 Describe the following, and the global perspectives they reflect: multinational corporations; transnational corporations; and borderless corporations.

European economic and monetary union (Emu) An economic integration which, in 1999, saw the advent of a single currency —the euro—for 11 of the countries in the European Union.

European Union (EU) A union of 15 European nations created to eliminate national barriers to travel, employment, investment and trade.

The European Union. January 1, 1999, marked the birth of a new currency in the world—the euro. The new currency is the result of the forming of the **European economic and monetary union (Emu)**. Emu has come from the creation of the **European Union (EU)**. The Emu encompasses all EU members except Greece—which did not meet economic criteria on time—and the UK, Sweden and Denmark—which did not join Emu in 1999 for political reasons, but will likely do so in the next couple of years. The single currency—the euro—is presently used in non-cash transactions and, in 2002, euro bills and coins will be introduced to replace all national denominations.

The signing of the Maastricht Treaty (named for the Dutch town in which the treaty was signed) in February 1992 created the formation of a 12-nation European Union (EU). This treaty united the 380 million people of Belgium, Denmark, France, Greece, Ireland, Italy, Luxembourg, the Netherlands, Portugal, Spain, the United Kingdom and Germany. By 1995, three other countries—Austria, Finland and Sweden—had joined the group.[5] (See Figure 4-1.) Before the creation of the EU, each of these nations had border controls, border taxes, border subsidiaries, nationalistic policies and protected industries. Now, as a single market, there are no national barriers to travel, and there is employment, investment and trade. A driver hauling cargo from Amsterdam to Lisbon can clear four border crossings and five countries by showing a single piece of paper. Before the EU, this same driver would have needed numerous official documents. The ultimate goal of the EU is to have common customs duties and unified industrial and commercial policies, as well as a single currency and a regional central bank. However, many problems have been associated with full implementation and it will undoubtedly take many years to reach the point of full unification.

The primary motivation for the union of these 15 nations was to allow them to re-assert their position against the industrial strength of the United States and Japan. Working in separate countries that erected barriers against one another, European industries were unable to develop the economies of scale enjoyed by American and Japanese firms. The new EU, however, allows European firms to tap into what is now one of the world's single richest markets.

The European Union is furthering global competition by encouraging European MNCs and TNCs to consolidate and merge their operations, as well as to form alliances with new partners. US firms in such diverse industries as telecommunications, heavy equipment, pharmaceuticals, civilian aerospace, banking, automobiles, computers, electronics, food, and beverages now face vigorous challenges from their European counterparts.

The EU has plans to enlarge its membership to the former communist countries of central and eastern Europe by 2002-2003. This target date may be a bit early, as even the strongest candidates (such as Poland) will have to undergo vast economic reform before qualifying for EU single-market status. But integration is almost inevitable, and this will make the economic clout of the EU even greater. By 1997, the EU, with a population of 370 million, accounted for 38.3 percent of the total gross domestic product among the world's leading industrialised nations—making the EU the largest economic market in the world. These numbers will continue to grow as the EU expands.[6]

North American Free Trade Agreement (NAFTA) An agreement among the Mexican, Canadian and US governments in which all barriers to free trade will eventually be eliminated.

North American Free Trade Agreement (NAFTA). When agreements in a number of key areas covered under the **North American Free Trade Agreement (NAFTA)** were reached by the Mexican, Canadian and US governments on August 12, 1992, it opened a vast market of over 363 million consumers, and created an economic bloc exceeding $6 trillion. (See Figure 4-2.) By the end of the 1990s, the North American trading bloc is forecast to average an annual GDP of $8.7 trillion.

NAFTA came into effect in January 1994 and, eventually, all barriers to free trade such as tariffs, import licensing requirements and customs user fees among the three countries, will be eliminated.[7] The signing of NAFTA had both critics and champions.[8] Treaty advocates emphasized the long-term benefits of job creation, market development and increased standard of living for all three countries. Opponents warned that job loss to the US and Mexico would devastate many Canadian industries and would increase Canadian unemployment. Environmentalists feared increased water and air pollution and toxic dumping because of weaker standards by the Mexican and American governments.

Separating truth from fiction on such an agreement is not easy. Two predictions, however, seem relatively certain.[9] First, the treaty will have different effects on different industries. As

FIGURE 4-2 North American Free-Trade Areas

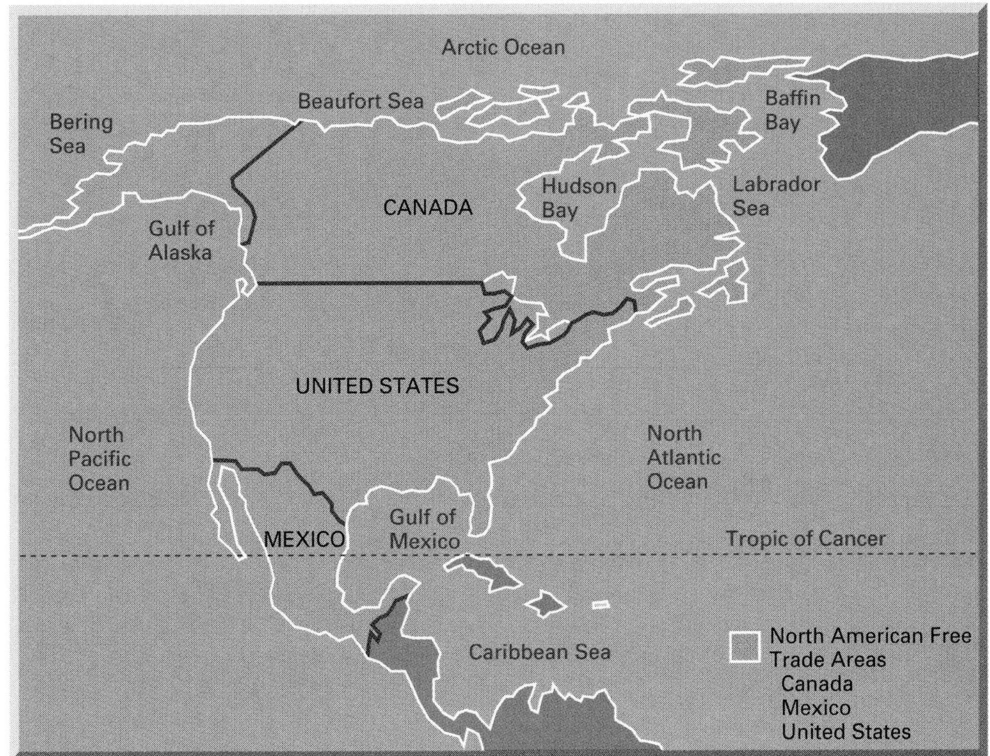

Mexico evolves into a developed economy, Canadian producers of telecommunications equipment, computers, machinery, pharmaceuticals, financial services and consumer goods are likely to benefit. The losers will most likely be low-tech, labour-intensive industries such as textiles, furniture, leather and glass. Second, a lot of labour-intensive industries such as clothing manufacturing will move production from Asia to Mexico. This will create manufacturing jobs for Mexican workers, as well as jobs in Canada in sales, warehousing and management.

In addition, other Latin American nations are clamouring to become part of free-trade blocs. Colombia, Mexico and Venezuela led the way with an economic pact signed in 1994 by all three governments, eliminating import duties and tariffs. Ecuador has asked to join the group and will probably become a part of it. Eventually, these countries hope to entice others in Latin America to join, in order to create a free-trade zone extending from Mexico to Argentina.[10]

There is another free-trade bloc, known as the **Southern Cone Common Market (Mercosur)**—(see Figure 4-3). Mercosur's members are Chile, Brazil, Argentina, Paraguay, Uruguay and Bolivia. As new trading blocs are created in this part of the globe, we are likely to see changes in how organizations—particularly those with significant business interests in these regions—are managed.

Mercosur
The Southern Cone Common Market, a free-trade bloc made up of South-American countries.

Association of Southeast Asian Nations (ASEAN) and Other Asian Developments. The trading alliance, the **Association of Southeast Asian Nations (ASEAN),** currently has 10 members: Brunei, Indonesia, Malaysia, the Philippines, Singapore, Thailand, Vietnam, Myanmar (formerly Burma), Cambodia and Laos (see Figure 4-4). The growth of Southeast Asia has been phenomenal over the past decade, and was obviously far ahead of itself in countries such as Thailand and Indonesia, which both had to be bailed out of economic collapse with tens of billions of dollars from the International Monetary Fund. Many of the ASEAN nations will have to undergo major economic restructuring, but the economic clout of an alliance with a population of around 500 million is very evident. The potential economic power of the Asian

Association of Southeast Asian Nations (ASEAN)
A trading alliance of 10 Southeast Asian nations.

FIGURE 4-3 Mercosur Members

Source: Based on C. Sims, "Chile Will Enter a Big South American Free-Trade Bloc," *New York Times*, June 26, 1996, p. C2.

region in the next century has some politicians in North America and Europe talking about creating a Transatlantic Free Trade Area (TAFTA). This would unite the European Union and NAFTA nations in a trade alliance. However, the proposal is simply speculative at this point.

Another significant historical and economic event in Asia was the return of Hong Kong from British to Chinese rule, back in the summer of 1997. The long-term effects of this transfer are uncertain, but there is no doubt that China will be an increasingly significant economic force in the future.

HOW ORGANIZATIONS GO INTERNATIONAL

How does an organization evolve into a global organization? It typically proceeds through three stages, as shown in Figure 4-5.

In Stage I, management makes its first push towards going international merely by exporting its products to other countries. This is a passive step towards international involvement, involving minimal risk because management makes no serious efforts to tap foreign markets. Rather, the organization fills foreign orders only when—or if—it gets them. For many firms in the mail-order business, this is the first and only international involvement they may have.

In Stage II, management makes an overt commitment to sell its products in foreign countries or to have them made in foreign factories. However, there is still no physical presence of company personnel outside the company's home country. On the sales side, Stage II typically involves either sending domestic employees on regular business trips to meet foreign cus-

Harley Davidson motorcycles symbolize a classic American image worldwide. The company gets approximately 25% of its revenue from global sales. Harleys are a big hit in Tokyo, where waiting lists for the bikes can be up to six months long.

tomers, or hiring foreign agents or brokers to represent the organization's product line. On the manufacturing side, management will contract with a foreign firm to produce its products.

Stage III represents a strong commitment by management to pursue international markets aggressively. As shown in Figure 4-5, this can happen in different ways. Management can *license* or *franchise* the right to use its brand name, technology or product specifications to

FIGURE 4-4 ASEAN Members, 1997

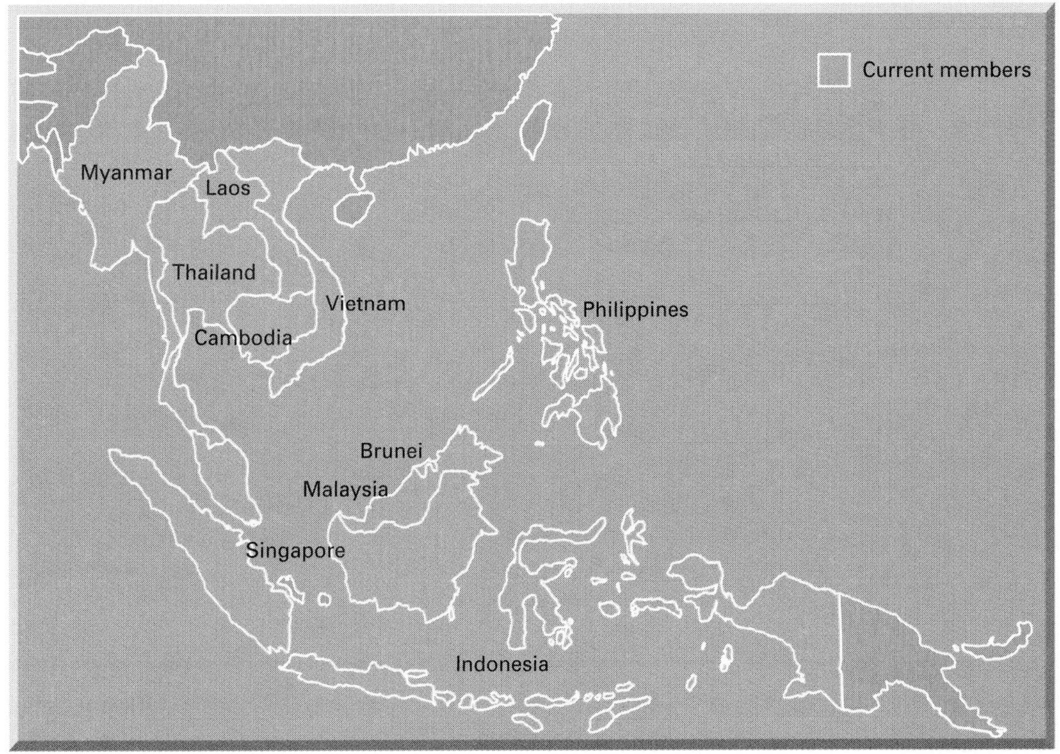

Source: Based on J. McClenahen and T. Clark, "ASEAN at Work," *IW*, May 19, 1997, p. 42.

Air Canada
www.aircanada.ca

another firm. This is a widely used approach among pharmaceutical companies and fast-food chains like Pizza Hut. *Joint ventures* involve a larger commitment since a domestic and a foreign firm share the cost of developing new products or building production facilities in a foreign country. These are also often called *strategic alliances*. These partnerships provide a fast and less expensive way for companies to compete globally. Air Canada co-founded the Star Alliance, a collection of international airlines including United (the largest in the world), Varig (Brazil), Thai Airways, and two major European airlines, Lufthansa and SAS. With this alliance, Air Canada can offer its customers increased connector flights and use of the booking services of all Star Alliance members. Moreover, passengers can earn Aeroplan frequent-flyer points by using any of the member airlines. Management makes its greatest commitment (and assumes the greatest risk) when it sets up a *foreign subsidiary*. As noted earlier in the chapter, this is achieved either through domestic control (multinational operations) or by decentralized control through foreign nationals (transnational operations).

MANAGING IN A FOREIGN ENVIRONMENT

Assume for a moment that you're a Canadian manager who is going to work for a branch of a Canadian multinational in a foreign country. You know that your environment will differ from the one at home, but how? What should you be on the lookout for?

Any manager who finds him or herself in a strange country faces new challenges. In this section, we will look at these challenges and offer some guidelines for responding. Since most readers of this text were raised in Canada, we'll present our discussion through the eyes of a Canadian manager. Of course, our analytical framework can be used by any manager, regardless of national origin, who has to manage in a foreign environment.

The Legal-Political Environment

Canadian managers are accustomed to stable legal and political systems. Changes are slow and procedures are well established. Elections are held within defined periods. Even changes in political parties after a federal election do not produce any quick, radical transformations. The stability of laws governing the actions of individuals and institutions allows for generally accurate predictions. The same cannot be said for all nations.

Some countries have a history of unstable governments. Some South American and African countries have had six different governments in as many years. With each new gov-

FIGURE 4-5 How Organizations Go International

Stage I
Passive Response
Exporting to foreign countries
→
Stage II
Initial Overt Entry
Hiring foreign representation or contracting with foreign manufacturers
→
Stage III
Established International Operations
Licensing/Franchising
Joint Ventures
Foreign Subsidiary

TESTING... TESTING...

3 What are the EU, NAFTA, Mercosur and ASEAN, and what effect might they have on global organizations?

4 Describe the three steps in how organizations go international.

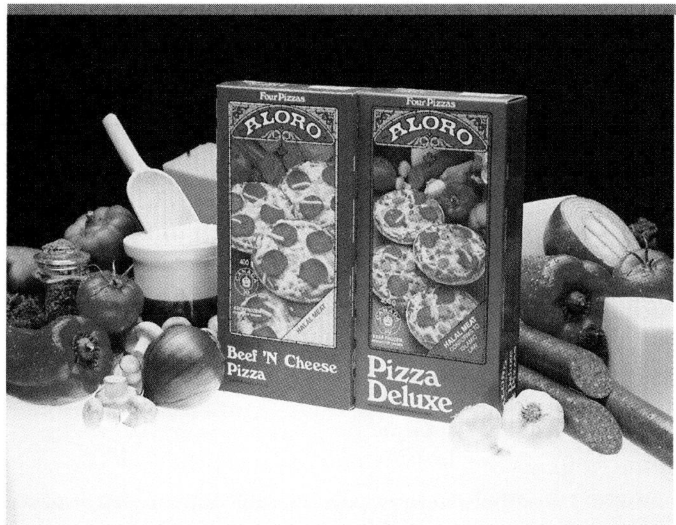

Aloro Foods of Ontario deals with the problems of foreign legal-political environments on a daily basis.

ernment have come new rules. The goal of one government may be to nationalize the country's key industries, while the goal of the next may be to stimulate free enterprise. Managers of business firms in these countries face dramatically greater uncertainty as a result of political instability. Political interference is a fact of life in many Asian countries as well. Political interference is also a factor of doing business in Mexico, as Bombardier found out in 1997, when the company suddenly lost a $500 million subway car contract.[11] Bombardier's technical bid was approved by the government, but then was suddenly refused. As it turned out, a picture published in a Mexican newspaper wrongly identified two men as Bombardier executives who were talking to a political figure of the previous administration—an administration which had been plagued by scandal. Eventually, the Mexican government relented and allowed Bombardier to bid for the contract again.

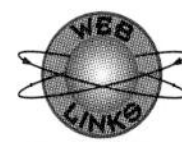

Bombardier Inc.
www.bombardier.com

However, it is not only in nations with unstable governments that politics interferes with business. Even in industrialized Western nations, changing rules can pose problems. A case in point is Aloro Foods of Mississauga, Ontario—a company that exports to countries as diverse as France and Japan. Aloro learned how the political climate can affect business when it tried to ship one of its biggest orders ever to a German supermarket chain. Roughly $100 000 worth of pepperoni pizzas were stopped at the border due to recent changes in meat inspection laws imposed by the European Union.[12]

The legal-political environment need not be unstable or revolutionary to be of concern to managers. Just the fact that a country's social and political system differs from that of Canada is important. Managers must recognize these differences if they are to understand the constraints under which they operate and the opportunities that exist. For example, Hong Kong imposes few legal constraints on business, while France imposes many. Laws differ between nations on industrial spying, restraint of trade, working conditions, payment of bribes, the rights of privacy, the rights of workers, and so forth.

The Economic Environment

The global manager has economic concerns which the manager who operates in a single country doesn't have. Three of the most obvious are fluctuating currency exchange rates, inflation rates and diverse tax policies.

A global firm's profits can vary dramatically depending on the strength of its home currency and the currencies of the countries in which it operates. The Rover Group, purchased by BMW of Germany in the mid-90s, is an automobile company based in England. The strength of the British pound during 1998 resulted in lay-offs, as the cost of production was too high.

Economic inflation rates can vary widely in different regions of the world. For example, in small nations such as Bolivia, annual inflation has been as high as 26 000 percent! Even in larger and more industrialized countries like Brazil, the rate of inflation has sometimes reached 2700 percent. The inflation rate influences prices paid for raw materials, labour and other supplies. In addition, it affects the price that a company can charge for its goods or services.

THINKING CRITICALLY ABOUT ETHICS

Foreign countries often have lax product-labelling laws. As a product manager for a Canadian drug company, you're responsible for the profitability of a new drug, the side effects of which can be serious, although not fatal. Adding this information to the label, or even putting an informational insert into the package, will add significantly to the product's cost, thereby threatening profit margins. What will you do? Why? What factors will influence your decision? ■

Finally, diverse tax policies are a major worry for a global manager. Some host countries are more restrictive than the corporation's home country. Others are far more lenient. The only certainty is that tax rules differ from country to country. Managers need precise knowledge of the various tax rules in countries in which they operate, in order to minimize their corporation's overall tax obligation.

The Cultural Environment

The final environmental force is the cultural differences between nations. As we know from Chapter 3, organizations have different internal cultures. Countries have cultures too, as anthropologists have been telling us for a long time. Like organizational culture, **national culture** is something that is shared by all, or most, inhabitants of a country and is something which shapes their behaviour and the way in which they see the world.[13]

national culture
The attitudes and perspectives shared by individuals from a specific country that shape their behaviour and the way in which they see the world.

Does national culture override an organization's culture? For example, is an IBM facility in Germany more likely to reflect German ethnicity or IBM's corporate culture? Research indicates that national culture has a greater effect on employees than their organization's culture.[14] German employees at an IBM facility in Munich will be influenced more by German culture than by IBM's culture. This means that, as influential as organizational culture may be on managerial practice, national culture is even more so.

Legal, political and economic differences among countries are fairly obvious. The Japanese manager who works in Canada, or his or her Canadian counterpart in Japan, can get information on their new country's laws or tax policies without too much difficulty. However, obtaining information about a new country's cultural differences is a lot harder. The primary

TABLE 4-2 How Alike Are Canadians and Americans?

The following is a list of traits that have been identified as being characteristic of Americans. When you listed what you thought were Canadian traits, did any of these appear on the list? How different do you think Canadians and Americans are? Some people say that all the traits apply, but to a lesser degree.

Americans:

are very informal. They don't tend to treat people differently even when there are great differences in age or social standing.
are direct. They don't talk around things. To some foreigners, this may appear as abrupt or even rude behaviour.
are competitive. Some foreigners may find Americans assertive or overbearing.
are achievers. They like to keep score, whether at work or play. They emphasize accomplishments.
are independent and individualistic. They place a high value on freedom and believe that individuals can shape and control their own destiny.
are questioners. They ask a lot of questions, even of someone they have just met. Many of these questions may seem pointless ("How ya' doing?") or personal ("What kind of work do you do?").
dislike silence. They would rather talk about the weather than deal with silence in a conversation.
value punctuality. They keep appointment calendars and live according to schedules and clocks.
value cleanliness. They often seem obsessed with bathing, eliminating body odours and wearing clean clothes.

Source: Based on Margo Ernest, ed., *Predeparture Orientation Handbook: For Foreign Students and Scholars Planning to Study in the United States* (Washington, DC: US Information Agency, Bureau of Cultural Affairs, 1984), pp. 103–05; Amanda Bennett, "American Culture Is Often a Puzzle for Foreign Managers in the US," *Wall Street Journal*, February 12, 1986, p. 29; "Don't Think Our Way's the Only Way," *The Pryor Report*, February 1988, p. 9; and Ben J. Wattenberg, "The Attitudes Behind American Exceptionalism," *US News & World Report*, August 7, 1989, p. 25.

Although it is an economically rich country, Japan scores high on collectivism. This helps explain the popularity of teams in Japanese automotive factories.

reason is that the "natives" are the least capable of explaining their culture's unique characteristics to someone else. If you're a Canadian raised in Canada, how would you characterize Canadian culture? Think about it for a moment and then look at the list in Table 4-2.

The most valuable framework to help managers better understand differences between national cultures was developed by Geert Hofstede. He surveyed over 116 000 employees in 40 countries who worked for a single multinational corporation. What did he find? His huge database revealed that national culture had a major effect on employees' work-related values and attitudes. In fact, it explained more of the differences than did age, sex, profession, or position in the organization. More importantly, Hofstede found that managers and employees varied on four dimensions of national culture: (1) individualism versus collectivism; (2) power distance; (3) uncertainty avoidance; and (4) quantity versus quality of life.[15] We don't have the space to review the results Hofstede obtained on each of the dimensions for each of the 40 countries, although 12 examples are presented in Table 4-3.

TABLE 4-3 Examples of Hofstede's Cultural Dimensions

Country	Individualism/ Collectivism	Power Distance	Uncertainty Avoidance	Quantity of Life[a]
Australia	Individual	Small	Moderate	Strong
Canada	Individual	Moderate	Low	Moderate
England	Individual	Small	Moderate	Strong
France	Individual	Large	High	Weak
Greece	Collective	Large	High	Moderate
Italy	Individual	Moderate	High	Strong
Japan	Collective	Moderate	High	Strong
Mexico	Collective	Large	High	Strong
Singapore	Collective	Large	Low	Moderate
Sweden	Individual	Small	Low	Weak
United States	Individual	Small	Low	Strong
Venezuela	Collective	Large	High	Strong

Source: Based on G Hofstede, "Motivation, Leadership, and Organization: Do American Theories Apply Abroad?" *Organizational Dynamics,* Summer 1980, pp. 42–63.

[a]A weak quantity score is equivalent to high quality of life.

individualism
A cultural dimension in which people are supposed to look after their own interests and those of their immediate family.

collectivism
A cultural dimension in which people expect others in their group to look after them and protect them when they are in trouble.

power distance
A cultural measure of the extent to which a society accepts the unequal distribution of power in institutions and organizations.

Individualism Versus Collectivism. The term **individualism** refers to a loosely knit social framework in which people are supposed to look after their own interests and those of their immediate family. This is made possible because of the large amount of freedom that such a society allows individuals. Its opposite is **collectivism**, which is characterized by a tight social framework in which people expect others in groups of which they are a part (such as a family or an organization) to look after them and protect them when they are in trouble. In exchange for this, they feel they owe absolute loyalty to the group.

Hofstede found that the degree of individualism in a country was closely related to that country's wealth. Wealthier countries, such as Canada, Great Britain and the Netherlands, are very individualistic. Poorer countries, such as Colombia and Pakistan, are very collectivistic.

Power Distance. People naturally vary in terms of physical and intellectual abilities. This, in turn, creates differences in wealth and power. How does a society deal with these inequalities? Hofstede used the term **power distance** as a measure of the extent to which a society accepts the fact that power in institutions and organizations is distributed unequally. A high power distance society accepts wide differences in power in organizations. Employees show a great deal of respect for those in authority. Titles, rank and status carry a lot of weight. When negotiating in high power distance countries, companies find it helps to send representatives whose titles are at least as impressive as those belonging to the people with whom they're bargaining. Countries high in power distance include the Philippines, Venezuela and India. In contrast, a low power distance society plays down inequalities as much as possible. Superiors still have authority, but employees are not fearful or in awe of their bosses. Denmark, Israel and Austria are examples of countries with low power distance scores.

uncertainty avoidance
A cultural measure of the degree to which people tolerate risk and unconventional behaviour.

quantity of life
A national culture attribute describing the extent to which societal values are characterized by assertiveness and materialism.

quality of life
A national culture attribute reflecting the emphasis placed on relationships and concern for others.

Uncertainty Avoidance. We live in a world of uncertainty. The future is largely unknown and always will be. Societies respond to this uncertainty in different ways. Some socialize their members into accepting it with equanimity. People in such societies are relatively comfortable with risks. They're also relatively tolerant of behaviour and opinions that differ from their own because they don't feel threatened by them. Hofstede describes such societies as having low **uncertainty avoidance**; their people feel quite secure. Countries that fall into this category include Singapore and Denmark.

A society that's high in uncertainty avoidance is characterized by an increased level of anxiety among its people, which manifests itself in greater nervousness, stress and aggression. Because people feel threatened by uncertainty and ambiguity in these cultures, mechanisms are created to provide security and reduce risk. Their organizations are likely to have more formal rules; there will be less tolerance for unusual ideas and behaviour; and members will strive to believe in absolute truths. Not surprisingly, in organizations in countries with high uncertainty avoidance, employees demonstrate relatively low job mobility, and lifetime employment is a widely practised policy. Countries in this category include Japan, Portugal and Greece.

Quantity Versus Quality of Life. The fourth dimension, like individualism and collectivism, is a dichotomy. Some cultures emphasize the **quantity of life** and value things such as assertiveness, and the acquisition of money and material goods. Other cultures emphasize the **quality of life**; the importance of relationships, and showing sensitivity and concern for the welfare of others.

Hofstede found that Japan and Austria scored high on the quantity dimension. In contrast, Norway, Sweden, Denmark and Finland scored high on the quality dimension.

5 **How do a country's legal-political and economic environments affect global managers?**

6 **Describe Hofstede's four cultural dimensions and how an understanding of them can make a manager more effective in the global marketplace.**

A Guide for Canadian Managers. We'll conclude this section by (1) reviewing how Canada ranked on Hofstede's four dimensions and (2) considering how a Canadian manager working in another country might be able to use Hofstede's research findings.

Comparing the 40 countries on the 4 dimensions, Hofstede found the Canadian culture to be high on individualism (although lower than the United States, which scored highest of all 40 countries on this dimension); below average on power distance; well below average on uncertainty avoidance; and above average on quantity of life (although, once again, not as high as the United States). These conclusions are not inconsistent with the world image of Canada. That is, Canada is seen as fostering the individualistic ethic, having a representative government with democratic ideals, being relatively free from threats of uncertainty, and having a capitalistic economy that values material achievement, though this is somewhat balanced by social concerns.

Into which countries are Canadian managers likely to fit best? Which are likely to create the biggest adjustment problems? All we have to do is identify those countries that are most and least like Canada on the four dimensions.

Canada is strongly individualistic but fairly low on power distance. A similar pattern was exhibited by Great Britain, Australia, the United States, the Netherlands and New Zealand. Those least similar to Canada on these dimensions were Venezuela, Colombia, Pakistan, Singapore and the Philippines.

Canada scored low on uncertainty avoidance and fairly high on quantity of life. Similar patterns were shown by Ireland, Great Britain, the Philippines, the United States, New Zealand, Australia, India and South Africa. Those least similar to Canada on these dimensions were Chile and Portugal.

These results empirically support part of what many of us suspected—that the Canadian manager transferred to Chicago, London, Melbourne, or a similar city in an English-speaking country, would have to make the fewest adjustments. The results also identify the countries in which culture shock is likely to be the greatest and the need to modify one's managerial style, the most imperative.

Is Global Assignment for You?

How do organizations decide which individuals will be sent overseas? Typically, the decision is based on selection criteria that are influenced by the company's experience and commitment to global operations. Table 4-4 lists several specific criteria that have been used by MNCs from

TABLE 4-4 Criteria for Making Global Employee Selection Decisions

	Australian Managers $n = 47$	Expatriate Managers[a] $n = 52$	Asian Managers $n = 15$
1. Ability to adapt	1	1	2
2. Technical competence	2	3	1
3. Spouse and family adaptability	3	2	4
4. Human relations skill	4	4	3
5. Desire to serve overseas	5	5	5
6. Previous overseas experience	6	7	7
7. Understanding of host country culture	7	6	5
8. Academic qualifications	8	8	8
9. Knowledge of language of country	9	9	9
10. Understanding of home country culture	10	10	10

Source: Raymond J Stone, "Expatriate Selection and Failure," *Human Resource Planning,* Vol. 14, No. 1, 1991, p. 10. Used with permission.

[a] American, British, Canadian, French, New Zealand or Australian managers working for an MNC outside their home countries.

Australia, the United States, Britain, Canada, France, New Zealand and Asia in making global employee selection decisions. Obviously, technical skills are important for success in overseas assignments, but other skills such as language skills, flexibility and family adaptability are needed as well. You can see by this list that usually technical **and** human factors are considered. Firms that don't consider both often find that their rate of failure in sending employees on global assignments is quite high.[16]

Once an employee has been selected as a good candidate for a managerial position in a foreign country, several individual and organizational factors determine whether or not the person can effectively adjust to an overseas assignment. Figure 4-4 shows some typical adjustment factors.

As the figure shows, a person makes two major types of adjustments when being transferred to another country: anticipatory adjustment and in-country adjustment. The anticipatory adjustment period is affected by a number of factors. For one thing, it's important that, prior to taking an overseas assignment, an individual has accurate expectations of the realities of the proposed position and the country to which he or she is being transferred. A person's expectations are affected by their level of predeparture training and previous experience with the assigned country or countries with similar cultures. Predeparture training, such as cross-cultural seminars or workshops that provide information about the culture and work life of the country to which a person is being transferred, can help smooth the anticipatory adjustment period. Also, if a person has prior experience with the cultural characteristics of the country to which he or she is going, the adjustment will be easier than for a person who has no experience with that culture.

There are certain other things that an organization can do to make the anticipatory adjustment smoother. For instance, the organization should have appropriate selection criteria (like those shown in Table 4-6) and mechanisms in place for choosing individuals for global assignments. By carefully selecting people for overseas assignments, the organization can alleviate many of the problems associated with the transition.

FIGURE 4-6 Factors Affecting International Adjustment

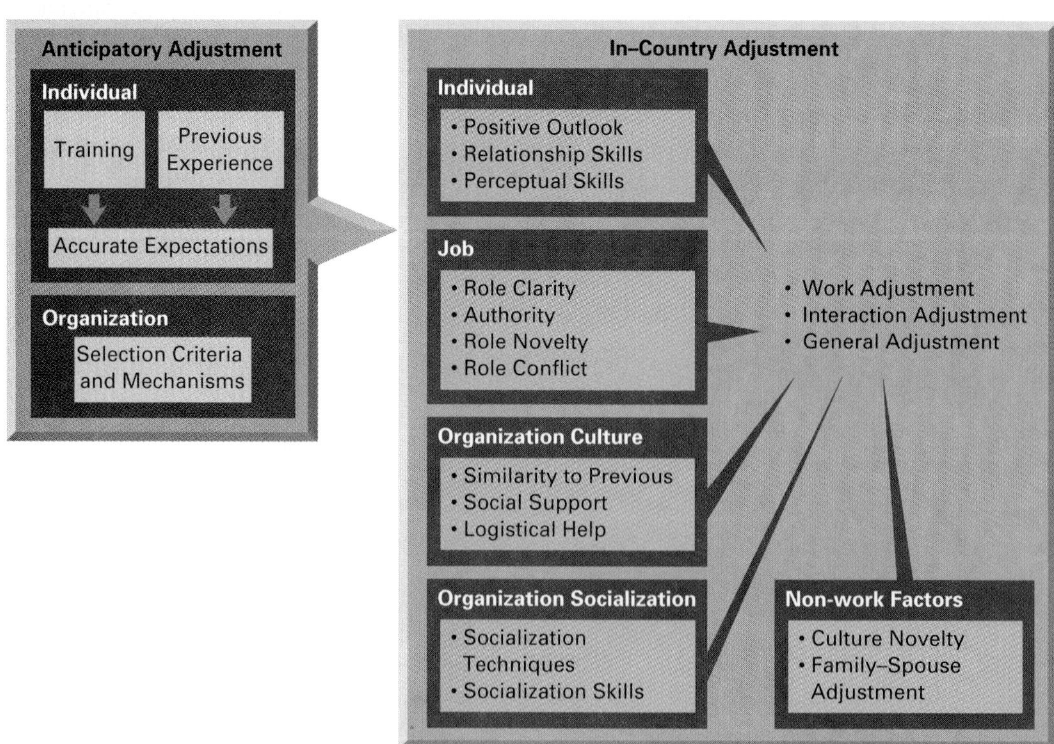

Source: Adapted from J Stewart Black, Mark Mendenhall, and Gary Oddou, "Toward a Comprehensive Model of International Adjustment: An Integration of Multiple Theoretical Perspectives," *Academy of Management Review,* April, 1991, p. 303.

Once the person has been transferred to the foreign location, there is a period of in-country adjustment, which also involves individual and organizational factors. Individual factors include the person's ability to remain positive and productive, even in new situations that may be pressurized and stressful; to interact effectively with host country co-workers; and to accurately perceive and adapt to the country's cultural values and norms.

Organizational factors include the job that the person will be doing; the organization's culture; and the level of organizational socialization. We can see from the figure that the important job factors for successful adjustment to a new country relate to the clarity of the job expectations, the authority the individual has to make decisions, the newness of the work-related activities, and the amount of role conflict that exists. If these job factors are not properly considered, a person transferred to another country faces a long period of adjustment or perhaps even an unsatisfactory adjustment.

Organizational culture factors that should be considered for successful transition include how similar the organizational culture is to those which the individual has experienced in the past; the social support provided by the organizational culture; and the amount of logistical help provided by the organization to make the adjustment easier. Again, if these factors are not properly addressed, a person transferred to another country may not adjust to being a productive employee as quickly or effectively.

Another factor in adjustment to an overseas assignment is an individual's organizational socialization skills. The term **organizational socialization** refers to the process that employees go through to adapt to an organization's culture. The cultural transition will be easier if the individual develops effective socialization skills and quickly learns the "way things are done around here".

organizational socialization
The process that employees go through to adapt to an organization's culture.

Finally, it is important to note that non-work considerations are also identified in the figure. These include individual personal adjustment to the novelty of the culture, as well as family-spouse adjustment, which can be a major source of problems. The realities of living in a different culture, where simple tasks such as grocery shopping, driving a car or going to a movie can be logistical challenges, create stresses for individuals and their families. **Culture shock**—the confusion, disorientation and emotional upheaval caused by being immersed in a new culture—is a real and normal reaction. However, studies have shown that, after about four to six months, most people adjust to the new culture.[17]

culture shock
The feelings of confusion, disorientation and emotional upheaval caused by being immersed in a new culture.

ANSWERS TO IN-CHAPTER QUIZ

1. **c.** Labatt, Canada's largest beer company, was acquired by the Belgian company, Interbrew SA, in 1995.
2. **a.** Tim Horton's was bought by Wendy's, the American fast-food corporation.
3. **b.** Tropicana was owned by the Canadian company, Seagram, until 1998, when it was sold to PepsiCo.
4. **b.** BC Tel—the British Columbian phone company—is a subsidiary of BC Telecom, which is owned by Anglo-Canadian Telephone which, in turn, is a subsidiary of GTE.
5. **a.** DuMaurier is made by Imperial Tobacco, has its headquarters in Montreal, and is owned by Imasco—which is owned by BAT Industries plc of England.
6. **b.** The *Telegraph*, the best-selling "quality" newspaper—as broadsheets are called in Britain—surpassed the *Times* to become number one in England. It is owned by Hollinger, the newspaper empire headed by Conrad Black.
7. **c.** Bic is a French company.
8. **d.** Seagram owns Universal Studios (the subject of Chapter 8's case study).
9. **b.** Despite the name, the Hong Kong Bank of Canada is owned by HSBC Holdings, UK.
10. **a.** Again, despite the name, the Yogen Fruz yoghurt and ice cream chain has its headquarters in Markham, Ontario.

SUMMARY

This summary is organized by the learning objectives found at the beginning of the chapter.

1. Competitors and markets are no longer defined within national borders. New competitors can suddenly appear at any time from anywhere in the world. New markets are opening up in countries around the world. Managers must think globally if their organizations are to succeed over the long term.
2. National parochialism prevents people from recognizing that people in other countries have different ways of living and working. Parochial people rigidly apply their own values and customs to foreign cultures. The result is that they fail to understand foreigners and reduce their ability to work effectively with such people.
3. The European Union (EU) is a 15-nation trading alliance whose purpose is to have common customs duties and unified industrial and commercial policies. The North American Free Trade Agreement (NAFTA) is a 3-nation trading alliance between Canada, the US and Mexico. The Association of Southeast Asian Nations (ASEAN) is a 10-nation trading alliance.
4. Multinational corporations have significant operations functioning in two or more countries simultaneously, but primary decision making and control is based in the company's home country. Transnationals also have significant operations in multiple countries but decision making is decentralized to the local level.
5. Regional trading alliances create more powerful economic entities. Many countries have joined these alliances in order to compete more effectively. For instance, countries joined the European Union to compete more aggressively against such economically powerful countries as the United States and Japan.
6. The typical stages by which organizations go international are (a) exporting to foreign countries, (b) hiring foreign representation or contracting with foreign manufacturers, and (c) establishing international operations through licensing and franchising, joint ventures and strategic alliances, and/or foreign subsidiaries.
7. The four primary dimensions on which nations' cultures differ are individualism versus collectivism, power distance, uncertainty avoidance, and quantity versus quality of life.
8. Canadian culture is characterized as being quite high on individualism, below average on power distance, well below average on uncertainty avoidance, and fairly balanced on quantity versus quality of life.
9. A manager on global assignment faces two periods of adjustment: the time prior to going to a foreign country and the period in the new country. Both individual ***and*** organizational factors influence the successful adjustment of managers to overseas assignments.

THINKING ABOUT MANAGEMENT ISSUES

1. What do you think is meant by the term "borderless organization"? What are the managerial implications of such an organization?
2. Can the Hofstede framework presented in this chapter be used to guide managers in a South Korean hospital or a government agency in Peru? Discuss.
3. Compare the advantages and drawbacks of the various approaches to going international.
4. What could managers do to avoid making mistakes when performing any of the managerial activities (planning, organizing, leading and controlling) while in a foreign culture?
5. In what ways do you think the global environment has changed or will change regarding the way in which organizations select and train managers?

SELF-ASSESSMENT EXERCISE

WHAT ARE YOUR CULTURAL ATTITUDES?

How well you would adapt and function in a different country depends to some extent on your cultural attitudes. If you are to succeed in the global economy, you'll need to develop a certain degree of cultural sensitivity. Take this self-assessment exercise to measure your cultural attitudes.

Instructions: Indicate the extent to which you agree or disagree with each of the following statements. Answer each statement by circling the appropriate number; for example, if you strongly agree with a particular statement, you would circle the "5" next to that statement.

5 = Strongly agree
4 = Agree
3 = Neither agree nor disagree
2 = Disagree
1 = Strongly disagree

	Strongly Agree				**Strongly Disagree**
1. It is important to have job requirements and instructions spelled out so people always know what they are expected to do.	5	4	3	2	1
2. Managers expect workers to closely follow instructions and procedures.	5	4	3	2	1
3. Rules and regulations are important because they inform workers what the organization expects of them.	5	4	3	2	1
4. Standard operating procedures are helpful to workers on the job.	5	4	3	2	1
5. Instructions for operations are important for workers on the job.	5	4	3	2	1
6. Individual rewards are not as important as group welfare.	5	4	3	2	1
7. Group success is more important than individual success.	5	4	3	2	1
8. Being accepted by the group is more important than working on your own.	5	4	3	2	1
9. An individual should not pursue his or her own objectives without considering the welfare of the group.	5	4	3	2	1
10. It is important for a manager to encourage loyalty and a sense of duty to the group.	5	4	3	2	1
11. Managers should make most decisions without consulting subordinates.	5	4	3	2	1
12. It is often necessary for a supervisor to emphasize his or her authority and power when dealing with subordinates.	5	4	3	2	1
13. Managers should be careful not to ask the opinions of subordinates too frequently.	5	4	3	2	1
14. A manager should avoid socializing with his or her subordinates off the job.	5	4	3	2	1
15. Subordinates should not disagree with their manager's decisions.	5	4	3	2	1
16. Managers should not delegate difficult and important tasks to their subordinates.	5	4	3	2	1
17. Meetings are usually run more effectively when they are chaired by a man.	5	4	3	2	1

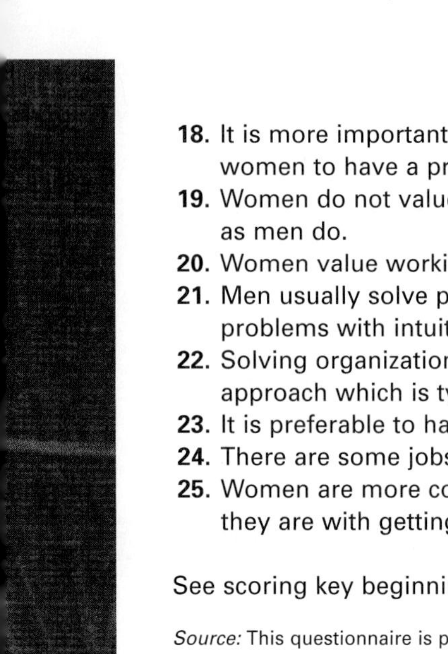

	Strongly Agree				Strongly Disagree
18. It is more important for men to have a professional career than it is for women to have a professional career.	5	4	3	2	1
19. Women do not value recognition and promotion in their work as much as men do.	5	4	3	2	1
20. Women value working in a friendly atmosphere more than men do.	5	4	3	2	1
21. Men usually solve problems with logical analysis; women usually solve problems with intuition.	5	4	3	2	1
22. Solving organizational problems usually requires the active, forcible approach which is typical of men.	5	4	3	2	1
23. It is preferable to have a man in a high-level position than a woman.	5	4	3	2	1
24. There are some jobs which a man can always do better than a woman.	5	4	3	2	1
25. Women are more concerned with the social aspects of their job than they are with getting ahead.	5	4	3	2	1

See scoring key beginning on page SK-1.

Source: This questionnaire is part of a larger instrument currently under development by Professors Peter W Dorfman and Jon P Howell, both of New Mexico State University. Reprinted by permission of the authors.

for your IMMEDIATE action

Delaney Environmental Services

TO: Sandy Collins, Director of Operations
FROM: J. Yamada, Managing Director
SUBJECT: Global expansion

Sandy, as we talked about last week at some length, I think it is important that DES starts looking carefully at expanding its global market opportunities. We have developed a successful track record for providing environmental consulting and design services here in Victoria and I believe that, with our experience, we have a lot to offer the American market, particularly the California market.

I would like you to do some research into the problems we might face in moving into the California market. Specifically, I would like you to cover (1) cultural differences we would need to consider, (2) the current currency rate of exchange and how it's changed over the last three years, and (3) any legal-political situations we need to be aware of. Since this is just an initial analysis for us to study, please keep your report to two pages or less.

This is a fictionalized account of a potentially real problem, written for academic purposes only.

TAKE IT TO THE NET

We invite you to visit the Robbins/Coulter/Stuart-Kotze Companion Website at www.prenticehall.ca/robbins for this chapter's Internet resources.

CASE APPLICATION

A Canadian Clothing Colossus? Club Monaco Inc., Toronto

Club Monaco Inc.'s head office may be located in Toronto, but this clothing company has its sights set on global expansion. In 1998, with 141 locations in the chain throughout North America (65) and Asia (76), CEO Joseph Mimran was planning to double his Asian total. He was also planning a major expansion throughout Canada and the US, while looking into opportunities in places as diverse as England, Kuwait and Saudi Arabia. But his plans hit a snag—nothing short of a gigantic economic collapse in much of Asia. Club Monaco's outlets in this part of the world are in Japan and South Korea and, while the former is a major economic power, the latter is not, and has not been able to weather the financial crisis easily. Club Monaco's stores, especially in Southeast Asian countries like South Korea, Thailand and Indonesia were hit hard by the currency crisis. Mimran said, in 1998, "Once this Asian thing is behind us, we'll be firing on all pistons again". Now, one must obviously take into account the fact that, when he said this, he had stockholders' fears to allay. Major currency collapses do not generally disappear in a short while.

This has meant that Club Monaco has decided to focus its expansion on the US. With 57 stores in Canada but only 8 in the States, Club Monaco does not have much of a presence down south. The first Club Monaco outlets were opened 10 years ago in San Francisco and Los Angeles. From there, Club Monaco went to New York, opening three stores in Manhattan. And here it is apparent what Club Monaco's challenge in the US will be—CM's flagship store in Manhattan is on the shopping Mecca of Fifth Avenue, and just a few doors down is the company's main competitor, The Gap. Whereas Club Monaco is a $100 million revenue company, The Gap has revenues of $6.5 billion. With The Gap's massive capital comes a lot of competitive clout.

Club Monaco does have some advantages. Its clothing generally gets very good reviews, such as "The Gap with panache" or "what Benetton could have been". And Mimran, for one, believes that Club Monaco not only has lower prices than its competitors, it also has better quality merchandise. So the plan is to focus on major US cities with suitable markets such as Seattle and Boston, and to build stores of 7000 square feet (the originals were less than a third the size). By 2001, Club Monaco plans to have up to 30 stores.

Whereas the huge currency drops in the Southeast Asian countries will continue to hurt Club Monaco, the low Canadian dollar will benefit the company in its move into the US. This is an interesting time for Club Monaco's global aims. We will have to wait to see whether Mimran and company can pull it off.

QUESTIONS

1. What legal-political, economic, and cultural differences do you think might be significant for Club Monaco considering its objectives in the US and Asia, as well as its further aims in other countries? How would you deal with these differences?
2. Suppose you were working for Club Monaco and were assigned a position in Saudi Arabia, overseeing the company's expansion there. What would you do to make a successful adjustment both personally and professionally?
3. If Club Monaco decided to embark upon a major expansion within the European Union (say, the major city of each member nation), how might recent changes make doing business there easier? What sort of preparation would Club Monaco want to make before embarking on such an expansion? What kinds of problems might Club Monaco face in its growth within this market?

Source: Showwei Chu, "Not Quite Wrinkle-Free", Canadian Business, April 10, 1998, pp. 57–61.

LEARNING OBJECTIVES

After Reading This Chapter, You Should Be Able To:

1 Explain the classical and socioeconomic views of social responsibility

2 List the arguments for and against business being socially responsible

3 Differentiate between social responsibility and social responsiveness

4 Explain the relationship between corporate social responsibility and economic performance

5 Define stakeholders, and describe their role in social responsibility

6 Explain what the "greening" of management is and how organizations are "going green".

7 Describe values-based management and how it relates to organizational culture

8 Define ethics

9 Differentiate four views of ethics

10 Identify the factors that affect ethical behaviour

11 Describe the stages of moral development

12 Discuss various ways in which organizations can improve the ethical behaviour of their employees

A MANAGER'S CHALLENGE

Pierre Lacombe, Le Commensal, Quebec

If you're in the food industry, one of the worst possible ways to start your day is with a call from the Health Department. Pierre Lacombe, vice-president of Le Commensal, had to listen as the voice on the other end of the line asked him: "Have you received any complaints about diners suffering from diarrhea?". And thus began a nightmarish few months for Pierre Lacombe, his three partners, and the company's franchisees.[1]

Le Commensal is a vegetarian-food enterprise which divides its operation's production among three markets: institutional markets such as hospitals; franchised restaurants, of which there are currently nine; and prepared products for retail outlets such as the large Quebec grocery chain Provigo, and Club Price. The institutional market at present only accounts for roughly five percent of Le Commensal's business, but the company has major plans for expansion in this area, through contracts with major organizations such as Marriot, Nortel and Air Canada. The retail market presently represents 55 percent of Commensal's sales. The remaining 40 percent of business comes from Commensal's franchised restaurants, and this is the part of the operation which threatened to ruin the company.

Two of the restaurants were implicated by the Health Department in an epidemic that had sent people to hospital because of an outbreak of the bacteria shigella. Since two different outlets were involved, this meant that the source of the bacteria was undoubtedly the central kitchen in Boisbriand. The owner-operators called an emergency meeting. The implications were huge, not only for the future of the company, but also for the finances of the owners who had personally guaranteed loans of several hundred thousand dollars. Tensions were high, but ultimately the owners decided that there was only one ethical course of action. The production facility was shut down, as were all of the restaurants. The company notified over 300 stores carrying their products and everything was thrown out. Then a sterilization operation was begun on the production facility, which would go on for 10 days. Over 25 tonnes of food was disposed of, and costs to Le Commensal were in the range of three-quarters of a million dollars.

The next step for the company was the most dangerous in terms of Commensal's future. The public had to be notified. Le Commensal's press release found its way into front-page stories in both of Montreal's major newspapers, *The Gazette* and *La Presse.* Eventually, over a hundred reports were produced on radio and in newspapers. But luckily for Le Commensal, most of the stories were sympathetic, recognizing the ethical manner in which the company had handled the situation.

Obviously, Commensal's customers also appreciated the company's integrity. Just two months after re-opening, sales levels at the restaurants had returned to their previous levels. This was a very impressive recovery considering the magnitude of the incident. Today, the company continues to grow steadily, even with setbacks such as the ice-storm of January, 1998, which cost the company $150 000.

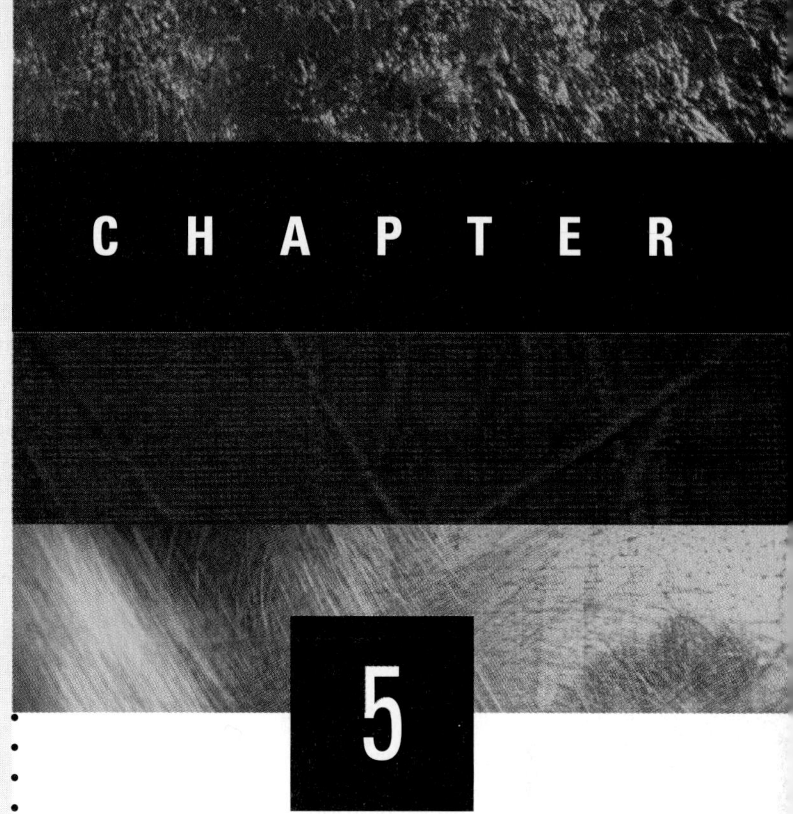

Social Responsibility and Managerial Ethics

As managers and organizations go about their business, social factors can and do influence their actions. This fact is abundantly clear in the dilemma faced by managers at Le Commensal. In this chapter we'll establish a foundation for understanding social responsibility and managerial ethics. The discussion of these topics is placed at this point in the text to link them to the preceding and following subjects. Specifically, we'll show that social responsibility is a response to a changing environment and that ethical considerations should be an important criterion in managerial decision making (the topic of Chapter 6).

WHAT IS SOCIAL RESPONSIBILITY?

Before the 1960s, the issue of corporate social responsibility drew little attention. However, social activists at that time began to question the singular economic objective of business firms. Were large corporations irresponsible because they discriminated against minorities and women, as shown by the obvious absence of female and minority managers? Did pulp and paper manufacturers across the country ignore their social responsibilities by allowing their effluent—often high in mercury—to pollute the water around them? Did International Nickel have a responsibility not to let emissions kill much of the vegetation around Sudbury, Ontario?

Before the 1960s, few people asked such questions. But times have changed. Managers are now regularly faced with decisions that have a dimension of social responsibility—philanthropy, pricing, employee relations, resource conservation, product quality and safety, and operations in countries that violate human rights are some of the more obvious. To help you understand how managers make such decisions, let's begin by defining social responsibility.

Two Opposing Views

Few terms have been defined in as many different ways as *social responsibility*. Some of the more popular meanings include "profit making only", "going beyond profit making", "voluntary activities", "concern for the broader social system", and "social responsiveness".[2] Most of the debate has focused on the extremes. On one side, there is the classical—or purely economic—view that management's only social responsibility is to maximize profits. On the other side is the socioeconomic position, which holds that management's responsibility goes well beyond making profits to include protecting and improving society's welfare.

classical view
The view that management's only social responsibility is to maximize profits.

The Classical View. The most outspoken advocate of the **classical view** is economist and Nobel laureate Milton Friedman.[3] He argues that most managers today are professional managers, which means that they don't own the business they run. They're employees, responsible only to the shareholders. Their primary responsibility is therefore to operate the business in the best interests of the shareholders. And what are those interests? Friedman contends that the shareholders have a single concern: financial return.

According to Friedman, when managers decide on their own to spend their organization's resources for the "social good", they undermine the market mechanism. Someone must pay for this redistribution of assets. If socially responsible actions reduce profits and dividends, shareholders lose. If wages and benefits have to be reduced to pay for social actions, employees lose. If prices are raised to pay for social actions, consumers lose. If higher prices are rejected by consumers and sales drop, the business might not survive—in which case, *all* the organization's constituencies lose. Moreover, Friedman argues that when professional managers pursue anything other than profit, they implicitly appoint themselves as non-elected policymakers. He questions whether managers of business firms have the expertise for deciding how society *should* be. That, Friedman says, is what we elect political representatives to decide.

Friedman's argument is probably best understood by using microeconomics. If socially responsible acts add to the cost of doing business, those costs either have to be passed on to consumers in the form of higher prices or absorbed by shareholders through a smaller profit margin. If management raises prices in a competitive market, it will lose sales. In a purely competitive market where competitors have not assumed the costs of social responsibility, prices can't be raised without losing the entire market. Such a situation means that the costs have to be absorbed by the business, which results in lower profits.

The classical view also contends that there are pressures in a competitive market for investment funds to go where they'll get the highest return. If the socially responsible firm can't pass on its higher social costs to consumers and must absorb them internally, it will generate a lower rate of return. Over time, investment funds will gravitate away from socially responsible firms towards those that aren't, because the latter will provide higher rates of return. That might even mean that if all the firms in a particular country—such as Canada—incurred additional social costs because management perceived this to be one of business's goals, the survival of entire domestic industries could be threatened by foreign competitors who chose not to incur such social costs.

The Socioeconomic View. The socioeconomic position counters that times have changed, and with them society's expectations of business. This is best illustrated in the legal formation of corporations. Corporations are chartered by state governments. The same government that grants a charter can take it away. So corporations are not independent entities responsible only to shareholders. They also have a responsibility to the larger society that creates and supports them.

One author, in supporting the **socioeconomic view**, reminds us that "maximizing profits is a company's second priority, not its first. The first is ensuring its survival".[4]

socioeconomic view
The view that management's social responsibility goes well beyond the making of profits to include protecting and improving society's welfare.

Over 50 years ago, senior managers at the Manville Corporation were given evidence that one of the company's products—asbestos—caused fatal lung disease. Managers kept the information from workers, to the point of concealing chest X-ray results—all in pursuit of short-term profit. In the long-run, the company had to pay for its despicable policies. Manville was forced into bankruptcy protection in the face of thousands of lawsuits. It has since emerged from bankruptcy, but will be paying up to 20 percent of the company's annual profits to a personal injury settlement trust fund until the year 2015. Another example of why companies must act responsibly in order to ensure their survival can be seen in the major controversy that has erupted over whether or not tobacco company executives knew several years ago about the dangers of smoking and secondhand smoke.

A major flaw in the classicist's view, as seen by socioeconomic proponents, is their time frame. Supporters of the socioeconomic view contend that managers should be concerned with maximizing financial returns in the *long run*. To do that, they must accept some social obligations and the costs that go with them. They must protect society's welfare by *not* polluting, *not* discriminating, *not* engaging in deceptive advertising, and so on. They must also play an activist role in improving society by involving themselves in their communities and contributing to charitable organizations.

A final point made by proponents of the socioeconomic position is that the classical view flies in the face of reality.[5] Modern business organizations are no longer merely economic institutions. They lobby, form political action committees, and engage in other activities to influence the political process for their benefit. Society accepts and even encourages business to become involved in its social, political and legal environment. That might not have been true 40 years ago, but it is the reality of today. In fact, a survey of business owners found that 68 percent of them said that they *would* continue socially responsible practices even if they found out these activities were cutting into profits.[6]

Arguments For and Against Social Responsibility

What are the specific arguments for and against businesses assuming social responsibilities? In this section, we'll outline the major points that have been presented.[7]

1 Why is the social responsibility of business receiving so much attention these days?

2 According to the socioeconomic view of social responsibility, what are the flaws in the classical view?

Office furniture maker, Herman Miller, buys old office panels that would otherwise be sent to landfills, and remakes them to sell again. The company also powers its corporate headquarters using a cogenerator that burns wood scraps for fuel, saving $450 000 a year in gas costs.

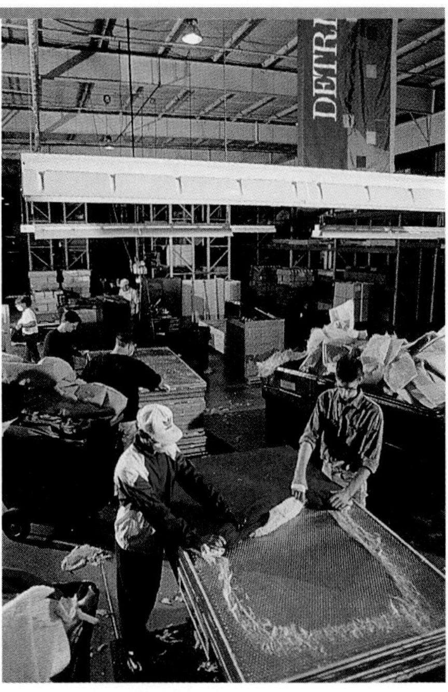

Arguments For. The major arguments supporting businesses being socially responsible are:

1. *Public expectations*. Social expectations of business have increased dramatically since the 1960s. Public opinion now supports business pursuing social as well as economic goals.

2. *Long-run profits*. Socially responsible businesses tend to have more secure long-run profits. This is the normal result of the better community relations and the improved business image that responsible behaviour brings.

3. *Ethical obligation*. A business firm can and should have a social conscience. Businesses should be socially responsible because responsible actions are *right* for their own sake.

4. *Public image*. Firms seek to enhance their public image to get increased sales, better employees, access to financing and other benefits. Since the public considers social goals important, business can create a favourable public image by pursuing social goals.

5. *Better environment*. Business involvement can help solve difficult social problems, helping create a better quality of life and a more desirable community in which to attract and keep skilled employees.

6. *Discouragement of further government regulation*. Government regulation adds economic costs and restricts management's decision flexibility. By becoming socially responsible, business can expect less government regulation.

7. *Balance of responsibility and power*. Business holds a large amount of power in society. An equally large amount of responsibility is required to balance it. When power is significantly greater than responsibility, the imbalance encourages irresponsible behaviour that works against the public good.

8. *Shareholder interests*. Social responsibility will improve a business's stock price in the long run. The stock market will view the socially responsible company as less risky and open to public criticism. Therefore, it will award its stock a higher price-earnings ratio.

9. *Possession of resources*. Business organizations have the financial resources, technical experts, and managerial talent to support public and charitable projects that need assistance.

10. *Superiority of prevention over cures*. Social problems must be addressed at some time. Business should act before these problems become more serious and costly to cor-

rect, taking management's energy away from accomplishing its goal of producing goods and services.

Arguments Against. The major arguments against business assuming social responsibility are:

1. *Violation of profit maximization.* This is the essence of the classical viewpoint. Business is being socially responsible when it attends strictly to its economic interests and leaves other activities to other institutions.
2. *Dilution of purpose.* The pursuit of social goals dilutes business's primary purpose: economic productivity. Society may suffer if both economic and social goals are poorly accomplished.
3. *Costs.* Many socially responsible activities don't cover their costs. Someone has to pay these costs. Business must absorb the costs or pass them on to consumers through higher prices.
4. *Too much power.* Business is already one of the most powerful sectors of our society. If it pursues social goals, it would have even more power. Society has given business enough power.
5. *Lack of skills.* The outlook and abilities of business leaders are oriented primarily towards economics. Business people are poorly qualified to address social issues.
6. *Lack of accountability.* Political representatives pursue social goals and are held accountable for their actions. Such is not the case with business leaders. There are no direct lines of social accountability from the business sector to the public.
7. *Lack of broad public support.* There is no broad mandate or outcry from society for business to become involved in social issues. The public is divided on the issue of business's social responsibility. In fact, it is a topic that typically generates heated debate. Actions taken under such divided support are likely to fail.

From Obligations to Responsiveness

Now it's time to narrow in on precisely what *we* mean when we talk about **social responsibility**. It is a business firm's obligation, beyond that required by the law and economics, to pursue long-term goals that are good for society.[8] Note that this definition assumes that business obeys laws and pursues economic interests. We assume that all business firms—those which are socially responsible and those which aren't—will obey all relevant laws that society enacts. Also note that this definition views business as a moral agent. In its effort to do *good* for society, it must differentiate between right and wrong.

We can understand social responsibility better if we compare it with two similar concepts: social obligation and social responsiveness.[9] As Figure 5-1 illustrates, social obligation is the foundation of business's social involvement. A business has fulfilled its **social obligation** when it meets economic and legal responsibilities, and no more. It does the minimum required by law. A firm pursues social goals only to the extent that they contribute to its economic goals. In contrast to social obligation, both social responsibility and social responsiveness go beyond merely meeting basic economic and legal standards.

Social responsibility adds an ethical imperative to do those things that make society better and *not* to do those that could make it worse. **Social responsiveness** is the capability of a firm to adapt to changing societal conditions.[10]

social responsibility
The obligation, beyond that required by the law and economics, of a firm to pursue long-term goals that are good for society.

social obligation
The obligation of a business to meet its economic and legal responsibilities.

social responsiveness
The capability of a firm to adapt to changing societal conditions.

THINKING CRITICALLY ABOUT ETHICS

In an effort to be (or at least appear to be) socially responsible, many organizations donate money to philanthropic and charitable causes. In addition, many organizations ask their employees to make individual donations to these causes. Suppose you're the manager of a work team, and you know that several of your employees can't afford to pledge money right now because of various personal and financial problems. You've also been told by your supervisor that the CEO has been known to check the list of individual contributors to see who is and who is not "supporting these very important causes". What do you do? What ethical guidelines might you suggest for individual and organizational contributions to philanthropic and charitable causes? ■

As Table 5-1 describes, social responsibility requires business to determine what is right or wrong, thus seeking fundamental ethical truths. Social responsiveness is guided by social norms. The value of social norms is that they can provide managers with a more meaningful guide for decision making. The following might make the distinction clearer:

Suppose, for example, that a multiproduct firm's social responsibility is to produce reasonably safe products. Similarly, the same firm is responsive every time it produces an unsafe product: it withdraws the product from the market as soon as the product is found to be unsafe. After, say, 10 recalls, will the firm be recognized as socially responsible? Will the firm be recognized as socially responsive? The likely answers to these questions are no to the first, but yes to the second.[11]

Toronto Dominion Bank
www.tdbank.ca/tdbank/

IBM
www.ibm.com/

Ontario Hydro
www.hydro.on.ca/

AGT Advanced Communications
www.agtac.net/

When a company meets pollution control standards established by the federal government or doesn't discriminate against employees over the age of 40 in promotion decisions, it is meeting its social obligation and nothing more. In the mid-1990s, when the Toronto Dominion Bank began offering same-sex benefits for its employees, management said it was to "recognize the diversity in our work force". TD was acting in a socially responsive manner, following in the footsteps of other organizations like Bell Canada, IBM Canada and Ontario Hydro, all of which have offered benefits for gay and lesbian couples. Why have these companies chosen to act socially responsively? They have felt pressurized to do so. They have recognized a social shift in attitude and decided it would be in their best interests to align themselves with current social standards. If these companies had instituted these measures 30 years ago, they could have been characterized as socially responsible actions.[12]

Advocates of social responsiveness believe that the concept replaces philosophical talk with practical action. They see it as a more tangible and achievable objective than social responsibility.[13] Rather than assessing what is good for society in the long term, a socially responsive management identifies the prevailing social norms and then changes its social involvement to respond to changing societal conditions. For example, AGT, the privately owned Alberta telephone company, has received approval for a plan to begin a workplace school in one of the company's buildings, educating children from kindergarten up to Grade Three. The Calgary school board will, of course, have control over the curriculum, and will supply teachers, desks, books, and other supplies while AGT provides the space (spending $200 000 to renovate) and $30 000 a year to keep the school running. With the increasing number of working parents in Canada, companies feel great pressure to take some sort of action, and practices such as this one by AGT are extremely pragmatic. This is an example of a company being socially responsive.[14]

SOCIAL RESPONSIBILITY AND ECONOMIC PERFORMANCE

In this section, we seek to answer the question: "Do socially responsible activities lower a company's economic performance?"

More than a dozen studies have looked at this question.[15] All have some methodological limitations related to measures of "social responsibility" and "economic performance".[16] Most

FIGURE 5-1 Levels of Social Involvement

TABLE 5-1 Social Responsibility Versus Social Responsiveness

	Social Responsibility	Social Responsiveness
Major consideration	Ethical	Pragmatic
Focus	Ends	Means
Emphasis	Obligation	Responses
Decision framework	Long-term	Medium- and short-term

Source: Adapted from Steven L. Wartick and Philip L. Cochran, "The Evolution of the Corporate Social Performance Model," *Academy of Management Review*, October 1985, p. 766.

determine a firm's social performance by analyzing the content of annual reports, citations of social actions in articles on the company, or public perception "reputation" indexes. Such criteria certainly have drawbacks as reliable measures of social responsibility. Although measures of economic performance (such as net income, return on equity, or per-share stock prices) are more objective, they are generally used to indicate only short-term financial performance. It may well be that the effect of social responsibility on a firm's profits—either positive or negative—takes a number of years to manifest itself. Assuming there is a time lag, studies that use short-term financial data aren't likely to show valid results. And there is also the issue of causation. If, for example, the evidence showed that social involvement and economic performance were positively related, this wouldn't mean that social involvement *caused* higher economic performance. It very well could be the opposite. That is, it might show that high profits permit firms the luxury of being socially involved.[17]

Given these cautions, what do the various research studies find? The majority show a *positive* relationship between corporate social involvement and economic performance. One review of 13 studies found only 1 negative association. In this instance, the price of socially responsible firms' stocks didn't do as well as national stock indices.[18] A recent stock evaluation index known as the Domini Index has, since its creation in May 1991, gone up by 62 percent, compared to 51 percent for the Standard & Poor's 500 Index.[19] The logic behind these positive relationships appears to be that social involvement provides a number of benefits to a firm that more than offset their costs. These would include a positive consumer image, a more dedicated and motivated workforce, and less interference from regulators.[20]

There is also another way to look at this issue. A number of socially conscious equity mutual funds have been started in recent years; these funds do not invest in companies that are involved in liquor, gambling, tobacco, nuclear power, weapons, price fixing or criminal fraud. These mutual funds provide a way for individual investors to support socially responsible companies in yet another way.

What conclusion can we draw from all this? In sum, the most meaningful conclusion we can make is that there is little substantive evidence to say that a company's socially responsible actions significantly reduce its long-term economic performance. Given the current political and social pressures on business to pursue social goals, this may have the greatest significance for managerial decision making. So, to answer our opening question—do socially responsible activities lower a company's economic performance? The answer appears to be no!

IS SOCIAL RESPONSIBILITY JUST PROFIT-MAXIMIZING BEHAVIOUR?

It can easily be argued that social responsibility is nothing more than a public relations benefit to a company while it pursues profit maximization. There is no question that some social actions taken by companies are motivated primarily by profit. In fact, the practice has required a descriptive label: **cause-related marketing**. The idea behind it is to determine a social cause that fits well with a company's product or service and then tie them together for mutual benefit.

cause-related marketing Performing social actions that are motivated directly by profits.

VALUES-BASED MANAGEMENT

values-based management An approach to managing in which managers establish, promote, and practise an organization's shared values.

Values-based management is an approach to managing in which managers establish, promote and practise an organization's shared values. An organization's values reflect what it stands for and what it believes in. As we discussed in Chapter 3, the shared organizational values form the organization's culture and influence the way in which the organization operates and the employees behave.[21]

Purposes of Shared Values

A company's shared values act as guideposts for managerial decisions and actions.[22] At clothing manufacturer, Blue Bell, Inc., a strong tradition of corporate values guides managers as they plan, organize, lead and control organizational activities. Their shared values were developed through a series of participative discussions and are expressed in the acronym *PRIDE*: profitability through excellence, respect for the individual, involved citizenship, dedication to fairness and integrity, and existing for the customer. In fact, any new manager participating in Blue Bell's management training programs learns that an important part of being a manager for this firm is sharing and following the beliefs expressed by *PRIDE*.

Another purpose of shared values is the impact they have on shaping employee behaviour and communicating what the organization expects of its members.[23] Robert Haas, Chairman and CEO of blue jeans maker, Levi Strauss & Company, is committed to bringing social values into the way he runs the business. During the late 1980s, Haas guided the development of the Levi Strauss Aspirations Statement (see Figure 5-2), a major endeavour designed to define the shared corporate values that would guide both management and the company's large and diverse workforce. The document provides a clear and concise description of expectations for employee behaviour.[24]

Shared corporate values also influence marketing efforts.[25] At Hanna Andersson, a children's clothing catalogue retailer, sales and customer loyalty increased when it developed a marketing program called Hannadowns. Hannadowns originated from one of the company's core corporate values—social action—that stated, "We will research specific opportunities for Hanna to contribute to the community." The program gives Hanna's customers a 20 percent credit for mailing back clothes their infants have outgrown. The clothes are cleaned and given to local women's shelters and other families in need. Consistent with cause-related marketing, Hanna's has found a way to link its business to a pressing social concern and improve its marketing efforts, at the same time.

Finally, shared values are a way to build team spirit in organizations.[26] When employees embrace the stated corporate values, they develop a deeper personal commitment to their work and feel obligated to take responsibility for their actions. Because the shared values influence the way work is done, employees become more enthusiastic about doing things they support and believe in. At companies like Hanna Andersson, Levi Strauss and numerous others, employees know what's expected of them on the job. They use the shared corporate values to shape the way they work. But how do organizations develop a set of shared values?

Developing Shared Values

As any company that uses values-based management will tell you, it's not easy to establish the shared corporate values. At Tom's of Maine, a manufacturer of natural personal care products, the process involved everyone in the company. All the employees, working in groups of four to six, took a hard look at defining "who we are " and "what we are about". But the commitment by Tom's employees to developing shared corporate values didn't stop there. The company's employees realized that as they made business decisions, they were to use the values they had helped define and develop; that those shared values really mattered. They began to under-

TESTING... TESTING...

3 Contrast social responsibility and social responsiveness. Which is more theoretical? Why?

4 What is cause-related marketing? Is it socially responsible according to the classical view?

FIGURE 5-2 Levi Strauss Company's Aspirations Statement

Aspirations Statement

We all want a company that our people are proud of and committed to, where all employees have an opportunity to contribute, learn, grow, and advance based on merit, not politics or background. We want our people to feel respected, treated fairly, listened to, and involved. Above all we want satisfaction from accomplishments and friendships, balanced personal and professional lives, and to have fun in our endeavors.

When we describe the kind of Levi Strauss & Co. we want in the future, what we are talking about is building on the foundation we have inherited: affirming the best of our company's traditions, closing gaps that may exist between principles and practices, and updating some of our values to reflect contemporary circumstances.

What type of leadership is necessary to make our Aspirations a Reality?

New Behaviors: Leadership that exemplifies directness, openness to influence, commitment to the success of others, willingness to acknowledge our own contributions to problems, personal accountability, teamwork, and trust. Not only must we model these behaviors but we must coach others to adopt them.

Diversity: Leadership that values a diverse workforce (age, sex, ethnic group, etc.) at all levels of the organization, diversity in experience, and diversity in perspectives. We have committed to taking full advantage of the rich backgrounds and abilities of all our people and to promoting a greater diversity in positions of influence. Differing points of view will be sought; diversity will be valued and honesty rewarded, not suppressed.

Recognition: Leadership that provides greater recognition—both financial and psychic—for individuals and teams that contribute to our success. Recognition must be given to all who contribute: those who create and innovate and also those who continually support the day-to-day business requirements.

Ethical Management Practices: Leadership that epitomizes the stated standards of ethical behavior. We must provide clarity about our expectations and must enforce these standards through the corporation.

Communications: Leadership that is clear about company, unit, and individual goals and performance. People must know what is expected of them and receive timely honest feedback on their performance and career aspirations.

Empowerment: Leadership that increases the authority and responsibility of those closest to our products and customers. By actively pushing responsibility, trust, and recognition into the organization we can harness and release the capabilities of all our people.

Source: Robert Howard, *Harvard Business Review,* September–October 1990, pp. 133–144.

TABLE 5-2 Suggestions for Creating a Good Corporate Values Statement

1. Involve everyone in the company.
2. Allow customizing of the values by individual departments or units.
3. Expect and accept employee resistance.
4. Keep it short.
5. Avoid trivial statements.
6. Leave out religious references.
7. Challenge it.
8. Live it.

Source: Based on Alan Farnham, *Fortune,* April 19, 1993, pp. 117–24.

At Tom's of Maine, CEO Tom Chappell struggled to find a way to bring his values into running the multimillion dollar business he had founded with his wife, Kate. In his autobiographical book *The Soul of a Business*, Chappell describes his self-awareness journey and states, "I confessed how confused I was about what I should be doing with the rest of my life…I had to make a real go of something I'd started. What more could I do in life except make more money? Where were the purpose and direction for the rest of my life?"

stand that they were part of a unique corporate culture where values shaped the business strategy.[27] Also, training programs like those used at Blue Bell are an important way to develop employees' sense of ownership of the corporate values.

A survey of Fortune 1000 companies found that 95 percent of the respondents were convinced they would have to adopt more socially responsible business practices in coming years to preserve their competitive edge.[28] Getting employees to buy into a set of core values that emphasize a commitment to doing good requires strong corporate leadership. Corporate executives are responsible for shaping the organization so that its values, norms and ideals appeal strongly to employees. Some specific suggestions for developing a good corporate values statement are listed in Table 5-2.

Companies that practise values-based management have accepted a broad perspective regarding their commitment to being socially responsible. However, as we describe in the next section, companies can have different levels of social responsibility.

THE "GREENING" OF MANAGEMENT

Until the late 1960s, people (and organizations) paid little attention to the environmental consequences of their decisions and actions. A number of highly visible ecological problems and environmental disasters brought about a new awareness and spirit of environmentalism. Increasingly, managers began to confront questions about the natural environment and its impact on organizations. This recognition of the close link between an organization's decisions and activities and its impact on the natural environment is referred to as the **greening of management**. Let's look at some issues managers may have to address as they "go green".

How Organizations Go Green

There are many things that managers and organizations can do to protect and preserve the natural environment. Some organizations do no more than what is required by law (that is, they fulfill their social obligation); others have made radical changes in the ways they do business. Products and production processes have become cleaner. Dr. Margaret Kerr's work for Northern Telecom (the subject of Chapter 5's Managers Who Make a Difference section) is an excellent example. Many other companies have also made efforts to make their businesses more environmentally friendly. Canadian Pacific Hotels & Resorts developed an environmental program that has been adopted by other hotels all over the world. The chain reduced waste by 50 percent simply by putting recycling boxes in rooms. A host of other changes, such as energy-saving light bulbs, have formed an overall strategy that won the company the 1996 Green Hotelier of the Year Award from the International Hotel Association. There are numerous other examples of environmentally friendly actions taken by global organizations—but

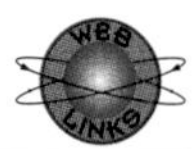

Canadian Pacific Limited
www.cp.ca

Canadian Pacific has developed an award-winning environmental program in their efforts to "go green".

how do these organizations "go green"? One approach to organizational roles in environmental responsibility uses the term *shades of green* to describe different approaches that organizations may embrace.

There are at least four approaches organizations can take with respect to environmental issues. The first approach is simply doing what is required legally: *the legal approach*. Under this approach, organizations exhibit little environmental sensitivity. They will obey laws, rules and regulations willingly and without legal challenge, but that is the extent of their being green. For example, many durable product manufacturers and oil refiners have taken the legal approach and comply with the relevant environmental laws and regulations, but these organizations are simply following their legal obligations of pollution prevention and environmental protection.

As an organization becomes more aware of, and sensitive to, environmental issues, it may adopt the *market approach*. Under this approach, organizations respond to the environmental preferences of their customers. Whatever customers demand in terms of environmentally-friendly products will be what the organization provides. For example, when you buy laundry detergent, you will be given a choice of phosphate-free products (at a premium price, mind you); and some coffee shops offer an organic variety of coffee, the beans of which have been produced in an environmentally friendly manner.

Under the next approach, the *stakeholder approach*, the organization chooses to respond to multiple demands made by **stakeholders** (any group in the organization's external environment that is affected by its decisions and actions). Under the stakeholder approach, the green organization will work to meet the environmental demands of groups such as employees, suppliers, investors, customers or the community. As an example, Ford Motor Company and Daimler-Benz AG have invested in British Columbia-based Ballard Power Systems, who are developing a fuel-cell technology that will allow automobiles to be run on hydrogen, methanol and natural gas without any pollutants. Both the market approach and the stakeholder approach are good illustrations of social responsiveness.

stakeholders
Any constituency in the external environment that is affected by an organization's decisions and policies.

Finally, if an organization pursues an *activist* (also called dark green) *approach*, it looks for ways to respect and preserve the earth and its natural resources. The subject of this chapter's Case Application is a good example. The activist approach exhibits the highest degree of environmental sensitivity and is a good illustration of social responsibility.

A GUIDE THROUGH THE MAZE

To this point, we've presented a number of themes related to social responsibility. Unfortunately, they don't lead us down a straight and clear path. In this section, we'll provide a modest guide through the maze to try and clarify the key issues.

The path will become easier to follow if we can identify the people to whom business managers are responsible. Classicists would say that shareholders or owners are their only legitimate concern. Progressives would respond that managers are responsible to any individual or group who is affected by the organization's decisions and policies—the stakeholders.

Figure 5-3 illustrates a four-stage model of the expansion of an organization's social responsibility.[29] What you do as a manager in terms of pursuing social goals depends on the person or persons to whom you believe you're responsible. A Stage 1 manager will promote the shareholders' interests by seeking to minimize costs and maximize profits. At Stage 2, managers will accept their responsibility to their employees and focus on human resource concerns. Because they'll want to get, keep and motivate good employees, they'll improve working conditions, expand employee rights, increase job security, and the like.

At Stage 3, managers will expand their goals to include fair prices, high-quality products and services, safe products, good supplier relations, and similar practices. Stage 3 managers perceive that they can meet their responsibilities to shareholders only indirectly, by meeting the needs of their other constituents.

Finally, Stage 4 characterizes the extreme socioeconomic definition of social responsibility. At this stage, managers are responsible to society as a whole. Their business is seen as public property and they are responsible for advancing the public good. The acceptance of such responsibility means that managers actively promote social justice, preserve the environment, and support social and cultural activities. They take these stances even if such actions negatively affect profits.

Each stage implies an increasing level of managerial discretion. As managers move to the right along the continuum in Figure 5-3, they have to make more judgment calls. At Stage 4, they are required to impose their values of right and wrong on society. For example, when is a product dangerous to society? Is Imasco doing "right" for society when it markets food products but "wrong" when it sells cigarettes? Or perhaps producing some food products that are not "healthy" is also wrong? Is Ontario Hydro, which operates nuclear power plants, or Atomic Energy of Canada (AECL) which sells them, behaving irresponsibly towards society? Is it wrong for a company to take advantage of all legal tax loopholes even if this means paying little or no tax on billions of dollars in profits?

Ontario Hydro
www.hydro.on.ca

Atomic Energy of Canada Ltd.
www.aecl.ca

There's no simple right-wrong dichotomy that can help managers make socially responsible decisions. Clearly, managers of business firms have a basic responsibility to obey the laws and make a profit. Failure to achieve either of these goals threatens the organization's survival. Beyond that, managers need to identify the people to whom they believe they're responsible. We suggest that by focusing on their stakeholders and their expectations of the organization, managers can make responsible choices, and they reduce the likelihood that they will ignore their responsibilities to crucial constituencies or alienate them.

MANAGERIAL ETHICS

Is it ethical for a salesperson to offer a bribe to a purchasing agent as an inducement to buy? What if the bribe comes out of the salesperson's commission? Does that make any difference? Is it ethical for someone to understate his or her educational qualifications in order to get a job during an economic slump if that person would ordinarily be considered overqualified for the job? Is it ethical for someone to use company gasoline for private use? How about using the company telephone for personal long-distance calls? Is it ethical to ask a company secretary to type personal letters?[30]

ethics
Rules and principles that define right and wrong conduct.

The term **ethics** commonly refers to the rules or principles that define right and wrong conduct.[31] In this section, we want to look at the ethical dimension of managerial decisions. Many decisions that managers make require them to consider who may be affected—in terms

FIGURE 5-3 To Whom Is Management Responsible?

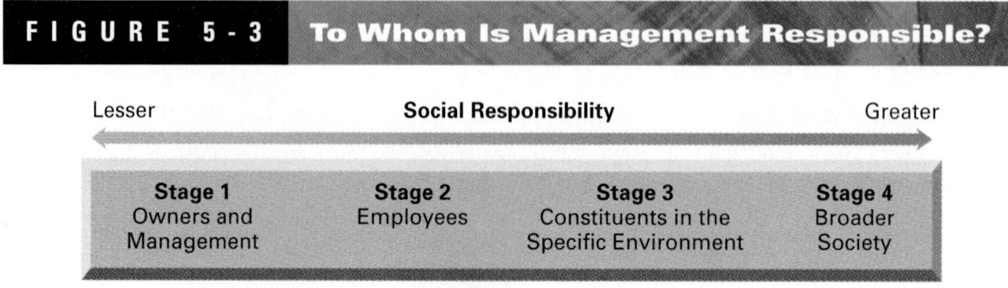

of the result as well as the process.[32] We'll present four different views of ethics and look at the factors that influence a manager's ethics. We'll conclude by offering some suggestions for what organizations can do to improve the ethical behaviour of employees.

Four Different Views of Ethics

There are four different perspectives on business ethics.[33] The first is the **utilitarian view of ethics**, in which decisions are made solely on the basis of their outcomes or consequences. The goal of utilitarianism is to provide the greatest good for the greatest number. Following the utilitarian view, a manager might conclude that laying off 20 percent of the workforce in her plant is justified because it will increase the plant's profitability, improve job security for the remaining 80 percent, and be in the best interest of shareholders. On the one hand, utilitarianism encourages efficiency and productivity and is consistent with the goal of profit maximization. On the other hand, it can result in biased allocations of resources, especially when some of those affected by the decision lack representation or a voice in the decision. Utilitarianism can also result in the rights of some stakeholders being ignored.

utilitarian view of ethics Decisions are made solely on the basis of their outcomes or consequences.

Another ethical perspective is the **rights view of ethics**. This position is concerned with respecting and protecting individual liberties and privileges, including the rights to privacy, freedom of conscience, free speech and due process. This would include, for example, protecting the rights of employees to free speech when they report violations of laws by their employers. The positive side of the rights perspective is that it protects individuals' freedom and privacy. But it has a negative side in organizations. It can present obstacles to high productivity and efficiency by creating a work climate that is more concerned with legally protecting individuals' rights than with getting the job done.

rights view of ethics Decisions are concerned with respecting and protecting basic rights of individuals.

The next view is the **theory of justice view of ethics**. This calls for managers to impose and enforce rules fairly and impartially. A manager would be using a theory-of-justice perspective in deciding to pay a new entry-level employee $1.50 an hour over the minimum wage, because he or she believes that the minimum wage is inadequate to allow employees to meet their basic financial obligations. Imposing standards of justice also comes with pluses and minuses. It protects the interests of those stakeholders who may be underrepresented or who may lack power; but it can encourage a sense of entitlement that might make employees reduce risk taking, innovation and productivity.

theory of justice view of ethics Decision makers seek to impose and enforce rules fairly and impartially.

The final perspective is the **integrative social contracts theory** view, which proposes combining empirical (what is) and normative (what should be) approaches to business ethics. This view of ethics is based on the integration of two "contracts": the general social contract among economic participants that defines the ground rules for doing business, and a more specific contract among specific members of a community that covers acceptable ways of behaving. This view of business ethics differs from the other three in that it suggests that managers need to look at existing ethical norms in industries and corporations in order to determine what is right and wrong.

integrative social contracts theory A view that proposes decisions should be based on both empirical (what is) and normative (what should be) factors.

Studies have shown that most business people continue to hold utilitarian attitudes towards ethical behavior.[34] This shouldn't be a total surprise, because utilitarianism is consistent with such goals as efficiency, productivity and high profits. By maximizing profits, for instance, an executive can argue that he or she is gaining the greatest good for the greatest number.

Because of the changing world of management, that perspective needs to change. Because utilitarianism tends to downplay the satisfaction of individual and minority interests for the benefit of the majority, new trends towards individual rights and social justice mean that managers need ethical standards based on non-utilitarian criteria. This is an obvious challenge to today's manager because making decisions using such criteria as individual rights, social justice and community standards involves far more ambiguities than using utilitarian criteria such as effects on efficiency and profits. The result, of course, is that managers increasingly find themselves struggling with ethical dilemmas.

5 **How does values-based management relate to the concepts of social responsibility and social responsiveness?**

6 **Which of the four views on business ethics is most popular among business people? Why?**

MANAGERS WHO MAKE A DIFFERENCE

Dr. Margaret Kerr, Senior Vice-President of Human Resources and Environment, Nortel Networks

As the heading states, Dr. Margaret Kerr is senior vice-president of human resources and environment for Nortel Networks, the biggest equipment manufacturer in the Canadian telecommunications industry. Dr. Kerr is a strong proponent of total quality management, but she has adopted TQM's ideals to her specific area of expertise: environmental management. Dr. Kerr joined Nortel Networks back in 1987 and, for the past 12 years, has devoted her efforts to developing and implementing new manufacturing processes that do not harm the environment. Her strategy is to attack problems at the root.[35]

To this effect, Dr. Kerr first tackled Nortel Network's massive use of chlorofluorocarbons (CFCs). The company was using solvents loaded with CFCs in the production of circuit boards. However, Dr. Kerr did not simply attempt to remedy the situation by replacing the solvents, as this would probably only result in switching one poison for another. Instead she developed an alternative to the manufacturing process itself—one in which no solvents whatsoever would be used. A pleasant side-benefit of this new process was a significant reduction in manufacturing costs. The company gladly instituted the changes. Nortel Networks became the first multinational telecommunications company to remove CFCs from its production processes, doing so nine years before an international agreement took effect banning the substances.

Northern Telecom Limited
www.nortel.com

Dr. Kerr then developed an environmental life-cycle program at Nortel Networks, the mandate of which is to reduce waste in every area of the manufacturing process. In true TQM fashion, Kerr's team now works with Nortel Network's employees, suppliers and customers to achieve its goals. And changes have been taken beyond the manufacturing processes to the design stage, where engineers now take environmental issues into account in their design of new products, such as a lead-free phone, which was developed in 1997.

Dr. Kerr's influence on Nortel Networks has been enormous. And luckily for the rest of the world, she has helped found a group—with other manufacturers—known as the International Co-operative for Ozone Layer Protection. Through this organization, Nortel's environmental advances are shared with other companies, and governments are given training on environmental issues. ■

Factors Affecting Managerial Ethics

Whether a manager acts ethically or unethically is the result of a complex interaction between the manager's stage of moral development and several moderating variables including individual characteristics, the organization's structural design, the organization's culture and the intensity of the ethical issue.[36] (See Figure 5-4.) People who lack a strong moral sense are much less likely to do the wrong things if they are constrained by rules, policies, job descriptions, or strong cultural norms that disapprove of such behaviour. Conversely, very moral individuals can be corrupted by an organizational structure and culture that permits or encourages unethical practices. Moreover, managers are more likely to make ethical decisions on issues where high moral intensity is involved. Let's look more closely at the various factors that influence whether managers behave ethically or unethically.

Stage of Moral Development. Substantial research confirms the existence of three levels of moral development, each composed of two stages.[37] At each successive stage, an individual's moral judgment becomes less and less dependent on outside influences. The three levels and six stages are described in Table 5-3.

FIGURE 5-4 Factors Affecting Ethical and Unethical Behaviour

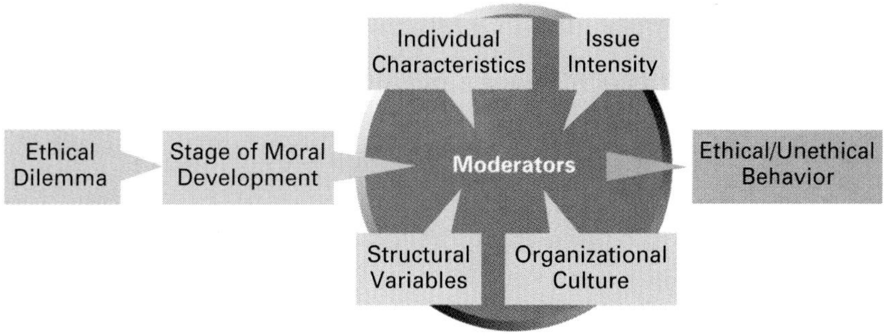

The first level is labeled *preconventional*. At this level, individuals respond to notions of right or wrong when there are personal consequences involved, such as physical punishment, reward or exchange of favours. Reasoning at the *conventional* level indicates that moral values reside in maintaining the conventional order and the expectations of others. At the *principled* level, individuals make a clear effort to define moral principles apart from the authority of the groups to which they belong, or of society in general.

Research on these stages allows us to draw several conclusions.[38] First, people proceed through the six stages in lockstep fashion. They gradually move up a ladder, stage by stage. Second, there is no guarantee of continued development. Development can terminate at any stage. Third, the majority of adults are at Stage 4. They are limited to obeying the rules and will be predisposed to behave ethically. For instance, a Stage 3 manager is likely to make decisions that will receive peer approval; a Stage 4 manager will seek to be a "good corporate citizen" by making decisions that respect the organization's rules and procedures; and a Stage 5

TABLE 5-3 Stages of Moral Development

Level	Stage Description
Preconventional Influenced exclusively by personal interest. Decisions are made in terms of self-benefit as defined by the rewards and punishments that come from different types of behaviour.	1. Sticking to rules to avoid physical punishment 2. Following rules only when it's in your immediate interest
Conventional Influenced by the expectations of others. Includes obedience to the law, response to the expectations of significant others, and a general sense of what is expected.	3. Living up to what is expected by people close to you 4. Maintaining the conventional order by fulfilling obligations to which you have agreed
Principled Influenced by personal ethical principles of what is right. These may or may not be in accordance with rules or laws of society.	5. Valuing rights of others; and upholding non-relative values and rights regardless of the majority's opinion. 6. Following self-chosen ethical principles even if they violate the law

Source: Based on Lawrence Kohlberg, "Moral Stages and Moralization: The Cognitive-Developmental Approach," in T. Lickona, ed., *Moral Development and Behavior: Theory, Research, and Social Issues* (New York: Holt, Rinehart & Winston, 1976), pp. 34–35.

manager is more likely to challenge organizational practices that he or she believes are wrong. Many of the recent efforts by universities to raise students' ethical awareness and standards are focused on helping them move to the principled level.

values
Basic convictions about what is right and wrong.

Individual Characteristics. Every person enters an organization with a relatively entrenched set of **values**. Developed in an individual's early years—from parents, teachers, friends and others—these values represent basic convictions about what is right and wrong. Thus, managers in an organization often have very different personal values.[39] Note that although *values* and *stage of moral development* may seem similar, they aren't. The former are broad and cover a wide range of issues, while the latter is specifically a measure of independence from outside influences.

Two personality variables have also been found to influence an individual's actions according to his or her beliefs about what is right or wrong: ego strength and locus of control.

ego strength
A personality characteristic that measures the strength of a person's convictions.

Ego strength is a personality measure of the strength of a person's convictions. People who score high on ego strength are likely to resist impulses and follow their convictions more than those who are low in ego strength. That is, individuals high in ego strength are more likely to do what they think is right. We would expect managers with high ego strength to demonstrate more consistency between moral judgment and moral action than those with low ego strength.

locus of control
A personality attribute that measures the degree to which people believe they control their own fate.

Locus of control is a personality attribute that measures the degree to which people believe they control their own fate. People with an internal locus of control believe that they control their own destinies, while those with an external locus of control believe that what happens to them in life is due to luck or chance. From an ethical perspective, externals are less likely to take personal responsibility for the consequences of their behaviour and are more likely to rely on external forces. Internals are more likely to take responsibility for consequences and rely on their own internal standards of right and wrong to guide their behaviour.[40] Managers with an internal locus of control will probably demonstrate more consistency between their moral judgments and moral actions than will "external" managers.

Structural Variables. An organization's structural design helps to shape the ethical behaviour of managers. Some structures provide strong guidance, while others only create ambiguity for managers. Structural designs that minimize ambiguity and continuously remind managers of what is "ethical" are more likely to encourage ethical behaviour.

Formal rules and regulations reduce ambiguity. Job descriptions and written codes of ethics are examples of formal guides that promote consistent behaviour. Research continues to show, though, that the behaviour of superiors is the strongest single influence on an individual's own ethical or unethical behaviour.[41] People check to see what those in authority are doing and use that as a benchmark for acceptable practices and for what is expected of them. Some performance appraisal systems focus exclusively on outcomes. Others evaluate means as well as ends. Where managers are evaluated only on outcomes, there will be increased pressures to do "whatever is necessary" to look good on the outcome variables. Closely associated with the appraisal system is the way rewards are allocated. The more rewards or punishment depend on specific goal outcomes, the more pressure there is on managers to do whatever they must to reach those goals and perhaps compromise their ethical standards. Structures also differ in the amount of time, competition, cost, and similar pressures that are placed on job holders. The greater the pressure, the more likely it is that managers will compromise their ethical standards.

Organization's Culture. The content and strength of an organization's culture also influence ethical behaviour.[42]

An organizational culture most likely to shape high ethical standards is one that's high in risk tolerance, control and conflict tolerance. Managers in such a culture are encouraged to be aggressive and innovative, are aware that unethical practices will be discovered, and feel free to openly challenge demands or expectations they consider unrealistic or personally undesirable.

A strong organizational culture will exert more influence on managers than a weak one. If the culture is strong and supports high ethical standards, it should have a very powerful and positive influence on a manager's ethical behaviour.

Daniel Green of Quebec's La Société pour vaincre la pollution is an example of a person operating at Stage 6 of moral development; his group fights to change laws and practices which they see as being detrimental to the earth's environment.

Issue Intensity. A student who would never consider breaking into an instructor's office to steal an introductory accounting exam doesn't think twice about asking a friend who took the same accounting course from the same instructor last year what questions were on the exam. Similarly, an executive might think nothing of taking home a few office supplies, yet be highly concerned about the possible embezzlement of company funds.

These examples illustrate the final factor that affects a manager's ethical behaviour—the characteristics of the ethical issue itself.[43] As Figure 5-5 shows, six characteristics have been identified as being relevant in determining issue intensity:[44]

1. How great a harm (or benefit) is done to victims (or beneficiaries) of the ethical act in question? *Example:* An act that puts 1000 people out of work is more harmful than one affecting only 10 people.

2. How much consensus is there that the act is evil (or good)? *Example:* More Canadians agree that it is wrong to bribe a customs official in Toronto than agree it is wrong to bribe a customs official in Mexico.

3. What is the probability that the act will actually take place and will actually cause the harm (or benefit) predicted? *Example:* Selling a gun to a known armed robber has greater probability of harm than selling a gun to a law-abiding citizen.

4. What's the length of time between the act in question and its expected consequences? *Example:* Reducing the retirement benefits of current retirees has greater immediate consequences than reducing the retirement benefits of current employees who are between the ages of 40 and 50.

5. How close does the person feel (socially, psychologically or physically) to the victims (or beneficiaries) of the evil (beneficial) act in question? *Example:* Layoffs in one's own work unit hit closer to home than do layoffs in a remote city.

6. How large is the concentrated effect of the ethical act on the people involved? *Example:* A change in the warranty policy denying coverage to 10 people with claims of $10 000 each has a more concentrated effect than a change denying coverage to 10 000 people with claims of $10 each.

Following these guidelines, the larger the number of people harmed, the greater the consensus that an act is evil; the higher the probability that an act will take place and actually cause harm, the shorter the length of time until the consequences of the act surface; and the closer the observer feels to the victims of the act, the greater the issue intensity. In sum, these

FIGURE 5-5 Characteristics Determining Issue Intensity

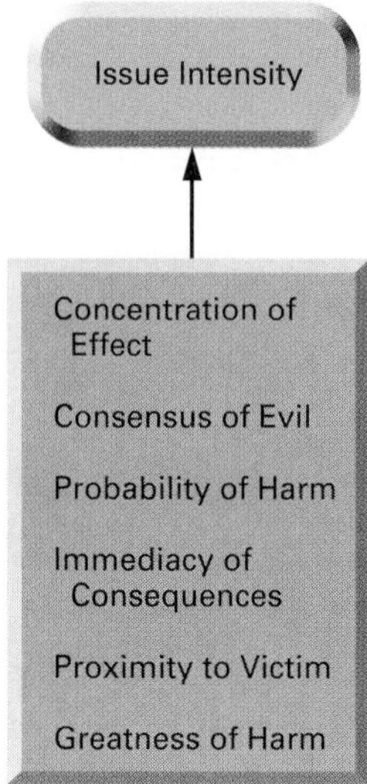

six factors determine how important an ethical issue is. And we would expect managers to behave more ethically when a moral issue is important to them than when it is not.

Ethics in an International Context

Are ethical standards universal across the globe? Hardly! Social and cultural differences between countries are important environmental factors that determine ethical and unethical behaviour. For example, the manager of a Mexican firm bribes several high-ranking government officials in Mexico City to secure a profitable government contract for his firm. Such a practice would be seen as unethical, if not illegal, in Canada. But it's a standard business practice in Mexico.

Companies in Canada are seen by the international community to be relatively corruption-free. In a 1997 ranking established by the organization Transparency International, Canada was listed as the fifth-most corruption-free country out of a list of fifty-two (one to four were Denmark, Finland, Sweden and New Zealand, respectively). The US was ranked sixteenth. [45]

It's important for managers working in foreign cultures to recognize the various social, cultural and political-legal influences on what is appropriate and acceptable behaviour. This adds another dimension to making ethical judgments.

Towards Improving Ethical Behaviour

Top managers can do a number of things if they are serious about reducing unethical practices in their organization. They can seek to select individuals with high ethical standards, establish

TABLE 5-4 The Ten Most Corrupt Nations in the World

1. Nigeria	6. Mexico
2. Bolivia	7. Indonesia
3. Columbia	8. India
4. Russia	9. Venezuela
5. Pakistan	10. Vietnam

Source: Transparency International's Corruption Perception Index 1997, cited in "Grease", *Report on Business* Magazine, March 1998.

codes of ethics and decision rules, lead by example, delineate job goals and provide ethics training. Taken individually, these actions will probably not have much effect. But when all or most of them are implemented as part of a comprehensive program, they have the potential to significantly improve an organization's ethical climate. The key term here, however, is *potential*. There are no guarantees that a well-designed program will lead to the outcome desired. Dow Corning, for instance, has long been recognized as a pioneer in corporate ethics, and its ethics program has been cited as being among the most elaborate in corporate North America.[46] However, this didn't stop the company from covering up and misrepresenting the results of studies on its silicone gel breast implants.

Selection. Given that individuals are at different stages of moral development and have different personal value systems and personalities, an organization's employee selection process—interviews, tests, background checks, and the like—should be used to eliminate ethically undesirable applicants. This is no easy task. Even under the best of circumstances, individuals with questionable standards of right and wrong will be hired. That is to be expected and needn't pose a problem if other controls are in place. But the selection process should be viewed as an opportunity to learn about an individual's level of moral development, personal values, ego strength and locus of control.[47]

Codes of Ethics and Decision Rules. We have already seen how ambiguity about what is ethical can be a problem for employees. Codes of ethics are an increasingly popular response for reducing that ambiguity.[48] For instance, Canada doesn't have the legislation on whistle blowing that exists in the United States, but codes of ethics are being supported and proposed by organizations like the Conference Board of Canada.

A **code of ethics** is a formal document that states an organization's primary values and the ethical rules it expects employees to follow. It has been suggested that codes should be specific enough to show employees the spirit in which they're supposed to do things, yet loose enough to allow for freedom of judgment.[49] These suggestions seem to have been applied at McDonnell Douglas, as shown in Figure 5-6.

code of ethics
A formal statement of an organization's primary values and the ethical rules it expects its employees to follow.

What do most codes of ethics look like? A survey of business ethics found that their content tended to fall into three categories: (1) be a dependable organizational citizen, (2) do not do anything unlawful or improper that will harm the organization, and (3) be good to customers.[50] Table 5-6 lists directives included in each of these clusters in order of their frequency of mention. However, another study of over 200 corporations suggested that many codes of ethics aren't as effective as they might be because they omit important issues.[51] Seventy-five percent, for example, fail to address personal character matters, product safety, product quality, environmental affairs, or civic and community affairs. In contrast, more than three-quarters mentioned issues such as relations with government, customer-supplier relations, political contributions, and conflicts of interest. The authors of this study concluded that "codes are really dealing with infractions against the corporation, rather than illegalities on behalf of the corporation."[52] That is, codes tend to give most attention to areas of illegal or unethical conduct that are likely to decrease a company's profits.[53]

In isolation, ethical codes are not likely to be much more than window dressing. Their effectiveness depends heavily on how strongly management supports them and on how employees who break the codes are treated. When management considers them important, regularly reaffirms their content, and publicly reprimands rule breakers, codes can supply a strong foundation for an effective corporate ethics program.

Another approach that uses formal written statements to guide behaviour has been suggested by Laura Nash.[54] She proposes 12 questions to guide managers in making decisions with ethical dimensions.

7 **What conditions are relevant in determining the degree of intensity a person is likely to have on an ethical issue?**

8 **What behaviours are most likely to be mentioned as being prohibited by an organization's code of ethics? Which are most likely not to be mentioned?**

FIGURE 5-6 McDonnell Douglas's Code of Ethics

MCDONNELL DOUGLAS
Code of Ethics

Integrity and ethics exist in the individual or they do not exist at all. They must be upheld by individuals or they are not upheld at all. In order for integrity and ethics to be characteristics of McDonnell Douglas, we who make up the corporation must strive to be

- Honest and trustworthy in all our relationships.
- Reliable in carrying out assignments and responsibilities.
- Truthful and accurate in what we say and write.
- Cooperative and constructive in all work undertaken.
- Fair and considerate in our treatment of fellow employees, customers, all other persons.
- Law abiding in all our activities.
- Committed to accomplishing all tasks in a superior way.
- Economical in utilizing company resources.
- Dedicated in service to our company and to improvement of the quality of life in the world in which we live.

Integrity and high standards of ethics require hard work, courage, and difficult choices. Consultation among employees, top management, and the Board of Directors will sometimes be necessary to determine a proper course of action. In the long run, however, we will be better served by doing what is right than what is expedient.

A recent survey found that 90 percent of Canadian companies with revenue of over $1 billion (all of which are almost certainly operating on a global scale, due to their size) have a stated code of ethics.[55] Moreover, in 1997 a coalition of 14 Canadian companies formed the International Code of Ethics for Canadian Business. Mind you, these efforts could be driven by Public Relations motives (as Warren Allmand, president of the International Centre for Human

TABLE 5-5 Exporting Countries Most Likely to Use Bribery

1. Belgium/Luxembourg	**7.** Spain
2. France	**8.** China/Hong Kong
3. Italy	**9.** Germany
4. Netherlands	**10.** Singapore
5. South Korea	**11. Canada**
6. United Kingdom	**12.** Japan

Source: Transparency International ranking, cited *Report on Business* Magazine, March 1998, p. 66.

TABLE 5-6 Clusters of Variables Found in 83 Corporate Codes of Business Ethics

Cluster 1. Be a Dependable Organizational Citizen

1. Comply with safety, health, and security regulations.
2. Demonstrate courtesy, respect, honesty and fairness.
3. Illegal drugs and alcohol at work are prohibited.
4. Manage personal finances well.
5. Exhibit good attendance and punctuality.
6. Follow directives of supervisors.
7. Do not use abusive language.
8. Dress in businesslike attire.
9. Firearms at work are prohibited.

Cluster 2. Do Not Do Anything Unlawful or Improper That Will Harm the Organization

1. Conduct business in compliance with all laws.
2. Payments for unlawful purposes are prohibited.
3. Bribes are prohibited.
4. Avoid outside activities that impair duties.
5. Maintain confidentiality of records.
6. Comply with all antitrust and trade regulations.
7. Comply with accounting rules and controls.
8. Do not use company property for personal benefit.
9. Employees are personally accountable for company funds.
10. Do not propagate false or misleading information.
11. Make decisions without regard for personal gain.

Cluster 3. Be Good to Customers

1. Convey true claims in product advertisements.
2. Perform assigned duties to the best of your ability.
3. Provide products and services of the highest quality.

Source: Fred R. David, "An Empirical Study of Codes of Business Ethics: A Strategic Perspective." Paper presented at the 48th Annual Academy of Management Conference, Anaheim, California; August 1988.

Rights and Democratic Development, has suggested). As it turns out, Canada is not quite as pure as the discussion so far might suggest. Take a look at Table 5-5. We're just barely staying out of the top 10.

Top Management's Leadership. Codes of ethics require a commitment from top management. Why? Because it's the top managers who set the cultural tone. They are role models in terms of both words and actions—though what they *do* is probably more important than what they *say*. If top managers, for example, use company resources for their personal use, inflate their expense accounts, or give favoured treatment to friends, they imply that such behaviour is acceptable for all employees.

Top management also sets the cultural tone by its reward and punishment practices. The choice of whom and what are rewarded with pay increases and promotions sends a strong message to employees. The promotion of a manager for achieving impressive results in an ethically questionable manner indicates to everyone that those questionable ways are acceptable. When wrongdoing is uncovered, management must not only punish the wrongdoer but publicize the fact, and make the outcome visible to everyone in the organization. This sends another message: "Doing wrong has a price, and it's *not* in your best interest to act unethically!"

Job Goals. Employees should have tangible and realistic goals. Explicit goals can create ethical problems if they make unrealistic demands on employees. Under the stress of achieving unrealistic goals, otherwise ethical employees often take the attitude that "anything goes". When goals are clear and realistic, they reduce ambiguity for employees and motivate rather than punish.

Ethics Training. More and more organizations are setting up seminars, workshops and similar ethics training programs to try to increase ethical behaviour. Recent estimates indicate that 33 percent of companies provide some ethics training.[56] But these training programs aren't without controversy. The primary debate is whether or not you can actually teach ethics. Critics, for instance, stress that the effort is pointless since people establish their individual value systems when they are very young.[57] Proponents, however, note that several studies have found that values can be learned after early childhood.[58] In addition, they cite evidence that shows that teaching ethical problem solving can make an actual difference in ethical behaviour;[59] that training has increased individuals' levels of moral development;[60] and that, if it does nothing else, ethics training increases awareness of ethical issues in business.[61]

How do you teach ethics? Let's examine how it's done at one large organization, Citicorp. There, as part of the company's comprehensive corporate ethics training program, managers participate in a game that allows them to practise their understanding of the company's ethical standards.[62] Players move markers around a game board when they correctly answer multiple-choice questions presented on cards. Each card poses an ethical dilemma a bank employee might encounter. As the game progresses, players are "promoted" from entry-level employee to supervisor and eventually to senior manager.

Ethical training sessions can provide a number of benefits.[63] They reinforce the organization's standards of conduct. They're a reminder that top management wants employees to consider ethical issues in making decisions. They clarify which practices are permissible and which are not. Finally, when managers discuss common concerns among themselves, they are reassured that they aren't alone in facing ethical dilemmas. This can strengthen their confidence when they have to take unpopular but ethically correct stances.

Comprehensive Performance Appraisal. When performance appraisals focus only on economic outcomes, ends will begin to justify means. If an organization wants its managers to uphold high ethical standards, it *must* include this dimension in its appraisal process. For example, a manager's annual review might include a point-by-point evaluation of how his or her decisions measured against the company's code of ethics, as well as on the more traditional economic criteria. Needless to say, if the manager looks good on the economic criteria but scores poorly on ethical conduct, appropriate action needs to be taken.

TABLE 5-7 Canadian Managers' 10 Most Important Issues of Ethical Risk

1. Integrity of books and records
2. Worker health and safety
3. Security of internal communications
4. Quality and safety of products and services
5. Receipt of inappropriate gifts, favours, entertainment and bribes
6. Security and use of proprietary knowledge and intellectual property
7. Discrimination on the basis of sex, race or religion
8. Privacy, confidentiality, and appropriate use of employee records
9. Sexual harassment
10. Reports of fraud or compliance failures

Source: Globe and Mail, February 21, 1997, p. B11.

Independent Social Audits. An important element of unethical behaviour is fear of being caught. Independent audits, which evaluate decisions and management practices in terms of the organization's code of ethics, increase the likelihood of detection. These audits can be routine evaluations, performed on a regular basis just like financial audits, or they can occur randomly with no prior announcement. An effective ethical program should probably include both. To maintain integrity, the auditors should be responsible to the company's board of directors, and present their findings directly to the board. This not only gives the auditors clout, but also reduces the opportunity for retaliation from those being audited.

Formal Protective Mechanisms. Our last recommendation is for organizations to provide formal mechanisms so that employees who face ethical dilemmas can do something about them without fear of reprimand.

An organization might, for instance, designate ethical counsellors. When employees face a dilemma, they could go to these advisers for guidance. The ethical counsellor's first role would be a sounding board; a channel to let employees openly verbalize the ethical problem, the problem's cause, and their own options. Then, after the options are clear, the adviser's second role might be that of an advocate who champions the "right" alternatives. In fact, according to the director of the Center for Business Ethics at Bentley College, around 20 percent of corporations now have ethics officers. The organization might also create a special appeals process that employees could use without risk to themselves, to raise ethical issues or blow the whistle on violators.[64]

A FINAL THOUGHT

If you looked through a management text from 20 years ago, you'd probably not find a chapter on social responsibility and ethics. If you even found the topics in the text, they wouldn't have had more than a passing mention. What has happened to bring about this increased focus?

One line of thinking is that the recent attention to these topics is a response to a *decline* in business's willingness to accept its societal responsibilities and in the ethical standards of managers. In a poll of 1500 Canadians, taken in 1997, only one company—Bombardier—was respected by more than 10 percent of participants.[65] There is a significant distrust of companies amongst the general population. However, experts on the role of business in society give another explanation for the increased focus on social responsibility.

They contend that today's managers *are* more socially conscious and ethical than their counterparts of a generation ago. What has happened is that the demands on business and the expectations of what is considered "proper conduct" have risen faster than the ability of business to raise its standards.

Cornelius Vanderbilt's famous phrase "the public be damned" was accepted by many in the 1890s. It certainly is not acceptable in the 1990s. It was acceptable for Hamilton steel plants to pollute Lake Ontario in the 1950s, but it is not today.

This observation has implications for managers. Since society's expectations of its institutions are regularly changing, managers must continually monitor these expectations. What is ethically acceptable today may be a poor guide for the future.

9 **How could independent social audits be used to encourage ethical behaviour?**

10 **Over the last 25 years, has business become less willing to accept its social responsibility?**

SUMMARY

This summary is organized by the learning objectives found at the beginning of the chapter.

1. According to the classical view, business's only social responsibility is to maximize financial returns for shareholders. The opposing socioeconomic view holds that business has a responsibility to the larger society.
2. The arguments for business being socially responsible include public expectations, long-run profits, ethical obligations, public image, a better environment, fewer government regulations, balancing of responsibility and power, shareholders' interests, possession of resources, and the superiority of prevention over cures. The arguments against hold that social responsibility violates the profit maximization objective, dilutes the organization's purpose, costs too much, gives business too much power, requires skills that business doesn't have, lacks accountability, and lacks wide public support.
3. Social responsibility refers to business's pursuit of long-term goals that are good for society. Social responsiveness refers to the capacity of a firm to respond to social pressures. The former requires business to determine what is right or wrong, thus seeking fundamental ethical truths, while the latter is guided by social norms.
4. Most research studies show a positive relationship between corporate social involvement and economic performance. The evidence does *not* show that acting in a socially responsible way significantly reduces a corporation's long-term economic performance.
5. A stakeholder is any constituency in an organization's environment that is affected by the organization's decisions and policies. By focusing on the organization's stakeholders and their expectations of the organization, management is less likely to ignore its responsibilities to crucial constituencies.
6. The term *values-based management* refers to an approach to managing in which managers establish, promote and practise the organization's shared values. The shared values make up the organization's culture and influence the way the organization operates and the way employees behave.
7. The "greening of management" is the recognition of the close link between an organization's decisions and activities, and the impact they have on the natural environment. Organizations might go green using any of four approaches: the legal approach, the market approach, the stakeholder approach, and the activist approach.
8. The term *ethics* refers to rules or principles that define right and wrong conduct.
9. The utilitarian view makes decisions based on their outcomes or consequences. The rights view seeks to respect and protect the basic rights of individuals. The theory of justice view seeks to impose and enforce rules fairly and impartially. The integrative social contracts view recognizes the implicit contracts between organizations and the ethical standards of the community within which they operate.
10. Whether a manager acts ethically or unethically is the result of a complex interaction between the manager's stage of moral development, his or her individual characteristics, the organization's structural design, the organization's culture, and the intensity of the ethical issue.
11. There are three levels of moral development, each composed of two stages. The first two stages are influenced exclusively by an individual's personal interests. Stages 3 and 4 are influenced by the expectations of others. Stages 5 and 6 are influenced by personal ethical principles of what is right.
12. A comprehensive ethics program would include selection in order to weed out ethically undesirable job applicants, a code of ethics and decision rules, a commitment by top management, clear and realistic job goals, ethics training, comprehensive performance appraisals, independent social audits, and formal protective mechanisms.

THINKING ABOUT MANAGEMENT ISSUES

1. What does social responsibility mean to you? Do you think business firms should be socially responsible? Why?
2. "The business of business is business." Critique this statement from (a) the classical view and (b) the socioeconomic view.
3. What are some problems that could be associated with employee whistle blowing for (a) the whistle blower and (b) the organization?
4. Do you think values-based management is just a "do-gooder" ploy? Explain your answer.
5. Discuss this statement: "In the long run, those who do not use power in a way that society considers responsible will tend to lose it."

SELF-ASSESSMENT EXERCISE

ATTITUDES TOWARDS BUSINESS ETHICS QUESTIONNAIRE

Here are 18 statements about business ethics. Indicate your level of agreement with these statements using the scale of 1 ("strongly disagree") to 5 ("strongly agree"). When you have finished, turn to the scoring key to compare your scores with those of other management and liberal arts students.

5 = Strongly agree
4 = Agree
3 = Neither agree nor disagree
2 = Disagree
1 = Strongly disagree

	Strongly Agree				Strongly Disagree
1. The only moral of business is making money.	5	4	3	2	1
2. A person who is doing well in business does not have to worry about moral problems.	5	4	3	2	1
3. Every business person acts according to moral principles, whether he or she is aware of it or not.	5	4	3	2	1
4. Act according to the law, and you can't go wrong morally.	5	4	3	2	1
5. Ethics in business is basically an adjustment between expectations and the ways in which people behave.	5	4	3	2	1
6. Business decisions involve a realistic economic attitude and not a moral philosophy.	5	4	3	2	1
7. Moral values are irrelevant to the business world.	5	4	3	2	1
8. "Business ethics" is a concept for public relations only.	5	4	3	2	1
9. Competitiveness and profitability are important values.	5	4	3	2	1
10. Conditions of a free economy will best serve the needs of society. Limiting competition can only hurt society and actually violates basic natural laws.	5	4	3	2	1
11. As a consumer, when making an auto insurance claim, I try to get as much as possible regardless of the extent of the damage.	5	4	3	2	1
12. While shopping at the supermarket, it is appropriate to switch price tags on packages.	5	4	3	2	1
13. As an employee, I can take home office supplies; it doesn't hurt anyone.	5	4	3	2	1
14. I view sick days as vacation days that I deserve.	5	4	3	2	1
15. Employees' wages should be determined according to the laws of supply and demand.	5	4	3	2	1
16. If you want a specific goal, you have to take the necessary steps to achieve it.	5	4	3	2	1
17. The business world has its own rules.	5	4	3	2	1
18. A good business person is a successful business person.	5	4	3	2	1

See scoring key beginning on page SK-1.

Source: Arie Reichel and Yoram Neumann, *Journal of Instructional Psychology,* March 1988, pp. 25–33. Reprinted with permission of authors.

for your IMMEDIATE action

TO: Frank Flokstra, Director of Corporate Legal Affairs
FROM: Van Sifferman, CEO
SUBJECT: Protecting Whistleblowers

The Dawn Reddy "whistle blower" case has been a terrible embarrassment to this company. She argued in court that we would have ignored her claims that several executives in our Laboratory Division, where she worked, were taking payoffs from clients to falsify research findings, in order to expedite government approval of those clients' drugs. She said she also feared reprisal from her direct superiors if she informed on them. This was her defence for going directly to the regulatory body with her allegations.

The loss of this case (and the $2.5 million settlement) makes it very clear that we have a serious problem. It is not enough that we fired the three managers involved in this scheme. We must do something immediately to change the ethical climate around here. No employee should need to go to outside authorities if he or she perceives wrongdoing. Employees must feel secure in knowing that we maintain high ethical standards and will protect any employee who reports unethical practices.

As a first step, I have spoken to Ms. Reddy and her attorneys. I told them that it is now evident that her superior's claim that he fired her for "unsatisfactory performance" was a total fabrication. I told her that her superior had been terminated, as had his superior and another associate. I offered Ms. Reddy her job back and told her I personally hoped she would return. She accepted my offer.

This case is now closed. But we must ensure that something like this never happens again! I want you to give me a written plan (not to exceed two pages in length) that describes specifically what we can do to (1) encourage employees to speak out if they see wrongdoings and (2) protect them when they do so.

This organization has been disguised for obvious reasons.

TAKE IT TO THE NET

We invite you to visit the Robbins/Coulter/Stuart-Kotze Companion Website at www.prenticehall.ca/robbins for this chapter's Internet resources.

CASE APPLICATION

Zero Emissions Research Initiative, Tokyo, Japan

Gunter Pauli, a native of Belgium now living in Tokyo, represents a whole new breed of business person: the social entrepreneur. Pauli has written eight management books and is fluent in six languages—any organization would love to have him working for them. But he considers himself more of a social crusader than a business leader. Since 1992, he has championed an ambitious program challenging how conventional companies work. He wants to create manufacturing facilities that function as closed-loop systems—that is, factories that completely eliminate waste by reusing or recycling all the raw materials they take in. Pauli calls this approach "zero-emission manufacturing" and believes it is the next big breakthrough in business productivity. Total quality management meant zero defects. Just-in-time manufacturing meant zero inventories. In zero emissions, you're striving for zero waste; you use everything. You completely eliminate waste. Pauli says, "This is part of the drive for higher productivity of raw materials. Zero emissions sounds radical today. In 20 years it will be standard operating procedure."

This "radical" operating concept is already in effect in a few places around the globe. Pauli is former CEO of Ecover, a small Belgian company that produces cleaning products from natural soaps and renewable raw materials. Ecover opened a near-zero-emissions factory in October 1992, in Malle, Belgium. What is unique about this factory is that it's a "green" marvel. A huge grass roof keeps the factory cool in summer and warm in winter. The water treatment system runs on wind and solar energy. The bricks in the factory walls are made of recycled clay from coal mines. But Pauli doesn't even like the term *green* to describe Ecover's products or its factory. He says that most people assume that "green" means lousy performance at a high price. Instead, what Ecover does is develop high-technology products based on a mastery of the chemistry of renewable resources. It's in the business of pioneering sustainable economic and social development.

Pauli believed that the media sensation created by Ecover's green factory was a prime opportunity to create a global product brand by opening more factories around the world, but his lead investor and partner preferred a more cautious approach. So he left Ecover and moved to Tokyo to work for the United Nations University and the Zero Emissions Research Initiative (ZERI). From there he co-ordinates a global network of scientists, corporate executives and political leaders, who are piecing together zero-emissions technology and documenting its performance benefits. In 1998, Pauli was developing a $60 million investment fund (to be financed by various world governments) that would underwrite zero-emissions factories in different industries around the world. In fact, construction was completed in mid-1997 on the world's most unconventional brewery in Namibia, in southern Africa. The brewery was designed as a model of what zero-emissions factories would be like. Pauli describes it as a fully integrated biosystem. Water (the brewing process wastes massive amounts of water) flows from the brewery into ponds designed for fish farming. Mushrooms grow on piles of used grain (brewing also requires huge supplies of grain) from the fermentation process. Chickens feed on earthworms turned loose in the grain. The waste from the chickens is put into a machine called the digester, which generates methane gas that produces steam for the fermentation process. As Pauli has said: "Does it make sense—morally, environmentally, economically—just to waste those resources? Is there no food shortage in the world?"

QUESTIONS

1. What view of social responsibility would you call Gunter Pauli's approach, and at what stage of social responsibility would you place his activities? Explain your choices.
2. What stakeholders would be most important to ZERI? Explain your choices.
3. What do you think ZERI's Statement of Values might include? Keep it brief (one page or less).
4. What is your opinion of Gunter Pauli's crusade for zero-emissions production? Is it smart business? Do you agree with it? Do you disagree? Why?

Source: S. Butler, "Green Machine", Fast Company Web Page, <http://www.fastcompany.com>, April 16, 1997.

LEARNING OBJECTIVES

After Reading This Chapter, You Should Be Able To:

1 Outline the steps in the decision-making process
2. Describe the rational decision maker
3. Explain the limits to rationality
4. Describe the perfectly rational decision-making process
5. Describe the boundedly rational decision-making process
6. Identify the two types of decision problems and the two types of decisions that are used to solve them
7. Describe the different decision-making styles
8. Differentiate the decision conditions of certainty, risk and uncertainty
9. Identify the advantages and disadvantages of group decisions
10. Describe four techniques for improving group decision making

A MANAGER'S CHALLENGE

Pierre H. Lessard, CEO, Metro-Richelieu, Quebec

Pierre Lessard is not a man to take decision-making lightly. By nature, he is meticulous about details—no doubt due to his accounting background (he has a Masters degree in accounting science, as well as one in business administration). As CEO of Metro-Richelieu, one of the two dominant grocery store chains in Quebec, Lessard is one of the most detail-driven decision makers in the country. At one time, Lessard was president and Chief Operating Officer of Metro's main rival, Provigo Inc. But ironically, it was what was seen as his cautious managerial style that ended his career with Provigo—he was passed over for the CEO position and a more flamboyant candidate was brought in from outside the organization. When Lessard resigned, he left the grocery business for five years before being wooed back by Metro.[1]

Metro was in trouble when Lessard came aboard. The company had been mirroring Provigo's growth strategies (following Provigo in acquiring a sporting goods chain, a pharmacy chain and a restaurant chain). As it transpired, Lessard's cautious strategy at Provigo proved prescient. Many of Provigo's moves,

such as expansion into California, had been costly mistakes (and let's not forget the purchase of Consumers Distributing, which went under in the late 90s). But Provigo was much larger than Metro and could afford some setbacks. Metro was not in quite such an enviable position. As the board chairman at Metro put it: "Our business began to suffer as our vice-presidents were devoting time and energy to salvaging non-core operations". When Lessard took over the reins, he quickly shed $15 million in expenses from the budget and eliminated one in ten head office jobs. He shifted the focus of the company to become more consumer-oriented.

Lessard is an avid number-cruncher, pouring over statistics before making strategic decisions. He never makes a move without first being certain that the outcome will be favourable, and information is his ammunition. One such successful manoeuvre occurred when the Steinberg grocery chain went on the auction block seven years ago. Metro was bidding against Provigo (the two chains were dividing the Steinberg stores), and managed to come up with the best locations—all strategically picked by Lessard and the Metro management, who had studied the statistics of each store. These acquisitions proved to be a great victory for Metro.

The company's market share has grown from 25 percent to 35 percent, and by 1998, Metro-Richelieu had sales of $3.4 billion.

There has been much talk of expansion by Metro into Ontario, with the purchase of an existing chain. But nothing has yet occurred. Metro's chief financial officer has said: "We will expand when the match and the price are right". With Lessard's strict attention to detail, you can be assured that all of Metro's decisions will be well thought out.

A manager's effectiveness is largely defined by his or her decision-making capabilities. Pierre Lessard's decision-making skills have contributed significantly to Metro-Richelieu's recent successes. In this chapter, we will examine the concept of decision making.

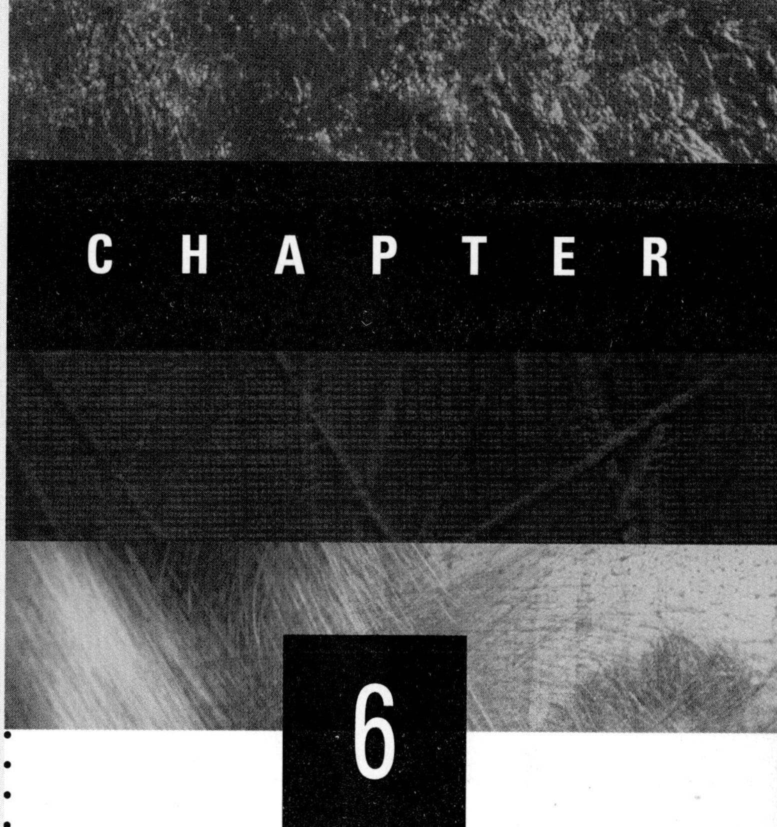

CHAPTER 6

Decision Making: The Essence of the Manager's Job

THE DECISION-MAKING PROCESS

Decision making is typically described as "choosing among alternatives". But this view is too simple. Why? Because decision making is a comprehensive *process,* not just a simple act of choosing among alternatives.

decision-making process
A set of eight steps which includes identifying a problem, selecting an alternative, and evaluating the decision's effectiveness.

Figure 6-1 illustrates the **decision-making process** as a set of eight steps which begins with identifying a problem and decision criteria, and allocating weights to those criteria; moves to developing, analyzing and selecting an alternative that can resolve the problem; implements the alternative; and concludes with evaluating the decision's effectiveness. This process is as relevant to your personal decision about where you're going to take your summer vacation as it is to a corporate action such as the Edmonton Oilers moving to a new arena. The process can also be used to describe both individual and group decisions. Let's take a closer look at the process in order to understand what each step involves.

Step 1: Identifying a Problem

problem
A discrepancy between an existing and a desired state of affairs.

The decision-making process begins with the existence of a **problem** or, more specifically, a discrepancy between an existing and a desired state of affairs.[2] Let's develop an example that illustrates this point, that we can use throughout this section. To keep it simple, let's make the example something most of us can relate to: the decision to buy a new notebook computer. Take the case of a sales manager whose sales representatives need new notebook computers because their old ones just don't have enough memory, or aren't fast enough to handle the volume of work any more. Again, for simplicity's sake, assume that it's not economical to add memory to the old ones and that corporate headquarters requires the managers to purchase new computers rather than lease them. So, we have a problem, and a decision to make.

Unfortunately, this example doesn't tell us much about how managers identify problems. In the real world, most problems don't come with neon signs in bright, bold colours flashing "problem". The sales representatives' complaints about computers being slow, when operating at capacity limits, gives the sales manager a clear signal that she needs to get them new notebook computers—but few problems are quite so obvious. For example, is a 5 percent decline in sales a *problem?* Or are declining sales merely a *symptom* of another problem, such as product obsolescence or poor advertising? Also, keep in mind that one manager's "problem" is another manager's "satisfactory state of affairs". Problem identification is subjective. Furthermore, the manager who mistakenly solves the *wrong* problem perfectly is likely to perform just as poorly as the manager who fails to identify the *right* problem and does nothing. Problem identification is neither a simple nor an insignificant step of the decision-making process.[3]

Before something can be characterized as a problem, managers have to be aware of the discrepancy, they have to be under pressure to take action, and they must have the resources necessary to take action.[4] (See Figure 6-2.)

How do managers become aware that they have a discrepancy? They obviously have to make a comparison between their current state of affairs and some predetermined standard. What is that standard? It can be past performance, previously set goals, or the performance of some other unit within the organization or in other organizations. In our computer-buying example, the standard is past performance—having a computer that holds all the necessary information and efficiently runs the desired programs.

But a discrepancy without pressure becomes a problem that can be put off until some future time. To initiate the decision process, then, the problem must be such that it exerts some type of pressure on the manager to act. Pressure might include organizational policies, deadlines, financial crises, expectations from the boss, or an upcoming performance evaluation.

Finally, managers aren't likely to characterize something as a problem if they perceive that they don't have the authority, budget, information, or other resources necessary to act on it. When managers perceive a problem and are under pressure to act, but feel they have inadequate resources, they usually describe the situation as one in which unrealistic expectations are being placed on them.

FIGURE 6-1 The Decision-Making Process

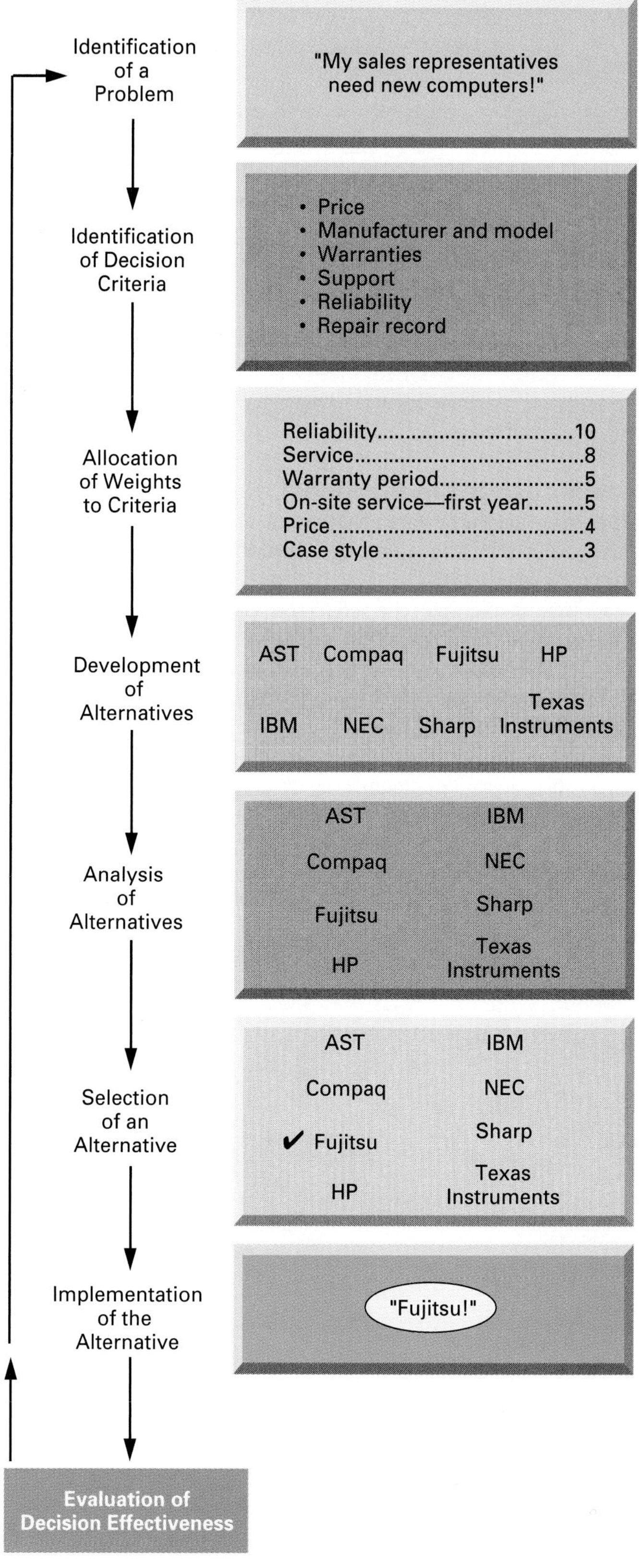

FIGURE 6-2 Characteristics of a Problem

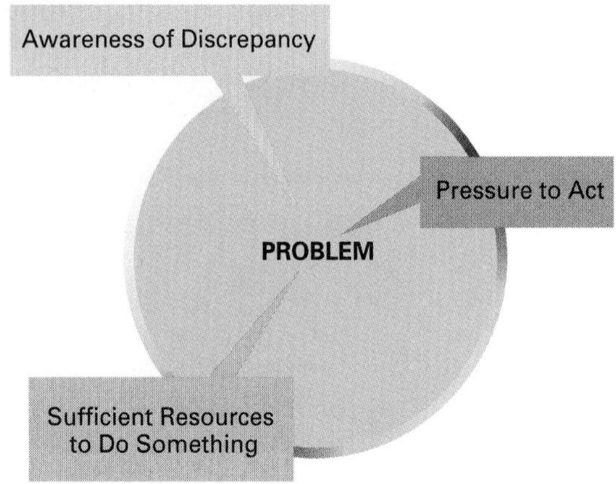

Step 2: Identifying Decision Criteria

decision criteria
Criteria that define what is relevant in a decision.

Once a manager has identified a problem that needs attention, the **decision criteria** important to resolving the problem must be identified. That is, managers must determine what is relevant when making a decision.

In our computer-buying example, the sales manager must assess what factors are relevant to her decision. These might include criteria such as price, product model and manufacturer, standard features, optional equipment, service warranties, repair record, and service support after purchase. These criteria reflect what the sales manager thinks is relevant to her decision.

Whether explicitly stated or not, every decision maker has criteria that guide his or her decision. Note that in this step in the decision-making process, what is *not* identified is as important as what *is*. If the sales manager doesn't consider a service warranty to be a criterion, then it will not influence her final choice of a computer. Thus, if a decision maker does not identify a particular criterion in this second step, it's treated as being irrelevant.

When making decisions, as in our computer purchase example, managers must identify the criteria—model, brand, price, warranty period—that are important.

TESTING... TESTING...

1. **In the first step of the decision-making process, how do managers know there is a problem?**
2. **What are decision criteria, and why are they important to the decision-making process?**

Step 3: Allocating Weights to the Criteria

The criteria listed in the previous step are not all equally important, so the items must be weighted in order to give them the correct priority in the decision.

How does the decision maker weight criteria? A simple approach is merely to give *the* most important criterion a weight of 10 and then assign weights to the rest against this standard. Thus, in contrast to a criterion that you gave a 5, the highest factor would be twice as important. Of course, you could use 100 or 1000 or any number you select as the highest weight. The idea is to use your personal preferences to assign a priority to the relevant criteria in your decision, as well as to indicate their degree of importance by assigning a weight to each.

Table 6-1 lists the criteria and weights that our sales manager developed for her computer replacement decision. Reliability is the most important criterion in her decision, with such factors as case style and price having low weights.

Step 4: Developing Alternatives

The fourth step requires the decision maker to list the viable alternatives that could resolve the problem. No attempt is made in this step to evaluate these alternatives, only to list them. Let's assume that our sales manager has identified eight notebook computer models as viable choices. These are: AST Ascentia A42; Compaq Armada 4100; Fujitsu LifeBook 555T; Hewlett Packard OmniBook 5500CT; IBM ThinkPad 760ED; NEC Versa 2435CD; Sharp WideNote W-100T; and Texas Instruments TravelMate 6050.

Step 5: Analyzing Alternatives

Once the alternatives have been identified, the decision maker must critically analyze each one. The strengths and weaknesses of each alternative become evident as they are compared with the criteria and weights established in Steps 2 and 3.

Each alternative is evaluated by appraising it against the criteria. Table 6-2 shows the assessed values that the sales manager gave each of her eight alternatives after she had talked to computer experts and read the latest information from computer magazines.

Keep in mind that the ratings given the eight computer models shown in Table 6-2 are based on the personal assessment made by the sales manager. We are again using a 1-to-10 scale. Some assessments can be achieved in a relatively objective fashion. For instance, the purchase price represents the best price the manager can get from local retailers, and consumer magazines report performance data from users. But the assessment of reliability is clearly a personal judgment. The point is that most decisions contain judgments. They are reflected in the criteria chosen in Step 2, the weights given to the criteria, and the evaluation of alternatives. This explains why two computer buyers with the same amount of money may look at two totally different sets of alternatives, or may even look at the same alternatives and rate them so differently.

Table 6-2 represents only an assessment of the eight alternatives against the decision criteria. It does not reflect the weighting done in Step 3. If one choice had scored 10 on every criterion, you wouldn't need to consider the weights. Similarly, if the weights were all equal, you

TABLE 6-1 Criteria and Weights for Computer Replacement Decision

Criteria	Weight
Reliability	10[a]
Service	8
Warranty period	5
On-site service—first year	5
Price	4
Case style	3

[a] In this example, the highest rating for a criterion is 10 points.

TABLE 6-2 Assessed Values of Notebook Computer Alternatives against Decision Criteria

Model	Reliability	Service	Warranty	On-site Service	Price	Case Style
AST Ascentia A42	8	3	5	10	3	5
Compaq Armada 4100	8	5	10	5	6	5
Fujitsu LifeBook 555T	10	8	5	10	3	10
HP OmniBook 5500CT	8	5	5	10	3	10
IBM ThinkPad 760ED	6	8	5	10	6	10
NEC Versa 2435CD	10	8	5	5	3	10
Sharp WideNote W-100T	2	10	5	10	10	10
Texas Instruments TravelMate 6050	4	10	5	10	10	5

could evaluate each alternative merely by summing up the appropriate lines in Table 6-2. For instance, the AST Ascentia A42 would have a score of 34, and the IBM ThinkPad 760ED would have a score of 45. The sum of these scores represents an evaluation of each alternative against the previously established criteria and weights. Notice that the weighting of the criteria has significantly changed the ranking of alternatives in our example.

Step 6: Selecting an Alternative

The sixth step is the crucial act of choosing the best alternative from among those listed and assessed. Since we have determined all the pertinent factors in the decision, weighted them appropriately, and identified the viable alternatives, we merely have to choose the alternative that generated the highest score in Step 5. In our computer-purchase example, Table 6-3, the decision maker would choose the Fujitsu LifeBook 555T computer. On the basis of the criteria identified, the weights given to the criteria, and the decision maker's assessment of each computer company's ranking on the criteria, the Fujitsu computer scored highest (281 points) and thus became the "best" alternative.

Step 7: Implementing the Alternative

While the choice process is completed in the previous step, the decision may still fail if it isn't implemented properly. Therefore, Step 7 is concerned with putting the decision into action.

TABLE 6-3 Evaluation of Notebook Computer Alternatives against Criteria and Weights

Model	Reliability	Service	Warranty	On-site Service	Price	Case Style	Total
AST Ascentia A42	80	24	25	50	12	15	206
Compaq Armada 4100	80	40	50	25	24	15	234
Fujitsu LifeBook 555T	100	64	25	50	12	30	281
HP OmniBook 5500CT	80	40	25	50	12	30	237
IBM ThinkPad 760ED	60	64	25	50	24	30	253
NEC Versa 2435CD	100	64	25	25	12	30	256
Sharp WideNote W-100T	20	80	25	50	40	30	245
Texas Instruments TravelMate 6050	40	80	25	50	40	15	250

Implementation includes conveying the decision to those affected and getting their commitment to it. As we'll demonstrate later in this chapter, groups or teams can help a manager achieve commitment. If the people who must carry out a decision participate in the process, they are more likely to enthusiastically support the outcome. For instance, if our decision example had been the purchase of several dozen computers for an entire department, having members of that department participate in the decision would increase the likelihood that they would enthusiastically accept the new machines and any new training necessary. (Parts Three through Five of this book detail how decisions are implemented by effective planning, organizing and leading.)

implementation
Conveying a decision to those affected and getting their commitment to it.

Step 8: Evaluating Decision Effectiveness

The last step in the decision-making process appraises the result of the decision, to see whether the problem has been resolved. Did the alternative chosen in Step 6 and implemented in Step 7 accomplish the desired result? The evaluation of such results is detailed in Part Six of this book, where we look at the control function.

What happens if, as a result of this evaluation, the problem is found to still exist? The manager then needs to carefully dissect what went wrong. Was the problem incorrectly defined? Were errors made in evaluating the various alternatives? Was the right alternative selected but incorrectly implemented? Answers to such questions might send the manager back to one of the earlier steps. They might even require her to start the whole decision process over again.

THE PERVASIVENESS OF DECISION MAKING

The importance of decision making in every aspect of a manager's job cannot be overstated. As Table 6-4 illustrates, decision making is part of all four managerial functions. In fact, this explains why managers—when they plan, organize, lead and control—are frequently called *decision makers*. So it is correct to say that decision making is synonymous with managing.[5]

The fact that almost everything a manager does involves decision making does not mean that decisions are always long, involved, or even clearly evident to an outside observer. Much of a manager's decision-making activity is routine. Every day of the year, you make a decision

TABLE 6-4 Decisions in the Management Functions

Planning
What are the organization's long-term objectives?
What strategies will best achieve these objectives?
What should the organization's short-term objectives be?
How difficult should individual goals be?

Organizing
How many subordinates should I have reporting directly to me?
How much centralization should there be in the organization?
How should jobs be designed?
When should the organization implement a different structure?

Leading
How do I handle employees who appear to be low in motivation?
What is the most effective leadership style in a given situation?
How will a specific change affect worker productivity?
When is the right time to stimulate conflict?

Controlling
What activities in the organization need to be controlled?
How should these activities be controlled?
When is a performance deviation significant?
What type of management information system should the organization have?

about the problem of when to eat lunch. It's no big deal. You've made the decision thousands of times before. It offers few problems and can usually be handled quickly. It's the type of decision you almost forget *is* a decision. Managers make dozens of these routine decisions every day. Keep in mind that even though a decision seems easy to make or has been faced by a manager a number of times before, it's a decision nonetheless.

THE RATIONAL DECISION MAKER

rational
Describes choices that are consistent and value-maximizing within specified constraints.

Managerial decision making is assumed to be **rational**. By that, we mean that managers make consistent, value-maximizing choices within specified constraints.[6] In this section, we want to take a close look at the underlying assumptions of rationality and then determine how valid these assumptions actually are.

Assumptions of Rationality

A decision maker who was perfectly rational would be fully objective and logical. He or she would define a problem carefully and would have a clear and specific goal. Moreover, the steps in the decision-making process would consistently lead towards selecting the alternative that maximizes that goal. Figure 6-3 summarizes the assumptions of rationality:

- *Problem clarity.* In rational decision making, the problem is clear and unambiguous. The decision maker is assumed to have complete information regarding the decision situation.
- *Goal orientation.* In rational decision making there is no conflict over the goal. Whether the decision involves purchasing a new computer, selecting a college to attend, choosing the proper price for a new product, or picking the right job applicant to fill a vacancy, the decision maker has a single, well-defined goal that he or she is trying to reach.
- *Known options.* It is assumed that the decision maker is creative, can identify all the relevant criteria, and can list all the viable alternatives. Further, the decision maker is aware of all the possible consequences of each alternative.
- *Clear preferences.* Rationality assumes that the criteria and alternatives can be ranked according to their importance.
- *Constant preferences.* In addition to a clear goal and preferences, it is assumed that the specific decision criteria are constant and that the weights assigned to them are stable over time.
- *No time or cost constraints.* The rational decision maker can obtain full information about criteria and alternatives because it is assumed that there are no time or cost constraints involved.
- *Maximum payoff.* The rational decision maker always chooses the alternative that will yield the maximum economic payoff.

These assumptions of rationality apply to any decision. However, since we're concerned with managerial decision making in an organization, we need to add one further assumption. Rational managerial decision making assumes that decisions are made in the best economic interests of the organization. That is, the decision maker is assumed to be maximizing the *organization's* interests, not his or her own interests.

How realistic are these assumptions about rationality? Managerial decision making can follow rational assumptions if the following conditions are met: the manager is faced with a simple problem in which the goals are clear and the alternatives are limited; in which the time pressures are minimal and the cost of seeking out and evaluating alternatives is low; where the organizational culture supports innovation and risk-taking; and where the outcomes are rela-

3 Why is the allocation of weights to criteria important to decision making?

4 How do managers develop, analyze, select and implement alternatives, and then assess whether the decision was effective?

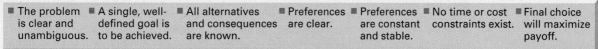

FIGURE 6-3 Assumptions of Rationality

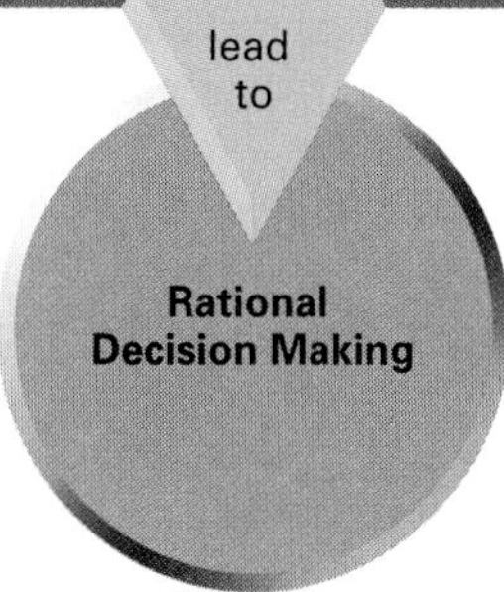
The problem is clear and unambiguous.
A single, well-defined goal is to be achieved.
All alternatives and consequences are known.
Preferences are clear.
Preferences are constant and stable.
No time or cost constraints exist.
Final choice will maximize payoff.
lead to
Rational Decision Making

tively concrete and measurable. But most decisions that managers face in the real world don't meet all those tests. So how are most decisions in organizations actually made? The concept of bounded rationality can help to answer that question.

Bounded Rationality

Despite the limits to perfect rationality, managers are expected to appear to follow the rational process when making decisions. Managers know that "good" decision makers are *supposed* to do certain things: identify problems, consider alternatives, gather information, and act decisively but prudently. Managers can thus be expected to exhibit the correct decision-making

MANAGERS SPEAK OUT

Interview with Graham Jones, Owner of GLA Interiors, Toronto

Describe your job.

I'm the owner of a custom millwork and cabinetry shop that specializes in commercial office interiors. My personal responsibilities include sales, estimating costs, project management and, of course, general management.

What is your opinion of the statement that decision making is the essence of management?

The group follows the leader. The ability to make effective decisions allows work to flow smoothly and be uninterrupted from start to finish, always moving forward with momentum. This results in high-quality work being done on time and within the budget.

What suggestions do you have for making effective decisions?

Information! To make effective decisions, you must know and understand the product you're selling. You must know what resources you have and the strengths and weaknesses of those resources so they may be used to their maximum potential. You must know the full status of any given project, not just your portion. Your work affects the other parts of the main project and vice versa. The most important key to effective decision making *is* information and having it as up-to-date as possible. ■

behaviours. By doing so, managers signal to their superiors, peers,and subordinates that they are competent and that their decisions are the result of intelligent and rational deliberation.

Table 6-5 summarizes how the perfectly rational manager should proceed through the eight-step decision-making process. It also describes an alternative model—one followed by a manager operating under the assumptions of **bounded rationality**.[7] In bounded rationality, managers construct simplified models that extract the essential features from problems without capturing all their complexity. Then, given information-processing limitations and constraints imposed by the organization, managers attempt to behave rationally within the parameters of the simple model. The result is a **satisficing** decision rather than a maximizing one; that is, a decision in which the solution is satisfactory or "good enough". Let's look at an example. Suppose that you're a finance major and, upon graduation, you want a job—preferably as a personal financial planner—with a minimum salary of $28 000 and within a hundred miles of your hometown. When you get a job offer as a business credit analyst—not exactly a personal financial planner but still within the finance field—at a bank 30 kilometres from home, at a starting salary of $28 500, you'd probably be strongly inclined to accept it. However, a more comprehensive job search would have revealed a job in personal financial planning at a trust company only 15 kilometres from your home and offering a starting salary of $30 000. Because the first decision was satisfactory (or "good enough") to you, you behaved in a boundedly rational manner by accepting the first job although, according to the assumptions of perfect rationality, you didn't maximize your decision by searching all possible alternatives.

bounded rationality
Behaviour that is rational within the parameters of a simplified model that captures the essential features of a problem.

satisficing
Acceptance of solutions that are "good enough".

The implications of bounded rationality on the manager's job can't be overlooked. In situations in which the assumptions of perfect rationality don't apply (including most of the important and far-reaching decisions a manager makes), the details of the decision-making process are strongly influenced by the decision maker's self-interest, the organization's culture, internal politics and power considerations.

Role of Intuition. Managers regularly use their intuition, which may actually help to improve their decision making. **Intuitive decision making** is an unconscious process of making decisions on the basis of experience and accumulated judgment. Making decisions on the basis of "gut feeling" doesn't necessarily happen independently of rational analysis; rather, the two complement each other. A manager who has had experience with a particular, or even similar type of problem or situation, can often act quickly with what appears to be limited information. Such a manager doesn't rely on a systematic and thorough analysis of the problem, or on identification and evaluation of alternatives, but instead uses his or her experience and judgment to make a decision. How common is intuitive decision making? One survey of managers and other organizational employees revealed that almost one-third of them emphasized "gut feeling" over cognitive problem solving and decision making.[8]

intuitive decision making
An unconscious process of making decisions on the basis of experience and accumulated judgment.

Whether managers use perfect rationality, bounded rationality, or intuition in making decisions, the organizational reality is that they're likely to face different types of problem situations. We will now look at the types of problems a manager might face in decision making.

PROBLEMS AND DECISIONS: A CONTINGENCY APPROACH

The *type* of problem a manager faces in a decision-making situation often determines how that problem is treated. In this section we present a categorization scheme for problems and for types of decisions. Then we show how the type of decision a manager uses should reflect the characteristics of the problem.

Types of Problems

Some problems are straightforward. The goal of the decision maker is clear, the problem familiar, and information about the problem is easily defined and complete. Examples might include

TESTING... TESTING...

5 Describe decision making from the rationality viewpoint.

6 Describe decision making from the bounded rationality perspective.

TABLE 6-5 Two Views of the Decision-Making Process

Decision-Making Step	Perfect Rationality	Bounded Rationality
1. Problem formulation	An important and relevant organizational problem is identified.	A visible problem that reflects the manager's interests and background is identified.
2. Identification of decision criteria	All criteria are identified.	A limited set of criteria are identified.
3. Allocation of weights to criteria	All criteria are evaluated and rated in terms of their importance to the organization's goal.	A simple model is constructed to evaluate and rate the criteria; the decision maker's self-interest strongly influences the ratings.
4. Development of alternatives	A comprehensive list of all alternatives is developed creatively.	A limited set of similar alternatives is identified.
5. Analysis of alternatives	All alternatives are assessed against the decision criteria and weights; the consequences for each alternative are known.	Beginning with a favoured solution, alternatives are assessed, one at a time, against the decision criteria.
6. Selection of an alternative	*Maximizing decision:* the one with the highest economic outcome (in terms of the organization's goal) is chosen.	*Satisficing decision:* the search continues until a solution is found that is satisfactory and sufficient, at which time the search stops.
7. Implementation of alternative	Since the decision maximizes the single, well-defined goal, all organizational members will embrace the solution.	Politics and power considerations will influence the acceptance of, and commitment to, the decision.
8. Evaluation	The outcome of the decision is objectively evaluated against the original problem.	Measurement of the decision's results are rarely so objective as to eliminate self-interests of the evaluator; possible escalation of resources to prior commitments in spite of both previous failures and strong evidence that allocation of additional resources is not warranted.

a customer wanting to return a purchase to a retail store, a supplier being late with an important delivery, a TV station news team responding to an unexpected and fast-breaking news event, or a college's handling of a student wanting to drop a class. Such situations are called **well-structured problems**. They align closely with the assumptions of perfect rationality.

well-structured problems Straightforward, familiar, easily defined problems.

Many situations faced by managers, however, are **ill-structured problems**. They are new or unusual. Information about such problems is ambiguous or incomplete. The selection of an architect to design a new corporate headquarters building is one example. So, too, is the decision to invest in a new, unproven technology.

ill-structured problems New problems in which information is ambiguous or incomplete.

Types of Decisions

Just as problems can be divided into two categories so, too, can decisions. As we will see, *programmed*, or routine decision making is the most efficient way to handle well-structured problems. However, when problems are ill structured, managers must rely on *non-programmed* decision making in order to develop unique solutions.

Antoine Paquin's company, Skystone Systems, was founded in his basement. With an innovative product—technology to carry data in optical networks—Paquin and his partner, Stefan Dralski, hand-picked the company's 50 employees, creating a highly effective team by instilling a shared vision, as well as by offering members the opportunity to share in the profit. In three years, still with sales of only $4 million. the company was seen to be so promising that the U.S. giant Cisco Systems paid $150 million for it.

Programmed Decisions. A server in a restaurant spills a drink on a customer's coat. The restaurant manager has an upset customer. What does the manager do? Since such occurrences aren't infrequent, there's probably some standardized routine for handling the problem. For example, if it is the server's fault, if the damage is significant, and if the customer has asked for a remedy, the manager offers to have the coat cleaned at the restaurant's expense. This is a **programmed decision**.

programmed decision
A repetitive decision that can be handled by a routine approach.

Decisions are programmed to the extent that they are repetitive and routine, and to the extent that a definite approach has been worked out for handling them. Because the problem is well structured, the manager need not go to the trouble and expense of working out an involved decision-making process. Programmed decision making is relatively simple and tends to rely heavily on previous solutions. The "develop-the-alternatives" stage in the decision-making process either doesn't exist or is given little attention. Why? Because once the structured problem is defined, its solution is usually self-evident, or is at least reduced to very few alternatives that are familiar and that have proven successful in the past. In many cases, programmed decision making becomes decision making by precedent. Managers simply do what they and others have done previously in the same situation. The spilled drink on the customer's coat does not require the restaurant manager to identify and weight decision criteria, nor to develop a long list of possible solutions. Rather, the manager falls back on a systematic procedure, rule or policy.

procedure
A series of interrelated sequential steps that can be used to respond to a structured problem.

A **procedure** is a series of interrelated sequential steps that a manager can use for responding to a structured problem. The only real difficulty is in identifying the problem. Once the problem is clear, so is the procedure. For instance, a purchasing manager receives a request from the sales department for 15 cellular phones for use by the company's sales representatives. The purchasing manager knows that there is a definite procedure for handling this decision. The decision-making process in this case merely involves executing a simple series of sequential steps.

Information technology is being used to further simplify the development of organizational procedures. Some powerful new software programs are being designed that automate routine and complex procedures. For example, at Hewlett-Packard, a comprehensive software program has automated a quarterly wage review process of over 13 000 salespeople.

rule
An explicit statement that tells managers what they ought or ought not to do.

A **rule** is an explicit statement that tells a manager what he or she ought or ought not to do. Rules are frequently used by managers when they confront a well-structured problem because they are simple to follow and ensure consistency. For example, rules about lateness and absenteeism permit supervisors to make disciplinary decisions rapidly and with a relatively high degree of fairness.

policy
A guide that establishes parameters for making decisions.

A third guide for making programmed decisions is a **policy**. It provides guidelines to channel a manager's thinking in a specific direction. In contrast to a rule, a policy establishes parameters for the decision maker, rather than specifically stating what should or should not be done.

Policies typically contain an ambiguous term that leaves interpretation up to the decision maker. For instance, each of the following is a policy statement:

- The customer shall always be *satisfied*.
- We promote from within, *whenever possible*.
- Employee wages shall be *competitive* for the community in which our plants are located.

Notice that *satisfied, whenever possible,* and *competitive* are terms that require interpretation. The policy to pay competitive wages does not tell a given plant's human resources manager the exact amount he or she should pay, but it does give direction to the decision he or she makes.

Non-programmed Decisions. Deciding whether or not to merge with another organization, how to re-engineer to improve processes, what type of marketing strategy is needed for a new product, or whether to shut down a money-losing division are examples of **non-programmed decisions**. Such decisions are unique and non-recurring. When a manager confronts an ill-structured problem, or one that is unique, there is no cut-and-dried solution. It requires a custom-made response.

non-programmed decisions
Unique decisions that require a custom-made solution.

Integration

Figure 6-4 describes the relationship among the types of problems, the types of decisions, and the manager's level in the organization. Well-structured problems are resolved with programmed decision making. Ill-structured problems require non-programmed decision making. Lower-level managers confront familiar and repetitive problems; therefore, they most typically rely on programmed decisions such as standard operating procedures, rules, and organizational policies. However, the problems confronting managers are likely to become more ill structured as they move up the organizational hierarchy. Why? Because lower-level managers handle the routine decisions themselves and only send decisions that they find unusual or difficult up the chain of command. Similarly, higher-level managers pass along routine decisions to their subordinates so that they can deal with more problematic issues.

Few managerial decisions in the real world are either fully programmed or non-programmed. These are extremes, and most decisions fall somewhere in between. Few programmed decisions are designed to eliminate individual judgment completely. At the other extreme, even the most unique situation requiring a non-programmed decision can be helped by programmed routines. It is best to think of decisions as *mainly* programmed or *mainly* non-programmed, rather than as completely one or the other.

A final point on this topic is that organizational efficiency is facilitated by the use of programmed decision making, which may explain its wide popularity. Wherever possible, management decisions are likely to be programmed. Obviously, this isn't too realistic at the top of the organization, because most of the problems that top management confronts are of a non-recurring nature. But there are strong economic incentives for top management to create standard operating procedures (SOPs), rules and policies in order to guide other managers.

FIGURE 6-4 Types of Problems, Types of Decisions, and Manager's Level in the Organization

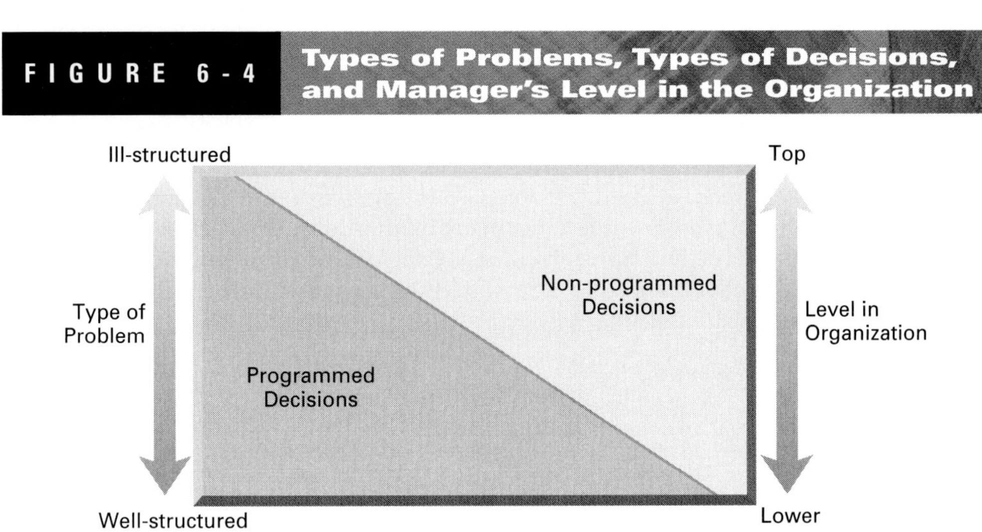

Programmed decisions minimize the need for managers to exercise discretion. This is relevant because discretion can cost money. The more non-programmed decision making a manager is required to do, the greater the judgment needed. Since sound judgment is an uncommon quality, it costs more to acquire the services of managers who have this ability.

Of course, some organizations try to economize by hiring less-skilled managers, without developing programmed decision guides for them to follow. Take, for example, a small women's clothing store chain whose owner, because he chooses to pay low salaries, hires store managers with little experience and with a limited ability to make good judgments. This, by itself, might not be a problem. The trouble is that the owner provides neither training nor explicit rules and procedures to guide his store managers' decisions. The result has been continual complaints by customers about things such as promotional discounts, processing credit sales, and the handling of returns.

DECISION-MAKING STYLES

problem avoider
An approach to problems in which the person avoids or ignores information that points to a problem.

problem solver
An approach to problems in which the person tries to solve problems as they come up.

problem seeker
An approach to problems in which the person actively seeks out problems to solve or new opportunities to pursue.

directive style
A decision-making style characterized by a low tolerance for ambiguity and a rational way of thinking.

analytic style
A decision-making style characterized by a high tolerance for ambiguity and a rational way of thinking.

conceptual style
A decision-making style characterized by a high tolerance for ambiguity and an intuitive way of thinking.

behavioural style
A decision-making style characterized by a low tolerance for ambiguity and an intuitive way of thinking.

Suppose you're a new manager in a large financial services organization or at the local YMCA. How would you tackle problems that arise? Managers have different styles when it comes to decision making and solving problems. One view holds that there are three different ways managers approach problems in the workplace: problem avoidance, problem solving, and problem seeking.[9] What are the characteristics of each of these approaches?

Problem avoiders ignore information that points to a problem. These types are inactive and do not want to confront problems. **Problem solvers** try to solve problems when they come up. They are reactive in dealing with problems after they occur. **Problem seekers** actively seek out problems to solve or new opportunities to pursue. They take a proactive approach to anticipating problems before they occur. Managers can, and do, use each approach. For example, there are times when avoiding a problem is the best response. At other times, being reactive is the only option because the problem happens so quickly. Innovative, creative organizations need managers who proactively seek opportunities and ways to do things better.

Another perspective on decision-making styles proposes that people differ along two dimensions in the way they approach decision making.[10] One of these dimensions is an individual's way of *thinking*. Some of us tend to be more rational and logical in the way we think or process information. A rational type looks at information in order and makes sure that it's logical and consistent before proceeding to make a decision. In contrast, some of us tend to be more creative and intuitive. Intuitive types don't have to process information in a certain order but are comfortable looking at it as a whole.

The other dimension describes an individual's *tolerance for ambiguity*. Again, some of us have a low tolerance for ambiguity and must have consistency and order in the way we structure information so that ambiguity is minimized. In contrast, some of us can tolerate high levels of ambiguity and can process many thoughts at the same time. When we show these two dimensions as a diagram, four decision-making styles are formed. (See Figure 6-5.) These styles include directive, analytic, conceptual and behavioural. Let's look closer at each of these styles.

- *Directive style.* People using the **directive style** have low tolerance for ambiguity and are rational in their way of thinking. They are efficient and logical. Directive types make fast decisions and focus on the short term. Their efficiency and speed in making decisions often results in their making decisions with minimal information and after assessing few alternatives.
- *Analytic style.* **Analytic style** decision makers have much greater tolerance for ambiguity than do directive types. They want more information before making a decision and consider more alternatives than a directive-style decision maker does. Analytic decision makers are best characterized as careful decision makers with the ability to adapt or cope with unique situations.
- *Conceptual style.* Individuals with a **conceptual style** tend to be very broad in their outlook and will look at many alternatives. They focus on the long term and are very good at finding creative solutions to problems.
- *Behavioural style.* **Behavioural style** decision makers work well with others. They're concerned about the achievement of subordinates and are receptive to suggestions from

THINKING CRITICALLY ABOUT ETHICS

You're in charge of hiring a new employee to work in your area of responsibility. One of your friends needs a job. You think he's qualified for the position, but you feel that you could find a better qualified and more experienced candidate if you kept looking. What do you do? Why? What factors will influence your decision? What will you tell your friend? ■

others. They often use meetings to communicate, although they try to avoid conflict. Acceptance by others is important to the behavioural-style decision maker.

Although these four decision-making styles are distinct, most managers have characteristics of more than one style. It's probably more realistic to think of a manager's *dominant* style and his or her alternate styles. Although some managers will rely almost exclusively on their dominant style, others are more flexible and can shift their style depending on the situation.

How do decision-making styles vary from country to country? For example, Huang Yantian, president of Guangdong International Trust and Investment Corporation, makes all key decisions, like the chief executives of most Chinese companies. We find that philosophies and practices differ in other countries as well.

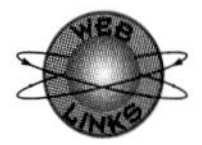

Guangdong Investment Limited
www.gdi.com/hk/gdi/default.htm

ANALYZING DECISION ALTERNATIVES

One of the more challenging tasks facing a manager is analyzing decision alternatives (Step 5 in the decision-making process). This section discusses approaches for analyzing alternatives under three different conditions: certainty, risk and uncertainty.

Certainty

The ideal situation for making decisions is one of **certainty**; that is, the manager can make perfectly accurate decisions because the outcome from every alternative is known. For example, when the treasurer of Alberta is deciding which bank to deposit excess government funds in, he knows exactly how much interest is being offered by each bank, and how much will be earned on the funds. He is certain about the outcomes of each alternative. As you might expect, this is *not* the situation in which most managerial decisions are made. It's more idealistic than pragmatic.

certainty
A situation in which a manager can make accurate decisions because the outcome of every alternative is known.

FIGURE 6-5 Decision-Making Styles

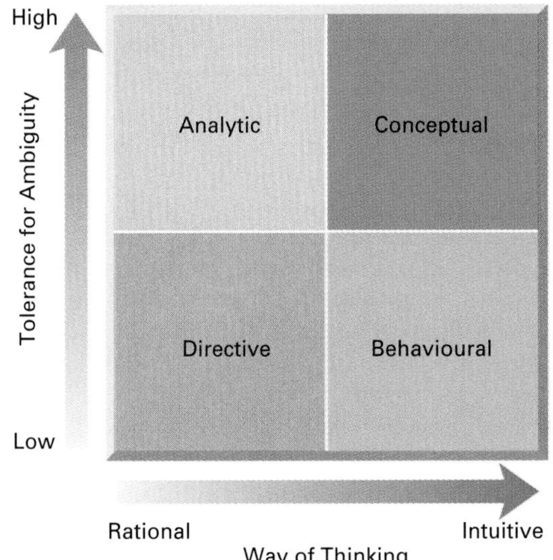

Source: Stephen P. Robbins, *Supervision Today* (Englewood Cliffs, NJ: Prentice Hall, 1995), p. 111.

Huang Yantian (on the left), president of GITIC, makes all key decisions in his company, the asset value of which has been estimated at $5.5 billion.

Risk

risk
Those conditions in which the decision maker is able to estimate the likelihood of certain outcomes.

A far more common situation is one of **risk**. By risk, we mean those conditions in which the decision maker is able to estimate the likelihood of certain alternatives or outcomes. This ability to assign probabilities to outcomes may be the result of personal experience or secondary information. However, under the conditions of risk, the manager has historical data that allow him or her to assign probabilities to different alternatives. Let's use an example.

Suppose that you manage a ski resort in the Alberta Rockies. You are thinking about adding another lift to your current facility. Obviously, your decision will be significantly influenced by the amount of additional revenue that the new lift will generate, and this will depend on the level of snowfall in that area. The decision is made somewhat clearer when you are reminded that you have reasonably reliable past data on snowfall levels in your area. The data show that, during the past 10 years, you had 3 years of heavy snowfall, 5 years of normal snow, and 2 years of light snow. Can you use this information to determine the expected future annual revenue if the new lift is added? If you have good information on the amount of revenue for each level of snow, the answer will be yes.

You can create an expected value formulation; that is, you can compute the conditional return from each possible outcome by multiplying expected revenues by snowfall probabilities. The result is the average revenue you can expect over time if the given probabilities hold. As Table 6-6 shows, the expected revenue from adding a new ski lift is $687 500. Of course, whether that justifies a yes or no decision depends on the costs involved in generating this revenue—factors such as the cost of building the lift, the additional annual operating expenses for another lift, the interest rate for borrowing money, and so forth.

Uncertainty

uncertainty
A situation in which a decision maker has neither certainty nor reasonable probability estimates available.

What happens if you have to make a decision when you're not certain about the outcomes and can't even make reasonable probability estimates? We call such a condition **uncertainty**. Many decision-making situations that managers face are ones of uncertainty. In conditions of uncertainty, alternative choice is influenced by the limited amount of information available to the decision maker.

Another factor that influences choice under conditions of uncertainty is the psychological orientation of the decision maker. The optimistic manager will follow a *maximax* choice (maximizing of the maximum possible payoff), the pessimist will pursue a *maximin* choice (maximizing the minimum possible payoff), while the manager who desires to minimize his maximum "regret" will opt for a *minimax* choice. Let's look at these different choice approaches using an example.

Bank of Montreal
www.bmo.com

Consider the case of a marketing manager at the Bank of Montreal in Toronto. He has determined four possible strategies for promoting the Bank of Montreal's MasterCard throughout the Eastern provinces. But the marketing manager is also aware that his major competitor, the CIBC, has three competitive actions of its own for promoting its Visa card in the same

MANAGING WORKFORCE DIVERSITY

Decision-Making Styles of Diverse Populations

Research shows that, to some extent, decision-making philosophies and practices differ from country to country.[11] For example, most British organizations are highly decentralized because many upper-level managers do not understand the technical details of the business. Therefore, top-level managers rely on their middle managers, who deal more closely with day-to-day technical details in order to make decisions. It's quite different in French firms, however. In France, many top managers graduated from the Grandes Écoles (universities), and they often lack confidence in their middle managers' ability to make good decisions. As a result, decision making tends to be quite centralized. In Germany, decision making tends to be fairly centralized, autocratic and hierarchical. Managers in German businesses place a greater emphasis on productivity and quality of goods than on managing subordinates, so there is no great pressure to involve workers in decisions or even to seek out their input. Swedish companies, in contrast, focus more on quality of work life and the importance of the individual in the organization. As you can guess, decision making tends to be very decentralized and participative. The Japanese approach to decision making is also different from the Europeans. In Japan, a decision-making process called *ringisei*, or decision making by consensus, is used a lot. Consensus decision making means that getting agreement from everyone involved with the decision and the process is very time consuming, but it results in a high degree of commitment and acceptance by all affected parties. Although the approach combines both centralized and decentralized decision making, top-level Japanese managers still exercise a great deal of authority over what issues are examined at lower levels of the organization.

Hofstede's cultural dimensions (discussed in Chapter 4) can also be used to help us understand differences in global decision-making styles. Our knowledge of power distance differences, for example, helps to explain why, in high power-distance cultures such as India, only very senior-level managers make decisions. However, in low power-distance cultures such as Sweden, even low-ranking employees are expected to make most of their own decisions about day-to-day operations. Also, our knowledge of time orientation helps us to understand why managers in Egypt will make decisions at a much slower and more deliberate pace than their Canadian counterparts. And why Italians, who value the past and traditions, tend to rely on tried and proven alternatives to resolve problems. Lastly, some cultures emphasize solving problems while others focus on accepting situations as they are. This helps to explain why managers in countries such as Thailand and Indonesia may take longer to identify a problem than managers in other countries.

As managers deal with employees from diverse cultures, they need to recognize what is common and accepted behaviour to employees when asking them to make decisions. Some individuals may not be as comfortable being closely involved in decision making as others, or may not be willing to experiment with something radically different. Managers should accommodate the diversity in decision-making philosophies and practices. The payoff is: capturing the perspectives and strengths that a diverse workforce offers! ■

region. In this case, we'll assume that the Bank of Montreal executive has no previous knowledge that would allow him to place probabilities on the success of any of his four strategies. With these facts, the Bank of Montreal manager has formulated the matrix in Table 6-7 to show the various Bank of Montreal strategies, and the resulting profit to the Bank of Montreal, depending on the competitive action chosen by CIBC.

In this example, if our Bank of Montreal manager is an optimist he'll choose S_4, because that could produce the largest possible gain: \$28 million. Note that this choice maximizes the maximum possible gain.

If our manager is a pessimist, though, he'll assume that only the worst can occur. The worst outcome for each strategy is as follows: $S_1 = 11$; $S_2 = 9$; $S_3 = 15$; $S_4 = 14$. These are the most pessimistic outcomes from each strategy. Following the maximin choice, he would maximize the minimum payoff—in other words, he'd select S_3.

TABLE 6-6 Expected Value for Revenues from the Addition of One Ski Lift

Event	Expected Revenues	×	Probability	=	Expected Value of Each Alternative
Heavy snowfall	$850 000		0.3		$255 000
Normal snowfall	725 000		0.5		362 500
Light snowfall	350 000		0.2		70 000
					$687 500

In the third approach, managers recognize that once a decision is made, it will not necessarily result in the most profitable payoff. This suggests that there may be a regret of profits forgone (given up)—regret referring to the amount of money that *could* have been made had a different strategy been used. Managers calculate regret by subtracting all possible payoffs in each category from the maximum possible payoff for each given event, in this case for each competitive action. For our Bank of Montreal manager, the highest payoff, given that CIBC engages in CA_1, CA_2 and CA_3, is $24 million, $21 million, and $28 million, respectively (the highest number in each column). Subtracting the payoffs in Table 6-7 from these figures produces the results shown in Table 6-8.

The maximum regrets are $S_1 = 17$; $S_2 = 15$; $S_3 = 13$; and $S_4 = 7$. Since the minimax choice minimizes the maximum regret, our Bank of Montreal manager would choose S_4. By making this choice, he'll never have a regret of profits forgone of more than $7 million. This contrasts, for example, with a regret of $15 million had he chosen S_2 and had CIBC taken CA_1.

Although managers will try to analyze the numbers, when possible, by using payoff and regret matrices, uncertainty often forces them to rely more on hunches, intuition, creativity and "gut feel".

GROUP DECISION MAKING

Many decisions in organizations, especially important ones that have far-reaching effects on organizational activities and personnel, are made in groups or teams. As we pointed out in Chapter 2, teams are often used in organizations in many different ways. It's a rare organiza-

TABLE 6-7 Payoff Matrix (in millions of dollars)

Bank of Montreal Marketing Strategies	CIBC's Response		
	CA_1	CA_2	CA_3
S_1	13	14	11
S_2	9	15	18
S_3	24	21	15
S_4	18	14	28

TESTING... TESTING...

7 What are the characteristics of decision making under the condition of certainty? Of risk?

8 How might a manager make decisions under conditions of uncertainty?

TABLE 6-8 Regret Matrix (in millions of dollars)

Bank of Montreal Marketing Strategies	CIBC's Response		
	CA_1	CA_2	CA_3
S_1	11	7	17
S_2	15	6	10
S_3	0	0	13
S_4	6	7	0

tion that doesn't at some time use committees, task forces, review panels, study teams, or similar groups as vehicles for making decisions. Studies tell us that managers spend up to 40 percent of their time in group meetings.[12] Undoubtedly, a large portion of that time is spent formulating problems, arriving at solutions to those problems, and determining the means for implementing the solutions. It's possible, in fact, for groups to be assigned any of the eight steps in the decision-making process.

In this section, we'll look at the advantages and disadvantages of both group and individual decision making, identify when groups should be preferred, and review the more popular techniques for improving group decision making.

Advantages and Disadvantages

Individual and group decisions each have their own set of strengths. Neither is ideal for all situations. Let's review the *advantages* that group decisions have over individual decisions.

1. *Provides more complete information.* There is often truth to the saying that two heads are better than one. A group brings a diversity of experience and perspectives to the decision-making process that an individual, acting alone, cannot.

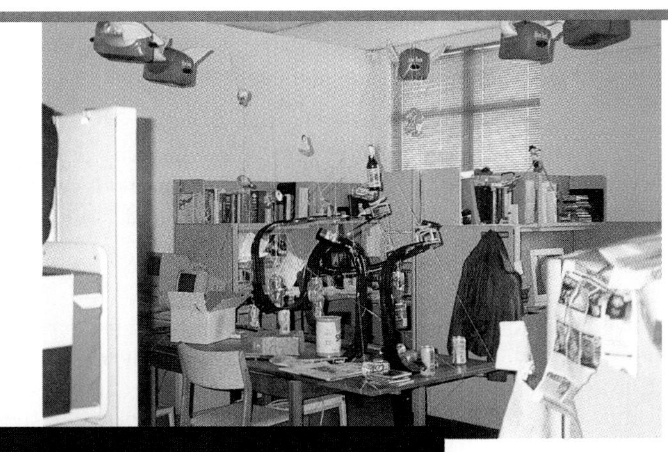

We've all seen 'em—the wonderfully captivating and unique flying toasters! The company behind the popular screen saver is just as quirky as its popular creation. At Berkeley Systems Inc.'s headquarters, most workers slither down a winding, plastic slide to get from the second floor to the first. Needless to say, imagination and creativity are highly encouraged and valued at this company!

2. *Generates more alternatives.* Because groups have a greater amount and diversity of information, they can identify more alternatives than an individual. This is particularly evident when group members represent different specialties. For instance, a team made up of representatives from engineering, accounting, production, marketing and personnel will generate alternatives that reflect their diverse specialties. Such a multiplicity of "world views" often yields a greater array of alternatives.

3. *Increases acceptance of a solution.* Many decisions fail after the final choice has been made because people do not accept the solution. However, if the people who will be affected by a certain solution and who will help implement it get to participate in the process itself, they will be more likely to accept it and to encourage others to accept it as well. Group members are reluctant to fight or undermine a decision they have helped to develop.

4. *Increases legitimacy.* The group decision-making process is consistent with democratic ideals and therefore decisions made by groups may be perceived as more legitimate than decisions made by one person. The fact that the individual decision maker has complete power and has not consulted others can create the perception that a decision was made autocratically and arbitrarily.

If groups are so good, how did the phrase, "A camel is a racehorse put together by a committee" become so popular? The answer, of course, is that group decisions are not without their drawbacks. The major *disadvantages* of group decision making are as follows.

1. *Time consuming.* It takes time to assemble a group. In addition, the interaction that takes place once the group is in place is frequently inefficient. The result is that groups almost always take more time to reach a solution than it would take an individual making the decision alone.

2. *Minority domination.* Members of a group are never perfectly equal. They may differ in the organization in rank, experience, knowledge about the problem, influence with other members, verbal skills, assertiveness, and the like. This creates the opportunity for one or more members to use their advantages to dominate others in the group. A dominant minority frequently can have an excessive influence on the final decision.

groupthink
The withholding by group members of different views in order to appear in agreement.

3. *Pressures to conform.* Social pressures to conform in groups can lead to a phenomenon called **groupthink**.[13] This is a form of conformity in which group members withhold deviant, minority, or unpopular views in order to give the appearance of agreement. Groupthink undermines critical thinking in the group and eventually harms the quality of the final decision.

4. *Ambiguous responsibility.* Group members share responsibility, but who is actually responsible for the final outcome? In an individual decision, it is clear who is responsible. In a group decision, the responsibility of any single member is diluted.

Effectiveness and Efficiency

Whether groups are more effective than individuals depends on the criteria you use for defining effectiveness. Group decisions tend to be more *accurate*. The evidence indicates that, on average, groups make better decisions than individuals. This doesn't mean, of course, that *all* groups outperform *every* individual. But group decisions are almost always superior to those made by individuals alone.[14]

If decision effectiveness is defined in terms of *speed*, individuals are superior. Group decision processes are characterized by give and take, which consumes time.

Effectiveness may mean the degree to which a solution demonstrates *creativity*. If creativity is important, groups tend to be more effective than individuals.[15] This requires, however, that the forces which encourage groupthink be constrained. In the next section, we'll review several remedies for the groupthink problem.

The final criterion for effectiveness is the degree of *acceptance* that the final decision achieves. As we previously noted, because group decisions have input from more people, they are likely to result in solutions that will be more widely accepted.

The effectiveness of group decision making is also influenced by the size of the group. The larger the group, the greater the opportunity for heterogeneous representation. In contrast, a larger group requires more co-ordination and more time to allow all members to contribute. What this means is that groups probably should not be too large: a minimum of five to a maximum of about fifteen. Evidence indicates, in fact, that groups of five and, to a lesser extent seven, are the most effective.[16] Because five and seven are odd numbers, deadlocks are avoided. These groups are large enough for members to shift roles and withdraw from unfavourable positions, but still small enough for quieter members to participate actively in discussions.

Effectiveness should not be considered without also assessing efficiency. Groups almost always come in a poor second in efficiency to the individual decision maker. With few exceptions, group decision making consumes more work time than does individual decision making. Exceptions occur when, to achieve comparable quantities of diverse input, the individual decision maker must spend a great deal of time reviewing files and talking to people. Because groups can include members from different areas, they can spend less time searching for information. However, as we noted, such decisions tend to be the exception. Generally, groups are less efficient than individuals. In deciding whether to use groups, then, primary consideration must be given to assessing whether increases in effectiveness are enough to offset the losses in efficiency.

Techniques for Improving Group Decision Making

When members of a group meet face to face and interact with one another, they create the potential for groupthink. They can censor themselves and pressure other group members into agreement. Four ways of making group decisions more creative have been suggested: brainstorming, the nominal group and Delphi techniques, and electronic meetings.

1. **Brainstorming** is a relatively simple technique for overcoming pressures for conformity that hinder the development of creative alternatives. It does this by utilizing an idea-generating process that specifically encourages any and all alternatives while withholding any criticism of those alternatives. In a typical brainstorming session, a group of six to twelve people sits around a table. The group leader states the problem in a clear manner that is understood by all participants. Members then "free-wheel" as many alternatives as they can in a given time period. No criticism is allowed, and all the alternatives are recorded for later discussion and analysis.

brainstorming
An idea-generating process that encourages alternatives while withholding criticism.

2. **Nominal group technique (NGT)** is a group decision-making technique in which discussion is restricted during the decision-making process. Although group members must be present, they are required to operate independently. Members meet as a group and

nominal group technique
A decision-making technique in which group members are physically present but operate independently.

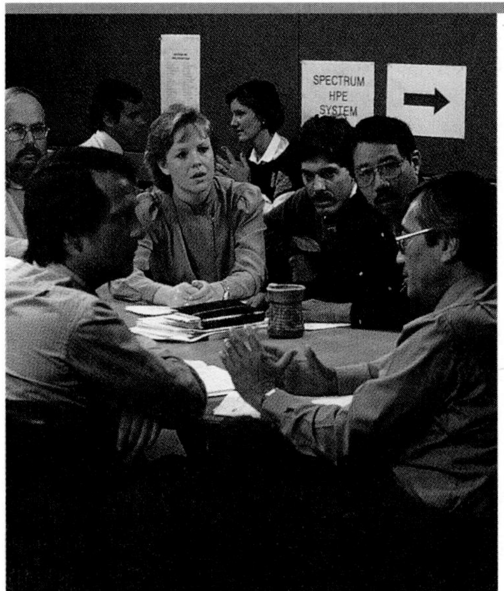

Groups and teams can be effective decision makers if the size is limited.

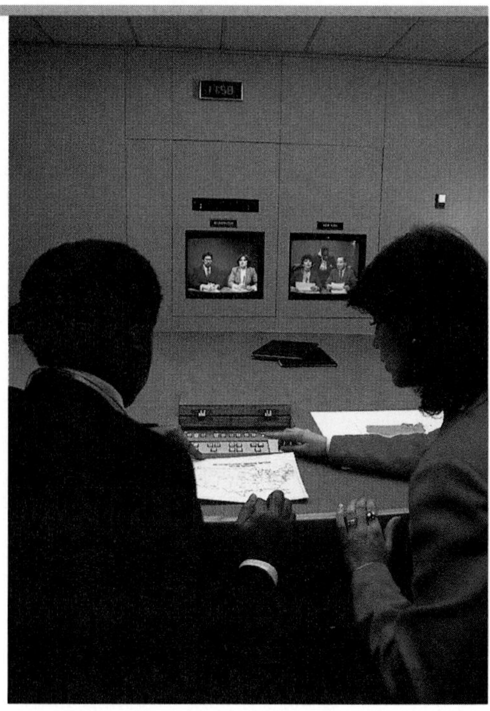

In an electronic meeting, all participants "communicate" by computer. The technology is relatively simple but organizations need to be aware of the technique's drawbacks as well.

are presented with a problem. Before any discussion takes place, each member independently writes down his or her ideas on the problem. After this silent period, each member presents one idea at a time until all ideas have been presented and recorded (typically on a flip chart or chalkboard). No discussion takes place until all ideas have been recorded. The group now discusses the ideas for clarity and evaluates them. Each group member silently and independently ranks the ideas. The final decision is determined by the idea with the highest aggregate ranking.

Delphi technique
A group decision-making technique in which members never meet face to face.

3. The **Delphi technique** is similar to NGT except that it does not allow group members to meet face to face and therefore does not require the physical presence of the group members. In the Delphi technique, the problem is identified and members are asked to provide possible solutions through a series of carefully designed questionnaires. Each member anonymously and independently completes the first questionnaire. Results of the first questionnaire are compiled at a central location, transcribed and then copied. Each member receives a copy of the results. After viewing the results, members are again asked for their solutions. The initial results typically trigger new solutions or cause changes in the original position. This process goes on until a consensus is reached.

electronic meeting
Decision-making groups that interact by way of linked computers.

4. **Electronic meetings** are the most recent approach to group decision making and they blend NGT with sophisticated computer technology. Once the technology for the meeting is in place, the concept is simple. Up to 50 people sit around a horseshoe-shaped table outfitted with computer terminals. Issues are presented to participants and they type their responses onto the computer screens. Individual comments, as well as aggregate votes, are displayed on a projection screen in the room. Experts claim that electronic meetings are as much as 55 percent faster than traditional face-to-face meetings.

SUMMARY

This summary is organized by the learning objectives found at the beginning of the chapter.

1. Decision making is an eight-step process: (a) formulation of a problem, (b) identification of decision criteria, (c) allocation of weights to the criteria, (d) development of alternatives, (e) analysis of alternatives, (f) selection of an alternative, (g) implementation of the alternative, and (h) evaluation of decision-making effectiveness.
2. The rational decision maker is assumed to have a clear problem, have no goal conflict, know all options, have a clear preference ordering, keep all preferences constant, have no time or cost constraints, and select a final choice that maximizes his or her economic payoff.
3. Rationality assumptions don't apply in many situations because (a) an individual's information-processing capacity is limited, (b) decision makers tend to intermix solutions with problems, (c) perceptual biases distort problem identification, (d) information may be selected more for its accessibility than for its quality, (e) decision makers often have favourite alternatives that bias their assessment, (f) decision makers sometimes increase commitment to a previous choice to confirm its original correctness, (g) prior decision precedents constrain current choices, (h) there is rarely agreement on a single goal, (i) decision makers must face time and cost constraints, and (j) most organizational cultures discourage risk taking and searching for innovative alternatives.
4. In the perfectly rational decision-making process: (a) the problem is identified as important and relevant, (b) all criteria are identified, (c) all criteria are evaluated, (d) a comprehensive list of alternatives is generated, (e) all alternatives are assessed against the decision criteria and weights, (f) the decision with the highest economic outcome is chosen, (g) all organizational members embrace the chosen solution, and (h) the decision's outcome is objectively evaluated against the original problem.
5. In the boundedly rational decision-making process: (a) the problem chosen is visible and reflects the manager's interests and background, (b) a limited set of criteria is identified, (c) a simple model is constructed to evaluate criteria, (d) a limited set of similar alternatives is identified, (e) alternatives are assessed one at a time, (f) the search continues until a satisfactory solution is found, (g) politics and power influence decision acceptance, and (h) the decision's outcome is evaluated against the self-interests of the evaluator.
6. Managers face well- and ill-structured problems. Well-structured problems are straightforward, familiar, easily defined, and are solved using programmed decisions. Ill-structured problems are new or unusual, involve ambiguous or incomplete information, and are solved using non-programmed decisions.
7. One description of decision-making styles says there are problem avoiders, problem solvers and problem seekers. Another view is that there are analytic, conceptual, directive, and behavioural decision makers.
8. The ideal situation for making decisions occurs when the manager can make accurate decisions because he or she knows the outcome from every alternative. Such certainty, however, rarely occurs. A far more relevant situation is one of risk, when the decision maker can estimate the likelihood of certain alternatives or outcomes. If neither certainty nor reasonable probability estimates are available, uncertainty exists, and the decision maker's choice will be influenced by intuition or by a hunch.
9. Groups offer certain advantages: more complete information, more alternatives, increased acceptance of a solution and greater legitimacy. However, groups are time consuming, can be dominated by a minority, create pressures to conform, and cloud responsibility.
10. Four ways of improving group decision making are brainstorming, the nominal group technique, the Delphi technique and electronic meetings.

THINKING ABOUT MANAGEMENT ISSUES

1. Why would decision making be described as the "essence of a manager's job"?
2. How might an organization's culture influence the way in which managers make decisions?
3. Suppose you are the chairperson of a community taskforce asked to come up with ideas for getting residents to recycle. What approaches might you use to get the group to generate creative ideas? Why would you use these approaches?
4. Why do you think organizations have increased the use of groups and teams to make decisions during the past 20 years? When would you recommend using groups or teams to make decisions?
5. Why do you think organizations need both systematic and intuitive thinkers?

SELF-ASSESSMENT EXERCISE

WHAT IS YOUR DECISION-MAKING STYLE?

Instructions:

1. Use the following numbers to answer each question:
   8 = when the question is MOST like you
   4 = when the question is MODERATELY like you
   2 = when the question is SLIGHTLY like you
   1 = when the question is LEAST like you
2. Rate the four answers to each question by inserting one of those numbers into each box in columns I–IV.
3. DO NOT repeat any number in a given row. For example, the numbers you might use to answer a given question could read across as 8 2 1 4, BUT NOT 8 8 1 4.
4. In answering the questions, think of how you NORMALLY act in your work situation.
5. Use the first thing that comes to your mind when answering the question. Your responses should reflect how you feel about the questions and what you prefer to do, not what you think might be the right thing to do.
6. There is no time limit in answering the questions, and there are no right or wrong answers.

	I		II		III		IV	
1. My prime objective is to:	Have a position with status		Be the best in my field		Achieve recognition for my work		Feel secure in my job	
2. I enjoy jobs that:	Are technical and well defined		Have considerable variety		Allow independent action		Involve people	
3. I expect people working for me to be:	Productive and fast		Highly capable		Committed and responsive		Receptive to suggestions	
4. In my job, I look for:	Practical results		The best solutions		New approaches or ideas		Good working environment	
5. I communicate best with others:	On a direct one-to-one basis		In writing		By having a group discussion		In a formal meeting	
6. In my planning, I emphasize:	Current problems		Meeting objectives		Future goals		Developing people's careers	
7. When faced with solving a problem, I:	Rely on proven approaches		Apply careful analysis		Look for creative approaches		Rely on my feelings	
8. When using information, I prefer:	Specific facts		Accurate and complete data		Broad coverage of many options		Limited data that are easily understood	

	I	II	III	IV
9. When I am not sure about what to do, I:	Rely on intuition	Search for facts	Look for a possible compromise	Wait before making a decision
10. Whenever possible, I avoid:	Long debates	Incomplete work	Using numbers or formulas	Conflict with others
11. I am especially good at:	Remembering dates and facts	Solving difficult problems	Seeing many possibilities	Interacting with others
12. When time is important, I:	Decide and act quickly	Follow plans and priorities	Refuse to be pressured	Seek guidance or support
13. In social settings, I generally:	Speak with others	Think about what is being said	Observe what is going on	Listen to the conversation
14. I am good at remembering:	People's names	Places we met	People's faces	People's personalities
15. The work I do provides me:	The power to influence others	Challenging assignments	Achievement of my personal goals	Acceptance by the group
16. I work well with those who are:	Energetic and ambitious	Self-confident	Open-minded	Polite and trusting
17. When under stress, I:	Become anxious	Concentrate on the problem	Become frustrated	Am forgetful
18. Others consider me:	Aggressive	Disciplined	Imaginative	Supportive
19. My decisions typically are:	Realistic and direct	Systematic or abstract	Broad and flexible	Sensitive to the needs of others
20. I dislike:	Losing control	Boring work	Following rules	Being rejected

See scoring key on page SK–3. Your score reflects how you see yourself, not what you believe is correct or desirable. This assessment is related to your work situation. It covers typical decisions that you make in your work environment.

Source: A.J. Rowe, R. Mason, and K. Dickel, *Strategic Management and Business Policy* (Reading, MA: Addison-Wesley, 1982), p. 217. Reprinted by permission of Dr. Alan J. Rowe.

for your IMMEDIATE action

Magic Carpet
Software
We'll take you away . . .

TO: Salman Dutta
From: Barbara Schrenk, VP Operations
RE: Software Design Decisions

For some time I've been aware of a problem that's been brewing in our software design unit. As you're well aware, we have a diverse pool of extremely talented and skilled designers. These individuals are, undoubtedly, our organization's most important asset. However, I'm concerned that in the creative process, an individual designer's strong emotional attachment to software that he or she has created can overshadow other important factors—especially concerning whether or not the program design should proceed. At this point, I'm not sure how to approach this issue with the design teams. The last thing I want to do is stifle the creativity of these individuals, but I fear the problem could get out of hand.

Please research the role of emotions in decision making. What do the "experts" say? What's the best way to deal with emotions in decision making? Please provide me with a one-page list of the important points you find from your research. And be sure to cite your sources in case I need to do some further investigation.

This is a fictionalized account of a potentially real problem. It was written for academic purposes only.

TAKE IT TO THE NET

We invite you to visit the Robbins/Coulter/Stuart-Kotze Companion Website at www.prenticehall.ca/robbins for this chapter's Internet resources.

CASE APPLICATION

SMK Speedy, Toronto

In early 1997, Toronto-based Speedy Muffler King Inc. seemed to be getting set to take a large slice out of worldwide markets. Speedy had been a presence in France for some time, but two new major takeovers seemed to position the company for even greater things there. Speedy had also moved into Germany, and set up franchise licensing agreements in Switzerland, Austria and South Korea. The corporate strategy called for major growth in undeveloped markets. At the same time, Speedy had been moving away from its traditional muffler installation business. Better quality mufflers and longer parts warranties from automobile companies meant that the market for mufflers was steadily declining. Speedy spread itself into new services like oil-and-lube jobs, tires and brakes. The CEO at the time declared that Speedy would "become the international brand name of customer-focused car service excellence".

What, in fact, occurred, was that Speedy had a rude awakening. By 1998, Speedy was swamped in debt from its rapid expansion, and had to be bailed out of technical default by a $10 million infusion from its parent company, Goldfarb. In France, the economy was suffering from massive strikes, and Speedy was not integrating its new acquisitions as quickly as it had anticipated. The added administrative costs were not helping Speedy's bottom line. Moreover, stores in the US had been underperforming for some time. Plans for expansion into other global markets had to be halted (in a way this was lucky timing, as South Korea's economy crumbled shortly thereafter). The money from Goldfarb was essential. New Speedy CEO, James Sardo, stated: "The cash will help us improve our liquidity during the slow winter months, while we develop a new strategic plan".

Speedy sold 205 of its US stores, allowing the company to reduce its debt. These US stores were not helping Speedy's bottom line and, with the sale, it was hoped that the company could "focus on key markets", as Sardo put it. Just what these key markets are remains to be seen. Apparently Sardo believes that operations in France—which were the cause of most of Speedy's losses—will turn around and account for most of the company's profit in the years to come. In Canada, Speedy hopes to focus on offering a more comprehensive list of services, including fast service. The company changed its name from Speedy Muffler King to SMK Speedy International, Inc., in a move to distance itself from the perception that it was solely a muffler specialist.

QUESTIONS

1. What sorts of problems and decisions do you think Sardo and company are dealing with? Explain your choices.
2. How might each of the following have been used in Speedy's decisions to expand into France: (a) perfectly rational decision making; (b) bounded rational decision making; and (c) intuition?
3. Would you characterize Speedy's new services focus in Canada as certainty, risk or uncertainty? Explain your choice.
4. What kind of decision-making style do you think Sardo exhibits? Explain your answer in relation to all four management styles.

Sources: Michael Posner, "Juicing a Lemon", *Report on Business* Magazine, April 1998, pp. 37–41; Greg Keenan, "Speedy Sells 205 US Stores", *Globe and Mail*, April 14, 1998, p. B4; and Casey Mahood, "Speedy Sinks in Red Ink", *Globe and Mail*, March 12, 1998, p. B1.

VIDEO CASE APPLICATION

Spar Aerospace

When Colin Watson took over at the helm of Spar after more than two decades at Rogers Cable, he obviously knew that this would not be a simple task. However, he must have been more disheartened when Spar's woes continued through 1997 and into 1998. Not only did Watson have to report Spar's quarterly loss after only two weeks on the job, he also had to report three successively worse ones for the rest of the year. Saving a sinking ship is a challenge that charismatic managers love to embark upon, but the problems facing Spar have been substantial. Watson has stated that he expects revenue of $1 billion by the year 2000. In the meantime, he has been dealing with major change at Spar.

"The challenge is to wean the company away from the dependency it once had on government contracts," Watson says in the video. During the 1990s, the federal government has undergone a process of downsizing, mirroring actions that have been occurring throughout the business world. When the government decided that funding multi-million dollar technology projects wasn't in its best interests fiscally, Spar was left to re-think its very existence. An extensive strategic re-focusing was required. Spar now has to determine where its strengths lie, and make those strengths the focus of its business. If Spar cannot compete without the safety of government contracts, it will have to adjust. For instance, Watson has said, "We were building a satellite every two years. The big boys were building one a month". Watson therefore repositioned Spar as a supplier of satellite parts for the major contractors. Listening to Watson, it seems as though he is building an entirely new company. In this endeavour, he is attempting to create a new corporate culture for Spar. As he says in this interview, it will be one that is more "exciting and energized".

QUESTIONS

1. "Clearly if things haven't improved in a couple of years I'm going to be very unhappy with myself, and I'm sure others will share that view." Discuss this comment of Colin Watson's in relation to the omnipotent and symbolic views of management.
2. How would you rate the level of environmental uncertainty at Spar? Explain.
3. What conditions in Spar's specific environment have had significant effects on it in recent years? How so? What about conditions in the general environment?
4. "You start by having a person at the top [who's] committed to the kind of culture you want to have in the company and then he or she migrates that down with their various hires and you seed in enough new people that you can start a new culture. But spreading it throughout the company certainly takes some time." In the light of this statement by Watson, how difficult do you think it will be for him to change the culture at Spar? What difficulties could you foresee?

Video source: "Spar Turnaround," *Venture* #647 (June 22, 1997).

PART THREE

Planning

LEARNING OBJECTIVES

After Reading This Chapter, You Should Be Able To:

1. Define *planning*
2. Explain the potential benefits of planning
3. Distinguish between strategic and operational plans
4. State when directional plans are preferred over specific plans
5. Differentiate between single-use and standing plans
6. Identify three contingency factors in planning
7. Explain the commitment concept
8. Explain why an organization's stated objectives might not be its real objectives
9. Describe a typical MBO program
10. Contrast the traditional approach to setting objectives with management by objectives (MBO)

A MANAGER'S CHALLENGE

Mark Chamberlain, President and CEO, Wescam Inc., Flamborough, Ontario

Wescam Inc. of Flamborough, Ontario, designs and produces camera systems. In fact, it designs and produces the world's best camera systems for use in unstable environments. When scenes in movies are shot from helicopters, boats, or any other unstable platform, Wescam's sphere-shaped camera systems are used. When news helicopters followed O.J. Simpson down the L.A. freeway, they were equipped with Wescam's high-technology camera systems. Wescam is the industry leader with its technology, and the company's newest camera system—the Model 20—promises to be another major advancement in stabilizing camera systems.[1]

Mark Chamberlain graduated from the University of Waterloo with a master's degree in mechanical engineering, and soon afterwards took a job with a company called Istec Ltd. Two years later, Chamberlain had put together a management buyout plan. He took

over the company from the existing owner who wanted to retire, renamed it Wescam, and turned it into an industry dynamo. Well, a dynamo that happened to record losses in 1997, but was back to profitability and record revenues in 1998.

In Chamberlain's 11 years as CEO, Wescam has seen seriously significant growth. In order to stay on top of technology, Wescam went on an acquisitions binge back in 1995 and 1996, buying five companies. In the process, the company doubled in size but also faced the challenges of dealing with a larger entity; handling increased operating expenses; and integrating the corporate cultures of five new subsidiaries into the whole. Chamberlain believes that Wescam has dealt with these issues through a major restructuring, and is now on target to tackle the challenges of new markets and greater growth. Approximately 30 percent of the company's business is in supplying camera systems for media and entertainment services. The remaining 70 percent of Wescam's revenues come from government agencies, military forces, airborne law enforcement agencies, and the electronic news-gathering industry. Chamberlain sees vast global opportunities in these areas although the majority of current revenue is generated from the United States. Moreover, Wescam is growing in new markets with technology that allows their camera systems to be used on high-speed aircraft. By continuing to develop new technology, Wescam plans to consolidate and, in fact, expand its presence in existing fields, while continually venturing into new ones.

In this chapter we discuss the basics of planning—concepts that Mark Chamberlain at Wescam is dealing with in his efforts to make his company a worldwide success. In the following pages, you'll learn the difference between formal and informal planning, why managers plan, the various types of plans that managers use, the key contingency factors that influence the types of plans that managers use in different situations, and the important role that objectives play in planning.

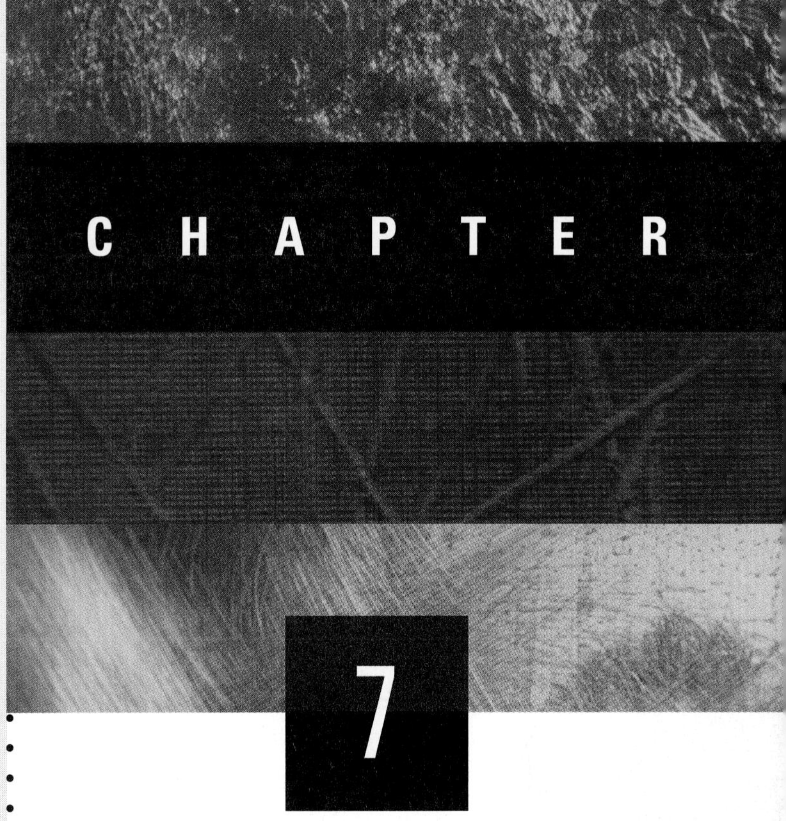

CHAPTER 7

Foundations of Planning

THE DEFINITION OF PLANNING

What do we mean by the term *planning*? As we stated in Chapter 1, planning involves defining the organization's objectives or goals, establishing an overall strategy for achieving these goals, and developing a comprehensive hierarchy of plans to integrate and co-ordinate activities. It is concerned with both *ends* (what is to be done) and *means* (how it is to be done).

Planning can be further defined in terms of whether it is informal or formal. All managers engage in planning, but it might be only informally. In informal planning, nothing is written down, and there is little or no sharing of objectives with others in the organization. This describes how planning is done in many small businesses; the owner-manager has a vision of where he or she wants to go and how to get there. The planning is general and lacks continuity. Of course, informal planning exists in some large organizations as well, and some small businesses have very sophisticated formal plans.

When we use the term planning in this book, we mean *formal* planning. Specific objectives are defined covering a period of years. These objectives are written and made available to organization members. Finally, specific action programs exist for the achievement of these objectives; that is, management clearly defines the path it wants to take to get from where it is to where it wants to be.

PURPOSES OF PLANNING

Why should managers plan? It gives direction, reduces the impact of change, minimizes waste and redundancy, and sets the standards used in controlling.

Planning establishes co-ordinated effort. It gives direction to managers and non-managers alike. When employees know where the organization is going and what they must contribute to reach the objective, they can co-ordinate their activities, co-operate with each other, and work in teams. Without planning, departments could be working at cross purposes and preventing the organization from moving efficiently towards its objectives.

By forcing managers to look ahead, anticipate change, consider the impact of change, and develop appropriate responses, planning reduces uncertainty. It also clarifies the consequences of actions managers might take in response to change.

Planning also reduces overlapping and wasteful activities. Co-ordination before the fact is likely to pinpoint waste and redundancy. Furthermore, when means and ends are clear, inefficiencies become obvious.

Finally, planning establishes objectives or standards that are used in controlling. If we are unsure of what we are trying to achieve, how can we determine whether or not we have achieved it? In planning, we develop the objectives. In the controlling function, we compare actual performance against the objectives, identify any significant deviations, and take the necessary corrective action. Without planning, there would be no way to control.

At Wascana Energy, identifying the resources that will best generate future growth is a critical first step in the planning process. Systematic assessment of potential gas and oil sites is necessary in order for other steps in the planning process to be carried out effectively.

PLANNING AND PERFORMANCE

Do managers and organizations that plan outperform those that don't? Intuitively, you would expect the answer to be a resounding yes. Reviews of performance in organizations that plan are generally affirmative, but we shouldn't take that as a blanket endorsement of formal planning. We cannot say that organizations that formally plan *always* outperform those that don't.

Numerous studies have been done to test the relationship between planning and performance.[2] Based on these, we can draw the following conclusions. First, generally speaking, formal planning is associated with higher profits, higher return on assets, and other positive financial results. Second, the *quality* of the planning process and the appropriate *implementation* of the plans probably contribute more to high performance than the *extent* of planning. Finally, in those studies in which formal planning didn't lead to higher performance, the environment was the culprit. When government regulations, powerful labour unions, and similar environmental forces constrain managers' options, planning will have less effect on an organization's performance. Why? Because management will have fewer choices for planning viable alternatives. For example, planning might indicate that a manufacturing firm should produce a number of its key parts in Taiwan in order to compete effectively against low-cost foreign competitors. But if the firm's labour union contract specifically forbids transferring work overseas, the value of the firm's planning effort is significantly reduced. Dramatic shocks from the environment can also undermine an organization's best-laid plans. In conditions of such environmental uncertainty, there is no reason to expect that firms which plan will outperform those which don't.

MYTHS ABOUT PLANNING

There is no shortage of myths and misconceptions about planning. We want to identify some of these common myths and try to clarify the misunderstandings behind them.

1. *Planning that proves inaccurate is a waste of management's time.* The end result of planning is only one of its purposes. The process itself can be valuable even if the results miss the target. Planning requires management to think through what it wants to do and how it is going to do it. This clarification can be important in and of itself. Management that does a good job of planning will have direction and purpose, and planning is likely to minimize wasted effort. All this can occur even if the objectives being sought are missed.

2. *Planning can eliminate change.* Planning cannot eliminate change. Changes will happen no matter what management does. Managers engage in planning in order to *anticipate* changes and to develop the most effective response to them.

3. *Planning reduces flexibility.* Planning implies commitments, but this is a constraint only if management stops planning after doing it once. Planning is an ongoing activity. The fact that formal plans have been thoroughly discussed and clearly articulated can make them easier to revise than an ambiguous set of assumptions carried around in some executive's head. Also, some plans can be made to be more flexible than others.

TYPES OF PLANS

The most popular ways to describe organizational plans are by their breadth (strategic versus operational), time frame (short versus long term), specificity (specific versus directional), and frequency of use (single use versus standing). However, keep in mind that these planning classifications aren't independent. For instance, short- and long-term plans are closely related to strategic and operational ones. And single-use plans typically are strategic, long term, and directional. Table 7-1 outlines all these types of plans according to category.

strategic plans
Plans that are organization-wide, establish overall objectives, and position an organization in terms of its environment.

Strategic Versus Operational Plans

Plans that apply to the entire organization, establish the organization's overall objectives, and seek to position the organization in terms of its environment are called **strategic plans**. Plans that specify the details of how the overall objectives are to be achieved are called **operational plans**. How do strategic and operational plans differ? Three differences have been identified: time frame, scope, and whether or not they include a known set of organizational objectives.[3]

operational plans
Plans that specify details on how overall objectives are to be achieved.

TABLE 7-1 Types of Plans

Breadth	Time Frame	Specificity	Frequency of Use
Strategic	Long term	Directional	Single use
Operational	Short term	Specific	Standing

short-term plans
Plans that cover less than one year.

long-term plans
Plans that extend beyond five years.

specific plans
Plans that are clearly defined and leave no room for interpretation.

directional plans
Flexible plans that set out general guidelines.

single-use plan
A one-time plan that's specifically designed to meet the needs of a unique situation and is created in response to non-programmed decisions that managers make.

Operational plans tend to cover shorter periods of time. For instance, an organization's monthly, weekly, and day-to-day plans are almost always operational. Strategic plans tend to include an extended time period—usually five years or more. They also cover a broader view of the organization and deal less with specific areas. Finally, strategic plans include the formulation of objectives, while operational plans assume the existence of objectives. Operational plans define ways to attain the objectives.

Short-Term Versus Long-Term Plans

Financial analysts traditionally describe investment returns as *short, intermediate,* and *long term.* The short term covers less than one year. Any time frame past five years is considered long term. The intermediate term is any period in between. Managers typically use the same terminology to describe plans, although an organization can designate any time frame it wants. For clarity, we'll use **short-term** plans and **long-term** plans in our discussions.

Specific Versus Directional Plans

Intuitively it seems right that specific plans would be preferable to directional, or loosely guided, plans. **Specific plans** have clearly defined objectives. There is no ambiguity, no problem with misunderstandings. For example, a manager who seeks to increase his or her firm's sales by 20 percent over a given 12-month period might establish specific procedures, budget allocations, and schedules of activities to reach that objective. These represent specific plans.

However, specific plans do have drawbacks. They require clarity and a sense of predictability that often doesn't exist. When uncertainty is high and management must be flexible in order to respond to unexpected changes, then it is preferable to use directional plans.[4] (See Figure 7-1.)

Directional plans identify general guidelines. They provide focus but do not lock managers into specific objectives or courses of action. Instead of following a specific plan to cut costs by four percent and increase revenues by six percent in the next six months, a directional plan might suggest improving corporate profits by five to ten percent over the next six months. The flexibility inherent in directional plans is obvious. However, this advantage must be weighed against the loss of clarity provided by specific plans.

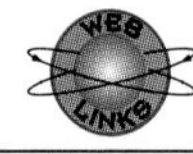

The Seagram Company Ltd.
www.seagram.com

standing plans
Ongoing plans that provide guidance for activities repeatedly performed in the organization and that are created in response to programmed decisions that managers make.

Frequency of Use

Some organizational plans that managers develop are ongoing while others are used only once. A **single-use plan** is a one-time plan specifically designed to meet the needs of a unique situation and one created in response to non-programmed decisions that managers make. For instance, in 1990, when Matsushita Electric Industrial Company acquired MCA Inc. (the film, television and record company), top-level executives devised a single-use plan to guide the acquisition. It was a one-time, unique situation that corporate managers were unlikely to repeat. And, in early 1995, Matsushita sold its interest in MCA to a Canadian company, Seagram—another example of a single-use plan.

In contrast, **standing plans** are ongoing plans that provide guidance for activities repeatedly performed in the organization. Standing plans are created in response to programmed decisions that managers make and include the policies, rules, and procedures that we defined in the previous chapter on managerial decision making. An example of a standing plan is the sexual harassment policy developed by the University of British Columbia. It provides guidance to university administrators as they perform their work activities.

FIGURE 7-1 Specific Versus Directional Plans

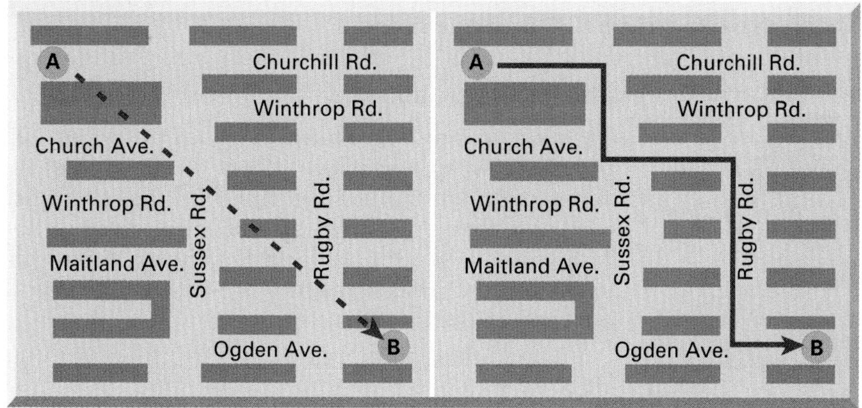

CONTINGENCY FACTORS IN PLANNING

In some situations, long-term plans make sense; in others they do not. Similarly, in some instances, directional plans are more effective than specific ones. What are these situations? In this section, we describe several contingency factors that affect planning.[5]

Level in the Organization

Figure 7-2 shows the general relationship between a manager's level in the organization and the type of planning done. For the most part, operational planning dominates the planning activities of lower-level managers. As managers move up the hierarchy, their planning role becomes more strategy oriented. The planning effort by top executives in large organizations is mostly strategic. In a small business, of course, the owner-manager does both.

FIGURE 7-2 Planning in the Hierarchy of Organizations

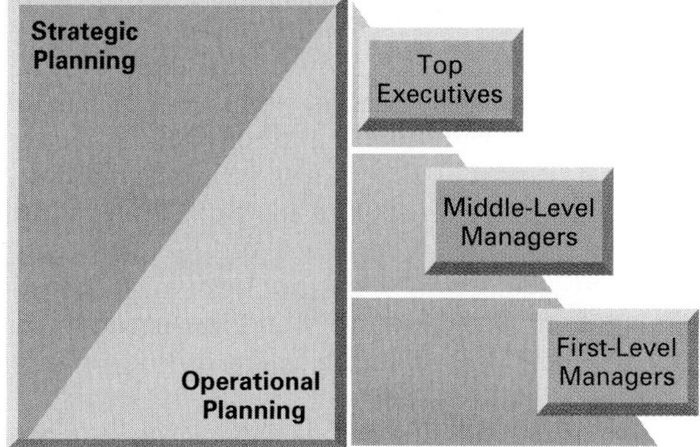

1 What are the potential benefits of formal planning?

2 Identify and rebut some common myths about planning.

MANAGERS SPEAK OUT

Interview with Geoff Gilpin, Director of Affinity Marketing, GTE Communications Corporation

Describe your job.

My job is to bring in profitable revenue through working with organizations to jointly market my company's communication products to the end customer. Our goal is to decrease customer acquisition costs and increase retention. To reach these goals, I seek out organizations that have a tight relationship with their constituency or similar target markets and business objectives.

How do you use planning in your job?

Planning is an ongoing process. It's our road map, but the destination is constantly changing due to dynamic market conditions. In an industry like telecommunications, where things change daily, planning is critical in keeping our team informed and co-ordinated in our efforts. In addition, planning is an element in our continuous improvement process as we measure our actual performance against the plan and learn from the gaps.

How important are objectives to what you do?

Objectives provide direction for our group. The focus on meeting our objectives drives results. It's critical to carefully craft objectives that fit in with the business plan and to communicate them well throughout the company. ■

Degree of Environmental Uncertainty

The greater the environmental uncertainty, the more plans need to be directional and the more emphasis needs to be placed on the short term.

If rapid or important technological, social, economic, legal, or other environmental changes are occurring, well-defined and precisely charted courses of action are more likely to hinder an organization's performance than help it. When environmental uncertainty is high, specific plans must be altered to accommodate the changes—often at high cost and decreased efficiency. For example, Air Canada operates in a very uncertain environment. The airline industry is cyclical and years of losses can easily follow years of profit (or in Canadian Airlines' case, years of losses following years of losses). In the mid-90s, Air Canada had a broad and general goal of reducing costs (largely through downsizing) and improving efficiency, while staying on top of the constantly changing business. In the late '90s, the company's directional plan has been to take advantage of a bigger market through more trans-border flights and ties with other international airlines (and in the process having to add thousands to the workforce).

Air Canada
www.aircanada.ca/

Also, the greater the change, the less likely it is that plans are accurate. For example, one study found that one-year revenue plans tended to achieve 99 percent accuracy in comparison to 84 percent for five-year plans.[6] Therefore, if an organization is facing a rapidly changing environment, managers should be flexible in planning.

We'd like to add a final thought on the importance of flexibility. Even as little as 20 years ago, the "best managed" corporations had large planning departments.[7] They generated numerous five- and ten-year plans, updated annually, of course. General Electric, for example, once had a planning staff of 350 who churned out hundreds of meticulously detailed reports. Now, however, planning is increasingly being done by divisional or unit managers as part of their management responsibilities, and the plans cover shorter periods of time and are more likely to consider a broader range of options. GE's formal planning group is down to about 20 and their only role is to advise operating managers. The heads of each of GE's business units

GE Canada
www.ge.com/canada

Galen Weston of George Weston Ltd., Canada's 11th largest company, believes in the flexibility of directional plans. He does not want his managers to make plans that count on sales volume and prices increasing by a certain percentage each year. Rather, he emphasizes being flexible and adapting to environmental factors.

George Weston Ltd.
www.weston.ca

now develop five one-page reports each year that identify possible opportunities and obstacles they see in their industries during the next two years.

In a volatile world, only the foolish are cocky enough to believe that they can accurately forecast the future. But that doesn't diminish the importance of plans. Well-managed organizations are spending less time coming up with highly detailed, quantitative plans and instead are developing multiple scenarios of the future. For example, Southern California Edison, an electric utility serving over 4 million customers in California, has created 12 possible versions of the future based on an economic boom, a Middle East oil crisis, expanded environmentalism efforts, and other developments. This approach to flexible planning came about after the utility's managers realized that every long-range plan they had painstakingly constructed during the 1970s and 1980s had been rendered virtually useless by unexpected events—from the Gulf War to nuclear accidents such as Chernobyl to new regulatory restrictions on sulphur emissions. And, of course, Southern California Edison is not unique in facing an increasingly uncertain world. As we pointed out in Chapter 3, most businesses, including for-profit and non-profit businesses, are finding their environments becoming more dynamic and uncertain. These forces require managers to develop more flexible plans. You can be sure, for example, that every major corporation in Quebec has been devising and revising corporate strategies to take into account the possibility of Quebec leaving the Canadian federation.

Length of Future Commitments

The other contingency factor again relates to the time frame of plans. The more that current plans affect future commitments, the longer the time frame for which managers should plan. This **commitment concept** means that plans should extend far enough to meet those commitments made today. Planning for too long or for too short a period is inefficient.

commitment concept
Plans should extend far enough to see through current commitments.

Managers are not planning for future decisions. Rather, they are planning for the future impact of the decisions they are currently making. Decisions made today become a commitment to some future action or expenditure. Tenure decisions in colleges and universities are an excellent example of how the commitment concept should work.

When a university grants tenure to a faculty member, it's making a commitment to provide lifelong employment for that person. The tenure decision must reflect an assessment by administrators that there will be a need for that individual's teaching expertise through his or her lifetime. If a university gives tenure to a 30-year-old art history professor, it should have a plan that covers at least the 30 or more years that this person could be teaching at that institution. Most importantly, the plan should demonstrate the need for a permanent art history professor throughout that time period.

To see how important the commitment concept is to planning, let's travel across Lake Erie to the Cleveland side where, on the shore, several distinct geometric forms are combined into an impressive building designed by IM Pei. The building houses the Rock and Roll Hall of Fame and Museum, opened in 1995. Back in 1983, a group of record industry professionals founded the Hall to honour musical greats, but there was no actual residence. In '86, the board of the

Cleveland's Rock and Roll Hall of Fame and Museum represents an example of the commitment concept in planning. A 1986 decision committed the governing board to a nine-year design and construction process that exceeded original time and budget estimates but could not be cut back or rescinded.

Hall of Fame decided to build a site in Cleveland. Initial plans were made, but cost estimates for construction proved to be too low, and delays plagued the project. For instance, the ground-breaking project, originally scheduled for 1990, didn't take place until 1993. By that time, it wasn't feasible to back out of the project, even with the delays and higher costs. Instead, construction went ahead. How does this example illustrate the commitment concept? The decision made back in the early '80s became a commitment for future actions and expenditures. Once the Hall of Fame board decided to build a facility, it had to plan for the increased costs and the construction delays. The future impact of the decision to build the Rock and Roll Hall of Fame and Museum was that it committed the board to live with the decision and all its consequences, good and bad.

OBJECTIVES: THE FOUNDATION OF PLANNING

objectives
Desired outcomes for individuals, groups or entire organizations.

Objectives are goals. We use the two terms interchangeably. What do these terms mean? They refer to desired outcomes for individuals, groups or entire organizations.[8] They provide the direction for all management decisions and form the criterion against which actual accomplishments can be measured. This is why they are the foundation of planning.

Multiplicity of Objectives

At first glance, it might appear that organizations have a single objective—for business firms to make a profit; and for non-profit organizations to efficiently provide a service. But closer analysis reveals that all organizations have multiple objectives. Businesses also seek to increase market share and satisfy employee welfare. A church provides a place for religious practices but it also assists the underprivileged in its community and acts as a social gathering place for church members. No one measure can evaluate effectively whether an organization is successful. Emphasis on one goal, such as profit, ignores other goals that must also be reached if long-term profits are to be achieved. Also, as we discussed in Chapter 5, the use of a single objective (such as profit) almost certainly will result in unethical practices, because managers will ignore other important parts of their jobs in order to look good on that one measure.

Table 7-2 lists a sampling of both financial and strategic goals from some well-known corporations.[9] The financial objectives relate to the financial performance of the firm while the strategic objectives relate to other areas of a firm's performance. Except for a few of the financial objectives, these goals could apply to a non-profit organization as well. Notice, too, that

3 How does environmental uncertainty affect planning?

4 What is the commitment concept, and how does it affect planning?

The Role of Planning in Developing a Productive Diverse Workforce

We already know that the composition of the workforce is changing drastically. A study done by the Hudson Institute pointed out that by the year 2000: (1) the average age of workers will rise while the pool of younger workers will shrink; (2) two-thirds of new entrants to the workforce will be women, minorities and immigrants; (3) single parents will account for more employees; and (4) a smaller pool of literate, skilled workers will be available at a time when many jobs require a more skilled workforce.[10] Managers will have to cope with these monumental human resource changes. What role can planning play as organizations attempt to develop a productive and effective diverse workforce? A very important role indeed!

For one thing, planning establishes coordinated organizational effort. It provides the foundation for developing organization-wide policies, practices, and training for an organization that is committed to cultural diversity. Organizational activities, from employee recruitment to meet workplace diversity goals to product development that encompasses diverse perspectives to purchasing supplies and materials from diverse sources, can be looked at from the perspective of incorporating diversity into everyday activities. For example, at Union Gas in Ontario, recruitment of diverse employees is an important objective. And Reebok International Ltd. actively seeks minority-owned businesses as supply sources.[11] At JP Morgan, company managers developed a diverse summer intern program for undergraduate and graduate students, with the intent of attracting some of these people to join the company after completing their degrees.[12]

Another way planning can be valuable is in reducing the uncertainty associated with the changing demographics of the workforce. Labour force participation statistics already show us that the workforce is aging and that more women, minorities and immigrants are entering the workplace. As managers consider the impact of these changes, they can plan ways to fully use the talents, skills, and abilities of their diverse employees. As part of this planning process, managers might establish short- and long-term targets or objectives for recruiting, training and promoting diverse individuals. Also, they might develop a long-range diversity development plan that outlines the steps their organization will take to become culturally diverse. ■

Union Gas Limited
www.uniongas.com

although survival is not specifically mentioned by the firms, it's of utmost importance to all organizations. Some of the objectives listed in Table 7-2 contribute directly to profits, but it is obvious that all organizations must survive if other objectives are to be achieved.

Real Versus Stated Objectives

Table 7-2 is a list of stated objectives. **Stated objectives** are official statements of what an organization says—and what it wants its various stakeholders to believe—are its objectives. However, stated objectives—which can be found in an organization's charter, annual report, public relations announcements, or in public statements made by managers—are often conflicting and excessively influenced by what society believes organizations *should* do.

stated objectives
Official statements of what an organization says—and what it wants various people to believe—are its objectives.

The overall objectives stated by top management should be treated for what they are: "fiction produced by an organization to account for, explain, or rationalize to particular audiences, rather than as valid and reliable indications of purpose."[13] The content of objectives is substantially determined by what those audiences want to hear. Moreover, it is simpler for management to state a set of consistent, understandable objectives than to explain a multiplicity of objectives. If you want to know what an organization's **real objectives** are, closely observe what members of the organization actually do. Actions define priorities. For example, the university that proclaims the objective of limiting class size, facilitating close student-faculty relations, and actively involving students in the learning process, and then puts its students into lecture classes of 300 or more, is pretty common! So, too, is the automobile service centre that promises fast, low-cost repairs and then provides mediocre service at high prices. An awareness that real and stated objectives differ is important, if for no other reason than helping you to explain what might otherwise seem to be management inconsistencies.

real objectives
Objectives that an organization actually pursues, as defined by the actions of its members.

TABLE 7-2 Stated Objectives from Some Large Companies

Financial Objectives	Strategic Objectives
• Faster revenue growth	• A bigger market share
• Faster earnings growth	• A higher, more secure industry rank
• Higher dividends	• Higher product quality
• Wider profit margins	• Lower costs relative to key competitors
• Higher returns on invested capital	• Broader or more attractive product line
• Stronger bond and credit ratings	• A stronger reputation with customers
• Bigger cash flows	• Superior customer service
• A rising stock price	• Recognition as a leader in technology and/or product innovation
• Recognition as a "blue chip" company	• Increased ability to compete in international markets
• A more diversified revenue base	• Expanded growth opportunities
• Stable earnings during recessionary periods	

Source: Arthur A. Thompson, Jr., and A. J. Strickland III, *Strategic Management* (Homewood, IL: Irwin, 1992), p. 28.

Traditional Objective Setting

The traditional role of objectives is one of control imposed by an organization's top management. The president of a manufacturing firm *tells* the production vice president what he or she expects manufacturing costs to be for the coming year. The president *tells* the marketing vice president what level he or she expects sales to reach for the coming year. The city mayor *tells* his or her chief of police how much the departmental budget will be. Then, at some later point, performance is evaluated to determine whether or not the assigned objectives have been achieved.

traditional objective setting Objectives are set at the top and then broken down into sub-goals for each level in an organization. Top management imposes its standards on everyone below.

The central theme in **traditional objective setting** is that objectives are set at the top and then broken down into sub-goals for each level of an organization. This traditional perspective assumes that top management knows what's best because only they can see the "big picture". Thus, the objectives that are established and "passed down" to each succeeding level of the organization serve to direct and guide, and in some ways to constrain, individual employees' work behaviours. Employees' work efforts at the various organizational levels are then geared to meet the objectives that have been assigned in their areas of responsibility.

means-ends chain An integrated network of organizational objectives in which higher-level objectives, or ends, are linked to lower-level objectives, which serve as the means for their accomplishment.

In addition to being imposed from above, traditional objective setting is often largely non-operational.[14] If top management defines the organization's objectives in broad terms such as achieving "sufficient profits" or "market leadership", these ambiguities have to be turned into specifics as the objectives flow down through the organization. At each level, managers supply operational meaning to the goals. Specificity is achieved by each manager applying his or her own set of interpretations and biases. The result is that objectives often lose clarity and unity as they make their way down from the top of the organization to lower levels. (See Figure 7-3.)

However, when the hierarchy of organizational objectives is clearly and properly defined, it forms an integrated network of objectives or a **means-ends chain**. What this means is that higher-level objectives or ends are linked to lower-level objectives that serve as the means for their accomplishment. In other words, the goals at the lower levels (means) must be achieved in order to reach the goals at the next level (end). And the accomplishment of goals at that level becomes the means to achieve the goals at the next level (end). And so forth and so on, up through the different levels of the organization.

management by objectives (MBO) A system in which specific performance objectives are jointly determined by subordinates and their superiors, progress towards objectives is periodically reviewed, and rewards are allocated on the basis of this progress.

Management by Objectives

Instead of traditional objective setting, many organizations use **management by objectives (MBO)**. It's a management system in which specific performance objectives are jointly determined by subordinates and their superiors, progress towards objectives is periodically reviewed, and rewards are allocated on the basis of this progress. Rather than using goals only as controls, MBO uses them to motivate employees as well.

FIGURE 7-3 Traditional Objective Setting

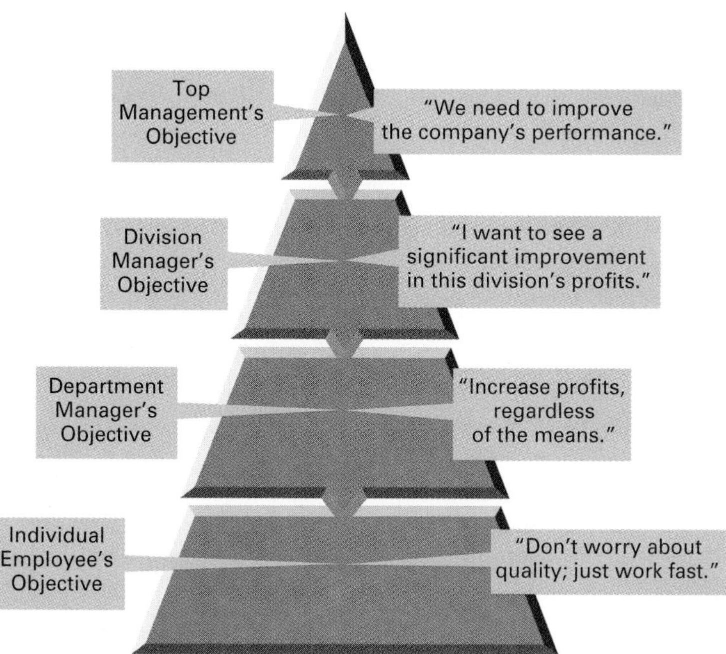
Top Management's Objective
"We need to improve the company's performance."
Division Manager's Objective
"I want to see a significant improvement in this division's profits."
Department Manager's Objective
"Increase profits, regardless of the means."
Individual Employee's Objective
"Don't worry about quality; just work fast."

Management by objectives was first described by Peter Drucker. It consists of four elements: goal specificity; participative decision making; an explicit time period; and performance feedback.[15] Its appeal lies in its emphasis on converting overall objectives into specific objectives for organizational units and individual members. Table 7-3 lists the steps in a typical MBO program.

Do MBO programs work? Studies of actual MBO programs confirm that MBO effectively increases employee performance and organizational productivity. A review of 70 programs, for example, found organizational productivity gains in 68 of them.[16] The same review identified top management commitment and involvement as important conditions for MBO to succeed. When top management had a high commitment to MBO and was personally involved in its implementation, the average gain in productivity was 56 percent. When commitment and involvement were low, the average gain in productivity dropped to only 6 percent.

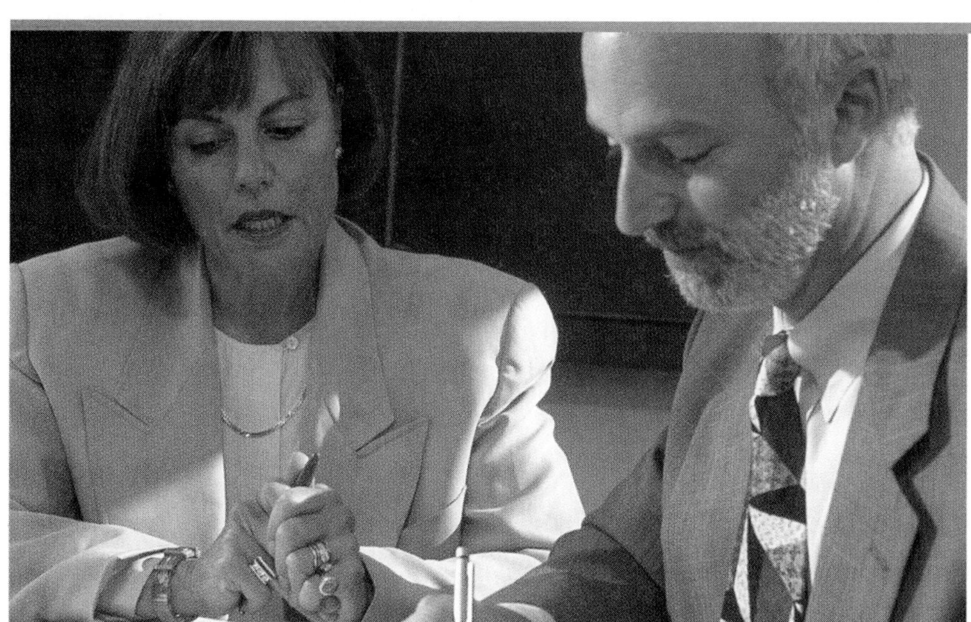

One of the defining characteristics of management by objectives, or MBO, is that the employee's performance goals are set jointly by the employee and the manager.

TABLE 7-3 Steps in a Typical MBO Program

1. The organization's overall objectives and strategies are formulated.
2. Major objectives are allocated among divisional and departmental units.
3. Unit managers collaboratively set specific objectives for their units with their superiors.
4. Specific objectives are collaboratively set for all department members.
5. Action plans, defining how objectives are to be achieved, are specified and agreed upon by managers and subordinates.
6. The action plans are implemented.
7. Progress towards objectives is periodically reviewed, and feedback is provided.
8. Successful achievement of objectives is reinforced by performance-based rewards.

THINKING CRITICALLY ABOUT ETHICS

"I'm telling you. After my talk with my manager today about my work goals for the next quarter, I think our company's MBO program actually stands for 'manipulating by objectives' rather than 'managing by objectives'," Kathy complained to her friend Joe. Kathy continued that her manager "came in and outlined what she thought I should be working on and then asked me what I thought about it—I guess her way of getting me to participate in the goal setting".

Is it unethical for a manager to enter a participative goal-setting session with a pre-established set of goals that he or she wants the employee to accept? Why or why not? Is it unethical for a manager to use his or her formal position to impose specific goals on an employee? Why or why not? ■

TESTING... TESTING...

5 **How would you identify an organization's stated objectives? Its real objectives? What happens when an organization has conflicting objectives?**

6 **Contrast traditional objective setting and MBO.**

7 **What are the steps in a typical MBO program?**

SUMMARY

This summary is organized by the learning objectives found at the beginning of the chapter.

1. Planning is the process of determining objectives and assessing the way these objectives can best be achieved.
2. Planning gives direction, reduces the impact of change, minimizes waste and redundancy, and sets the standards for use in controlling.
3. Strategic plans cover an extensive time period (typically five or more years), cover broad issues, and include the formulation of objectives. Operational plans cover shorter periods of time, focus on specifics, and assume that objectives are already known.
4. Directional plans are preferred over specific plans when uncertainty is high and when the organization is in the formative and the decline stages of its life cycle.
5. A single-use plan is a one-time plan that's specifically designed to meet the needs of a unique situation and is created in response to non-programmed decisions that managers make. Standing plans are ongoing plans that provide guidance for activities repeatedly performed in the organization and are created in response to programmed decisions that managers make.
6. Three contingency factors in planning include a manager's level in the organization, the degree of environmental uncertainty, and the length of future commitments.
7. The commitment concept concerns the fact that a manager should plan just far enough ahead to see that those commitments he or she makes today are kept.
8. An organization's stated objectives might not be its real objectives because management might want to tell people what they want to hear, and because it is simpler to state a set of consistent, understandable objectives than to explain a multiplicity of objectives.
9. In traditional objective setting, objectives are set at the top of the organization and then broken down into sub-goals for each level of an organization. The objectives are established and passed down to each succeeding level. In management by objectives (MBO), specific performance objectives are jointly determined by subordinates and their superiors, progress towards objectives is periodically reviewed, and rewards are allocated on the basis of this progress.

THINKING ABOUT MANAGEMENT ISSUES

1. What relationship do you see between planning and traditional objective setting? And between planning and controlling?
2. Explain how planning involves making decisions today that will have an impact later.
3. How might planning in a non-profit organization like the Heart and Stroke Foundation of Ontario differ from planning in a for-profit organization like Maple Leaf Foods?
4. What types of planning do you do in your personal life? Describe these plans in terms of being (a) strategic or operational, (b) short- or long-term, and (c) specific or directional.

SELF-ASSESSMENT EXERCISE

HOW WELL DO I SET GOALS?

How well do you plan in your personal life and, if you're employed, in your organizational setting? The following questions are designed to help you assess how well goal-setting processes are working in your personal and work lives. Indicate how much you agree or disagree with each statement. When you finish, review the items that received the lowest scores.

5 = Strongly agree
4 = Agree
3 = Neither agree nor disagree
2 = Disagree
1 = Strongly disagree

At school and in my personal life:

_____ **1.** I am proactive rather than reactive.
_____ **2.** I set aside enough time and resources to study and complete projects.
_____ **3.** I am able to budget money to buy the things I really want without going broke.
_____ **4.** I have thought through what I want to do in school.
_____ **5.** I have a plan for completing my major.
_____ **6.** My goals for the future are realistic.

At work (complete only if you have work experience):

_____ **1.** We are proactive rather than reactive.
_____ **2.** Policies, programs and procedures are developed in an integrated fashion.
_____ **3.** Time and resources are committed to set goals and objectives.
_____ **4.** We work on forecasting future opportunities and threats.
_____ **5.** The overall mission is clear to all.
_____ **6.** Goal-setting processes take place at both the organizational unit and individual level.
_____ **7.** There are written goals and objectives.
_____ **8.** There are long-range goals and objectives.
_____ **9.** There is short-range objective setting.
_____ **10.** Goals and objectives are realistic.
_____ **11.** Goals and objectives are challenging.
_____ **12.** Goals and objectives are reviewed and modified on a regular cycle.
_____ **13.** Accomplishment of goals and objectives is tied to a reward system.
_____ **14.** Pursuing goals and objectives is a productive activity.

For scoring, turn to the scoring key beginning on page SK-1.

Source: Robert E. Quinn, Sue R. Faerman, Michael P. Thompson, and Michael R. McGrath, *Becoming a Master Manager: A Competency Framework* (New York: Wiley, 1990), pp. 33–34.

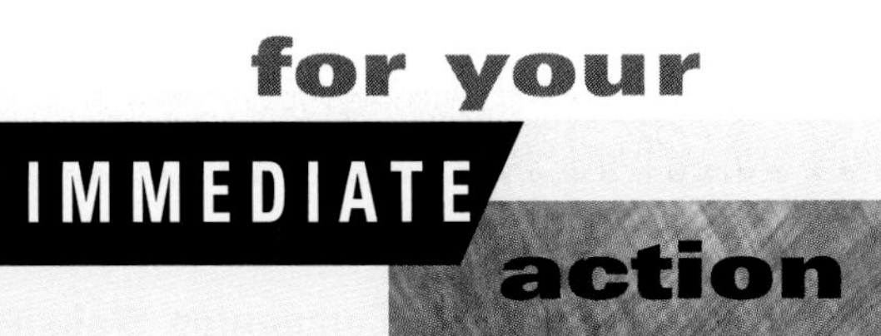

SERVING ALL YOUR HUMAN RESOURCE NEEDS

TO: Alpha Team Members
FROM: Jerome Lawrence, Alpha Team Leader
SUBJECT: Objectives for Developing the New Training Module

Hey, Alpha Team! Congratulations! We've been assigned the task of developing People Power's new Internet/World Wide Web training module. The overall objective of this new project is to design a training module for using the Internet to research information. The sales reps say we've already had several requests from our various corporate customers for this type of training program. So we're on an accelerated development schedule.

I'm asking each Alpha Team member to identify three or four specific goals for each of the three stages of the project: (1) researching customer needs; (2) researching the Internet/World Wide Web for specific information sources and techniques we want to use in our training module; and (3) designing and writing specific training modules. Please have these written by next week. We'll have a team meeting to share ideas and finalize the specific objectives for this project. Then we'll be able to get to work!

This is a fictionalized account of a potentially real problem. It was written for academic purposes only and is not meant to reflect either positively or negatively on management practices at People Power.

TAKE IT TO THE NET

We invite you to visit the Robbins/Coulter/Stuart-Kotze Companion Website at www.prenticehall.ca/robbins for this chapter's Internet resources.

CASE APPLICATION

Computervision Corporation, Bedford, Massachusetts

"The most important thing for any organization is to have everyone focused on the same objectives and to have the objectives clearly defined." So says Kathleen Cote, CEO of Computervision Corporation. Her company is a leading supplier of product design and development software and services. Its vision is to be the partner of choice for the most important thing its customers do—product development. The company pioneered CAD/CAM (computer-aided design/computer-aided manufacturing) hardware and software back in 1971, and was flying high during the 1980s, as revenues and profits soared. Then, the once-profitable company posted losses of nearly $1.3 billion from 1991 to 1993. Cote headed the operating committee that developed the strategic plan for Computervision's turnaround and ultimate survival.

The company had to clearly define its objectives, and Cote had to make sure that everyone was focused on those objectives. The first thing Cote did was to have her senior managers identify where Computervision was winning business and where it was losing business. On the basis of that analysis, they decided to shift the company's focus to providing product development solutions through software and services, while putting less of an emphasis on hardware. The top managers then established corporate objectives and communicated them throughout the organization. These objectives were then used to clearly define individual performance objectives. In addition, Cote was firmly committed to sticking to the objectives. She has said, "I'm a firm believer that if you stay on course and never get off, you will have great success. There really is no surprise if you have a plan in place".

Cote isn't just focused on establishing and communicating common objectives for organizational employees. She is also strongly committed to making sure objectives are met. Managers (and all employees) are held accountable for meeting their respective objectives. Says Cote, "I don't like surprises. If something isn't going right, let me know what you can do about it to work through the issues and the problem". According to Cote, achieving these objectives entails showing employees how they are a part of making the plans happen and making them feel that they play an important role in helping the company meet its goals. The company totalled 11 straight profitable quarters with Cote at the helm, but then a brief aberration—a $6 million loss in the fourth quarter of 1996. Surely that wasn't according to plan? No need to worry though, Computervision quickly recovered and you can bet that they plan to remain profitable in the future.

QUESTIONS

1. What is your reaction to Cote's philosophy that the most important thing for any organization is to have everyone focused on the same objectives and to have the objectives clearly defined? Do you agree? Why or why not? What could the drawbacks be of such a philosophy?
2. What role did strategic plans play in Computervision's turnaround? What role should they play in the company's future? What role should operational plans play?
3. One of the major criticisms of formal planning is that planning may create rigidity, particularly in a creative environment. How do you think Kathleen Cote would respond to that criticism?
4. How might the commitment concept affect planning at Computervision?
5. Would you call Computervision's approach to setting objectives a more traditional approach or more of an MBO approach? Explain your choice.

Source: M.A. Verespej, "Future Vision", *IW*, February 17, 1997, pp. 50-55. And http://www.cv.com.

LEARNING OBJECTIVES

After Reading This Chapter, You Should Be Able To:

1 Explain the importance of strategic planning

2 Differentiate corporate-, business-, and functional-level strategies

3 Describe the steps in the strategic management process

4 Explain SWOT analysis

5 Differentiate the various grand strategies

6 Describe the four business groups in the BCG matrix

7 Describe how to assess an organization's competitive advantage

8 Describe how TQM is used as a strategic weapon

9 Identify the various competitive strategies

A MANAGER'S CHALLENGE

Kevin O'Leary, President, and Michael Perik, CEO, The Learning Co.

One of the great Canadian success stories in the early 1990s was Softkey Software Products of Mississauga, Ontario. Softkey's business strategy as a software provider was to sell other companies' programs under the Softkey name. Softkey sold programs cheaply, and on a mass scale—something new at that time. In 1986, the company's revenue was $375 000. By 1991, it was $36.9 million. In 1992, it had ballooned to $61.4 million. But the founders of the company, Kevin O'Leary and Michael Perik, realized that their phenomenal growth could not continue, due to the way the industry was changing. With the fast rise of the Internet, packaged software was being replaced by the easier method of simply downloading it. Softkey saw an obvious problem: they didn't produce any of their own software, they only packaged it.[1]

It was time for a major shift in strategy. O'Leary and Perik took the company on an acquisitions binge, gobbling up as many software producers as they could buy. The biggest

of these acquisitions was The Learning Co., and Softkey took this as its company name while it completed the move from distributor to producer. The company had decided to focus on education software (the other major growth market Softkey was looking at; the entertainment industry was dominated by big guns like Time Warner and Disney). No market leader had yet emerged from the education software industry—it was basically a field of hundreds of software companies. So Softkey set out to become the biggest player in the market.

The acquisitions strategy eventually led Softkey to move its headquarters from Mississauga to Cambridge, Mass., a better strategic location to operate from. According to O'Leary, "We had to be in the States, access to capital is crucial in a consolidating industry". With the acquisition of The Learning Company (TLC) in 1995, they were the biggest educational software producer in the world. However, with this rapid growth has come growing pains such as having to write off losses of $400 million for both '96 and '97. The turnaround to profit for TLC began in 1998. The company has gone through a major shift in the past seven years, but now TLC is firmly established as the market leader in its field. And O'Leary and Perik are prepared for possible new shifts in the industry, such as the growth of direct satellite and cable, which may lead to a situation where customers don't actually have to own software, but instead simply pay to receive it in their homes, like cable TV.

Strategic planning has been a widely recognized contributor to organizational success for less than three decades. However, the benefits of strategic planning are clearly evident in The Learning Co.'s success. This chapter will emphasize how strategy affects organizational performance.

Chapter 8 Strategic Management

THE INCREASING IMPORTANCE OF STRATEGIC PLANNING

Before the early 1970s, managers who made long-range plans generally assumed that better times were ahead. Plans for the future were merely extensions of what the organization had done in the past. However, environmental shocks during the 1970s and 1980s, such as energy crises, deregulation of many industries, accelerating technological change, and increasing global competition, undermined this approach to long-range planning. These changes in the "rules of the game" forced managers to develop a systematic approach to analyzing the environment, assessing their organization's strengths and weaknesses, and identifying opportunities where the organization could have a competitive advantage. The value of thinking strategically began to be recognized.[2]

Why is strategic management considered so important? It's involved in many of the decisions that managers make. For example, Loblaw's decision to launch banking services in its grocery stores under the President's Choice moniker is an example of strategic management; so is Sears Canada's move into the furniture market with their new Sears Home Furniture stores. Also, one survey of business owners found that 69 percent had strategic plans and, among those owners, 89 percent responded that they had found their plans to be effective.[3] They stated, for example, that strategic planning gave them specific goals and provided their staff with a unified vision. Other studies of the effectiveness of strategic planning and management have found that, generally speaking, companies with formal strategic management systems had higher financial returns.[4]

Today, strategic management has moved beyond the private sector to include government agencies, hospitals and educational institutions. For example, the skyrocketing costs of a university education, cutbacks in government aid for students and research, and the decline in the absolute number of high school graduates have forced many university administrators to assess their organizations' aspirations and identify a market niche in which they can survive and prosper.[5]

LEVELS OF STRATEGY

If an organization produced a single product or service, managers could develop a single strategic plan that covered everything it did. But many organizations are in diverse lines of business. Bombardier is a good example, with three distinct divisions: aerospace, ski-doo/sea-doo, and mass transit. Each of these different businesses typically demands a separate strategy. Moreover, these multibusiness companies also have diverse functional departments, such as finance and marketing, that support each of their businesses. As a result, we need to differentiate between corporate-level, business-level, and functional-level strategies. (See Figure 8-1.)

corporate-level strategy Seeks to determine what businesses a corporation should be in.

Corporate-Level Strategy

If an organization is in more than one type of business, it will need a **corporate-level strategy**. This strategy seeks to answer the question: What business or businesses should we be in?

FIGURE 8-1 Levels of Strategy

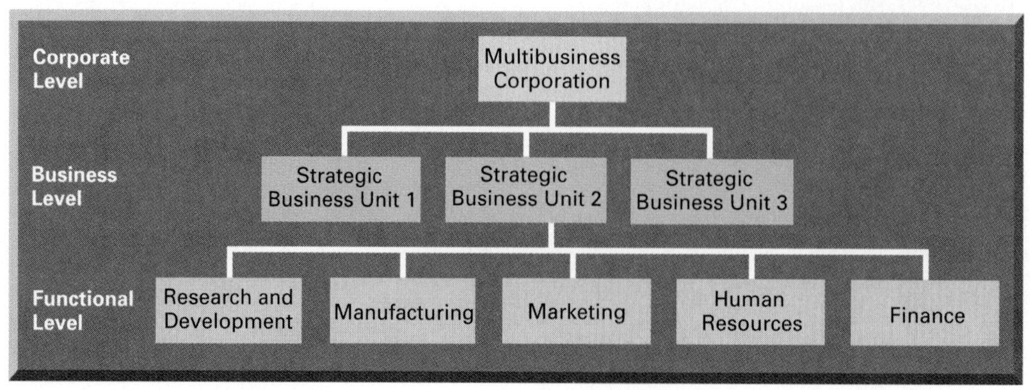

Corporate-level strategy determines the roles that each business unit in the organization will play. At a company such as Imasco, top management's corporate level strategy integrates the strategies of the company's various divisions. Imasco sets corporate level strategy for Imperial Tobacco (makers of Dumaurier, Players, and other brands); CT Financial Services (operating Canada Trust and other financial companies); Genstar Development (a company that develops planned residential communities); and Shoppers Drug Mart/Pharmaprix (Canada's largest drugstore chain). In 1998, Imasco made a major change in its corporate level strategy and decided that it should sell its Fast Food Merchandisers (FFM) subsidiary (a company with $1.3 million in annual revenue). Corporate level strategy thereby changed at Imasco to focus on its other four primary businesses.

Business-Level Strategy

Business-level strategy seeks to answer the question: How should we compete in each of our businesses? For the small organization in only one line of business, or the large organization that has not diversified into different products or markets, the business-level strategy is typically the same as the organization's corporate strategy. For organizations in multiple businesses, each division will have its own strategy that defines the products or services it will offer, the customers it wants to reach, and the like. So, Imasco will therefore have different business level strategies for each of its divisions. Imperial Tobacco, which controls 68 percent of the Canadian tobacco market, has its own business level strategy, as does Shoppers Drug Mart.

business-level strategy Seeks to determine how a corporation should compete in each of its businesses.

When an organization is in a number of different businesses, planning can be facilitated by creating strategic business units. A **strategic business unit (SBU)** represents a single business or group of related businesses. Each SBU will have its own unique mission, competitors and strategy. This distinguishes an SBU from the other businesses of the parent organization. In a company like Bombardier, which has many diverse lines of business, management might create a dozen or more SBUs.

strategic business unit (SBU) A single business or collection of businesses that is independent and formulates its own strategy.

The SBU concept of planning separates business units based on the following principles:

- The organization is managed as a "portfolio" of businesses, each business unit serving a clearly defined product and market segment with a clearly defined strategy.
- Each business unit in the portfolio develops a strategy tailored to its capabilities and competitive needs, but consistent with the overall organization's capabilities and needs.
- The total portfolio is managed to serve the interests of the organization as a whole—to achieve balanced growth in sales, earnings, and asset mix at an acceptable and controlled level of risk.[6]

Functional-Level Strategy

Functional-level strategy seeks to answer the question: How do we support the business-level strategy? For organizations that have traditional functional departments such as manufacturing, marketing, human resources, research and development, and finance, these strategies need to support the business-level strategy. For instance, when PepsiCo's Taco Bell unit decided to open a new chain of full-service—Mexican-style restaurants—its marketing department developed a promotional strategy for the new concept, the research and development department created new product selections for the restaurants, and the human resources department developed new training programs for the management teams that would staff the new facilities.

functional-level strategy Seeks to determine how to support the business-level strategy.

We focus on corporate-level and business-level strategies in the rest of this chapter. This is not to diminish the importance of functional-level strategies. Rather, it reflects the emphasis that researchers and practitioners have placed on developing strategic frameworks.

1 **Differentiate between the three levels of strategy.**

2 **What is an SBU, and how is it distinguished from the parent corporation?**

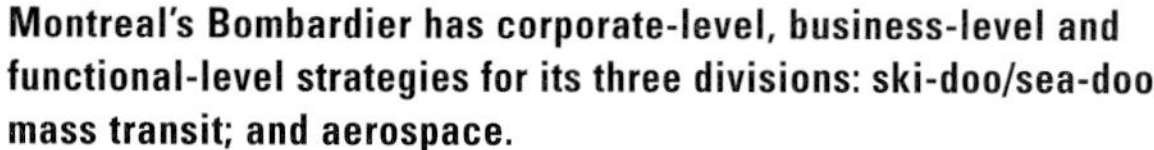

Montreal's Bombardier has corporate-level, business-level and functional-level strategies for its three divisions: ski-doo/sea-doo; mass transit; and aerospace.

THE STRATEGIC MANAGEMENT PROCESS

strategic management process
An eight-step process encompassing strategic planning, implementation and evaluation.

The **strategic management process**, as illustrated in Figure 8-2, is an eight-step process that encompasses strategic planning, implementation and evaluation. Although the first six steps describe the planning that must take place, implementation and evaluation are just as important. Even the best strategies can fail if management doesn't implement or evaluate them properly. In this section we'll examine in detail the various steps in the strategic management process.

Step 1: Identifying the Organization's Current Mission, Objectives and Strategies

mission
The purpose of an organization.

Every organization needs a **mission** that defines its purpose and answers the question: What is our reason for being in business? Defining the organization's mission forces management to

FIGURE 8-2 The Strategic Management Process

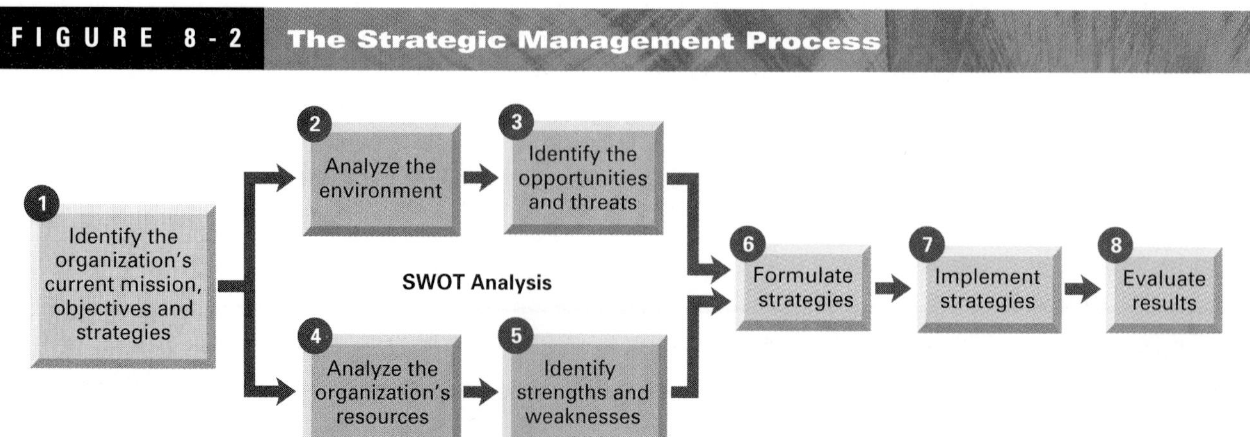

identify the scope of its products or services carefully. For instance, the mission of Canadian Tire Corp. is: "To be the first choice for Canadians in automotive, sports and leisure, and home products by providing total customer value through customer-driven service, focused assortments and competitive operations."[7] This statement provides clues as to what this organization sees as its reason for being in business. (See Figure 8-3 for a further description of the typical components of mission statements.) When a company does a poor job of defining its purpose and scope of purpose, the results can be disastrous. For instance, Eaton's had dominated the Canadian retailing scene for over a century, but the changing face of the industry—led by Wal-Mart—forced Eaton's into bankruptcy. Many retail analysts believe that Eaton's problems stemmed from an inability to clearly define its mission—the company lost its focus and couldn't compete with retailers who had clearly defined missions.

At R R Donnelley & Sons Co., the world's largest commercial printer, CEO John Walter says his company isn't in the business of just slapping ink on paper.[8] Instead he describes Donnelley's business as delivering information from publishers to consumers in many different formats. Some of their newest formats have included compact discs, data bases, and other forms of software. Specifying Donnelley's mission in this way may seem a minor point, but it isn't—it provides guidance to management. As technology and customer demands change, Donnelley can move in those directions because it is not strictly limited to "printing" in the traditional sense.

Determining the purpose or reason for one's business is as important for non-profit organizations as it is for business firms. For example, is a college seeking students from the top five percent of high school graduates, students with low academic grades but high aptitude test scores, or students in the vast middle ground? Is it training students for the professions, training students for particular jobs, or educating students through a well-rounded liberal education?

Answers to questions like these clarify the organization's current purpose. Some Canadian colleges have formed links with business to achieve the goals of their current missions. The

FIGURE 8-3 Mission Statement Components

1. Customer market	We believe our first responsibility is to the doctors, nurses and patients, to mothers and all others who use our products and services. (Johnson & Johnson)
2. Product and service	AMAX's principal products are molybdenum, coal, iron ore, copper, lead, zinc, petroleum and natural gas, potash, phosphates, nickel, tungsten, silver, gold, and magnesium. (AMAX)
3. Geographical domain	We are dedicated to the total success of Corning Glass Works as a worldwide competitor. (Corning Glass)
4. Technology	Control Data is in the business of applying microelectronics and computer technology in two general areas: computer-related hardware and computing-enhancing services, which include computation, information, education, and finance. (Control Data)
5. Concern for survival	In this respect, the company will conduct its operations prudently and will provide the profits and growth which will assure Hoover's ultimate success. (Hoover Universal)
6. Philosophy	We believe human development to be the worthiest of goals of civilization and independence to be the superior condition for nurturing growth in the capabilities of people. (Sun Company)
7. Self-concept	Hoover Universal is a diversified, multi-industry corporation with strong manufacturing capabilities, entrepreneurial policies, and individual business unit autonomy. (Hoover Universal)
8. Concern for public image	Also, we must be responsive to the broader concerns of the public, including especially the general desire for improvement in the quality of life, equal opportunity for all and the constructive use of natural resources. (Sun Company)

Source: J A Pearce, II, and F. R. David, "Corporate Mission Statements: The Bottom Line," *Academy of Management Executive,* May 1992, pp. 109–116.

In establishing links with high-tech businesses, Algonquin College in Ontario is pursuing its purpose of graduating students skilled in the latest technology.

Chrysler Canada
www.chrysler.com/

Algonquin College
www.algonquinc.on.ca/

Baldwin-Cartier school in Pierrefonds, Quebec, has formed an alliance with Chrysler Canada Ltd. to train students for high-tech auto mechanics work at Chrysler dealerships. Algonquin College in Ontario has formed an alliance with two software companies and Bell Canada to provide the tools necessary to graduate students skilled in the latest technology.[9]

It is also important for management to identify the objectives and strategies currently being used. As we explained in Chapter 7, objectives are the foundation of planning. A company's objectives provide the measurable performance targets that workers strive to reach. Knowing the company's current objectives gives managers a basis for deciding whether or not these objectives need to be changed. For the same reasons, it's important for managers to identify the strategies currently being used.

Step 2: Analyzing the External Environment

In Chapter 3, we described the external environment as a primary constraint on a manager's actions. Analyzing that environment is a crucial step in the strategy process. Why? Because an organization's environment, to a large degree, defines management's available options. A successful strategy will be one that aligns well with the environment.[10]

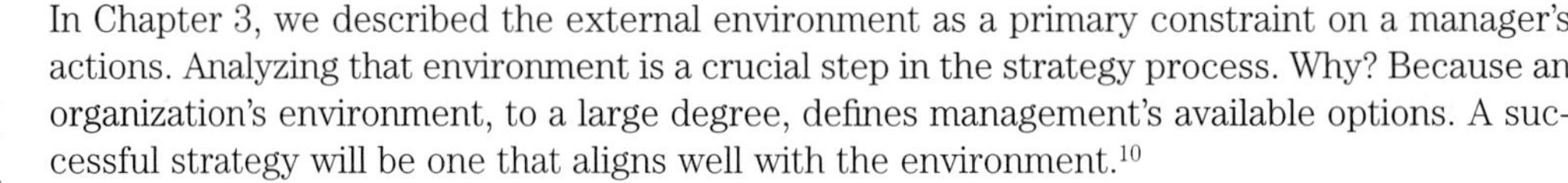

JDS Fitel Inc.
www.jdsfitel.com

JDS Fitel Inc. of Nepean, Ontario, makes components for the fibre-optics industry. It is an industry that is estimated to grow from its 1999 level of $5 billion to around $40 billion in the next eight years.[11] JDS Fitel is taking advantage of this, supplying components to major fibre-optics companies like Northern Telecom here, and others like Lucent Technologies (US), Alcatel Alsthom SA (France), and Pirelli Cable Corp. (Italy), worldwide. With revenue growing from $74.8 million in 1996 to around $200 million today, JDS Fitel has been able to keep pace with, and take advantage of, the vast expansion of the industry.

Managers in every organization need to analyze the environment. They need to know, for instance, what the competition is doing, what pending legislation might affect the organization, and what the labour supply is like in locations where it operates.

Step 2 of the strategic management process is complete when management has an accurate grasp of what is taking place in its environment, and is aware of important trends that might affect its operations.

Step 3: Identifying Opportunities and Threats

opportunities
Positive external environmental factors.

threats
Negative external environmental factors.

After analyzing the environment, management needs to assess what it has learned in terms of opportunities that the organization can exploit and the threats it faces.[12] **Opportunities** are positive external environmental factors while **threats** are negative.

Keep in mind that the same environment can present opportunities to one organization and pose threats to another in the same industry, because of their different management of resources. While a multitude of small operations have come and gone in the turbulent

After carefully analysing opportunities and threats, Clive Beddoe of Westjet has managed exceptional growth in the Canadian west, where many before have failed.

Canadian airline industry, Westjet Airlines has managed to succeed very profitably in the regional sectors of the Canadian West.

Step 4: Analyzing the Organization's Resources

Now we move from looking outside the organization to looking inside. For example, what skills and abilities do the organization's employees have; has it been successful at innovating new products; what is the organization's cash flow; and how do consumers perceive the organization and the quality of its products or services?

This step forces management to recognize that every organization, no matter how large or powerful, is constrained in some way by the resources and skills it has available. The internal analysis provides important information about an organization's specific assets, skills and work activities. If any of these organizational skills or resources are exceptional or unique, they're called the organization's **core competencies**. The core competencies are the organization's major value-creating skills, capabilities and resources that determine the organization's competitive weapons. When Montreal-based Arrow Manufacturing Inc., a maker of men's belts, decided to move into the luggage business, the results were disastrous. Arrow discovered that belts and luggage were two very different businesses. Since luggage is sold in leather-goods stores rather than clothing stores, it requires a completely different sales force. Handling luggage also requires great amounts of storage space to keep large inventories. And Arrow found that it could not control the quality of the luggage products. Simply put, Arrow did not have the resources to move into this new field and it cost the company over a million dollars in losses. Now Arrow is back to its successful business of producing men's belts.[13]

core competencies
An organization's major value-creating skills, capabilities and resources that determine its competitive weapons.

Step 5: Identifying Strengths and Weaknesses

The analysis in Step 4 should lead to a clear assessment of the organization's internal resources (such as capital, technical expertise, skilled workforce, and experienced management). It

3 What is a mission and why is it important?

4 What are (a) external analyses? (b) core competencies?

should also point out the organization's abilities in performing the different functional activities (such as marketing, production and operations, research and development, finance and accounting, information systems, and human resources management). Any activities the organization does well or any resources that it has available are called **strengths**. **Weaknesses** are activities the organization doesn't do well or resources it needs but doesn't possess. If any of these organizational skills or resources are exceptional or unique, they're called the organization's **distinctive competence**. Management can use these unique or exceptional skills and resources to determine the organization's competitive weapons. For instance, when Black & Decker bought General Electric's small appliances division—which made coffee makers, toasters, irons, and so on—it renamed them and capitalized on B&D's reputation for quality and durability, to make these appliances far more profitable than they had been under the GE name.

strengths
Activities the firm does well or resources it controls.

weaknesses
Activities the firm doesn't do well or resources it needs but doesn't have.

distinctive competence
The exceptional or unique skills and resources that determine the organization's competitive weapons.

An understanding of the organization's culture and the strengths and drawbacks it offers management is a crucial part of Step 5 that's often overlooked.[14] Specifically, managers should be aware that strong and weak cultures have different effects on strategy and that the content of a culture has a major effect on the chosen strategy.

As we discussed in Chapter 3, an organization's culture is its personality. It reflects the values, beliefs, attitudes and valued behaviours that embody the "way things are done around here". In a strong culture almost all employees will have a clear understanding of what the organization is about. This should make it easier for management to convey to new employees the organization's distinctive competence. At a department store chain such as The Bay, which has a very strong culture that emphasizes customer service and satisfaction, managers are able to instill cultural values in new employees in a much shorter time than a competitor with a weak culture. The negative side of a strong culture, of course, is that it's more difficult to change. A strong culture may act as a significant barrier to acceptance of a change in the organization's strategies. Successful organizations with strong cultures can become prisoners of their own past successes.

Cultures differ in the degree to which they encourage risk taking, exploit innovation and reward performance. Since strategic choices encompass such factors, cultural values influence managerial preference for certain strategies. In a risk-aversive culture, for example, management is more likely to favour strategies that are defensive, that minimize financial exposure, and that react to changes in the environment rather than trying to anticipate those changes. Where risk is avoided, you shouldn't be surprised to find management's strategies emphasizing cost cutting and improving established product lines. Conversely, where innovation is highly valued, management is likely to favour new technology and product development instead of more service locations or a superior sales force. Corel's CEO, Michael Cowpland, realizes this, and has never shied away from the risks of new markets. Mind you, when a company is forced to stay ahead of industry changes in an ever-changing industry such as computer software, not all moves will turn out to be successes. Corel (and specifically Cowpland) began to come under major pressure from stockholders after unsuccessful forays into the CD-ROM market and word processing software.

Corel Corporation
www.corel.com

Organizational culture also can promote or hinder an organization's strategic actions. One study showed that firms with "strategically appropriate cultures" outperformed selected other corporations with less appropriate cultures.[15] Just what is a strategically appropriate culture? It's one that supports the firm's chosen strategy. For instance, Longo Brothers Fruit Markets Inc. of Mississauga concentrates on excellent produce, knowledgeable staff, and a more personal relationship with customers from the family-owned grocery chain (they also have a 1-800 number which is answered by staff armed with a binder of information and which operates seven days a week to handle any enquiries). The chain of stores has an organizational culture that supports the strategic emphasis on customer service.[16] The merging of Steps 3 and 5 results in an assessment of the organization's internal resources and abilities, and its opportunities and threats in its external environment. (See Figure 8-4.) This is frequently called **SWOT analysis** because it brings together the organization's **S**trengths, **W**eaknesses, **O**pportunities, and **T**hreats in order to identify a strategic niche that the organization might exploit. For instance, as prices for pulp and paper products started to rise drastically in 1995—after a major drop during the recessionary years of the early 1990s—Repap started up a new mill in northern New Brunswick. Although advised against the move, Repap managers knew that they had to take advantage of the opportunity in the external environment.

SWOT analysis
Analysis of an organization's strengths and weaknesses, and its environmental opportunities and threats.

In light of the SWOT analysis, management also re-evaluates its current mission and objectives. Are they realistic? Do they need modification? Are we where we want to be right

FIGURE 8-4 Identifying the Organization's Opportunities

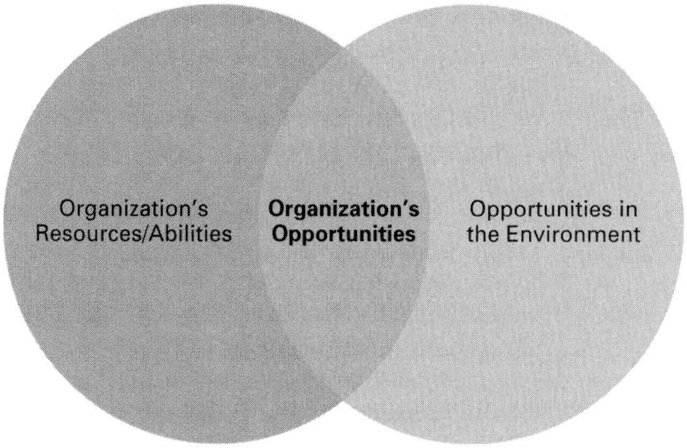

now? If changes are needed in the overall direction, this is where they're likely to originate. If no changes are necessary, management is ready to begin the actual formulation of strategies.

Step 6: Formulating Strategies

Strategies need to be established for the corporate, business, and functional levels. The formulation of these strategies follows the decision-making process we discussed in Chapter 6. Specifically, management needs to develop and evaluate strategic alternatives and then select strategies that are compatible at each level, and which allow the organization to best capitalize on its strengths and environmental opportunities.

Step 6 is complete when management has developed a set of strategies that will give the organization a competitive advantage. That is, management will seek to position the organization so that it can gain a relative advantage over its rivals. As you'll see later in the chapter, this requires a careful evaluation of the competitive forces that dictate the rules of competition within the organization's industry. Successful managers will choose strategies that give their organization the most favourable competitive advantage; then they will try to sustain that advantage over time. The strategy of Casket Royale (based in New Hampshire) is to offer burial caskets at a far cheaper rate than the funeral homes. Casket Royale manufactures caskets and sells them through its outlets (over 200 of them) such as the 11 it has in Toronto.

Step 7: Implementing Strategies

The next-to-last step in the strategic management process is implementation. A strategy is only as good as its implementation. No matter how effectively a company has planned its strategies, it cannot succeed if the strategies aren't implemented properly. The rest of the chapters in this book address a number of issues related to strategy implementation.

For instance, in Chapter 10, we'll discuss the strategy-structure relationship. We'll show how successful strategies require a properly matched organizational structure. If an organization significantly changes its strategy, it needs to make appropriate changes in its overall structural design. In fact, we'll show that many of the new designs for organizational structure are ways in which organizations can cope with environmental and strategic changes.

Management might need to recruit, select, train, discipline, transfer, promote and possibly even lay off employees to achieve the organization's strategic objectives. In Chapter 2, we discussed the impact that downsizing is having on management's actions. In Chapter 11, we'll show that, if new strategies are to succeed, they will often require hiring new people with different skills, transferring some current employees to new positions, or laying off some employees. Also, since more and more organizations are using teams, the ability to build and manage effective teams is an important part of implementing strategy. Chapter 14 describes how managers can develop effective teams.

Doing a Personal SWOT Analysis

A SWOT analysis can be a useful tool for examining your own skills, abilities, career preferences and career opportunities. Doing a personal SWOT analysis involves taking a hard-nosed look at what your individual strengths and weaknesses are and then assessing the opportunities and threats of various career paths that you might be interested in.[17]

Step 1: Assessing personal strengths and weaknesses. All of us have special skills, talents and abilities. Also, each of us enjoys doing certain activities and not others. For example, some people hate sitting at a desk all day; others panic at the thought of having to interact with strangers. Make a list of those activities you enjoy and the things you are good at. (The Self-Assessment Exercise found at the end of every chapter can help you to define some of your strengths.) Also, identify some things you're not so good at and don't enjoy. It's just as important to recognize our weaknesses so we can either try to correct them or to stay away from careers in which those things would be important. Make a list of your important individual strengths and weaknesses. Highlight those which you think are particularly significant.

Step 2: Identifying Career Opportunities and Threats. We know from this chapter and Chapter 3 that different industries (and the companies in those industries!) face different external opportunities and threats. It's important to identify these external factors for the simple reason that your initital job offer(s) and future career advancement can be significantly influenced by these opportunities and threats. A company that's in an industry filled with several negative factors will offer few job openings and career advancement opportunities. In contrast, job prospects will be brighter in industries where there are abundant positive external factors. List two or three industries you have an interest in (for example, health care, financial services, or telecommunications) and critically evaluate the opportunities and threats facing these industries.

Step 3: Outlining five-year career objectives. Taking your SWOT assessments, make a list of four or five career objectives that you would like to accomplish within five years of graduation. These objectives might include things such as type of job you'd like to have, how many people you might be supervising, or the type of salary you'd like to be making. Keep in mind that, ideally, you should try to match your individual strengths with industry opportunities.

Step 4: Outline a five-year career action plan. Now it's time to get specific! Write a specific career action plan for accomplishing each of the career objectives you identified in the previous step. State exactly what you will need to do, and by when, in order to meet each objective. If you think you will need special assistance, state what it is and how you will get it. For example, your personal SWOT analysis may indicate that to achieve your desired career objective, you need to take more courses in management. Your career action plan should indicate when you will take these courses. Your specific career action plan will provide you with guidance for making decisions, just like an organization's plans provide direction to managers.

Doing this type of personal SWOT analysis takes effort, yet the payoff will be a coherent, realistic career strategy that you can pursue. Having a challenging, rewarding and fun career doesn't just happen (at least not to most of us!). By spending some time in identifying what's personally important, you can develop a strategic plan and assure that it's effectively implemented to your satisfaction. ■

Top management leadership is a necessary ingredient in a successful strategy. So, too, is a motivated group of middle- and lower-level managers who carry out senior management's specific plans. Chapters 15 and 16 discuss ways in which to motivate people, and offer suggestions for improving leadership effectiveness.

Step 8: Evaluating Results

The final step in the strategic management process is evaluating results. How effective have our strategies been? What adjustments, if any, are necessary? At IBM, CEO Lou Gerstner made strategic adjustments to improve his company's competitiveness in the computer industry.

These strategic actions were developed after assessing the results of previous strategies and determining that changes were needed.

In Chapter 17 we'll review the control process. The concepts and techniques that we introduce in that chapter can be used to assess the results of strategies and to correct significant deviations.

CORPORATE-LEVEL STRATEGIC FRAMEWORKS

We defined corporate-level strategy as asking the question: What business or businesses do we want to be in? Two popular approaches for answering this question are the grand strategies framework and the corporate portfolio matrix.

Grand Strategies

Irving Oil and BCE are both large companies that have enjoyed profitability. However, in recent years, each one seems to be going in a different direction. Essentially, Irving Oil's management seems to be maintaining the status quo. BCE continues to expand its operations and develop new businesses; recently it entered Britain's cable TV market. These different directions can be explained in terms of grand or all-encompassing strategies.[18] Figure 8-5 shows each of the grand strategies in relation to the SWOT analysis.

stability strategy
A corporate-level strategy characterized by an absence of significant change.

Stability. A **stability strategy** is characterized by an absence of significant change. Examples of this strategy include continuing to serve the same clients by offering the same

FIGURE 8-5 SWOT Analysis and Grand Strategies

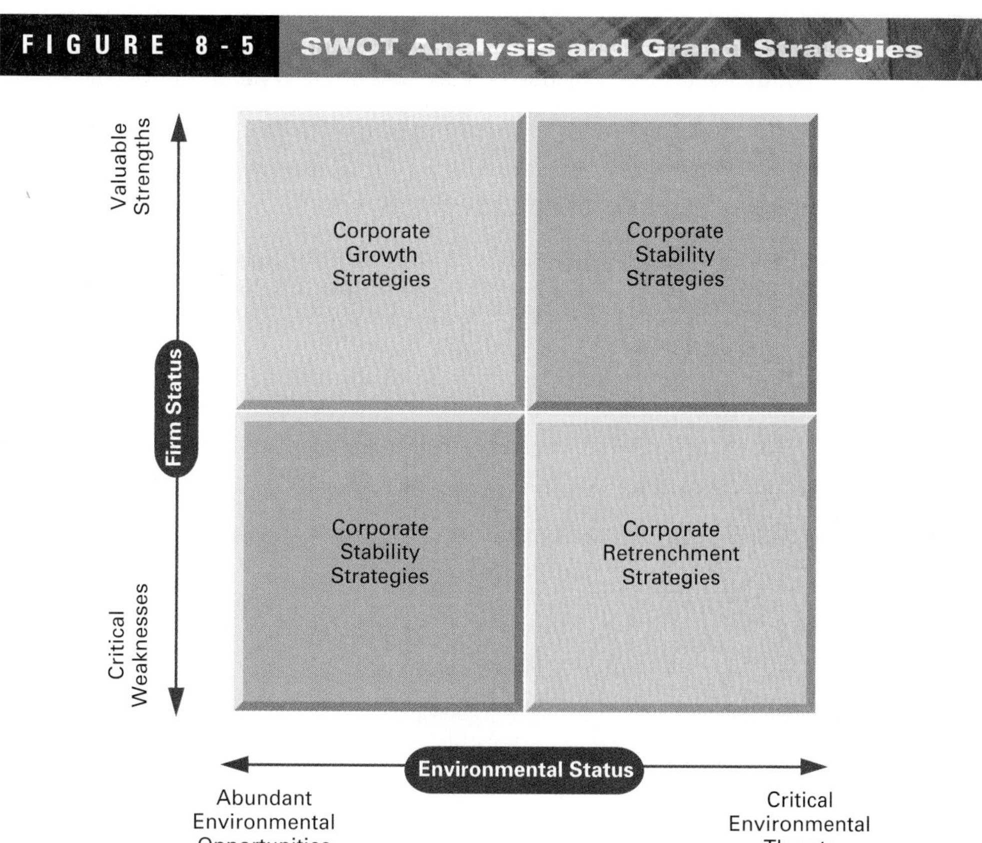

Source: P Wright, C D Pringle and M J Kroll, *Strategic Management*, 2d ed. (Boston: Allyn and Bacon, 1994), p. 82.

5 List the eight steps in the strategic management process.

6 Why is a SWOT analysis important?

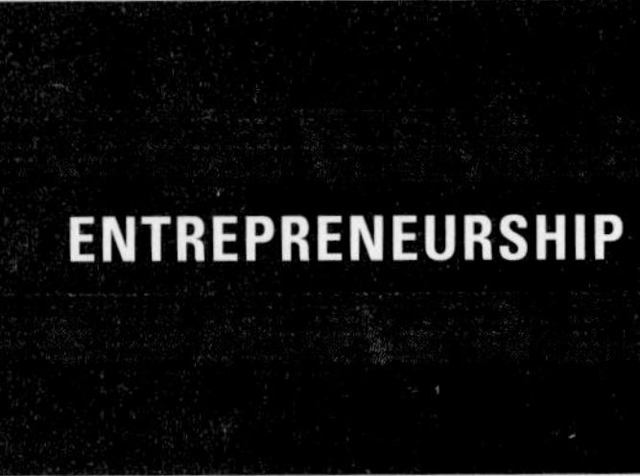

Strategy and the Entrepreneur

Strategic planning carries a "big business" bias. It implies a formalization and structure that fits well with large, established organizations that have abundant resources. Yet many strategic planning concepts can be applied directly to those who wish to pursue the entrepreneurial route in management, but with a different emphasis.[19]

Entrepreneurs approach strategy differently from the way typical bureaucratic managers do. This can be seen in the way in which they address key strategic questions. The typical bureaucratic managers ask strategic questions in the following order: What resources do I control? What structure determines our organization's relationship to its market? How can I minimize the impact of others on my ability to perform? What opportunity is appropriate? In contrast, the typical entrepreneur will ask: Where is the opportunity? How do I capitalize on it? What resources do I need? How do I gain control over them? What structure is best?

The entrepreneur's strategic emphasis is driven by *perception of opportunity* rather than by *availability of resources*. The entrepreneur's inclination is to monitor the environment closely in search of opportunities. The resources at his or her disposal take a back seat to identifying an idea that can be pursued.

Once an opportunity is identified, the entrepreneur begins to look for ways in which to take advantage of it. Because an entrepreneur's personality characteristics typically include hard work, self-confidence, optimism, determination and a high energy level, he or she is confident that the opportunity can be exploited. Moreover, the entrepreneur is not afraid to risk financial security, career opportunities, family relations or psychic well-being, in order to get the new venture off the ground. Entrepreneurs tend to ignore the cold hard facts about a new business's chances for success. (One study found that 40 percent of new businesses fail in the first year, 60 percent fail by the end of the second year, and 90 percent fail by the end of the tenth year. ■

product or service, maintaining market share, and sustaining the organization's past return-on-investment record.

When should management pursue stability? When it views the organization's performance as satisfactory and the environment appears stable and unchanging—that is, the firm has no valuable strengths or critical weaknesses and there are no abundant environmental opportunities to pursue, but also no critical threats to avoid.

It's not easy to identify organizations pursuing a stability strategy, if for no other reason than the fact that few top executives are willing to admit it. In North America, for instance, growth tends to have universal appeal, and retrenchment is often accepted as a necessary evil. The active pursuit of stability can result in management being considered complacent or even smug.

We mentioned Irving Oil as an example of a firm using this strategy. The company seems to have little interest in changing its operations and, instead, seems content to maintain what it has.

growth strategy
A corporate-level strategy that seeks to increase the level of the organization's operations. This typically includes increasing revenues, employees, and/or market share.

Growth. The pursuit of growth has traditionally had a magical appeal for North American firms. Supposedly, bigger is better and biggest is best, of course! For us, **growth strategy** means increasing the level of the organization's operations. (Refer again to Figure 8-5.) This includes such popular measures as more sales revenues, more employees and more market share. Growth can be achieved through direct expansion, a merger with or acquisition of similar firms, or diversification.

Growth through direct expansion (or concentration) is achieved by internally increasing a firm's sales, its production capacity or its workforce. No other firms are acquired or merged with; instead the company chooses to grow by itself through its own business operations. For instance, McDonald's had always pursued a growth strategy by way of direct expansion, until 1998 when, for the first time, the company invested in another restaurant chain (Chipotle Mexican Grill).

A company might also choose to grow directly by creating (not acquiring or merging with) new businesses that operate in the same business as the original firm, in related businesses, or

Montreal-based Seagram Co. Ltd.'s latest foray into diversification was the 1998 purchase of music industry colossus, PolyGram. The company's previous major acquisition outside of its traditional liquor business was the purchase of Universal, the giant entertainment company, the film division of which has contracts to work with Steven Spielberg and David Geffen's Dreamworks.

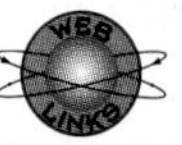

Universal
http://www.mca.com/

in unrelated businesses. As an example, the western Canadian restaurant chain, Earl's, created a new chain of restaurants named Joey Tomatoes.

Finally, a company could grow directly by creating businesses within its own vertical channel of distribution. For instance, the trucking company OTR Express set up its own fuel depots to supply its trucks.

Another popular way that many companies choose to grow is by merging with or acquiring *similar* firms in a strategic move known as **related diversification**. A **merger** occurs when two or more firms, usually of similar size, combine into one through an exchange of shares. The proposed merger of the Bank of Montreal with the Royal Bank was huge news when it was announced in 1998. The idea behind it was to create a bank that could compete more effectively in the rapidly consolidating global banking industry.

Growth can also occur by **acquisition**, which occurs when one company acquires another company through a payment of cash or shares, or some combination of the two. In 1998, Maple Leaf Gardens Ltd., owners of the Toronto Maple Leafs, acquired the National Basketball Association's Toronto Raptors—with plans to have both teams play their games under one roof.

Finally, a company can choose to grow by **unrelated diversification**—merging with or acquiring *unrelated* firms, or firms that are not directly related to what the company does. The subject of this chapter's Case Application—Montreal's Seagram Co.—shows how this company has had a long history of such growth.

Retrenchment. Until the 1980s, retrenchment was a dirty word to North American managers. No one wanted to admit that he or she was pursuing a **retrenchment strategy**—reducing the size or diversity of their operations. However, in the last decade, managing decline has become one of the most actively investigated issues in the field of management.[20] There has been no shortage of Canadian firms that have recently pursued a retrenchment strategy. Molson Cos. Ltd. has been following a retrenchment strategy which focuses on its brewing interests, shedding non-core assets like Home Depot Canada.

related diversification
A way that companies choose to grow that involves merging with or acquiring *similar* firms.

merger
When two or more firms, usually of similar size, combine into one through an exchange of shares.

acquisition
When one company acquires another company through a payment of cash or shares or some combination of the two.

unrelated diversification
A way that companies choose to grow that involves merging with or acquiring *unrelated* firms, or firms whose business is not directly related to what the company does.

retrenchment strategy
A corporate-level strategy that seeks to reduce the size or diversity of an organization's operations.

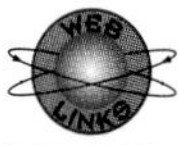

Molson Cos. Ltd.
www.molson.com

THINKING CRITICALLY ABOUT ETHICS

You're an assistant store manager for a discount store chain, and you are opening a new store in Moncton, New Brunswick. You are being helped by five people who have been transferred from other locations and have been told that this was a "management training" program. Everyone works hard getting the store ready on time. One week after the store opens, your boss tells you to find a reason to let three of the five people go, because there is only room for two management trainees. Do you think that it is wrong to let these people go? What ethical dilemmas do you see? How would you handle this situation? ■

combination strategy
A corporate-level strategy that simultaneously pursues two or more of the strategies of stability, growth and retrenchment.

BCG matrix
Strategy tool to guide resource allocation decisions based on market share and growth of SBUs.

cash cows
Products that demonstrate low growth but have a high market share.

stars
Products that demonstrate high growth and have high market share.

question marks
Products that demonstrate high growth but have low market share.

dogs
Products that demonstrate low growth and have low market share.

cumulative experience curve
Assumes that when a business increases the amount of product manufactured, the per-unit cost of the product will decrease.

Combination. A **combination strategy** is the simultaneous pursuit of two or more of the previous strategies. The Case Study from Chapter 6—SMK Speedy International Inc.—is an example of a company pursuing a combination strategy. The company is following a retrenchment strategy in its US division, a stability strategy in Canada, and a growth strategy in France.

Corporate Portfolio Matrix

One of the most popular approaches to corporate-level strategy has been the corporate portfolio matrix.[21] Developed by the Boston Consulting Group in the early 1970s, this approach introduced the idea that each of an organization's SBUs could be evaluated and plotted on a 2 × 2 matrix to identify which ones offered high potential and which were a drain on organizational resources.[22] Their **BCG matrix** is shown in Figure 8-6. The horizontal axis represents market share and the vertical axis indicates anticipated market growth. For definitional purposes, high market share means that a business is the leader in its industry and high market growth is defined as at least 10 percent annual growth in sales (after adjusting for inflation). The matrix defines four business groups:

Cash cows (low growth, high market share). Products in this category generate large amounts of cash, but their prospects for future growth are limited.

Stars (high growth, high market share). These products are in a fast-growing market and hold a dominant share of that market but might or might not produce a positive cash flow, depending on the need for investment in new plant and equipment or product development.

Question marks (high growth, low market share). These are speculative products that entail high risks. They may be profitable but they hold a small percentage of market share.

Dogs (low growth, low market share). This category doesn't produce much cash, nor does it require much. These products hold no promise for improved performance.

It's important to understand that the BCG matrix assumes the existence of a **cumulative experience curve**. This is the assumption that if a company is producing a product and managing its production process properly, every significant *increase* in the cumulative amount of product manufactured will bring about a predictable *decrease* in the per-unit cost of manu-

FIGURE 8-6 The BCG Matrix

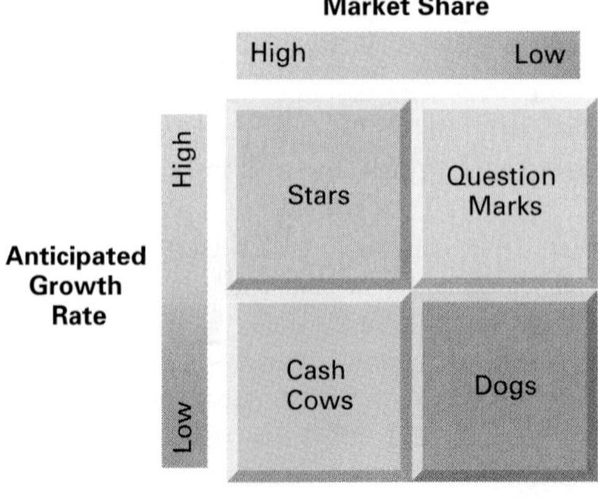

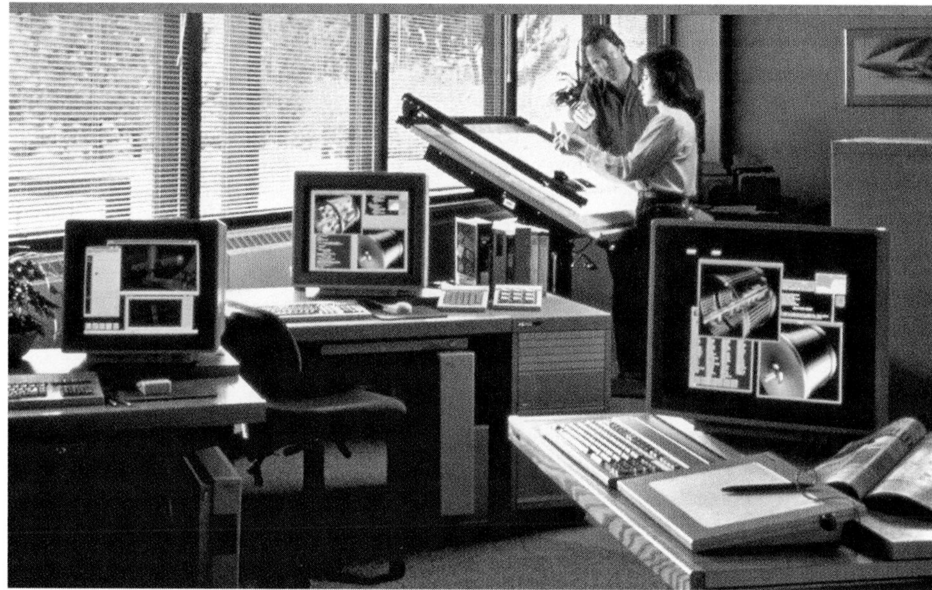

Hewlett-Packard manufactures medical equipment, analytical instruments for the chemical and food industries, equipment for environmental monitoring, business and scientific calculators, personal computers, scanners, palmtops, and printers. One way it could evaluate the operations of each of its strategic business units is to use the Boston Consulting Group matrix.

facturing the product. Specifically, the Boston Consulting Group contends that doubling manufacturing volume typically leads to a 20 to 30 percent reduction in unit cost. The obvious conclusion then is that businesses with the largest market share should have the lowest costs.

Now let's turn specifically to the strategic implications of the BCG matrix. What strategy should management pursue with each group?

BCG's research shows that organizations that sacrifice short-term profits to gain market share yield the highest long-term profits. So management should "milk" cash cows for as much as they can, limit any new investment in them to the minimal maintenance level, and use the large amounts of cash generated by them to invest in stars. Heavy investment in stars pays high dividends. The stars, of course, will eventually develop into cash cows as their markets mature and sales growth slows. The hardest decision relates to the question marks. Some should be sold off and others turned into stars, which requires substantial investment of resources. But question marks are risky, so management wants to have only a limited number of these speculative ventures. The dogs pose no strategic problems—they should be sold off or liquidated at the earliest opportunity. There is little to recommend dogs remaining in the corporate portfolio or receiving further company resources. Money obtained from selling off dogs can be used to buy or finance question marks. For example, the BCG matrix might indicate to McGraw-Hill management that it should sell off its trade book business because it's a dog, milk its cash cow college textbook business, and invest in a star such as *Business Week* or a question mark such as database information products.

In the 1990s, the portfolio concept (and the BCG matrix in particular) has lost much of its lustre. Why? There are at least four reasons.[23] First, not every organization has found that increased market share leads to lower costs. To successfully move down the experience curve, management must tightly control costs. Intel is an example of an organization that has been able to take advantage of volume and experience curve economies in its production of computer memory chips. Its sizable production volume (in 1993, over 40 million 486 chips alone) makes it possible for Intel to invest heavily in research and development and in new plant capacity, and still earn huge profits. Unfortunately, not all organizations have been able to do this. Second, the portfolio concept assumes that an organization's businesses can be divided into a reasonable number of independent units. For large, complex organizations, this has been a lot easier in theory than in practice. Third, contrary to predictions, many so-called dogs have shown consistently higher levels of profitability than their growing competitors with dominant market shares. For example, according to the BCG matrix, Rolex would be considered a dog. Yet it has been a highly profitable company. Finally, given the rate at which the economy has been growing in recent years and the fact that a market can have only one leader, well over half of all businesses by definition fall into the dog category. Following the corporate portfolio concept, most organizations' businesses today are cash cows and dogs and there are few stars and question marks in which to invest.

Despite these problems, the corporate portfolio matrix can be a useful concept. It provides a framework for understanding disparate businesses and establishes priorities for making resource allocation decisions. However, it has definite limitations as a device for guiding management in establishing corporate-level strategy.

BUSINESS-LEVEL STRATEGIC FRAMEWORKS

Now we move to the business level, where managers decide how they want their business units to compete in the marketplace. In discussing the business-level strategies, we need to look at the role that competitive advantage plays, and then at the various competitive strategies.

The Role Of Competitive Advantage

competitive advantage What sets an organization apart; its competitive edge.

Competitive advantage is a key concept in strategic management. It is what sets an organization apart—its distinctive edge. That edge might be in the form of organizational capabilities (the organization does something that others cannot do, or does it better than others can do it), or it might arise from organizational assets or resources (the organization has something that its competitors do not have). Every organization has the resources and work systems to do whatever it's in business to do, but not every organization is able to effectively exploit its resources or capabilities, or to develop the core competencies that can provide it with a competitive advantage. And it's not enough for an organization to simply create a competitive advantage, it must be able to sustain it. A sustainable competitive advantage enables the organization to keep its edge despite competitors' actions or changes in the industry.

Competitive Strategies

Many important ideas in strategic planning have come from the work of Michael Porter of the Harvard Business School.[24] His competitive strategies framework identifies three generic strategies that managers can choose from. Success depends on selecting the right strategy—the one that fits the competitive strengths of the organization and the industry it's in. Porter's major contribution has been to carefully outline how management can create and sustain a competitive advantage that will give the company above-average profitability.

Industry Analysis. Porter proposes that some industries are inherently more profitable (and therefore more attractive to enter or remain in) than others. For example, the pharmaceutical industry is one with historically high profit margins and the airline industry has notoriously low ones. However, this doesn't mean that a company can't make a lot of money in a "dull" industry. The key is to exploit a competitive advantage. Consistent with this logic, we would expect that firms can lose money in so-called glamour industries like personal computers and cable television, while making it big in mundane industries such as manufacturing fire trucks and selling remanufactured auto parts.

In any industry, five competitive forces dictate the rules of competition:

1. *Barriers to entry*: Factors such as economies of scale, brand loyalty and capital requirements determine how easy or hard it is for new competitors to enter an industry.
2. *Threat of substitutes*: Factors such as switching costs and buyer loyalty determine the degree to which customers are likely to buy a substitute product.
3. *Bargaining power of buyers*: Factors such as number of buyers in the market, buyer information, and the availability of substitutes determine the amount of influence buyers have in an industry.
4. *Bargaining power of suppliers*: Factors such as the degree of supplier concentration and availability of substitute inputs determine the amount of power that suppliers have over firms in the industry.
5. *Existing rivalry*: Factors such as industry growth, increasing or falling demand, and product differences determine how intense the competitive rivalry will be among firms in the industry.

FIGURE 8-7 Forces in the Industry Analysis

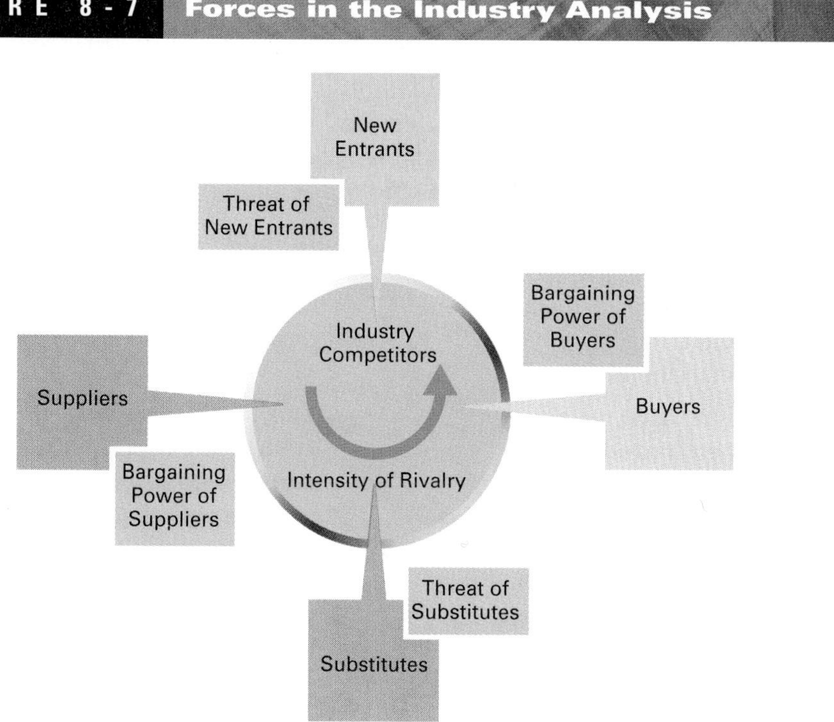

Source: Based on M E Porter, *Competitive Strategy: Techniques for Analyzing Industries and Competitors* (New York: The Free Press, 1980).

These five forces, in total (see Figure 8-7), determine industry profitability because they directly influence the prices that a firm can charge, its cost structure, and its investment requirements. Management should assess its industry's attractiveness by evaluating it in terms of these five factors. According to this framework, in 1993, the aluminum-window manufacturing business tended to look unattractive, while the pharmaceuticals industry looked enormously attractive. Of course, industry dynamics are always changing. An industry that is favourable one day can become unfavourable the next. Managers need to re-evaluate the status of their industry regularly.

Selecting a Competitive Advantage. According to Porter, no firm can successfully perform at an above-average level by trying to be all things to all people. He suggests that managers select a strategy that will give the organization a competitive advantage. A competitive advantage arises out of having either lower costs or being different. Based on these, managers can choose one of three strategies: cost leadership, differentiation and focus. Which of these management selects depends on the organization's strengths and distinctive competences, and on its competitors' weaknesses. (See Figure 8-8.)

When an organization sets out to be *the* low-cost producer in its industry, it's following a **cost leadership strategy**. A low cost leader aggressively searches out efficiencies in production, marketing and other areas of operation. Overhead is kept to a minimum, and the firm does everything it can to cut costs. You won't find expensive art or interior decor at offices of low-cost leaders! At Wal-Mart's headquarters in Bentonville, Arkansas, office furnishings are sparse and drab, but functional. Although low-cost leaders don't place a lot of emphasis on "frills", the product or service being sold must be perceived as being comparable to that offered by rivals, or should at least be acceptable to buyers. Examples of firms that have used the low-cost leader strategy include Wal-Mart, Union Carbide and Hyundai (the Korean automobile manufacturer).

cost leadership strategy
The strategy an organization follows when it wants to be the lowest-cost producer in its industry.

The firm that seeks to be unique in its product offering and in its industry in ways that customers widely value is following a **differentiation strategy**. Sources of differentiation might be high quality, extraordinary service, innovative design, technological capability, or an unusually positive brand image. The key to this strategy is that whatever product or service

differentiation strategy
The strategy a firm follows when it wants to be unique in its industry along dimensions widely valued by buyers.

FIGURE 8-8 Common Requirements for Successfully Pursuing Porter's Competitive Strategies

Generic Strategy	Commonly Required Skills and Resources	Common Organizational Requirements
Overall cost leadership	Sustained capital investment and access to capital Process engineering skills Intense supervision of labour Products designed for ease in manufacture Low-cost distribution system	Tight cost control Frequent, detailed control reports Structured organization and responsibilities Incentives based on meeting strict quantitative targets
Differentiation	Strong marketing abilities Product engineering Creative flair Strong capability in basic research Corporate reputation for quality or technological leadership Long tradition in the industry or unique combination of skills drawn from other businesses Strong co-operation from channels	Strong coordination among functions in R&D, product development, and marketing Subjective measurement and incentives instead of quantitative measures Amenities to attract highly skilled labour, scientists, or creative people
Focus	Combination of the above policies directed at the particular strategic target	Combination of the above policies directed at the particular strategic target

Source: Reprinted from Michael E Porter, *Competitive Strategy: Techniques for Analyzing Industries and Competitors* (New York: Free Press, 1980), pp. 40–41.

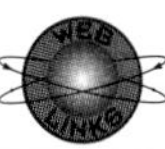

The Body Shop
www.the-body-shop.ca/

Maytag
www.maytag.com/

Mary Kay Cosmetics
www.marykay.com/

L L Bean
www.llbean.com/

attribute is chosen for differentiating must set the firm apart from its competitors and be significant enough to justify a price premium that exceeds the cost of differentiating.

Practically any successful consumer product or service can be identified as an example of the differentiation strategy—CAE (technology), The Body Shop (environmental responsibility), Maytag (reliability), Mary Kay cosmetics (distribution), and L L Bean (service) are a few. Sharp Corporation and Sanyo Electric illustrate how an effective differentiation strategy can lead to success, and how a poor definition of differentiation can lead to dismal results. Although the two companies are similiar in size and origin and have partly overlapping product lines, Sharp has profitably capitalized on its differentiation strategy. It uses unusual devices such as colour liquid crystal displays to distinguish its products. In contrast, Sanyo's products have few differentiating features and the company hasn't had nearly the level of success that Sharp has.

focus strategy
The strategy a company follows when it pursues a cost or differentiation advantage in a narrow industry segment.

The first two of Porter's strategies seek a competitive advantage in a broad range of markets and industry segments. The **focus strategy** aims at a cost advantage (cost focus) or a differentiation advantage (differentiation focus) in a narrow segment. That is, management selects a market segment or group of segments in an industry to the exclusion of others. These segments can be based on product variety, type of end buyer, distribution channel, or geographic location of buyers. At Cia. Chilena de Fosforos, a large Chilean wood products manufacturer, vice chairman Gustavo Romero devised a focus strategy to sell chopsticks in Japan. Competitors, and even some managers in his own company, thought he was crazy. However, by focusing on this narrow segment, Romero's strategy managed to create more demand for his company's chopsticks than it had mature trees to make the products with.

The goal of a focus strategy is to exploit a narrow segment of a market. Of course, whether a focus strategy is feasible or not depends on the size of the segment and whether it can sup-

Every day at Gillette's south Boston headquarters, 200 volunteers test and evaluate new razors as part of the company's ongoing product research effort. Its emphasis on innovation and quality enables Gillette to differentiate itself in the crowded personal care products market.

port the additional cost of focusing. Recent research suggests that the focus strategy may be the most effective for small businesses.[25] This is because they typically don't have the economies of scale or internal resources to successfully pursue one of the other two strategies.

Porter uses the term **"stuck in the middle"** to describe organizations that are unable to gain a competitive advantage by any one of the preceding strategies. Such organizations find it very difficult to achieve long-term success. When they do, it's usually a result of competing in a highly attractive industry or because all competitors are similarly stuck in the middle. Porter goes on to note that successful organizations frequently get into trouble by reaching beyond their competitive advantage and ending up stuck in the middle.

stuck in the middle
Descriptive of organizations that cannot compete through cost leadership, differentiation, or focus strategies.

A growing number of studies show that a dual emphasis on low costs and differentiation can result in high performance.[26] To be successful though, an organization must be strongly committed to quality products or services, and consumers of those products or services must value quality. By providing high-quality products or services, an organization differentiates itself from its rivals. Consumers who value the high quality will purchase more of these goods, and the increased demand leads to economies of scale and lower per-unit costs. For instance,

Originally targeted at a narrow segment of the market, cuddly Beanie Babies took off in 1996. Their cute names and low price appeal to more than just preschoolers. Ty Warner, who creates and produces Beanie Babies, profited from the biggest toy of the year as a result of his successful focus strategy.

Using a focus strategy, James Lindsay has made Rap Snacks profitable. Though the overall market is dominated by Frito-Lay, Lindsay has been successful by marketing his chips to consumers in US inner cities.

companies such as Molson, Federal Express and Coca-Cola differentiate their products, while at the same time maintaining low-cost operations.

Sustaining a Competitive Advantage. Long-term success with any one of Porter's competitive strategies requires that the advantage be sustainable. That is, it must withstand actions of competitors or evolutionary changes in the industry. This isn't easy. Technology changes and so do consumers' tastes. Most importantly, some advantages can be easily imitated by competitors. Management needs to create "barriers" that make imitation difficult or that reduce competitive opportunities. For instance, Glaxo, the British pharmaceutical maker, has been able to sustain its successful product innovations because it effectively protects its products from imitation. How can a company do this? Well, one thing a company can do is to have strong economies of scale so it can reduce price to gain volume. Also, it can lock in suppliers with exclusive contracts and thus limit competitors' access to these sources of supply. Or it can lobby for government policies that impose import tariffs, thus limiting foreign competition. Yet, whatever actions management takes to sustain a competitive advantage, it cannot become complacent. Sustaining a competitive advantage requires constant action by management to stay one step ahead of the competition.

TQM AS A STRATEGIC WEAPON

As mentioned earlier, emphasizing quality can be a way for a company to create a competitive advantage and an increasing number of companies are applying total quality management (TQM) concepts to their operations. As we first discussed in Chapter 2, TQM focuses on quality and continuous improvement. To the degree that an organization can satisfy a customer's need for quality, it can differentiate itself from competitors and attract a loyal customer base. Moreover, constant improvement in the quality and reliability of an organization's products or services can result in a competitive advantage that can't be taken away.[27] Product innovations, for example, offer little opportunity for sustained competitive advantage. Why? Because usually, as soon as they hit the market, they are copied by competitors. But incremental improvement, which is an essential element of TQM, is something that becomes an integrated part of an organization's operations and can develop into a considerable competitive advantage.

To illustrate how TQM can be used as a strategic tool, let's look at four companies—AMP of Canada Ltd., Cargill Limited, Pratt and Whitney Canada Ltd., and Steelcase Canada Limited.

AMP, a manufacturer and distributor of electric and electronic connecting products, as well as being original equipment manufacturers of computers and telecommunications equipment, has created an environment that is organized around processes rather than functions and it has done this by not filling vacancies as they arise. This forces people to wear more than one hat and focus their activities on what the customer wants, rather than on what the function wants. A cross-functional team that exemplifies this flexibility and customer focus is the "on-time delivery" team, made up of people from quality, inside sales, warehouse, and inventory control. They have achieved 98–99 percent delivery "as promised."

Pratt and Whitney Canada, a manufacturer of small gas turbines for corporate and commuter aircraft and helicopters, and auxiliary power units for jumbo jets, has integrated the efforts of marketing, engineering, manufacturing, procurement, customer support and finance to cut the product development cycle from five to two-and-a-half years.

Steelcase Canada Ltd.
www.steelcase.com/

Steelcase Canada is a manufacturer and distributor of office furniture and equipment. Its "focus factories", which integrate all functions in production, inventory, ordering, procurement and production scheduling, have cut cycle times from 8 to 10 weeks down to 4 weeks, and have decreased inventory by 50 percent in two manufacturing areas. Their "Quick Shop" program ensures delivery of items in 12 days or less.

Cargill is a diversified agricultural company with operations across Canada in grain, fertilizers and farm chemicals, livestock, feed and seed. A computer linked to the finished goods scanning system tells the fabrication line when orders from sales for any given product have been filled; the system has improved production accuracy by 15 to 20 percent.

However, the TQM attempts have not had a good record overall. According to an American survey reported in *Canadian Business Review*, only 13 percent of CEOs state that TQM efforts resulted in higher profits or greater operating income. A British study showed that, in the UK, 80 percent of TQM efforts fail. A Canadian study showed that while 80 percent of Canadian companies were making an effort to implement TQM programs, only a third of them had achieved tangible positive results.[28]

7 Describe the BCG matrix and why the portfolio concept is not as popular as it once was.

8 What does the five-forces model show?

9 Describe three possible competitive strategies.

SUMMARY

This summary is organized by the learning objectives found at the beginning of the chapter.

1. In a dynamic and uncertain environment, strategic planning is important because it can provide managers with a systematic and comprehensive means for analyzing the environment, assessing their organization's strengths and weaknesses, and identifying opportunities for which they could develop and exploit a competitive advantage.
2. Corporate-level strategy seeks to determine what set of businesses the organization should be in. Business-level strategy is concerned with how the organization should compete in each of its businesses. Functional-level strategy is concerned with how functional departments can support the business-level strategy.
3. The strategic management process includes eight steps: (a) identifying the organization's current mission, objectives and strategies; (b) analyzing the environment; (c) identifying opportunities and threats in the environment; (d) analyzing the organization's resources; (e) identifying the organization's strengths and weaknesses; (f) formulating strategies; (g) implementing strategies; and (h) evaluating results.
4. The term SWOT analysis refers to analyzing the organization's internal strengths and weaknesses as well as external opportunities and threats, in order to identify a niche market that the organization can exploit.
5. The various corporate grand strategies include stability, growth, retrenchment and combination. A firm that's pursuing a stability strategy is not making any significant changes. A growth strategy means that the firm is increasing the level of its operations. When a firm is following a retrenchment strategy, it's reducing the size and diversity of its operations. A combination strategy is the simultaneous pursuit of two or more of the other corporate strategies.
6. The BCG matrix identifies four business groups: stars, cash cows, question marks, and dogs.
7. Management assesses its organization's competitive advantage by analyzing the forces that dictate the rules of competition within its industry (barriers to entry, substitutes, bargaining power of buyers and suppliers, and current competitive rivalry) and then by selecting a strategy (cost leadership, differentiation, or focus) that best exploits its competitive advantage.
8. TQM (total quality management) can be used as a competitive weapon to ensure continuing differentiation on grounds of quality.

THINKING ABOUT MANAGEMENT ISSUES

1. Arie P DeGeus, head of planning for the Royal Dutch/Shell Group Companies, suggests that the ability to "learn faster than competitors" may be the only sustainable competitive advantage. Do you agree? Why or why not?
2. As we've seen in previous chapters, high-, mid-, and low-level managers make different types of decisions. How do you think this hierarchy applies to the three levels of strategic planning?
3. Perform a SWOT analysis on a local business you feel you know well. What, if any, competitive advantage has this organization staked out?
4. Walt Disney Companies successfully employed a growth strategy during the 1990s as it expanded its theme parks and resorts division with new parks in Tokyo and Paris, and added attractions at its US parks. It also aggressively pursued the movie market with its Touchstone film division, its new Disney releases aimed at the family market and its re-releases of old Disney classics, and it beefed up its consumer products division through global licensing agreements and aggressively opening new Disney stores and Mic-Kids. However, experts say that the company will find it difficult to continue this kind of growth. Do you agree? Explain. What strategies would you recommend for Disney to pursue?
5. How might the processes of strategy formulation and implementation differ for (a) large businesses; (b) small businesses; (c) non-profit organizations; and (d) global businesses?

SELF-ASSESSMENT EXERCISE

ARE YOU A RISK TAKER?

Formulating and implementing strategies typically involves taking risks. Whether the strategy is moving into a new market or divesting a "dog", there are risks involved. Not everyone is comfortable taking risks. This assessment exercise examines your level of comfort with risk taking.

Instructions: As a decision maker, do you tend to steer clear of risky situations, or do you find them tantalizing and invigorating? For example, if you had saved $20 000 would you keep it in the bank or invest it in a friend's new business venture? This quiz measures how likely you are to take risks with finances and your career. Answer true or false for each question.

	True	False
1. I'd rather start my own business than work for someone else.	_____	_____
2. I would never take a job that requires lots of travelling.	_____	_____
3. If I were to gamble, I would be a high roller.	_____	_____
4. I like to improve on ideas.	_____	_____
5. I would never give up my job before I was certain I had another one.	_____	_____
6. I'd never invest in highly speculative stocks.	_____	_____
7. I'd be willing to take risks just to broaden my horizons.	_____	_____
8. Thinking about investing in stocks doesn't excite me.	_____	_____
9. I'd consider working strictly on a commission basis.	_____	_____
10. Knowing that any new business can fail, I'd always avoid investing in one, even if the potential payoff was high.	_____	_____
11. I would like to experience as much of life as possible.	_____	_____
12. I don't feel that I have a strong need for excitement.	_____	_____
13. I have a lot of energy.	_____	_____
14. I can easily generate lots of money-making ideas.	_____	_____
15. I'd never bet more money than I had at the time.	_____	_____
16. I enjoy proposing new ideas or concepts when the reactions of others—my boss, for example—are unknown or uncertain.	_____	_____
17. I have never written cheques without having enough money in the bank to cover them.	_____	_____
18. A less secure job with a large income is more to my liking than a more secure job with an average income.	_____	_____
19. I'm not very independent-minded.	_____	_____

For scoring directions, turn to page SK-3.

Source: Frank Farley, 1025 West Johnson Street, University of Wisconsin, Madison, WI 53706.

for your IMMEDIATE action

BRADFORD

FINANCIAL FUNDS

TO: Aretha Stamelos, Research Associate
FROM: Sandra Bradford, President
RE: New Investments

As you know, we are continually on the lookout for new additions to our technology-based fund. At a dinner meeting last night, the speaker was talking about the Fredericton, New Brunswick-based company, Star Choice Communications Inc. I'd like you to check out the information at its Web site <http://www.starchoice.com>. Then put together a list of what you feel are Star Choice's key strengths and potential weaknesses. Keep this list short (one page). After I've had a chance to look at it, I may have you do more indepth research on this company. Please get this information to me as soon as possible.

This is a fictionalized account of a potentially real problem. It was written for academic purposes only and is not meant to reflect either positively or negatively on management practices at Bradford Financial.

TAKE IT TO THE NET

We invite you to visit the Robbins/Coulter/Stuart-Kotze Companion Website at www.prenticehall.ca/robbins for this chapter's Internet resources.

CASE APPLICATION

Seagram Co. Ltd., Montreal

Montreal-based Seagram Co. Ltd. has been one of Canada's great success stories through generations of the Bronfman family, who founded and control it. Seagram moved successfully from its foundation in the spirits business into chemicals, with the acquisition of DuPont, which then grew to account for 65 percent of the company's earnings. The latest member of the Bronfman family to head the company is Edgar Bronfman Jr., who, between 1993 and 1995, moved the company into the entertainment industry with a $2 billion investment in Time Warner. Also in 1995 Bronfman, as CEO, sold DuPont to pay for the purchase of Universal Studios (then called MCA), taking Seagram even more heavily into the entertainment industry.

In 1998, Seagram sold its remaining Time Warner stock for $1 billion (it had sold off some of its investment previously to pay for the purchase of Turner Broadcasting System Inc. in 1997, and later in the year had divested itself of $1.4 billion in Time Warner stock). At the time of the sale, Edgar Bronfman, Jr. stated: "As we have said before, our position in Time Warner is non-strategic". At one time, Seagram had been Time Warner's largest shareholder. Time Warner had never been a very successful venture for Seagram, but the company managed to come out with proceeds of $2.4 billion from an initial investment of $2 billion.

Seagram also bought Tropicana Beverages Group back in the late 1980s, and this investment turned into a stellar performer for the company. Tropicana had sales of $2.1 billion in 1997, virtually all in North America. In 1998, Edgar Bronfman, Sr. (who had handed the reins of Seagram over to his son, but remained as chairman) secured a joint venture with a Chinese company to produce and distribute Tropicana in China. Sales were projected to be $100 million in the first year, with one-third growth every year subsequently. But later in the year, Edgar Jr. announced the sale of Tropicana. Seagram was going into another new venture, this time with the $10.6 billion acquisition of the music industry giant, PolyGram NV. PolyGram was merged with Seagram's Universal Music Group.

Through all of this, Seagram's liquor division has accounted for less and less of the company's total revenues (one-quarter of its revenue in 1998). Today, investments in motion pictures, music, theme parks and media account for most of Seagram's business. Meanwhile, critics have noted a few facts: DuPont's share price has more than doubled since Seagram sold it; Tropicana—the world's biggest juice company—was a star performer; and PolyGram reported a steep fall in second quarter net income for 1998, going down to $11.4 million compared to $75 million for 1997's second quarter. But Edgar Bronfman, Jr. is intent on turning his company into an entertainment industry giant.

QUESTIONS

1. What is Seagram's competitive strategy? Explain your choice.
2. What kinds of competitive advantages do you think Seagram might have? Explain your choices.
3. Try to take Seagram through the strategic management process with regard to its music and film industry purchases.
4. Describe what types of grand strategies you see in the case of Seagram.

Sources: Alice Rawsthorn, "PolyGram Tumbles To Fl 23m in Quarter", *Financial Times* (U.K.), August 2, 1998; Peter Waal, "V.O. - Better Make it a Double", *Canadian Business*, June 26/July 10, 1998, pp. 25-26; Brian Milner, "Seagram Sells Half Time Warner Stake", *Globe and Mail*, February 6, 1998, p. B1; Kathy Chen, "Seagram Takes Fresh Approach to Orange Juice Sales in China", *Globe and Mail*, January 12, 1998, p. B5.

LEARNING OBJECTIVES

After Reading This Chapter, You Should Be Able To:

1 Describe techniques for scanning the environment
2 Contrast quantitative and qualitative forecasting
3 Explain why budgets are popular
4 Describe benchmarking
5 Differentiate Gantt charts from load charts
6 Identify the steps in a PERT network
7 State the factors that determine a product's breakeven point
8 Describe the requirements for using linear programming
9 Discuss how simulation can be a planning tool
10 Explain the concept of project management

A MANAGER'S CHALLENGE

The Canadian Bookselling Industry

In the US, two major chains—Barnes & Noble and Borders—dominate the book retailing market, and their superstore formula of bookselling has revolutionized the market. In Canada, Chapters has emulated the big-box style of retailing, and has changed the industry here. Formed from the merger of Smithbooks and Coles, Chapters' huge stores, containing coffee bars, a vast selection of books, and comfy chairs, have been extremely successful. From 1996 to 1998, profits quadrupled, and the company plans to have 75 superstores open by the end of 2000. But Chapters was not the first in Canada to recognize the shifts in the industry. Bollum's Books in Vancouver opened the country's first mega-bookstore. Winnipeg's McNally Robinson Booksellers saw the writing on the wall, and opened a superstore in 1996,

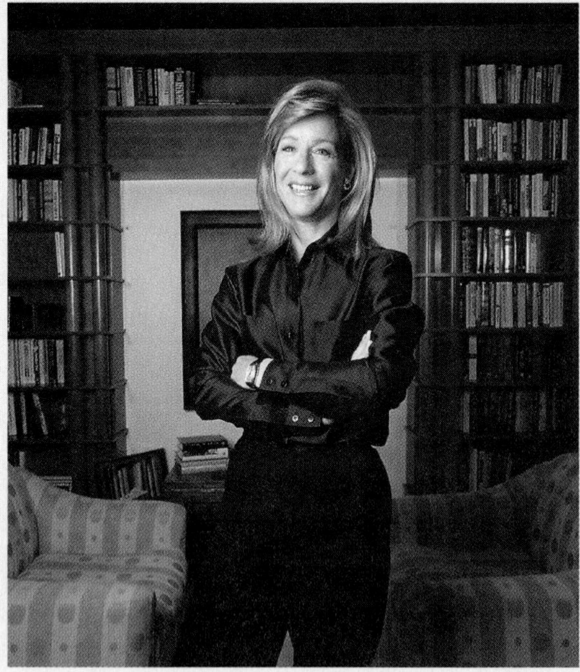

beating Chapters to the Winnipeg market. Now, Toronto entrepreneur Heather Reisman is challenging Chapters with a bid to take Indigo Books Music Cafes nationwide, with its own chain of superstores.[1]

The small, independent bookstores are having a tough time struggling for market share against this new onslaught of big-box stores. In an attempt to compete more effectively, 35 small stores in the Ottawa area have formed an alliance known as The Independents. They are concentrating their marketing efforts, promoting their hassle-free atmospheres, emphasizing a focus on quality of product over quantity, and stressing the advantages of their knowledgeable staff. The industry is undergoing such rapid change that it is difficult to predict who will have survived when the dust settles. Yet another major factor is the advent of on-line, Internet bookselling. Amazon.com calls itself the world's biggest bookstore, with 2.5 million titles.

With the shape of the Canadian bookselling industry redefining itself at such a rapid pace, all of these organizations will have to concentrate on developing plans that will allow them to survive in the marketplace.

This chapter discusses many of the basic planning tools and techniques that could be useful for organizations operating in the changing Canadian bookselling industry. In this chapter, we will be looking at three planning techniques to assist managers in assessing their environment—environmental scanning, forecasting and benchmarking. Then we'll review the most popular planning tool used by managers—budgets. We'll end the chapter by looking at some ideas to help you in your personal, day-to-day planning by presenting key things that you need to know about time management.

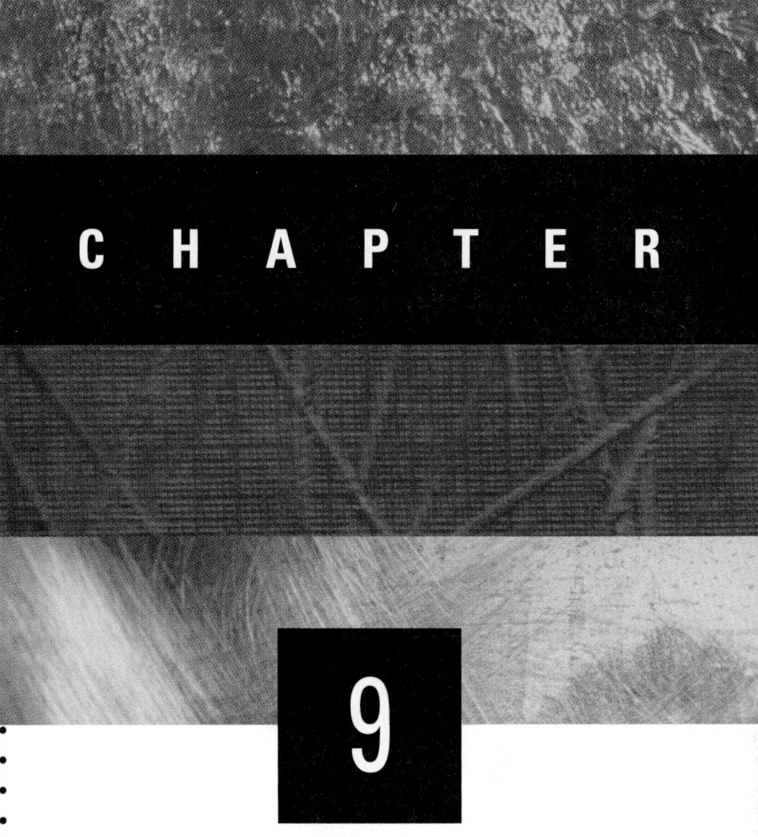

CHAPTER 9

Planning Tools and Techniques

Calgary-based Poco Petroleum has experienced rapid growth through careful attention to its dynamic environment, under the leadership of its CEO, C W Stewart.

TECHNIQUES FOR ASSESSING THE ENVIRONMENT

In our last chapter, we examined the strategic management process in detail. In this section, we want to review several techniques that have been developed to help managers with one of the most challenging aspects of the process: assessing their organization's environment. Today's managers can more accurately analyze their organization's environment by using structured techniques such as environmental scanning, forecasting and benchmarking.

Environmental Scanning

environmental scanning
The screening of large amounts of information to detect emerging trends and create scenarios.

Managers in both small and large organizations are increasingly using **environmental scanning** to anticipate and interpret changes in their environment. In fact, one study found that companies with advanced environmental scanning systems had higher profits and revenue growth.[2] Poco Petroleums of Calgary, Alberta, has developed from a small producer and marketer of gas to one of the top three non-aggregator exporters to the United States, along with Shell and Mobil. (Non-aggregators principally sell the gas they produce; aggregators sell gas they acquire.) It accomplished this by carefully scanning the environment and recognizing the changes needed to survive and prosper. In the complex world of gas marketing, management has to understand the altered market environment created by regulatory changes affecting pipelines, the evolving relationships with customers, and the opportunities that now exist to buy and sell gas in either the Canadian or American market, wherever prices warrant it. By taking into account all these factors, Poco has developed a strong customer base and knowledge that now make it very difficult for competitors to catch up with it.

competitor intelligence
Environmental scanning activity that seeks to identify who competitors are, what they're doing, and how their actions will affect the focus organization.

One of the fastest-growing areas of environmental scanning is **competitor intelligence**.[3] It seeks basic information about competitors: Who are they? What are they doing? How will what they're doing affect us? Accurate information on what competitors are doing can allow managers time to *anticipate* competitor actions rather than just *react* to them.

One person who has closely studied the process of competitive intelligence suggests that 95 percent of the competitor-related information an organization needs to make crucial strategic decisions is available and accessible to the public.[4] In other words, competitive intelligence doesn't have to involve organizational spying. Advertisements, promotional materials, press releases, reports filed with government agencies, annual reports, want ads, newspaper reports and industry studies are examples of readily accessible sources of information. Trade shows and debriefing your own sales force can be other good sources of information on competitors. Many firms even regularly buy competitors' products and have their own engineers break them down (through a process called *reverse engineering*) to learn about new technical innovations.

Shell
www.shellus.com/

Mobil
www.mobil.com

Another type of environmental scanning that has become increasingly important is global scanning. The value of global scanning to management, of course, largely depends on the extent of the organization's international activities. For a company that has significant inter-

Bill Gates, founder and CEO of Microsoft Corporation, describes his vision for the future as one in which information is available at your fingertips. What implications would this type of capability have for environmental scanning?

national operations, global scanning can provide a wealth of information. Because world markets are complex and dynamic, managers have expanded the scope of their scanning efforts in order to gain vital information on those global forces that might affect their organizations.[5] Just consider what the Japanese firm Mitsubishi Trading Company does. It has over 60 000 market analysts around the world whose principal job is to identify and feed back information to the parent company.

The sources that managers have used for scanning the domestic environment are too limited for global scanning. Managers need to internationalize their perspectives and information sources. For instance, they can subscribe to information clipping services that review newspapers and business periodicals throughout the world and provide summaries. An increasing number of electronic services can provide topic searches and automatic updates in areas of special interest to managers.

Extensive environmental scanning is likely to reveal a number of issues and concerns that could affect your organization's current or planned operations. Not all of these are likely to be equally important, so it's usually necessary to focus on a limited set—say three or four—that are most important, and to develop scenarios based on each of these.

scenario
A consistent view of what the future is likely to be.

A **scenario** is a consistent view of what the future is likely to be. If, for instance, scanning uncovers increasing interest within the government of Alberta in raising the minimum wage, managers at Tim Horton's could create a multiple set of scenarios to assess the possible consequences of such an action. What would the implications be for its labour supply if the minimum wage were raised to $7.00 an hour? How about $8.00 an hour? What effect would these changes have on labour costs and on the bottom line? How might competitors respond? Different assumptions would lead to different outcomes. The intent of this exercise is not to try to predict the future, but to reduce uncertainty by playing out potential situations under different specified conditions.[6] Tim Horton's could, for example, develop a set of scenarios ranging from optimistic to pessimistic in terms of the minimum-wage issue. It would then be better prepared to initiate strategic changes in order to gain and keep a competitive advantage.

THINKING CRITICALLY ABOUT ETHICS

The following are some techniques that have been suggested for gathering competitor information: (1) Access public records of lawsuits filed against competitors, for useful information; (2) Ask Better Business Bureau about any complaints filed against competitors; (3) Ask questions of competitors, under the guise of being a reporter; (4) Get hold of competitors' in-house newsletters; (5) Buy a share in competitors' stock in order to receive annual reports, etc.; and (6) Gain information by pretending to go through a job interview. Which, if any, of these do you think are unethical? Defend your choices. What ethical guidelines would you suggest for competitor intelligence activities?

Forecasting

forecasts
Predictions of future outcomes.

Environmental scanning creates the foundation for forecasts. Information obtained through scanning is used to develop scenarios. These, in turn, establish premises for **forecasts**, which are predictions of future outcomes.

Future Shop
futureshop.com

Types of Forecasts. Two specific outcomes managers attempt to forecast are future revenues and new technological breakthroughs. However, virtually any component in the organization's general and specific environment can receive forecasting attention.

revenue forecasting
Predicting future revenues.

Future Shop's sales level drives the company's purchasing requirements, production goals, employment needs, inventories and numerous other decisions. Similarly, the University of Alberta's income from tuition and grants will determine course offerings, staffing needs, salary increases for the faculty, and the like. Both of these examples illustrate that predicting future revenues—**revenue forecasting**—is a crucial element of planning for both profit and non-profit organizations.

Where does management get the data for developing revenue forecasts? Typically, it begins by looking at historical revenue figures. For example, what were last year's revenues? This figure can then be adjusted for any significant trends discovered during environmental scanning. What revenue patterns have evolved over recent years? What changes in social, economic, or other factors in the general environment might alter the pattern in the future? In the specific environment, what might our competitors be doing? Answers to such questions provide the basis for revenue forecasts.

technological forecasting
Predicting changes in technology and when new technologies are likely to be economically feasible.

Technological forecasting seeks to predict changes in technology and the time frame in which new technologies are likely to be economically feasible. The rapid pace of technological change has brought us innovations in lasers, biotechnology, robotics, and data communications, and has dramatically changed surgery techniques, pharmaceutical products, manufacturing processes used for almost every mass-produced product, and the use of cellular phones. The environmental scanning techniques discussed in the previous section can provide data on potential technological innovations.

quantitative forecasting
Applies a set of mathematical rules to a series of past data to predict future outcomes.

qualitative forecasting
Uses the judgment and opinions of knowledgeable individuals to predict future outcomes.

Forecasting Techniques. Forecasting techniques fall into two categories: quantitative and qualitative. **Quantitative forecasting** applies a set of mathematical rules to a series of past data to predict future outcomes. These techniques are preferred when management has enough "hard" data. **Qualitative forecasting**, in contrast, uses the judgment and opinions of knowledgeable people. Qualitative techniques are typically used when precise data are limited or hard to obtain.

Table 9-1 lists some of the better-known quantitative and qualitative forecasting techniques.

Forecasting Effectiveness. Despite the importance to strategic planning, managers have mixed success in forecasting trends and outcomes accurately.[7] Forecasting techniques are most accurate when the environment is not rapidly changing. The more dynamic the environment, the more likely management is to develop inaccurate forecasts. Forecasting is also relatively unimpressive in predicting non-seasonal events such as recessions, unusual occurrences, discontinued operations, and the actions or reactions of competitors.

Although forecasting has a mixed record, various research studies have proposed some suggestions for improving forecasting effectiveness.[8] First, use simple forecasting techniques. They tend to do as well as, and often better than, complex methods, which tend to mistakenly confuse random data for meaningful information. Second, compare every forecast with "no change". A no-change forecast is very accurate approximately half the time. Third, don't rely on a single forecasting method. Make forecasts with several models and average them, especially when making long-range forecasts. Fourth, don't assume that you can accurately identify turning points in a trend. What is typically perceived as a significant turning point often turns out to be an unusual, random event. And last, shorten the length of forecasts to improve their accuracy, because accuracy declines the further into the future you're trying to predict.

benchmarking
The search for the best practices among competitors or non-competitors that lead to their superior performance.

Benchmarking for TQM

A third strategic planning tool is **benchmarking**. This is the search for the best practices among competitors or non-competitors that lead to their superior performance.[9] The basic

TABLE 9-1 Forecasting Techniques

Techniques	Description	Application
Quantitative		
Time series analysis	Fits a trend line to a mathematical equation and projects into the future by means of this equation	Predicting next quarter's sales based on four years of previous sales data
Regression models	Predicts one variable on the basis of known or assumed other variables	Seeking factors that will predict a certain level of sales (for example, price, advertising expenditures)
Econometric models	Uses a set of regression equations to simulate segments of the economy	Predicting change in car sales as a result of changes in tax laws
Economic indicators	Uses one or more economic indicators to predict a future state of the economy	Using change in GNP to predict discretionary income
Substitution effect	Uses a mathematical formula to predict how, when, and under what circumstances a new product or technology will replace an existing one	Predicting the effect of microwave ovens on the sale of conventional ovens
Qualitative		
Jury of opinion	Combines and averages the opinions of experts	Polling all the company's personnel managers to predict next year's college recruitment needs
Sales force composition	Combines estimates from field sales personnel of customers' expected purchases	Predicting next year's sales of industrial lasers
Customer evaluation	Combines estimates from established purchases	Surveying of major dealers by a car manufacturer to determine types and quantities of products desired

idea behind benchmarking is that management can improve quality by analyzing and then copying the methods of the leaders in various fields. Even small companies are finding that benchmarking can bring them big benefits. As such, benchmarking is a very specific form of environmental scanning.

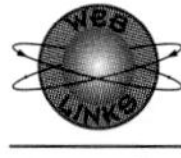

Xerox Canada
www.xerox.ca

Xerox Corporation is widely recognized as the first North American company to systematically attempt benchmarking. Up to 1979, Japanese firms had been aggressively copying the successes of others by travelling around the world, watching what others were doing, then applying their new knowledge to improve their products and processes. Xerox's management couldn't figure out how Japanese manufacturers could sell midsize copiers in North America for considerably less than Xerox's production costs. So the company's head of manufacturing took a team to Japan to make a detailed study of their competitors' costs and processes. They got most of their information from Xerox's own joint venture partner, Fuji-Xerox, since it knew the competition well. What the team found was shocking. Their Japanese rivals were light-years ahead of Xerox in efficiency. Benchmarking those efficiencies marked the beginning of Xerox's turnaround in the copier industry. Today, all kinds of organizations use benchmarking as a standard tool in their quest for quality improvement—for example, manufacturing companies such as Magna and Bombardier, firms such as the telephone companies that deal in services, and non-profit organizations such as hospitals.

What does the benchmarking process involve? It typically follows four steps:

1. A benchmarking planning team is formed, and the team's initial task is to identify what is to be benchmarked, identify comparative organizations, and determine data collection methods.

2. Data are collected internally on the organization's own operations and externally from other organizations.
3. The data are analyzed to identify performance gaps and to determine the cause of differences.
4. An action plan is prepared and implemented that will result in meeting or exceeding the standards of others.

To illustrate its use in practice, let's look at how Alcoa, one of the world's leading aluminum companies, used benchmarking to improve its manufacturing processes. The company used employee benchmarking teams to identify benchmarking opportunities throughout its worldwide facilities. These teams focused on the following criteria in identifying possible areas for benchmarking improvement: Is the topic important to our customers? Is the topic consistent with our mission, values and milestones? Does the topic reflect an important business need? Is the topic significant in terms of costs or key non-financial indicators? Is the topic in an area where additional information could influence plans and actions? Once specific benchmarking areas had been identified, an overall plan was developed that described how external and internal information was going to be gathered on the key criteria, and what companies were going to be used as benchmarking targets. The teams then gathered the information and analyzed the data they collected. Performance gaps between the organization being studied and the specific Alcoa unit looking to improve its processes were quantified and studied for implications. Suggested changes were implemented, and the teams were asked what other units in the organization could potentially benefit from the work they had done. Alcoa's corporate managers have been satisfied with the benchmarking process and the changes that came about because of it.

How can managers ensure that their benchmarking efforts are effective? Table 9-2 lists some suggestions for improving the process.

BUDGETS

Most of us have had some experience, as limited as it might be, with budgets. We probably learned about them at a very early age when we discovered that unless we allocated our "revenues" carefully, our weekly allowance was gone before the week was half over.

TABLE 9-2 Suggestions for Improving Benchmarking Efforts

1. Link benchmarking efforts to strategic objectives.
2. Have the right-sized team—between 6 and 8 people is the most effective.
3. Involve those individuals who will be directly affected by benchmarking efforts.
4. Focus on specific, targeted issues rather than broad, general ones.
5. Set realistic timetables.
6. Choose benchmarking targets carefully.
7. Observe proper protocol when gathering benchmarking information by dealing with the appropriate individuals.
8. Don't collect excessive, unnecessary data.
9. Look at the processes behind the numbers, not just at the numbers themselves.
10. Identify benchmarking targets and then be sure to take action.

Source: Based on John H Sheridan, "Where Benchmarkers Go Wrong," *Industry Week,* March 15, 1993, pp. 28–34.

TESTING... TESTING...

1 Describe the different types of forecasting.

2 What does the benchmarking process involve?

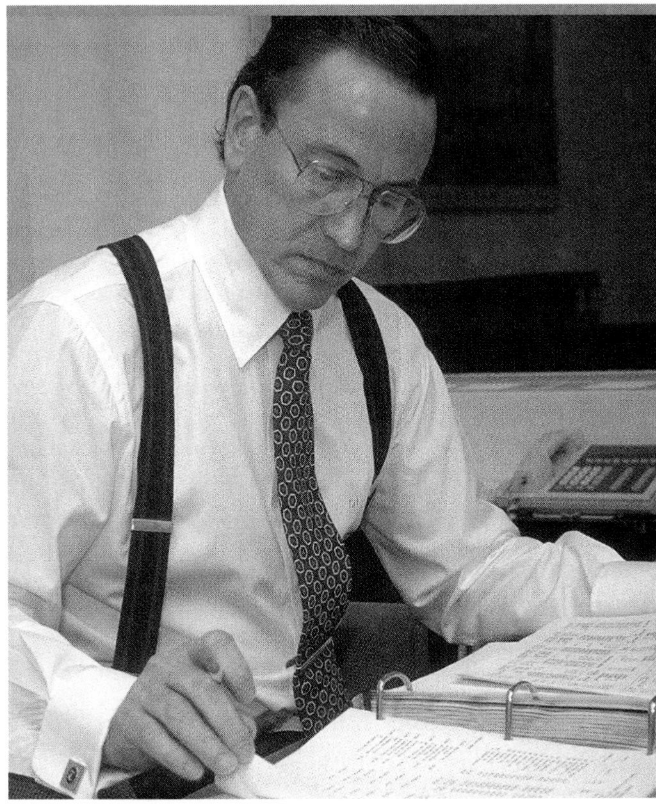

Each department within a company assumes responsibility for its own budget. The manager then assumes responsibility for co-ordinating the departmental budgets and making changes as new business demands require.

A **budget** is a numerical plan for allocating resources to specific activities. Managers typically prepare budgets for revenues, expenses, and large capital expenditures such as machinery and equipment. It's not unusual, though, for budgets to be used for improving time, space and the use of material resources. These latter types of budgets substitute non-dollar numbers for dollar amounts. Such items as person-hours, capacity utilization, or units of production can be budgeted for as daily, weekly, or monthly activities. However, we'll emphasize dollar-based budgets in this section.

budget
A numerical plan for allocating resources to specific activities.

Why are budgets so popular? Probably because they are applicable to a wide variety of organizations and units within an organization. We live in a world in which almost everything is expressed in monetary units. Even human life has a monetary value. Insurance actuaries compute the value of a lost eye, arm or leg, and Canadian insurance companies and trial juries regularly convert the loss of human body parts, or life itself, into dollars. It seems logical, then, that monetary budgets make a useful common denominator for directing activities in such diverse departments as production and marketing research, or at various levels in an organization. Budgets are one planning device that most managers, regardless of organizational level, help to formulate.

Types of Budgets

Budgets can be used for a number of areas or items. The following represent the ones managers are most likely to use.

Revenue Budgets. The **revenue budget** is a specific type of revenue forecast. It's a budget that projects future sales. If the organization could be sure of selling everything it produced, revenue budgets would be very accurate. Managers would need only to multiply the sale price of each product by the quantity that could be produced. However, such situations rarely exist. Managers must take into account their competitors, planned advertising expenditures, sales force effectiveness, and other relevant factors, and must make an estimate of sales volume. Also, on the basis of estimates of product demand at various prices, managers must select an appropriate sales price. Then they can multiply sales volume times sales price for each product in order to get the revenue budget.

revenue budget
A budget that projects future sales.

Expense Budgets. While revenue budgets are essentially a planning device for marketing and sales activities, expense budgets are found in all units of profit and non-profit organizations. **Expense budgets** list the primary activities undertaken by a unit to achieve its goals, and allocate a dollar amount to each. Lower expenses, when accompanied by stable quantity and quality of output, lead to greater efficiency. In times of intense competition, economic recession, or the like, managers typically look first at the expense budget as a place to make cuts and improve economic inefficiencies. Because not all expenses are linked to volume, they do not all decline at the same rate when product demand drops. Managers pay particular attention to so-called fixed expenses—those that remain relatively unchanged regardless of volume. As production levels fall, the variable expenses tend to control themselves because they decrease with volume.

expense budget
A budget that lists the primary activities undertaken by a unit and allocates a dollar amount to each.

Profit Budgets. Organizational units that have easily determined revenues are often designated as profit centres and use profit budgets for planning and controlling. **Profit budgets** combine revenue and expense budgets into one. They are typically used in large organizations that have multiple facilities and divisions. Each manufacturing plant in a corporation, for instance, might measure its monthly expenses (including a charge for corporate overhead) against its monthly billing revenues. In fact, some organizations create artificial profit centres by developing transfer prices for intraorganizational transactions. For instance, the exploration division of Texaco produces oil only for Texaco's refining division, so the exploration unit has no "real" sales. However, Texaco turned the exploration unit into a profit centre by establishing prices for each barrel of oil the division drills, and then "sells" to the refining division. The internal transfers create revenue for the exploration division and allow managers in that division to formulate, and be evaluated against, their profit budget.

profit budget
A budget used by separate units of an organization that combines revenue and expense budgets to determine the unit's profit contribution.

Cash Budgets. **Cash budgets** are forecasts of how much cash the organization will have on hand and how much it will need to meet expenses. This budget can reveal potential cash flow shortages or surpluses.

cash budget
A budget that forecasts how much cash an organization will have on hand and how much it will need to meet expenses.

Capital Expenditure Budgets. Investments in property, buildings and major equipment are called *capital expenditures*. These are typically substantial expenditures both in terms of magnitude and duration. For example, when Kraft decides to build a new cheese processing production facility, it represents a commitment of hundreds of millions of dollars. Such a project would require an outlay of funds over several years and would take many years for the company to recoup its investment. The magnitude and duration of these investments justifies the development of separate budgets for these expenditures. Such **capital expenditure budgets** allow management to forecast future capital requirements, to keep on top of important capital projects, and to ensure that adequate cash is available to meet these expenditures as they become due.

capital expenditure budget
A budget that forecasts investments in property, buildings and major equipment.

Variable Budgets. The budgets just described are based on the assumption of a single specified volume—that is, they are **fixed budgets**. They assume a fixed level of sales or production volume. Most organizations, however, are not able to predict volume accurately. Moreover, a number of costs—such as labour, material, and some administrative expenses—vary with volume. **Variable budgets** are designed to deal with these facts. Since plans can change, standards need to be flexible in order to adapt to these changes. Variable budgets represent flexible standards. They can help managers to better plan costs by specifying cost schedules for varying levels of volume.

fixed budget
A budget that assumes a fixed level of sales or production.

variable budget
A budget that takes into account those costs that vary with volume.

OPERATIONAL PLANNING TOOLS

Jeanine and Jeff Spencer own a Tim Horton's store in Lloydminster, Alberta. Much of their time is spent setting up work schedules for their 30 full- and part-time employees, as well as decid-

TESTING... TESTING...

3 Describe the five types of budgets and what each is designed to do.

4 What is the difference between a variable and a fixed budget?

ing how much inventory to order, and doing other day-to-day planning tasks. In the following pages, we'll discuss some operational planning tools that can help managers in a small business like Tim Horton's (as well as managers in larger organizations) to be more effective.

Scheduling

scheduling
A listing of necessary activities, their order of accomplishment, who is to do each, and the time needed to complete them.

The Gantt Chart. As discussed in Chapter 2, the Gantt chart was developed during the early 1900s by Henry Gantt, a protégé of Frederick Taylor. The idea behind a Gantt chart is simple. It is essentially a bar graph with time on the horizontal axis, and the activities to be scheduled on the vertical axis. The bars show output, both planned and actual, over a period of time. The Gantt chart visually shows when tasks are supposed to be done and compares this to the actual progress on each. It is a simple but important device that lets managers easily detail what has yet to be done to complete a job or project, and to assess whether an activity is ahead of, behind, or on schedule.

Figure 9-1 depicts a simplified Gantt chart that was developed for book production by a manager in a publishing firm. Time is expressed in months across the top of the chart. The major activities are listed down the left side. The planning comes in deciding what activities need to be done to get the book finished, the order in which these activities need to be completed, and the time that should be allocated to each activity. Where a box sits within a time frame reflects its planned sequence. The shading represents actual progress. The chart becomes a control tool when the manager looks for deviations from the plan. In this example, everything has been accomplished on schedule except the printing of galley proofs. This activity is two weeks behind schedule. Given this information, the manager of the project might want to take some corrective action, either to make up for the two lost weeks or to ensure that no further delays will occur. At this point, the manager can expect that the book will be published at least two weeks later than planned, if no corrective action is taken.

load chart
A modified Gantt chart that schedules capacity by workstations.

The Load Chart. A **load chart** is a modified Gantt chart. Instead of listing activities on the vertical axis, load charts list either whole departments or specific resources. This allows managers to plan and control for capacity utilization. In other words, load charts schedule capacity by work stations.

For example, Figure 9-2 shows a load chart for six production editors at the same publishing firm. Each editor supervises the production and design of a number of books. By reviewing a load chart like the one shown in Figure 9-2, the executive editor, who supervises

FIGURE 9-1 A Gantt Chart

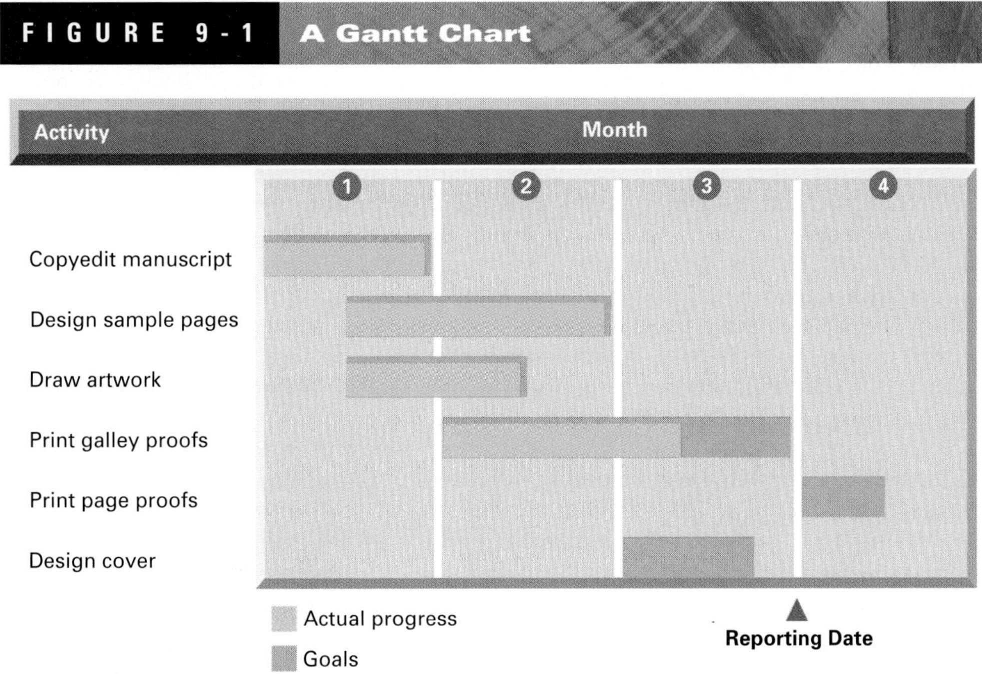

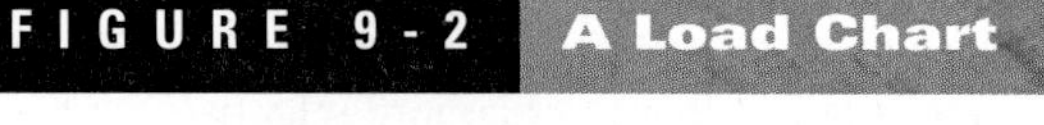

FIGURE 9-2 A Load Chart

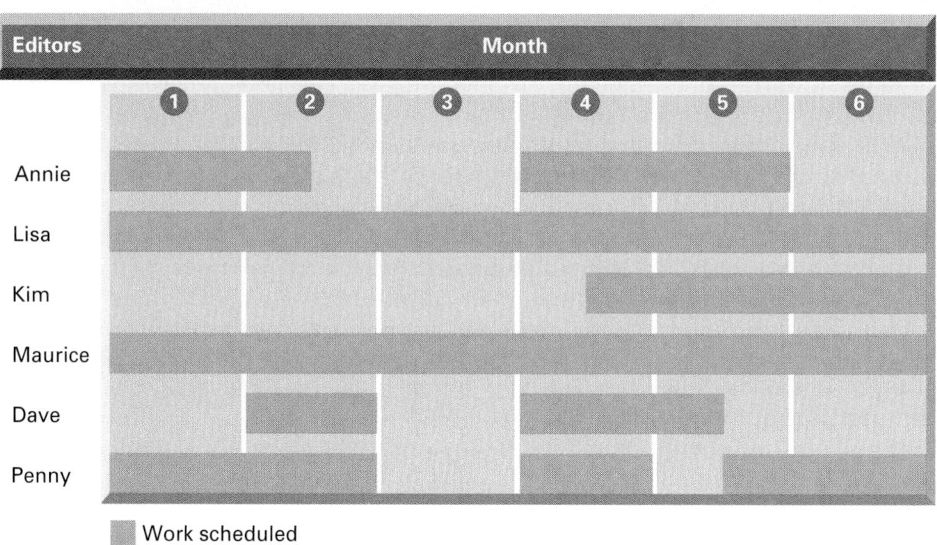

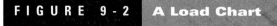

the six production editors, can see who is free to take on a new book. If everyone is fully scheduled, the executive editor might decide not to accept any new projects, to accept new projects and delay others, to ask the editors to work overtime, or to employ more production editors. In Figure 9-2, only Lisa and Maurice are completely booked for the next six months. Since the other editors have some unassigned time, they might be able to accept one or more new projects.

PERT Network Analysis. Gantt and load charts are useful as long as the activities being scheduled are few in number, and are independent of each other. But, what if a manager had to plan a large project such as a unit re-organization, the implementation of a cost reduction campaign, or the development of a new product that required co-ordinating inputs from marketing, production, and product design personnel? Such projects require co-ordinating hundreds—even thousands—of activities, some of which must be done simultaneously and some of which cannot begin until earlier activities have been completed. If you're constructing a building, you obviously can't start putting up the walls until the foundation is laid. How, then, can you schedule such a complex project? The Program Evaluation and Review Technique (PERT) is highly appropriate for such projects.

Program Evaluation and Review Technique (PERT) A technique for scheduling complicated projects comprising many activities, some of which are interdependent.

PERT network A flowchart-like diagram showing the sequence of activities needed to complete a project, and the time or cost associated with each.

The **Program Evaluation and Review Technique**—usually just called PERT or PERT network analysis—was originally developed in the late 1950s for co-ordinating the more than 3000 contractors and agencies working on the *Polaris* submarine weapon system.[10] This project was incredibly complicated, involving hundreds of thousands of activities that had to be co-ordinated. PERT is reported to have cut two years off the completion date of the project.

A **PERT network** is a flowchart-like diagram that depicts the sequence of activities needed to complete a project, and the time or costs associated with each activity. With a PERT network, a project manager must think through what has to be done, determine which events depend on one another, and identify potential trouble spots. PERT also makes it easy to compare the effects which alternative actions will have on scheduling and costs. Thus, PERT allows managers to monitor a project's progress, identify possible bottlenecks, and shift resources as necessary, to keep the project on schedule. For instance, Pacific Gas and Electric company uses PERT to schedule projects varying in cost from $5000 to more than $50 million. The technique has been used to design and construct facilities, prepare environmental studies, and conduct research and development.[11]

To understand how to construct a PERT network, you need to know three terms: *events*, *activities* and *critical path*. Let's define these terms, outline the steps in the PERT process, and then look at an example.

Events are end points that represent the completion of major activities. **Activities** represent the time or resources required to progress from one event to another. The **critical path** is the longest or most time-consuming sequence of events and activities in a PERT network.

events
End points that represent the completion of major activities in a PERT network.

activities
The time or resources needed to progress from one event to another in a PERT network.

critical path
The longest sequence of activities in a PERT network.

Developing a PERT network requires that a manager identify all key activities needed to complete a project, rank them in order of dependence, and estimate each activity's completion time. This can be translated into five specific steps, which are outlined in Table 9-3.

As we noted at the beginning of this section, most PERT projects are quite complicated and may be composed of hundred or thousands of events. Such complicated computations are best done with a computer using specialized PERT software.[12] But, for our purposes, let's work through a simplified example. Assume that you're the superintendent at a construction company. You've been assigned to oversee the construction of an office building. Because time really is money in your business, you must determine how long it will take to get the building built. You've carefully broken down the entire project into activities and events. Table 9-4 outlines the major events in the construction project and your estimate of the expected time required to complete each activity. Figure 9-3 shows the PERT network based on the data in Table 9-4. You've also calculated the length of time that each path of activities will take: A–B–C–D–I–J–K (44 weeks); A–B–C–D–G–H–J–K (50 weeks); A–B–C–E–G–H–J–K (47 weeks); and A–B–C–F–G–H–J–K (47 weeks).

Your PERT network shows that if everything goes as planned, it will take 50 weeks to complete the building. This is calculated by tracing the project's critical path: A–B–C–D–G–H–J–K. Any delay in completing the events on this path will delay the completion of the entire project. For example, if it took six weeks instead of four to put in the floor covering and panelling (Event I), this would have no effect on the final completion date. Why? Because C–D + D–I + I–J takes only 13 weeks while C–E + E–G + G–H + H–J equals 16 weeks. However, if you wanted to cut the 50-week completion time frame, you would concentrate on those activities along the critical path that could be speeded up.

Breakeven Analysis

How many units of a product must an organization sell in order to break even—that is, to have neither profit nor loss? A manager might want to know the minimum number of units that must be sold to achieve his or her profit objective or whether a current product should continue to be sold or be dropped from the organization's product line. **Breakeven analysis** is a widely used technique for helping managers to make profit projections.[13]

breakeven analysis
A technique for identifying the point at which total revenue is just sufficient to cover total costs.

TABLE 9-3 Steps in Developing a PERT Network

1. Identify every significant activity that must be achieved for a project to be completed. The accomplishment of each activity results in a set of events or outcomes.
2. Determine the order in which these events must be completed.
3. Draw a diagram showing the flow of activities from start to finish, identifying each activity and its relationship to all other activities. Use circles to indicate events and arrows to represent activities. This results in a flowchart diagram called a **PERT network**.
4. Compute a time estimate for completing each activity. This is done with a weighted average that uses an optimistic time estimate (t_o) of how long the activity would take under ideal conditions, a most-likely estimate (t_m) of the time the activity normally should take, and a pessimistic estimate (t_p) that represents the time that an activity should take under the worst possible conditions. The formula for calculating the expected time (t_e) is then

$$t_e = \frac{t_o + 4t_m + t_p}{6}$$

5. Using the network diagram that contains time estimates for each activity, determine a schedule for the start and finish dates of each activity and for the entire project. Any delays that occur along the critical path require the most attention because they can delay the whole project.

TABLE 9-4 A PERT Network for Erecting an Office Building

Event	Description	Expected Time (in weeks)	Preceding Event
A	Approve design and get permits	10	None
B	Dig subterranean garage	6	A
C	Erect frame and siding	14	B
D	Construct floor	6	C
E	Install windows	3	C
F	Put on roof	3	C
G	Install internal wiring	5	D, E, F
H	Install elevator	5	G
I	Put in floor covering and panelling	4	D
J	Put in doors and interior decorative trim	3	I, H
K	Turn over to building management group	1	J

Breakeven analysis is a simple formulation, yet it is valuable to managers because it points out the relationship between revenues, costs and profits. To compute the breakeven point (*BE*), the manager needs to know the unit price of the product being sold (*P*), the variable cost per unit (*VC*), and the total fixed costs (*TFC*).

An organization breaks even when its total revenue is just enough to equal its total costs. But total cost has two parts: a fixed component and a variable component. *Fixed costs* are expenses that do not change, regardless of volume. Examples include insurance premiums, rent, and property taxes. Fixed costs, of course, are fixed only in the short term because, in the long run, commitments terminate and could change as they are renegotiated. *Variable costs* change in proportion to output and include raw materials, labour costs and energy costs.

The breakeven point can be computed graphically or by using the following formula:

$$BE = \frac{TFC}{P - VC}$$

This formula tells us that (1) total revenue will equal total cost when we sell enough units at a price that covers all variable unit costs, and (2) the difference between price and variable costs, when multiplied by the number of units sold, equals the fixed costs.

FIGURE 9-3 A Pert Network for Erecting an Office Building

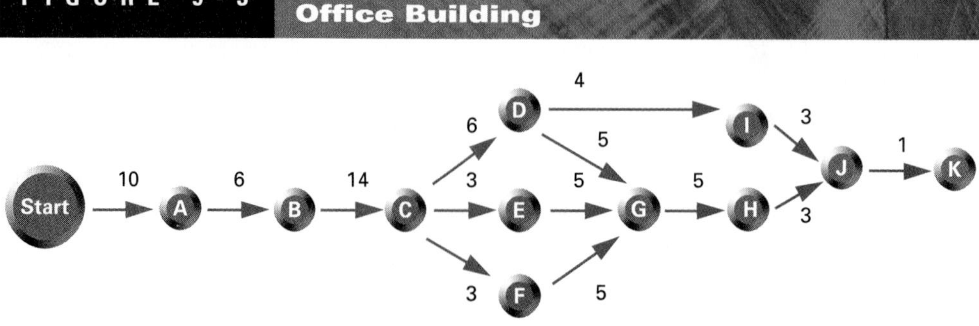

TESTING... TESTING...

5 Compare a Gantt chart with a load chart.

6 How would a manager construct a PERT network?

For example, assume that Mike's Photocopying Service charges \$0.10 per photocopy. If fixed costs are \$27 000 a year and variable costs are \$0.04 per copy, Mike can compute his breakeven point as follows: \$27 000/(\$0.10 – \$0.04) = 450 000 copies, or when annual revenues are \$45 000, 450 000 copies × \$0.10. This same relationship is shown graphically in Figure 9-4.

As a planning tool, breakeven analysis could help Mike to set his sales objective. For example, he could determine the profit he wants and then work backwards to see what sales level is needed to reach that profit. Breakeven analysis could also tell Mike how much volume has to increase to break even, if he's currently running at a loss, or how much volume he can afford to lose and still break even, if he's currently operating profitably. In some cases, such as the management of professional sports franchises, breakeven analysis has shown the projected volume of ticket sales required to cover all costs to be so unrealistically high that the best action for management is to get out of the business.

Linear Programming

Dan Collier has a manufacturing plant that produces two kinds of high quality stereo components—a CD deck and a tape deck. Business is good. He can sell all the stereo equipment he can produce. This is his problem: Given that both components go through the same production departments, how many of each type should he manufacture to maximize his profits?

A closer look at Dan's operation tells us that he can use a mathematical technique called **linear programming** to solve his resource allocation dilemma. As we'll show, linear programming is applicable to Dan's problem, but it can't be applied to all resource allocation situations. Besides requiring limited resources and the objective of optimization, it requires that there be alternative ways of combining resources to produce a number of output mixes. There must also be a linear relationship between variables.[14] This means that a change in one variable will be accompanied by an exactly proportional change in the other. For Dan's business, this condition would be met if it took exactly twice the amount of raw materials and hours of labour to produce two of a given component, that it took to produce one.

linear programming
A mathematical technique that solves resource allocation problems.

FIGURE 9-4 Breakeven Analysis

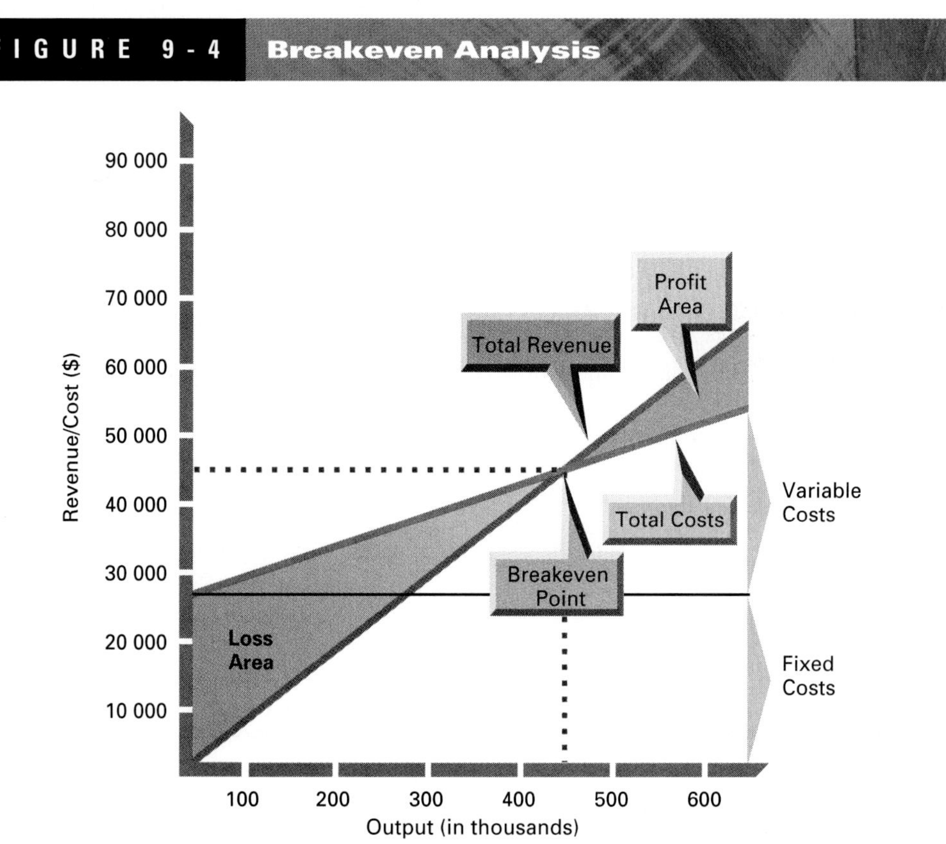

TABLE 9-5 Production Data for Stereo Components

	Number of Hours Required (per unit)		
Department	***Tape decks***	***CD Decks***	***Monthly Production Capacity (in hours)***
Manufacturing	2	4	1 200
Assembly	2	2	900
Profit per unit	$100	$180	

What kinds of problems can be solved with linear programming? Some applications would include selecting transportation routes that minimize shipping costs, allocating a limited advertising budget among various product brands, making the optimum assignment of personnel among projects, and determining how much of each product to make with a limited number of resources. Let's return to Dan's problem and see how linear programming could help him solve it. Fortunately, Dan's problem is relatively simple, so we can solve it rather quickly. For complex linear programming problems, a number of computer software programs are designed specifically to help develop optimizing solutions.

First, we need to establish some facts about Dan's business. Dan has computed the profit margins on the components at $100 for the tape deck and $180 for the CD deck. These numbers establish the basis for Dan to be able to express his *objective function* as: maximum profit = $\$100T + \$180C$, where T is the number of tape decks produced and C is the number of CD decks produced. The objective function is simply a mathematical equation that can predict the outcome of all proposed alternatives. In addition, Dan knows the time each component must spend in each department and the monthly production capacity (1 200 hours in manufacturing and 900 hours in assembly) for the two departments (see Table 9-5). The production capacity numbers act as *constraints* on his overall capacity. Now Dan can establish his constraint equations:

$$2T + 4C \leq 1\,200$$

$$2T + 2C \leq 900$$

Of course, since neither component can be produced in a volume less than zero, Dan can also state that $T \geq 0$ and $C \geq 0$.

Dan has made a graph of his solution, as shown in Figure 9-5. The shaded area represents the options that don't exceed the capacity of either department. What does this mean? Well, let's first look at the manufacturing constraint line BE. We know that total manufacturing capacity is 1 200 hours, so if Dan decides to produce all tape decks, the maximum he can produce is 600 (1 200 hours ÷ 2 hours required to produce a tape deck). If he decides to produce all CD decks, the maximum he can produce is 300 (1 200 hours ÷ 4 hours required to produce a CD deck). The other constraint Dan faces is that of assembly, shown by line DF. If Dan decides to produce all tape decks, the maximum he can assemble is 450 (900 hours production capacity ÷ 2 hours required to assemble). Likewise, if Dan decides to produce all CD decks, the maximum he can assemble is also 450 since the CD decks also take 2 hours to assemble. The constraints imposed by these capacity limits establishes Dan's *feasibility region*. Dan's optimal resource allocation will be defined at one of the corners within this feasibility region. Point C is the furthest from the origin and thus provides the maximum profits within the constraints stated. How do we know? At point A, profits would be 0 (no production of either tape decks or CD decks). At point B, profits would be $54 000 (300 CD decks produced × $180 profit and 0 tape decks produced = $54 000). At point D, profits would be $45 000 (450 tape decks × $100 profit and 0 CD decks produced = $45 000). At point C, however, profits would be $57 000 (150 CD decks produced × $180 profit and 300 tape decks produced × $100 profit = $57 000).

IGA
www.igainc.com/

Queuing Theory

You are the manager of an IGA grocery store in St. John's, Newfoundland. One of the decisions you have to make is how many of the 12 checkout counters you should keep open at any given

FIGURE 9-5 **Graphic Solution to Linear Programming Problem**

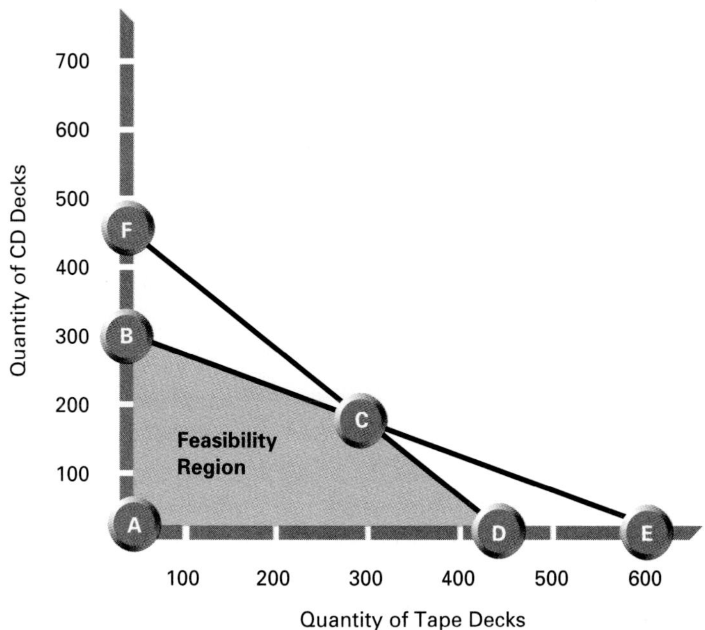

time. Queuing theory, or as it is frequently called, *waiting-line theory*, could assist you with this problem.

Whenever a decision involves balancing the cost of having a waiting line against the cost of service to maintain that line, it can be made easier with **queuing theory**. This includes such common situations as determining how many gas pumps are needed at gas stations, tellers at bank windows, or check-in lines at airline ticket counters. In each situation, management wants to minimize cost by having as few stations open as possible, yet not so few as to test the patience of customers. For instance, L L Bean, the outdoor products firm, developed a queuing model for handling customers' calls that resulted in a $10 million annual savings for the company, because resources in its telemarketing program were more effectively allocated. Looking back at our grocery example, at peak shopping hours you could open all counters and keep waiting time to a minimum or you could open only one, thereby minimizing staffing costs, but risking having shoppers walk out, leaving their ice cream and frozen pizza to thaw in the carts.

queuing theory
A technique that balances the cost of having a waiting line against the cost of service to maintain that line.

The mathematics behind queuing theory is beyond the scope of this book. But you can see how the theory works in a simple example. Assume that you're a bank supervisor and one of your responsibilities is assigning tellers. Your bank branch has five teller windows, but you want to know whether you can get by with only one window open during an average morning. You consider 12 minutes to be the longest you would expect any customer to wait patiently in line. If it takes 4 minutes, on average, to serve each customer, the line should not be permitted to get longer than 3 deep (12 minutes/4 minutes per customer = 3 customers). If you know from past experience that, during the morning, people arrive at the average rate of one every 2 minutes, you can calculate the probability that the line will become longer than any number (n) of customers as follows:

$$P_n = \left(1 - \frac{\textit{arrival rate}}{\textit{service rate}}\right) \times \left(\frac{\textit{arrival rate}}{\textit{service rate}}\right)^n$$

where n = 3 customers, *arrival rate* = 2 minutes and *service rate* = 4 minutes per customer. Putting these numbers into this formula generates the following:

$$P_3 = \left(1 - \frac{2}{4}\right) \times \left(\frac{2}{4}\right)^3 = \left(\frac{1}{2}\right)\left(\frac{8}{64}\right) = \frac{8}{128} = .0625$$

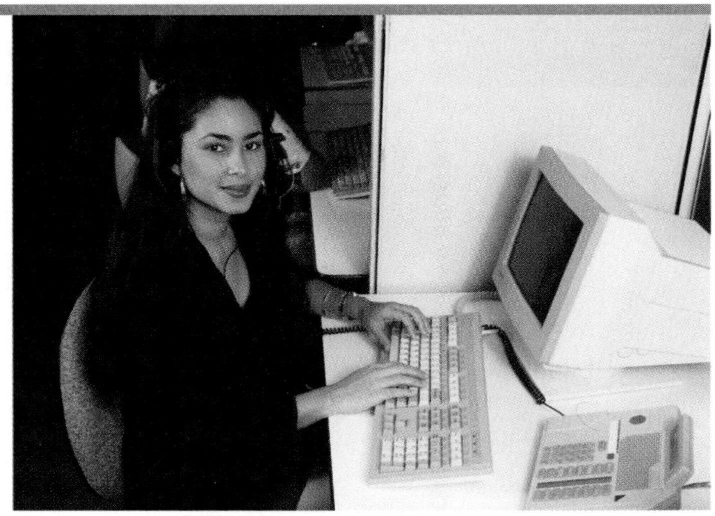
A queuing model developed for promptly handling customers' calls ensures that this representative handles customers efficiently and doesn't keep them waiting too long.

What does a P_3 of .0625 mean? It tells you that the likelihood of having more than 3 customers in line during the morning is one chance in 16 ($1 \div 16 = .0625$). Are you willing to live with 4 or more customers in line 6 percent of the time? If so, keeping 1 teller window open will be enough. If not, you'll need to open additional windows and assign personnel to staff them.

Probability Theory

probability theory
The use of statistics to analyze past predictable patterns and to reduce risk in future plans.

With the help of **probability theory**, managers can use statistics to reduce the amount of risk in plans. By analyzing past predictable patterns, a manager can improve current and future decisions. It makes for more effective planning when, for example, the marketing manager at Porsche/North America, who is responsible for the 968 product line, knows that the mean age of her customers is 35.5 years, with a standard deviation of 3.5. If she assumes a normal distribution of ages, the manager can use probability theory to calculate that 95 of every 100 customers are between 28.6 and 42.4 years of age ($1.96 \times$ standard deviation of $3.5 = 6.86$; then 35.5 ± 6.86). If she were developing a new marketing program, she could use this information to target available marketing dollars more effectively.

Marginal Analysis

marginal analysis
A planning technique that assesses the incremental costs or revenues in a decision.

The concept of marginal, or incremental, analysis helps decision makers to optimize returns or minimize costs. **Marginal analysis** deals with the additional cost in a particular decision, rather than the average cost. For example, the commercial dry cleaner who wonders whether he should take on a new customer would not consider the total revenue and the total cost that would result after the order was taken, but rather what additional revenue and costs would be generated by this particular order. If the incremental revenues exceeded the incremental costs, total profits would be increased by accepting the order. Managers also use marginal analysis for determining whether or not to add new product features. For instance, before Volvo decided to install its newly developed multilink suspension system, supplemental restraint system, and anti-lock braking system on its cars, managers analyzed the marginal costs and revenues generated by these product additions.

Simulation

simulation
A model of a real-world phenomenon that contains one or more variables that can be manipulated in order to assess their impact.

Managers are increasingly turning to simulation as a means for trying out various planning options. They are using **simulation** to create a model of a real-world event, and are then manipulating one or more variables in the model to assess their impact. Simulation can deal with problems addressed by linear programming, but it can also deal with more complex situations.

How might a manager use simulation? Let's see how Merck used simulation as it considered the proposed $6.6 billion acquisition of Medco, the mail-order pharmacy company. The problem it wanted to simulate was how Merck's performance would be in the future, with and without Medco. Managers in the finance department built a model with a vast number of vari-

These software designers at Coopers & Lybrand are perfecting a computer simulation technique called "agent-based simulation", which offers insights into real-life business decisions by allowing hundreds, thousands, or even millions of virtual humans to interact and make buying decisions. The current project simulates 50 000 imaginary CD buyers.

ables including, among other things, information about the US health care system and health care reform possibilities, profit margins, possible future changes in the mix of generic and brand-name drugs, and how the company's competitors might react to the merger. Needless to say, with the number of variables involved in this complex model, a computer was used to change the variables at random, and to test to see how the proposed merger would perform under different business and economic scenarios. The numerous simulations helped Merck managers to decide that the Medco acquisition made sense and they proceeded with their acquisition plan.

PROJECT MANAGEMENT

Project management is the task of getting project activities completed on time, within budget, and according to specifications. More and more organizations are using project management, because its approach fits well with a dynamic environment and with the need for flexibility and rapid response. Organizations are increasingly undertaking projects that are somewhat unusual or are unique, have specific deadlines, contain complex interrelated tasks requiring specialized skills, and are temporary in nature. These types of projects do not fit neatly into the standardized planning and operating procedures that guide an organization's other routine and ongoing work activities.

project management
The task of getting a project's activities done on time, within budget, and according to specifications.

In a typical project, the work is done by a project team whose members are temporarily assigned to the project, and who report to a project manager. The project manager co-ordinates the project's activities with other departments and often reports directly to upper-level management.

The planning process begins by first clearly defining the project's objectives. Second, all activities in the project and the resources needed to accomplish them must be identified—that is, the labour and materials needed to complete the project. This step may be time-consuming and complex, particularly if the project is unique, and there is none of the history or experience that typically exists in planning tasks to refer to.

TESTING... TESTING...

7 What is the value of breakeven analysis as a planning tool?

8 For what types of planning situations would linear programming be appropriate?

9 Describe how the following are used in planning: queuing theory; probability theory; marginal analysis; and simulation.

Once the activities have been identified, the third step is to determine their sequential relationship. What activities must be completed before others can begin? Which can be undertaken simultaneously? This step is usually done using flow-chart diagrams.

Fourth, the project activities need to be scheduled. The manager estimates the time required for each activity and then uses these estimates to develop an overall project schedule and completion date. Fifth, the project schedule is compared with the objectives, and any necessary adjustments are made. If the project time is too long, the manager might assign more resources to critical activities so that they can be completed more quickly. The project manager may choose to use any of the scheduling techniques that we described earlier in the chapter, such as a Gantt chart, a load chart, or a PERT network.

SUMMARY

This summary is organized by the learning objectives found at the beginning of the chapter.

1. Techniques for scanning the environment include reading newspapers, magazines, books, and trade journals; reading competitors' ads, promotional materials, and press releases; attending trade shows; debriefing sales personnel; and reverse engineering of competitors' products.
2. Quantitative forecasting applies a set of mathematical rules to a set of past data in order to predict future outcomes. Qualitative forecasting uses judgments and the opinions of knowledgeable individuals to predict future outcomes.
3. Benchmarking is the search for the best practices among competitors or non-competitors that lead to superior performance.
4. Gantt and load charts are scheduling devices. Both are bar graphs. Gantt charts monitor planned and actual activities over time; load charts focus on capacity utilization by monitoring whole departments or specific resources.
5. The five steps in developing a PERT network are (a) identifying every significant activity that must be achieved for a project to be completed, (b) determining the order in which these activities must be completed, (c) diagramming the flow of activities in a project from start to finish, (d) estimating the time needed to complete each activity, and (5) using the network diagram to determine a schedule for the start and finish dates of each activity and for the entire project.
6. A product's breakeven point is determined by the unit price of the product, its variable cost per unit, and its total fixed costs.
7. For linear programming to be applicable, a problem must have limited resources, constraints, an objective function to optimize, alternative ways of combining resources, and a linear relationship between variables.
8. Simulation is an effective planning tool because it allows managers to simulate, on a computer, thousands of potential options at very little cost. By simulating a complex situation, managers can see how changes in variables will affect outcomes.
9. Project management involves getting a project's activities done on time, within budget, and according to specifications. A project is a one-time-only set of activities that has a definite beginning and ending point.

THINKING ABOUT MANAGEMENT ISSUES

1. Assume that you manage a large fast-food restaurant in downtown Montreal and you want to know the amount of each type of sandwich to make, and the number of cashiers to have on each shift. What type of planning tool(s) do you think will be useful to you? What type of environmental scanning, if any, would you be likely to do in this management job?
2. *Canadian Business Magazine* and other business periodicals often carry reports of companies that have not met their sales forecasts. What are some reasons a company might not meet its forecasts? What suggestions could you make for improving the effectiveness of forecasting?
3. "People can use statistics to prove whatever it is they want to prove." What do you think of this statement? What are the implications for managers?
4. Some experts believe that the personal computer, additional improvements in information systems technology, and the highly competitive environment of most Canadian firms are leading to an increased use of planning tools and techniques by managers. Do you agree? Why or why not?

SELF-ASSESSMENT EXERCISE

AM I A GOOD PLANNER?

Planning is an important skill for managers. The following assessment is designed to help you understand your planning skills.

Instructions: Answer either Yes or No to each of the following questions.

	Yes	No
1. My personal objectives are clearly spelled out in writing.	_____	_____
2. Most of my days are hectic and disorderly.	_____	_____
3. I seldom make any snap decisions and usually study a problem carefully before acting.	_____	_____
4. I keep a desk calendar or appointment book as an aid.	_____	_____
5. I use "action" and "deferred action" files.	_____	_____
6. I generally establish starting dates and deadlines for all my projects.	_____	_____
7. I often ask others for advice.	_____	_____
8. I believe that all problems have to be solved immediately.	_____	_____

See scoring key on page SK–3.

for your IMMEDIATE action

FOUR MEN & A TRUCK

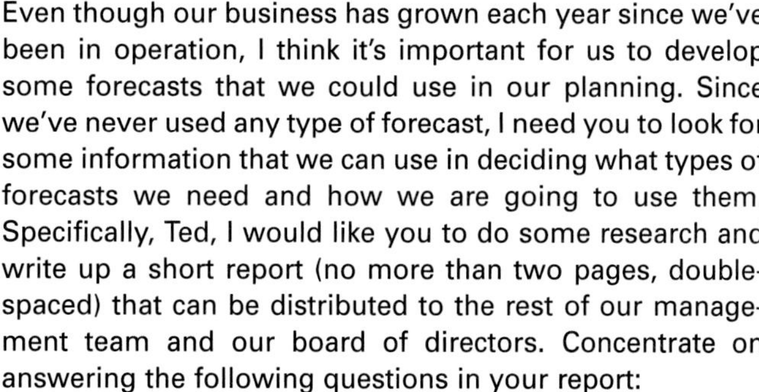

TO: Ted Smith, VP of Marketing
FROM: Sam Gianelli, President
RE: Forecasting for 1999

Even though our business has grown each year since we've been in operation, I think it's important for us to develop some forecasts that we could use in our planning. Since we've never used any type of forecast, I need you to look for some information that we can use in deciding what types of forecasts we need and how we are going to use them. Specifically, Ted, I would like you to do some research and write up a short report (no more than two pages, double-spaced) that can be distributed to the rest of our management team and our board of directors. Concentrate on answering the following questions in your report:

1. What types of forecasts are common? Which do you think would be most appropriate for our use? Why?
2. Where would we get the information to make these forecasts?
3. What would be the disadvantages of using these forecasts?
4. Are there any other planning tools that we could use? What are they and why do you think they would be useful?

I look forward to seeing what you come up with. If you have any questions, don't hesitate to let me know.

This is a fictionalized account of a potentially real problem. It was written for academic purposes only and is not meant to reflect either positively or negatively on management practices at Four Men & a Truck.

TAKE IT TO THE NET

We invite you to visit the Robbins/Coulter/Stuart-Kotze Companion Website at www.prenticehall.ca/robbins for this chapter's Internet resources.

CASE APPLICATION

Oticon Holding A/S, Denmark

Oticon Holding A/S is a Danish manufacturer of hearing aids. Founded in 1905, the company was an ultra-traditional, hierarchical, conservative organization. Then reality set in, as the market changed and new competitors like Sony, Siemens and Philips entered the market. Oticon had to undergo revolutionary change in order to stay competitive with these global giants. CEO Lars Kolind led the company in its metamorphosis into what he calls "the ultimate flexible organization".

To begin with, all organizational departments and employee job titles disappeared. Instead, all work activities became project-based and were implemented by informal groups of interested individuals. Employee "jobs" were reconfigured into unique and fluid combinations of work activities that fit each employee's own specific capabilities and needs. Today, project teams form, disband, and form again as the work requires. Project "leaders" are basically anyone in the company with a good idea who is willing to pursue it. Project leaders compete to attract whatever resources and people they need to complete the project. Project "owners", members of Oticon's 10-person management team, provide advice and support, but they make few actual decisions.

The company's offices have been redesigned to be conducive to relaxed, informal team groups. Paper is virtually obsolete. Open spaces with desks on wheels and computers typify the office areas—these can be pulled together by any group. Coffee bars provide informal meeting places. Large and small "dialogue rooms" with circular sofas and small tables are scattered throughout the building. Kolind estimates that there are, at any one time, approximately 100 projects of various magnitude in progress. He feels strongly that the company can respond quickly to any opportunities that emerge anywhere around the globe. Kolind has said: "We're developing products twice as fast as anybody else. But when you look around, you see a very relaxed atmosphere. We're not fast on the surface, we're fast underneath".

QUESTIONS

1. Given the unusual ways in which work is done at Oticon, what planning tools and techniques might be useful? Explain your choices.
2. Suppose that some organization wanted to use Oticon as a benchmark. What types of things might it learn from Oticon?
3. Compare Oticon's approach to project management with what was described in the chapter. What similarities do you see? What differences? Is one approach better than the other? Explain.

Sources: P LaBarre, "The Dis-organization of Oticon", *Industry Week,* July 18, 1994, pp. 22-38; T. Peters, "Successful Electronic Change-overs Depend on Daring", *Springfield Business Journal,* August 8, 1994, p.15; and LaBarre, "This Organization Is Dis-Organization", Fast Company Web Page <http://www.fastcompany.com>, April 16, 1997.

VIDEO CASE APPLICATION

Canadians in Cuba

Canada is Cuba's number one trading partner. Not a situation one might have predicted three-and-a-half decades ago when Cuba was very much part of the communist world and was the scene of anxious brinkmanship between the Soviet Union and the US. The cold war may be over, but the US has certainly not forgotten the Cuban Missile Crisis, and isn't comfortable with the idea of having a government that is ostensibly communist only ninety miles from its shores. The Helms-Burton Law in the US seeks to punish any companies that trade with Cuba. Canadian executives with companies trading in Cuba are forbidden entry into the US Moreover, US law allows American interests to sue companies operating in Cuba, using the argument that US assets appropriated by the Cuban government are being acquired by Canadian and other interests.

Joint-ventures between the Cuban government and the foreign investor typify how international companies do business with Castro's nation. Operations are left in the hands of the foreign investor, while the Cuban government retains controlling interest. State-run organizations handle all hiring for the operations. This obviously results in a lack of control over human-resources for Canadian companies in Cuba. But perhaps this is an ideal world in which companies can operate: strikes are non-existent and labour shortages are never hard to fill. Canadian managers operating in Canada with its multitude of labour laws might find the Cuban situation an enviable one. Canadian workers, on the other hand, probably couldn't imagine having to work in an environment in which they would have virtually no rights.

QUESTIONS

1. Cuban workers receive an average salary of $15 a month. Is it ethical for a Canadian company to pay such low wages for the same job that they might pay a Canadian $1500 a month to do? At Canada's Delta Hotels' operations in Cuba, employees are provided with free meals, monthly supplies such as soap and toothbrushes and, of course, employees receive tips (in foreign currencies, often heavily outweighing their actual salaries). Does this have any effect on the ethical dimensions of the situation? What ethical responsibilities, if any, do Canadian companies have in regard to Cuban employees?
2. Should businesses concern themselves at all with international political situations? Explain your position.
3. Is it ethical for a Canadian company to have one set of ethical standards at home, and a different one abroad?

Video source: "Congressman" and "Ambassador," *The National* (April 27, 1998).

VIDEO CASE APPLICATION

Skeet and Ikes, Vancouver

Skeet and Ikes is a great entrepreneurial story. The story of Jason Dorland ("Skeet") forming the idea for the business from a packaging design project for his art school graduation thesis, is the sort of business story that the media loves to report on. When a company is created out of a mixture of inspiration, chance, enthusiasm and guts, this always makes an interesting tale. But, of course, the realities of the world of business soon create many obstacles for a business to overcome. As Dorland himself says, he "hates the serious side" of the business. In many ways, he is a problem avoider. Hopefully, therefore, Ian Walker, President of Skeet and Ikes, is a problem seeker and problem solver. Skeet and Ikes has created a niche for itself in the marketplace; now it must find the best ways in which it can exploit that niche. Determining how best to market its products, and to whom, is one major challenge. In the video, we see that Dorland and Walker have decided to focus on the nearby US market, specifically on the Seattle-based "Larry's" chain. "We feel that just in five stores in Larry's we're going to sell almost as much as in thirty stores in Vancouver," says Walker. Although the size of these stores is obviously a major factor, perhaps the more important aspect is the type of store in which Skeet and Ikes products are sold. In order to make a profit, they will obviously want to market to a specific type of customer. Larry's carries many high-end products and therefore its clientele may be more likely to purchase this kind of upmarket product.

When Skeet and Ikes determine what its target market is, it will need further financial backing in order to reach it. How to attract investors in order to expand the company is another challenge for Dorland and Walker. Right now, the company is obviously in its infant stages. There will be many changes and decisions to be made in the immediate future, as Skeet and Ikes attempts to grow into a profitable enterprise.

QUESTIONS

1. What sort of non-programmed decisions would Dorland and Walker have had to face when forming Skeet and Ikes? What sorts of decisions do they face now and in the future?
2. What do you think would be the most effective decision-making style (analytic, conceptual, behavioural or directive) for Ian Walker at this stage of the business? Why?
3. Use Table 6-4 to discuss the kinds of decisions that Skeet and Ikes face.

Video source: "Skeet and Ikes," *Venture* #646 (June 15, 1997).

VIDEO CASE APPLICATION

Conrad Black

As chairman of the international newspaper empire, Hollinger (which owns Canadian-based Southam Inc.'s chain), Conrad Black's strategy thus far has always followed a specific formula: buying newspapers that are facing financial difficulty, and turning them into efficient profit-generators. When Black announced his intention to form a daily national newspaper in Canada, the news was met with some shock by media analysts. Black had never before built a newspaper from the ground up. In the final interviews in this video, we see Chris Dornan commenting that: "The pressure has just ratcheted up on *The Financial Post* to sell themselves or come over to the Southam camp". As it turns out, he was quite right. Southam did buy controlling interest in *The Financial Post*, giving up four of its fifty-eight Canadian daily newspapers to finance the acquisition.

Now Black has his national paper, the *National Post* in circulation, and is competing head-to-head with the *Globe and Mail* for the national market. The coming years will prove very interesting in the Canadian newspaper industry. The American daily national newspaper, *USA Today,* suffered losses of roughly $800 million in its first decade. Of course, it is perhaps a poor example for comparison considering the size of that market versus the Canadian market. Black's track record would suggest that he knows what he is doing, and the *National Post* does have some significant weapons in its arsenal. The base of newspapers Southam controls across the country will be an advantage for the *Post*, and the expertise of *The Financial Post* on business reporting should provide the new paper with one major selling point from the outset. But it will take years to determine whether it has won enough of the Canadian advertising market to justify the expense Black has poured into the project.

QUESTIONS

1. What role would specific plans play in the planning of this launch? What role would directional plans play?
2. To what degree and in what ways is environmental uncertainty a factor here? How would this affect planning for the new paper?
3. How would the commitment concept affect planning at the new paper?

Video Source: "Newspapers" and "2x1 Canadian," *The National* (April 8, 1998).

Additional Sources: A. Wilson-Smith, "The Scoop on Black", *Maclean's,* March 30, 1998, pp. 14-17; D Berman, "Black's Big Bet", *Canadian Business,* May 8, 1998, pp. 33-36; and E Alden, "Hollinger buys Financial Post in swap deal", *Financial Times (UK).*

P A R T F O U R

Organizing

LEARNING OBJECTIVES

After Reading This Chapter, You Should Be Able To:

1. Define organizational structure and organizational design
2. Explain why structure and design are important to an organization
3. Describe the six key elements of organizational structure
4. Differentiate between mechanistic and organic organizational designs
5. Identify the four contingency factors that influence organizational design
6. Describe bureaucracy and its strengths
7. Explain team-based structures and why organizations use them
8. Describe matrix organizations, project structures, and autonomous internal units
9. Identify the characteristics of a boundaryless organization and this structure's appeal
10. Explain the concept of a learning organization and how it influences organizational design
11. Describe the role that technology plays in organizational design

A MANAGER'S CHALLENGE

Abitibi-Consolidated, Montreal

The headquarters of the world's largest producer of newsprint was moved to Montreal after the merger of Abitibi-Price and Stone Consolidated created what is now known as Abitibi-Consolidated. Since the merger back in 1997, Chairman Ronald Oberlander has been faced with the task of leading the integration of the two mammoth companies into one corporate culture. This entails combining 18 newsprint mills, seven sawmills, and a total of 14 500 employees. Oberlander believes that the merger has allowed Abitibi-Consolidated to become far more efficient than the two companies were separately. He has said, "The purpose of the merger was to get $200 million in synergies back. It won't happen if we each

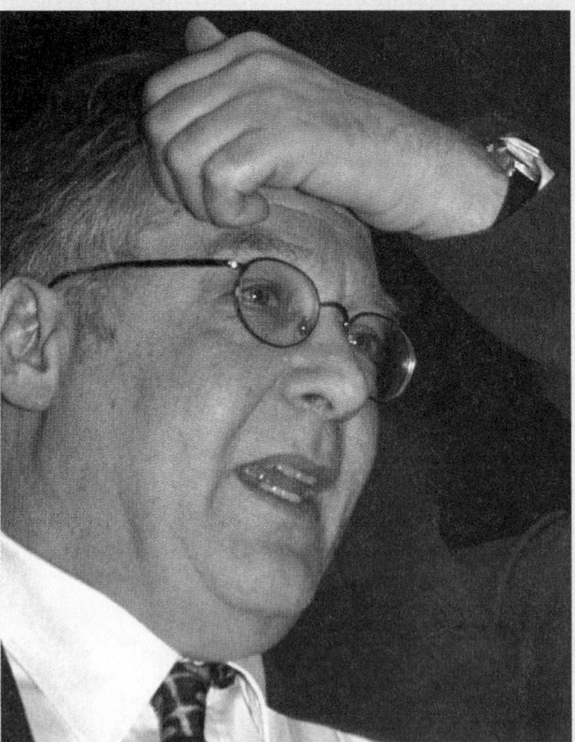

hide in our own corners". To achieve this, Oberlander focuses on "improving communication" laterally between plants. After the merger, 150 managers took three months to determine what the new vision for the company should be. Abitibi is now focusing on new product development, as well as expanding its global reach.[1]

The company is fostering a global outlook amongst its employees, and providing greater opportunities in career development through programs such as formal mentoring. Oberlander states: "We must give challenges to people before they think they are ready". To further this aim, Abitibi encourages movement of its employees throughout the organization, wherein a person can move into different departments to gain a greater knowledge of the organization as a whole. In Oberlander's words: "If the requirement to become CEO is that you have to run a mill, and only engineers can run mills, then we will lose very good people". Abitibi-Consolidated's commitment to furthering employees' career aims seems to be having an impressive effect on employee attitudes. An internal memo designed to discover how many people would be willing to devote three years to working in a Chinese operation, found that 200 managers and lower-level employees were willing to take the plunge.

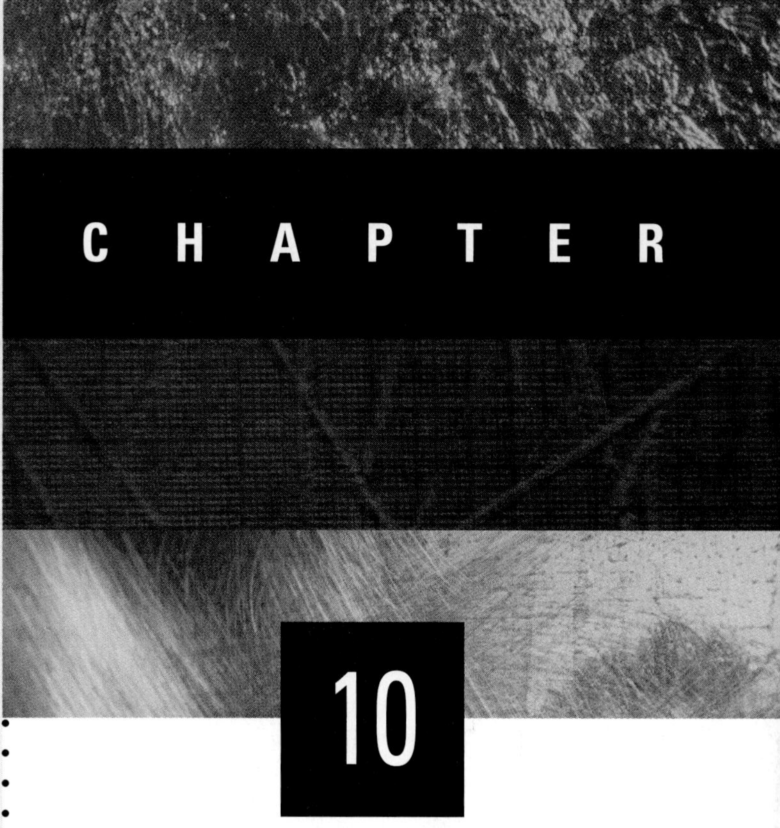

Organizational Structure and Design

In this chapter we'll present information about designing appropriate organizational structures. We'll look at the various dimensions of organizational structure and what contingency factors influence the design. Finally, we'll look at how organizational structures evolve and at some of the newest concepts in organizational design. By the end of the chapter, you should have a better sense of the issues facing organizations like Abitibi-Consolidated, with regard to structure and design.

DEFINING ORGANIZATIONAL STRUCTURE AND DESIGN

No other topic in management has undergone as much change in the past few years as that of organizing and organizational structure. Traditional approaches to organizing work are being questioned and re-evaluated, as managers search out structural designs that will best support and facilitate employees doing the organization's work. Remember, from Chapter 1, that **organizing** is defined as the process of creating an organization's structure. This process is important and serves many purposes (see Table 10-1). The challenge for managers is to design an organizational structure that allows employees to do their work effectively and efficiently, while accomplishing organizational objectives.

organizing
The process of creating an organization's structure.

Just what is an organization's structure? An **organizational structure** is the formal framework by which job tasks are divided, grouped and co-ordinated. Just as humans have skeletons that define their shapes, organizations have strucures that define theirs. When managers develop or change an organization's structure, they are engaged in **organizational design**—a process that involves decisions about six key elements: work specialization; departmentalization; chain of command; span of control; centralization and decentralization; and formalization.[2] Let's take a closer look at each of these six elements of structure.

organizational structure
The organization's formal framework, by which job tasks are divided, grouped, and co-ordinated.

organizational design
The developing or changing of an organization's structure.

Work Specialization

The concept of work specialization can be traced back a couple of centuries to Adam Smith's discussion of division of labour, and his conclusion that it contributed to increased employee productivity (refer to Chapter 2 if you'd like to refresh your memory). A well-known application of the division-of-labour concept is Henry Ford's assembly line in the early 1900s. Every Ford worker was assigned a specific, repetitive task. One person would put on the right front wheel, someone else would install the right front door, another worker would install the bench seat, and so on. By breaking jobs up into small, standardized tasks that could be performed over and over again, Ford was able to produce cars at a rate of one every 10 seconds, while using employees who had relatively limited skills.

Today we use the term **work specialization**, or division of labour, to describe the degree to which tasks in an organization are divided into separate jobs. The essence of work specialization is that an entire job is not done by one individual but, instead, is broken down into steps, and each step is completed by a different person. Individual employees specialize in doing part of an activity rather than the entire activity.

work specialization
The degree to which tasks in an organization are divided into separate jobs. Also known as division of labour.

By the late 1940s, most manufacturing jobs in industrialized countries were being done with the use of high work specialization. Managers saw it as a way to make the most efficient use of employees' skills. How? In most organizations, some work tasks require high levels of skills and others can be performed by unskilled workers. If all workers were engaged in every step of, say, the manufacturing process, all would need the skills necessary to perform both the most demanding and the least demanding jobs. The result would be that, except when performing the most skilled or highly sophisticated work tasks, employees would be working below their skill levels. Because skilled workers are paid more than unskilled workers and their wages tend to reflect their highest level of skills, this use of organizational resources would be inefficient—a company would be paying highly skilled workers to perform simple tasks.

TABLE 10-1 Some Purposes of Organizing

Divides work to be done into specific jobs and departments
Assigns tasks and responsibilities associated with individual jobs
Coordinates diverse organizational tasks
Clusters jobs into units
Establishes relationships among individuals, groups, and departments
Establishes formal lines of authority
Allocates and deploys organizational resources

The prestige of the Mayo Clinic, renowned for its expertise in every branch of medicine, is largely due to the specializations of its 1150 physicians, 1000 residents, and 15 000 nurses, technicians, students and staff.

Managers also found that other efficiencies could be achieved through work specialization. It stands to reason that employees' skills at performing a task would improve through repetition. In addition, less time would be spent in changing tasks, in putting away tools and equipment from a prior step in the work process, and in getting ready for another. Equally important is the fact that employee training in specialization is more efficient from the organization's perspective, because it is easier and less costly to find and train workers to do specific, repetitive, limited tasks than to find and train workers to do all the tasks. The difference is especially true of highly sophisticated and complex operations. Could Bombardier produce one of its planes if one person was building it alone? Also, work specialization increases efficiency and productivity by encouraging the creation of special inventions and machinery to perform work tasks.

During the first half of the twentieth century, managers viewed work specialization as an unending source of increased productivity. Because it wasn't highly practised, its implementation in an organization almost always generated higher employee productivity. By the 1960s, however, it was becoming evident that a good thing could be carried too far. The point had been reached in some jobs at which the human diseconomies from work specialization (such as boredom, fatigue, stress, low productivity, poor quality of work, increased absenteeism, and higher job turnover) more than offset the economic advantages. In such instances, worker productivity could be increased by enlarging, rather than narrowing, the scope of job activities. In addition, several organizations found that employees who were given a variety of work activities to do were allowed to do the work activities necessary to complete a whole job. They were put into teams with interchangeable skills, and often achieved significantly higher output and were more satisfied with their jobs than were specialized workers.

Most managers today see work specialization as an important organizing mechanism but not as a source of endlessly increasing productivity. They recognize the economies it provides in certain types of jobs, but they also recognize the problems it creates when it's carried to extremes.

Departmentalization

Does your school have a financial aid department or an administrative department? If you are employed, does your organization have an advertising department or regional sales divisions?

THINKING CRITICALLY ABOUT ETHICS

Changes in technology have cut the shelf life of most employees' skills. A factory worker or clerical employee used to be able to learn one job and be reasonably sure that the skills learned to do that job would be enough for most of his or her working life. This is no longer the case. What ethical obligation do organizations have to assist workers whose skills have become obsolete? What about employees? Do they have an obligation to keep their skills from becoming obsolete? What ethical guidelines might you suggest for dealing with employee skill obsolescence? ■

FIGURE 10-1 Functional Departmentalization

Plant Manager

Manager, Engineering | Manager, Accounting | Manager, Manufacturing | Manager, Human Resources | Manager, Purchasing

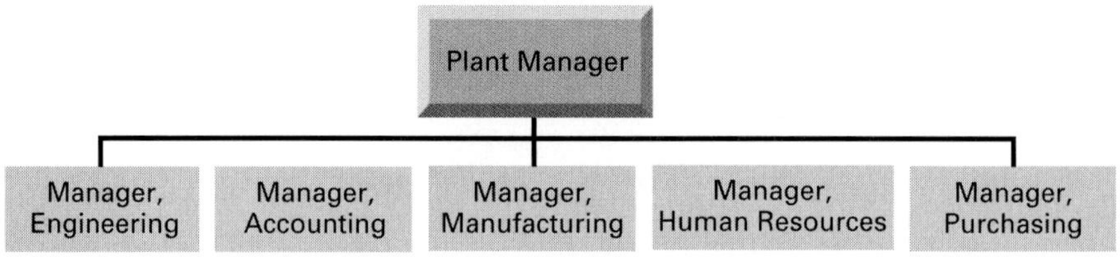

departmentalization
The basis on which jobs are grouped in order to accomplish organizational goals.

Once jobs have been divided up through work specialization they then have to be grouped back together so that common tasks can be co-ordinated. The basis on which jobs are grouped in order to accomplish organizational goals is called **departmentalization**. Every organization will have its own specific way of classifying and grouping work activities.

functional departmentalization
Grouping jobs by functions performed.

Historically, one of the most popular ways to group work activities has been by function performed, or **functional departmentalization** (see Figure 10-1). For instance, a manufacturing manager might organize his or her plant by separating engineering, accounting, manufacturing, human resources, and purchasing specialists into common departments. A hotel might be organized around housekeeping, front desk, maintenance, restaurant operations, reservations, human resources, and accounting. Of course, departmentalization by function can be used in all types of organizations, although the functions change to reflect the organization's objectives and work activities. The major advantage of this type of grouping is obtaining efficiencies from putting similar specialities and people with common skills, knowledge, and orientations together into common units.

product departmentalization
Grouping jobs by product line

Work activities can also be departmentalized by the type of product the organization produces—that is, by **product departmentalization**. Figure 10-2 illustrates this type of grouping as used by Montreal's Bombardier Ltd. Each major product area in the corporation is placed under the authority of an executive who is a specialist in, and is responsible for, everything having to do with his or her product line. If an organization's activities were service-related rather than product-related, each service would be grouped separately. For instance, an accounting firm could have departments for tax preparation, management consulting, auditing, and the like. Each department would offer an array of related services under the direction of a service manager.

geographical departmentalization
Grouping jobs on the basis of territory or geography.

Another way to departmentalize is on the basis of geography or territory—called **geographical departmentalization** (see Figure 10-3). The sales function, for instance, may

FIGURE 10-2 Product Departmentalization

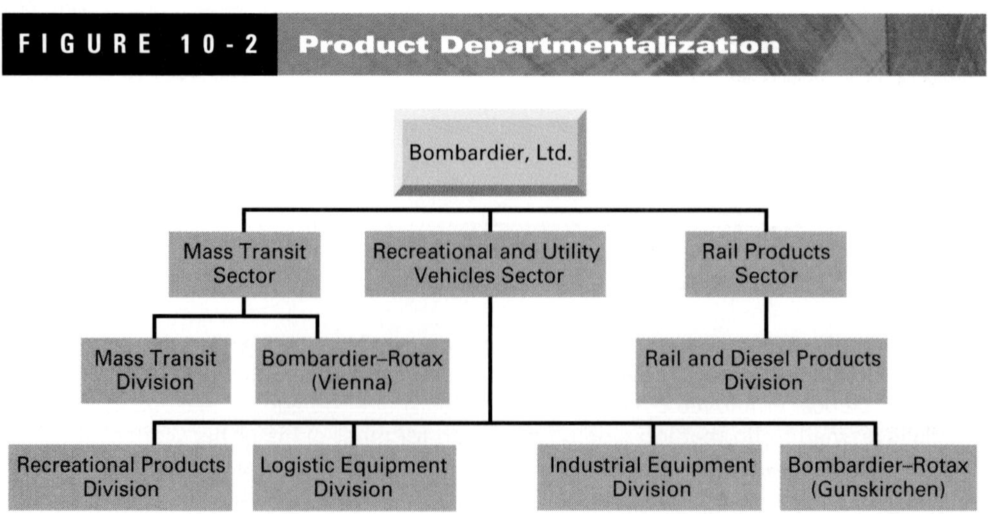

Source: Bombardier Annual Report.

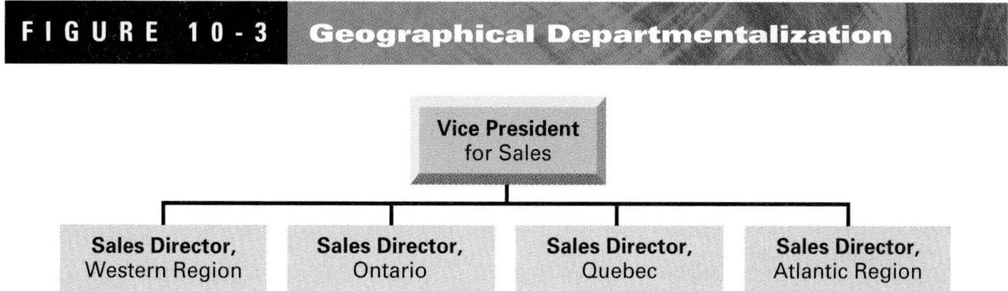

FIGURE 10-3 Geographical Departmentalization

have regions divided into western Canada, Ontario, Quebec, and the Atlantic provinces. Each of these regions is, in effect, a department organized around geography. If an organization's customers are scattered over a large geographical area, this form of departmentalization can be valuable.

At a wood cabinet manufacturing plant in Dartmouth, Nova Scotia, production is organized around six departments: sawing; planing and milling; assembling; lacquering and sanding; finishing; and inspection and shipping. This is an example of **process departmentalization**, which is grouping activities on the basis of product or customer flow. Figure 10-4 illustrates the process form of departmentalization. Because each process requires particular skills, this approach offers a basis for the homogeneous categorizing of work activities. Process departmentalization can be used for processing customers as well as products. For instance, if you've ever been in a provincial motor vehicle office to get a driver's licence, you probably went through several departments before receiving your licence. A common scenario would be to go through three steps: validation by the motor vehicle division; processing by the licensing department; and payment collection by the treasury department.

process departmentalization Grouping jobs on the basis of product or customer flow.

A final means of departmentalizing is to use the particular type of customer the organization seeks to reach (see Figure 10-5). This is known as **customer departmentalization**. For instance, the sales activities in an office supply firm can be broken down into three departments that service retail, wholesale, and government customers. Or a large law office might segment its staff on the basis of whether they serve corporate or individual clients. The assumption underlying customer departmentalization is that customers in each department have a common set of problems and needs that can best be met by having specialists for each.

customer departmentalization Grouping jobs on the basis of common customers.

Large organizations often combine most or all of these forms of departmentalization. For example, a major Japanese electronics firm organizes each of its divisions along functional lines and organizes its manufacturing units around processes. It departmentalizes sales around seven geographical regions, and it divides each sales region into four customer groups.

FIGURE 10-4 Process Departmentalization

Plant Superintendent

Sawing Department Manager | Planing and Milling Department Manager | Assembling Department Manager | Lacquering and Sanding Department Manager | Finishing Department Manager | Inspection and Shipping Department Manager

1 What are the advantages and drawbacks of work specialization?

2 Describe the ways in which managers can departmentalize work activities.

FIGURE 10-5 Customer Departmentalization

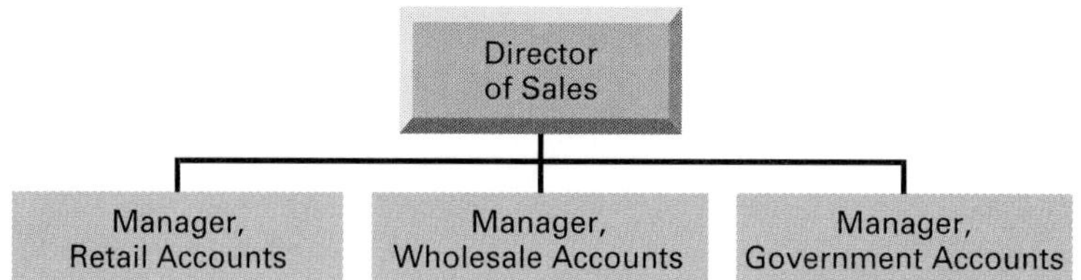

L L Bean
www.llbean.com

Today, two general departmentalization trends seem to have taken hold. First, customer departmentalization remains highly popular as an approach to departmentalizing. In order to be more able to respond to changes in those needs, many organizations have emphasized customer departmentalization. For example, L L Bean restructured around six customer groups on the basis of what its customers generally purchased from the company. This arrangement allowed the company to better understand its customers and respond more quickly to their requirements. The second trend is that rigid functional departmentalization is being complemented by the use of cross-functional teams that cross over traditional departmental lines. In many organizations, rigid departmental divisions have been replaced by a hybrid grouping of individuals who are experts in various specialities, and who work together in an organizational arrangement known as a **cross-functional team**. What is unique about cross-functional teams is that they bring together diverse experts who might never cross paths in a traditional organization, although their work might be highly interdependent. Today, we find cost accountants teaming up with operations managers, product designers collaborating with purchasing department employees, and marketing professionals working with research engineers. We'll discuss the use of cross-functional teams more fully in Chapter 14.

cross-functional teams
A hybrid grouping of individuals who are experts in various specialities (or functions) and who work together.

Chain of Command

During the 1960s and 1970s, the chain of command concept was a basic cornerstone of organizational design. As you'll see, it has far less importance today, but managers still need to consider its implications when they decide how best to structure their organizations.

The **chain of command** is an unbroken line of authority that extends from the upper levels of an organization down to the lowest levels, and clarifies who reports to whom. It helps employees determine to whom they should go if they have a problem and also to whom they are responsible.

chain of command
An unbroken line of authority that extends from the upper levels of the organization to the lowest levels, and clarifies who reports to whom.

We can't discuss the chain of command without discussing three analogous concepts: authority; responsibility; and unity of command. **Authority** refers to the rights inherent in a managerial position to give orders and to expect the orders to be obeyed. To facilitate decision making and co-ordination, the organization provides each managerial position in the organizational structure with a place in the chain of command and "grants" each manager a certain degree of authority to meet his or her responsibilities. When one is given the "right" to do something, one assumes a corresponding obligation to perform those assigned activities. This obligation or expectation to perform is known as **responsibility**. Finally, the **unity of command** principle (one of Henri Fayol's 14 principles of management) helps to preserve the concept of an unbroken line of authority. It states that a person should have one and only one superior to whom he or she is directly responsible. If the unity of command is broken, a subordinate might have to cope with conflicting demands or priorities from several superiors.

authority
The rights inherent in a managerial position to give orders and to expect the orders to be obeyed.

responsibility
The obligation or expectation to perform.

unity of command
The management principle that a subordinate should have one and only one superior to whom he or she is directly responsible.

The classical management theorists (Fayol, Weber, Taylor, and others) were enamoured with the concepts of chain of command, authority, responsibility, and unity of command—but times change and so has the relevance of these basic tenets of organizational design. The concepts are substantially less relevant today because of advancements in computer technology and the trend towards empowering employees. A low-level employee today can access information that used to be available only to top managers, in a matter of seconds. Similarly, computer technology increasingly allows employees anywhere in an organization to communicate with anyone else, without going through formal channels—that is, through the chain of command. Moreover, the concepts of authority, responsibility, and maintaining the chain of command have become less relevant as operating employees are being empowered to make decisions that previously were reserved for management. Add the popularity of self-managed and cross-functional teams, and the creation of new structural designs that include multiple bosses, and you can begin to see why the chain-of-command concept has become less relevant. Of course, many organizations still find that they are most productive when enforcing the chain of command, but the number of such companies is dwindling.

Span of Control

span of control
The number of subordinates a manager can supervise effectively and efficiently.

The concept of **span of control** refers to how many subordinates a manager can effectively and efficiently supervise. The question of span of control received a great deal of attention from early management writers. Although they achieved no consensus on a specific ideal number, these writers favoured small spans—typically no more than six—in order to maintain close control.[3] Several writers did acknowledge, however, that the level in the organization was a contingency variable that could affect the number. They argued that as a manager rose in the organizational hierarchy, he or she would have to deal with a greater variety of complex and ill-structured problems, so top executives should have a smaller span of control than did middle managers. And, likewise, middle managers required a smaller span than supervisors. We now recognize and understand that the most effective and efficient span of control is increasingly determined by looking at several contingency variables. For instance, it's obvious that the more training and experience subordinates have, the less direct supervisors they'll need. Therefore, managers who have well-trained and experienced employees can function quite well with a wider span. Other contingency variables that will determine the appropriate span include similarity of subordinate tasks; the complexity of those tasks; the physical proximity of subordinates; the degree to which standardized procedures are in place; the sophistication of the organization's management information system; the strength of the organization's culture; and the preferred style of the manager.[4]

Why is the span-of-control concept important? To a large degree, it determines how many levels and managers an organization will have. All things being equal, the wider or larger the span of control, the more efficient the organizational design. Let's look at an example to illustrate the validity of that statement.

Assume that we have 2 organizations, and each has approximately 4100 operative employees. As Figure 10-6 shows, if one organization has a uniform span of 4 and the other a span of

FIGURE 10-6 Contrasting Spans of Control

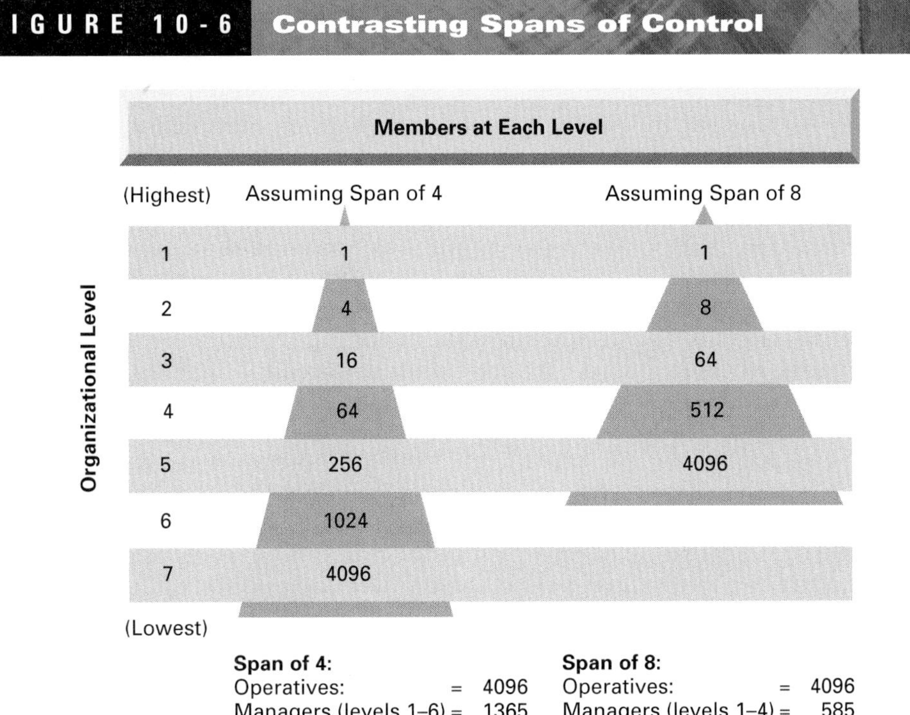

Although he maintains a close personal involvement in every aspect of his successful men's clothing business, Karl Kani of Karl Kani Infinity also sees the need to delegate some control. "It's very hard to be an expert at designing, marketing, manufacturing and distribution,... the smartest thing to do was to enlist experts so that I could attend to the thing I do best"—designing the clothes that carry his name.

8, the wider span will have 2 fewer levels and approximately 800 fewer managers. If the average manager made $40 000 a year, the organization with the wider span would save $32 million a year in management salaries alone! Obviously, wider spans are more efficient in terms of cost. But at some point, wider spans reduce effectiveness. The contemporary view of span of control recognizes that many factors influence the appropriate number of subordinates that a manager can efficiently *and* effectively manage.

The trend in recent years has been towards larger spans of control. Wide spans of control are consistent with efforts by organizations to reduce costs, cut overhead, speed up decision making, increase flexibility, get closer to customers, and empower employees. However, to ensure that performance doesn't suffer because of these wider spans, organizations have been investing heavily in employee training. Managers recognize that they can handle a wider span when employees know their jobs inside out, or can turn to their co-workers if they have any questions.

Centralization and Decentralization

In some organizations, top managers make all the decisions and the lower-level managers merely carry out the directives. At the other extreme, there are organizations in which decision making is pushed down through the levels of management to the managers who are closest to the action. The former organizations are described as highly centralized, and the latter as decentralized.

centralization
The degree to which decision making is concentrated in the upper levels of the organization.

decentralization
The handing down of decision-making authority to lower levels in an organization.

Centralization describes the degree to which decision making is concentrated in the upper levels of the organization. If top management makes the organization's key decisions with little or no input from lower-level employees, then the organization is highly centralized. In contrast, the more that lower level employees provide input or are actually given the discretionary power to make decisions, the more **decentralized** the organization is. Keep in mind that the concept of centralization-decentralization is a relative, not an absolute one. What we mean by *relative* is that an organization is never completely centralized or decentralized. Few organizations could function effectively if all decisions were made only by a select group of top managers; nor could they function effectively if all decisions were delegated to the lowest employee levels.

Consistent with recent management efforts to make organizations more flexible and responsive, there has been a distinct trend towards decentralizing decision making. In large companies especially, lower-level managers are "closer to the action" and typically have more detailed knowledge about problems and how best to solve them, than top managers do. An example of the trend towards decentralization can be found at the Bank of Montreal whose 1164 branches have been organized into 236 "communities"—each community being a group

TABLE 10-2 Factors That Influence the Amount of Centralization and Decentralization

More Centralization	More Decentralization
• Environment is stable.	• Environment is complex, uncertain.
• Lower-level managers are not as capable or experienced at making decisions as upper-level managers.	• Lower-level managers are capable and experienced at making decisions.
• Lower-level managers do not want to have a say in decisions.	• Lower-level managers want a voice in decisions.
• Decisions are significant.	• Decisions are relatively minor.
• Organization is facing a crisis or the risk of company failure.	• Corporate culture is open to allowing managers to have a say in what happens.
• Company is large.	• Company is geographically dispersed.
• Effective implementation of company strategies depends on managers' retaining say over what happens.	• Effective implementation of company strategies depends on managers' having involvement and flexibility to make decisions.

of branches within a limited geographical area. Each community is led by a community area manager, who typically works within a 20-minute drive of all the community's branches. This area manager can respond faster and more knowledgeably to problems in his community than can someone at the bank's national headquarters.[5]

What determines whether an organization will move towards more centralization or more decentralization? A number of influencing factors have been identified. Table 10-2 lists some of them.

Formalization

Formalization refers to the degree to which jobs within the organization are standardized and the extent to which employee behaviour is guided by rules and procedures. If a job is highly formalized, then the person doing that job has a minimum amount of discretion over what is to be done, when it's to be done, and how it should be done. Employees can be expected to always handle the same input in exactly the same way, resulting in a consistent and uniform output. In organizations with high formalization, there are explicit job descriptions, a lot of organizational rules, and clearly defined procedures covering work processes. Where formalization is low, job behaviours are relatively non-structured and employees have a great deal of freedom in how they do their work. An individual's discretion on the job is inversely related to the amount of behaviour in that job which is pre-programmed by the organization. Therefore, the greater the standardization, the less input the employee has into how his or her work is done. Standardization not only eliminates the possibility that employees will engage in alternative behaviours, it also removes the need for employees to consider alternatives.

formalization
The degree to which jobs within an organization are standardized and the extent to which employee behaviour is guided by rules and procedures.

The degree of formalization can vary widely between organizations and even within organizations. For instance, at an organization that publishes newspapers, news reporters often have a great deal of discretion in their job. They may be told what news topic to write about, but they have the freedom to find their own stories, research them in the way that they want, and write them up with only minimal guidelines. On the other hand, the compositors and typesetters who lay out the newspaper pages don't have that type of freedom. They have constraints—both of time and space—that standardize how they do their work.

3 How is the chain-of-command concept used in organizing?

4 Describe the advantages and drawbacks of centralization and decentralization.

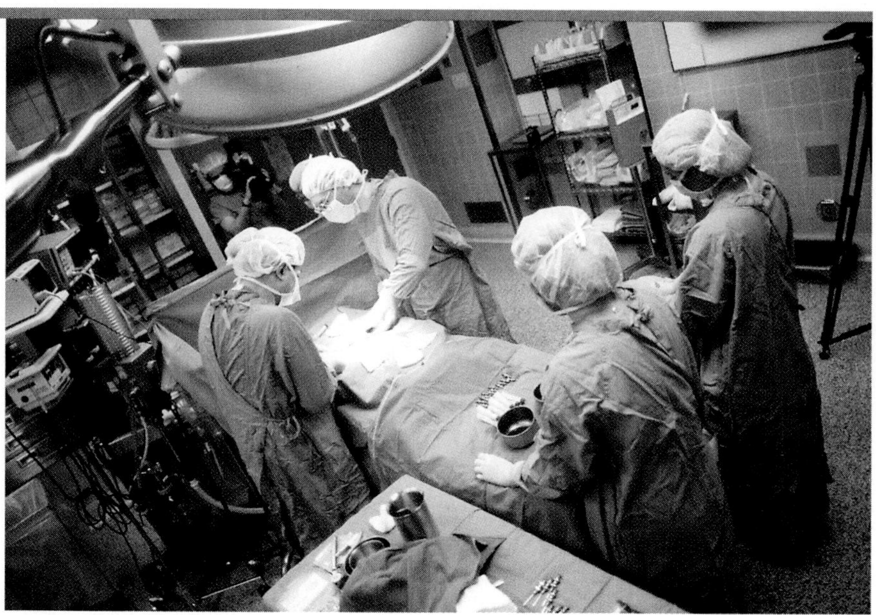

Queen Elizabeth II Hospital in Halifax is a good example of an organization in which job descriptions are highly *formalized.*

THE CONTINGENCY APPROACH TO ORGANIZATIONAL DESIGN

If we combine the classical principles, we arrive at what most of the early management writers believed to be the "ideal" structural design: the mechanistic or bureaucratic organization. Today, we recognize that there's no single ideal organizational design for all situations. As we discovered with planning and most other management concepts, the ideal organizational design depends on contingency factors. In this section, we'll look at two generic models of organizational design and then look at the contingency factors that favour each.

Mechanistic and Organic Organizations

mechanistic organization (bureaucracy)
A structure that is high in complexity, formalization and centralization.

Figure 10-7 describes two diverse organizational forms.[6] The **mechanistic organization** (or **bureaucracy**) was the natural result of following the classical principles. Adherence to the unity of command principle ensured the existence of a formal hierarchy of authority, with each person controlled and supervised by one superior. Keeping the span of control small at increasingly higher levels in the organization created tall, impersonal structures. As the distance between the top and the bottom of the organization expanded, top management would increasingly impose rules and regulations. Because top managers couldn't control lower-level activities through direct observation and ensure the use of standard practices, they substituted rules and regulations. The classical writers' belief in a high degree of division of labour

FIGURE 10-7 Mechanistic Versus Organic Organizations

Mechanistic	Organic
• High Specialization	• Cross-Functional Teams
• Rigid Departmentalization	• Cross-Hierarchical Teams
• Clear Chain of Command	• Free Flow of Information
• Narrow Spans of Control	• Wide Spans of Control
• Centralization	• Decentralization
• High Formalization	• Low Formalization

created jobs that were simple, routine, and standardized. Further specialization through the use of departmentalization increased impersonality and the need for multiple layers of management to co-ordinate the specialized departments.

In terms of our definition of organizational structure, we find the classicists advocating that *all* organizations be high in complexity, formalization, and centralization. Organizational structures would be efficiency machines, well oiled by rules, regulations and routines. The impact of personalities and human judgments, which impose inefficiencies and inconsistencies, would be minimized. Standardization would lead to stability and predictability. Confusion and ambiguity would be eliminated.

In direct contrast to the mechanistic form of organization is the **organic organization** (also referred to as an **adhocracy**). It's low in complexity and formalization, and is decentralized.

organic organization (adhocracy)
A structure that is low in complexity, formalization and centralization.

The organic organization is a highly adaptive structure that's as loose and flexible as the mechanistic organization is rigid and stable. Rather than having standardized jobs and regulations, the adhocracy's loose structure allows it to change rapidly as needs require. Organic organizations have division of labour, but the jobs people do are not standardized. Employees tend to be professionals who are technically proficient and trained to handle diverse problems. They need very few formal rules and little direct supervision because their training has prepared them to deal with the demands of the situation. For instance, a computer engineer is given an assignment. He doesn't need to be given procedures on how to do it. He can solve most problems himself, or can resolve them after conferring with colleagues. Professional standards and conduct guide his behaviour. The organic organization is low in centralization, to allow the professional to respond quickly to problems and to ensure decisions are made by those with relevant expertise.

When is a mechanistic organizational structure preferable, and when is an organic one more appropriate? Let's look at the key contingency factors that influence the structure decision.

Strategy and Structure

An organization's structure is a means to help management achieve its objectives. Since objectives are derived from the organization's overall strategy, it's only logical that strategy and structure should be closely linked. More specifically, structure follows strategy. If management significantly changes its strategy, it will need to modify the structure to accommodate and support this change.

The initial research on the strategy-structure relationship was a study conducted by Alfred Chandler of several large US companies.[7] He traced the development of organizations such as Du Pont, General Motors, Standard Oil of New Jersey, and Sears over a period of 50 years and concluded that changes in corporate strategy precede and lead to changes in an organization's structure. Specifically, Chandler found that organizations usually begin with a single product or line. The simplicity of the strategy requires only a simple or loose form of structure to carry it out. Decisions can be centralized in the hands of a single senior manager while complexity and formalization are low. As organizations grow, their strategies become more ambitious and elaborate, and the structure changes to support the chosen strategy. Recent research has generally confirmed the strategy-structure relationship but has used the strategy terminology presented in Chapter 8.[8] For instance, organizations pursuing a prospector strategy must innovate to be successful. An organic organization matches best with this strategy because it's flexible and maximizes adaptability. In contrast, a defender strategy seeks stability and efficiency, and this can best be achieved with a mechanistic form.

Size and Structure

There's considerable historical evidence that an organization's size significantly affects its structure.[9] For instance, large organizations—typically those employing 2000 or more employees—tend to have more specialization, horizontal and vertical differentiation, and rules and regulations than do small organizations. However, the relationship isn't linear. Rather, size affects structure at a decreasing rate.What we mean by this is that the impact of size becomes less important as an organization expands. Why? Essentially, once an organization has around 2000 employees, it is already fairly mechanistic. An additional 500 employees won't have much of an impact. In contrast, adding 500 employees to an organization that has only 300 members is likely to result in a shift towards a more mechanistic structure.

Technology and Structure

Kinko's Inc.
www.kinkos.com

Every organization uses some form of technology to convert its inputs into outputs. To reach its objectives, the organization uses equipment, materials, knowledge and/or experienced individuals, and combines them into certain types and patterns of activities. For instance, Maytag uses workers on assembly lines to build the washers, dryers, and other home appliances that it manufactures and sells. Kinko's Copies custom-produces jobs for individual customers. And Miles, Inc. uses a continuous-flow production line for manufacturing its vitamins. Each of these organizations represents a different type of technology.

The initial interest in technology as a determinant of structure can be traced to the work of a British scholar—Joan Woodward—in the 1960s.[10] Her research was the first major attempt to view organizational structures from a technological perspective. She demonstrated that organizational structures adapt to their technology. Although few organizational design researchers would argue today that technology is the *sole* determinant of structure, clearly it's an important contributor.[11]

Woodward studied several small manufacturing firms in southern England to determine the extent to which structural design principles, such as unity of command and span of control, were related to organizational success. She was unable to derive any consistent pattern from her data until she segmented the firms into three categories, based on the size of their production runs. The three categories, representing three distinct technologies, had increasing levels of complexity and sophistication. The first category, **unit production**, comprised unit or small-batch producers that manufactured custom products such as tailor-made suits, or turbines for hydroelectric dams. The second category, **mass production**, included large-batch or mass-production manufacturers that made items such as refrigerators or automobiles. The third and most technically complex group, **process production**, included continuous process producers such as oil and chemical refiners.

unit production
The production of items in units or small batches.

mass production
Large-batch manufacturing.

process production
Continuous-process production.

What did Woodward find in her studies of these three groups? She found that (1) distinct relationships existed between these technology classifications and the subsequent structure of the firms; and (2) the effectiveness of the organizations was related to the "fit" between technology and structure. A summary of her findings is shown in Table 10-3.

After carefully analyzing her findings, Woodward concluded that specific structures were associated with each of the three categories, and that successful firms met the requirements of their technology by adopting the proper structural arrangements. She found that there was no one best way in which to organize a manufacturing firm. Unit and process production were most effective when matched with an organic structure, and mass production was most effective when matched with a mechanistic structure.

Since Woodward's initial work, numerous studies have been conducted on the technology-structure relationship. These studies generally demonstrate that organizational structures

Merck Frosst, one of Canada's foremost pharmaceutical companies, relies on new technology to keep its business practices current.

TABLE 10-3 Woodward's Findings on Technology, Structure, and Effectiveness

	Unit Production	Mass Production	Process Production
Structural characteristics	Low vertical differentiation Low horizontal differentiation Low formalization	Moderate vertical differentiation High horizontal differentiation High formalization	High vertical differentiation Low horizontal differentiation Low formalization
Most effective structure	Organic	Mechanistic	Organic

adapt to their technology.[12] The processes or methods that transform an organization's inputs into outputs differ by their degrees of routine involved. In general, the more routine the technology, the more standardized the structure can be. We would expect organizations with routine technologies to be mechanistic, and organizations with non-routine technologies to be organic.[13] Because technology has had—and continues to have—a significant impact on communication flow and organizational design, we include a separate section on those topics at the end of the chapter.

Environment and Structure

In Chapter 3 we introduced the organization's environment as a constraint on managerial discretion. Research has shown that environment is also a major influence on the structure.[14] Essentially, mechanistic organizations are most effective for stable environments. Organic organizations are best matched with dynamic and uncertain environments.

The evidence on the environment-structure relationship helps to explain why so many managers are restructuring their organizations to be lean, fast and flexible. Global competition, accelerated product innovation by all competitors, and increased demands from customers for higher quality and faster deliveries are examples of dynamic environmental forces. Mechanistic organizations tend to be ill-equipped to respond to rapid environmental change. As a result, we're seeing more managers redesigning their organizations in order to make them more organic.

APPLICATIONS OF ORGANIZATIONAL DESIGN

What types of organizational design are companies such as McCain Foods Ltd., Canadian Tire Corp., Loblaws, and Big Rock Breweries using? Let's look at various organizational designs that you might see in today's organizations.

Loblaws
www.loblaws.ca/

Simple Structure

Most organizations start as entrepreneurial ventures with a simple structure consisting of owner(s) and employees. A **simple structure** is defined more by what it is *not* than what it *is*. It is not an elaborate structure.[15] If you work in, or have dealt with, an organization that appears to have almost no structure, it's probably a simple structure. By that we mean that it's low in complexity, has little formalization, and has authority centralized in a single person. The simple structure is a "flat" organization since it usually has only two or three vertical levels, an informal arrangement of employees, and one individual in whom decision-making authority is centralized.

simple structure
An organizational design that is low in complexity and formalization but high in centralization.

5 Describe the differences between mechanistic and organic organizations.

6 What is the relationship between the degree of routine technology and organizational structure?

The simple structure is most widely used by small businesses in which the owner and manager are one and the same. The strengths of the simple structure are obvious: it's fast, flexible, and inexpensive to maintain, and accountability is clear. One major weakness is that it's effective only in small organizations. It becomes increasingly inadequate as an organization grows because its low formalization and high centralization result in information overload at the top. As the organization increases in size, decision making becomes slower and can eventually come to a standstill as the single executive tries to continue making all the decisions. If the structure isn't changed and made more elaborate, the firm is likely to lose market momentum and eventually fail. The simple structure's other weakness is that it's risky; everything depends on one person. If anything happens to that person, the organization's information and decision-making centre is lost.

Bureaucracy

Many organizations do not, by choice or by design, remain simple structures. As a company increases its sales and production volume, it generally reaches a point where it must add employees to help cope with the additional duties and requirements of operating at that volume. As the number of employees rises, the organizational structure tends to become more formalized. Rules and regulations are introduced, jobs become specialized, departments are created, levels of management are added, and the organization becomes increasingly bureaucratic.

We first described the characteristics of a bureaucracy in Chapter 2. Remember that bureaucracy is an organizational arrangement based on order, logic, and the legitimate use of authority. When contingency factors, including growth in size, favour a bureaucratic or mechanistic design, one of two options is most likely to be used. One is a *functional structure,* whose primary focus is on achieving the efficiencies of division of labour by grouping like specialists

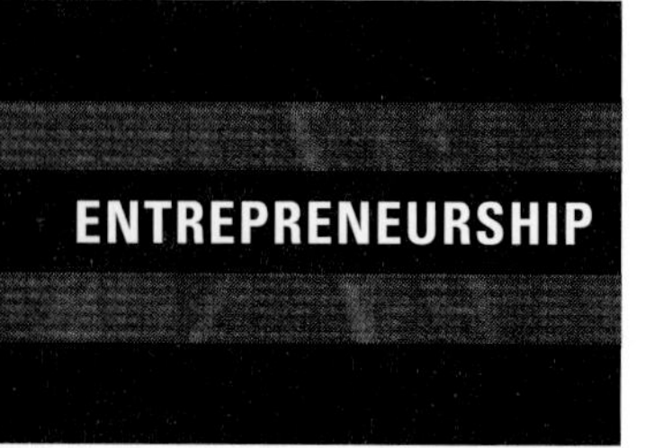

Structuring the Entrepreneurial Firm

At some point, the successful entrepreneur finds that he or she can't do everything alone. More people must be added to the firm. And the entrepreneur must decide the most appropriate structural arrangement for effectively carrying out the firm's activities.[16] Without some type of suitable organizational structure, the entrepreneurial firm can soon find itself in a chaotic situation.

In small firms, the organizational structure tends to evolve with very little conscious and deliberate planning on the part of the founder or owner. For the most part, it looks like a simple structure. As the entrepreneurial firm grows and the owner or founder finds it increasingly difficult to go it alone, employees are brought on board to perform certain functions or duties that the entrepreneur can't handle. These individuals tend to keep doing those same functions as the company matures. Thus is born the functional structure in which each or most of the functional aspects of the venture—such as accounting, marketing, human resources, and so on—is handled by a manager. And it's normal for this functional structure to gradually evolve rather than being created in one bold move.

With the evolution to a more deliberate structure comes a whole new set of challenges for the entrepreneur. All of a sudden, he or she must delegate authority and operating responsibility to others. This is typically one of the most difficult things for an entrepreneur to do—to let someone else make decisions. After all, he or she reasons, how can anyone know this business as well as I do? Also, what might have been a fairly informal, loose, and flexible atmosphere that worked well when the firm was a certain size, now is no longer effective. Many entrepreneurs are intensely concerned about keeping the "small company" atmosphere alive, even as their organization evolves into a more structured arrangement. However, having a "structured" organization doesn't mean having to give up flexibility, adaptability and freedom. In fact, many of the newest organizational designs such as the team-based structure and the boundaryless organization, are particularly well suited to small firms. The fluid designs and arrangements of these contemporary structural designs may provide the entrepreneurial firm with both the openness and the rigidity it needs. ■

together in functional groupings. The other is the *divisional structure,* which creates self-contained, autonomous units or divisions. Let's look at each of these variations more closely.

The **functional structure** expands the concept of functional departmentalization—which we talked about earlier—to the entire organization. Under a functional structure, management designs an organization based on grouping together similar or related occupational specialties. The strength of the functional structure lies in the cost-saving advantages that accrue from specialization. Putting similar specialties together results in economies of scale, minimizes duplication of people and equipment, and makes employees more comfortable because they are with others who "talk the same language". However, the biggest weakness of the functional structure is that the organization can lose sight of its best overall interests, in the pursuit of functional goals. No one function is totally responsible for end results, so functional specialists become insulated and have little understanding of what people in other functions are doing.

functional structure
An organizational design that groups similar or related occupational specialties together.

The **divisional structure** is an organizational structure made up of autonomous, self-contained units or divisions. Each unit or division in a divisional structure is generally autonomous, with a division manager responsible for performance and holding complete strategic and operational decision-making authority over his or her unit. In most divisional structures, a central headquarters provides support services, such as financial and legal services, to the various units. Of course, central headquarters also acts as an external overseer to co-ordinate and control the various divisions. So the divisions are autonomous within given parameters.

divisional structure
An organizational structure made up of autonomous self-contained units.

The strength of the divisional structure is that it focuses on results. Division executives have full responsibility over what happens to their products or services. The major disadvantage of this approach is the duplication of activities and resources. Since each division has its own functional departments, such as marketing, research and development, and production, the duplication of functions increases the organization's costs and reduces efficiency.

Many contemporary organizations are finding that the traditional hierarchical organizational designs, including functional and divisional structures, aren't appropriate for the increasingly dynamic and complex environments they face. In response to marketplace demands for being lean, flexible and innovative, many managers are finding creative ways to structure and organize work, and to make their organizations more responsive to the needs of customers, employees, and other organizational constituents.[17] In the remaining part of this chapter, we want to tell you about two of the newest concepts in organizational design.

Team-Based Structures

In a **team-based structure**, the entire organization is made up of work groups or teams that perform the organization's work.[18] Needless to say, in a team-based structure, employee empowerment is crucial, because there's no rigid line of managerial authority flowing from top to bottom. Rather, the employee teams are free to design work in the way they think best. However, the teams are also held responsible for all work activity and performance results in their respective areas. In Chapter 14, we will cover the practical details of working with teams more thoroughly.

team-based structure
An organizational structure made up of work groups or teams that perform that organization's work.

Project and Matrix Structures

During the 1960s, an unusual organizational arrangement known as the **matrix structure** was developed by companies in the US aerospace industry to help them cope with the demands of efficiently and effectively managing a number of concurrent projects. A matrix organization was a structural design that assigned specialists from different functional departments to work on one or more projects being led by a project manager. Look at Figure 10-8 and you will see, along the top, the familiar organizational functions of engineering, accounting, human resources, and so forth. Along the vertical dimension, however, you'll see that the various projects the aerospace firm is currently working on have been added. Each project is directed by a manager who staffs his or her project with people from each of the functional departments. The addition of this vertical dimension to the traditional horizontal functional departments, in effect, wove together elements of functional and product departmentalization—hence the term *matrix*. One other unique aspect of the matrix structure was that it created a *dual chain of command*. It explicitly violated the classical organizing principle of unity of command. Functional departmentalization was used to gain the economies from specialization but, over-

matrix structure
An organizational structure that assigns specialists from different functional departments to work on one or more projects being led by project managers.

FIGURE 10-8 A Matrix Organization in an Aerospace Firm

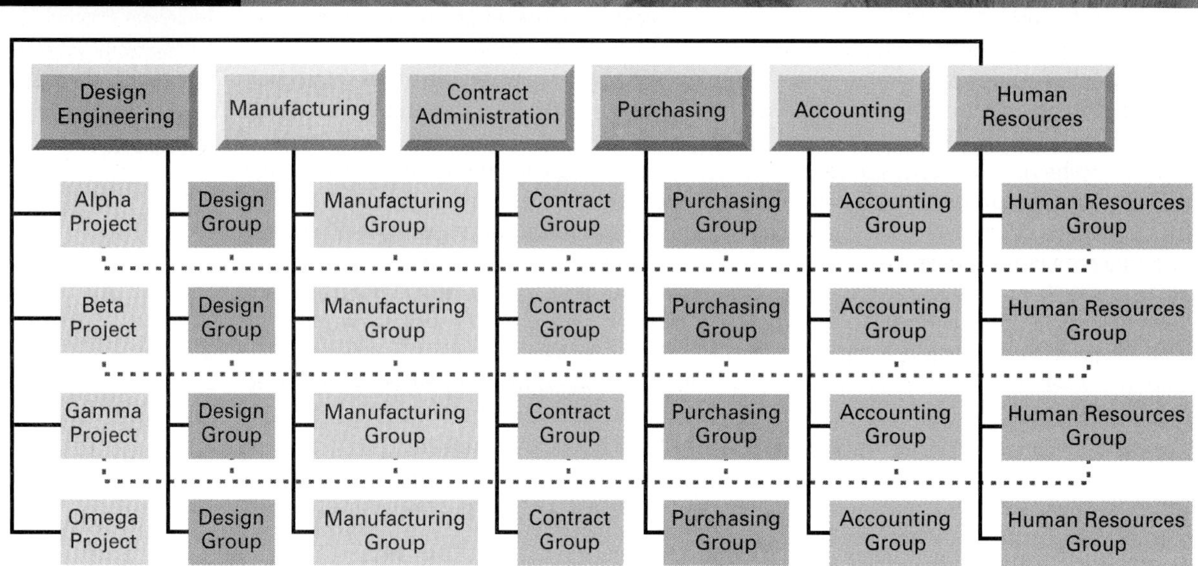

lying the functional departments, was another set of managers responsible for specific projects within the organization.

How does the matrix work in reality? Employees in the matrix have two bosses: their functional departmental manager and their product or project manager. The project managers have authority over functional members, who are part of that manager's project team. Authority is shared between two managers. Typically, this sharing is done by giving the project manager authority over project employees, relative to the project's goals. However, decisions such as promotions, salary recommendations, and annual reviews remain the functional manager's responsibility. To work effectively, project and functional managers have to communicate regularly and co-ordinate the demand among the common employees.

project structure
An organizational structure in which employees are permanently assigned to projects.

Although the matrix structure worked well—and continues to be an effective structural design choice for many organizations—some organizations are using a more "advanced" type of **project structure**, in which employees (and the work they do) are permanently assigned to projects. Unlike the matrix structure, a project structure has no formal departments that employees return to at the completion of a project. Instead, employees take their specific skills, capabilities and experiences to other work projects. In addition, all work activities in project structures are performed by teams of employees who become part of a project team, because they have the appropriate work skills and abilities.

Project structures tend to be very fluid and flexible organizational designs. There is no departmentalization or rigid organizational hierarchy to slow down decision making or taking actions. In this type of structure, managers serve as facilitators, mentors and coaches. They "service" the project teams by eliminating or minimizing organizational obstacles, and by ensuring that the teams have the resources they need to effectively and efficiently complete their work.

Autonomous Internal Units

autonomous business units
Separate decentralized business units, each with its own products, clients, competitors, and profit goals.

Some large organizations with numerous business units or divisions have adopted an organizational structure that's nothing more than a collection of **autonomous business units**. These are separate decentralized business units, each with its own products, clients, competitors, and profit goals. Through a market-oriented infrastructure of performance measures, financial incentives, and communication systems, top-level managers evaluate these units as if they were free-standing companies. Although this may sound very similar to the divisional structure that we discussed earlier under bureaucratic organizational design, the key difference is that these business units are *autonomous*. There is neither the centralized control nor the resource allocation that you would find in the divisional structure arrangement. It has been

MANAGING WORKFORCE DIVERSITY

The Feminine Organization: Myth or Reality?

A number of research studies have generally concluded that men and women do manage differently, and do use different styles of leadership. But, do men and women also have different approaches when it comes to organizational design?[19]

An organizational sociologist who has studied this area closely proposes that gender differences in values and moral principles often lead women to prefer an organizational form that is very different from the traditional, hierarchically rigid bureaucratic structure. What does this "feminine model of organization" look like? We can identify six characteristics:

1. *It values organizational members as individual human beings.* People are treated as individuals, with individual values and needs, rather than as just someone doing a job or filling a position. In fact, a recent US survey of women-owned businesses by the National Foundation for Women Business Owners, found that these firms are more likely to provide flexible work schedules, tuition reimbursement, and job-sharing arrangements.
2. *It's non-opportunistic.* Organizational relationships are seen as being valuable in themselves, not just as a formal means to achieve organizational objectives.
3. *Careers are defined in terms of service to others.* In the bureaucratic model, organizational members define career success in terms of promotions, amount of power acquired, and salary increases. In the feminine model, organizational members measure success in terms of service to others.
4. *There's a commitment to employee growth.* Feminine organizations create extensive personal growth opportunities for their members. Rather than emphasizing specialization and the development of a narrow range of expertise, these organizations expand members' skills and broaden employee competencies by offering new learning experiences.
5. *A caring community is fostered.* Organizational members become closely bound in a "community" sense, and they learn to trust and care for each other, much like neighbours in a small town.
6. *There's a sharing of power.* In the traditional bureaucratic organization, information and decision-making authority are highly coveted and hierarchically allocated. In the feminine organization, information is generously shared. All members who will be affected by a decision are given the opportunity to participate in the making of that decision.

This feminine model may be more effective and may be the organizational design of choice in organizations that are essentially managed by and for women. This might include, but is certainly not limited to, battered women's shelters, rape crisis centers, women's health care clinics, and entrepreneurial firms that sell products directly to the female market. ■

National Foundation for Women Business Owners
www.nfwbo.org

estimated that about 15 percent of large corporations have moved to this structural form. The giant Canadian auto parts manufacturer, Magna, is one of them.[20]

The Boundaryless Organization

The final concept in organizational design that we want to cover is the idea of the boundaryless organization. Just what *is* a "boundaryless" organization? A **boundaryless organization** is one whose design is not defined by, or limited to, the boundaries imposed by a predefined structure. This may sound pretty odd or strange, yet many of today's most successful organizations are finding that they can operate most effectively in today's environment by remaining flexible and *un*structured; that the ideal structure for them is *not* having a rigid, predefined structure. Instead, they want a structure that lets them meet the demands of each situation as it arises.

boundaryless organization An organization whose design is not defined by, or limited to, the boundaries imposed by a predefined structure.

7 Contrast functional structures and divisional structures.

8 Compare and contrast a matrix structure and a project structure.

The boundaryless organization has discovered that it can function efficiently and effectively by breaking down the artificial boundaries created by a fixed structural design. What do we mean by "boundaries"? Think of the horizontal boundaries imposed by departmentalization, the vertical boundaries that separate employees into organizational levels and hierarchies, and the external boundaries that separate the organization from its all-important suppliers, customers and other stakeholders. Ideally, by minimizing or eliminating these artificial boundaries, the boundaryless organization streamlines its work activities so that it can respond quickly to the tumultuous and fast-moving marketplace.

What factors have contributed to the rise of the boundaryless organization (also referred to as a *network organization, modular corporation,* or a *virtual corporation*)?[21]

Undoubtedly, one factor that has contributed to the evolution of a boundaryless organization is the increasing globalization of markets and competitors. The need to respond to complex, rapidly changing, and highly competitive global environments has created the necessity for an organization that can adapt quickly, in order to take advantage of opportunities that arise anywhere in the world. Also, the changing face of global trade has opened up new doors for organizations. No longer is a company limited to manufacturing and/or selling in a limited territory. So, we find organizations moving towards a fluid, flexible structure that is, in effect, custom designed as situations arise. For instance, Nike has found that it can sell billions of dollars of shoes every year and earn a competitive profit even though it has no shoe-manufacturing facilities of its own. Instead, it has chosen to outsource its manufacturing to suppliers in Asia.

VeriFone, Inc.
www.verifone.com

Another factor that has contributed to the rise in boundaryless organizations is the rapidly changing technology that permits the boundaryless organization to work. Without advanced computing power, software, and telecommunications capabilities, the boundaryless organization couldn't exist. For instance, at VeriFone, the world leader in credit card authorization systems, there are no corporate headquarters, secretaries, or paper mail. CEO Hatim Tyabji calls his organizational structure the "blueberry pancake model, very flat, with all blueberries equal".[22] Even without a rigid, defined structure, VeriFone employees have fast information at their fingertips through the company's electronic mail network. This type of organizational arrangement wouldn't be possible without the advanced technology that is the backbone of the information network.

Finally, the need for rapid innovation has contributed to the evolution and development of the boundaryless organization. Rapidly changing marketplace needs and brief "windows" of opportunity demand that organizations be able to respond quickly and effectively to these situations. A boundaryless organization, with its flexible and fluid structure which might include employee teams, outside contracts with other "specialist" organizations, or sophisticated electronic information networks, can respond with the rapid innovation that the global marketplace requires.

The Learning Organization

We first introduced the concept of a learning organization back in Chapter 2, as we looked at some of the current trends and issues facing management. The concept of a learning organization doesn't involve a specific organzational design per se but, instead, describes an organizational mind-set or philosophy that has significant design implications. A **learning organization** is an organization that has developed the capacity to continuously adapt and change because all members take an active role in identifying and resolving work-related issues.[23] In a learning organization, employees are continually acquiring and sharing new knowledge and are willing to apply that knowledge in making decisions or performing their work. Some organizational design theorists even go so far as to say that an organization's ability to do this may be the only sustainable source of competitive advantage.[24]

What would a learning organization look like? As you can see in Figure 10-9, the important characteristics of a learning organization revolve around organizational design, information sharing, leadership, and culture. Let's take a closer look at each.

What types of organizational design elements would be necessary for organizational learning to take place? In a learning organization, it's critical for members to share information and collaborate on work activities throughout the entire organization— across different specialities and even at different organizational levels. What is the best way of doing this? By eliminating or, at the very least, minimizing, the existing structural and physical boundaries in the organization. In this type of boundaryless environment, employees are free to work together

FIGURE 10-9 Characteristics of a Learning Organization

Source: Based on P M Senge, *The Fifth Discipline: The Art and Practice of Learning Organizations* (New York: Doubleday, 1990); and R M Hodgetts, F Luthans and S M Lee, "New Paradigm Organizations: From Total Quality to Learning to World Class," *Organizational Dynamics*, Winter 1994, pp. 4–19.

and collaborate in doing the organization's work the best way they can, and to learn from each other. Because of this need to share and collaborate, teams also tend to be an important feature of a learning organization's structural design. Employees work in teams on whatever activities need to be done, and these employee teams are empowered to make decisions about doing their work or resolving issues. With empowered employees and teams in place, there is little need for "bosses" to control and direct. Instead, managers serve as facilitators, supporters, and advocates for employee teams. One of their most important functions is facilitating the creation of a shared vision for the organization's future and then keeping organizational members aligned with that vision. In addition, leaders should support and encourage the collaborative environment. The organizational culture is an important aspect of a learning organization, wherein everyone agrees on a shared vision and feels free to openly communicate and experiment, without fear of criticism.

TECHNOLOGY, COMMUNICATIONS, AND ORGANIZATIONAL DESIGN

Although changing technology has obviously contributed to much of the environmental uncertainty facing organizations, these same technological advances have enabled managers to organize work in new ways to become more efficient and effective. We will discuss two ways in which technology has affected organizations: the effect on the way information is communicated in organizations; and technology's effect on the way in which organizations are structured.

How Technology Affects Communications

Technology, and more specifically information technology, has radically changed the ways in which organizational members communicate. For example, it has significantly improved a manager's ability to monitor individual or team performance, and it has allowed employees to have more complete information to make faster decisions. Two developments in information technology seem to have had the most impact on organizational communication: networked computer systems and wireless capabilities.[25]

Networked Computer Systems. In a networked computer system, an organization links its computers together through compatible hardware and software, creating an organizational network. Organizational members can communicate with each other and tap into information whether they're down the hall, across the city, or on the other side of the world. Electronic mail—or e-mail—is a quick and convenient way for organizational members to share information. A voice mail system is another convenient communication tool. And facsimile (fax) machines allow the easy transmission of text and graphics. **Teleconferencing** allows a group of people to confer simultaneously using telephone or e-mail group communications software. If meeting participants can see each other over video screens, the simultaneous conference is called **videoconferencing**.

teleconferencing
A communication system that allows a group of people to confer simultaneously using telephone or e-mail.

videoconferencing
A communication system that allows a group of people to confer simultaneously and see each other over video screens.

Electronic data interchange (EDI) is a way for organizations to exchange standard business transaction documents, such as invoices or purchase orders, using direct computer-to-computer networks. Organizations often use EDI with vendors, suppliers and customers, because it saves time and money. Transactions are transmitted from one organization's information system to another through a telecommunications network. The printing and handling of paper documents at one organization are eliminated, as is the inputting of data at the other organization.

electronic data interchange (EDI)
A communications system that allows organizations to exchange standard business transaction documents.

Finally, network computer systems have allowed the development of organizational **intranets**—internal organizational communication systems that use Internet technology and are accessible only by organizational employees. An intranet is not only an effective way to share information, it is also proving to be a convenient way for employees to collaborate on documents and projects at different locations.

intranets
Internal organizational communication systems that use Internet technology and are accessible only by organizational employees.

Wireless Capabilities. Wireless products—such as personal pagers, cellular telephones and specially equipped laptop computers—are making it possible for people in organizations to be fully accessible to each other, at any time or any place. Employees don't have to be at their desks with their computers plugged in, in order to communicate with colleagues.

How Communications Affects Organizational Design

Communications and the exchange of information among organizational members are no longer constrained by geography or time. And the elimination of these physical and time constraints means that organizations no longer need to be structured solely to support and facilitate information flows and work activities horizontally or vertically. What are the implications for organizational design?

Technological advances have led to numerous improvements in organizational communication methods. Videoconferencing is one such method, linking people in different locations and allowing them to carry out virtually face to face meetings.

Several of the contemporary organizational designs—such as team-based, boundaryless, project, and learning designs—would not be feasible without the availability and accessibility of information made possible by technology. Collaborative work efforts among widely dispersed individuals and teams, the sharing of information, and the integration of decisions and work throughout an entire organization, have the potential to increase the efficiency and effectiveness of organizations. In addition, work design options such as **telecommuting**—in which employees do their work at home on a computer that is linked to the office—and **virtual workplaces**—which are offices characterized by open spaces, moveable furniture, portable phones, laptop computers and electronic files—are possible only because of information technology.

telecommuting
A work design option in which workers are linked to the workplace by computers and modems.

virtual workplace
Offices that are characterized by open spaces, moveable furniture, portable phones, laptop computers and electronic files.

9 What are some of the advantages and disadvantages of a boundaryless organization?

10 Describe the characteristics of a learning organization.

11 How has technology affected communications?

SUMMARY

This summary is organized by the learning objectives found at the beginning of the chapter.

1. An organizational structure is the organization's formal framework by which job tasks are divided, grouped, and coordinated. When managers develop or change an organization's structure, they are engaged in organizational design.
2. Structure and design are important to an organization because they clarify expectations of what is to be done; divide work to avoid duplication, wasted effort, conflict, and misuse of resources; provide for logical flow of work activities; establish communication channels; provide co-ordinating mechanisms; focus work efforts on accomplishing objectives; and enhance planning and controlling.
3. The six key elements of organizational structure are work specialization, departmentalization, chain of command, span of control, centralization and decentralization, and formalization. Work specialization describes the degree to which tasks in the organization are divided into separate jobs. Departmentalization describes the way in which jobs are grouped in order to accomplish organizational goals. The chain of command is an unbroken line of authority that extends from the upper levels of the organization down to the lowest levels and clarifies who reports to whom. Span of control refers to how many subordinates a manager can effectively and efficiently supervise. Centralization describes the degree to which decision making is concentrated in the upper levels of the organization. Decentralization is when lower-level employees provide input or are actually given the discretion to make decisions. Formalization refers to the degree to which jobs within the organization are standardized and the extent to which employee behaviour is guided by rules and procedures.
4. Mechanistic organizations are rigid and tightly controlled structures. They are characterized by high specialization, extensive departmentalization, narrow spans of control, high formalization, a limited information network (mostly downward), and little participation in decision making by lower-level employees. On the other hand, organic organizations are highly adaptive and flexible. There is division of labour, but jobs are not highly standardized. Formalization and tight managerial controls are unnecessary because employees are highly trained.
5. The four contingency factors that influence an organization's design are strategy, size, technology, and environment.
6. A bureaucracy is an organizational design with high levels of work specialization, hierarchical levels, and formalization. One of its strengths is that it helps an organization cope with increasing size. In addition, it is based on order, logic, and legitimate use of authority.
7. In a team-based structure, the entire organization is made up of work groups or teams that perform the organization's work. More and more organizations are using teams because it breaks down departmental barriers and decentralizes decision making to the level of the work team.
8. A matrix organization is a structural design that assigns specialists from different functional departments to work on one or more projects being led by a project manager. A project structure is a design in which employees are permanently assigned to projects. Autonomous internal units are autonomous decentralized business units, each with its own products, clients, competitors, and profit goals.
9. The boundaryless organization is an organizational design in which the structure is not defined by, or limited to, the boundaries imposed by traditional structures. It is a structure that is flexible and adaptable to environmental conditions. This structure is appealing because it allows organizations to respond efficiently and effectively to global markets and competition, technology advancements, and the need for rapid innovation.
10. A learning organization is an organization that has developed the capacity to continuously adapt and change because all members take an active role in making decisions or performing their work. It influences organizational design because an organization's ability to learn is enhanced (or hindered) by its structural and physical boundaries and the amount of collaborative work efforts.
11. Technology plays an important role in organizational design because it influences how organizational employees communicate, share information, and collaborate on work.

THINKING ABOUT MANAGEMENT ISSUES

1. Can an organization's structure be changed quickly? Why or why not?
2. What types of skills would a manager need to work effectively in (a) a project structure; (b) a boundaryless organization; and (c) a learning organization?
3. Would you rather work in a mechanistic or an organic organization? Why?
4. The boundaryless organization has the potential to create a major shift in our living and working patterns. Do you agree or disagree? Explain.
5. With the availability of advanced information technology that allows an organization's work to be done anywhere and at any time, is organizing still an important managerial function? Why or why not?

SELF-ASSESSMENT EXERCISE

HOW WILLING ARE YOU TO DELEGATE?

As a manager, you must be willing to delegate work to different people under your supervision. This self-assessment will help you to determine your willingness to delegate work to others.

Instructions: This instrument is designed to help you understand the assumptions you make about people and human nature. Ten pairs of statements follow. Assign a weight from 0 to 10 to each statement to show the relative strength of your belief in the statement. The points assigned for each pair must always total 10. Be as honest with yourself as you can and resist the tendency to respond as you would like to think things are. This instrument is not a test: there are no right or wrong answers. It is designed to stimulate personal reflection and discussion.

1. ______ a. It's only human nature for people to do as little work as they can get away with.
   ______ b. When people avoid work, it's usually because their work has been deprived of meaning.
2. ______ c. If employees have access to any information they want, they tend to have better attitudes and behave more responsibly.
   ______ d. If employees have access to more information than they need to do their immediate tasks, they will usually misuse it.
3. ______ e. One problem in asking for the ideas of employees is that their perspective is too limited for their suggestions to be of much practical value.
   ______ f. Asking employees for their ideas broadens their perspective and results in the development of useful suggestions.
4. ______ g. If people don't use much imagination and ingenuity on the job, it's probably because relatively few people have much of either.
   ______ h. Most people are imaginative and creative but may not show it because of limitations imposed by supervision and the job.
5. ______ i. People tend to raise their standards if they are accountable for their own behaviour and for correcting their own mistakes.
   ______ j. People tend to lower their standards if they are not punished for their misbehaviour and mistakes.
6. ______ k. It's better to give people both good and bad news because most employees want the whole story, no matter how painful.
   ______ l. It's better to withhold unfavourable news about business because most employees really want to hear only the good news.
7. ______ m. Because a supervisor is entitled to more respect than those below her in the organization, it weakens her prestige to admit that a subordinate was right and she was wrong.
   ______ n. Because people at all levels are entitled to equal respect, a supervisor's prestige is increased when he supports this principle by admitting that a subordinate was right and he was wrong.
8. ______ o. If you give people enough money, they are less likely to be concerned with such intangibles as responsibility and recognition.
   ______ p. If you give people interesting and challenging work, they are less likely to complain about such things as pay and supplemental benefits.

9. ______ q. If people are allowed to set their own goals and standards of performance, they tend to set them higher than the boss would.

______ r. If people are allowed to set their own goals and standards of performance, they tend to set them lower than the boss would.

10. ______ s. The more knowledge and freedom a person has regarding her job, the more controls are needed to keep her in line.

______ t. The more knowledge and freedom a person has regarding her job, the fewer controls are needed to ensure satisfactory job performance.

For scoring information, turn to page SK-3.

Source: David A Whetten and Kim S Cameron, *Developing Management Skills* (Glenview, IL: Scott, Foresman, 1984), pp. 351–352.

for your IMMEDIATE action

ONTARIO ELECTRONICS LIMITED

TO: Claude Fortier, Special Assistant to the President
FROM: Ian Campbell, President
SUBJECT: Using Cross-Functional Teams for New Product Development

As you know, last week I was attending the Canadian Electronics Manufacturers Industry Association annual meeting. Our luncheon speaker on the final day talked about how important it is for organizations to be responsive to customer and marketplace needs. One of the approaches for accomplishing this crucial need that she described in her speech was using crossfunctional teams in the new product development process. I came away from this talk convinced that this might be something that we want to try in our facilities.

What I would like for you to do is to find some current information on the use of cross-functional teams in organizations. Although I'm sure you will be able to find numerous articles about it, limit your report to five of what you consider to be the best possible sources of information on the topic. Write a one-paragraph summary for each of these five articles, being sure to note all the bibliographic information in case we need to refer back to the article itself later.

Since I would like the executive team to move on this fairly quickly, please have your report back to me by the end of the week.

This is a fictionalized account of a potentially real management issue. It is meant for academic purposes only and is not meant to reflect positively or negatively on Ontario Electronics Ltd. or any of its employees.

TAKE IT TO THE NET

We invite you to visit the Robbins/Coulter/Stuart-Kotze Companion Website at www.prenticehall.ca/robbins for this chapter's Internet resources.

CASE APPLICATION

Magna International, Inc., Aurora, Ontario

Frank Stronach is founder and chairman of Aurora Ontario's Magna International, a giant in the global auto parts manufacturing industry. The company supplies parts and systems to such clients as Honda, GM, Ford, Chrysler, Daimler-Benz, BMW, Volkswagen and Toyota. Annual revenue is more than $7 billion, and the company operates over 130 manufacturing centres in 12 countries, with 30 years' experience behind it. Stronach downplays his own role in Magna's success, stressing that the organization's structure accounts for its profitability. Management and labour operate in what Stronach calls a "fair enterprise system". All employees benefit from a profit and equity participation plan, giving them a greater sense of commitment to the organization. Managers and labour are also given a good deal of decision-making authority, providing them with a greater sense of personal involvement in the company's success. Stronach has stated that "the system is stronger than any one person or group of people".

Magna has managed to stay ahead of industry trends by understanding where the automotive industry is going, and by adjusting the organization to fit these changes. The global automobile manufacturers are now demanding more from their suppliers— instead of dealing with many suppliers, they want to deal with a few, in order to make their operations more efficient. Therefore, suppliers must have versatile manufacturing systems in order to produce a wide variety of parts to satisfy auto makers. Magna moved into this type of manufacturing long ago, anticipating the coming changes. Now Magna wants to solidify its position in the global market. Nineteen ninety-eight was marked by a series of international acquisitions by Magna, such as big purchases in countries like Austria and Italy.

QUESTIONS

1. Would you describe Magna as more of a mechanistic or organic organization? Explain.
2. What would you think the relationship is between strategy and structure at Magna?
3. How could the following structures work at Magna: team-based; project structure; autonomous internal units?
4. How could Magna use the ideals of a boundaryless organization in its worldwide operations?

Sources: Simon Avery, "Magna Extends European Reach", *Financial Post*, January 10, 1998, p. 1; David Berman "Car and Striver", *Canadian Business*, September 1996, pp. 92–101; Greg Keenan, "Magna Buying Italian Parts Maker", *Globe and Mail*, February 3, 1998, p. B3.

LEARNING OBJECTIVES

After Reading This Chapter, You Should Be Able To:

1 Describe the human resource management process

2 Discuss the influence of government regulations on human resource decisions

3 Differentiate between job descriptions and job specifications

4 Contrast recruitment and decruitment options

5 Explain the importance of validity and reliability in selection

6 Describe the selection devices that work best with various kinds of jobs

7 Identify the various training methods

8 Describe the various types of compensation and how compensation decisions are made

9 Describe how HRM practices can facilitate workforce diversity

10 Explain why harassment is a growing concern of management

11 Discuss how organizations are meeting the challenges of employee family concerns and AIDS in the workplace

A MANAGER'S CHALLENGE

Robert Schad, Founder and CEO, Husky Injection Molding Systems, Bolton, Ontario

Husky Injection Molding Systems is a manufacturer of injection molding machines, used by manufacturers to produce plastic products like car parts, toys, and food containers. The company is the third largest of its kind in the world, with consistently growing revenues at the $850 million level in 1998. But what truly makes Husky unique is its incredible dedication to its human resources. Founder Robert Schad has created an environment geared towards hiring the right people, getting the most out of them, and keeping them happy. According to Schad, "You build something to last if you treat workers well".[1]

Schad instituted a rotating employee council—consisting of employees from all levels—

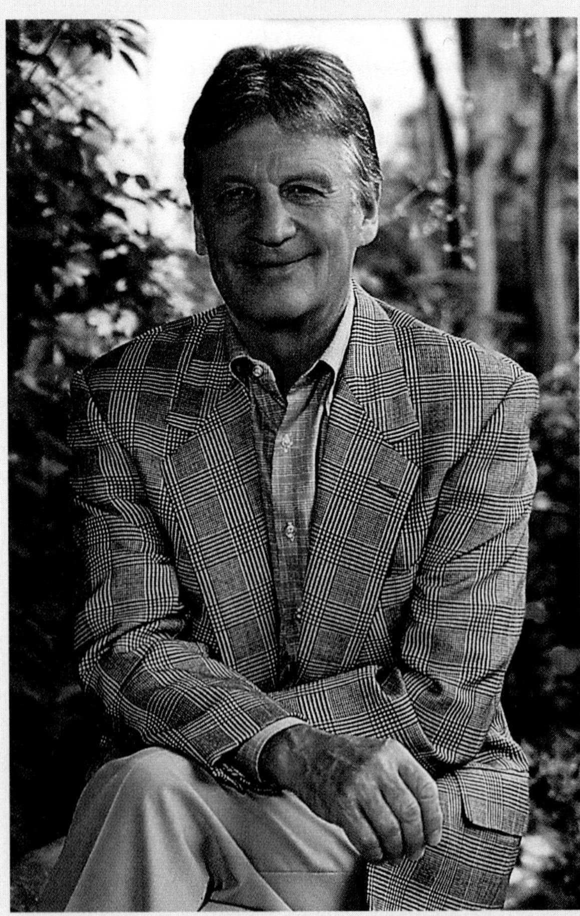

which meets every month. Representatives poll fellow workers to determine what should be discussed, and transcripts of the meetings' minutes accompany everyone's paycheque. Every employee is included in a profit-sharing plan, and people holding specialized jobs are allowed to purchase shares in the company (Schad and his family presently hold 65 percent). Salaries are above the industry average, and employees are kept informed of the company's performance through annual reports and monthly newsletters.

Physical health is a primary concern at Husky. Employees have a state-of-the-art fitness centre at their disposal, as well as a medical doctor, nurse, naturopath, chiropractor and massage therapist. What's more, employees get a $500 credit every year for vitamins. These investments in Husky's workforce pay off on the bottom line. The company spends only a third of the industry average in drug costs for employees, and absenteeism is roughly a quarter of that in other manufacturing companies.

Employees seem content, and why wouldn't they be? Husky's facilities include a $5 million child-care centre, and company perks include full payment of tuition and books for any employee wishing to go to university or college. Obviously, Robert Schad believes that keeping his workers happy is good for business, and Husky's incredible success certainly seems to support that view.

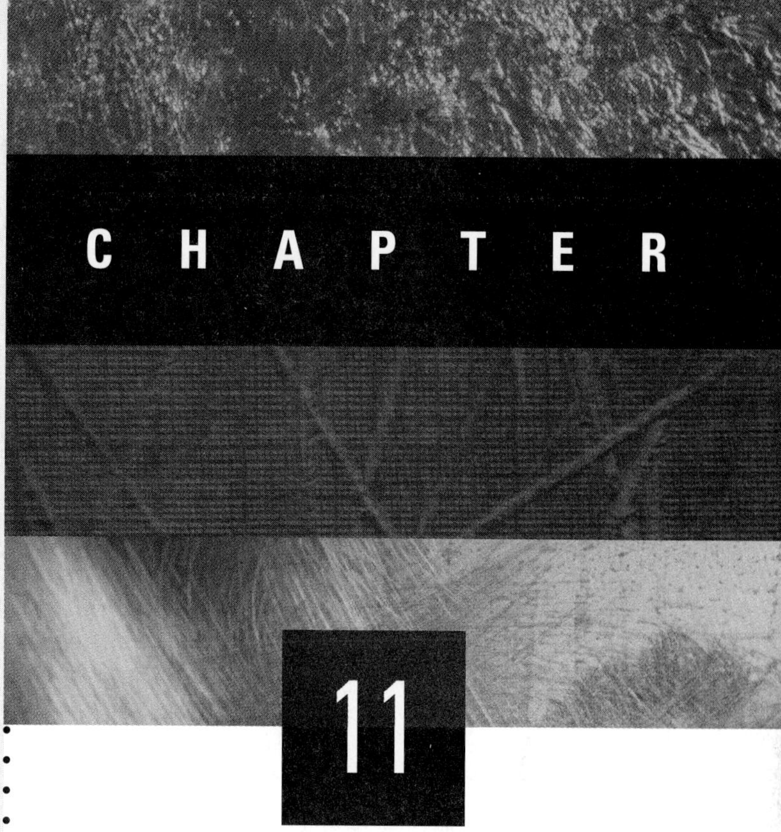

Human Resource Management

Getting and keeping competent employees is crucial to the success of every organization, whether the organization is just starting or has been in business for a number of years. Therefore, part of every manager's job in the organizing function is filling job positions—that is, putting the right person into the right job. Husky's human resource department may well have an advantage over other organizations, in that recruitment and motivation is made easier due to the company's excellent HR policies. But not all organizations have such an enlightened view—and human resource management is not always an easy task.

MANAGERS AND HUMAN RESOURCES DEPARTMENTS

Some readers may be thinking, "Sure, personnel decisions are important, but aren't they made by people in human resources departments? These aren't decisions that *all* managers are involved in".

It's true that, in large organizations, a number of the activities grouped under the label *human resource management* (HRM) are often done by specialists in personnel or human resources. However, not all managers work in organizations that have formal human resource departments, and even those who do, must still engage in some human resource activities.

Small-business managers are an obvious example of individuals who frequently do their hiring without the assistance of a human resources department. But even managers in billion-dollar corporations are involved in recruiting employee candidates, reviewing application forms, interviewing applicants, orienting new employees, appraising employee performance, making decisions about employee training, and providing career advice to subordinates. In addition, many organizations have begun to recognize the important role that employees play in organizational success, and have committed themselves to strong HRM departments. The HRM departments in these organizations are moving away from their traditional responsibilities of simple personnel administration to a more central role in establishing and implementing organizational strategy. Studies that have looked at the link between HRM policies and organizational performance have found that certain HRM policies and practices have a significant positive impact on performance. The term used to describe these types of HRM policies and practices is **high-performance work practices** (see Table 11-1).

high-performance work practices
Human resource policies and practices that lead to high levels of performance.

THE HUMAN RESOURCE MANAGEMENT PROCESS

Figure 11-1 introduces the key components of an organization's **human resource management process**. It consists of eight activities or steps, that, if properly done, will staff an organization with competent, high-performing employees who are capable of sustaining their performance level over the long term.

human resource management process
Activities necessary for staffing the organization and sustaining high employee performance.

The first four steps represent *human resource planning*, the addition of staff through *recruitment*, the reduction of staff through *decruitment*, and *selection*, resulting in the identification and selection of competent, skilled employees. Once you've got competent people, you need to help them adapt to the organization, ensure that their job skills and knowledge are kept current, develop appropriate career development activities, and provide an efficient and effective reward system. You do this through *orientation, training*, *career development*, and *compensation and benefits*. The last step in the HRM process is designed to identify performance problems and correct them. This activity is called *performance appraisal* and since it's part of the manager's controlling activities, we'll cover it in Chapter 19.

Notice in Figure 11-1 that the entire HRM process is influenced by the external environment. In Chapter 3 we elaborated on the constraints that the environment puts on management. These constraints are probably most severe in the management of human resources.

TABLE 11-1 Examples of High-Performance Work Practices

- Self-directed work teams
- Job rotation
- High levels of skills training
- Problem-solving groups
- Total quality management procedures and processes
- Encouragement of innovative and creative behaviour
- Extensive employee involvement and training
- Implementation of employee suggestions
- Contingent pay based on performance
- Coaching and mentoring
- Significant amounts of information sharing
- Use of employee attitude surveys
- Cross-functional integration
- Comprehensive employee recruitment and selection procedures

Source: Based on M Huselid, "The Impact of Human Resource Management Practices on Turnover, Productivity, and Corporate Financial Performance," *Academy of Management Journal*, June 1995, p. 635; and B Becker and B Gerhart, "The Impact of Human Resource Management on Organizational Performance: Progress and Prospects," *Academy of Management Journal*, August 1996, p. 785.

FIGURE 11-1 The Human Resource Management Process

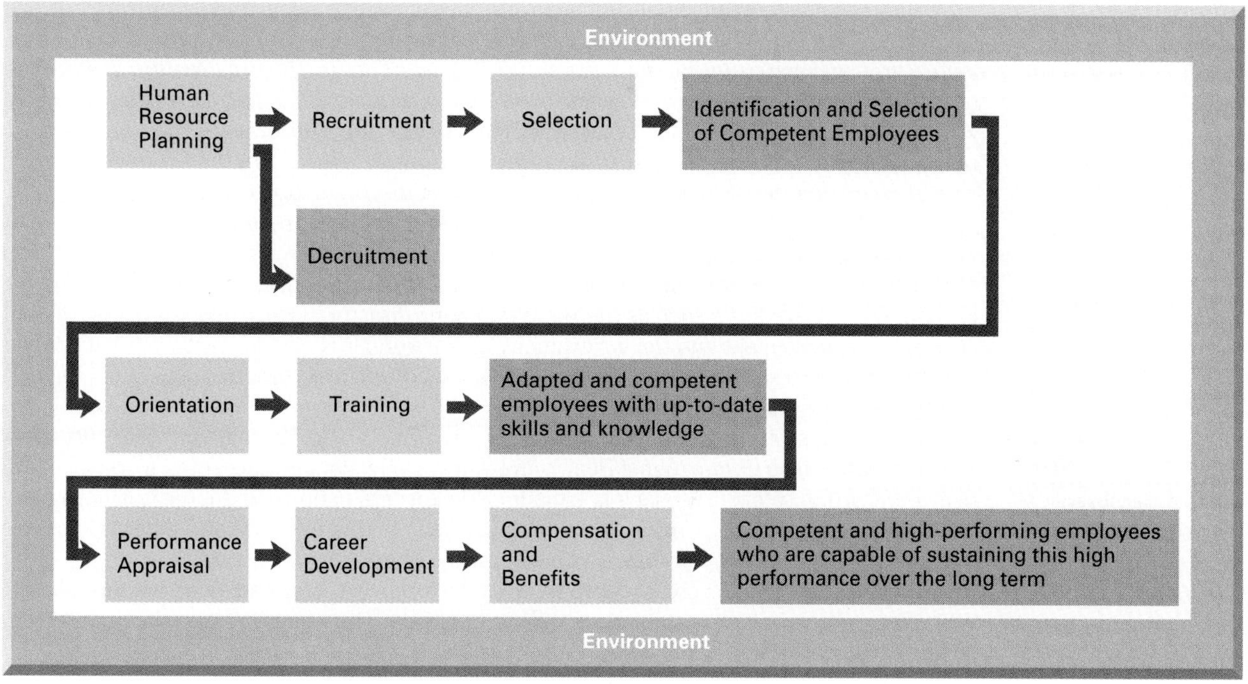

Before we review the steps in the HRM process, therefore, let's briefly examine how environmental forces influence it.

IMPORTANT ENVIRONMENTAL CONSIDERATIONS

Numerous environmental forces affect human resource management activities. For instance, approximately 37 percent of the Canadian workforce is unionized, excluding the agricultural sector.[2] Canada is on a par with some countries, such as Germany, but the percentages in other nations can be much lower, like Mexico (30 percent), Japan (24 percent) and the United States (14.5 percent).[3]

A **labour union** represents workers and seeks to protect and promote members' interests through collective bargaining. In unionized organizations, many key personnel decisions are regulated by the terms of collective bargaining agreements. These agreements usually define such things as recruitment sources; criteria for hiring, promotions and layoffs; training eligibility; and disciplinary practices. For many managers in unionized organizations, good **labour-management relations** are important. The development of good labour-management relations can produce a number of positive outcomes for management during contract negotiations: for instance, work rules that don't place unreasonable constraints on managerial decision options, and reduced threats of costly strikes and work stoppages.[4]

But no environmental constraint can match the influence of governmental laws and regulations.

Since the mid-1960s, government has greatly expanded its influence over HRM decisions by enacting new laws and regulations. All employers in Canada are covered by human rights legislation. (See Table 11-2.) As a result of this legislation, employers today must ensure that equal employment opportunities exist for job applicants and current employees. Decisions regarding who will be hired, for example, or which employees will be chosen for a management training program must be made without regard to race, sex, religion, age, colour or national origin. Exceptions can occur only for requirements that are **bona fide occupational qualifications (BFOQ)**. This explains why, for instance, airlines today have flight attendants of both sexes and of varying ages. In the early 1960s, airlines hired flight attendants who were, almost exclusively, young, attractive females. But age, beauty and gender are not BFOQs for

labour union
An organization that represents workers and seeks to protect their interests through collective bargaining.

labour-management relations
The formal interactions between unions and an organization's management.

bona fide occupational qualifications (BFOQ)
A criterion such as sex, age, or national origin that may be used as a basis for hiring because it can be clearly demonstrated to be job related.

this job, so these criteria had to be dropped. However, in hiring models for a men's clothing catalogue, a mail order firm can legitimately limit the job to males. Keep in mind that there are very few legitimate BFOQs that an organization can use in hiring or promoting.

employment equity programs
Programs that enhance the organizational status of members of protected groups, which include women, visible minorities, persons with disabilities, and aboriginals. Francophones are also a protected group in some jurisdictions.

Many Canadian organizations have **employment equity programs** to ensure that decisions and practices enhance the employment, upgrading, and retention of members of protected groups, such as visible minorities and females. That is, the organization goes beyond non-discrimination and actively seeks to enhance the status of members from protected groups. Why are organizations taking this stance? On the ethical side, they have a social responsibility to improve the status of protected group members. On the economic side, the cost of defending the organization against charges of discrimination can be enormous.

Workplace safety is another area in which violations of laws and regulations can be expensive. Workplace fatalities don't appear to be lessening. Each year in Canada, approximately 1000 people die in work-related incidents. This number has remained constant for the past decade. When tragedies—such as the Westray mining disaster in Nova Scotia—occur, the public turns to management and the government for answers. It is obvious that what happened at Westray could and should have been avoided. A tragedy such as this cries out for better safety controls in the workplace.

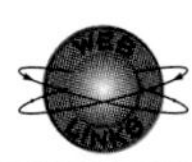

Westray Mining Disaster
geocities.com/Athens/3116/commen16.html

Canada Labour Code Review
labour.hrdc-drhc.gc.ca/labour/labstand/toc.html

In Canada, safety legislation is at work on two levels—provincially and federally. Every province has its own Occupational Health and Safety Code, detailing accepted workplace practices in regard to safety. The Canada Labour Code governs national and interprovincial industries. One of the main provisions of the national Code is that a Health and Safety Committee must be in place in every workplace with 20 or more employees. The costs of workplace injury for a business include decreased productivity, insurance costs, and poor labour relations. When the injury results from violations of laws or regulations, heavy fines can be imposed and, in severe cases, jail sentences.

Organizations in other countries also face environmental constraints that affect management's decision discretion in the area of human resources management and labour relations. For example, in Germany, unions are quite powerful although unions and management have had a more co-operative relationship there than in Canada. In Denmark, workers participate in the management of their firms, both directly and indirectly. They're actively involved in making workplace decisions. In China, however, worker participation in decision making is less open, and the number of employees who participate in workplace decisions isn't very high. Because the laws and regulations governing human resources vary by country, managers of global companies need to familiarize themselves with the relevant information for those countries in which they operate.

Our conclusion is that managers aren't completely free to choose whom they hire, promote or lay off; nor are they free to operate their workplace any way they like. Although governmental regulations have significantly helped to reduce discrimination, unfair employment practices, and unsafe workplaces in organizations, they have, at the same time, also reduced management's discretion over human resource decisions.

HUMAN RESOURCE PLANNING

human resource planning
The process by which management ensures that it has the right personnel who are capable of completing those tasks that help the organization to reach its objectives.

Human resource planning is the process by which management ensures that it has the right number and kinds of people in the right places, and at the right times, who are capable of effectively and efficiently completing those tasks that will help the organization achieve its overall objectives. In other words, human resource planning translates the organization's objectives into terms of the workers needed to meet those objectives.[5]

Human resource planning can be condensed into three steps: (1) assessing current human resources, (2) assessing future human resource needs, and (3) developing a program to meet future human resource needs.

Current Assessment

Management begins by reviewing its current human resource status. This is typically done by generating a *human resource inventory*. Because of the availability of sophisticated computer information systems, it's not too difficult a task for most organizations to generate a human resource inventory report. The input for this report is derived from forms completed by employees. Such reports might include the name, education, training, prior employment, languages spoken, special capabilities, and specialized skills of each employee in the organization. This inventory allows management to assess what talents and skills are currently available.

TABLE 11-2 Prohibited Grounds of Discrimination in Employment*

Prohibited Grounds	Fed.	B.C.	Alta.	Sask.	Man.	Ont.	Que.	N.B.	P.E.I.	N.S.	Nfld.	N.W.T.	Y.T.
Race or colour	•	•	•	•	•	•	•	•	•	•	•	•	•
Religion or creed	•	•	•	•	•	•	•	•	•	•	•	•	•
Age	•	• (19–65)	• (18+)	• (18–64)	•	• (18–65)	•	•	•	•	• (19–65)	•	•
Sex (includes pregnancy or childbirth)	•	•[1]	•	•	•[2]	•	•	•	•[1]	•	•[1]	•[1]	•
Marital status	•	•	•	•	•	•	•[3]	•	•	•	•	•	•
Physical/Mental handicap or disability	•	•	•	•	•	•	•	•	•	•	•	•	•
Sexual orientation	•[4]	•		•	•	•	•	•	•[1]	•	•[1]		•
National or ethnic origin (includes linguistic background)	•			•[5]	•	•[6]	•	•	•	•	•	•[5]	•
Family status	•	•		•	•	•	•[3]			•		•	•
Dependence on alcohol or drug	•	•[7]	•[1]	•[1]	•[1]	•[1]		•[1,7]	•[1]	•[7]			
Ancestry or place of origin		•	•	•	•	•		•				•[5]	•
Political belief		•			•		•		•	•	•		•
Based on association					•	•			•	•			•
Pardoned conviction	•	•				•	•					•	
Record of criminal conviction		•					•						•
Source of income				•[8]	•					•			
Place of residence												•	
Assignment, attachment, or seizure of pay										•			
Social condition/origin							•				•		
Language							•						

Harassment on any of the prohibited grounds is considered a form of discrimination.
*Any limitation, exclusion, denial, or preference may be permitted if a bona fide occupational requirement can be demonstrated.
[1] Complaints accepted based on policy.
[2] Includes gender-determined characteristics.
[3] Quebec uses the term "civil status."
[4] Pursuant to a 1992 Ontario Court of Appeal decision, the Canadian Human Rights Commission now accepts complaints on the grounds of sexual orientation.
[5] Defined as nationality.
[6] Ontario's Code includes only "citizenship."
[7] Previous dependence only.
[8] Defined as "receipt of public assistance."

Source: Reprinted with permission of the Canadian Human Rights Commission, Cat. No. HR21-44/1993, August 1993.

Another part of the current assessment is the **job analysis**. Although the human resource inventory is concerned with telling management what individual employees can do, job analysis is more fundamental. It defines the *jobs* within the organization and the *behaviours* that are necessary to perform those jobs. For instance, what are the duties of a purchasing specialist, Grade 3, who works for Abitibi Price? What minimal knowledge, skills and abilities are necessary to be able to adequately perform this job? How do the requirements for a purchas-

job analysis
An assessment that defines jobs and the behaviours necessary to perform them.

Each and every employee brings special capabilities and specialized skills to an organization. By keeping an inventory of an organization's human resources, managers will know which talents and skills are currently available and which might be in short supply.

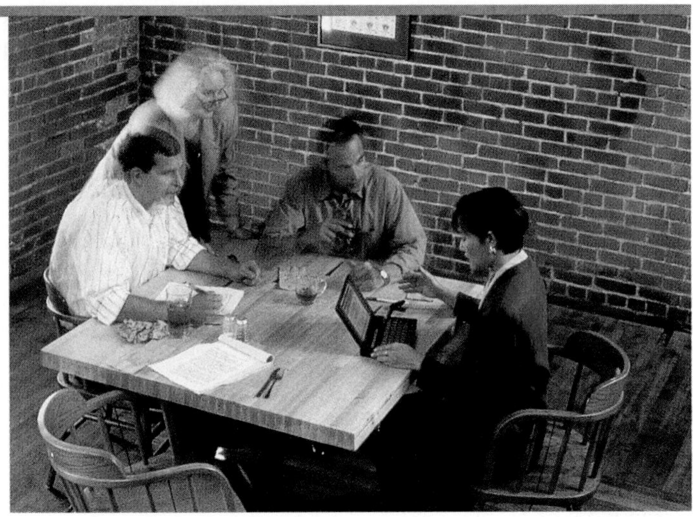

ing specialist, Grade 3, compare with those for a purchasing specialist, Grade 2, or for a purchasing analyst? These are questions that job analysis can answer. It seeks to determine the kind of people needed to fill each job and provides information for preparing job descriptions and job specifications.

job description
A written statement of what a jobholder does, how it is done, and why it is done.

job specification
A statement of the minimum acceptable qualifications that an incumbent must possess in order to perform a given job successfully.

A **job description** is a written statement of what a jobholder does, how it's done, and why it's done. It typically describes job content, environment, and conditions of employment. It focuses on the *job*. In contrast, a **job specification** focuses on the *person*. It states the minimum acceptable qualifications that a jobholder must possess in order to perform a given job successfully. The job specification identifies the knowledge, skills and abilities needed to do the job effectively.

The job description and job specification are important documents when managers begin recruiting and selecting. The job description can be used to describe the job to potential candidates. The job specification keeps the manager's attention focused on the list of qualifications necessary for a person to be able to perform a job, and assists in determining whether or not candidates are qualified.

How is information gathered in a job analysis? There are several methods for analyzing a job. There's the observation method, in which employees are either watched directly or are filmed on the job. Employees can also be interviewed individually or in a group. A third method is the use of structured questionnaires on which employees check or rate the items they perform in their jobs from a long list of possible task duties. Another method is the use of a technical conference, at which "experts"—usually supervisors with extensive knowledge of a job—identify its specific characteristics. A final method is to have employees record their daily activities in a diary or notebook, which can then be reviewed and structured into job activities.

Future Assessment

Future human resource needs are determined by the organization's objectives and strategies. Demand for human resources (employees) is a result of demand for the organization's products or services. On the basis of its estimate of total revenue, management can attempt to establish the number and mix of human resources needed to reach these revenues. In some cases, the situation may be reversed. This might be the case, for example, in a tax consulting firm that finds it has more business opportunities than it can handle. Its only limiting factor in building revenues might be its ability to find and hire staff with the needed qualifications to satisfy the consulting firm's clients. In most cases, however, the overall organizational goals and the resulting revenue forecast provide the major input for determining the organization's human resource requirements.

Developing a Future Program

After it has assessed both current capabilities and future needs, management is able to estimate shortages—both in number and in type—and to highlight areas in which the organization will be overstaffed. A program can then be developed to match these estimates with forecasts of future labour supply. So human resource planning not only provides information to guide current staffing needs, but also provides projections of future human resource needs and availability.

RECRUITMENT AND DECRUITMENT

Once managers know their current personnel status (whether they're understaffed or overstaffed), they can begin to do something about it. If one or more vacancies exist, they can use the information gathered through job analysis to guide them in **recruitment**—that is, the process of locating, identifying, and attracting capable applicants.[6] If human resource planning indicates a surplus of employees, management may want to reduce the labour supply within the organization. This activity is called **decruitment**.[7]

recruitment
The process of locating, identifying, and attracting capable applicants.

decruitment
Techniques for reducing the labour supply within an organization.

Where can a manager recruit potential job candidates? Table 11-3 offers some guidance. The source that is used should reflect the local labour market, the type or level of position, and the size of the organization.

No matter the type of position or its attractiveness, it's generally easier to recruit in large labour markets than in small ones, if for no other reason than that large labour markets, such as Toronto or Montreal, have a greater supply of workers. Of course, this generalization needs to be moderated by unemployment levels, wage rates, needed skills and other factors. But, in large markets, recruitment efforts can be directed locally—to newspapers, employment agencies, colleges, or referrals by current employees.

TABLE 11-3 Major Sources of Potential Job Candidates

Source	Advantages	Disadvantages
Internal search	Low cost; builds employee morale; candidates are familiar with organization	Limited supply; may not increase proportion of employees from protected groups
Advertisements	Wide distribution; can be targeted to specific groups	Generates many unqualified candidates
Employee referrals	Knowledge about the organization provided by current employee; can generate strong candidates because a good referral reflects on the recommender	May not increase the diversity and mix of employees
HRD Canada (Canada Employment Centres)	Free	Candidates tend to be unskilled or minimally trained
Private employment agencies	Wide contacts; careful screening; short-term guarantees often given	High cost
School placement	Large, centralized body of candidates	Limited to entry-level positions
Temporary help services	Fills temporary needs	Expensive; may have limited understanding of organization's overall goals and activities

TESTING... TESTING...

1 List the eight steps of the human resource management process and explain how the external environment affects it.

2 Why is a job analysis important for job description and job specification?

The type or level of a position influences recruitment methods. The greater the skill required in the job or the higher the position in the organization's hierarchy, the more the recruitment process will expand to become a regional or national search.

The scope of recruitment and the amount of effort devoted to it will also be influenced by the size of the organization. Generally, the larger the organization, the easier it is to recruit job applicants. Larger organizations have a larger pool of internal candidates to choose from to fill positions above the lowest level. Larger organizations also have more visibility and, typically, more prestige. In addition, larger organizations may be perceived as offering greater opportunities for job promotions and increased responsibility.

Are certain recruiting sources better than others? More specifically, do certain recruiting sources produce superior candidates? The answer is yes. The majority of studies find that current employee referrals prove to be superior.[8] This finding is not surprising. First, applicants referred by current employees are prescreened by these employees. Because the recommenders know both the job and the person being recommended, they tend to refer applicants who are better qualified for the position. Also, because current employees often feel that their reputation in the organization is at stake with a referral, they tend to refer others only when they are reasonably confident that the referral won't make them look bad.

The other approach to controlling labour supply is the process of decruitment. In the past decade, most large Canadian corporations, many government agencies, and even small businesses have been forced to engage in some decruitment activities. These cutbacks can be traced to market changes, foreign competition, mergers, and the overall decline in many manufacturing industries.

Decruitment is not a pleasant task for any manager to perform. However, since many organizations are forced to shrink the size of their workforce or restructure their skill composition, decruitment is becoming an increasingly important part of human resource management.

What are a manager's decruitment options? Obviously, people can't be fired indiscriminately. But other choices may be more beneficial to the organization and/or the employee.[9] Table 11-4 summarizes these major options.

At a later point in the chapter, we'll discuss the human resources challenges associated with downsizing and how managers can deal with the traumas and stresses of these activities.

SELECTION

A new university graduate with a degree in accounting walked into the human resources office of a medium-sized corporation not long ago, in search of a job. Immediately, she was face to face with two doors, one of which displayed the sign "Applicants with University Degree" and the other, "Applicants without University Degree". She opened the first door. As soon as she

TABLE 11-4 Decruitment Options

Option	Description
Firing	Permanent involuntary termination
Layoffs	Temporary involuntary termination; may last only a few days or extend to years
Attrition	Not filling openings created by voluntary resignations or normal retirements
Transfers	Moving employees either laterally or downward; usually does not reduce costs but can reduce intra-organizational supply-demand imbalances
Reduced workweeks	Having employees work fewer hours per week, share jobs, or perform their jobs on a part-time basis
Early retirements	Providing incentives to older and more senior employees for retiring before their normal retirement date

did so, she found two more doors. The first said, "Applicants with Overall A Average" and the other, "Applicants with Less Than A Average Overall". Since she had an 85.6 percent average, she again chose the first door and was once again facing two doors. One read, "Applicants with Management Majors" and the other, "Applicants Without Management Majors". Since she had an accounting degree, she opened the second of these doors—and found herself out in the street.[10]

Although this story is fictitious, it does convey the essence of the selection process. When human resource planning identifies a personnel shortage and develops a pool of applicants, managers need some method for screening the applicants to ensure that the most appropriate candidate is hired. That screening method is the **selection process**.

selection process
The process of screening job applicants to ensure that the most appropriate candidates are hired.

What Is Selection?

Selection is an exercise in prediction. It seeks to predict which applicants will be successful if hired. "Successful" in this case means performing well on the criteria which the organization uses to evaluate employees. In filling a sales position, for example, the selection process should be able to predict which applicants would be likely to generate a high volume of sales; for a position as a high school teacher, it should predict which applicants will be effective educators.

Prediction. Consider, for a moment, that any selection decision can result in four possible outcomes. As shown in Figure 11-2, two of these outcomes would be correct decisions, but two would be errors.

A decision is correct when the applicant was predicted to be successful and later proved to be successful on the job, or when the applicant was predicted to be unsuccessful and, indeed, would have been unsuccessful. In the first case, we have successfully accepted; in the second case, we have successfully rejected.

Problems arise when we make errors by rejecting candidates who would have later performed successfully on the job (reject errors) or accepting those who subsequently perform poorly (accept errors). These problems are, unfortunately, far from insignificant. Prior to governmental hiring laws and regulations, reject errors meant only that the costs of selection would be increased because more candidates would have to be screened. Today, however, selection techniques that result in reject errors can open the organization to charges of discrimination, especially if applicants from protected groups are disproportionately rejected. Accept errors also mean obvious costs to the organization, including the cost of training the employee, the costs generated or profits lost because of the employee's incompetence, the cost of severance, and the subsequent costs of further recruiting and selection screening. The major thrust of any selection activity should be to reduce the probability of making reject errors or accept errors, while increasing the probability of making correct decisions.

FIGURE 11-2 Selection Decision Outcomes

Later Job Performance	Selection Decision: Accept	Selection Decision: Reject
Successful	Correct decision	Reject error
Unsuccessful	Accept error	Correct decision

The potential employee must identify and match his or her skills to a specific job or career path. The employer must be able to test job applicants and determine their suitability. Computers can assist at both ends of the procedure; this INFOBUSINESS Job Power Source multimedia CD-ROM trains job seekers for the application and interview procedures they will be facing.

validity
The proven relationship that exists between a selection device and some relevant criterion.

Validity. Any selection device that a manager uses—such as application forms, tests, interviews, or background investigations—must demonstrate **validity**. That is, there must be a proven relationship between the selection device and some relevant criterion. For example, the law prohibits management from using a test score as a selection device unless there is clear evidence that, once on the job, individuals with high scores on this test outperform individuals with low test scores.

The burden is on management to support the claim that any selection device it uses to differentiate applicants is related to job performance. While management can give applicants an intelligence test and use the results to help make selection decisions, it must be prepared to show, if challenged, that this intelligence test is a valid measure. That is, the scores on the test must be shown to be positively related to later job performance.

reliability
The ability of a selection device to measure the same thing consistently.

Reliability. In addition to being valid, a selection device must also demonstrate reliability. **Reliability** indicates whether the device measures the same thing consistently. For example, if a test is reliable, any single individual's score should remain fairly consistent over time, assuming that the characteristics it is measuring are also stable.

The importance of reliability should be evident. No selection device can be effective if it's not reliable. This is equivalent to weighing yourself every day on an erratic scale. If the scale is unreliable—randomly fluctuating, say, 10 to 15 kilograms every time you step on it—the results will not mean much. To be effective predictors, selection devices must possess an acceptable level of consistency.

Selection Devices

Managers can use a number of selection devices to reduce accept and reject errors. The best-known devices include an analysis of the job candidate's completed application form, written and performance simulation tests, interviews, and background investigations. Let's briefly review each of these devices, paying particular attention to the validity of each in predicting job performance. After we review the devices, we'll discuss when each should be used.

The Application Form. Almost all organizations require job candidates to fill out an application form. It may only be a form on which the person gives his or her name, address, and telephone number. Or it might be a comprehensive personal history profile, detailing the person's activities, skills and accomplishments.

Relevant biographical data and facts that can be verified—for example, rank in high school graduating class or university final average—have been shown to be valid performance measures for some jobs.[11] In addition, when application form items have been appropriately

THINKING CRITICALLY ABOUT ETHICS

Prospective employees commonly provide a resumé, summarizing background, education, work experiences, and accomplishments. Should it be 100 percent truthful? Is it wrong to embellish—to give a previous job a better title or to increase a past salary? What deviations from the truth, if any, might be acceptable when writing a resume? ■

weighted to reflect job relatedness, this selection device has proved a valid predictor for such diverse groups as sales clerks, engineers, factory workers, district managers, clerical employees, and technicians.[12] But typically, only a couple of items on the application form prove to be valid predictors of job performance, and then only for a specific job. Use of weighted applications for selection purposes is difficult and expensive because the weights have to be validated for each specific job, and must be continually reviewed and updated to reflect changes in job relatedness over time.

Written Tests. Typical types of written tests include tests of intelligence, aptitude, ability and interest. Such tests have been used for a number of years although their popularity tends to run in cycles. Written tests were widely used for 20 years following World War II. Beginning in the late 1960s, however, the use of tests went out of favour. Written tests were frequently characterized as discriminatory and many organizations couldn't validate their written tests as being job related.[13] But since the late 1980s, written tests have made a comeback.[14] Managers have become increasingly aware that poor hiring decisions are costly, and that properly designed tests can reduce the likelihood of poor decisions occurring. In addition, the cost of developing and validating a set of written tests for a specific job has decreased significantly. What used to take six months and cost $100 000 now takes only a couple of weeks and costs around $6000.[15]

A review of research in this area shows that tests of intellectual ability, spatial and mechanical ability, perceptual accuracy, and motor ability are moderately valid predictors for many semi-skilled and unskilled operative jobs in industrial organizations.[16] And intelligence tests are reasonably good predictors for supervisory positions.[17] However, an enduring criticism of written tests is that intelligence, and other tested characteristics, can be somewhat removed from the actual performance of a job. For example, a high score on an intelligence test is not necessarily a good indicator that the applicant will perform well as a computer programmer. This criticism has led to an increased use of performance simulation tests.

Boeing–McDonnell-Douglas
www.boeing.com

Performance Simulation Tests. What better way to find out whether an applicant for a technical writing position at Boeing–McDonnell-Douglas can write technical manuals than by having him or her do it? The logic of this question has led to an expanding interest in performance simulation tests as selection devices. Undoubtedly, the enthusiasm for these tests is due to the fact that they are based on job analysis data and, therefore, should more easily meet the requirement of job relatedness than do written tests. Performance simulation tests are made up of actual job behaviours rather than surrogates.

The best-known performance simulation tests are work sampling and assessment centres. The former is appropriate for routine jobs, and the latter for selecting people for managerial positions.

work sampling
A personnel selection device in which job applicants are presented with a miniature replica of a job and are asked to perform tasks central to that job.

Work sampling involves presenting applicants with a miniature model of a job and having them perform a task or set of tasks that are central to it. Applicants demonstrate that they have the necessary skills and abilities by actually doing the tasks. By carefully devising work samples based on job analysis data, managers can determine the knowledge, skills and abilities needed for each job. Each work sample element is then matched to a corresponding job performance element. For instance, a work sample for a job that involves computing figures on a calculator would require applicants to make similar computations.

The results from work sample experiments generally have been impressive. They have almost always yielded validity scores that are superior to those of written aptitude, personality or intelligence tests.[18]

assessment centres
Places in which job candidates undergo performance simulation tests that evaluate managerial potential.

A more elaborate set of performance simulation tests, specifically designed to measure a job candidate's managerial potential, is administered in **assessment centres**. In assessment centres, line executives, supervisors or trained psychologists evaluate candidates as they go

The more sophisticated testing done at assessment centres helps identify those individuals who have management capabilities.

through two to four days of exercises which simulate real problems they would confront on the job. Based on a list of descriptive dimensions that the actual job incumbent has to meet, activities might include interviews, in-basket problem-solving exercises, group discussions and business decision games. The evidence on the effectiveness of assessment centres as a selection device is extremely impressive. They've consistently demonstrated results that predict later job performance in managerial positions.[19] Although they're not cheap to administer, selecting an ineffective manager can be significantly more costly.

Interviews. The interview, along with the application form, is an almost universal selection device.[20] Not many of us have ever got a job without one or more interviews. The irony is that the value of the interview as a selection device has been the subject of considerable debate.[21]

Interviews *can* be valid and reliable selection tools, but often they're not. When interviews are structured and well organized, and when interviewers are held to common questioning, interviews are effective predictors.[22] But most interviews don't meet those conditions. The typical interview—in which applicants are asked a varying set of essentially random questions in an informal setting—usually provides little in the way of valuable information.

All kinds of potential biases can creep into interviews if they're not well structured and standardized. To illustrate, a review of the research on interviews leads us to the following conclusions:

1. Prior knowledge about the applicant will bias the interviewer's evaluation.
2. The interviewer tends to hold a stereotype of what represents a "good" applicant.
3. The interviewer tends to favour applicants who share his or her own attitudes.
4. The order in which applicants are interviewed will influence evaluations.
5. The order in which information is elicited during the interview will influence evaluations.
6. Negative information is given unduly high weight.
7. The interviewer often makes a decision concerning the applicant's suitability within the first four or five minutes of the interview.
8. The interviewer forgets much of the interview's content within minutes after its conclusion.
9. The interview is most valid in determining an applicant's intelligence, level of motivation, and interpersonal skills.
10. A "cold" interviewer (i.e., one who's extremely formal and serious) can have a devastating effect on the verbal and non-verbal behaviours of applicants with low self-esteem.[23]

TABLE 11-5 Suggestions for Interviewing

1. Structure a *fixed set of questions* for all applicants.
2. Have *detailed information about the job* for which applicants are being interviewed.
3. *Minimize any prior knowledge* of applicants' background, experience, interests, test scores, or other characteristics.
4. *Ask behavioural questions* that require applicants to give detailed accounts of actual job behaviours.
5. Use a *standardized evaluation form.*
6. *Take notes* during the interview.
7. *Avoid short interviews* that encourage premature decision making.

Source: Based on David A DeCenzo and Stephen P Robbins, *Human Resource Management*, 4th ed. (New York: Wiley, 1994), pp. 208-09.

What can managers do to make interviews more valid and reliable? Table 11-5 lists some specific suggestions.

Background Investigation. Background investigations are of two types: verifications of application data and reference checks. Both can be valuable sources of selection information.

Several studies indicate that verifying "facts" given on the application form is worthwhile. A significant percentage of job applicants—upward of 15 percent—exaggerate or misrepresent dates of employment, job titles, past salaries, or reasons for leaving a prior position.[24] Confirmation of hard data given on the application with prior employers is a worthwhile endeavour.

Over two-thirds of Canadian employers use reference checks when hiring people for some jobs.[25] Not only are more companies checking references, they are asking for more than the standard three references. Some are asking for as many as 15 from a variety of people who have interacted with the candidate: superiors, subordinates, peers and clients. In addition, private companies that check references for a fixed fee are growing. References should be checked after a tentative hiring decision has been made, or a short list prepared. The best way to check references is by phone, preferably by two people using an extension phone. The two-person check, while not infallible, tends to eliminate untruthful interviews; signed, dated notes by both interviewers provide a record that protects the recruiter.[26] Questions should relate to job requirements. Reference letters are less useful because they tend to be inflated, and former employers are often reluctant to put unfavourable comments in writing, for fear of legal repercussions. Personal references are likely to provide biased information. Doesn't each of us have three or four friends who will speak in glowing terms about our integrity, work habits, positive attitudes, knowledge and skills?

Physical Examination. A medical examination should be conducted only after an offer of employment has been made. The offer can be conditional on the candidate's physical ability to perform the essential tasks of the job, based on the examination. The examination also provides a baseline against which future medical information can be compared—which can be important if the employee claims workers' compensation for a work-caused disability.

Any inquiries about health or physical ability must be related directly to the candidate's ability to perform the essential duties of the job. Screening out applicants with disabilities or health problems has been found to be discriminatory. The interviewer may ask about disabilities that would require accommodation to enable job performance, but should not probe for details, so as not to give the impression that the hiring decision would be based on this information. The employer is required to accommodate the needs of disabled people. Prior to human rights legislation, it was common for employers to have standards—often arbitrary—of height, weight, or strength. Such standards often discriminate against women or designated minority groups, and are very rarely defensible as bona fide occupational requirements.

What Works Best and When?

Many selection devices are of limited value to managers in making selection decisions. An understanding of the strengths and weaknesses of each will help you to determine when each should be used. We offer the following advice to guide your choices.

Since the validity of selection devices varies for different types of jobs, you should use only those devices that predict suitability for a given job. (See Table 11-6.) The application form offers limited information. Traditional written tests are reasonably effective devices for routine jobs. Work samples, however, are clearly preferable to written tests. For managerial selection, the assessment centre is strongly recommended. If the interview has a place in the selection decision, it is most likely to be among less routine jobs, particularly middle- and upper-level managerial positions.The interview is a reasonably good device for discerning intelligence and interpersonal skills.[27] These are more likely to be related to job performance in non-routine activities, especially in senior managerial positions. Verification of application data is valuable for all jobs.

ORIENTATION

Did you participate in some type of organized introduction to college or university life when you started school? If you did, you may have been told about the school's rules and regulations, and the procedures for activities such as applying for financial aid, cashing a cheque or registering for classes. And you were probably introduced to some of the college administrators. A person starting a new job needs the same type of introduction to his or her job and the organization. This introduction is called **orientation**.

orientation
The introduction of a new employee to his or her job and the organization.

The major objectives of orientation are to reduce the initial anxiety which all new employees feel as they begin a new job; to familiarize new employees with the job, the work unit and the organization as a whole; and to facilitate the outsider-insider transition. Job orientation expands on the information the employee received during the recruitment and selection stages. The new employee's specific duties and responsibilities are clarified, as well as how his or her performance will be evaluated. This is also the time to resolve any unrealistic expectations new employees might hold about the job. Work unit orientation familiarizes the employee with the goals of the work unit, clarifies how his or her job contributes to the unit's goals, and includes

TABLE 11-6 Validity of Selection Devices as Predictors

	Position			
Selection Device	***Senior Management***	***Middle And Lower Management***	***Complex Non-managerial***	***Routine Operative***
Application form	2	2	2	2
Written tests	1	1	2	3
Work samples	—	—	4	4
Assessment centre	5	5	—	—
Interviews	4	3	2	2
Verification of application data	3	3	3	3
Reference checks	1	1	1	1
Physical exam	1	1	1	2

Note: Validity is measured on a scale from 5 (highest) to 1 (lowest).

TESTING... TESTING...

3 Why are validity and reliability important in selection?

4 Describe the advantages and disadvantages of the various selection devices.

an introduction to co-workers. Organization orientation informs the new employee about the organization's objectives, history, philosophy, procedures and rules. This should include relevant personnel policies such as work hours, pay procedures, overtime requirements, and benefits. A tour of the organization's work facilities is often part of organization orientation.

Many organizations, particularly large ones, have formal orientation programs. Such a program might include a tour of the offices or plant, a video describing the history of the organization, and a short discussion with a representative of the human resources department who describes the organization's benefit programs. Other organizations use a more informal orientation program in which, for instance, the manager assigns the new employee to a senior member of the unit, who then introduces the new employee to immediate co-workers and shows him or her the locations of the copy room, coffee machine, rest rooms, cafeteria, and the like.

Management has an obligation to make the integration of the new employee into the organization as smooth and as free of anxiety as possible. There should be open discussion of the employee's beliefs regarding the obligations of both the organization and the employee.[28] It's in the organization's, and the new employee's, best interests to get the person up and running in the job as soon as possible. Successful orientation, whether formal or informal, results in an outsider-insider transition that makes the new member feel comfortable and fairly well adjusted, lowers the likelihood of poor work performance, and reduces the probability of a surprise resignation a week or two into the job.

EMPLOYEE TRAINING

On the whole, planes don't cause airline accidents—people do. Most collisions, crashes and other mishaps—about 74 percent to be exact—result from errors made by the pilot or air traffic controller, or through inadequate maintenance. Weather and structural failures cause only 15 percent of accidents.[29] We point out these statistics to show the importance of employee training in the airline industry. These maintenance and human errors could be significantly reduced, if not prevented, by better employee training.

MANAGERS WHO MAKE A DIFFERENCE

Terry McBride, Nettwerk Records, Vancouver

Managing an independent record label has never been an easy occupation. Without the muscle of the large labels, independents have always had to gamble on acts which the big companies wouldn't touch.[30] Nettwerk Records was formed in 1985 by Terry McBride with two partners—Ric Arboite and Mark Jowett. As the label signed artists, it found that these unknowns were not represented by any management, so McBride took it upon himself to perform this role. As it turned out, this strategy led to a company philosophy that has paid off greatly for Nettwerk. The do-it-yourself ethic has led to the development of different arms in the business, such as a publishing entity, a multimedia division, and a merchandising department. McBride's views on human resources can be seen in this statement: "Whenever we do something new, we bring the other key people in the company into the ownership of that new entity. Because a lot of growing a young company and keeping it dynamic is keeping the key people there. If in essence they're working for themselves, in the end there's probably a better chance that we're still gonna be around here in 10 or 15 years". Nettwerk has tried to develop a familial relationship with both its employees and its clients, such as Sarah McLachlan. The company obviously has as much faith in its clients as it does in its employees: Nettwerk supported McLachlan's highly successful Lilith Fair tour, when many in the industry believed it could never succeed. ■

Nettwerk Records
www.nettwerk.com

As job demands change, employee skills have to be altered and updated. It has been estimated, for instance, that North American business firms spend more than $50 billion on formal courses and training programs to build workers' skills.[31] Management, of course, is responsible for deciding when subordinates are in need of training, and what form that training should take.

Skill Categories

We can group employee skills into three categories: technical, interpersonal, and problem solving. Most employee training activities seek to modify one or more of these skills.

Technical. Most training is directed at upgrading and improving an employee's technical skills. This includes basic skills—the ability to read, write, and perform math computations—as well as job-specific competencies.[32]

The majority of jobs today have become more complex than they were a decade ago. Computerized factories and offices, digitally controlled machines, and other types of sophisticated technology require employees to have math, reading, and computer skills. How, for example, can employees master statistical process control or the careful measurement and self-inspection needed for tool changes in flexible manufacturing systems, if they can't make basic math calculations or read detailed operating manuals? Or how can most clerical personnel do their jobs effectively without the ability to understand word-processing programs and e-mail systems?

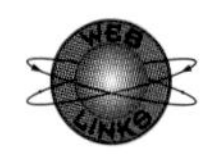

Honeywell Ltd
www.honeywell.com

Interpersonal. Almost every employee belongs to a work unit. To some degree, work performance depends on the employee's ability to interact effectively with his or her co-workers and boss. Some employees have excellent interpersonal skills. Others require training to improve theirs. This includes learning how to be a better listener, how to communicate ideas more clearly, and how to reduce conflict. For instance, Honeywell Limited's Scarborough, Ontario, plant underwent a re-engineering recently in order to implement just-in-time inventory systems, total quality management, and self-directed work teams. Honeywell provided training in these areas, but faced a more fundamental problem. Most employees had less than Grade 12 education and half did not speak English as their first language. Yet, for the plant's new operating methods to work, it was imperative that employees be able to communicate effectively. The company found it had to offer more basic training. It now offers courses in English, mathematics, computers, communications, team skills, and a variety of other subjects.[33]

Strengthening employees' broad management skills and building their commitment to their firm's mission are two of the goals of such off-site training programs as the Well Team Course. A firm can reap many benefits and even develop its competitive advantage when its human resource management includes such a strong focus on its people.

Problem Solving. Many employees find that they have to solve problems in their jobs. This is particularly true in jobs that are of the non-routine variety. When the problem solving skills of employees are deficient, management might want to improve these skills through training. This would include participating in activities to sharpen logic, reasoning, creativity and skills in defining problems, as well as assessing causation, developing and analyzing alternatives, and selecting solutions.

Training Methods

Most training takes place on the job since this approach is simple to implement and is usually less expensive. However, on-the-job training can disrupt the workplace and result in an increase in errors while learning takes place. Also, some skills training is too complex to learn on the job. In such cases, it should take place outside the work setting.

On-the-Job Training. Popular on-the-job training methods include job rotation and understudy assignments. **Job rotation** involves lateral transfers that enable employees to work at different jobs. Employees get to learn a wide variety of jobs, while gaining increased insight into the interdependency between jobs, and a wider perspective on organizational activities. New employees frequently learn their jobs by studying under a seasoned veteran. In the trades, this is called an *apprenticeship*. In white-collar jobs, it is called a *coaching* or *mentor* relationship. In both cases, the understudy works under the observation of an experienced worker, who acts as a model.

job rotation
On-the-job training that involves lateral transfers in which employees get to work at different jobs.

Both job rotation and understudy assignments apply to the learning of technical skills. Interpersonal and problem-solving skills are acquired more effectively by training that takes place off the job.

mentor
A person who sponsors or supports another employee who is lower in the organization.

Off-the-Job Training. There are a number of off-the-job training methods that managers may want to use. The more popular ones are classroom lectures, films or video, and simulation

Getting the Most Out of a Mentor Relationship

Acquiring a mentor who provides advice, assistance and support can be one of the smartest career moves a young manager makes. A **mentor** is someone in the organization who is usually older, more experienced, typically higher up in the organizational levels, and who can help another person achieve his or her career goals. A mentor is someone from whom you can learn, who can encourage and help you, and who serves as adviser, coach, counsellor and guide. One study of managers and professionals in Belgium who were in the early stages of their careers found that career mentoring was positively related to early career promotions, general satisfaction with work, and overall satisfaction with career choice. How can you get the most out of a mentor relationship?[34]

If your organization has no formal mentoring program, you'll need to find your own mentor—someone in the organization whom you trust, respect and like. Ask this person if he or she would be willing to serve as your mentor. Building a strong partnership with your mentor is like building any interpersonal relationship. First, honest and open communication by both of you is absolutely essential. If you're going to benefit from your mentor's accumulated years of experience and knowledge, he or she must be willing to level with you in "telling it like it is". And, as the protégé, you must exhibit a willingness to listen and learn, which also implies a willingness to ask questions and challenge statements your mentor might make. Also, treat your mentor with the respect he or she deserves. After all, your mentor has more years of experience as a manager than you and has, undoubtedly, learned much in those years. And, of course, effective work performance is absolutely essential. Having an excellent mentor is no substitute or excuse for poor work performance. Finally, when you get to a point in your career where you have experience and insights to offer younger organizational members, consider becoming a mentor yourself. It helps the organization to develop its managerial talent. And there can be a great deal of personal satisfaction in helping develop others. ■

FIGURE 11-3 Steps to a Successful Management Career

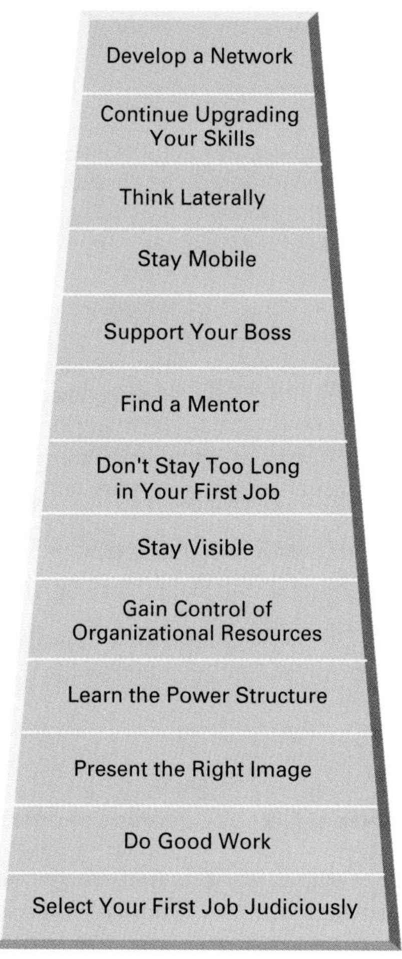

exercises. *Classroom lectures* are well suited for conveying specific information. They can be used effectively for developing technical and problem-solving skills. *Films* and *videos* can also be used to explicitly demonstrate technical skills that aren't easily presented by other methods. Interpersonal and problem-solving skills may be best learned through *simulation exercises* such as case analyses, experiential exercises, role playing, and group interaction sessions. However, complex computer models, such as those used by airlines in pilot training, are another kind of simulation exercise—used in this case to teach technical skills. So, too, is **vestibule training**, in which employees learn their jobs on the same equipment they'll be using, but in a simulated work environment rather than in the actual work setting. Many airplane maintenance trainees learn to repair engines in specially created vestibule labs, containing actual aircraft that simulate real working conditions. This provides for careful control of learning experiences—allowing trainees to deal with every conceivable problem—while minimizing interference with an airline's actual ongoing maintenance operations.

vestibule training
Training in which employees learn on the same equipment they will be using but in a simulated work environment.

TESTING... TESTING...

5 What is the goal of orientation?

6 Identify three skill categories for which organizations use employee training.

TABLE 11-7 Components of a Compensation System

- Base wages and salaries
- Wage and salary add-ons
- Incentive payments
- Benefits and services

Source: Based on Richard I Henderson, *Compensation Management*, 6th ed. (Englewood Cliffs, NJ: Prentice Hall, 1994), p. 16.

COMPENSATION AND BENEFITS

Would you work 40 hours a week (or more) for an organization for no pay and no benefits? Although we might consider doing this for some "cause" organizations, most of us expect to receive some form of reward from our employer. Developing an effective and efficient system of employee rewards is an important part of the human resources management process.[35]

The purpose of having an effective reward system is to attract and retain competent and talented individuals who can help the organization accomplish its mission and goals. Organizational rewards can include many different types of compensation and benefits. Table 11-7 provides a brief description of the typical compensation components which an organization can provide.

How does management determine who receives $7.00 an hour and who receives $250 000 a year? There are several factors that influence the differences in compensation and benefit packages for different employees. (See Figure 11-4.)

The primary determinant of rate of pay is the *kind of job an employee performs.* Different jobs require different kinds and levels of skills, and these skills have varying levels of value to the organization. Typically, the higher the skill level, the higher the pay.

Because employees' levels of skills tend to affect work efficiency and effectiveness, many organizations have implemented **skill-based pay** systems which reward employees for the job skills and competencies they can demonstrate. In a skill-based pay system, an employee's job

skill-based pay
A pay system that rewards employees for the job skills and competencies they can demonstrate.

FIGURE 11-4 Factors Influencing Compensation and Benefits Packages

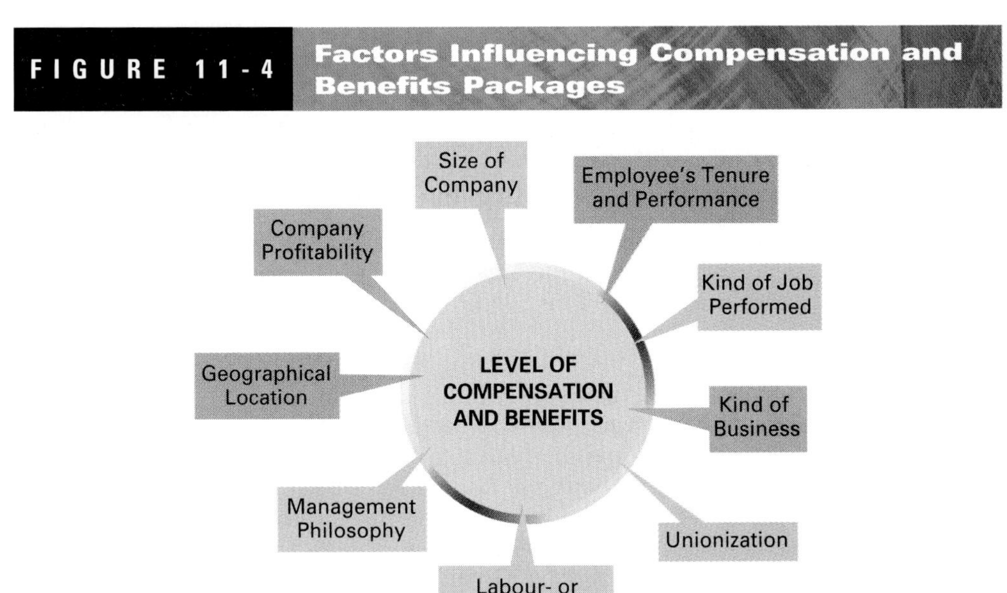

Source: Richard I Henderson, *Compensation Management,* 6th ed. (Englewood Cliffs, NJ: Prentice Hall, 1994), pp. 3–24; and Alan Murray, "Mom, Apple Pie, and Small Business," *Wall Street Journal,* 8/15/94, p. A1.

Some of the many factors that influence employee compensation are the kind of business, its size, and the level of skill required. Equally important are the individual's tenure, job performance, and level of skill attained.

title doesn't define his or her pay category—skills do. The more skills a worker has (such as operating forklifts or using computer controls), the higher the wage. Skill-based pay systems seem to mesh nicely with the changing nature of jobs and the new world of work. As one expert has noted: "Slowly, but surely, we're becoming a skill-based society where your market value is tied to what you can do and what your skill set is. In this new world where skills and knowledge are what really count, it doesn't make sense to treat people as jobholders. It makes sense to treat them as people with specific skills and to pay them for those skills".[36]

Another factor that influences an employee's pay is the *kind of business the organization is in*. Private-sector jobs typically provide higher rates of pay than public sector or non-profit jobs. The nature of the business and its impact on compensation also applies to different industries. For example, restaurants and other retail businesses have notoriously low salaries for operative employees and first-line managers.

Also, whether or not an organization or particular business unit is *unionized*, can influence an employee's pay. We find that the wages of unionized workers tend to be higher than those of non-unionized employees for comparable jobs, but this is true mainly in heavy manufacturing industries (for example, steel, mining and oil). However, the economics of global competition have forced organizations to look for ways to reduce their labour costs. As a result, unionization doesn't affect pay levels as it once did.

Another industry characteristic that influences the rate of pay is whether or not the business is *labour or capital intensive*. As businesses have become more capital intensive, it doesn't take as many workers to do the organization's work, but these employees need higher levels of knowledge and skills. Thus, highly skilled employees usually demand higher rates of pay.

Another factor that influences pay levels is *management's philosophy*. Some organizations have the philosophy that, "We don't pay employees any more than we absolutely have to", while others are committed to a philosophy of paying their employees at, or above, area standards in order to attract and retain the best pool of talent.

Geographical location is another of the factors that influences pay. Usually, the geographical regions where the cost of living is highest offer the highest wages. Also, the supply and demand for labour and the prevailing unemployment rate in a particular area of a country affect the level of pay that must be offered to attract and retain competent employees.

The *profitability of the company* also influences employee pay levels. If a company is experiencing declining profits, its ability to offer high levels of pay and benefits will be affected. However, if the company is profitable, it may be able to provide higher pay levels or some type of profit-sharing system.

Studies also show that the *size of a company* affects pay levels. The hourly pay of workers at companies with more than 500 employees is greater than the pay of workers at smaller companies.[37]

The final factor that affects pay is an *employee's tenure and performance* at his or her job. In most cases, an employee's rate of pay increases with each year worked at an organization. But, we also find that organizations may reward employees who have achieved high levels of performance by increasing their pay through some type of merit or pay-for-performance system. Taking all these factors into account, management hopes to establish a fair, equitable and motivating reward system that allows the organization to recruit and keep a productive workforce.

CURRENT ISSUES IN HUMAN RESOURCE MANAGEMENT

We conclude this chapter by looking at several contemporary human resource issues facing today's managers. These include managing workforce diversity, harassment, family concerns, AIDS in the workplace, and downsizing.

Managing Workforce Diversity

We've discussed the changing makeup of the Canadian workforce in several places throughout the book. Let's now look at how workforce diversity affects such basic HRM concerns as recruitment, selection, and orientation and training.

Recruitment. Improving workforce diversity means that managers need to widen their recruiting net. For example, the popular practice of relying on current employee referrals as a source of new job applicants tends to result in hiring candidates who have similar characteristics to present employees. So, managers must look for job applicants in places where they might not have looked before.

To increase diversity, managers are increasingly turning to non-traditional recruitment sources. For example, they might contact women's job networks, over-50 clubs, urban job banks, training centres for persons with disabilities, ethnic newspapers and gay rights organizations. This type of outreach should enable the organization to broaden its pool of diverse applicants.

Selection. Once a diverse set of applicants exists, efforts must be made to ensure that the selection process isn't discriminatory. Moreover, applicants need to be made comfortable with the organization and with any interview or testing situation. They also need to be made aware of management's desire to accommodate their needs. For instance, at Microsoft Corporation,

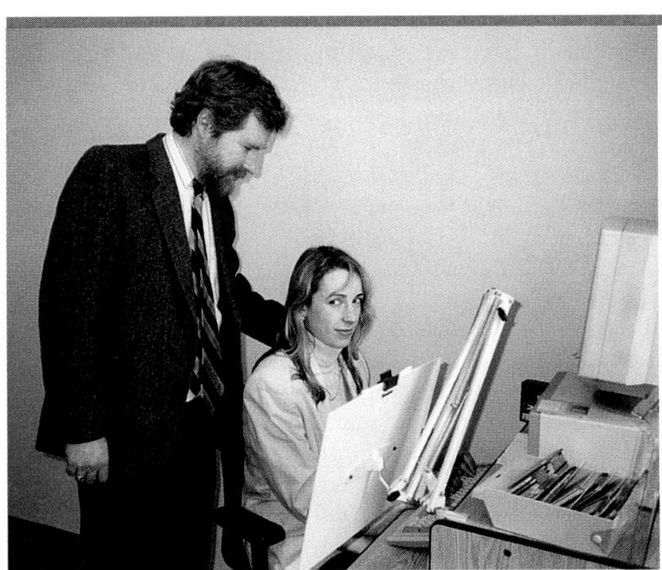

The issue of harassment in the workplace only began to be given attention by the Canadian courts in the 1980s. Today every organization should have a clearly defined set of policies defining proper behaviour.

only a small number of women apply for its technical jobs. However, the company makes every effort to hire a higher percentage of the female applicants, and strives to make sure that these women have a successful experience once they're on the job.[38]

Rogers Communications Inc.
www.rogers.com

Orientation and Training. The outsider-insider transition is often more challenging for women entering a largely male workforce, or for people whose ethnic background is different from that of most of their co-workers. Many organizations provide special workshops to raise diversity awareness among current employees, as well as programs for new employees that focus on diversity issues. Rogers Communications, for example, has a formal Diversity Management program which all business units are expected to include in their plans. The Bank of Montreal actually has a Vice-President of Workplace Equality, and attempts to integrate diversity programs into the fabric of the organization. This goal includes everything from adapting branch decor to appeal to the culture in each community to promoting the advancement of women. In the five years since the introduction of a Task Force for the Advancement of Women, the percentage of Bank of Montreal executives who are women rose from 6 to 16 percent.[39] A number of companies have special mentoring programs to deal with the reality that lower-level female and minority managers have fewer role models with whom to identify.

Harassment

sexual harassment
Behaviour marked by sexually aggressive remarks, unwanted touching and sexual advances, requests for sexual favours, or other verbal or physical conduct of a sexual nature.

Before 1980, Canadian courts did not recognize sexual harassment as a form of sex discrimination. This changed permanently with the case of Cherie Bell in Ontario provincial court; since then legislation has begun to catch up with the issues of the times. Today, **sexual harassment** covers a vast array of situations. Virtually any type of behaviour that an individual considers offensive in a sexual manner can be construed as sexual harassment. This may include sexually suggestive remarks, unwanted touching and sexual advances, requests for sexual favours, degrading comments or jokes, mandatory work uniforms that are deemed sexually provocative, or sexual images in the workplace.[40] Behaviours such as these are a violation of human rights legislation in every Canadian jurisdiction. Yet, according to Status of Women Canada, only 40 percent of Canadian women who suffer sexual harassment at work take any formal action, and only 50 percent of women believe that a complaint would be taken seriously in their workplace.[41]

Status of Women Canada
www.swc-cfc.gc.ca

From management's standpoint, harassment is a concern because it intimidates employees, interferes with job performance, and exposes the organization to legal liability. On this last point, human rights case rulings have made it clear that, if the employee who is guilty of sexual harassment is a supervisor or agent for an organization, then the organization is liable for sexual harassment, regardless of whether the act was authorized or forbidden by the organization, or whether or not the organization knew of the act.

To avoid liability, management must establish a clear and strong policy against harassment.[42] That policy should then be reinforced by regular discussion sessions in which managers are reminded of the rule, and are carefully instructed that unwelcome sexual overtures to another employee will not be tolerated. Studies have shown that the best training on harassment or discrimination gives participants a chance to talk to each other, instead of just listening to a lecture or watching a film on the subject.[43]

Family Concerns

Organizations are beginning to recognize that employees can't (and don't) just leave their family problems behind when they walk into work. An organization hires a person who has feelings, personal problems and family commitments. Although we're not trying to imply that an organization should be sympathetic with each and every detail of an employee's family life, we *are* seeing organizations become more attuned to the fact that employees have sick children or elderly parents who need care, and experience other family issues that may require special arrangements.[44] Many companies have implemented such family-friendly policies as flexible work hours; job sharing; in-house day cares; and allowing employees to work from home via e-mail.

dual-career couples
Couples in which both partners have a professional, managerial, or administrative occupation.

Another family concern that arises is the large number of **dual-career couples**—couples in which both partners have a professional, managerial, or administrative occupation.[45] An organization's human resource management policies need to reflect the special problems this situation creates for couples. Special attention needs to be given to the organization's policies regarding nepotism, relocations and transfers, and conflicts of interest.[46]

AIDS in the Workplace

AIDS is an issue in human resource management because of the profound impact it can have on the workplace and employees. Although many don't want to confront it, managers need to be prepared to deal with HIV/AIDS-related issues in the workplace.

There have been many cases in Canada of employees refusing to work with people infected with the virus. One of the early cases involved two prison guards working in a prison hospital, who refused to work for fear that they would contract AIDS from inmates. The Public Service Staff Relations Board found that, with adequate protection, there was no risk to the guards.[47] In many subsequent cases, human rights hearings have confirmed that being HIV positive is not valid grounds for firing an employee or for rejecting a job applicant. (There are a few rare exceptions, such as when an employee in a health care setting performs invasive procedures that result in exposure to blood or blood products, or when the job involves international travel to countries that prohibit entry to HIV-positive individuals.)[48] But what if colleagues refuse to work with an HIV-positive person? What if a supervisor expresses concern about the employee's contact with customers? To be prepared for such issues, managers need policies, employee training and education programs.

Public Service Staff Relations Board
www.pssrb-crtfp.gc.ca

Procter & Gamble Canada
www.pg.com

A number of Canadian companies are implementing such programs. For example, Procter & Gamble produced an employee magazine supplement entitled, "It's Time for Education, Not Denial", outlining corporate policy on AIDS and providing information about the disease, including interviews with leading experts from Canadian hospitals.[49] However, a recent survey found that, while more than 80 percent of Canadian companies believed they needed an AIDS awareness program, fewer than 30 percent had actually set one up.[50]

The goal of any workplace AIDS program should be to create an environment in which HIV-positive employees are not afraid to reveal their condition; in which they can continue to lead useful and productive lives; and in which co-workers can ask questions, express concerns and overcome their fear of working with individuals who are HIV positive. To do this, what should a comprehensive AIDS program include? Experts suggest that it have the following components: (1) a workplace policy that stresses human rights entitlements and provides guidelines for dealing with employees who may be HIV positive; (2) training for managers, supervisors, and union leaders who may have HIV-positive employees within their work groups; (3) employee education on AIDS-related issues; (4) family education programs and materials on AIDS and AIDS prevention; and (5) community involvement in AIDS education. Any type of AIDS program requires the full commitment and support of top-level management in order to be effective.

7 Why is managing workforce diversity an important HRM issue?

8 How can companies minimize the occurrences of sexual harassment?

9 How can organizations make their HRM programs and practices more family-friendly?

SUMMARY

This summary is organized by the learning objectives at the beginning of the chapter.

1. The human resource management process seeks to staff the organization and sustain high employee performance through human resource planning, recruitment or decruitment, selection, orientation, training, career development, compensation and benefits, and performance appraisal.
2. Since the mid-1960s, government has greatly expanded its influence over HRM decisions by enacting new laws and regulations. Because of governments' efforts to provide equal employment opportunities, management must ensure that key HRM decisions—such as recruitment, selection, training, promotions and terminations —are made without regard to race, sex, religion, age or national origin. Extensive financial penalties can be imposed on organizations that fail to follow these laws and regulations. In addition, companies doing business globally must know and adhere to the applicable human resources laws and regulations in the countries in which they are operating.
3. A job description is a written statement of what a jobholder does, how it's done, and why it's done. A job specification states the minimum acceptable qualifications that a jobholder must possess to perform a given job successfully.
4. Recruitment seeks to develop a pool of potential job candidates. Typical sources include an internal search, advertisements, employee referrals, HRD, employment agencies, school placement centres and temporary help services. Decruitment reduces the labour supply within an organization through options such as firing, layoffs, attrition, transfers, reduced workweeks and early retirements.
5. The quality of a selection device is determined by its validity and reliability. If a device is not valid, then no proven relationship exists between it and relevant job criteria. If a selection device isn't reliable, then it cannot be assumed to be a consistent measure.
6. Selection devices must match the job in question. Work samples work best with low-level jobs. Assessment centres work best for managerial positions. The validity of the interview as a selection device increases for progressively higher levels of management.
7. Employee training can be on the job or off the job. Popular on-the-job methods include job rotation, understudying, and apprenticeships. The more popular off-the-job methods are classroom lectures, films, and simulation exercises.
8. The various types of compensation include base wages and salaries, wage and salary add-ons, incentive payments, and benefits and services. Compensation decisions are typically based on the following factors: kind of job and skills required, nature of the business, whether the company is unionized or non-unionized, how labour- or capital-intensive the business is, management's philosophy towards compensation, a company's geographical location, company profitability, company size, and employee's tenure and performance on the job.
9. HRM practices can facilitate workforce diversity by widening the recruitment net, eliminating any discriminatory selection practices, communicating to applicants the company's willingness to accommodate their needs, and providing employee training and education programs that focus on diversity.
10. Harassment is a growing concern for management because it intimidates employees, interferes with job performance, and exposes the organization to liability.
11. Companies are meeting the challenges of employee family concerns by developing policies and programs that are family-friendly. Companies are developing employee education programs on AIDS and related issues.

THINKING ABOUT MANAGEMENT ISSUES

1. What is the relationship between selection, recruitment, and job analysis?
2. Do you think there are moral limits on how far a prospective employer should delve into an applicant's life by means of interviews and tests? Explain.
3. Assume that you're the director of new product research for a company that has 75 employees and is expanding rapidly. What specific practices would you implement to facilitate the hiring of diverse individuals?
4. Should an employer have the right to choose employees without governmental interference? Support your conclusion.
5. Studies have shown that women's salaries still lag behind those of men; even with equal opportunity laws and regulations, women are paid about 70 percent of what men are paid. How would you design a compensation system that would address this issue?

SELF-ASSESSMENT EXERCISE

DIVERSITY QUESTIONNAIRE

Instructions: Place a number next to each question that best describes your own actions and beliefs.

1 = Almost always
2 = Frequently
3 = Sometimes
4 = Seldom
5 = Almost never

_____ 1. Do you recognize and challenge the perceptions, assumptions, and biases that affect your thinking?
_____ 2. Do you think about the impact of what you say or how you act before you speak or act?
_____ 3. Do you do everything you can to prevent the reinforcement of prejudices, including avoiding using negative stereotypes when you speak?
_____ 4. Do you demonstrate your respect for people who are not from the dominant culture by doing things that show you feel they are as competent and skilled as others, including handing them responsibility as often as you do others?
_____ 5. Do you encourage people who are not from the dominant culture to speak out on their concerns and respect those issues?
_____ 6. Do you speak up when someone is making racial, sexual, or other derogatory remarks or is humiliating another person?
_____ 7. Do you apologize when you realize you might have offended someone by inappropriate behaviour or comments?
_____ 8. Do you try to know people as individuals not as representatives of specific groups and include different types of people in your peer group?
_____ 9. Do you accept the notion that people from all backgrounds need to socialize with and reinforce one another?
_____ 10. Do you do everything that you can to understand your own background and try to educate yourself about other backgrounds, including different communication styles?

See scoring key on page SK–4.

Source: Based on W Sonnenschein, *The Practical Executive and Workforce Diversity* (Lincolnwood, IL: NTC Business Books, 1997).

for your IMMEDIATE action

North River Public Utilities Commission

To: Sandra Gillies, Director of Human Resources
From: William Mullane, Chair
Subject: Sexual Harassment

It has come to my attention that some of our people are not clear on what practices do or do not constitute sexual harassment. This is an area that cannot be ambiguous. We need to take immediate action towards developing training for all our employees and developing a workable procedure to handle complaints.

I want to make the issue of sexual harassment the primary topic of next month's executive board meeting. To facilitate discussion, I'd like you to develop a working paper (no longer than two pages in length) that would describe (1) the content of an initial two-hour employee workshop on sexual harassment and (2) an appropriate procedure that all employees could follow if they believe that they have been the victims of sexual harassment.

This is a fictionalized account of a potentially real problem, written for academic purposes only.

TAKE IT TO THE NET

We invite you to visit the Robbins/Coulter/Stuart-Kotze Companion Website at www.prenticehall.ca/robbins for this chapter's Internet resources.

CASE APPLICATION

Rhino Foods, Burlington, Vermont

Rhino Foods is a small but successful speciality-dessert producer that takes HRM seriously. The company's purpose statement reads:

> The employees and families of Rhino Foods are its greatest assets. The company's relationship with its employees is founded on a climate of mutual trust and respect within an environment for listening and personal expression. Rhino Foods declares that it is a vehicle for people to get what they want.

The emphasis on mutual trust and respect is evident in Rhino's recognition of its employees' home lives, and its support of employees' goals, both in their personal and professional lives. Employees are encouraged to meet with "wants co-ordinators" to discuss professional and personal goals, on company time. The point of this is to challenge employees and show them that they can achieve things on their own. Worker empowerment is a key ingredient at Rhino.

When Rhino was forced to downsize during the mid-1990s, managers came to employees for ideas on how to handle the situation. The employees came up with a very innovative solution. They partnered with local businesses who needed extra help. Workers volunteered to leave Rhino and, when business picked up, they were taken back into the Rhino fold. The employees came back with a renewed sense of commitment to the organization because Rhino had not just thoughtlessly laid people off. Since then, Rhino has doubled its workforce to 80 people.

QUESTIONS

1. What do you think Rhino's philosophy might be regarding the role of strategic human resource management? Explain.
2. On the basis of information included in the case, create a recruitment advertisement for a production line position that Rhino might use.
3. How is Rhino Foods dealing with work-family issues? How might they further their work-family commitment?
4. Would Rhino Foods' approach to HRM work in a company with 20 000 employees? Why or why not?

Sources: T H Naylor, W H Willimon, and R Osterberg, "The Search for Community in the Workplace", *Business and Society Review*, Spring 1995, pp. 42-47; and G Flynn, "Why Rhino Won't Wait 'Til Tomorrow", *Personnel Journal*, July 1996, pp. 36-43.

LEARNING OBJECTIVES

After Reading This Chapter, You Should Be Able To:

1 Contrast the "calm waters" and "white-water rapids" metaphors of change
2 Explain why people are likely to resist change
3 List techniques for reducing resistance to change
4 Describe what managers can change in organizations
5 Describe the situational factors that facilitate cultural change
6 Explain how management should go about enacting cultural change
7 Describe how managers can implement TQM
8 Explain how re-engineering relates to change
9 Describe techniques for reducing employee stress
10 Explain how organizations can stimulate innovation

A MANAGER'S CHALLENGE

Paul Ivanier, CEO, Ivaco Inc., Montreal

Sometimes it takes an economic shock like a recession to make a company aware of the need for change. The recession Canada faced in the early years of the past decade had this affect on Montreal's Ivaco Inc. This is how CEO Paul Ivanier describes the business climate that the steelmaker suddenly found itself facing: "I remember one February evening, the whole market had crashed. I gathered the company executives into my office to figure out what we were doing wrong". While Ivaco remained the country's top producer of wire-rod products, its

revenues were nearly cut in half. The company had to adapt quickly in the face of the rapidly changing environment. "We realized that although we were modern and had good products, it was not enough for survival. We needed imagination," says Ivanier. Ivaco embarked on a mission to find innovative ways to improve efficiency throughout the organization. Ivaco has come up with over 100 such innovations—some of which have been patented by the company.[1]

Ivaco decided it had to focus on its core business and invest heavily in modernization, to make it a technology leader in its industry. The company sold a dozen companies that were outside of what it defined as its main focus. Ivanier's opinion was that these non-core businesses would be a drag on the company: "The point is to be the best in your kingdom". Ivaco's modernization process has been expensive for the company, but it now runs the largest wire-rod plant in the world, producing more, and at greater speeds, than any of its competitors. The last word belongs to Ivanier: "If you're modern, you pay your bills. If you're not modern, you don't".

The situation faced by Ivaco is by no means rare in today's business world. While change has always been a part of the manager's job, it's become even more so in recent years. We'll describe why in this chapter. We'll also discuss ways in which managers can stimulate innovation and increase their organization's adaptability.

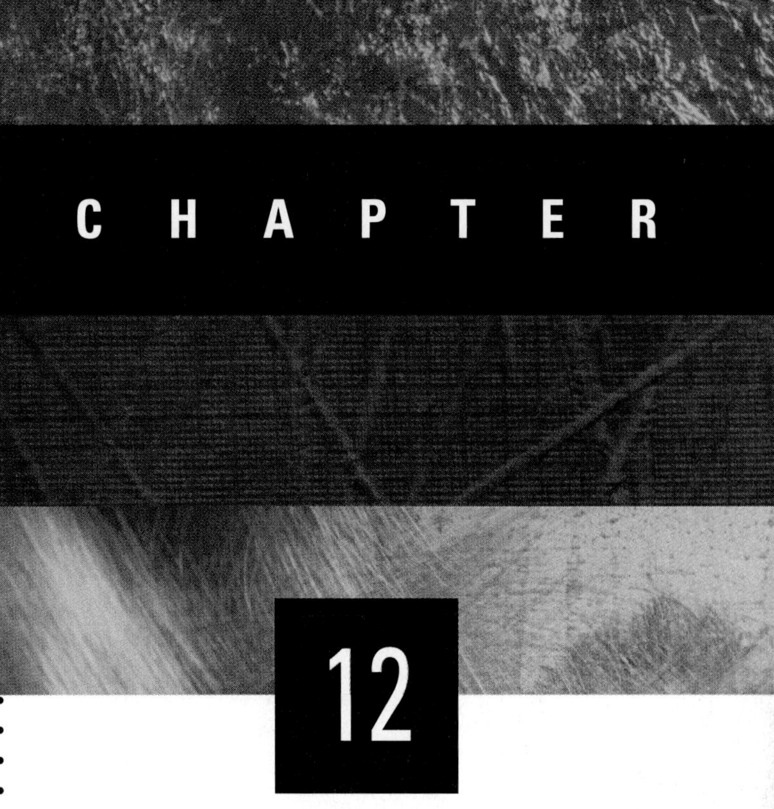

CHAPTER 12

Managing Change and Innovation

WHAT IS CHANGE?

change
An alteration in people, structure, or technology.

If it weren't for **change**, the manager's job would be relatively easy. Planning would be simplified, because tomorrow would be no different from today. The issue of effective organizational design would also be solved, since the environment would be free from uncertainty and there would be no need to adapt. Similarly, decision making would be dramatically streamlined because the outcome of each alternative could be predicted with almost certain accuracy. It would indeed simplify the manager's job if, for example, competitors didn't introduce new products or services, if customers didn't demand new and improved products, if government regulations were never modified, or if employees' needs didn't change.

However, that isn't the way it is. Change is an organizational reality. Handling change is an integral part of every manager's job. In this chapter of the book, we address the key issues related to managing change.

FORCES FOR CHANGE

In Chapter 3, we pointed out that there are both external and internal forces that constrain managers. These same forces also bring about the need for change. Let's briefly look at the factors that can create the need for change.

External Forces

The external forces that create the need for change come from various sources. The *marketplace* creates the need for change in many industries, such as when the Canadian restaurant industry suddenly faced a new competitor in 1998 as Loblaw's grocery stores installed areas where high-quality, made-to-order take-out meals could be cooked on the spot for time-constrained consumers.

Government laws and regulations are a frequent impetus for change. For example, the passage of various legislation has required thousands of organizations (profit and non-profit) to reconfigure restrooms, add ramps, widen doorways, and take other actions to improve access for persons with disabilities.

Technology also creates a need for change. For example, recent developments in sophisticated and extremely expensive diagnostic equipment have created significant economies of scale for hospitals and medical centres. Assembly-line technology in other industries is undergoing dramatic changes, as organizations replace human labour with robots. The fluctuation in *labour markets* forces managers to change. For instance, the continuing demand for health care technicians and specialists has meant that organizations needing those kinds of employees have had to change their human resource management activities in order to attract and retain skilled employees in those areas of greatest need.

Economic changes, of course, affect almost all organizations. For instance, recessionary pressures force organizations to become more cost efficient, as is shown in our Manager's Challenge section. Also, during the early 1990s, falling interest rates stimulated an unprecedented demand for the services of mortgage brokers and other financial service firms.

Internal Forces

In addition to the external forces just described, internal forces can also stimulate the need for change. These internal forces tend to originate primarily from the internal operations of the organization, or from the impact of external changes.

When management redefines or modifies its *strategy*, it often introduces a host of changes. For instance, when Bombardier's sea-doo business was dormant, Pierre Beaudoin was forced to implement a turnaround strategy that involved changes in production, strict product quality control processes, and modernization of factories. In addition, an organization's *workforce* is rarely static. Its composition changes in terms of age, education, gender, and so forth. In a stable organization with an increasing number of older executives, there might be a need to restructure jobs in order to retain the younger and more ambitious managers who occupy lower ranks. The compensation and benefits system might also need to be adapted to reflect the needs of an older workforce. The introduction of new *equipment* represents another internal force for change. Employees may have their jobs redesigned, need to undergo training on how to operate the new equipment, or be required to establish new interaction patterns within their work group. *Employee attitudes,* such as increased job dissatisfaction, may lead to increased absenteeism, more voluntary resignations, and even strikes. Such events will, in turn, often lead to changes in management policies and practices.

The Manager as Change Agent

Changes within an organization need a catalyst. People who act as catalysts and assume the responsibility for managing the change process are called **change agents**.

change agents
People who act as catalysts and manage the change process.

Any manager can be a change agent. As we review the information on change, we assume that it's initiated and carried out by a manager within the organization. However, the change agent could be a non-manager—for example, an internal staff specialist or outside consultant whose expertise is in change implementation. For major system-wide changes, internal management will often hire outside consultants to provide advice and assistance. Because they're from the outside, they can offer an objective perspective that insiders usually lack. However, outside consultants are usually at a disadvantage because they have an inadequate understanding of the organization's history, culture, operating procedures and people. Outside consultants are also often prone to initiate more drastic change than insiders—which can be either a benefit or a disadvantage—because they don't have to live with the repercussions after the change is implemented. In contrast, internal managers who act as change agents may be more thoughtful (and possibly overly cautious) because they must live with the consequences of their actions.

TWO DIFFERENT VIEWS OF THE CHANGE PROCESS

We can use two very different metaphors to describe the change process.[2] One envisions the organization as a large ship crossing a calm sea. The ship's captain and crew know exactly where they're going because they've made the trip many times before. Change comes in the form of an occasional storm—a brief distraction in an otherwise calm and predictable trip. In the other metaphor, the organization is seen as a small raft navigating a raging river with uninterrupted white-water rapids. Aboard the raft are half a dozen people who've never worked together before, who are totally unfamiliar with the river, who are unsure of their eventual destination and, as if things weren't bad enough, who are travelling in pitch-dark night. In the white-water rapids metaphor, change is a natural stage and managing change is a continual process.

These two metaphors present very different approaches to understanding and responding to change. Let's take a closer look at each one.

The "Calm Waters" Metaphor

Until very recently, the "calm waters" metaphor dominated the thinking of academics and practising managers. It's best illustrated in Kurt Lewin's three-step description of the change process[3] (see Figure 12-1).

According to Lewin, successful change requires *unfreezing* the status quo, *changing* to a new state, and *refreezing* the new change to make it permanent. The status quo can be considered an equilibrium state. To move from this equilibrium, unfreezing is necessary. It can be achieved in one of three ways:

1. Increase the *driving forces*, which direct behaviour away from the status quo.
2. Decrease the *restraining forces*, which hinder movement from the existing equilibrium.
3. Combine the two approaches.

Once unfreezing has been accomplished, the change itself can be implemented. However, the mere introduction of change doesn't ensure that it will take hold. The new situation needs to be *refrozen* so that it can be sustained over time. Unless this last step is done, there's a very strong chance that the change will be short-lived, and employees will revert to the original equilibrium state. The objective of refreezing, then, is to stabilize the new situation by balancing the driving and restraining forces.

Note how Lewin's three-step process treats change as a break in the organization's equilibrium state. The status quo has been disturbed, and change is necessary to establish a new equilibrium state. This view was probably appropriate to the relatively calm environment that most organizations faced from the 1950s to the early 1970s. However, this "calm waters"

FIGURE 12-1 The Change Process

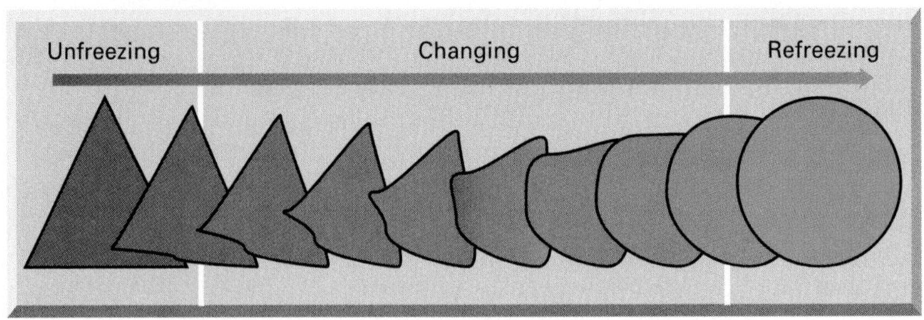

metaphor is becoming increasingly obsolete as a way to describe the kind of seas that managers in today's organizations have to navigate.

The "White-Water Rapids" Metaphor

The "white-water rapids" metaphor is consistent with our discussion of uncertain and dynamic environments in Chapter 3. It's consistent with Mintzberg's observation, discussed in Chapter 1, that the manager's job is one of constant interruptions. It's also consistent with the dynamics that are characteristic of going from an industrial society to a world dominated by information and ideas.

To get a feeling for what managing change might be like when you have to continually manoeuvre in uninterrupted rapids, consider attending a university that had the following rules: Courses vary in length. Unfortunately, when you sign up, you don't know how long a course will last. It might go on for two weeks or thirty weeks. Furthermore, the instructor can end a course at any time he or she wants to, with no prior warning. If that isn't bad enough, the length of the class changes each time it meets—sometimes it lasts twenty minutes, while at other times it runs for three hours—and determination of the time of the next class meeting is set by the instructor during the previous class. Oh yes, there's one more thing. The exams are all unannounced, so you have to be ready for a test at any time.

To succeed in this university, you would have to be incredibly flexible and able to respond quickly to every changing condition. Students who were overly structured or slow to respond wouldn't survive.

A growing number of managers are coming to accept that their job is much like what a student would face in such a university. The stability and predictability of the "calm water" metaphor doesn't exist. Disruptions in the status quo aren't occasional and temporary, fol-

Louis Deveau and son, Jean-Paul, operate in a "white-water rapids" environment. Their company, Acadian Seaplants Ltd., a seaweed supplier in Dartmouth, Nova Scotia, was developing new seaweed products when they lost their sole customer. Acadian pushed ahead with product and market research, and eventually found a potentially huge market in Asia for one of their new seaweed products.

lowed by a return to calm waters. Many of today's managers never get out of the rapids. They face constant change, bordering on chaos. These managers are being forced to play a game they've never played before, and the game is governed by rules that are created as the game progresses.[4]

Putting the Two Views in Perspective

Does *every* manager face a world of constant and chaotic change? No, but the number of managers who don't is dwindling rapidly.

Managers in such businesses as computer software and women's high-fashion clothing have long confronted a world of white-water rapids. These managers used to look enviously at their counterparts in industries such as auto manufacturing, oil exploration, banking, publishing, and air transportation, who historically faced a stable and predictable environment. That might have been true in the 1960s, but it's certainly not correct today!

Few organizations today can treat change as the occasional disturbance in an otherwise calm and stable world. Those that do are running a great risk. Too much is changing too fast for any organization or its managers to be complacent.[5] Most competitive advantages last only a short time—often less than 18 months. A company like People Express Airlines—a no-frills, no-reservations-needed company—was once described in the business news as the model "new look" firm, then went bankrupt a short time later. As Tom Peters has aptly noted, the old saying, "If it ain't broke, don't fix it," no longer applies. In its place, he suggests, "If it ain't broke, you just haven't looked hard enough. Fix it anyway".[6]

ORGANIZATIONAL INERTIA AND RESISTANCE TO CHANGE

As change agents, managers should be motivated to initiate change because they're committed to improving their organization's effectiveness. However, change can be a threat to managers. Of course, change can be a threat to non-managerial people as well. Organizations can build up inertia that motivates people to resist changing their status quo, even though that change might be beneficial. In this section, we want to review why people in organizations resist change and what can be done to lessen this resistance.

Resistance to Change

It's been said that most people hate any change that doesn't jingle in their pockets. This resistance to change is well documented.[7] But why do people resist change? An individual is likely to resist change for three reasons: uncertainty, concern over personal loss, and the belief that the change is not in the organization's best interest.[8]

Changes substitute ambiguity and uncertainty for the known. Regardless of how much you may dislike attending university, at least you know what to do. You know what's expected of you. When you leave college for the world of full-time employment, regardless of how anxious you are to get out of college, you'll trade the known for the unknown. Employees in organizations hold the same dislike for uncertainty. For example, the introduction of quality control methods based on sophisticated statistical models into manufacturing plants means that many quality control inspectors will have to learn these new methods. Some inspectors may fear that they'll be unable to do so. They may, therefore, develop a negative attitude towards statistical control techniques or behave dysfunctionally if required to use them.

The second cause of resistance is the fear of losing something already possessed. Change threatens the investment you've already made in the status quo. The more people have invested in the current system, the more they resist change. Why? They fear the loss of status, money, authority, friendships, personal convenience, or other benefits they value. This explains why older employees resist change more than younger ones. Older employees have generally invested more in the current system and therefore have more to lose by changing.

A final cause of resistance is a person's belief that the change is incompatible with the goals and best interests of the organization. If an employee believes that a new job procedure proposed by a change agent will reduce productivity or product quality, that employee can be expected to resist the change. If the employee expresses his or her resistance positively (perhaps by clearly expressing it to the change agent, along with substantiation), this form of resistance can be beneficial to the organization.

Techniques for Reducing Resistance

When management sees resistance to change as dysfunctional, what actions can it take? Six tactics have been suggested for use by managers or other change agents in dealing with resistance to change.[9]

Education and Communication. Resistance can be reduced by communicating with employees to help them see the logic of a change. This tactic assumes that the source of resistance stems from misinformation or poor communication: If employees receive the full facts and have any misunderstandings clarified, they'll no longer resist the change. This can be achieved through one-on-one discussions, memos, group meetings or reports. Does it work? It does, provided that the source of resistance is inadequate communication and that management-employee relations are characterized by mutual trust and credibility. If these conditions don't exist, it's unlikely to succeed. Moreover, the time and effort that this approach requires must be weighed against its advantages, particularly when the change affects a large number of people.

Participation. It's difficult for individuals to resist a change decision in which they participate. Before a change is made, those who are opposed can be brought into the decision-making process. Assuming that the participants have the expertise to make a meaningful contribution, their involvement can reduce resistance, obtain commitment to seeing the change succeed, and increase the quality of the change decision. However, this technique has its disadvantages: the possibility of a poor solution and the amount of time it takes.

Facilitation and Support. Change agents can offer a range of supportive efforts to reduce resistance. When employees' fears and anxiety are high, employee counselling and therapy, new skills training, or a short paid leave of absence might facilitate adjustment. The drawback of this tactic, as in the others we've just discussed, is that it is time consuming. Furthermore, it's expensive, and its implementation offers no assurance of success.

Negotiation. Another way for the change agent to deal with potential resistance to change is to exchange something of value for a reduction in the resistance. For instance, if the resistance is centred in a few powerful individuals, a specific reward package can be negotiated that will meet their individual needs. Negotiation as a tactic may be necessary when resistance comes from a powerful source, such as a union. Yet you can't ignore its potentially high costs. There's also the risk that, once a change agent negotiates in exchange for lessened resistance, he or she is open to the possibility of being blackmailed by others with power.

Manipulation and Co-optation. The term *manipulation* refers to covert attempts to influence someone or something. Twisting and distorting facts to make them appear more attractive, withholding damaging information, and creating false rumours to get employees to accept a change are all examples of manipulation. For instance, if management threatens to

When profits at Federal Express Canada were suffering, a team of employees was given the task of formulating a new strategy for the company—in only six weeks. The team decided to temporarily refocus the company's business away from the Canadian domestic market, with its high price sensitivity and competition—and focus instead on shipping from Canada to the US. Thanks to the employees' efforts, FedEx Canada is today a highly profitable enterprise, and the change was handled with little resistance.

close a particular manufacturing plant if the employees don't accept an across-the-board pay cut—when it actually has no intention of doing so—it is using manipulation. *Co-optation* is a form of both manipulation and participation. It seeks to "buy off" the leaders of a resistance group by giving them a key role in the change decision. The leaders' advice is sought, not to arrive at a better decision, but to get their endorsement. Both manipulation and co-optation are relatively inexpensive and easy ways to gain the support of adversaries, but the tactics can fail miserably if the targets become aware that they're being tricked or used. Once the deception has been discovered, the change agent's credibility may drop to zero.

Coercion. Last on the list of tactics is *coercion*—that is, using direct threats or force on the resisters. Managers who are really determined to close a manufacturing plant if employees don't agree to a pay cut are using coercion. Other examples of coercion include threats of transfer, loss of promotions, negative performance evaluations, or a poor letter of recommendation. The advantages of coercion are approximately the same as those of manipulation and co-optation. However, the major disadvantage of this method is that coercion very often is illegal. Even legal coercion tends to be seen as bullying and can completely undermine a change agent's credibility.

TECHNIQUES FOR MANAGING CHANGE

What *can* a manager change? The manager's options essentially fall into one of three categories: structure, technology, or people. (See Figure 12-2.) Changing *structure* includes any alteration in authority relations, co-ordination mechanisms, degree of centralization, job redesign, or similar structural variables. Changing *technology* encompasses modifications in the way work is performed, or the methods and equipment that are used. Changing *people* refers to changes in employee attitudes, expectations, perceptions or behaviour.

Changing Structure

In Chapter 10, we discussed structural issues. Managers were described as having responsibility for such activities as choosing the organization's formal design, allocating authority, and determining the degree of decentralization that would prevail. Once those structural decisions have been made, however, they aren't set in concrete. Changing conditions demand changes in the structure. As a result, the manager, in his or her role as change agent, might need to modify the structure.

What options does the manager have for changing structure? Essentially the same ones we introduced in our discussion of structure and design. A few examples should make these options clearer.

An organization's structure is defined in terms of its degree of complexity, formalization, and centralization. Managers can alter one or more of these *structural components*. For instance, departmental responsibilities can be combined, vertical layers removed, and spans of control widened, to make the organization flatter and less bureaucratic. Or more rules and procedures could be implemented to increase standardization. An increase in decentralization can be used to speed up the decision-making process. For instance, AT&T's top management eliminated a fourth of the company's payroll, cut several levels out of the hierarchy, widened spans, and decentralized decision making into new operating units. Many organizational downsizing efforts involve changes in structure.

Another option would be to introduce major changes in the actual *structural design*. This might include a shift from a functional to a product structure, or the creation of a matrix design.

1 What internal and external forces create the need for organizations to change?

2 Contrast the "calm-waters" and "white-water rapids" metaphors for change.

3 Describe why people resist change, and some techniques for reducing this resistance.

FIGURE 12-2 Three Categories of Change

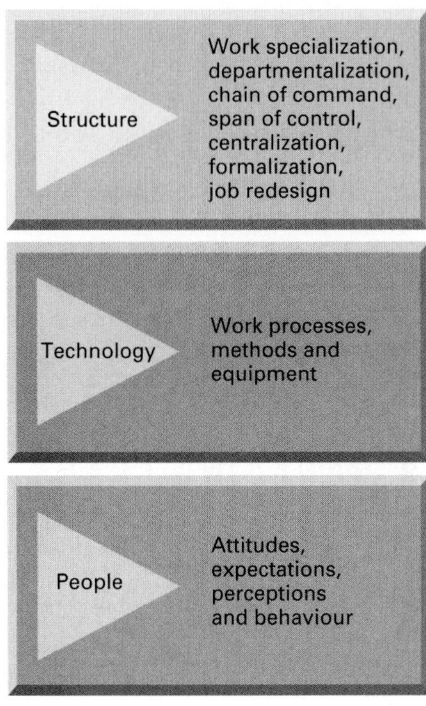

Changing Technology

Managers can also change the technology used to convert inputs into outputs. Most of the early studies in management—such as the work of Frederick W Taylor and Frank Gilbreth—dealt with efforts aimed at technological change. If you recall, scientific management sought to implement changes that would increase production efficiency based on time-and-motion studies. Today, major technological changes usually involve the introduction of new equipment, tools, or methods; automation; or computerization.

Competitive factors or new innovations within an industry often require management to introduce *new equipment, tools* or *operating methods*. For example, North American aluminum companies such as Alcoa and Reynolds have significantly modernized their plants in recent years, in order to compete more effectively against foreign manufacturers. More efficient handling equipment, furnaces and presses have been installed to reduce the cost of manufacturing aluminum.

Canada Post
www.canadapost.ca

Automation is a technological change that replaces people with machines. It began in the Industrial Revolution and continues today as a management option. Automation has been introduced (and sometimes resisted) in organizations such as Canada Post—where automatic mail sorters are used to sort mail—or in automobile assembly lines, where robots do some jobs that blue-collar workers used to perform.

Probably the most visible technological change in recent years has come through management's effort at expanding *computerization*. Most organizations now have sophisticated information systems. For instance, grocery stores and many other retailers use scanners linked to computers that provide instant inventory information. And it's very uncommon to find an office today that isn't computerized.

Changing People

organization development (OD)
Techniques to change people and the quality of interpersonal work relationships.

Since the 1960s, academic researchers and practising managers have increasingly been interested in helping individuals and groups within organizations to work together more effectively. The term **organization development (OD)**, though occasionally referring to all types of change, essentially focuses on techniques or programs to change people, and the nature and quality of interpersonal work relationships.[10] The more popular OD techniques are shown in

Figure 12-3. The common thread in these techniques is that each seeks to bring about changes in or among the organization's human resources.

Sensitivity training is a method of changing behaviour through unstructured group interaction. The group is made up of a professional behavioural scientist and a set of participants. There is no specified agenda. The professional, who doesn't function as the group leader, merely creates the opportunity for participants to express their ideas and feelings. The discussion is free and open. Participants can bring up any topic they like. What evolves is discussion that focuses on the individual participants and their interactive processes.

sensitivity training
A method of changing behaviour through unstructured group interaction.

The research evidence on the effectiveness of sensitivity training as a change technique shows mixed results. On the positive side, it appears to stimulate short-term improvement in communication skills, improve perceptual accuracy, and increase a person's willingness to use participation.[11] However, the impact of these changes on job performance is inconclusive,[12] and the technique is not immune from psychological risks.[13]

Survey feedback is a technique for assessing the attitudes of organizational members, identifying discrepancies in these attitudes and perceptions, and resolving the differences by communicating survey information in feedback groups. A questionnaire is typically completed by all members of the organization or unit. It asks members for their perceptions and attitudes on a broad range of topics such as decision-making practices, communication effectiveness, co-ordination among units, and satisfaction with the organization, job, peers, and immediate manager. The data from the questionnaire are tabulated and distributed to the relevant employees, and the information obtained becomes a catalyst for identifying problems and clarifying issues that may be creating difficulties for people.

survey feedback
A technique for assessing attitudes, identifying discrepancies between these attitudes and perceptions, and resolving the differences by using survey information in feedback groups.

In **process consultation**, an outside consultant helps the manager to "perceive, understand, and act on process events" with which he or she must deal.[14] These might include, for example, work flow, informal relationships among unit members, and formal communication channels. The consultant gives the manager insight into what's going on. The consultant is not there to solve the manager's problem. Rather, the consultant acts as a coach to help the manager diagnose which interpersonal processes need improvement. If the manager, with the help of the consultant, can't solve the problem, the consultant will help the manager locate an expert who has the appropriate knowledge to do so.

process consultation
Help given by an outside consultant to a manager in perceiving, understanding, and acting on process events.

In **team building**, work team members interact to learn how each member thinks and works. Through high interaction, team members learn to develop increased trust and openness. Activities that might be included in a team-building program include group goal setting, development of positive interpersonal relations among team members, role analysis to clarify each member's role and responsibilities, and team process analysis. This process has become particularly important in organizations that have moved to a team-based structure.

team building
Interaction among members of work teams to learn how each member thinks and works.

FIGURE 12-3 Organization Development Techniques

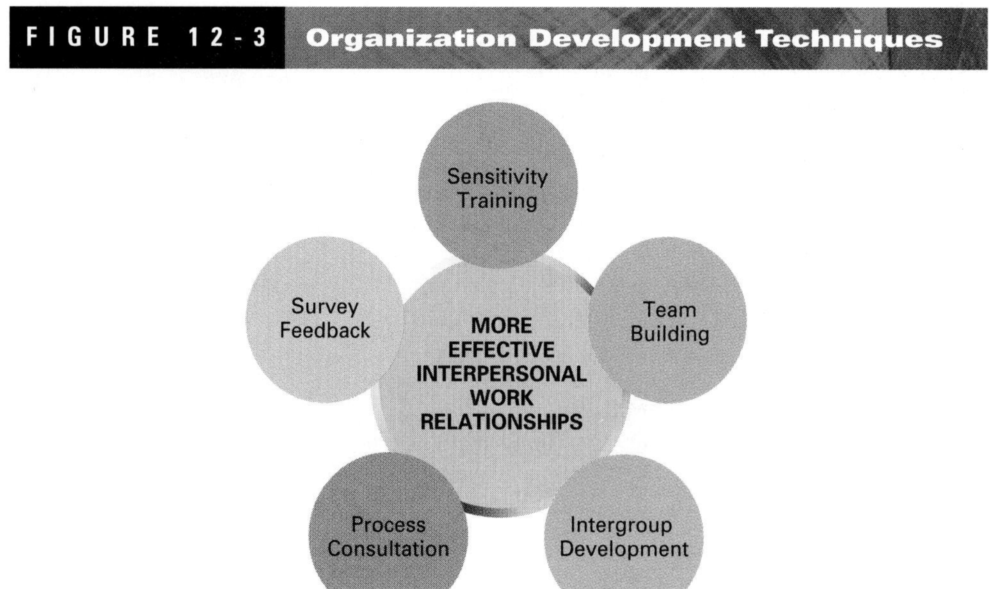

intergroup development Changing the attitudes, stereotypes and perceptions that work groups have of each other.

The attempt to change the attitudes, stereotypes and perceptions that members of work groups have about each other is called **intergroup development**. For example, if two groups have a history of strained work relationships, they can meet independently to develop lists of their perceptions of themselves, of the other group, and of how they believe the other group perceives them. The groups then share their lists, after which similarities and differences are discussed. Differences are clearly articulated, the groups look for the causes of the differences, and efforts are made to develop solutions that will improve relations between the groups.

CONTEMPORARY ISSUES IN MANAGING CHANGE

- What can management do to change an organizational culture when that culture no longer supports the organization's mission?
- How does management implement a continuous change program such as TQM?
- What implications for changing structure, technology, and people are associated with re-engineering efforts?
- Finally, today's competitive environment has made the workplace more stressful. What can managers do to help employees better handle this stress?

These change issues—changing organizational cultures, implementing TQM, re-engineering, and handling employee stress—will be crucial concerns to managers leading their organizations into the late 1990s. In this section, we'll look at each of these issues and discuss what actions managers should consider for dealing with them.

Changing Organizational Cultures

Royal Bank
www.royalbank.com/

IBM Canada
www.can.ibm.com

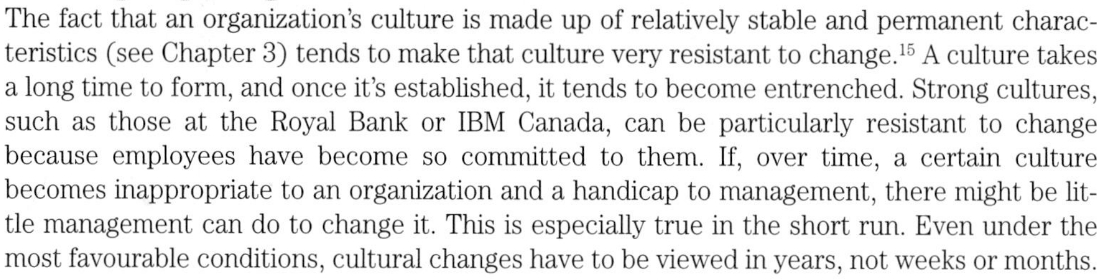

The fact that an organization's culture is made up of relatively stable and permanent characteristics (see Chapter 3) tends to make that culture very resistant to change.[15] A culture takes a long time to form, and once it's established, it tends to become entrenched. Strong cultures, such as those at the Royal Bank or IBM Canada, can be particularly resistant to change because employees have become so committed to them. If, over time, a certain culture becomes inappropriate to an organization and a handicap to management, there might be little management can do to change it. This is especially true in the short run. Even under the most favourable conditions, cultural changes have to be viewed in years, not weeks or months.

Understanding the Situational Factors. What "favourable conditions" *might* facilitate cultural change? The evidence suggests that cultural change is most likely to take place where most or all of the following conditions exist:

When John Cleghorn of Royal Bank and Matthew Barrett of Bank of Montreal announced their proposed merger in 1998, one of the major factors they had to prepare themselves for was handling the inevitable massive resistance to change from their workforces. They were dealing with two of the most deeply ingrained corporate cultures in Canada.

- *A dramatic crisis occurs.* This can be the shock that undermines the status quo and calls into question the relevance of the current culture. Examples are a surprising financial setback, the loss of a major customer, or a dramatic technological innovation by a competitor.
- *Leadership changes hands.* New top leadership, which can provide an alternative set of key values, may be perceived as being more capable of responding to the crisis. Top leadership includes the organization's chief executive, but might need to include all senior management positions.
- *The organization is young and small.* The younger the organization, the less entrenched its culture. Similarly, it's easier for management to communicate its new values when the organization is small.
- *The culture is weak.* The more widely held a culture and the higher the agreement among members on its overall value, the more difficult it will be to change. Conversely, weak cultures are more receptive to change than strong ones.[16]

These situational factors help to explain why companies with strong cultures like the Bank of Nova Scotia, Bell Canada or Canada Life Assurance Co. may have difficulty reshaping their culture. For the most part, employees at these companies don't see their company's day-to-day problems as being of crisis proportions. "New" leadership has, typically, been more in name than in substance. Traditionally, CEOs at IBM Canada, for instance, have been long-term veterans of the company, steeped in the organization's established culture.

How Can Cultural Change Be Accomplished? Now we ask the question: If conditions are right, how does management go about enacting the cultural change? The challenge is to unfreeze the current culture. No single action is likely to have the impact necessary to unfreeze something that is so ingrained and highly valued. Thus, there needs to be a comprehensive and co-ordinated strategy for managing cultural change, as shown in Table 12-1.

The best place to begin is with a cultural analysis.[17] This would include a cultural audit to assess the current culture, a comparison of the present culture with the culture that's

Preparing for a Changing Workplace

Face it. The only constant thing about change is that it's constant. These days, you don't have the luxury of dealing with change only once in a while. No—in fact, workplace changes seem to be almost a daily occurrence. How can you cope with, and take advantage of, what seems to a hopelessly chaotic situation?

Well, before you throw your hands up in frustration, let's look at some ways in which you can deal with the demands of a constantly changing workplace.[18]

Being prepared is not just a credo for the Boy Scouts—it should be your motto for managing your career. What do we mean by "being prepared"?

Well, being prepared means taking the initiative and responsibility for your own career development. Rather than depending on your organization to provide you with career development and training opportunities, do it yourself. Take advantage of continuing education or graduate courses at local colleges. Sign up for workshops and seminars that can help you to enhance your skills. Keeping your skills current and continually upgrading your skills is one of the most important career strategies you can follow.

It's also important for you to be a positive force when faced with workplace changes such as implementing cross-functional teams or work process improvements. And by this, we don't mean automatically accepting any change that's being implemented. If you feel a proposed change isn't appropriate or won't be effective, voice your opposition in a constructive manner. This may mean providing an alternative to what's being suggested. However, if you feel the change is beneficial, support it.

The changes that an organization makes in response to a dynamic environment, can be overwhelming and stressful. However, you can contend with a changing workplace by being prepared, and by being a positive force for change. ■

TABLE 12-1 The Road to Cultural Change

- Conduct a cultural analysis to identify cultural elements needing change.
- Make it clear to employees that the organization's survival is legitimately threatened if change is not forthcoming.
- Appoint new leadership with a new vision.
- Initiate a re-organization.
- Introduce new stories and rituals to convey the new vision.
- Change the selection and socialization processes and the evaluation and reward systems to support the new values.

desired, and an analysis of the "gap", in order to identify what cultural elements specifically need changing.

We've discussed the importance of a dramatic crisis as a means to unfreezing an entrenched culture. Unfortunately, crises are not always evident to all members of the organization. Management may need to make the crisis more visible. It's important that everyone clearly sees that the organization's survival is at stake. If employees don't see the urgency for change, it's unlikely that a strong culture will respond to change efforts.

The appointment of a new top executive is likely to dramatize the fact that major changes are going to take place. He or she can offer a new role model and new standards of behaviour. However, this executive needs to introduce his or her new vision of the organization quickly, and to fill key management positions with individuals who are loyal to this vision.

Along with a shake-up of key management personnel, it also makes sense to initiate a re-organization. The creation of new units, the combination of some, and the elimination of others conveys, in very visible terms, that management is determined to move the organization in new directions. For instance, Oy Nokia, a Finnish company best known for its toilet paper and galoshes, is now the second largest global seller of cellular phones (behind Motorola, Inc.).[19] To change from an old "smokestack" company to a high-tech telecommunications superpower required a major shake-up of its corporate culture. CEO Jorma Ollila ousted old-guard managers and brought in a new group of younger managers who were more in favour of change. Ollila also encouraged and rewarded a high level of entrepreneurial, risk-seeking ventures throughout the company. Without these drastic cultural changes, it's unlikely Nokia would be a strong competitor in a dynamic, high-tech industry.

The new leadership will also want to move quickly to create new stories and rituals, in order to replace those that were previously used to convey the organization's dominant values to employees.This needs to be done rapidly. Delays allow the old culture to become associated with the new leadership, thus closing the window of opportunity for change.

Finally, management will want to change the selection and socialization processes, and the evaluation and reward systems, to support employees who embrace the new values that are sought.

The previous suggestions, of course, provide no guarantee that change efforts will succeed. Organizational members don't easily let go of values that they understand and that have worked well for them in the past. Managers must, therefore, be patient. Change, if it comes, will be slow. And management must keep constantly alert to protect against any return to old, familiar practices and traditions.

Implementing TQM

Total quality management is essentially a continuous, incremental change program. It's compatible with the "calm-waters" metaphor, because TQM recognizes that organizations must continuously find ways to "navigate" the problems that arise as it strives to improve. In this section, we want to draw on our knowledge of change processes in order to consider how managers can effectively implement TQM.

First, let's briefly review the key components of TQM. You'll remember that it focuses on customer needs, emphasizes participation and teamwork, and seeks to create a culture in

MANAGING WORKFORCE DIVERSITY

The Paradox of Diversity

When organizations bring diverse individuals into an organization and socialize them into the organization's culture, a paradox is created.[20] Management wants these new employees to accept the organization's core cultural values, otherwise the employees may have a difficult time fitting in or being accepted. But, at the same time, management wants to openly acknowledge, embrace, and show support for, the diverse perspectives and ideas that these employees bring to the workplace.

Strong cultures put considerable pressure on employees to conform. The range of acceptable values and styles of behaviour is limited. Obviously, this creates a dilemma. Organizations hire diverse individuals because of the unique strengths these people have, yet these diverse behaviours and strengths are likely to diminish in strong organizational cultures as people attempt to fit in.

Management's challenge in this paradox of diversity is to balance two conflicting goals: get employees to accept the organization's dominant values, and encourage the acceptance of differences. When and if changes are made in the organization's culture, managers need to remember the importance of keeping diversity alive.

which all employees strive to continuously improve such activities and outputs as the quality of the organization's products or services, customer response time, or work processes. It might be helpful to look at TQM in terms of the three areas towards which management can direct its change efforts: structure, technology, and people. (See Figure 12-4.)

Focusing the Change Effort. The *structure* of an organization that expects to implement TQM successfully will be decentralized; will have reduced vertical differentiation, wider spans of control and reduced division of labour; and will support cross-functional teams. These structural components give employees the authority and means to implement process improvements. For instance, the creation of work teams that cut across departmental lines allows those people who are closest to a problem and understand it best to solve the problem. In addition, cross-functional teams encourage co-operative problem solving rather than an "us-versus-them" finger-pointing approach.

The primary focus on *technology* change in TQM is directed at developing flexible processes to support continuous improvement. Employees committed to TQM are constantly looking for things to fix. Thus, work processes must be adaptable to continual change and fine tuning. To achieve this, TQM requires an extensive commitment to educating and training workers. The organization must provide employees with training in skills such as problem solving, decision making, negotiation, statistical analysis, and team building.[21] For example, employees need to be able to analyze and interpret data. An organization with a TQM program should provide work teams with quality data such as failure rates, reject rates, and scrap rates. It should provide feedback data on customer satisfaction. It should give the teams the necessary information to create and monitor process control charts. And, of course, the structure

FIGURE 12-4 Factors That Facilitate Continuous Incremental Improvements

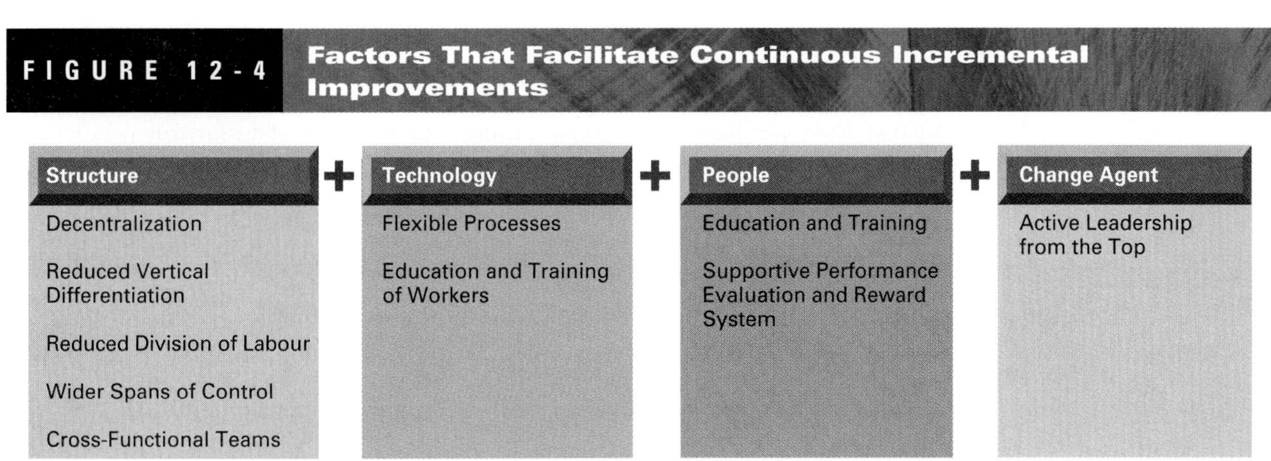

Structure
Decentralization
Reduced Vertical Differentiation
Reduced Division of Labour
Wider Spans of Control
Cross-Functional Teams
+
Technology
Flexible Processes
Education and Training of Workers
+
People
Education and Training
Supportive Performance Evaluation and Reward System
+
Change Agent
Active Leadership from the Top

Companies around the world are embracing the concept of quality. In Korea, Daewoo chairman Kim Woo-Chung (left) puts on a work uniform and checks out the quality efforts on the night shift at one of his company's auto plants.

should allow the work teams to make continual improvements in the operations, based on process control data.

The *people* dimension of TQM requires a workforce committed to the organization's objectives of quality and continual improvement. Again, this necessitates proper education and training. It also demands a performance evaluation and reward system that supports and encourages TQM objectives. In addition, successful programs put quality objectives into bonus plans for executives, and incentives for operating employees.[22] For instance, at LL Bean, the implementation of its TQM program was totally focused on employee development, the development of new roles for managers, and the creation of a system for communicating that role. Since the introduction of the TQM system, the company has improved its profitability, boosted customer satisfaction, enhanced safety, and reduced order backlogs.[23]

Role of the Change Agent. Studies of successful TQM programs consistently demonstrate that these programs require active and strong leadership from the CEO.[24] It's the CEO who sets the vision and continually conveys the message.

Re-engineering

The historical role of change agents in organizations was to fix and improve things bit by bit. When the environment changed slowly, organizations could respond to those changes in an orderly fashion. However, in today's dynamic "white-water rapids" world, where long-term marketplace success increasingly belongs to the flexible and adaptive organization, there's a need for a new kind of change agent: Someone who can throw out the conventional wisdom about how things "have always been done" and initiate radical change.[25]

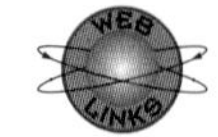

Numetrix Inc.
www.numetrix.com

Turbulent times require revolutionary, not orderly, change. Numetrix Inc., of Toronto, was the world's third-largest supply chain management software producer (software that controls the chain of supplies, production, and distribution for manufacturers) as of 1998, but CEO Josef Schengili decided that the market was about to be bombarded by big-guns like Germany's SAP. In the face of new competition from huge multinational corporations, Schengili decided that Numetrix should move into a new market—"extranet" software production (supply chain management systems using Internet capabilities). Examples like this are constantly occurring in the Canadian business world and, indeed, in companies all over the globe.[26]

TESTING...
TESTING...

4 Describe the different OD techniques.

5 How can cultural change be implemented?

6 What change efforts might be associated with implementing a TQM program?

TABLE 12-2 TQM Versus Re-engineering

TQM	Re-engineering
• Continuous, incremental change	• Radical change
• Fixing and improving	• Redesigning—starting over
• Mostly "as is"	• Mostly "what can be"
• Works from bottom up in organization	• Initiated by top management

Organizations worldwide are increasingly looking for managers who can introduce and successfully implement revolutionary change—managers who can direct re-engineering efforts.

We introduced the concept of re-engineering in Chapter 2.[27] Remember that it's a radical redesign of all or part of a company's work processes. In re-engineering, a company drastically changes its structure, technology and people, by starting from scratch in re-examining the way the organization's work is done. During re-engineering efforts, managers continually ask themselves, "How could this process be improved?" or "What's a better way of performing this activity?" For instance, at Imperial Oil's refinery in Dartmouth, Nova Scotia, managers and workers redesigned the way work schedules were composed, thus reducing contract work and overtime. This re-engineering cut 46 percent of labour costs while salvaging most of the refinery's full-time jobs.

How does the concept of re-engineering relate to the other change topics we've talked about? It's not a replacement for any change efforts that the organization may be implementing. Instead, for many companies, it's the first step in changing. Re-engineering provides the framework for making these changes. Whether it's marketplace changes, changes in the economic climate, or changes in organizational strategy that are creating the need to change, organizations that decide to re-engineer must first look at the way in which people work and interact within the organization. Once these processes have been identified and critically evaluated, managers and subordinates can look for ways to "do it better". Doing it better might involve total quality initiatives, changes in organizational culture, or any other types of changes that we've discussed in this chapter. However, the point of re-engineering is that the organization peels back its old way of doing things in deciding what types of other changes to implement.

You might be asking yourself by now whether or not *re-engineering* is just another term for TQM. The answer is definitely no. Although both are focused on organizational change, the goals and means they use are clearly different. TQM is a commitment to continuous, incremental change. It's about continually improving organizational activities that are basically okay. TQM works from the bottom up in the organization, emphasizing participative decision making in both planning and implementing the TQM program. In contrast, re-engineering is about dramatic and radical shifts in the way the organization performs its work. It's focused on quan-

A new approach to scheduling preserved most of the full-time jobs, while slashing labour costs, at this Imperial Oil refinery in Dartmouth, Nova Scotia.

tum changes and starting over, in redesigning the way work is done. Re-engineering is initiated by top management, although, once the process is complete, the workplace tends to be largely self-managed.

Handling Employee Stress

For many employees, change creates stress. A dynamic and uncertain environment characterized by mergers, restructurings, re-engineering efforts, forced retirements and downsizing has created a large number of employees who are overworked and stressed out.[28] In this section, we want to review what specifically is meant by the term *stress*, what causes it, how to identify it, and what managers can do to reduce it.

stress
A dynamic condition in which an individual is confronted with an opportunity, constraint, or demand related to what he or she desires and for which the outcome is perceived to be both uncertain and important.

What Is Stress? **Stress** is a dynamic condition in which an individual is confronted with an opportunity, constraint, or demand related to what he or she desires, and for which the outcome is perceived to be both uncertain and important.[29] This is a complicated definition, so let's look at its components more closely.

Stress is not necessarily bad in itself. Although stress is often discussed in a negative context, it also has a positive value, particularly when it offers a potential gain. Functional stress allows an athlete or stage performer to perform at his or her highest level in crucial situations.

However, stress is more often associated with constraints and demands. A constraint prevents you from doing what you desire; demands refer to the loss of something desired. When you take a test at school or undergo your annual performance review at work, you feel stressed because you confront opportunity, constraints and demands. A good performance review may lead to a promotion, greater responsibilities, and a higher salary. But a poor review may keep you from getting the promotion. An extremely poor review might lead to your being fired.

Because the conditions are right for stress to surface, doesn't mean it always will. Two conditions are necessary for *potential* stress to become *actual* stress.[30] There must be uncertainty over the outcome, and the outcome must be important. Regardless of the conditions, a stressful condition exists only when there is doubt or uncertainty regarding whether the opportunity will be seized, whether the constraint will be removed, or whether the loss will be avoided. That is, stress is highest for individuals who are uncertain whether they will win or lose, and lowest for individuals who think that winning or losing is a certainty. The importance of the outcome is also a crucial factor. If winning or losing is unimportant, there is no stress. If a subordinate feels that keeping a job or earning a promotion is unimportant, he or she will experience no stress before a performance review.

Causes of Stress. As illustrated in Figure 12-5, the causes of stress can be found in issues related to the organization, or in personal factors that evolve out of the employee's private life.

Clearly, change of any kind has the potential to cause stress. It can present opportunities, constraints, or demands. Moreover, changes are frequently created in a climate of uncertainty and around issues that are important to employees. It's not surprising, then, for change to be a major stressor.

FIGURE 12-5 Sources of Stress

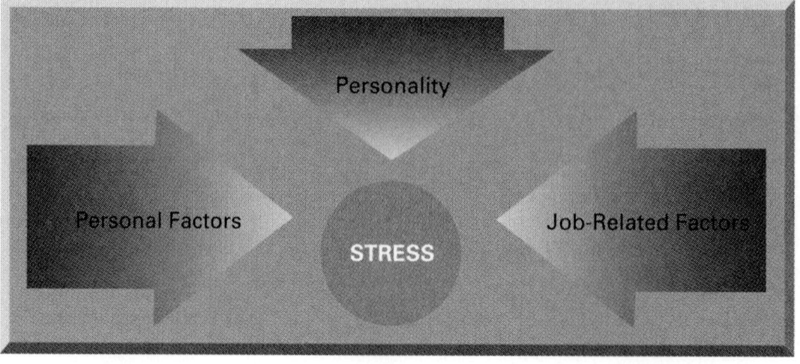

An employee's job and the organization's structure are also pervasive causes of stress. Excessive workloads create stress, as do pressures to maintain a machine-regulated pace. At the other extreme, job boredom can also create stress. Individuals with more challenging jobs have less anxiety, depression, and physical illness than those with less challenging jobs.[31] Role conflict and ambiguity over job expectations also create stress.[32] The former imposes contradictory demands on the employee, while the latter creates uncertainty over job requirements. A classic structural source of stress is when the unity of command is broken and employees must deal with more than one boss. Additional organizational factors that cause employee stress include excessive rules and regulations, an unresponsive and unsupportive boss, ambiguous communications, and unpleasant working conditions such as extreme temperatures, poor lighting, or distracting noises.

Personal factors that can create stress include the death of a family member, a divorce, and personal financial difficulties.[33] Because employees bring their personal problems with them to work, a full understanding of employee stress requires the consideration of these personal factors.

There is evidence that an employee's personality acts as a moderator to strengthen or diminish the impact of both organizational and personal stressors.[34] The most commonly used description is what is called the Type A–Type B dichotomy.[35] Individuals exhibiting **Type A behaviour** are characterized by a chronic sense of time urgency and an excessive competitive drive. They're impatient, do everything fast, and have great difficulty coping with leisure time. **Type B behaviour** is just the opposite—relaxed, easygoing, and non-competitive. Type As live with moderate to high levels of stress; they're more susceptible to heart disease than Type Bs. From a manager's perspective, Type As are more likely to show symptoms of stress, even if organizational and personal stressors are low.

type A behaviour
Behaviour marked by a chronic sense of time urgency and an excessive competitive drive.

type B behaviour
Behaviour that is relaxed, easygoing, and non-competitive.

Symptoms of Stress. What signs indicate that an employee's stress level might be too high? Stress shows itself in a number of ways. For instance, an employee who's experiencing a high level of stress may become depressed, accident prone, or argumentative, or may have difficulty making routine decisions, be easily distracted, and the like. These symptoms can be grouped under three general categories: physiological, psychological and behavioural.[36] (See Figure 12-6.)

Most of the early concerns over stress were directed at physiological symptoms. This was true primarily because the topic was researched by specialists in the health and medical sciences. Their research led to the conclusion that stress could create changes in metabolism, increase heart and breathing rates, raise blood pressure, cause headaches, and induce heart attacks.

The link between stress and certain physiological symptoms is not entirely clear. There are few, if any, consistent relationships.[37] This is attributed to the complexity of the symptoms and the difficulty in measuring them objectively. But physiological symptoms, although important, have the least direct relevance to managers.

Of greater importance are the psychological symptoms. Stress can cause dissatisfaction. Job-related stress can cause job-related dissatisfaction. Job dissatisfaction, in fact, is "the simplest and most obvious psychological effect" of stress.[38] But stress has other psychological

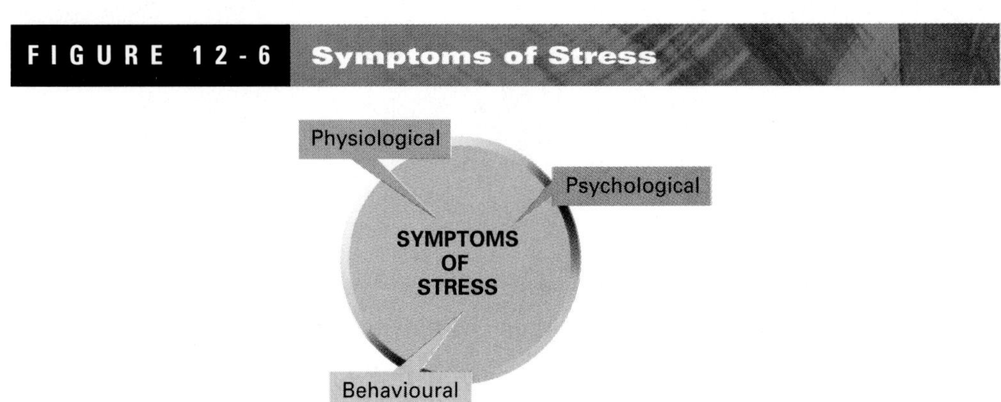

FIGURE 12-6 Symptoms of Stress

indications—for instance, tension, anxiety, irritability, boredom and procrastination. Behaviourally related stress symptoms include changes in productivity, increases in absenteeism, and a high job turnover rate, as well as changes in eating habits, increased smoking or consumption of alcohol, rapid speech, fidgeting, and sleep disorders.

Reducing Stress. As we mentioned earlier, not all stress is dysfunctional. Moreover, realistically, stress can never be totally eliminated from a person's life, either off the job or on. As we review stress reduction techniques, keep in mind that our concern is with reducing the part of stress that's dysfunctional.

In terms of organizational factors, any attempt to lower stress levels must begin with employee *selection*. Management needs to make sure that an employee's abilities match the requirements of the job. When employees are "in over their heads", their stress levels are typically high. A realistic job preview during the selection process will also minimize stress by reducing ambiguity over job expectations. Improved organizational communications will keep ambiguity-induced stress to a minimum. Similarly, a performance planning program such as MBO will clarify job responsibilities, provide clear performance objectives, and reduce ambiguity through feedback. Job redesign is also a way to reduce stress. If stress can be traced directly to boredom or work overload, jobs should be redesigned to increase challenge or reduce the workload. Redesigns that increase opportunities for employees to participate in decisions and to gain social support have also been found to lessen stress.[39]

Saskatchewan Research Council
www.src.sk.ca

Stress that arises from an employee's personal life raises two problems. First, it's difficult for the manager to control this type of stress directly. Second, there are ethical considerations. Specifically, does the manager have the right to intrude—even in the most subtle ways—in the employee's personal life? If a manager believes it's ethical and the employee is receptive, there are a few approaches which the manager can consider. Employee *counselling* can provide stress relief. Employees often want to talk to someone about their problems, and the organization—through its managers, in-house human resource counsellors, or free or low-cost outside professional help—can meet that need. The Saskatchewan Research Council is one organization that is committed to providing confidential counselling to all of its 250 employees and their families concerning any issues that may affect their workplace performance.[40] For employees whose personal lives suffer from a lack of planning and organization that, in turn, creates stress, the offering of a *time management program* may prove beneficial in helping them to sort out their priorities.[41] For instance, Honeywell provides such a service. And still

Good health contributes to work performance. This workplace gym at Husky Injection Molding Systems helps employees to alleviate stress and improve physical well-being.

TESTING... TESTING...

7 Contrast re-engineering and TQM as change efforts.

8 What signs might indicate to a manager that an employee's stress level is too high?

THINKING CRITICALLY ABOUT ETHICS

Although numerous organizations are providing stress reduction programs, many employees choose not to participate. Why? A number are reluctant to ask for help, especially if a major source of that stress is job insecurity. After all, there is still a stigma associated with stress. Employees don't want to be perceived as being unable to cope effectively with the demands of their jobs. Although they may need stress management now more urgently than ever, few employees actually want to admit that they're stressed. What can be done about this paradox? Do organizations even *have* an ethical responsibility to help employees deal with stress? ■

another approach is organizationally sponsored *physical activity programs*.[42] Husky Injection Molding Systems in Bolton, Ontario, has a glass-walled, state-of-the-art fitness facility in its Advanced Manufacturing Centre. At Apple Computer, employees are encouraged to go for lunchtime fitness walks and join the company's running club.

STIMULATING INNOVATION

"Innovate or die!" That has increasingly become the rallying cry of today's managers. In the dynamic, chaotic world of global competition, organizations must create new products and services and adopt state-of-the-art technology if they're going to compete successfully. Bombardier is a national leader in innovation. For more than two decades, the Montreal firm acquired technology from other companies rather than developing this technology itself. Now Bombardier has 6300 engineers and technicians in its workforce working on innovative new products for its ski-doo and sea-doo division, as well as in its aerospace and mass transit divisions. The company has built trains for the Channel tunnel connecting England and France, and it has also developed a new executive jet that uses innovative technology, making it the industry leader. This commitment to innovation has made Bombardier's aerospace division the sixth-largest civil aviation company in the world, in an incredibly short space of time. Innovation has also secured Bombardier's top spot in the ski-doo and sea-doo markets, as well as having landed the company contracts to build new cars for the subways of New York and Paris.[43]

Bombardier Inc.
www.bombardier.com

Many other Canadian companies are committed to innovation. Northern Telecom remained Canada's biggest spender on research and development as of 1999, with an annual R&D budget of over $3 billion. Atomic Energy of Canada and Merck Frosst Canada both spend over 40 percent of revenues on R&D.

Merck Frosst Canada
www.merckfrosst.ca

What's the secret to Bombardier's success? What, if anything, can other managers do to make their organizations more innovative? In the following pages, we'll try to answer these questions as we discuss the factors behind innovation.

Innovation Versus Creativity

The term **creativity** refers to the ability to combine ideas in a unique way or to make unusual associations between ideas.[44] An organization that stimulates creativity develops novel approaches to doing the work, or unique solutions to problems. **Innovation** is the process of taking a creative idea and turning it into a useful product, service, or method of operation. Thus, the innovative organization is characterized by the ability to channel its creativity into useful outcomes. When managers talk about changing an organization to make it more creative, they usually mean they want to stimulate innovation. Bombardier is aptly described as innovative because it takes novel ideas and turns them into profitable products. Another company that's innovative is Intel—the highly successful microchip manufacturer. It leads all chip manufacturers worldwide in miniaturization, and has had enormous success in developing smaller and faster technology. Intel is committed to staying ahead of its competition by continually introducing a stream of new and more powerful products.

creativity
The ability to combine ideas in a unique way or to make unusual associations between ideas.

innovation
The process of taking a creative idea and turning it into a useful product, service, or method of operation.

Fostering Innovation

By using the systems model we introduced in Chapter 2, we can better understand how organizations become more innovative[45] (see Figure 12-7). We see from the model that, in order to get our desired output (i.e., creative products), we have to look at the inputs and the transformation of those inputs. The inputs would include creative people and groups within the organization. But just having creative people isn't enough. It takes the right environment for

FIGURE 12-7 Systems View of Innovation

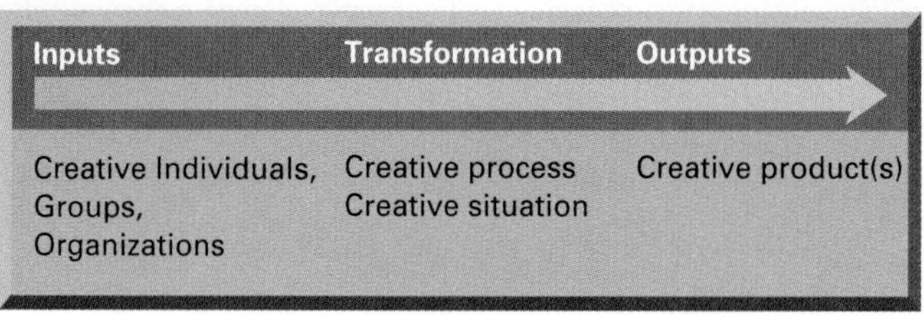

Source: Adapted from Richard W Woodman, John E Sawyer, and Ricky W Griffin, "Towards a Theory of Organizational Creativity," *Academy of Management Review,* April 1993, p. 309.

the innovation process to take hold and prosper, just as a flower requires the proper soil, watering, and light levels to grow. What does this "right" environment look like? We've identified three sets of variables that have been found to stimulate innovation. These include the organization's structure, culture, and human resource practices (see Figure 12-8).

Structural Variables. Based on extensive research, we can conclude three things about the effect of structural variables on innovation.[46] First, organic structures positively influence innovation. Because this type of organization is relatively low in formalization, centralization, and work specialization, organic structures facilitate the flexibility, adaptability and cross-fertilization that promote the adoption of innovations. Second, the easy availability of plentiful resources provides a key building block for innovation. An abundance of resources means

FIGURE 12-8 Innovation Variables

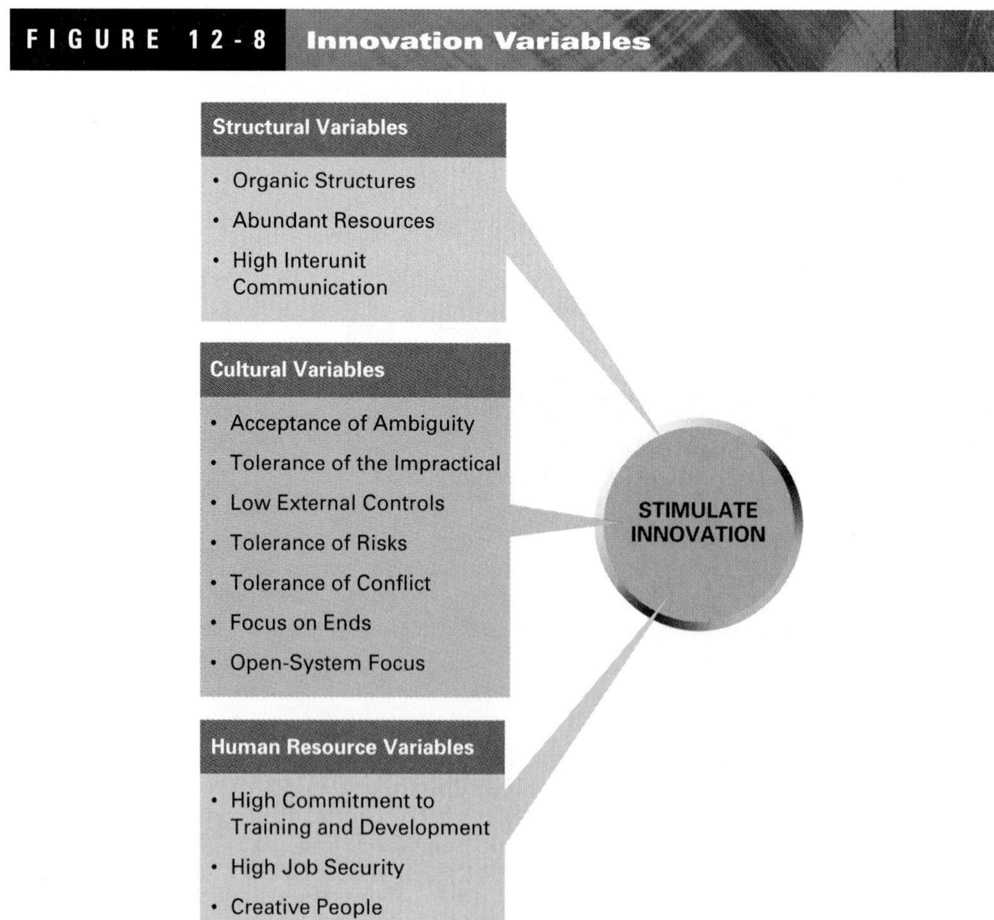

management can afford to purchase innovations, afford the cost of instituting innovations, and absorb failures. Finally, frequent interunit communication helps to break down possible barriers to innovation.[47] Cross-functional teams, task forces and other such organizational designs facilitate interaction across departmental lines and are widely used in innovative organizations. For instance, 3M, which thrives on extensive innovation, is highly decentralized and, although large, takes on many of the characteristics of small, organic organizations. The company also has the "deep pockets" needed to support its policy of allowing scientists and engineers to use up to 15 percent of their time on projects of their own choosing. At Syncrude Canada Ltd., employees are encouraged to actively participate in decision making, and they are given the freedom to customize their job descriptions. Ideas from employees have often turned out to be very innovative and profitable for the company.[48]

Syncrude Canada Ltd.
www.syncrude.com

Cultural Variables. Innovative organizations tend to have similar cultures.[49] They encourage experimentation; reward both successes and failures; and celebrate mistakes. An innovative culture is likely to have the following characteristics:

- *Acceptance of ambiguity.* Too much emphasis on objectivity and specificity constrains creativity.
- *Tolerance of the impractical.* Individuals who offer impractical, even foolish, answers to "what if" questions are not stifled. What seems impractical at first might lead to innovative solutions.
- *Low external controls.* Rules, regulations, policies, and similar controls are kept to a minimum.
- *Tolerance of risk.* Employees are encouraged to experiment without fear of consequences should they fail. Mistakes are treated as learning opportunities.
- *Tolerance of conflict.* Diversity of opinions is encouraged. Harmony and agreement between individuals and/or units are *not* assumed to be evidence of high performance.

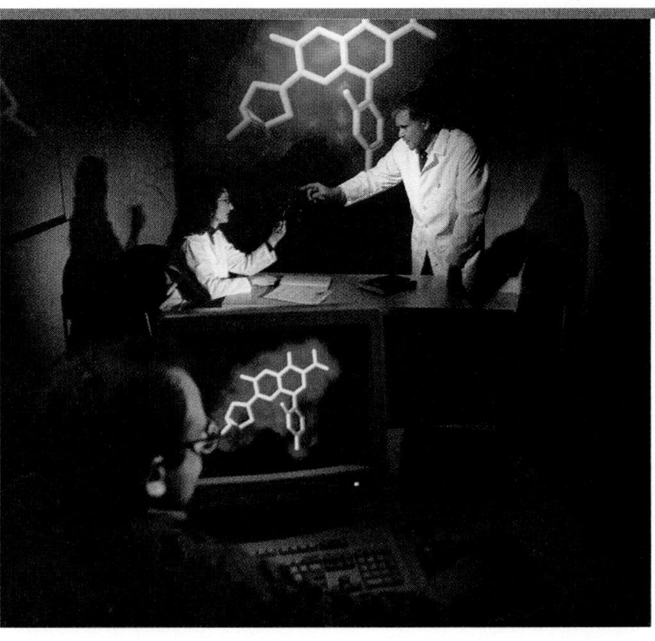

Innovation, such as the computer modelling of drugs shown here at Pfizer Corporation, thrives when creativity is encouraged and channelled into practical outcomes. The molecules shown here are an antibiotic.

TESTING... TESTING...

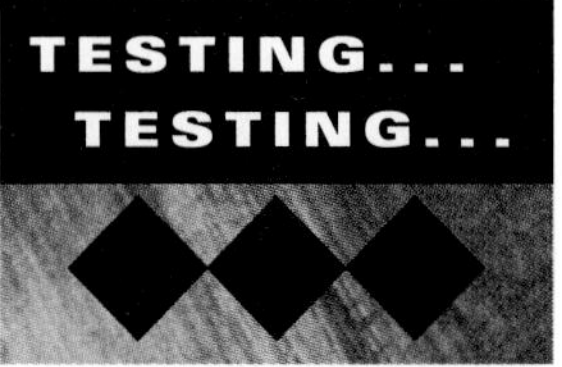

9 How can the systems model be used to help organizations become more innovative?

10 Describe the specific structural, cultural, and human resource variables associated with innovation.

- *Focus on ends rather than means.* Goals are made clear, and individuals are encouraged to consider alternative routes towards meeting the goals. Focusing on ends suggests that there might be several right answers to any given problem.
- *Open systems focus.* The organization closely monitors the environment and responds rapidly to changes as they occur.

Human Resource Variables. Within the *human resources* category, we find that innovative organizations actively promote the training and development of their members so that their knowledge remains current; offer their employees high job security to reduce the fear of getting fired for making mistakes; and encourage individuals to become "champions" of change. Once a new idea is developed, champions of change actively and enthusiastically promote the idea, build support, overcome resistance, and ensure that the innovation is implemented. Recent research finds that champions have common personality characteristics: extremely high self-confidence, persistence, energy, and a tendency towards risk-taking. Champions also display characteristics associated with dynamic leadership. They inspire and energize others with their vision of the potential of an innovation, and through their strong personal conviction in their mission. They're also good at gaining the commitment of others to support their mission. In addition, champions have jobs that provide considerable decision-making discretion. This autonomy helps them to introduce and implement innovations in organizations.[50]

SUMMARY

This summary is organized by the learning objectives found at the beginning of the chapter.

1. The "calm waters" metaphor views change as a break in the organization's equilibrium state. Organizations are seen as being stable and predictable, disturbed by an occasional crisis. The "white-water rapids" metaphor views change as continual and unpredictable. Managers must deal with ongoing and almost chaotic change.
2. Change is often resisted because of the uncertainty it creates, concern for personal loss, and a belief that it might not be in the organization's best interests.
3. Six tactics to reduce resistance to change include education and communication, participation, facilitation and support, negotiation, manipulation and co-optation, and coercion.
4. Managers can change the organization's *structure* by altering complexity, formalization, or centralization variables; changing the organization's *technology* by altering work processes, methods, and equipment; or changing *people* by altering attitudes, expectations, perceptions or behaviour.
5. Dramatic crises and changes in top leadership facilitate cultural change by providing major shocks to employees and the status quo. Having a small or young organization and a weak culture facilitates cultural change by providing a more impressionable base with which to work.
6. Management can enact cultural change by beginning with a cultural analysis. This can be followed by taking action to make a crisis more visible; appointing new people in top positions; re-organizing key functions; creating new stories, symbols, and rituals to replace old ones that reflect the old culture; and altering the organization's selection and socialization processes and its evaluation and reward systems to reflect the new cultural values.
7. Managers can implement TQM by providing the right structure, technology, and human resources. The structure should be decentralized, have reduced vertical differentiation and wide spans of control, and support cross-functional teams. The technology must be flexible to support continuous improvement. The workforce must be committed to the objectives of quality and continual improvement.
8. Re-engineering involves radically redesigning an organization's work processes. These activities involve changes in structure, technology, and human resources.
9. Techniques for reducing employee stress include carefully matching applicants with jobs in the selection process; having clear performance objectives; redesigning jobs to increase challenge and reduce the workload; counselling employees; providing time management programs; and sponsoring physical activity programs.
10. Organizations can stimulate innovation by having structures that are flexible; having easy access to resources; having fluid communication; fostering a culture that is relaxed, is supportive of new ideas, and encourages monitoring of the environment; and employing creative people who are well trained, current in their fields, and secure in their jobs.

THINKING ABOUT MANAGEMENT ISSUES

1. Do you think that a low-level employee could act as a change catalyst? Explain.
2. Contrast management practices in a retail electronics store where management followed the "calm waters" view of change versus one where management followed the "white-water rapids" view.
3. How can an innovative culture make an organization more effective? Could such an innovative culture make an organization less effective? Explain.
4. Do you think a TQM program could be developed that consisted of continual revolutionary change, as opposed to continual gradual change? Discuss.
5. Assuming that employees are well informed about the jobs they're getting themselves into, do you think it's the manager's responsibility to try to alleviate work-related stress on employees, or is this stress just a normal part of the job with which employees will just have to cope? Explain.

SELF-ASSESSMENT EXERCISE

HOW INNOVATIVE ARE YOU?

Organizations need innovative people to lead the way in making changes. In fact, much of the TQM movement is about innovation and change. And we know that quantum changes require innovative, risk-seeking personalities. Are you one of those innovative people? This self-assessment exercise will help you to find out.

Instructions: To find out how innovative you are, react to the following 18 statements. Remember that there is no right or wrong answer. Rather, we are interested in exploring your attitudes. Answer using the following scale.

(SA) = Strongly Agree
(A) = Agree
(?) = Undecided
(D) = Disagree
(SD) = Strongly Disagree

	Strongly Agree				Strongly Disagree
1. I try new ideas and new approaches to problems.	SA	A	?	D	SD
2. I take things or situations apart to find a new use for existing methods or existing equipment.	SA	A	?	D	SD
3. I can be counted on by my friends to find a new use for existing methods or existing equipment.	SA	A	?	D	SD
4. Among my friends, I'm usually the first person to try out a new idea or method.	SA	A	?	D	SD
5. I demonstrate originality.	SA	A	?	D	SD
6. I like to work on a problem that has caused others great difficulty.	SA	A	?	D	SD
7. I plan on developing contacts with experts in my field, located in different companies or departments.	SA	A	?	D	SD
8. I plan on budgeting time and money for the pursuit of novel ideas.	SA	A	?	D	SD
9. I make comments at meetings on new ways of doing things.	SA	A	?	D	SD
10. If my friends were asked, they would say I'm a wit.	SA	A	?	D	SD
11. I seldom stick to the rules or follow protocol.	SA	A	?	D	SD
12. I discourage formal meetings to discuss ideas.	SA	A	?	D	SD
13. I usually support a friend's suggestion on new ways to do things.	SA	A	?	D	SD
14. I probably will not turn down ambiguous job assignments.	SA	A	?	D	SD
15. People who depart from the accepted organizational routine should not be punished.	SA	A	?	D	SD
16. I hope to be known for the quantity of my work rather than the quality of my work when starting a new project.	SA	A	?	D	SD
17. I must be able to find enough variety of experience in my job or I will leave it.	SA	A	?	D	SD
18. I am going to leave a job that doesn't challenge me.	SA	A	?	D	SD

For scoring information, turn to page SK-4.

Source: J E Ettlie and R D O'Keefe, "Innovative Attitudes, Values, and Intentions in Organizations," *Journal of Management Studies*, 19, 1982, p. 176.

TO: Chuck Sangster, Director of Human Resources
FROM: Kathy Daw, CPA, Managing Partner
RE: Introduction of Audit Teams

Given the complexity of many of our clients' situations, the other partners and myself have decided that the best way to serve our clients' changing needs is to use audit teams, instead of doing audits with individual auditors as we've done in the past. Moving to a team-based approach is going to require changes on the part of our audit staff. Individuals who have been accustomed to working on their own will now need to work in a team.

What I need from you is some background information on team building. Would you review current literature on team building and provide me with a one-page, single-spaced list of the most important ideas about what an effective team is, and what it takes to build one? I will then share these ideas with the other partners. Once we've had a chance to digest the information, I'll meet with you to begin preparing our approach to implementing this change.

This is a fictionalized account of a potentially real problem. It was written for academic purposes only.

TAKE IT TO THE NET

We invite you to visit the Robbins/Coulter/Stuart-Kotze Companion Website at www.prenticehall.ca/robbins for this chapter's Internet resources.

CASE APPLICATION

Teleglobe Inc., Montreal

Nineteen ninety-eight was a big year for Teleglobe Inc. The telecommunications company's 50-year monopoly on overseas long-distance calls to and from Canada came to an end in October. The Canadian government's compliance with a World Trade Organization accord ended Teleglobe's monopoly, thereby forcing the company out of its long security and into a seriously turbulent environment. Faced with these changes, Teleglobe began to shift the focus of its business away from the wholesale Canadian market (Teleglobe supplied the country's major telephone companies with overseas calling services using its 240-country network) into global retail markets. The retail arm of the company, Teleglobe Communication Services (TCS), will be the vehicle for the new retail growth. Teleglobe's plan is to take TCS from a $10 million-a-year company to a $2 *billion-a-year* one, thereby accounting for half of total revenues. And CEO Charles Sirois believes that this can be accomplished by 2003. During the lead-up to the end of Teleglobe's monopoly, the company was already significantly reducing the percentage of revenues earned from Canadian operations and moving into new areas. Initially, efforts will be focused on three target markets: television broadcasting corporations; international companies; and specific groups of immigrants in cities throughout North America (such as the Russian, Korean and Chinese markets).

Sirois is not bemoaning the loss of the Canadian monopoly at all. As he has pointed out: "Canada is 30 million people, the rest of the world is 6 billion—and I am selling to the six billion people so, obviously, at the end of the day, I just need to grab a very small market share of the total worldwide market to replace the loss in Canada". Teleglobe is transforming its sales offices around the world into operating companies, in order to take advantage of the global opening-up of telecom markets. In the summer of 1998, Teleglobe announced a merger with Excel Communications Inc. in the US. Teleglobe's move into retail sales in the US was thereby a *fait accompli:* "With this merger, Teleglobe has reached its target for retail expansion four or five years ahead of schedule," said Sirois. The addition of Excel's large US telecommunications network to Teleglobe's intercontinental network has created a force to be reckoned with in the fight for the lucrative $200 billion market amongst G7 countries.

QUESTIONS

1. Explain what external and internal forces were creating the need for change at Teleglobe. Would you describe this situation as a "calm-waters" or "white-waters" situation? Why?
2. To what degree do you think Teleglobe will be going through cultural change? What sort of resistance to change would you expect from employees? How should Sirois handle resistance to change?
3. How might the end of Teleglobe's monopoly on intercontinental long-distance calling affect Stentor (the consortium of Canada's 10 largest phone companies, including Bell Canada), and a smaller company like Sprint Canada?

Sources: Lawrence Surtees, "Telecom Competition to Spread", *Globe and Mail,* January 3, 1998, p. B1; "Teleglobe Merging With US Telecom", *Globe and Mail,* June 15, 1998, p. B1; Andy Riga, "'Zero to $2billion in 5 Years'", *Montreal Gazette,* May 15, 1998, p. F1; and Jan Ravensbergen, "Teleglobe Enters the Fray", May 6, 1998, p. C1.

VIDEO CASE APPLICATION

Managing Workforce Absenteeism

The statistics mentioned in the video speak for themselves: an estimated $10 billion absenteeism problem in Canada; 75 percent of companies recognizing it as a major problem; and in the Toronto Hydro example, 100 people a day off work, creating a $5 million-a-year payment for no return. This program focused on attendance management programs as a method of combating absenteeism. As a control tool, these programs are certainly very useful. When 80 percent of absenteeism is accounted for by 20 percent of the workforce, it is apparent that much of the problem is from this particular group of employees who know how the system works and who take advantage of it. The example of workers consistently taking three consecutive days off work because they realize that after four days they need a doctor's certificate, shows how some employees seek to take as much advantage of the system as possible. The scenario which describes workers filling in their future sick leave at the start of the year, along with their vacations, is patently ridiculous. In these incidences, it is imperative that management has methods to keep track of employee behaviour. Toronto Hydro's reduction of absenteeism by 33 percent shows the value of attendance management programs.

However, these are often remedial efforts to combat the problem. It is important for management to look at the root causes of absenteeism in their organizations. This chapter's opening section, A Manager's Challenge, shows how Husky Injection Moulding deals with absenteeism. Husky's absenteeism is a quarter of that in other manufacturing companies. This obviously results in major cost savings for the company. Husky has invested in many techniques to control absenteeism, largely through the company's focus on employee health. Husky has an on-site fitness centre, a naturopath, a doctor and a massage therapist. Wouldn't you like to work there? Another major contributor towards avoiding worker absenteeism is the creation of a culture that stresses the importance of each individual employee. Allowing some flexibility in work schedules through things such as flextime, telecommuting and job sharing, can also alleviate some of the pressures put on workers.

QUESTIONS

1. What role could empowerment play in reducing worker absenteeism?
2. Is intimidating workers through scrutiny (which is often a major component of attendance management programs) an effective tool for curtailing absenteeism? Are motivational techniques a better method? What about a combination of the two approaches? Explain your reasoning.
3. At the CIBC, 75 percent of the workforce are women, and 72 percent of employees are parents. What kind of actions could the bank take to reduce work-family conflicts?
4. Is it possible that strict reductions in absenteeism could actually end up costing an organization, in terms of such things as injury compensation, employee health, insurance premiums, and employee morale and loyalty? How could such problems be avoided?

Video source: "No Place to Hide," *Venture* #646 (June 15, 1997).

VIDEO CASE APPLICATION

MBNA Challenges Canadian Banks

The Canadian banking industry is by no means what one would call a soft target. The large banks have been pulling in record profits throughout the 1990s, the biggest of them netting over $1 billion in revenue. But up until recently, they have only competed amongst themselves for the credit card market in Canada. Now, MBNA is challenging that oligopoly by vying for a large share of the 30 million credit cards in use in this country. Not only is MBNA a specialist in an area that represents a part of the banks' business, it also has a significant amount of economic clout and marketing savvy behind it. With excellent customer targeting knowledge, and the ability to compete fiercely on price, MBNA could pose a serious threat to the banks, who may have been lulled into a sense of complacency due to the modest competition they have faced thus far.

The reporter in this video mentions that the banks are counting on customer loyalty to protect them, but it is unlikely that the banks would be so naïve. However, it will be interesting to see how well they adjust to this new and very different kind of competition.

QUESTIONS

1. Would you consider this situation to be more of a "white water" or "calm waters" situation for the Canadian banks?
2. Describe the forces for change in this situation. How might the banks respond to the changes in their environment?
3. Do you think it is possible that competition of the sort MBNA represents could eventually lead to the Canadian banks reassessing their organizational cultures? If so, in what ways? And how might cultural change be effectively handled?

Video source: "MBNA," *Venture* #674 (January 13, 1998).

P A R T   F I V E

Leading

LEARNING OBJECTIVES

After Reading This Chapter, You Should Be Able To:

1 Define the focus and goals of organizational behaviour
2 Explain how an organization is like an iceberg
3 Describe the three components of an attitude
4 Identify the role that consistency plays in attitudes
5 Explain the relationship between satisfaction and productivity
6 Describe the Myers-Briggs personality type framework and its use in organizations
7 Explain Holland's personality-job fit theory
8 Describe attribution theory
9 Identify the types of shortcuts managers use in judging others
10 Explain how managers can shape employee behaviour

A MANAGER'S CHALLENGE

Canada Safeway Ltd., Alberta

In 1997, 10 000 Safeway employees from 74 stores across Alberta went on strike. The strike lasted two-and-a-half months and cost Safeway heavily—an estimated $24 million in lost revenue; loss of the workforce's trust; and, more importantly, loss of regular customers who are very difficult to win back. It could be said that all of this might easily have been avoided if management had had a better understanding of its employees.[1]

Four years earlier, Safeway was facing serious competition from new superstores. Management opened the books up to its workforce, showing them how losses were mounting in the face of this new threat. Market share had fallen from 70 to 30 percent. The workers agreed to take a wage rollback of $2.85 per-

hour. Management, in turn, promised wage increases when profits returned. Profits did indeed return, but the promise of compensation to employees did not materialize.

The strike became a very public issue throughout the province. Customers sympathized with the plight of the workers, who were believed to have been cheated by a lying management. In communities where most people knew someone who worked in the local Safeway, neighbours, friends, and even acquaintances were not going to cross a picket line to buy their groceries. Inevitably, both sides lost. The strike cost the union $10 million, and caused an even greater divide between management and labour at the Safeway stores. Safeway has had a hard, uphill battle to regain the losses to its customer base and its revenue. And it could all have been avoided if management had had a better understanding of employee behaviour.

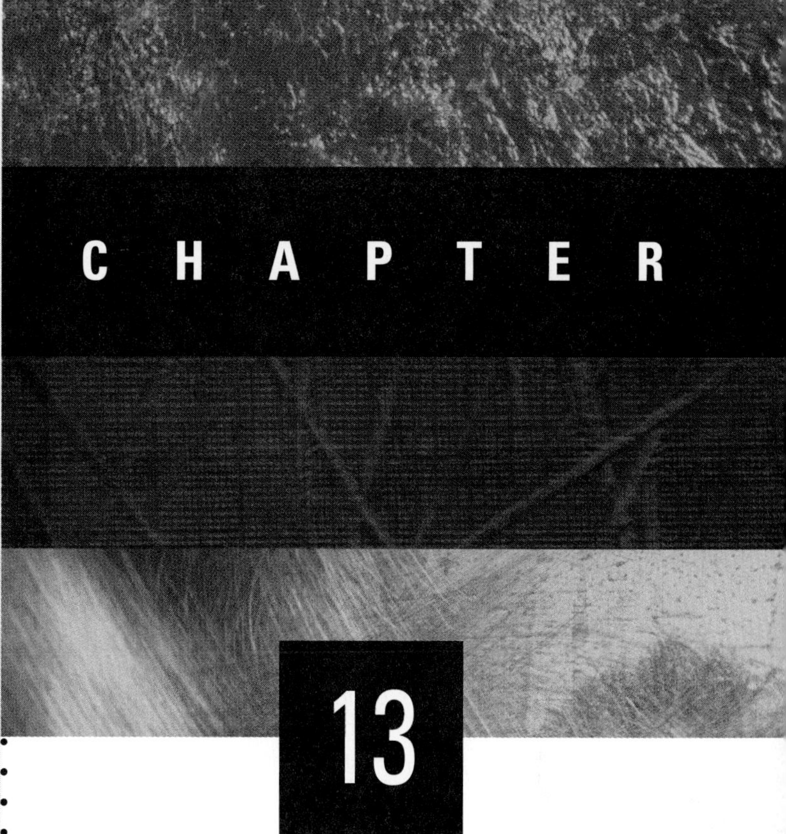

CHAPTER 13

Foundations of Behaviour

The Safeway example illustrates the difficulties many organizations have in understanding the behavioural aspects of their workforces. You're probably already aware of the fact that people differ in their actions or behaviour. For instance, you've regularly had to deal with people who have different types of personalities. And haven't you seen family members or friends engage in behaviour that prompted you to wonder: Why did they do that? As the opening challenge illustrates, effective managers need to understand their employees' behaviour. This chapter looks at several psychological factors that influence employee behaviour, and then considers the implications of each for management practice.

TOWARDS EXPLAINING AND PREDICTING BEHAVIOUR

behaviour
The actions of people.

organizational behaviour
The study of the actions of people at work.

The material in this and the following four chapters draws heavily on the field of study that is known as *organizational behaviour* (OB). Although it's concerned with the subject of **behaviour**—that is, the actions of people—**organizational behaviour** is concerned more specifically with the actions of people at work.

One of the challenges to understanding organizational behaviour is that it addresses a number of issues that aren't that obvious. Like an iceberg, a lot of organizational behaviour isn't visible. (See Figure 13-1.) What we tend to see when we look at organizations is their formal aspects—strategies, objectives, policies and procedures, structure, technology, formal authority, and chains of command. But just under the surface are a number of informal elements that managers need to understand. As we'll show, OB provides managers with considerable insights into these important, but hidden, aspects of the organization.

Focus of Organizational Behaviour

Organizational behaviour focuses primarily on two major areas. First, OB looks at *individual behaviour*. Based predominantly on contributions from psychologists, this area includes such topics as attitudes, personality, perception, learning and motivation. Second, OB is concerned with *group behaviour*, which includes norms, roles, team building and conflict. Our knowledge about groups basically comes from the work of sociologists and social psychologists. Unfortunately, the behaviour of a group of employees can't be understood by merely summing up the actions of each individual, because individuals in a group setting behave differently from individuals acting alone. You see this characteristic at its extreme, for instance, when a street gang harasses innocent citizens. The gang members, acting individually, might never engage in such behaviour. Put them together, and they act differently. Therefore, because employees in an organization are both individuals and members of groups, we need to study them at two levels. In this chapter, we'll provide the foundation for understanding individual behaviour. Then, in the next chapter, we'll introduce basic concepts related to understanding group behaviour.

Goals of Organizational Behaviour

The goals of OB are to *explain* and to *predict behaviour*. Why do managers need this skill? Simply, in order to manage their employees' behaviour. We know that a manager's success

FIGURE 13-1 The "Organization as an Iceberg" Metaphor

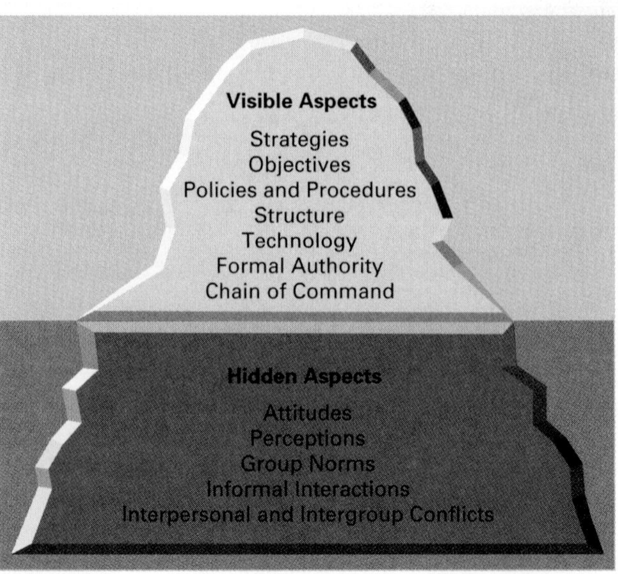

depends on getting things done through people. To do this, the manager needs to be able to explain why employees engage in some behaviours rather than others, and to predict how employees will respond to various actions the manager might take.

Which employee behaviours do we specifically want to explain and predict? We'll emphasize employee productivity, absenteeism, and turnover. In addition, we'll also look at job satisfaction. While job satisfaction is an attitude rather than a behaviour, it's an outcome many managers are concerned about.

In the following pages, we'll address how an understanding of employee attitudes, personality, perception, and learning can help us to predict and explain employee productivity, absence and turnover rates, and job satisfaction.

ATTITUDES

Attitudes are evaluative statements—either favourable or unfavourable—concerning objects, people, or events. They reflect how an individual feels about something. When a person says, "I like my job," he or she is expressing an attitude about work.

To better understand the concept of attitudes, we should look at an attitude as being made up of three components: cognition, affect and behaviour.[2] The **cognitive component of an attitude** makes up the beliefs, opinions, knowledge, or information held by a person. The belief that "discrimination is wrong" illustrates a cognition. The **affective component of an attitude** is the emotional or feeling part of an attitude. Using our example, this component would be reflected by the statement, "I don't like Jon because he discriminates against minorities." Finally, affect can lead to behavioural outcomes. The **behavioural component of an attitude** refers to an intention to behave in a certain way towards someone or something. To continue our example, I might choose to avoid Jon because of my feelings about him.

Looking at attitudes as being made up of three components—cognition, affect, and behaviour—helps to show the complexity of attitudes. But for the sake of clarity, keep in mind that the term *attitude* usually refers only to the affective component.

Naturally, managers aren't interested in every attitude an employee might hold. They're specifically interested in job-related attitudes. The three most commonly examined attitudes are job satisfaction, job involvement, and organizational commitment.[3] **Job satisfaction** is an employee's general attitude towards his or her job. When people speak of employee attitudes, they're usually referring to job satisfaction. **Job involvement** is the degree to which an employee identifies with his or her job, actively participates in it, and considers his or her job performance important to his or her self-worth. Finally, **organizational commitment** repre-

attitudes
Evaluative statements concerning objects, people or events.

cognitive component of an attitude
The beliefs, opinions, knowledge or information held by a person.

affective component of an attitude
The emotional or feeling segment of an attitude.

behavioural component of an attitude
An intention to behave in a certain way towards someone or something.

job satisfaction
A person's general attitude towards his or her job.

job involvement
The degree to which an employee identifies with his or her job, actively participates in it, and considers his or her job performance important to his or her self-worth.

organizational commitment
An employee's orientation towards the organization in terms of his or her loyalty to, identification with, and involvement in, the organization.

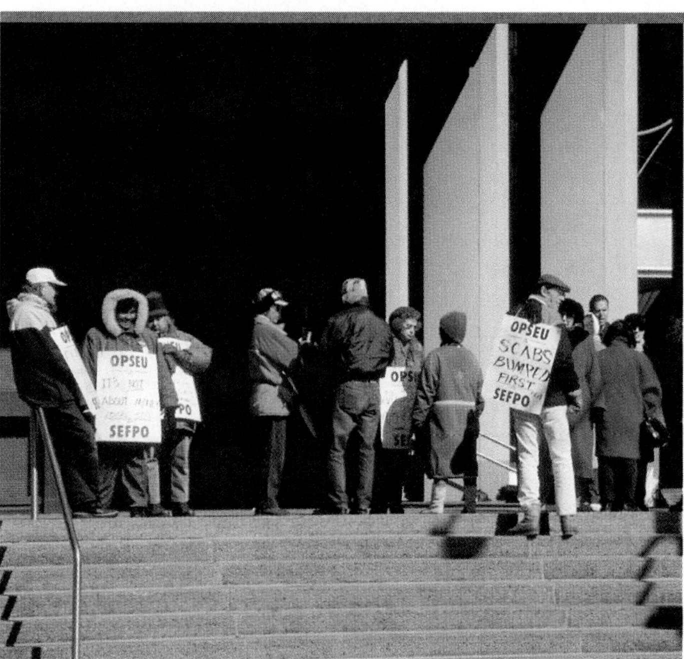

How would you analyze these people's attitude towards the issue they are protesting?

sents an employee's orientation towards the organization in terms of his or her loyalty to, identification with, and involvement in, the organization. In recent years, these topics have been popular ones for organizational researchers.[4]

Attitudes and Consistency

Did you ever notice how people change what they say so that it doesn't contradict what they do? Perhaps a friend of yours has continually argued that North American cars are poorly built and that he'd never own anything but a foreign car. But when his dad gives him a late-model North American-made car, suddenly they're not so bad. Or, when going through sorority rush, a new freshman believes that sororities are good and that pledging a sorority is important. However, if she isn't asked to join one, she may say that sorority life isn't all that great anyway.

Research has generally concluded that people seek consistency among their attitudes and between their attitudes and behaviour.[5] This means that individuals try to reconcile differing attitudes and align their attitudes and behavior, so that they appear rational and consistent. When there's an inconsistency, individuals will take steps to correct it. This can be done by altering either the attitudes or the behaviour, or by developing a rationalization for the inconsistency.

For example, a campus recruiter for Ontario Electronics Ltd. (OEL) who visits university campuses, identifies qualified job candidates, and sells them on the advantages of OEL as a good place to work would be in conflict if he personally believed that OEL had poor working conditions and few opportunities for recent university graduates. This recruiter could, over time, find his attitudes towards OEL becoming more positive. He may, in effect, convince himself by continually articulating the merits of working for the company. Another alternative would be for the recruiter to become overtly negative about OEL and its opportunities within the firm for prospective candidates. The original enthusiasm that the recruiter might have shown would dwindle, probably to be replaced by open cynicism towards the company. Finally, the recruiter might acknowledge that OEL is an undesirable place to work, but as a professional recruiter, his obligation is to present the positive aspects of working for the company. He might further rationalize that no workplace is perfect; therefore, his job isn't to present both sides of the issue, but rather to present a favourable picture of the company.

Cognitive Dissonance Theory

Can we, in addition, assume from this consistency principle that an individual's behaviour can always be predicted if we know his or her attitude on a subject? The answer to this question is, unfortunately, more complex than merely yes or no.

cognitive dissonance
Any incompatibility between two or more attitudes or between behaviour and attitudes.

Leon Festinger, in the late 1950s, proposed the theory of **cognitive dissonance**.[6] This theory sought to explain the relationship between attitudes and behaviour. Dissonance in this case means inconsistency. The term *cognitive dissonance* refers to any inconsistency someone might perceive between two or more of his or her attitudes, or between his or her behaviour and attitudes. Festinger argued that any form of inconsistency is uncomfortable and that people will try to reduce the dissonance and thus the discomfort. In other words, people seek a stable state with a minimum of dissonance.

Of course, no one can completely avoid dissonance. You know that cheating on your income tax is wrong, but you may "fudge" the numbers a bit every year and hope you're not audited. Or you tell your children to brush their teeth after every meal, but don't do it yourself. So how *do* people cope? Festinger proposed that the desire to reduce dissonance is determined by the *importance* of the factors creating the dissonance, the degree of *influence* the individual believes he or she has over those factors, and the *rewards* that may be involved in dissonance.

If the factors creating the dissonance are relatively unimportant, the pressure to correct the imbalance will be low. However, say that a corporate manager—Eliana Lopez—believes strongly that no company should pollute. Unfortunately, because of job requirements, Lopez is placed in the position of having to make decisions that would trade off her company's profitability against her attitudes on pollution. She knows that dumping the company's waste water into a local river is in her company's best economic interests (and for this example we'll assume it is legal). What will she do? Clearly, Lopez will be experiencing a high degree of cognitive dissonance. Because of the importance of the elements in this example, we can't expect Lopez to ignore the inconsistency. But there are several paths that she can follow to deal with her dilemma. She can change her behaviour (use her authority to have the dumping stopped), or she can reduce dissonance by concluding that the dissonant behaviour isn't so important after all ("I've got to have a job, and in my role as a corporate decision maker, I often have to place the good of my company above that of the environment or society"). A third alternative would be for Lopez to change her attitude ("There's nothing wrong with dumping waste water into the river"). Still another choice would be for her to identify compatible factors that outweigh the dissonant ones ("The benefits to society from our manufacturing our product more than offset the cost to society of the resulting water pollution").

The degree of influence that individuals believe they have over the factors will have an impact on how they'll react to the dissonance. If they perceive the dissonance to be an uncontrollable result—something in which they have no choice—they're less likely to be receptive to attitude change. If, for example, the dissonance-producing behaviour were required as a result of a boss's order, the pressure to reduce dissonance would be less than if the behaviour were performed voluntarily. While dissonance exists, it can be rationalized and justified by the lack of individual choice and control.

Rewards also influence the degree to which people are motivated to reduce dissonance. High dissonance, when accompanied by high rewards, tends to reduce the tension inherent in the dissonance. The reward acts to reduce dissonance by increasing the individual's belief that there is consistency.

These moderating factors suggest that just because people experience dissonance, they won't necessarily move directly towards consistency—that is, reducing the dissonance. If the issues contributing to the dissonance are of minimal importance, if an individual perceives that the dissonance is externally imposed and is substantially uncontrollable by him or her, or if rewards are significant enough to offset the dissonance, the person won't be under great tension to reduce the dissonance.

Attitude Surveys

An increasing number of organizations are regularly surveying their employees about their attitudes. Figure 13-2 shows what an attitude survey might look like. Typically, **attitude surveys** present the employee with a set of statements or questions. Ideally, the items are

attitude surveys
Eliciting responses from employees through questionnaires about how they feel about their jobs, work groups, supervisors, and/or the organization.

FIGURE 13-2 Sample Attitude Survey

Please answer each of the following statements using the following rating scale:

5 = Strongly agree
4 = Agree
3 = Undecided
2 = Disagree
1 = Strongly disagree

Statement	Rating
1. This company is a pretty good place to work.	_____
2. I can get ahead in this company if I make the effort.	_____
3. This company's wage rates are competitive with those of other companies.	_____
4. Employee promotion decisions are handled fairly.	_____
5. I understand the various fringe benefits the company offers.	_____
6. My job makes the best use of my abilities.	_____
7. My workload is challenging but not burdensome.	_____
8. I have trust and confidence in my boss.	_____
9. I feel free to tell my boss what I think.	_____
10. I know what my boss expects of me.	_____

Source: Based on Teri Lammers, "The Essential Employee Survey," *INC.,* December 1992, pp. 159–161.

Having employee meetings can be a good way to get a grip on what problems employees are facing. Open forums such as this can't replace employee attitude surveys, but they can be a useful communication tool.

designed to obtain the specific information that management desires. An attitude score is achieved by summing up responses to individual questionnaire items. These scores can then be averaged for job groups, departments, divisions, or the organization as a whole.

The Satisfaction-Productivity Controversy

From the 1930s to the mid-1960s, it was widely believed that happy workers were productive workers. As a result of the Hawthorne studies (discussed in Chapter 2), managers generalized that if their employees were satisfied with their jobs, they would then translate that satisfaction into high productivity. Many paternalistic actions by managers in the 1930s, 1940s and 1950s—such as forming company bowling teams and credit unions, having company picnics, and training supervisors to be sensitive to the concerns of subordinates—were supposed to make workers happy. But belief in the happy worker idea was based more on wishful thinking than on hard evidence.

A careful review of research indicates that, if satisfaction does have a positive effect on productivity, it's quite small.[7] However, looking at situational contingency variables has improved the relationship.[8] For example, the relationship is stronger when the employee's behaviour isn't constrained or controlled by outside factors. An employee's productivity on machine-paced jobs, for instance, is going to be more heavily influenced by the speed of the machine than by his or her level of satisfaction. Another important contingency variable seems to be job level. The satisfaction-performance correlations are stronger for higher-level employees. Thus, we might expect the relationship to be more relevant for individuals in professional, supervisory and managerial positions.

Unfortunately, most studies on the relationship between satisfaction and productivity used research designs that couldn't prove cause and effect. Studies that controlled for this possibility indicate that a more valid conclusion is that productivity leads to satisfaction, rather than the other way around.[9] If you do a good job, you intrinsically feel good about it. In addition, assuming that the organization rewards productivity, your higher productivity should increase verbal recognition, your pay level, and promotion opportunities. These rewards, in turn, increase your level of satisfaction with the job.

Implications for Managers

We know that employees will try to reduce dissonance. And, not surprisingly, there's relatively strong evidence that committed and satisfied employees have lower rates of job turnover and absenteeism.[10] Because most managers want to minimize the number of resignations and absences—especially among their most productive employees—they should do those things that will generate positive job attitudes. For instance, dissonance can be managed. If employees are required to do things that appear inconsistent to them or that are at odds with their attitudes, managers should remember that pressure to reduce the dissonance is minimized when the employee perceives that the dissonance is externally imposed and uncontrollable.

The pressure is also decreased if rewards are significant enough to offset the dissonance. What this means is that the manager might point to external forces such as competitors, customers, or other factors when explaining the need to perform some work activity that the individual may have some dissonance about. Or the manager can provide rewards that an individual desires, in order to decrease his or her attempts to eliminate the dissonance.

The findings about the satisfaction-productivity relationships have important implications for managers. They suggest that the goal of making employees happy on the assumption that this will lead to high productivity is probably misdirected. Managers who follow this strategy could end up with a very happy, but very unproductive, group of employees. Managers would get better results by directing their attention primarily to what will help employees become more productive. Then, successful job performance should lead to feelings of accomplishment, increased pay, promotions, and other rewards—all desirable outcomes—which then lead to job satisfaction.

PERSONALITY

Some people are quiet and passive, while others are loud and aggressive. When we describe people using terms such as *quiet*, *passive*, *loud*, *aggressive*, *ambitious*, *extroverted*, *loyal*, *tense*, or *sociable*, we're categorizing them in terms of *personality traits*. An individual's **personality** is the unique combination of the psychological traits we use to describe that person.

personality
A combination of psychological traits that classifies a person.

Predicting Behaviour from Personality Traits

There are, literally, dozens of personality traits. However, six have received most of the attention in the search to link personality traits to behaviour in organizations. These are *locus of control, authoritarianism, Machiavellianism, self-esteem, self-monitoring,* and *risk propensity*.

Locus of Control. Some people believe that they control their own fate. Others see themselves as pawns of fate, believing that what happens to them in their lives is due to luck or chance. The locus of control in the first case is *internal*; these people believe that they control their destiny. In the second case, it's *external*; these people believe that their lives are controlled by outside forces.[11] Research evidence indicates that employees who rate high in externality are less satisfied with their jobs, more alienated from the work setting, and less involved in their jobs than those who rate high in internality.[12] A manager might also expect to find that externals blame a poor performance evaluation on their boss's prejudice, their co-workers, or other events outside their control, whereas internals explain the same evaluation in terms of their own actions.

Authoritarianism. The term **authoritarianism** refers to a belief that there should be status and power differences among people in organizations.[13] The extremely high authoritarian personality is intellectually rigid, judgmental of others, deferential to those in higher-ranking positions, exploitative of those in lower-ranking positions, distrustful, and resistant to change. Because few people are extreme authoritarians, we need to be cautious in drawing conclusions. It seems reasonable to expect, however, that possessing a high authoritarian personality would be negatively related to the performance of a job that demands sensitivity to the feelings of others, tact, and the ability to adapt to complex and dynamic situations.[14] In contrast, in a job that's highly structured and where success depends on close conformance to rules and regulations, the highly authoritarian employee should perform quite well.

authoritarianism
A measure of a person's belief that there should be status and power differences among people in organizations.

Machiavellianism
A measure of the degree to which people are pragmatic, maintain emotional distance, and believe that ends can justify means.

Machiavellianism. Closely related to authoritarianism is the characteristic called **Machiavellianism** ("Mach"), named after Niccolò Machiavelli, who wrote in the sixteenth century on how to gain and manipulate power. An individual who is high in Machiavellianism—

1 **Explain how individuals reconcile inconsistencies between attitudes and behaviour.**

2 **Describe the relationship between job satisfaction and productivity.**

in contrast to someone who is low—is pragmatic, maintains emotional distance, and believes that ends can justify means.[15] "If it works, use it" is consistent with a high-Mach perspective. Do high Machs make good employees? That answer depends on the type of job and whether you consider ethical implications in evaluating performance. In jobs that require bargaining skills (such as labour negotiator or purchasing manager) or that have substantial rewards for winning (such as a commissioned salesperson), high Machs are productive. In jobs where ends do not justify the means or that lack absolute measures of performance, it's difficult to predict the performance of high Machs.

self-esteem
An individual's degree of like or dislike for himself or herself.

Self-Esteem. People differ in the degree to which they like or dislike themselves. This trait is called **self-esteem**.[16] The research on self-esteem (SE) offers some interesting insights into organizational behaviour. For example, self-esteem is directly related to expectations for success. High SEs believe that they possess more of the ability they need in order to succeed at work. Individuals with high SEs will take more risks in job selection and are more likely to choose unconventional jobs than people with low SEs.

The most common finding on self-esteem is that low SEs are more susceptible to external influence than are high SEs. Low SEs are dependent on receiving positive evaluations from others. As a result, they're more likely to seek approval from others and more prone to conform to the beliefs and behaviours of those they respect than are high SEs. In managerial positions, low SEs will tend to be concerned with pleasing others and, therefore, less likely to take unpopular stands than are high SEs.

Not surprisingly, self-esteem has also been found to be related to job satisfaction. A number of studies confirm that high SEs are more satisfied with their jobs than low SEs.

self-monitoring
A personality trait that measures an individual's ability to adjust his or her behaviour to external situational factors.

Self-Monitoring. Another personality trait that has received increasing attention is called **self-monitoring**.[17] It refers to an individual's ability to adjust his or her behaviour to external, situational factors.

Individuals high in self-monitoring show considerable adaptability in adjusting their behaviour to external, situational factors. They're highly sensitive to external cues and can behave differently in different situations. High self-monitors are capable of presenting striking contradictions between their public persona and their private selves. Low self-monitors can't deliberately vary their behaviour. They tend to display their true dispositions and attitudes in every situation, and there's high behavioural consistency between who they are and what they do.

The research on self-monitoring is in its infancy, thus predictions are hard to make. However, preliminary evidence suggests that high self-monitors tend to pay closer attention to the behaviour of others and are more capable of conforming than are low self-monitors.[18] We might also hypothesize that high self-monitors will be more successful in managerial positions

There are dozens of personality traits, but the search to link them to behaviour in organizations has focused primarily on locus of control, authoritarianism, Machiavellianism, self-esteem, self-monitoring, and risk propensity.

where individuals are required to play multiple, and even contradicting, roles. The high self-monitor is capable of putting on different "faces" for different audiences.

Risk Taking. People differ in their willingness to take chances. This propensity to assume or avoid risk has been shown to have an impact on how long it takes managers to make a decision, and how much information they require before making their choice. For instance, in one study, a group of managers worked on simulated personnel exercises that required them to make hiring decisions.[19] High risk-taking managers made more rapid decisions and used less information in making their choices than did the low risk-taking managers. Interestingly, the decision accuracy was the same for both groups.

To maximize organizational effectiveness, managers should try to align employee risk-taking propensity with specific job demands.[20] For instance, a high risk-taking propensity may lead to more effective performance for a commodities trader in a brokerage firm, since this type of job demands rapid decision making. However, this personality characteristic might prove a major obstacle to accountants auditing financial statements. This type of job might be better filled by someone with a low risk-taking propensity.

Personality Assessment Tests

How would you describe your personality? Have you ever taken a personality test to see what personality characteristics you have? Personality assessment tests are commonly used to reveal an individual's personality traits. One of the most popular personality tests—over 2 million people took it in one recent year—is the Myers-Briggs Type Indicator (or MBTI, as it's often called).

The MBTI is a personality test that asks people over 100 questions about how they usually act or feel in different situations.[21] The way you respond to these questions puts you at one end or another of four dimensions:

1. *Social interaction*: extrovert or introvert (E or I). An extrovert is someone who is outgoing, dominant, often aggressive, and who wants to change the world. The extrovert needs a work environment that is varied and action oriented, lets him or her be around and with others, and gives him or her a variety of experiences. An individual who's shy and withdrawn and focuses on understanding the world is described as an introvert. An introvert prefers a work environment that is quiet and concentrated, lets him or her be alone, and gives him or her a chance to explore in depth a limited set of experiences.

2. *Preference for gathering data*: sensing or intuitive (S or N). Sensing types dislike new problems unless there are standard ways to solve them, like an established routine, must usually work all the way through to reach a conclusion, show patience with routine details, and tend to be good at precise work. In contrast, intuitive types are individuals who like solving new problems, dislike doing the same thing over and over again, jump to conclusions, are impatient with routine details, and dislike taking time for precision.

3. *Preference for decision making*: feeling or thinking (F or T). Individuals who are feeling types are aware of other people and their feelings, like harmony, need occasional praise, dislike telling people unpleasant things, tend to be sympathetic, and relate well to most people. Thinking types are unemotional and uninterested in people's feelings, like analysis and putting things into logical order, are able to reprimand people and fire them when necessary, may seem hard-hearted, and tend to relate well only to other thinking types.

4. *Style of making decisions*: perceptive or judgmental (P or J). Perceptive types are curious, spontaneous, flexible, adaptable, and tolerant. They focus on starting a task, postpone decisions, and want to find out all about the task before starting it. Judgmental types are decisive, good planners, purposeful, and exacting. They focus on completing a task, make decisions quickly, and want only the essential information necessary to get a task done.

Then, the way these preferences are combined provide descriptions of sixteen different personality types. Table 13-1 illustrates four examples.

How could the MBTI help managers? Proponents of the test believe that it's important to know these personality types because they influence the way in which people interact and

TABLE 13-1 Examples of MBTI Personality Types

INFJ	(introvert, intuitive, feeling, judgmental): This personality type is quietly forceful, conscientious, and concerned for others. Such people succeed by perseverance, originality, and the desire to do whatever is needed or wanted. They're often highly respected for their uncompromising principles.
ESTP	(extrovert, sensing, thinking, perceptive): This personality type is blunt and sometimes insensitive. Such people are matter-of-fact and do not worry or hurry. They enjoy whatever comes along. They work best with real things that can be assembled or disassembled.
ISFP	(introvert, sensing, feeling, perceptive): This personality type is sensitive, kind, modest, shy, and quietly friendly. Such people strongly dislike disagreements and will avoid them. They're loyal followers and are quite often relaxed about getting things done.
ENTJ	(extrovert, intuitive, thinking, judgmental): This personality type is warm, friendly, candid, and decisive. Also, they're usually skilled in anything that requires reasoning and intelligent talk. However, they may sometimes be overly positive about what they're capable of doing.

Source: Based on Isabel Briggs-Myers, *Introduction to Type* (Palo Alto,CA: Consulting Psychologists Press, 1980), pp. 7–8.

solve problems. For instance, if your boss is an intuitor and you're a sensor, you'll gather information in different ways. An intuitor prefers gut reactions while a sensor prefers facts. To work well with your boss, you'd have to present more than just facts about a situation; you'd need to bring out how you feel about it. Also, it's been used to help managers select employees better matched to certain types of jobs. All in all, the MBTI can be a useful tool for understanding personality and predicting people's behaviour.

Personality Types in Different National Cultures

We know that there are certainly no common personality types for a given country. You can, for instance, find high risk takers and low risk takers in almost any culture. Yet a country's culture can influence *dominant* personality characteristics of its people. We can see this by looking at two personality traits—locus of control and authoritarianism.

National cultures differ in terms of the degree to which people believe they control their environment. For instance, North Americans believe that they can dominate their environment while other societies, such as those in Middle Eastern countries, believe that life is essentially preordained or predetermined. Notice how closely this distinction parallels the concept of internal and external locus of control. Based on this particular cultural characteristic, we should expect a larger proportion of internals in the Canadian and American workforces than in the workforces of Saudi Arabia or Iran.

Another personality trait that we can examine in relation to national culture is that of authoritarianism, which is closely related to the concept of power distance. In high-power-distance societies, such as Mexico or Venezuela, you'd expect to find a large proportion of people with authoritarian personalities, especially among the ruling class. In contrast, because Sweden rates below average on this dimension, we'd expect authoritarian personalities to be less prevalent than in the high-power-distance countries.

As we've seen throughout this section, personality traits influence employees' behaviour. For global managers, understanding how personality traits differ takes on added significance when looking at it from the perspective of national culture.

Matching Personalities and Jobs

Individual personalities differ. But so, too, do jobs. Following this logic, efforts have been made to match the proper personalities with the proper jobs.

The best documented personality-job fit theory has been developed by psychologist John Holland.[22] His theory states that an employee's satisfaction with his or her job, as well as his or her likelihood of leaving that job, depends on the degree to which the individual's personality matches his or her occupational environment. Holland identified six basic personality types that an organization's employees might exhibit. Table 13-2 describes each of the six types, their personality characteristics, and sample occupations.

Holland's research strongly supports the hexagonal diagram in Figure 13-3.[23] This figure illustrates that the closer two fields or orientations are in the hexagon, the more compatible they are. Adjacent categories are quite similar, while those diagonally opposite are highly dissimilar.

What does all this mean? The theory proposes that satisfaction is highest and turnover lowest where personality and occupation are compatible. Social individuals should be in "people" type jobs, and so forth. A realistic person in a realistic job is in a more congruent situation than is a realistic person in an investigative job. A realistic person in a social job is in the most incongruent situation possible. The key points of this model are that (1) there do appear to be intrinsic differences in personality among individuals, (2) there are different types of jobs, and (3) people in job environments compatible with their personality types should be more satisfied and less likely to resign voluntarily than should people in incongruent jobs.

TABLE 13-2 Holland's Typology of Personality and Sample Occupations

Type	Personality Characteristics	Sample Occupations
Realistic—Prefers physical activities that require skill, strength, and co-ordination	Shy, genuine, persistent, stable, conforming, practical	Mechanic, drill press operator, assembly-line worker, farmer
Investigative—Prefers activities involving thinking, organizing, and understanding	Analytical, original, curious, independent	Biologist, economist, mathematician, news reporter
Social—Prefers activities that involve helping and developing others	Sociable, friendly, co-operative, understanding	Social worker, teacher, counsellor, clinical psychologist
Conventional—Prefers rule-regulated, orderly and unambiguous activities	Conforming, efficient, practical, unimaginative, inflexible	Accountant, corporate manager, bank teller, file clerk
Enterprising—Prefers verbal activities where there are opportunities to influence others and attain power	Self-confident, ambitious, energetic, domineering	Lawyer, real estate agent, public relations specialist, small business manager
Artistic—Prefers ambiguous and unsystematic activities that allow creative expression	Imaginative, disorderly, idealistic, emotional, impractical	Painter, musician, writer, interior decorator

Source: Based on John L Holland, *Making Vocational Choices: A Theory of Vocational Personalities and Work Environments,* 2nd. ed. (Englewood Cliffs, NJ: Prentice Hall, 1985).

FIGURE 13-3 **Relationships Among Occupational Personality Types**

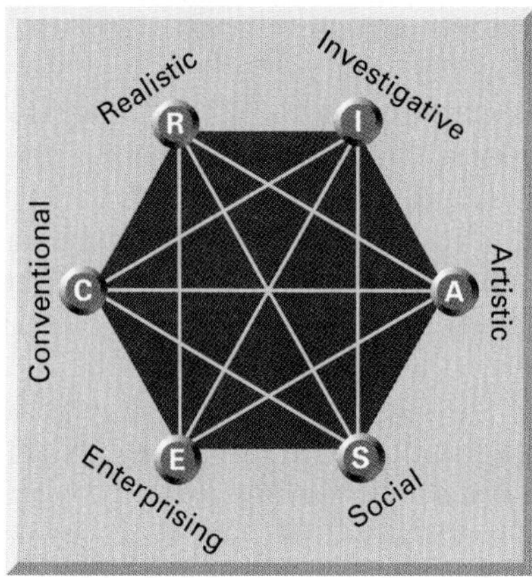

Source: J L Holland, *Making Vocational Choices: A Theory of Vocational Personalities and Work Environments,* 2nd ed. (Englewood Cliffs, NJ: Prentice Hall, 1985). Used by permission. This model originally appeared in J L Holland et al., "An Empirical Occupational Classification Derived from a Theory of Personality and Intended for Practice and Research," ACT Research Report No. 29 (Iowa City: The American College Testing Program, 1969).

Implications for Managers

The major value of a manager's understanding personality differences probably lies in employee selection. Managers are likely to have higher-performing and more satisfied employees if consideration is given to matching personality types with compatible jobs. In addition, there may be other benefits. By recognizing that people approach problem solving, decision making, and job interactions differently, a manager can better understand why, for instance, a subordinate is uncomfortable with making quick decisions, or why an employee insists on gathering as much information as possible before addressing a problem. Another example is that managers can expect that people with an external locus of control may be less satisfied with their jobs than internals, and also that they may be less willing to accept responsibility for their actions.

PERCEPTION

perception
The process of organizing and interpreting sensory impressions in order to give meaning to the environment.

Perception is a process by which individuals organize and interpret their sensory impressions in order to give meaning to their environment. Research on perception consistently demonstrates that people may look at the same thing, yet perceive it differently. One manager, for instance, can interpret the fact that her assistant regularly takes several days to make important decisions, as evidence that the assistant is slow, disorganized, and afraid to make decisions. Yet another manager, with the same assistant, might interpret the same action as evidence that the assistant is thoughtful, thorough, and deliberate. The first manager would probably evaluate her assistant negatively, while the second manager would probably evaluate the person positively. The point is that none of us sees reality. We interpret what we see and call it *reality*. And, of course, as the previous example shows, we act according to our perceptions.

Factors Influencing Perception

How do we explain the fact that people can perceive the same thing differently? A number of factors operate to shape and sometimes distort perception. These factors can reside in the *perceiver;* in the object, or *target*, being perceived; or in the context of the *situation* in which the perception occurs.

TESTING... TESTING...

3 **Describe the six personality traits that have proved to be the most powerful in explaining individual behaviour in organizations.**

4 **How can we use our knowledge of personality to match people to jobs?**

FIGURE 13-4 Perception Challenges: What Do You See?

Old woman or young woman? Two faces or an urn? A knight on a horse?

When an individual looks at a target and attempts to interpret what he or she sees, the individual's personal characteristics are going to heavily influence the interpretation. These personal characteristics include attitudes, personality, motives, interests, past experiences, and expectations.

The characteristics of the target being observed can also affect what's perceived. Loud people are more likely to be noticed in a group than quiet people. So, too, are extremely attractive or unattractive people. Because targets aren't looked at in isolation, the relationship of a target to its background also influences perception (see Figure 13-4 for some examples), as does our tendency to group similar things together.

The context in which we see objects or events is also important. The time at which an object or event is seen can influence perception, as can location, light, heat, colour, and any number of other situational factors.

The Entrepreneurial Personality

One of the most researched topics in entrepreneurship has been the search to determine what, if any, psychological characteristics entrepreneurs have in common.[24] A number of these characteristics have been identified. These include hard work, self-confidence, optimism, determination, and a high energy level. But three factors are regularly at the top of most lists profiling the entrepreneurial personality. Entrepreneurs have a high need for achievement, believe strongly that they can control their own destinies, and take only moderate risks.

The research allows us to draw a general description of entrepreneurs. They tend to be independent types who prefer to be personally responsible for solving problems, for setting goals, and for reaching these goals by their own efforts. They value independence and particularly don't like being controlled by others. Although they're not afraid of taking chances, they're not wild risk takers. They prefer to take calculated risks where they feel that they can control the outcome.

The evidence on entrepreneurial personalities leads us to two obvious conclusions. First, people with this personality makeup aren't likely to be contented, productive employees in the typical large corporation or government agency. The rules, regulations and controls that these bureaucracies impose on their members would frustrate entrepreneurs. Second, the challenges and conditions inherent in starting one's own business mesh well with the entrepreneurial personality. Starting a new venture that they control appeals to their willingness to take risks and determine their own destinies. But because entrepreneurs believe that their future is fully in their own hands, the risk they perceive as moderate is often seen as high by non-entrepreneurs. ■

Attribution Theory

Much of the research on perception is directed at inanimate objects. Managers, though, are more concerned with people. So our discussion of perception should focus on person perception.

Our perceptions of people differ from our perceptions of inanimate objects such as desks, machines, or buildings, because we make inferences about the actions of people that we don't make about objects. Objects don't have beliefs, motives, or intentions, whereas people do. The result is that when we observe people, we attempt to develop explanations of why they behave in certain ways. Our perception and judgment of a person's actions, therefore, will be significantly influenced by the assumptions we make about the person's internal state.

attribution theory
A theory used to develop explanations of how we judge people differently, depending on the meaning we attribute to a given behaviour.

Attribution theory has been developed to explain how we judge people differently, depending on what meaning we attribute to a given behaviour.[25] Basically, the theory suggests that when we observe an individual's behaviour, we attempt to determine whether it was internally or externally caused. Internally caused behaviours are those that are believed to be under the personal control of the individual. Externally caused behaviour results from outside factors; that is, the person is forced into the behaviour by the situation. This determination, however, depends on three factors: (1) distinctiveness, (2) consensus, and (3) consistency.

The term *distinctiveness* refers to whether an individual displays a behaviour in many situations or whether it's particular to only one situation. Is the employee who arrives late today also the source of complaints by co-workers for being a "goof-off"? What we want to know is if this behaviour is unusual or not. If it's unusual, the observer is likely to attribute the behaviour to external forces. However, if the action isn't unique, it will probably be judged as internal.

If everyone who's faced with a similar situation responds in the same way, we can say the behaviour shows *consensus*. A tardy employee's behaviour would meet this criterion if all employees who took the same route to work were also late. From an attribution perspective, if consensus is high, you'd be likely to give an external attribution to the employee's tardiness; but if other employees who took the same route made it to work on time, your conclusion about causation would be internal.

Finally, an observer looks for *consistency* in a person's actions. Does the person engage in the behaviours regularly and consistently? Does the person respond the same way over time? Coming in 10 minutes late for work isn't perceived in the same way if, for one employee, it represents an unusual case (she hasn't been late in months), while for another it's part of a routine pattern (she's regularly late two or three times a week). The more consistent the behaviour, the more the observer is inclined to attribute it to internal causes.

Figure 13-5 summarizes the key elements of attribution theory. It would tell us, for instance, that if an employee—let's call him Mr. Luke—generally performs at or about the same level on other related tasks as he does on his current task (low distinctiveness); if other employees frequently perform differently (better or worse) than Luke does on that current

FIGURE 13-5 Attribution Theory

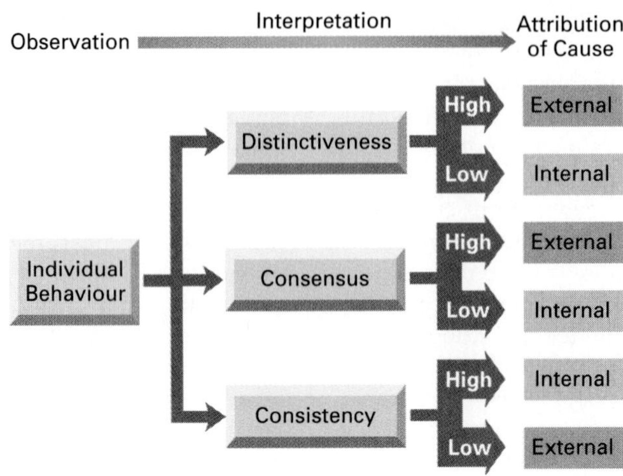

task (low consensus); and if Luke's performance on this current task is consistent over time (high consistency); then his manager or anyone else who is judging Luke's work is likely to hold him primarily responsible for his task performance (internal attribution).

One of the more interesting findings drawn from attribution theory is that there are errors or biases that distort attributions. For instance, there's substantial evidence to support the fact that when we make judgments about the behaviour of other people, we have a tendency to underestimate the influence of external factors, and overestimate the influence of internal or personal factors.[26] This is called the **fundamental attribution error** and it can explain why a sales manager may be prone to attribute the poor performance of her sales representatives to laziness, rather than to the innovative product line introduced by a competitor. There's also a tendency for individuals to attribute *their own* successes to internal factors like ability or effort, while putting the blame for personal failure on external factors, like luck. This is called the **self-serving bias** and suggests that feedback provided to employees in performance reviews will be predictably distorted by them, depending on whether it's positive or negative.

fundamental attribution error
The tendency to underestimate the influence of external factors and overestimate the influence of internal factors when making judgments about the behaviour of others.

self-serving bias
The tendency for individuals to attribute their own successes to internal factors, while putting the blame for failures on external factors.

Frequently Used Shortcuts in Judging Others

We use a number of shortcuts when we judge others. Perceiving and interpreting what others do is a lot of work. As a result, individuals develop techniques for making the task more manageable. These techniques are frequently valuable—they let us make accurate perceptions rapidly and provide valid data for making predictions. However, they're not foolproof. They can and do get us into trouble. An understanding of these shortcuts can be helpful for recognizing when they can result in significant distortions.

Individuals can't assimilate all they observe, so they engage in **selectivity**. They take in bits and pieces of the vast amounts of stimuli bombarding their senses. These bits and pieces aren't chosen randomly; rather, they are selectively chosen depending on the interests, background, experience, and attitudes of the observer. Selective perception allows us to "speed read" others, but not without the risk of drawing an inaccurate picture.

selectivity
The process by which people assimilate certain bits and pieces of what they observe, depending on their interests, background and attitudes.

It's easy to judge others if we assume they're similar to us. In **assumed similarity**, or the "like me" effect, the observer's perception of others is influenced more by the observer's own characteristics than by those of the person observed. For example, if you want challenges and responsibility in your job, you'll assume that others want the same. People who assume that others are like them can, of course, be correct, but most of the time they're wrong.

assumed similarity
The belief that others are like oneself.

When we judge someone on the basis of our perception of a group he or she is part of, we're using the shortcut called **stereotyping**. "Married people are more stable employees than single people" and "union people expect something for nothing" are examples of stereotyping. To the degree that a stereotype is based on fact, it may produce accurate judgments. However, many stereotypes have no foundation in fact. In such cases, stereotypes distort judgments.[27]

stereotyping
Judging a person on the basis of one's perception of a group to which he or she belongs.

When we form a general impression about a person based on a single characteristic such as intelligence, sociability or appearance, we're being influenced by the **halo effect**. This effect frequently occurs when students evaluate their classroom instructor. Students may isolate a single trait such as enthusiasm, and allow their entire evaluation to be slanted by their

halo effect
A general impression of an individual based on a single characteristic.

Stereotyping Keith Kocho by his age—as a member of the so-called slack Generation X—would result in a highly distorted judgment. Kocho started his multimedia company, Digital Renaissance, at the age of 21 and, 9 years later, it is among Canada's top 2000 companies.

perception of this one trait. An instructor might be quiet, assured, knowledgeable, and highly qualified, but if his classroom teaching style lacks zest, he might be rated lower on a number of other characteristics.

Implications for Managers

Managers need to recognize that their employees react to perceptions, not to reality. So, whether a manager's appraisal of an employee is *actually* objective and unbiased, or whether the organization's wage levels are *actually* among the highest in the industry, is less relevant than what employees *perceive* them to be. If individuals perceive appraisals to be biased or wage levels to be low, they'll behave as if these conditions actually exist. Employees organize and interpret what they see, and this creates the potential for perceptual distortion.

The message to managers should be clear: Pay close attention to how employees perceive both their jobs and management practices. Remember, the valuable employee who quits because of an *inaccurate perception* is just as great a loss to an organization as the valuable employee who quits for a *valid reason*.

LEARNING

The last individual behaviour concept we want to introduce in this chapter is learning. It's included for the obvious reason that almost all complex behaviour is learned. If we want to explain and predict behaviour, we need to understand how people learn.

What is learning? A psychologist's definition is considerably broader than the average person's view that "it's what we did when we went to school". In actuality, each of us is continually "going to school". Learning occurs all the time. We continuously learn from our experiences. A workable definition of **learning** is, therefore, any relatively permanent change in behaviour that occurs as a result of experience.

learning
Any relatively permanent change in behaviour that occurs as a result of experience.

Operant Conditioning

Operant conditioning argues that behaviour is a function of its consequences. People learn to behave in order to get something they want, or to avoid something they don't want. Operant behaviour describes voluntary or "learned" behaviour in contrast to reflexive or "unlearned" behaviour. The tendency to repeat such behaviour is influenced by the reinforcement or lack of reinforcement that happens as a result of the behaviour. Reinforcement, therefore, strengthens a behaviour and increases the likelihood that it will be repeated.

operant conditioning
A type of conditioning in which desired voluntary behaviour leads to a reward or prevents a punishment.

Building on earlier work in the field, B F Skinner's research has widely expanded our knowledge of operant conditioning.[28] Even his most outspoken critics, who represent a sizeable group, admit that his operant concepts work.

Behaviour is assumed to be determined from "without"—that is, learned—rather than from "within"—reflexive or unlearned. Skinner argued that if pleasing and desirable consequences follow specific forms of behaviour, the frequency of that behaviour will increase. People will most likely engage in desired behaviours if they're positively reinforced for doing so. And rewards are most effective if they immediately follow the desired response. In addition, behaviour that isn't rewarded, or is punished, is less likely to be repeated.

The B F Skinner Foundation
www.lafayette.edu/allanr/skinner.html

You see examples of operant conditioning everywhere. Any situation in which it's either explicitly stated or implicitly suggested that reinforcements (rewards) are contingent on some action on your part is an example of operant conditioning. Your instructor says that if you want a high grade in the course, you must give correct answers on the tests. A salesperson working on commission who wants to earn a sizeable income finds that this is contingent on generating high sales in his or her territory. Of course, the linkage between behaviour and reinforcement can also work to teach the individual to engage in behaviours that work against the best interests of the organization. Assume that your boss tells you that if you'll work overtime during the next three-week busy season, you'll be compensated for it at the next performance

5 What role does attribution theory play in perception?

6 Name four shortcuts used in judging others. What effect does each have on perception?

MANAGING WORKFORCE DIVERSITY

Challenging the Stereotypes of Women and Older Workers

What's your perception of women and older workers? Is it something like this: Women show less initiative than men on the job. They're less committed to their career and organization. And if you ask them to relocate, forget it. Typically, they won't, especially if they have children. And older workers! Older workers have higher absentee rates because they're often sick. That comes with age, you know. They're also slower, more accident prone, and tend to complain more than younger workers.

Well, if this fits your perception, you're wrong![29] Yet as long as these types of perceptions prevail, they hurt women and older workers and they hurt the organizations that need their skills.

The stereotype of women as uncommitted employees who won't stay with an organization or who won't relocate is just not true. The primary reason female professionals resign from their jobs is not because of home or child-rearing responsibilities—it's because of frustration with career progress. In fact, 73 percent of women who quit large companies moved to another company, while only 7 percent resigned to stay home.

Many young people's perceptions of older workers are also way off base. They stereotype them by describing workers over 55 in terms such as incompetent, past their prime, or slow to respond. The actual evidence suggests that they are, in reality, reliable, trained, and experienced. The facts confirm that older workers almost inevitably display significantly lower absenteeism than younger workers, have about half the accident rate of younger workers, and consistently score higher on job satisfaction. Moreover, there's no research evidence that age negatively affects job productivity.

Negative gender and ageist stereotypes not only adversely affect women and older workers, but are also likely to be a major handicap for organizations in the future. The projected shortage of skilled workers in North America and much of western Europe beginning in the early years of the next decade means that organizations will be desperately searching for employees who have skills and experience. Organizations that refuse to recognize that both women and older workers are a valuable labour resource will lose a large part of an increasingly smaller talent pool. ■

appraisal. However, when performance appraisal time comes, you find that you're given no positive reinforcement (such as praise for pitching in and helping out when needed). What will you do the next time your boss asks you to work overtime? You probably won't do it. Your behaviour can be explained by operant conditioning: If a behaviour isn't positively reinforced, the probability declines that the behaviour will be repeated.

Social Learning

Individuals can also learn by observing what happens to other people and just by being told about something, as well as by direct experiences. So, for example, much of what we've learned comes from watching models—parents, teachers, peers, television and movie performers, bosses, and so forth. This view that we can learn both through observation and direct experience has been called **social learning theory**.

social learning theory People can learn through observation and direct experience.

While social learning theory is an extension of operant conditioning—that is, it assumes that behaviour is a function of consequences—it also acknowledges the existence of observational learning and the importance of perception in learning. People respond to how they perceive and define consequences, not to the specific consequences themselves.

The influence of models is central to the social learning viewpoint. The amount of influence that a model will have on an individual is determined by four processes:

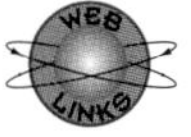

Albert Bandura's social learning theory
www.cmhc.com/psyhelp.chap4

1. *Attentional processes.* People learn from a model only when they recognize and pay attention to its crucial features. We tend to be most influenced by models who are attractive, who are repeatedly available, who we think are important, or who we see as similar to us.
2. *Retention processes.* A model's influence will depend on how well the individual remembers the model's action, even after the model is no longer readily available.

3. *Motor reproduction processes*. After a person has seen a new behaviour by observing the model, the watching must be converted to doing. This process then demonstrates that the individual can perform the modelled activities.

4. *Reinforcement processes*. Individuals will be motivated to exhibit the modelled behaviour if positive incentives or rewards are provided. Behaviours that are reinforced will be given more attention, learned better, and performed more often.

Shaping: A Managerial Tool

Because learning takes place on the job as well as prior to it, managers will be concerned with how they can teach employees to behave in ways that most benefit the organization. Thus, managers will often attempt to "mould" individuals by guiding their learning in graduated steps. This process is called **shaping behaviour**.

shaping behaviour
Systematically reinforcing each successive step that moves an individual closer to the desired response.

Consider the situation in which an employee's behaviour is significantly different from that sought by management. If management only reinforced the individual when he or she showed desirable responses, there might be very little reinforcement taking place. In such a case, shaping offers a logical approach towards achieving the desired behaviour.

We *shape* behaviour by systematically reinforcing each successive step that moves the individual closer to the desired response. If an employee who has chronically been a half-hour late for work comes in only twenty minutes late, we can reinforce this improvement. Reinforcement would increase as responses more closely reached the desired behaviour.

There are four ways to shape behaviour: positive reinforcement, negative reinforcement, punishment, or extinction. When a behaviour is followed with something pleasant, such as when a manager praises an employee for a job well done, it's called *positive reinforcement*. Rewarding a response with the elimination or withdrawal of something unpleasant is called *negative reinforcement*. Managers who habitually criticize their subordinates for taking extended coffee breaks are using negative reinforcement. The only way these employees stop the criticism is to shorten their breaks. *Punishment* penalizes undesirable behaviour. Suspending an employee for two days without pay for showing up at work drunk is an example of punishment. Eliminating any reinforcement that's maintaining a behaviour is called *extinction*. When a behaviour isn't reinforced, gradually it disappears. In meetings, managers who wish to discourage employees from continually asking irrelevant or distracting questions can eliminate this behaviour by ignoring these employees when they raise their hands to speak. Soon this behaviour will disappear.

Both positive and negative reinforcement result in learning. They strengthen a desired response and increase the probability of a behaviour being repeated. Both punishment and extinction also result in learning; however, they weaken behaviour and tend to decrease its frequency.

The mentoring relationship that we've discussed in earlier chapters is a good example of the role that social learning plays in organizations.

THINKING CRITICALLY ABOUT ETHICS

Is shaping behaviour a form of manipulative control? Suppose an employee does something that the organization judges to be wrong but that was motivated by a manager's control of rewards. Say, for instance, the employee fudges a sales report because bonuses are based on sales volume. Is that employee any less responsible for his or her actions than if such rewards had not been involved? Does management have any responsibility for the situation, due to the bonus policy? Explain your position. ■

Implications for Managers

Employees are going to learn on the job. The only issue then is whether managers are going to manage learning through the rewards they allocate and the examples they set, or allow it to occur haphazardly. If marginal employees are rewarded with pay raises and promotions, they'll have little reason to change their behaviour. In fact, other productive employees may see this and change their behaviour. If managers want behaviour A but reward behaviour B, it shouldn't surprise them to find employees "learning" to engage in behaviour B. Similarly, managers should expect that employees will look to them as models. Managers who are consistently late for work, take two hours for lunch, or help themselves to company office supplies for personal use should expect employees to read the message they're sending, and model their behaviour accordingly.

7 How could operant conditioning help a manager understand and predict behaviour?

8 What is social learning theory, and what are its implications for managing people at work?

9 How can managers"shape" employee behaviour?

SUMMARY

This summary is organized by the learning objectives found at the beginning of the chapter.

1. The field of organizational behaviour is concerned with the actions of people—managers and operatives alike—in organizations. By focusing on individual- and group-level concepts, OB seeks to explain and predict behaviour. Because they get things done through other people, managers will be more effective leaders if they have an understanding of behaviour.
2. An organization is like an iceberg because many of the behavioural issues are not obvious. What we tend to see when we look at organizations is their formal aspects such as strategies, objectives, policies, rules, and the like. However, there are also a number of "hidden" aspects that managers need to understand, such as attitudes and perceptions.
3. The three components of an attitude are cognitive, affective, and behavioural. The cognitive component consists of the beliefs, opinions, knowledge, or information held by a person. The affective component is the emotional or feeling segment of an attitude. Finally, the behavioural component is an intention to behave in a certain way towards someone or something.
4. People seek consistency among their attitudes and their behaviour. They seek to reconcile divergent attitudes, and to align their attitudes and behaviour so they appear rational and consistent.
5. The correlation between satisfaction and productivity tends to be low. The best evidence suggests that productivity leads to satisfaction rather than, as was popularly believed, the other way around.
6. The Myers-Briggs Type Indicator (or MBTI) is a personality assessment test that asks people how they usually act or feel in different situations. The way a person responds to the questions is combined into one of 16 different personality types. The MBTI can help managers to understand and predict people's behaviour.
7. Holland identified six basic personality types and six sets of congruent occupations. He found that when individuals were properly matched with occupations that were consistent with their personality types, they experienced high job satisfaction and exhibited lower job turnover rates.
8. Attribution theory can help to explain how we judge people differently depending on what meaning we attribute to a given behaviour. When we observe an individual's behaviour, we attempt to determine whether it was internally or externally caused. That determination is based on three factors: distinctiveness, consensus and consistency.
9. Managers use four shortcuts in judging others. Selectivity is the process by which people assimilate selected bits and pieces of what they observe, depending on their interests, background, and attitudes. Assumed similarity is the belief that others are like oneself. Stereotyping is judging a person on the basis of a group to which he or she belongs. The halo effect is a general impression of an individual based on a single characteristic.
10. Managers can shape or mould employee behaviour by systematically reinforcing each successive step that moves the employee closer to the desired behaviour.

THINKING ABOUT MANAGEMENT ISSUES

1. How could you use personality traits to improve employee selection?
2. Given that perception affects behaviour, do you think there's anything management can do to reduce employees' perceptual distortion?
3. How could managers minimize their tendency to stereotype individuals?
4. "Managers should never use discipline with a problem employee." Do you agree or disagree? Discuss.
5. How important do you think knowledge of OB is to low-, middle-, and upper-level managers? What type of OB knowledge do you think is most important to each? Why?

SELF-ASSESSMENT EXERCISE

WHAT'S YOUR PERSONALITY TYPE?

Here's a short, modified version of the MBTI. Mark your responses to the following questionnaire on a separate sheet of paper. Keep in mind that there are no right or wrong answers to any of these items.

Part I. Circle the response that comes closest to how you usually feel or act.

1. I am more careful about:
   A. People's feelings.
   B. Their rights.

2. I usually get on better with:
   A. Imaginative people.
   B. Realistic people.

3. It is a higher compliment to be called:
   A. A person of real feeling.
   B. A consistently reasonable person.

4. In doing something with many people, it appeals more to me:
   A. To do it in the accepted way.
   B. To invent a way of my own.

5. I get more annoyed with:
   A. Fancy theories.
   B. People who do not like theories.

6. It is higher praise to call someone:
   A. A person of vision.
   B. A person of common sense.

7. I more often let:
   A. My heart rule my head.
   B. My head rule my heart.

8. I think it is a worse fault:
   A. To show too much warmth.
   B. To be unsympathetic.

9. If I were a teacher, I would rather teach:
   A. Courses involving theory.
   B. Fact courses.

Part II. Which word in each of the following pairs appeals to you more? Circle a or b.

	a	b
10.	a. Compassion	b. Foresight
11.	a. Justice	b. Mercy
12.	a. Production	b. Design
13.	a. Gentle	b. Firm
14.	a. Uncritical	b. Critical
15.	a. Literal	b. Figurative
16.	a. Imaginative	b. Matter-of-fact

For scoring information, turn to page SK-4.

Source: Adapted from the Myers-Briggs Type Indicator, I Myers, *The Myers-Briggs Type Indicator* (Princeton, NJ: Educational Testing Service, 1962), cited in D. Hellriegel, J W Slocum, Jr., and R W Woodman, *Organizational Behaviour*, 3rd ed. (St. Paul, MN: West, 1983), pp. 128–143.

for your IMMEDIATE action

TO: Michelle DePriest, Executive Vice President, Finance
FR: Aaron Sigler, President
RE: Hiring a Corporate Controller

As we discussed last Friday, our revenues—and consequently our manufacturing operations—have grown to the point where we need to hire a person for a newly created position, Corporate Controller. This person will be responsible for establishing needed operational and financial standards (such as the number of labour hours and other standard costs to manufacture entertainment centre shelving or any other wood furniture) for our various work units. This person will be working with financial and manufacturing statistics to establish these standards, so he or she should have a background in accounting, finance, or operations management.

I recall something from my management class in university about how certain personality types fit best with certain types of jobs. would you do some research on this for me and write up a short report, describing the type of personality you think might be an appropriate match for this position and why? Please get this in to me by the end of the week.

This is a fictionalized account of a potentially real situation, written for academic purposes only.

TAKE IT TO THE NET

We invite you to visit the Robbins/Coulter/Stuart-Kotze Companion Website at www.prenticehall.ca/robbins for this chapter's Internet resources.

CASE APPLICATION

Petofi Printing & Packaging Co., Keckskemet, Hungary

Petofi is a manufacturer of cardboard boxes, wrappers, and other types of containers. Only a few years ago, the operation was running something like this: both managers and line workers would begin drinking schnapps in the morning and, by 11 a.m., "everyone was in the bag"; flies would be stuck all over the painted cardboard; containers were delivered to customers in the wrong colours and sizes; and worker absenteeism was ridiculously high. Obviously, Petofi needed to change. New top managers were brought in. With a $35 million cash infusion, new state-of-the-art production equipment was installed. But the biggest challenge was bringing the workforce in line with the new corporate culture that management was trying to create.

The workforce was whipped into shape by a combination of inducements and threats. The new managers offered workers huge incentives to improve their performance—a 40 percent pay raise, year-end bonuses and better working conditions. They also brought customers into the shop floor and took employees to trade shows to teach them about the importance of quality. If workers still didn't get the quality message, managers reminded them. If a customer rejected a product shipment, the mistake was traced back to the workers responsible and their wages were docked. If a worker was caught drinking alcohol on the job, a third of his or her monthly salary was deducted. If an offence was serious enough, the worker was fired—and this was a strong deterrent in a city with double-digit unemployment. All of these tactics have paid off handsomely. Petofi has won awards from the World Packaging Association, and its customers now include well-known, worldwide companies.

QUESTIONS

1. What do you think caused the original sloppy behaviour described at Petofi?
2. How have Petofi's managers used the process of shaping behaviour?
3. Can you see any use of social learning theory in this Case Application? Discuss.
4. Would you expect employees to exhibit higher or lower job satisfaction after the changes than before.

Source: D Millbank, "East Europe's Industry Is Raising Its Quality and Taking on The West", *Wall Street Journal,* September 21, 1994, pp. A1+.

LEARNING OBJECTIVES

After Reading This Chapter, You Should Be Able To:

1 Contrast formal and informal groups
2 Explain why people join groups
3 Describe the five stages of group development
4 Identify how roles and norms influence an employee's behaviour
5 Describe the key components in the group behaviour model
6 Explain the increased popularity of teams in organizations
7 Describe the different types of teams found in organizations
8 List the characteristics of effective teams
9 Identify how managers can build trust
10 Describe what activities are associated with managing teams
11 Explain the role of teams in TQM

A MANAGER'S CHALLENGE

Algoma Steel, Sault Ste. Marie, Ontario

In the early 1990s, Algoma Steel was a division of Dofasco, and was suffering under a debt of $800 million. The only way Dofasco was going to keep the plant open was if the workers agreed to major wage concessions. The union rejected Dofasco's proposal and countered with a novel one of its own: the workers would take a $10-million-a-year wage cutback in return for 60 percent ownership in Algoma. The plan was backed by a government restructuring of the company's debt.[1]

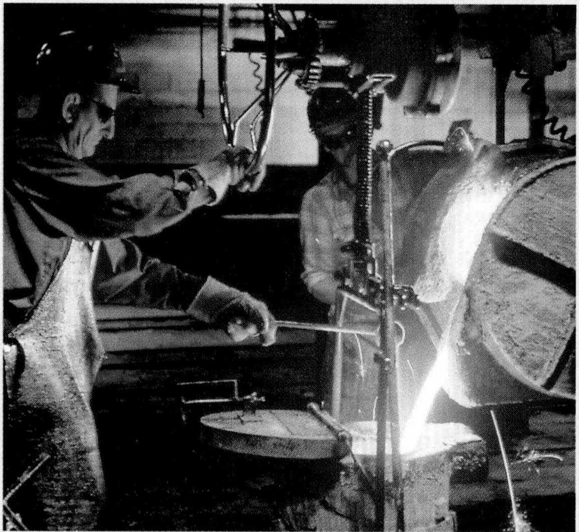

The Steelworkers Union decided that, while it would have four directors on the thirteen-member board, it did not actually want to manage Algoma. Steve Boniferro, a union leader, commented, "Somebody has to be looking after the business and, quite frankly, we aren't trained, prepared, or interested in looking after the business. We want to balance what's best for the company with what's best for the workers". The philosophy at Algoma today is based on the balance of a "strong, independent union and a strong, independent management".

Self-directed work groups have replaced the old command-and-control structure. These work teams are empowered to deal with everything from determining their own vacation schedules to redesigning their workplaces. Costs have been cut, productivity has increased, and the workforce has actually grown. After nearly being written off as bankrupt in the early 1990s, Algoma was reporting revenues of $1.2 billion as of 1998.

Thousands of organizations such as Algoma have made the move to restructure work around groups rather than individuals. Why has this occurred? What do these teams look like? How can interested managers build effective teams? These are some of the types of questions we'll be answering in this chapter. First, however, let's begin by developing our understanding of group behaviour.

CHAPTER 14

Understanding Groups and Teams

UNDERSTANDING GROUP BEHAVIOUR

The behaviour of individuals in groups is not merely the sum total of the behaviour of the individuals in that group. Why? Because people act differently in groups from the way they do when they're alone. Therefore, if we want to understand organizational behaviour more fully, we need to study groups.

What Is a Group?

group
Two or more interacting and interdependent individuals who come together to achieve particular objectives.

A **group** is defined as two or more interacting and interdependent individuals who come together to achieve particular objectives. Groups can be either formal or informal. *Formal groups* are work groups established by the organization that have designated work assignments and specific tasks. In formal groups, appropriate behaviours are stipulated by, and directed towards, organizational goals. Table 14-1 provides some examples of different types of formal groups used in organizations today.

In contrast, *informal* groups are of a social nature. These groups occur naturally in the work environment, in response to the need for social contact. Informal groups tend to form around friendships and common interests.

Stages of Group Development

Group development is a dynamic process. Most groups are in a continual state of change. But even though groups probably never reach complete stability, there's a general pattern that describes how most groups evolve. Research on groups shows that groups pass through a standard sequence of five stages.[2] As shown in Figure 14-1, these five stages include *forming, storming, norming, performing* and *adjourning*.

forming
The first stage in group development during which people join the group and then define the group's purpose, structure and leadership; characterized by uncertainty.

The first stage, **forming**, has two aspects. In the first, people are joining the group, either because of a work assignment in the case of a formal group, or because of some other benefit desired in the case of an informal group. Figure 14-2 depicts the reasons why people join groups.

Once the group's membership is in place, then the second part of the forming stage begins—the task of defining the group's purpose, structure and leadership. This phase is characterized by a great deal of uncertainty. Members are "testing the waters" to determine what types of behaviour are acceptable. This stage is complete when members begin to think of themselves as part of a group.

storming
The second stage of group development, characterized by intragroup conflict.

The **storming** stage is one of intragroup conflict. Members accept the existence of the group, but there's resistance to the control that the group imposes on individuality. Further, there's conflict over who will control the group. When this stage is complete, there will be a relatively clear hierarchy of leadership within the group, and agreement on the group's direction.

TABLE 14-1 Examples of Formal Groups

Command groups. These are the basic, traditional work groups determined by formal authority relationships and depicted on the organizational chart. They typically include a manager and those subordinates who report directly to him or her.

Cross-functional teams. These bring together the knowledge and skills of individuals from various work areas, in order to come up with solutions to operational problems. Cross-functional teams also include groups whose members have been trained to do each other's jobs.

Self-managed teams. These are essentially independent groups that, in addition to doing their operating jobs, take on traditional management responsibilities such as hiring, planning and scheduling, and performance evaluations.

Task forces. These are temporary groups created to accomplish a specific task. Once the task is complete, the group is disbanded.

FIGURE 14-1 Stages of Group Development

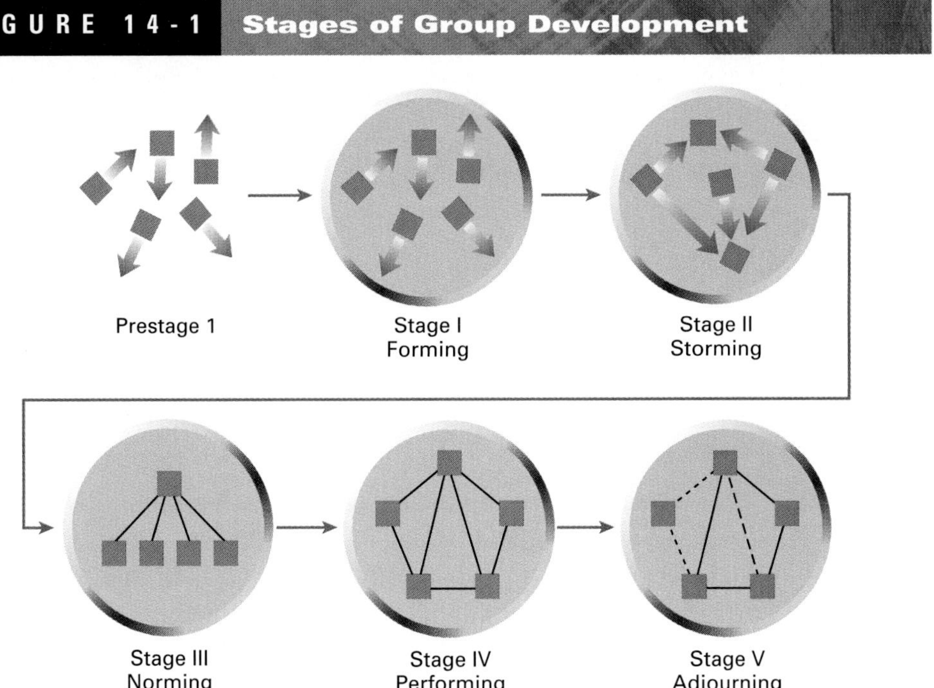

The third stage is one in which close relationships develop and the group demonstrates cohesiveness. There's now a strong sense of group identity and camaraderie. This **norming** stage is complete when the group structure solidifies, and the group has assimilated a common set of expectations of what defines correct member behaviour.

The fourth stage is **performing**. The group structure at this point is fully functional and accepted. Group energy has moved from getting to know and understand each other to performing the task at hand.

For permanent work groups, performing is the last stage in their development. However, for temporary committees, task forces teams, and similar groups that have a limited task to perform, there's an **adjourning** stage. In this stage, the group prepares for its disbandment. High levels of task performance are no longer the group's top priority. Instead, attention is directed towards wrapping up activities. Responses of group members vary at this stage. Some are upbeat, basking in the group's accomplishments. Others may be depressed over the loss of camaraderie and friendships gained during the work group's life.

Most of you have probably experienced each of these stages in a group project for a class. Group members are selected and then meet for the first time. There's a "feeling out" period to assess what the group is going to do and how it's going to do it. This is usually rapidly followed

norming
The third stage of group development, characterized by close relationships and cohesiveness.

performing
The fourth stage in group development, when the group is fully functional.

adjourning
The final stage in group development for temporary groups, characterized by concern with wrapping up activities rather than task performance.

FIGURE 14-2 Why People Join Groups

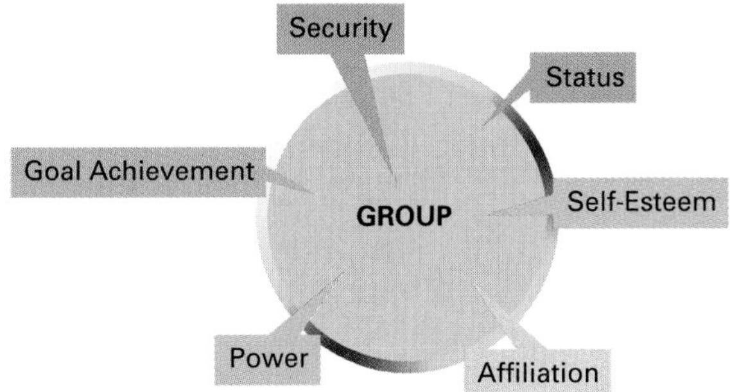

The organizing committee for the 1998 Olympic Winter Games held in Nagano, Japan, had a great deal of responsibility and needed to build cohesiveness quickly. Invitations to participate in the games were sent out in February 1997, shortly after this photo was made.

by a battle for control: Who's going to be in charge? Once this is resolved and a "hierarchy" is agreed on, the group identifies specific aspects of the task, who's going to do them, and dates by which the assigned work needs to be completed. General expectations are established and agreed on for each member. This forms the foundation for what you hope will be a co-ordinated group effort culminating in a job well done. Once the group project is complete and turned in, the group breaks up. Of course, groups occasionally don't get much beyond the first or second stage, which typically results in disappointing projects and grades.

Should you assume from the preceding discussion that a group becomes more effective as it progresses through the first four stages? Some argue that effectiveness of work groups increases at advanced stages, but it's not that simple.[3] Although this assumption may be generally true, what makes a group effective is a complex issue. Under some conditions, high levels of conflict are conducive to high levels of group performance. We might expect to find situations in which groups in Stage II outperform those in Stages III or IV. Similarly, groups don't always proceed clearly from one stage to the next. Sometimes, in fact, several stages may be going on simultaneously, as when groups are storming and performing at the same time. Groups even occasionally regress to previous stages. Therefore, one shouldn't always assume that all groups precisely follow this developmental process, or that Stage IV is always the most preferable. It's better to think of this model as a general framework. It reminds you that groups are dynamic entities and can help you to better understand the problems and issues that are most likely to surface during a group's life.

Basic Group Concepts

In this section we introduce a number of concepts to help you to begin to understand group behaviour. These are *roles, norms and conformity, status systems, group size,* and *group cohesiveness.*

Roles. We introduced the concept of roles in Chapter 1 when we discussed what managers do. Of course, managers aren't the only individuals in an organization who have roles. The concept of roles applies to all employees in organizations and to their life outside the organization as well.

role
A set of behaviour patterns expected of someone occupying a given position in a social unit.

A **role** refers to a set of expected behaviour patterns attributed to someone who occupies a given position in a social unit. Individuals play multiple roles, adjusting their roles to the group to which they belong at the time. In an organization, employees attempt to determine what behaviours are expected of them. They'll read their job descriptions, get suggestions from their boss, and watch what their co-workers do. An individual who's confronted by divergent role expectations experiences *role conflict.* Employees in organizations often face such role conflicts. The credit manager expects her credit analysts to process a minimum of 30 applications a week, but the work group pressures members to restrict output to 20 a week, so that everyone has work to do and no one gets laid off. A young professor's colleagues want him to give very few high grades in order to maintain the department's "tough standards" reputation, whereas students want him to give out lots of high grades to enhance their grade point averages. To the degree that the professor sincerely seeks to satisfy the expectations of both his colleagues and his students, he faces role conflict.

Norms and Conformity. All groups have established **norms**, or acceptable standards that are shared by the group's members. Norms dictate things like output levels, absenteeism rates, promptness or tardiness, and the amount of socializing allowed on the job.

norms
Acceptable standards shared by a group's members.

Norms, for example, dictate the "arrival ritual" among scheduling clerks at one national steel plant. The workday begins at 8 a.m. Most employees typically arrive a few minutes before and put their jackets, purses, lunch bags, or similar personal items on their chairs or desks, to prove they're "at work"; they then proceed down to the company cafeteria to get coffee and chat. Employees who violate this norm by starting work sharply at 8 are teased and pressured until their behaviour conforms to the group's standard.

Although each group will have its own unique set of norms, there are common classes of norms that appear in most organizations. These focus on effort and performance, dress, and loyalty.

Probably the most widespread norms relate to levels of effort and performance. Work groups typically provide their members with very explicit cues on how hard to work, what level of output to have, when to look busy, when it's acceptable to "goof off", and the like. These norms are extremely powerful in affecting an individual employee's performance. They're so powerful that performance predictions that are based solely on an employee's ability and level of personal motivation often prove to be wrong.

Some organizations have formal dress codes. However, even in their absence, norms frequently develop that dictate the kind of clothing that should be worn to work. University seniors, interviewing for their first postgraduate job, discover this norm very quickly. Every semester on university campuses, those interviewing for jobs can usually be spotted—they're the ones walking around in the dark gray or blue pinstriped suits. They're enacting the dress norms they've learned are expected in professional positions. Of course, what's acceptable dress in one organization may be very different from what's expected in another.

Few managers appreciate employees who belittle the organization. Similarly, professional employees and those in the executive ranks recognize that most employers view unfavourably those who actively look for another job while they are still employed at the current organization. If such people are unhappy, they know to keep their job searches secret. These examples demonstrate that loyalty norms are widespread in organizations. This concern for demonstrating loyalty, by the way, often explains why ambitious individuals who aspire to top management positions willingly take work home at night, come in on weekends, and accept transfers to cities where they'd otherwise prefer not to live.

Because people desire acceptance by the groups to which they belong, they're susceptible to conformity pressures. The impact that group pressures for conformity can have on an individual member's judgment and attitudes was demonstrated in the classic studies by Solomon Asch.[4] Asch made up groups of seven or eight people who sat in a classroom and were asked to compare two cards held by the experimenter. One card had one line, the other had three lines of varying length. As shown in Figure 14-3, one of the lines on the three-line card was identical to the line on the one-line card. Also, as shown in Figure in 14-3, the difference in line length was quite obvious. The object was to announce aloud which of the three lines matched the single line. Under ordinary conditions, fewer than 1 percent of subjects made errors in identifying which lines were the same length. But what would happen if all the members in the group began to give incorrect answers? Would the pressures to conform result in the unsuspecting subject (USS) altering his or her answers to align with the others? That's what Asch wanted to know. So he arranged the group so that only the USS was unaware that the experiment was "fixed". The seating was prearranged so the USS was the last to announce his or her decision.

The experiment began with several sets of matching exercises in which all the subjects gave the right answers. On the third set, however, the first subject gave an obviously wrong answer—for example, saying "C" in Figure 14-3. The next subject gave the same wrong answer, and so did the others until it was the USS's turn. He knew "B" was the same as "X", yet everyone had said "C". The decision confronting the USS was this: Do you state a percep-

FIGURE 14-3 Examples of Cards Used in the Asch Study

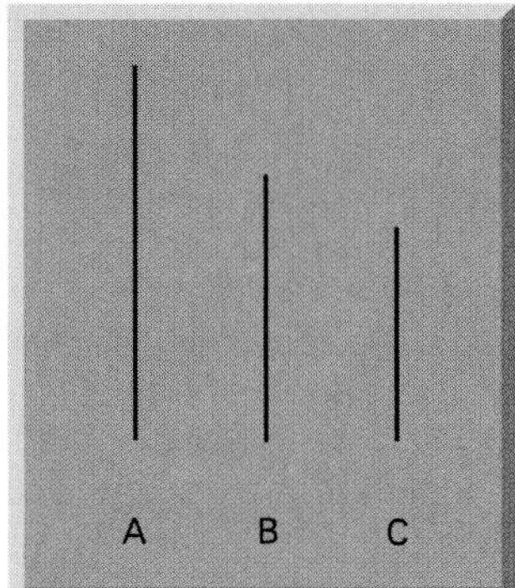

tion publicly that differs from the pre-announced position of the other group members? Or do you give an answer that you strongly believe is incorrect in order to be in agreement with the other group members?

The results demonstrated that over many experiments and trials, subjects conformed in about 35 percent of the trials; that is, the USS gave answers that he or she knew were wrong, but which were consistent with the replies of other group members.

What can we conclude from this study? The results suggest that there are group norms that pressurize us to conform. We desire to be one of the group and avoid being visibly different. We can generalize further to say that when an individual's opinion of objective data differs significantly from that of others in the group, he or she feels extensive pressure to align his or her opinion to conform with those of the others.

status
A prestige grading, position, or rank within a group.

Status Systems. **Status** is a prestige grading, position or rank within a group. As far back as researchers have been able to trace human groups, they've found status hierarchies. Status systems are an important factor in understanding behaviour. Status is a significant motivator, and has behavioural consequences when individuals see a disparity between what they perceive their status to be and what others perceive it to be.

Status may be informally conferred by characteristics such as education, age, skill or experience. Anything can have status value if others in the group evaluate it that way. Of course, just because status is informal doesn't mean that it's less important, or that there is less agreement on who has it or who doesn't. Members of groups have no problem placing people in status categories, and they usually agree closely about who is high, low, and in the middle.

It's important for employees to believe that the organization's formal status system is congruent. That is, there should be equity between the perceived ranking of an individual and the

THINKING CRITICALLY ABOUT ETHICS

You have been hired as a summer intern in the auditing section of an accounting firm. After working there for about a month, you conclude that the attitude in the office is that "anything goes". Employees know that supervisors won't discipline them for ignoring company rules. For example, employees have to turn in expense accounts, but the process is a joke—nobody submits receipts to verify reimbursement, and nothing is ever said. In fact, when you try to turn in your receipts with your expense report, you are told: "Nobody else turns in their receipts, and you don't need to either". No expense report has ever been denied because of failure to turn in a receipt, even though the employee handbook says that receipts are required. Also, your co-workers use company phones for personal long-distance calls, even though this is also "officially" prohibited. And one permanent employee tells you to take any office supplies you might need at home, such as paper, pens and folders.

What are the norms of this group? Suppose that you were the supervisor in this area. How would you go about changing the norms? ■

Their musical talent is undisputed. Combine it with extraordinary cohesiveness and you get the Tokyo String Quartet, one of the world's foremost musical ensembles. (Left to right: violinists Peter Oundjian and Kikuei Ikeda, cellist Sadao Harada, and violist Kazuhide Isomura.)

status symbols he or she is given by the organization. For instance, status incongruence occurs when a supervisor is earning less than his or her subordinates, a desirable office is occupied by a lower-ranking position, or paid country club membership is provided by the company for division managers but not for vice presidents. Employees expect the "things" an individual has and receives to be congruent with his or her status. When they're not, employees are likely to reject the authority of their superiors, the motivation potential of promotions decreases, and the general pattern of order and consistency in the organization is disturbed.

Group Size. Does the size of a group affect the group's overall behaviour? The answer to this question is a definite yes, but the effect depends on the outcomes on which you focus.[5]

The evidence indicates, for instance, that small groups are faster at completing tasks than are larger ones. However, if the group is engaged in problem solving, large groups consistently get better marks than smaller ones. Translating these results into specific numbers is a bit more troublesome, but we can offer some guidelines. Large groups—those with a dozen or more members—are good for gaining diverse input. Thus, if the goal of the group is finding facts, larger groups should be more effective. On the other hand, smaller groups are better at doing something productive with those facts. Groups of approximately seven members tend to be more effective for taking action.

One of the more disturbing findings related to group size is that, as groups get incrementally larger, the contribution of individual members often tends to decrease.[6] That is, while the total productivity of a group of four is generally greater than that of a group of three, the individual productivity of each group member declines as the group expands. Thus, a group of four will tend to produce at a level less than four times that of an average individual performance. The best explanation for this reduction of effort is a phenomenon known as the **free rider tendency**. The dispersion of responsibility within a group encourages individuals to slack off. When the results of the group can't be attributed to any one person, the relationship between

free rider tendency
The reduction of effort that individual members contribute to the group as it increases in size.

1 **Describe the five stages of group development.**

2 **What is the influence of roles on group behaviour?**

3 **How can group norms both help and hurt an organization?**

TESTING... TESTING...

an individual's input and the group's output is clouded. In such situations, individuals may be tempted to become "free riders" and coast on the group's efforts. In other words, there will be a reduction in efficiency when individuals think that their contributions can't be measured. The obvious conclusion from this finding is that when managers use work teams they should also provide means for identifying individual efforts.

group cohesiveness
The degree to which members are attracted to one another and share the group's goals.

Group Cohesiveness. Intuitively, it makes sense that groups in which there's a lot of internal disagreement and lack of co-operation are less effective in completing their tasks than groups in which members generally agree, co-operate, and like each other. Research in this area has focused on **group cohesiveness**, or the degree to which members are attracted to one another and share the group's goals. The more the members are attracted to one another and the more the group's goals align with their individual goals, the greater the group's cohesiveness.

Research has generally shown that highly cohesive groups are more effective than those with less cohesiveness,[7] but the relationship between cohesiveness and effectiveness is more complex. A key moderating variable is the degree to which the group's attitude aligns with its formal goals, or those of the larger organization of which it is a part.[8] The more cohesive a group is, the more its members will follow its goals. If these goals are desirable (for instance, high output, quality work, or co-operation with individuals outside the group), a cohesive group is more productive than a less cohesive group. But if cohesiveness is high and attitudes are unfavourable, productivity decreases. If cohesiveness is low and goals are supported, productivity increases—but not as much as when both cohesiveness and support are high. When cohesiveness is low and goals aren't supported, cohesiveness has no significant effect on productivity. These conclusions are summarized in Figure 14-4.

conflict
Perceived incompatible differences that result in interference or opposition.

traditional view of conflict
The view that all conflict is bad and must be avoided.

human relations view of conflict
The view that conflict is a natural and inevitable outcome in any group.

interactionist view of conflict
The view that some conflict is necessary for a group to perform effectively.

Conflict Management. As a group performs its assigned tasks, disagreements or conflicts will inevitably arise. When we use the term **conflict**, we're referring to *perceived* incompatible differences resulting in some form of interference or opposition. Whether the differences are real or not is irrelevant. If people in a group perceive that differences exist, then a conflict state exists. In addition, our definition includes the extremes, from subtle, indirect, and highly controlled forms of interference to overt acts such as strikes, riots and wars.

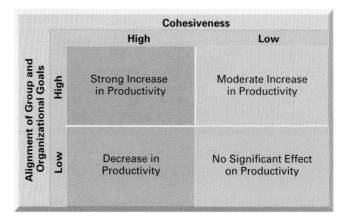

Over the years, three different views have evolved regarding conflict. One view argues that conflict must be avoided; that it indicates a malfunctioning or problem within the group. We call this the **traditional view of conflict**. A second view, the **human relations view of conflict**, argues that conflict is a natural and inevitable outcome in any group and that it need not be negative but, rather, has the potential to be a positive force in contributing to a work group's performance. The third and most recent perspective proposes not only that conflict can be a positive force in a group, but also that some conflict is *absolutely necessary* for a group to perform effectively. We label this third approach the **interactionist view of conflict**.

FIGURE 14-4 The Relationship Between Cohesiveness and Productivity

Alignment of Group and Organizational Goals	Cohesiveness: High	Cohesiveness: Low
High	Strong Increase in Productivity	Moderate Increase in Productivity
Low	Decrease in Productivity	No Significant Effect on Productivity

The interactionist view does not propose that all conflicts are good. Some conflicts are seen as supporting the goals of the work group; these are **functional conflicts**, and they're of a constructive nature. Other conflicts prevent a group from achieving its goals; these are **dysfunctional conflicts**, and are destructive forms.

functional conflicts Conflicts that support a group's goals.

dysfunctional conflicts Conflicts that prevent a group from achieving its goals.

Of course, it's one thing to argue that conflict can be valuable, but how does a manager tell whether group conflict is functional or dysfunctional? Unfortunately, the differentiation isn't clear or precise. No one level of conflict can be adopted as acceptable or unacceptable under all conditions. The type and level of conflict that will promote a healthy and positive involvement towards one group's goals may, in another group or in the same group at another time, be highly dysfunctional. Functionality or dysfunctionality, therefore, is a matter of judgment. Figure 14-5 illustrates the challenge facing managers. They want to create an environment in which group conflict is healthy but not allowed to run to extremes. Neither too little nor too much conflict is desirable. Managers should stimulate conflict to gain the full benefits of its functional properties, yet reduce its level when it becomes a disruptive force.[9] Because we have yet to devise a sophisticated measuring instrument for assessing whether a given conflict level is functional or dysfunctional, the manager must make intelligent judgments concerning whether conflict levels in work groups are either optimal, too high, or too low.

What resolution tools or techniques can a manager call upon to reduce conflict when it is too high? Managers can essentially draw upon five conflict-resolution options: avoidance, accommodation, forcing, compromise and collaboration.[10] Each has particular strengths and weaknesses, and no one option is ideal for every situation. You should consider each one a "tool" in your conflict-management "tool chest". Although you might be better at using some tools than others, the skilled manager knows what each tool can do, and when each is likely to be most effective.

FIGURE 14-5 Conflict and Group Performance

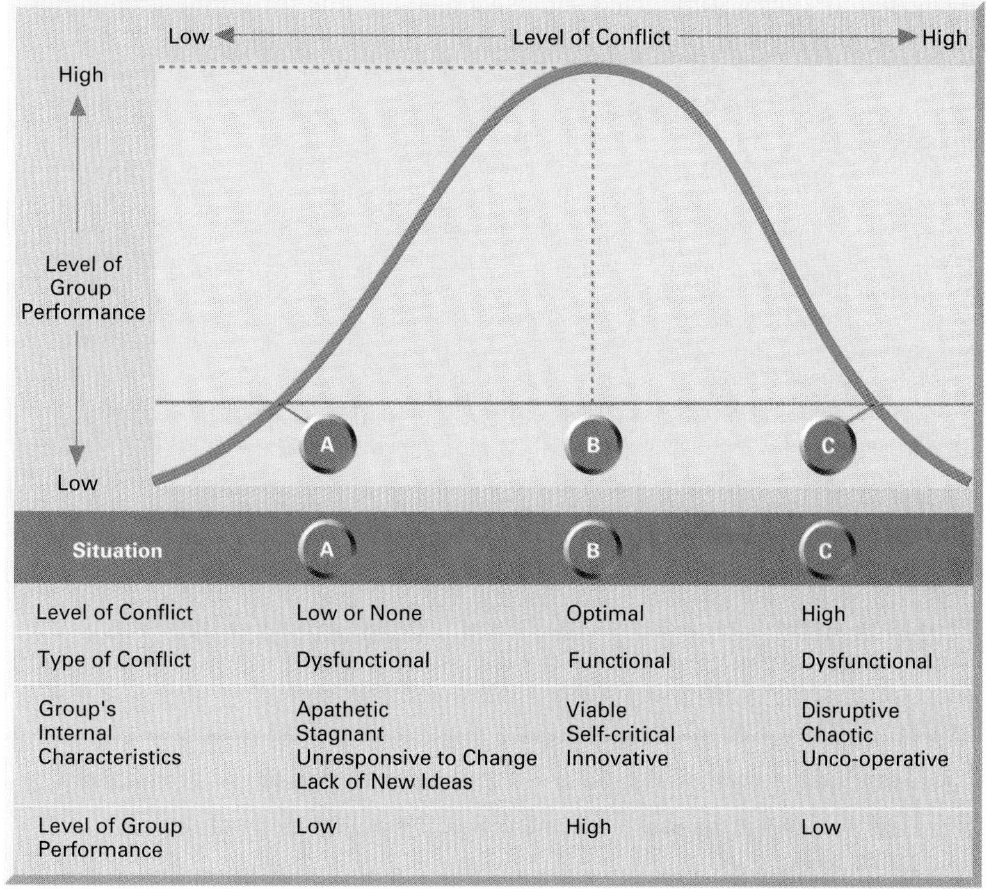

Situation	A	B	C
Level of Conflict	Low or None	Optimal	High
Type of Conflict	Dysfunctional	Functional	Dysfunctional
Group's Internal Characteristics	Apathetic Stagnant Unresponsive to Change Lack of New Ideas	Viable Self-critical Innovative	Disruptive Chaotic Unco-operative
Level of Group Performance	Low	High	Low

avoidance
Withdrawal from or suppression of conflict.

Not every conflict requires an assertive action. Sometimes **avoidance**—just withdrawing from or suppressing the conflict—is the best solution. Avoidance is most appropriate when conflict is trivial—when emotions are running high and time is needed for the conflicting parties to cool down, or when the potential disruption from an assertive action outweighs the benefits of resolution.

accommodation
Resolving conflicts by placing the needs and concerns of another above one's own.

The goal of **accommodation** is to maintain harmonious relationships by placing the needs of another above your own. You might, for example, yield to another person's position on an issue. This option is most viable when the issue under dispute isn't that important to you, or when you want to "build up credits" for later issues.

forcing
Satisfying one's own needs at the expense of another person's needs.

In **forcing**, you attempt to satisfy your own needs at the expense of the other party. In organizations, this is most often illustrated when a manager uses his or her formal authority to resolve a dispute. Forcing works well when you need a quick resolution on important issues for which unpopular actions must be taken, and when commitment by others to your solution isn't critical.

compromise
A solution to conflict in which each party gives up something of value.

A **compromise** requires each party to give up something of value. Typically, this is the approach taken by management and labour in negotiating a new labour contract. Compromise can be an optimal strategy when conflicting parties are about equal in power, when it is desirable to achieve a temporary solution to a complex issue, or when time pressures demand an expedient solution.

collaboration
Resolving conflict by seeking a solution advantageous to all parties.

Finally, **collaboration** offers the ultimate win-win solution. All parties in the conflict seek to satisfy their interests. Collaboration is typically characterized by open and honest discussion among the parties, active listening to understand differences, and careful deliberation over a full range of alternatives to find a solution that is advantageous to all. Collaboration is the best conflict option when time pressures are minimal, when all parties seriously want a win-win solution, and when the issue is too important to be compromised.

informal communication
Communication that exists outside the organization's formally authorized communication channels.

Informal Communication. How do work groups get the information they need to perform their tasks, and how do work groups communicate both within the group and with other work groups? Although there are formal communication channels that work groups may use, many times **informal communication**—that is, communication that exists outside the organization's formally authorized communication channels—is preferred. Informal communication serves two purposes for groups: (1) Employees can satisfy their need for social interaction; and (2) group performance can be improved through these alternative—and frequently faster and more efficient—communication channels.

the grapevine
The informal communication network.

The informal communication network is better known by the name **the grapevine**, and is active in almost every organization. Information, both within a work group and between work groups, will flow along the grapevine. Managers often find the grapevine valuable for identifying issues that employees consider important, and that are creating anxiety among them. The grapevine can also serve as both a filter and feedback mechanism for managers, by highlighting issues that employees consider relevant and by planting messages that managers want employees to hear.

Towards Understanding Work Group Behaviour

Why are some groups more successful than others? The answer to that question is complex, but it includes variables such as the abilities of the group's members, the size of the group, the level of conflict, and the internal pressures on members to conform to the group's norms. Figure 14-6 presents the major components that determine group performance and satisfaction.[11] It can help you to sort out the key variables and their interrelationships.

External Conditions Imposed on the Group. To begin to understand the behaviour of a formal work group, we need to view it as a subsystem of a larger system.[12] When we accept

4 **Describe the relationship between group cohesiveness and productivity.**

5 **How do conflict management and informal communication influence group behaviour?**

FIGURE 14-6 Group Behaviour Model

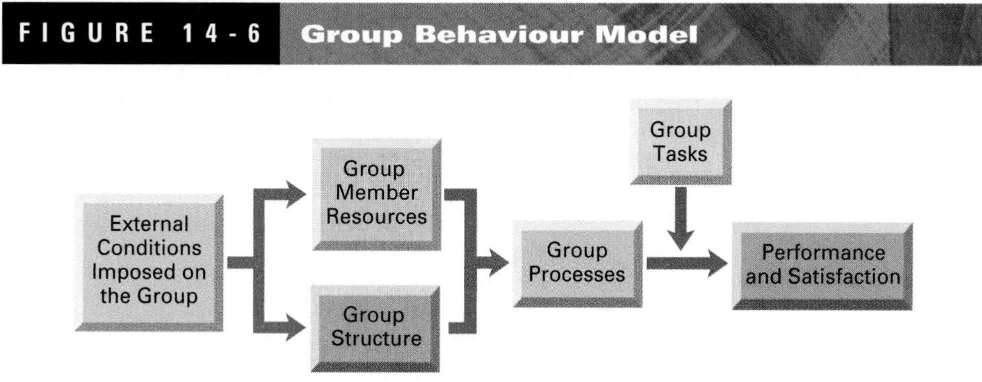

that formal groups are subsets of a larger organization system, we can extract part of the explanation of the group's behaviour from an explanation of the organization. For instance, a product quality control team at a food plant might have to live within the rules and policies dictated by the plant's management, by division headquarters in another city, and by corporate offices in another province. Every work group is influenced by external conditions imposed from outside.

What are some of these external conditions? They include the organization's overall strategy, authority structures, formal regulations, the availability or absence of organization-wide resources, employee selection criteria, the organization's performance evaluation and reward system, the organization's culture, and the general physical layout of the group's work space, set by the organization's industrial engineers and office designers.

Group Member Resources. A group's potential level of performance depends to a large extent on the resources that its members individually bring to the group. This would include members' abilities and personality characteristics.

Part of a group's performance can be predicted by assessing the task-relevant and intellectual abilities of its individual members. We do occasionally read about an athletic team composed of mediocre players who, because of excellent coaching, determination, and precision teamwork, beat a far more talented group of players. Such cases make the news precisely because they are aberrations. Group performance isn't merely the summation of its individual members' abilities. However, these abilities set parameters for what members can do, and for how effectively they will perform in a group.

There has been a great deal of research on the relationship between personality traits and group attitudes and behaviours. The general conclusion is that attributes that tend to have a positive connotation in our culture tend to be positively related to group productivity and morale. These include traits such as sociability, self-reliance and independence. In contrast, negative characteristics such as authoritarianism, dominance and unconventionality tend to be negatively related to productivity and morale.[13] These personality traits affect group performance by strongly influencing how the individual will interact with other group members.

Group Structure. Work groups aren't unorganized mobs. They have a structure that shapes members' behaviour and makes it possible to explain and predict a larger portion of individual behaviour within the group, as well as the performance of the group itself. These structure variables include roles, norms, status, group size and leadership. We've already discussed roles, norms, status and size in this chapter, and leadership will be covered in Chapter 16, so we don't need to elaborate on these variables here. Just keep in mind that every work group has an internal structure that defines member roles, norms, status, group size, and formal leadership positions.

Group Processes. The next component in our group behaviour model concerns the processes that go on within a work group—the communication patterns used by members to exchange information, group decision processes, leader behaviour, power dynamics, conflict interactions, and the like.

Why are processes important to understanding work group behaviour? Because in groups, one and one don't necessarily add up to two. Every group begins with a potential defined by the group's constraints, resources and structure. Then you need to add in process factors (gains and losses) created within the group itself. Four people on a research team, for instance, may be able to generate far more ideas as a group than the members could produce individually. This positive synergy results in a process gain. You also have to subtract process losses such as high levels of conflict, which may hinder group effectiveness.

To determine a group's *actual* effectiveness, you need to *add* in process gains and *subtract* process losses from the group's *potential* effectiveness.

Group Tasks. The final box in our model points out that the impact of group processes on the group's performance and member satisfaction depends on the task that the group is doing. More specifically, the *complexity* and *interdependence* of tasks influence the group's effectiveness.[14]

Tasks can be generalized as being either simple or complex. Simple tasks are routine and standardized. Complex tasks are ones that tend to be novel or non-routine. We would hypothesize that the more complex the task, the more the group will benefit from discussions among group members about alternative work methods. If the task is simple, group members don't need to discuss such alternatives. They can rely on standardized operating procedures. Similarly, if there's a high degree of interdependence among the tasks that group members must perform, they'll need to interact more. Effective communication and controlled levels of conflict should, therefore, be more relevant to group performance when tasks are interdependent.

TURNING GROUPS INTO EFFECTIVE TEAMS

A recent survey of Fortune 1000 companies found that 68 percent were using self-managed or high-performance teams in one way or another to perform work activities.[15] Many smaller organizations are also using teams to perform organizational tasks and solve problems. Teams are currently popular and are likely to continue that way. In this section, we'll discuss what a work team is, the different types of teams that organizations might use, why organizations are increasingly designing work around teams rather than individuals, and how to develop and manage work teams.

What Is a Team?

Most of us are already familiar with the idea of a team, especially if we've ever participated in or watched any type of organized sports activity. Although a sports team has many of the same characteristics as a work team, work teams are different and have their own unique traits. And just what are **work teams**? They're formal groups, made up of interdependent individuals, responsible for attaining a goal.[16] Thus, all work teams are groups, but only formal groups can be work teams.

work teams
Formal groups made up of interdependent individuals, responsible for attaining a goal.

Types of Teams

Although there are many ways to categorize teams, one convenient way is to look at teams in terms of four characteristics: their purpose, duration, membership and structure.[17] (See Figure 14-7.) Let's explain these characteristics in more detail.

Teams can vary in their purpose or goal. A team might be involved in product development, problem solving, as part of a re-engineering effort, or for any other number of work-related activities. For instance, at Esso, multidisciplinary teams are used in work process optimization projects throughout the facility.[18]

The duration of a team may be either permanent or temporary. Functional department teams and others that are part of the organization's formal structure are types of permanent teams. Temporary teams include task forces, project teams, problem-solving teams, and any other type of short-term team created to develop, analyze, or study a business or work-related issue.

Team membership can either be functional or cross-functional. A departmental team is functional because it pulls its members from a specific area. However, as we've already discussed previously in Chapter 10, many organizations are using cross-functional teams as a way

FIGURE 14-7 Categories of Teams

Purpose	Structure
• Product Development • Problem Solving • Re-engineering • Any Other Organizational Purposes Desired	• Supervised • Self-Managed

Membership	Duration
• Functional • Cross-Functional	• Permanent • Temporary

to foster innovation, co-operation and commitment. The cross-functional team has members from various functional areas and organizational levels.

Finally, teams can either be supervised or self-managed. A supervised team will be under the direction of a manager who's responsible for guiding the team in setting goals, in performing the necessary work activities, and in evaluating performance. In contrast, a self-managed team assumes the responsibilities for managing itself.

Given these four characteristics, what are some of the popular types of teams being used in organizations today? The three best known are functional teams, self-directed or self-managed teams, and cross-functional teams.[19]

Functional teams are composed of a manager and his or her direct subordinates, from a particular functional area. Within this functional team, issues such as authority, decision making, leadership, and interactions are relatively simple and clear. These functional teams are often involved in efforts to improve work activities or solve specific problems within that particular functional area. For example, at the California headquarters of Birkenstock Footprint Sandals, employees in sales, credit, production, warehousing and other functional areas now work in independent teams to complete tasks and solve customer problems.[20]

Another type of team commonly being used in organizations is the self-directed or self-managed team. A **self-directed** or **self-managed team** is a formal group of employees who operate without a manager, and who are responsible for a complete work process or segment that delivers a product or service to an external or internal customer. The self-directed work team is responsible for getting the work done *and* for managing themselves. For instance, at the Diesel Systems Division of Stanadyne Automotive Corporation, production workers are divided into self-directed teams assigned to a specific automotive component, such as drive shafts. These teams are given specific production goals, the responsibility to divide work within the team to see that these goals are met, and the obligation to control costs.[21] Even service companies such as Federal Express and IDS Financial Services use self-managed teams in deciding how best to do the work.

The last type of team we want to discuss is the **cross-functional team**, which we introduced back in Chapter 10, and defined as a hybrid grouping of individuals who are experts in various specialties and who come together across departmental lines to work on various organizational tasks. Many organizations are moving to using cross-functional teams. For instance, at Avcorp Industries in British Columbia, employees are involved in teams that span several functions and departments. Through this system, products are developed with input from a wide field of expertise. These teams are involved in various functional activities from

functional team
A type of work team that's composed of a manager and his or her subordinates from a particular functional area.

self-directed or self-managed team
A type of work team that operates without a manager and is responsible for a complete work process or segment that delivers a product or service to an external or internal customer..

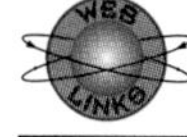

Federal Express
www.fedex.com

cross-functional team
A type of work team in which a hybrid grouping of individuals who are experts in various specialties (or functions) work together on various organizational tasks

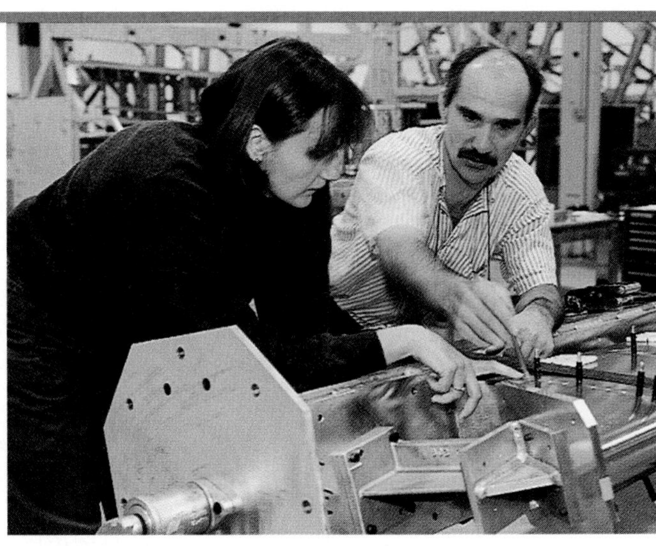

The idea of using cross-functional teams has been used with great success at BC's Avcorp Industries.

The Challenge of Co-ordinating Heterogeneous Groups

Understanding and managing groups that are similar in nature can be a difficult undertaking in and of itself. Add in diversity, and it can be even more of a challenge. But even though it may be more of a challenge, the benefits to be gained from the diverse perspectives, skills and abilities more than offset the extra effort expended.[22]

So how can you meet the challenge of co-ordinating a heterogeneous (diverse) work group? It's important in managing a diverse group to stress four crucial interpersonal behaviours: understanding, empathy, tolerance and communication.

You know that people aren't the same, yet they need to be treated fairly and equitably. And cultural differences can cause people to behave in different ways. Group leaders need to understand and accept these differences. Each and every group member should be encouraged to do the same.

Empathy is closely related to understanding. As a group leader, you should try to understand others' perspectives. Put yourself in their shoes, and encourage group members to empathize as well. For instance, suppose a Japanese woman joins a group made up of Caucasian and Hispanic men. They can make her feel more welcome and comfortable in the group by identifying with how she might feel. Is she disappointed or excited about her new work assignment? Has she had any experience in working with male colleagues? By putting themselves in her position, the existing group members can enhance their ability to work together as an effective group.

Tolerance is another important interpersonal behaviour in co-ordinating heterogeneous groups. Just because you understand that people are different and you empathize with them doesn't mean that it's any easier to accept different perspectives or behaviours. But it's important when dealing with diverse ages, gender, cultural behaviours, or any of the other dimensions of diversity to be tolerant—to allow group members the freedom to be themselves. Part of being tolerant is being open-minded about different values, attitudes and behaviours.

Finally, open communication is important when co-ordinating a diverse team. Diversity problems may intensify if people are afraid or otherwise unwilling to openly discuss issues that concern them. And for communication to work within a diverse group, it needs to be a two-way process. If a person wants to know whether or not a certain behaviour is offensive to someone else, it's best just to ask. Likewise, if someone is offended by a certain behaviour of another person, he or she should explain the concern to that person and ask him or her to stop it. As long as these communication exchanges are handled in a non-threatening, low-key and friendly way, they generally will have a beneficial outcome. And it helps to have a group atmosphere that supports and celebrates diversity. ■

production, to engineering, to marketing.[23] At Hallmark Cards, editors, writers, artists and production specialists join with employees from manufacturing, graphic arts, sales and distribution to work on everything from developing new product ideas to improving customer deliveries.[24]

Why Use Teams?

There's no *single* explanation for the recent increased popularity of teams. We propose that there are a number of reasons. Using teams:

Creates Esprit de Corps. Team members expect and demand a lot from each other. In so doing, they facilitate co-operation and improve employee morale. So we find that team norms tend to encourage members to excel and, at the same time, create a climate that increases job satisfaction.

Allows Management to Think Strategically. The use of teams, especially self-managed ones, frees managers to do more strategic planning. When jobs are designed around individuals, managers often spend an inordinate amount of their time supervising their people and "putting out fires". They're too busy to do much strategic thinking. By using work teams, managers can redirect their energy towards bigger issues such as long-term plans.

Speeds Up Decisions. Moving decision making vertically down to teams allows the organization greater flexibility for faster decisions. Team members frequently know more about work-related problems than do managers. Moreover, team members are closer to those problems. As a result, decisions are often made more quickly when teams exist than when jobs are designed around individuals.

Facilitates Workforce Diversity. We all know the old saying that two heads are better than one; this can be true of work teams. Groups made up of individuals from different backgrounds and with different experiences often see things that homogeneous groups don't. Therefore, the use of diverse teams may result in more innovative ideas and better decisions than might arise if individuals made the decision alone.

Increases Performance. Finally, all the preceding factors can combine to make team performance higher than might be achieved by the same individuals working alone. Organizations as varied as PetroCanada, Bombardier, Amoco Canada, and the Girl Guides have found that teams eliminate waste, slash bureaucratic overhead, stimulate ideas for improvements, and generate more output per worker-hour than more traditional individual-focused work designs.[25]

Amoco Canada Petroleum Company Ltd.
www.amoco.com

Girl Guides of Canada
www.girlguides.ca

DEVELOPING AND MANAGING EFFECTIVE TEAMS

Teams aren't automatic productivity enhancers. They can also be disappointments for management. We need to look more closely at how managers can develop and manage effective teams and how teams are used in TQM initiatives. But first, let's look at what characterizes an "effective" team.

Characteristics of Effective Teams

Recent research provides insights into the primary characteristics associated with effective teams.[26] Let's look at these characteristics as summarized in Figure 14-8.

6 **Compare groups and teams.**

7 **Contrast functional, self-directed or self-managed, and cross-functional teams.**

8 **Why have teams become so popular in organizations?**

FIGURE 14-8 Characteristics of Effective Teams

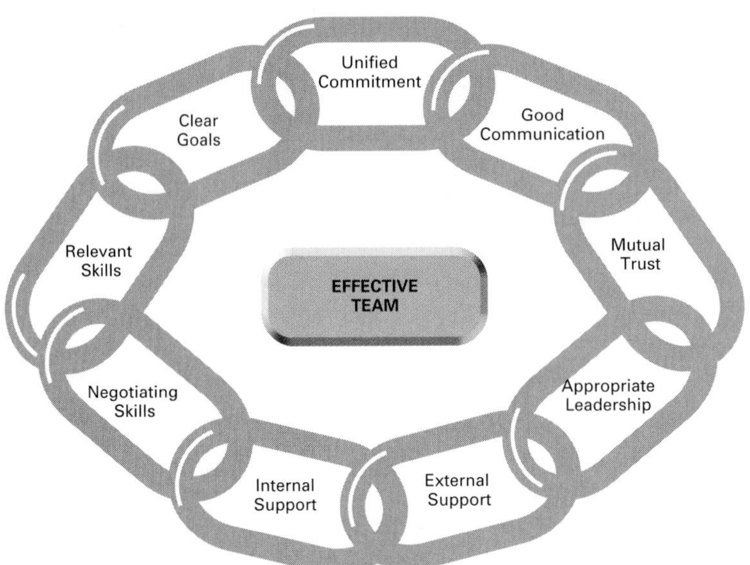

Clear Goals. High-performance teams have both a clear understanding of the goal to be achieved and a belief that the goal embodies a worthwhile or important result. Moreover, the importance of these goals encourages individuals to redirect personal concerns to these team goals. In effective teams, members are committed to the team's goals, know what they're expected to accomplish, and understand how they will work together to achieve these goals.

Relevant Skills. Effective teams are composed of competent individuals. They have the necessary technical skills and abilities to achieve the desired goals, and the personal characteristics required to achieve excellence while working well with others. This second point is important and often overlooked. Not everyone who is technically competent has the skills to work well as a team member. High-performing teams have members who possess both technical and interpersonal skills.

There are problem-solving teams, product-development teams, self-managed teams and virtual teams, to name a few. A manager must learn which team to fit to which task. This Boeing team, part of the new 777 jet project, solves sticky problems between members of other teams!

Mutual Trust. Effective teams are characterized by high mutual trust among members. That is, members believe in the integrity, character and ability of one another. But as you probably know from personal relationships, trust is fragile. It takes a long time to build and can easily be destroyed. Also, because trust begets trust and distrust begets distrust, maintaining trust requires careful attention by management.

The climate of trust within a group tends to be strongly influenced by the organization's culture and the actions of management. Organizations that value openness, honesty, and collaborative processes, and that encourage employee involvement and autonomy, are likely to create trusting cultures. Table 14-2 lists six recommended actions that can help managers to build and maintain trust.

Unified Commitment. Members of an effective team exhibit intense loyalty and dedication to the team. They're willing to do anything that has to be done to help their team succeed. We call this loyalty and dedication *unified commitment.*

Studies of successful teams have found that members identify with their teams.[27] Members redefine themselves to include membership in the team as an important aspect of the self. Unified commitment, then, is characterized by dedication to the team's goals, and a willingness to expend extraordinary amounts of energy to achieve it.

Good Communication. Not surprisingly, effective teams are characterized by good communication. Members are able to convey messages among each other in a form that is readily and clearly understood. This includes non-verbal as well as spoken messages. Good communication is also characterized by a healthy dose of feedback from team members and management. This helps to guide team members and to correct misunderstandings. Like a couple who have been together for many years, members on high-performing teams are able to share ideas and feelings quickly and efficiently.

Negotiating Skills. When jobs are designed around individuals, job descriptions, rules and procedures, and other types of formalized documentation clarify employee roles. Effective teams, on the other hand, tend to be flexible and are continually making adjustments. This

TABLE 14-2 Six Suggestions for Helping Managers To Build Trust

1. *Communicate.* Keep team members and subordinates informed by explaining decisions and policies and providing accurate feedback. Be candid about your own problems and limitations.
2. *Be supportive.* Be available and approachable. Encourage and support team members' ideas.
3. *Be respectful.* Delegate real authority to team members and listen to their ideas.
4. *Be fair.* Give credit where it's due, be objective and impartial in performance evaluations, and be generous with your praise.
5. *Be predictable.* Be consistent in your daily affairs. Make good on your explicit and implied promises.
6. *Demonstrate competence.* Develop the admiration and respect of team members by demonstrating technical and professional ability and good business sense.

Source: Adapted from Fernando Bartolomé, "Nobody Trusts the Boss Completely—Now What?" *Harvard Business Review,* March–April 1989, pp. 135–142.

requires team members to possess adequate negotiating skills. Problems and relationships are regularly changing in teams, requiring members to confront and reconcile differences.

Appropriate Leadership. Effective leaders can motivate a team to follow them through the most difficult situations. How? They help to clarify goals, and they demonstrate that change is possible by overcoming inertia. They increase the self-confidence of team members, helping members to realize their potential more fully. Most importantly, the best leaders aren't necessarily directive or controlling. Increasingly, effective team leaders are taking the role of coach and facilitator. They help to guide and support the team, but they don't control it. This obviously applies to self-managed teams, but also increasingly applies to task forces and cross-functional teams in which the members themselves are empowered. For some traditional managers, changing their role from boss to facilitator—from giving orders to working *for* the team—is a difficult transition. While most managers relish the new-found shared authority or come to understand its advantages through leadership training, some hard-nosed dictatorial managers are just ill-suited to the team concept and must be transferred or replaced.

Internal and External Support. The final condition necessary for an effective team is a supportive climate. Internally, the team should be provided with a sound infrastructure. This includes proper training, an understandable measurement system that team members can use to evaluate their overall performance, an incentive program that recognizes and rewards team activities, and a supportive human resource system. The right infrastructure should support members and reinforce behaviours that lead to high levels of performance. Externally, management should provide the team with the resources needed to get the job done.

Managing Teams

What's involved in managing a team? Well, we can look at the task of managing a team using the four basic management functions: planning, organizing, leading and controlling.[28]

The success of NASA's recent *Pathfinder* mission is a tribute to the effectiveness of its earth-bound team. The team exhibits many of the characteristics of effective teams.

Planning. Goal determination is an important part of the planning process. As we've pointed out previously, effective teams have clear goals. It's important that team members understand and accept the team's goals.[29] Whether these goals are provided for the team or whether the team develops its own goals every team member needs to know what the goals are. One easy way to check on the understanding of goals is to have each team member write down the team's goals, then collect and analyze the statements for accuracy and consistency. If there are misconceptions about the team's goals, a team meeting can be called to clear these up.

Organizing. Organizing tasks involved with managing a team include clarification of authority and structural issues. One of the key questions for any team is "how much authority do we have?" If the team is a self-directed or self-managed team, it's already been empowered with the authority to make certain decisions and perform specific work activities. However, even if the team isn't a self-managed team, questions about what it can and cannot do often come up. If the organizational culture is supportive of employee involvement and autonomy, then it's likely that work teams will have substantial authority over what they do and how they do it. But it's important that these authority issues be addressed early, so that a team knows its parameters and constraints. And, within the team itself, structural issues need to be resolved. Has a leader been appointed, or will the team designate one? What tasks need to be done in order to accomplish the team's goals? What are the most effective and efficient ways to do the work? Who's going to be assigned to the various tasks, and how will these assignments be made? These are the types of structural questions that teams must answer.

Leading. Important issues in leading that a team must address include, among others, what role the leader will play, how conflict will be handled, and which communication processes will be used. The team leader plays an important role in directing the efforts of the team. However, as we described in the section on effective teams, a team leader is increasingly becoming more of a facilitator and a coach than a "person in charge". Leading a team typically requires having sufficient technical knowledge so you can understand the team's work duties, *and* having strong interpersonal skills so you can facilitate individual participation, motivate outstanding performance, resolve conflicts, and gain consensus on key issues. Dealing with the human dynamics of the team is often the most difficult part of managing a team. Table 14-3 lists some people skills that are important in leading a team.

TABLE 14-3 Types of Interpersonal Skills Used in Managing Teams

- Ask appropriate questions to bring out ideas and stimulate discussion.
- Listen closely and intently to members' ideas and concerns.
- Manage group discussions to encourage shy team members to participate.
- Establish an informal and non-threatening climate so that members feel free to candidly speak their thoughts.
- Use the consensus method to reach decisions on key team issues.
- Involve team members in setting goals.
- Implement meeting guidelines to minimize wasted time in group meetings.
- Encourage respect for each other so that each member knows that his or her contributions are valued.
- Identify and deal with dysfunctional behaviours immediately.
- Celebrate the achievement of milestones and other team accomplishments.
- Use recognition, task assignments, and other techniques to motivate team members.

Source: Based on Glenn M Parker, *Cross-Functional Teams* (San Francisco: Jossey-Bass,1994), pp. 57–58.

Controlling. The final function we want to look at in relation to managing teams is that of controlling. Two of the most important controlling issues are how the team's performance will be evaluated, and what type of reward system will be used. As organizations begin to use teams more and more, their employee appraisal and reward systems will have to change to reflect this. What types of changes can we expect?

Performance criteria need to be modified to incorporate teamwork behaviour in employee evaluations.[30] Not only should individual performance be evaluated, but factors that indicate how well the individual works within the team context should also be considered. For instance, at Bull HN Information Systems, the North American division of France's Groupe Bull, one important performance evaluation criterion is how well individuals work in teams, get things done through people, and build teams.[31]

But changes in the appraisal process to incorporate team efforts are only half the story. We also need to look at how teams are rewarded for their efforts and performance levels. As organizations use teams more frequently, we are beginning to see an increased use of group incentive plans. One of the most popular approaches to group incentives is **gainsharing**, an incentive program that shares the gains of the efforts of employees with those employees. In gainsharing, rewards are directly related to performance. If the team succeeds, team members will be rewarded. Team-based organizations also use rewards such as one-time bonuses, team incentive systems, employee-based recognition programs, and informal team recognition. At the head office of Aid Association for Lutherans (AAL) insurance company, for instance, team members get pay increments as they acquire and use new skills. But at Dial Corporation, which uses regional teams consisting of a marketing person, a financial specialist, a customer service representative, and the salesperson, individuals are rewarded based on individual performance as measured by results against goals, and on team results as measured by sales volume, sales forecasting accuracy, and improved profitability.[32] Whatever approach is used, however, the team itself should be the primary force in deciding what types of rewards and recognition are important.

gainsharing
A group incentive program that shares the gains of the efforts of group members with those group members.

Teams and TQM

One of the central characteristics of total quality management is the use of teams. But why teams? The essence of TQM is process improvement—and employee participation is the cornerstone of process improvement. In other words, TQM requires management to give employees the encouragement to share ideas and act on what they suggest. Problem-solving teams provide the natural vehicle for employees to share ideas and to implement improvements. As stated by Gil Mosard, a TQM specialist at McDonnell-Douglas, "When your measurement system tells you your process is out of control, you need teamwork for structured problem solving. Not everyone needs to know how to do all kinds of fancy control charts for performance tracking, but everybody does need to know where their process stands so they can judge if it is improving."[33]

One team application of TQM is **quality circles**.[34] These are work groups of eight to ten employees and supervisors who share an area of responsibility. They meet regularly (typically once a week, on company time and on company premises) to discuss their quality problems, investigate causes of the problems, recommend solutions, and take corrective actions. They assume responsibility for solving quality problems, and they generate and evaluate their own feedback. However, management usually makes the final decision about the implementation of recommended solutions. Figure 14-9 describes a typical quality circle process.

quality circles
Work groups that meet regularly to discuss, investigate, and correct quality problems.

Finally, examples from Ford Motor Company and Amana Refrigeration Inc. illustrate how teams are being used in TQM programs.[35] Ford began its TQM efforts in the early 1980s with teams as the primary organizing mechanism. "Because this business is so complex, you can't make an impact on it without using a team approach," noted one Ford manager. In designing their quality problem-solving teams, Ford's management identified five goals. The teams should (1) be small enough to be efficient and effective; (2) be properly trained in the skills their members will need; (3) be allocated enough time to work on the problems they plan to address; (4) be given the authority to resolve the problems and implement corrective action; and (5) each have a designated "champion" whose job it is to help the team get around roadblocks that arise.

At Amana, task forces made up of people from different levels within the company are used to deal with quality problems that cut across various functional areas. The various task

FIGURE 14-9 How a Typical Quality Circle Operates

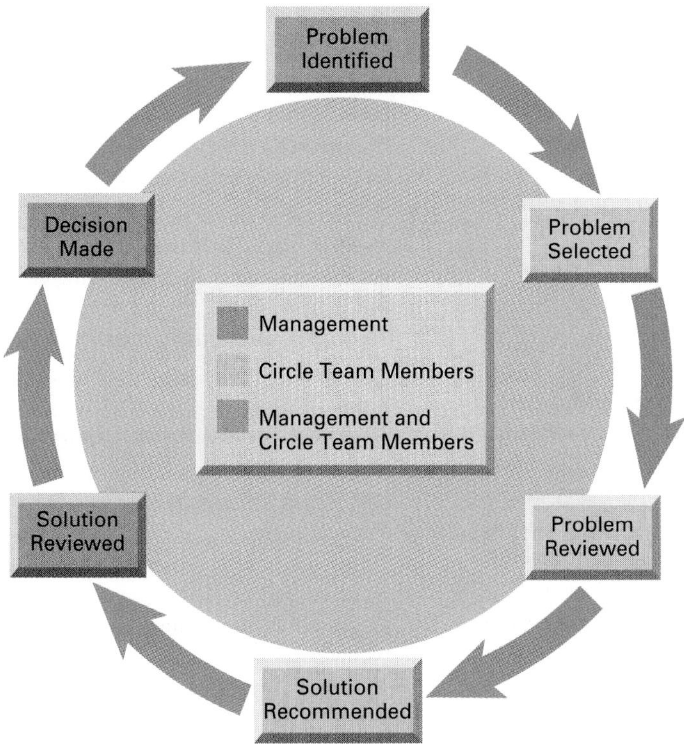

forces each have a unique area of problem-solving responsibility. For instance, one handles in-plant products, another deals with items that arise outside the production facility, and still another focuses its attention specifically on supplier problems. Amana claims the use of these task forces has improved vertical and horizontal communication within the company, and substantially reduced the number of units that don't meet company specifications and the number of service problems in the field.

9 What characteristics do effective teams exhibit?

10 What types of issues must be addressed when managing a team?

11 How are teams used in TQM programs?

SUMMARY

This summary is organized by the learning objectives found at the beginning of the chapter.

1. *Formal* groups are defined by the organization's structure, with designated work assignments establishing tasks. *Informal* groups are social alliances that are neither structured nor organizationally determined.
2. People join groups because of their needs for security, status, self-esteem, affiliation, power, or achievement.
3. The five stages of group development are forming, storming, norming, performing and adjourning. Forming includes people joining the group, and the task of defining the group's purpose, structure and leadership. Storming is a stage of intragroup conflict over control issues. During the norming stage, close relationships develop and the group demonstrates cohesiveness. Performing is the stage at which the group is doing the task at hand. Finally, adjourning is the stage when temporary committees, task forces, and teams with a limited task to perform prepare for disbandment.
4. A role is a set of behaviour patterns expected of someone occupying a given position in a social unit. At any given time, employees adjust their role behaviours to the group of which they're a part. Norms are standards shared by group members. They informally convey to employees which behaviours are acceptable and which are unacceptable.
5. There are five variables in the group behaviour model that, in total, explain the group's performance and satisfaction. First, a group is influenced by the larger organization of which it's a part. Second, a group's potential level of performance depends to a large extent on the resources that its members individually bring to the group. Third, there's a group structure that shapes the behaviour of members. Fourth, there are internal processes within the group that aid or hinder interaction and the ability of the group to perform. Finally, the impact of group processes on the group's performance and member satisfaction depends on the task that the group is doing.
6. Teams have become increasingly popular in organizations because they build esprit de corps, free management to do more strategic thinking, permit faster decision making, facilitate workforce diversity, and usually increase performance.
7. Teams can be categorized in terms of their purpose, duration, membership and structure. Some popular types of teams being used in organizations include functional teams, self-directed or self-managed teams, and cross-functional teams.
8. Effective work teams are characterized by clear goals, members with relevant skills, mutual trust among members, unified commitment, good communication, adequate negotiating skills, and appropriate leadership.
9. Managers can build trust by communicating openly; providing support to team members' ideas; being respectful, fair, and predictable; and demonstrating competence.
10. Managing teams involves the managerial functions of planning, organizing, leading and controlling. Planning issues for teams include having clear goals. Organizing issues involve clarification of authority and structural elements. Leading issues include what role the leader will play, how conflicts will be resolved, and what communication processes will be used. Controlling issues involve appraisal and reward systems.
11. Problem-solving teams provide a natural vehicle for employees to share ideas and to implement improvements, as part of the TQM process. Teams are particularly effective for resolving complex problems.

THINKING ABOUT MANAGEMENT ISSUES

1. Think of a group to which you belong (or have belonged). Trace its development through the stages of group development shown in Figure 14-1. Think of specific examples or instances of each of the stages.
2. Identify five roles you play. What behaviours do they require? Are any of these roles in conflict? If so, in what way? How do you resolve these conflicts?
3. How do you think scientific management theorists would react to the increased reliance on teams in organizations? How about the behavioural science theorists?
4. When might individuals, acting independently, outperform teams in an organization?
5. In North America, historically we have built organizations around individuals. What would happen if we used teams as the basic building block for an organization? What if we *selected* teams rather than individuals, *trained* teams rather than individuals, *paid* teams rather than individuals, *promoted* teams rather than individuals, *fired* teams rather than individuals, and so forth?

SELF-ASSESSMENT EXERCISE

ARE YOU A TEAM PLAYER?

This self-assessment exercise asks you to examine your behaviour as a team member. For each pair of items, place a checkmark in the space in the column that best defines your behaviour in class project groups, clubs or student groups, and in work groups (if you're employed).

	Very like me	Somewhat like me	Both describe me	Somewhat like me	Very like me	
1. Flexible in own ideas	____	____	____	____	____	Set in own ideas
2. Open to new ideas	____	____	____	____	____	Avoid new ideas
3. Listen well to others	____	____	____	____	____	Tune others out
4. Trusting of others	____	____	____	____	____	Not trusting of others
5. Readily contribute to group meetings	____	____	____	____	____	Hold back from contributing in meetings
6. Concerned for what happens to others	____	____	____	____	____	Not concerned for what happens to others
7. Fully committed to tasks	____	____	____	____	____	Have little commitment to tasks
8. Share leadership with group	____	____	____	____	____	Maintain full control of group
9. Encourage others to participate	____	____	____	____	____	Expect others to participate without encouragement
10. Put group needs before own individual needs	____	____	____	____	____	Put own individual needs before group needs

For scoring information, turn to page SK-4.

Source: Adapted from training materials for income maintenance supervisors, Special Topics Workshop: "Motivation, Teambuilding, and Enhancing Morale," Professional Development Program, Rockefeller College of Public Affairs and Policy, State University of New York at Albany. Used with permission.

for your IMMEDIATE action

★ The Edmonton News ★

TO: Diane diNardo, Director of Human Resources
FROM: John Steinberg, Editor-in-Chief
SUBJECT: Re-organization of Departments

It seems as if every business periodical I've picked up recently has had an article on work teams. Also, I just got back from a meeting of the Western Newspaper Publishers group and found that the issue of "using teams to improve productivity" was a major topic of cocktail-party conversation. I think it's time for us to consider whether we could benefit by re-organizing our departments—the national news desk, local news, editorial, sports, business, lifestyles, commercial advertising, classified, and operations—around teams rather than individuals. Please provide me with a two- or three-page concise summary of the advantages and disadvantages that might result from such a re-organization. You should also address whether teams make more sense in some departments than in others.

This is a fictionalized account of a potentially real problem. It was written for academic purposes only and is not meant to reflect either positively or negatively on actual management practices at any newspaper.

TAKE IT TO THE NET

We invite you to visit the Robbins/Coulter/Stuart-Kotze Companion Website at www.prenticehall.ca/robbins for this chapter's Internet resources.

CASE APPLICATION

The Evart Glass Plant

The Evart Glass plant, an automobile glass manufacturer, is a division of Chrysler Corporation. In 1994, as a result of an employee survey, Chrysler challenged each of its plants to improve organizational culture and climate. Evart Glass's culture committee decided to focus on improving interaction between employees on work teams, as well as between each work team. However, getting employees to function effectively and efficiently as team members, and getting teams to high levels of performance, doesn't just happen. That's why the decision was made to send the company's 257 employees through a team-building and team-training program.

The team-training experiences were made more challenging by combining the employees into cross-functional teams, not their normal work groups. For instance, one team consisted of a forklift driver, a maintenance person, a shift supervisor and a receptionist. After a full day of completing different types of team adventures, team members gathered together to discuss the experience and to compare it with the workplace challenges they faced. The company's human resources manager said that this experience allowed everyone to "get to know the people in different work areas, and to feel more comfortable about going to each other to talk and solve a work-related problem and share information".

Employees weren't immediately enamoured of the idea of team-building exercises. Some workers, primarily union members, initially resisted the mandatory team training. To ease the uncertainty over what the training was all about, the company provided information to workers well in advance of the training.

QUESTIONS

1. "You can't train people to be team players." Build an argument to support this statement, then refute it.
2. Describe the advantages and disadvantages of using cross-functional team training, rather than using the actual work teams which employees are part of.
3. How might the team-building exercises, such as the ones briefly described in this chapter, contribute towards making a team more effective?
4. Think of a team-building exercise that would help a team meet one of the characteristics of an effective team (use Figure 14-8, Characteristics of Effective Teams). Describe the characteristic you choose, then describe the exercise you would use to help a team practise or achieve that characteristic.

Source: H Campbell, "Adventures in Teamland", *Personnel Journal,* May 1996, pp. 56–62.

LEARNING OBJECTIVES

After Reading This Chapter, You Should Be Able To:

1. Describe the motivation process
2. Explain the hierarchy of needs theory
3. Differentiate Theory X from Theory Y
4. Explain the motivational implications of the motivation–hygiene theory
5. Identify the characteristics that high achievers seek in a job
6. Explain how goals motivate people
7. Differentiate reinforcement theory from goal-setting theory
8. Describe ways to design motivating jobs
9. Describe the motivational implications of equity theory
10. Explain the key relationships in expectancy theory
11. Identify management practices that are likely to lead to more motivated employees

A MANAGER'S CHALLENGE

The Canadian Information Technology Industry

In an industry with seemingly limitless potential for growth, one major factor continues to hamper Canada's burgeoning information-technology (IT) sector: employee availability. As of 1999, more than 16 000 companies continue to contribute double-digit growth in the Canadian IT industry. The sector is comprised of a wide range of companies, from major players such as Northern Telecom (which hires nearly a quarter of all Canadian computer science and engineering graduates every year) to small but rapidly growing firms like McGill Multimedia Inc. (five-year growth up to 1998: 3.274%). Worth an estimated $64 billion, new companies are constantly joining the Canadian IT industry. But the Software Human Resource Council estimates that there are 20 000 IT positions in Canada that are not filled. And it's not simply a Canadian situation. As George Cwynar of Kanata, Ontario's, Mosaid Technologies puts it: "The greatest challenge facing companies worldwide is finding enough skilled people to fulfill the growing needs of the high-tech industry."[1]

It's a seller's market for IT personnel and employees know it. Companies are facing the necessity of offering increasingly generous signing bonuses ($20 000 is not uncommon),

larger salaries, significant bonuses, stock options, profit-sharing plans, benefits packages, longer vacations (sometimes starting at eight weeks), flexible hours, free day care, and a wide array of perks. Companies are desperate; recruitment is a war, with competitors scrambling to acquire new employees before they even graduate. And as if the challenge of finding employees isn't enough, it is even more difficult to keep them. The IT industry's annual turnover rate has been estimated at between 10 and 20 percent. Companies are always at risk of losing their skilled employees to rival firms offering better incentives. One company that seems to be staving off the advances of competitor recruitment is Teranet Land Information Services, in Toronto. Teranet manages a turnover rate of less than one percent. CEO Aris Kaplanis has said: "My perspective is that the company has two assets—one is the customers, the other is our employees". The company provides a familial corporate culture (with monthly social events, annual picnics, etc.), and offers work arrangements to meet employee needs, such as flexible work times, and telecommuting. Marilyn Barber, VP of human resources, makes the point that "it's easy to leave a job, but it's not so easy to leave a family".

With educational institutions not being able to keep up with the demand for workers, the IT industry in Canada will continue to face the challenge of finding skilled employees amongst global competition, as well as the tougher challenge of keeping employees, in an industry where a company's skilled personnel base is constantly being plundered by the competition.

Motivating and rewarding employees are two of the most important yet difficult activities that managers perform. This is obvious in the Canadian IT industry, but these activities are essential aspects of a manager's job in any organization. Successful managers understand that what motivates them personally may have little or no effect on others. Just because you're motivated by being part of a cohesive work team, don't assume everyone else is. Effective managers who want their employees to make a maximum effort know that they need to tailor their motivational practices in order to satisfy the needs and wants of those employees.[2]

Motivating Employees

WHAT IS MOTIVATION?

To understand what motivation *is*, let's begin by pointing out what motivation *isn't*. Why? Because many people incorrectly view motivation as a personal trait—that is, some have it and others don't. In practice, this would characterize the manager who labels a certain employee as unmotivated. Our knowledge of motivation, though, tells us that this just isn't true. What we know is that motivation is the result of the interaction between the individual and the situation. Certainly, individuals differ in motivational drive, but overall motivation varies from situation to situation. As we analyze the concept of motivation, keep in mind that levels of motivation vary both between individuals and within individuals at different times.

motivation
The willingness to exert high levels of effort to reach organizational goals, conditioned by the effort's ability to satisfy some individual need.

We'll define **motivation** as the willingness to exert high levels of effort to reach organizational goals, conditioned by the effort's ability to satisfy some individual need. While general motivation refers to effort towards *any* goal, here it will refer to *organizational goals*, because our focus is on work-related behaviour. The three key elements in our definition are effort, organizational goals, and needs.

The *effort* element is a measure of intensity or drive. When someone is motivated, he or she tries hard. But high levels of effort are unlikely to lead to favourable job performance outcomes, unless the effort is channelled in a direction that benefits the organization.[3] Therefore we must consider the quality of the effort as well as its intensity. Effort that's directed towards, and is consistent with, the organization's goals, is the kind of effort that we should be seeking. Finally, we'll treat motivation as a need-satisfying process. This is depicted in Figure 15-1.

need
An internal state that makes certain outcomes appear attractive.

A **need**, in our terminology, means some internal state that makes certain outcomes appear attractive. An unsatisfied need creates tension that stimulates drives within an individual. These drives generate a search behaviour to find particular goals that, if attained, will satisfy the need and reduce the tension.

We can say that motivated employees are in a state of tension. To relieve this tension, they exert effort. The greater the tension, the higher the effort level. If this effort successfully leads to the satisfaction of the need, it reduces tension. Since we're interested in work behaviour, this tension-reduction effort must also be directed towards organizational goals. Therefore, inherent in our definition of motivation, is the requirement that the individual's needs be compatible and consistent with the organization's goals. When this doesn't occur, individuals may exert high levels of effort that run counter to the interests of the organization. Incidentally, this isn't so unusual. Some employees regularly spend a lot of time talking with friends at work in order to satisfy their social needs. That's a high level of effort, but it's unproductively directed.

EARLY THEORIES OF MOTIVATION

The 1950s were a fruitful time for the development of motivation concepts. Three specific theories were formulated during this period that, although heavily attacked and now considered only questionably valid, are probably still the best known explanations for employee motivation. These three theories are the *hierarchy of needs theory, Theories X and Y,* and the *motivation–hygiene theory*. Although more valid explanations of motivation have been developed, you should know these early theories for at least two reasons: (1) they represent the foundation from which contemporary theories of motivation were developed, and (2) practising managers regularly use these theories and their terminology in explaining employee motivation.

hierarchy of needs theory
Maslow's theory that there's a hierarchy of five human needs: physiological, safety, social, esteem, and self-actualization. As each need is substantially satisfied, the next becomes dominant.

Hierarchy of Needs Theory

The best-known theory of motivation is probably Abraham Maslow's **hierarchy of needs theory**.[4] He hypothesized that within every human being is a hierarchy of five needs:

FIGURE 15-1 The Motivation Process

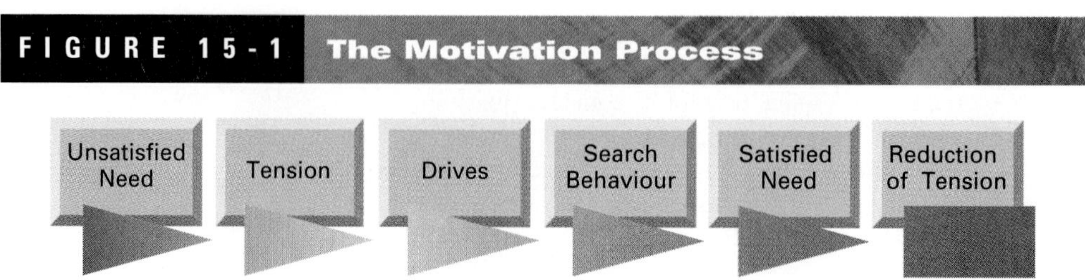

1. **Physiological needs:** food, drink, shelter, sexual satisfaction, and other physical requirements
2. **Safety needs:** security and protection from physical and emotional harm, as well as assurance that physical needs will continue to be met
3. **Social needs:** affection, sense of belonging, acceptance, and friendship
4. **Esteem needs:** internal esteem factors such as self-respect, autonomy and achievement; and external esteem factors such as status, recognition and attention
5. **Self-actualization needs:** growth, achieving one's potential, and self-fulfillment; and the drive to become what one is capable of becoming

As each need is substantially satisfied, the next need becomes dominant. In terms of Figure 15-2, the individual moves up the hierarchy. From the standpoint of motivation, the theory proposes that although no need is ever fully satisfied, a substantially satisfied need will no longer motivate an individual. If you want to motivate someone then, according to Maslow, you need to understand what level that person is on in the hierarchy, and focus on satisfying needs at or above that level.

Maslow separated the five needs into higher and lower levels. Physiological and safety needs were described as *lower-order needs*, while social, esteem, and self-actualization were described as *higher-order needs*. The differentiation between the two levels was made on the premise that higher-order needs are satisfied internally, whereas lower-order needs are predominantly satisfied externally. In fact, the natural conclusion from Maslow's classification is that, in times of economic prosperity, almost all permanently employed workers have their lower-order needs substantially met.

Maslow's need theory has received wide recognition, particularly among practising managers. This can be attributed to the theory's intuitive logic and ease of understanding. Unfortunately, however, research doesn't generally validate the theory. Maslow provided no empirical substantiation for his theory, and several studies that sought to validate it found no support.[5]

Theory X and Theory Y

As discussed in Chapter 2, Douglas McGregor proposed two distinct views about the nature of humans. One is a basically negative view, labelled **Theory X**, and the other is a basically pos-

physiological needs
Basic food, drink, shelter, and sexual needs.

safety needs
A person's needs for security and protection from physical and emotional harm.

social needs
A person's needs for affection, a sense of belonging, acceptance, and friendship.

esteem needs
Internal factors such as self-respect, autonomy and achievement; and external factors such as status, recognition and attention.

self-actualization needs
A person's drive to become what he or she is capable of becoming.

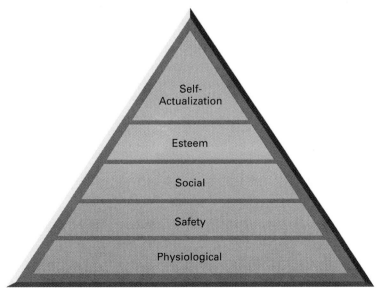

Theory X
The assumption that employees dislike work, are lazy, seek to avoid responsibility, and must be coerced to perform.

FIGURE 15-2 Maslow's Hierarchy of Needs

Theory Y
The assumption that employees are creative, seek responsibility, and can exercise self-direction.

itive view, labelled **Theory Y**.[6] Table 15-1 lists the assumptions about human nature for each of these perspectives.

What does McGregor's analysis imply about motivation? The answer is best expressed in the framework presented by Maslow. Theory X assumes that lower-order needs dominate individuals and Theory Y assumes that higher-order needs dominate. McGregor himself held the belief that the assumptions of Theory Y were more valid than those of Theory X. Therefore he proposed that participation in decision making, responsible and challenging jobs, and good group relations would maximize job motivation.

Unfortunately, there's no evidence to confirm that either set of assumptions is valid, that accepting Theory Y assumptions and altering your actions accordingly will motivate your employees more. In the real world, there are examples of effective managers who hold Theory X assumptions. An example of a manager who has essentially followed Theory X, is Robert Findlay at MacMillan Bloedel. His approach to managing is strict, stern, and focused on getting results. On the other hand, someone like Robert Schad, CEO of Husky Injection Molding Systems, would be classified as a Theory Y manager, who believes in decisions made on the spot, with employees encouraged to set high performance standards for themselves.

Husky Injection Molding Systems
www.husky.on.ca/

Motivation-Hygiene Theory

motivation–hygiene theory
The theory that intrinsic factors are related to job satisfaction, while extrinsic factors are associated with dissatisfaction.

The **motivation–hygiene theory** was proposed by psychologist Frederick Herzberg.[7] Believing that an individual's relation to his or her work is a basic one and that his or her attitude towards work can very well determine success or failure, Herzberg investigated the question "What do people want from their jobs?" He asked people to describe, in detail, situations in which they felt exceptionally good or bad about their jobs. Their responses were tabulated and categorized, and Herzberg's findings are shown in Figure 15-3.

From analyzing the findings, Herzberg concluded that the replies people gave when they felt good about their jobs differed significantly from the replies they gave when they felt bad. As shown in Figure 15-3, certain characteristics were consistently related to job satisfaction (factors on the left side of the figure), and others to job dissatisfaction (the right side of the figure). Intrinsic factors such as achievement, recognition, and responsibility were related to job satisfaction. When the people questioned felt good about their work, they tended to attribute these characteristics to themselves. When they were dissatisfied, they tended to cite extrinsic factors such as company policy and administration, supervision, interpersonal relationships, and working conditions.

Herzberg said that the data suggested that the opposite of satisfaction isn't dissatisfaction, as was traditionally believed. Removing dissatisfying characteristics from a job doesn't neces-

TABLE 15-1 Theory X and Theory Y Assumptions

Theory X	Theory Y
Employees inherently dislike work and will attempt to avoid it, whenever possible.	Employees view work as being as natural as rest or play.
Employees must be coerced, controlled, or threatened with punishment to achieve desired goals.	Employees will exercise self-direction and self-control if they are committed to the objectives.
Employees will shirk responsibilities and seek formal direction whenever possible.	The average person can learn to accept, and even seek, responsibility.
Most workers place security above all other factors associated with work and will display little ambition.	The ability to make good decisions is widely dispersed through the population and isn't necessarily the sole ability of managers.

FIGURE 15-3 Herzberg's Motivation-Hygiene Theory

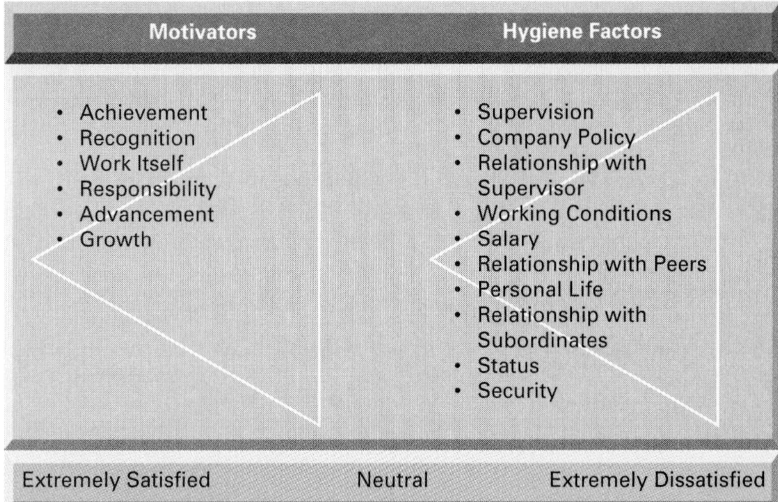

sarily make the job satisfying. As shown in Figure 15-4, Herzberg proposed that his findings indicated the existence of a dual continuum: The opposite of "satisfaction" is "no satisfaction," and the opposite of "dissatisfaction" is "no dissatisfaction".

Motivators
Hygiene Factors
• Achievement
• Recognition
• Work Itself
• Responsibility
• Advancement
• Growth
• Supervision
• Company Policy
• Relationship with Supervisor
• Working Conditions
• Salary
• Relationship with Peers
• Personal Life
• Relationship with Subordinates
• Status
• Security
Extremely Satisfied
Neutral
Extremely Dissatisfied

According to Herzberg, the factors leading to job satisfaction are separate and distinct from those that lead to job dissatisfaction. Therefore, managers who seek to eliminate factors that create job dissatisfaction can bring about workplace harmony, but not necessarily motivation. They're placating their workforce, rather than motivating it. Because they don't motivate employees, the factors that create job dissatisfaction were characterized by Herzberg as **hygiene factors**. When these factors are adequate, people won't be dissatisfied; however, they won't be satisfied either. To motivate people on their jobs, Herzberg suggested emphasizing **motivators**—the factors that increase job satisfaction.

hygiene factors
Factors that eliminate dissatisfaction.

motivators
Factors that increase job satisfaction.

The motivation–hygiene theory isn't without its critics. The criticisms of the theory include the following:

1. The procedure that Herzberg used was limited by its methodology. It's human nature to take personal credit when things are going well and to blame failure on extrinsic factors.
2. The reliability of Herzberg's methodology was questionable. Since raters had to make interpretations, they might have contaminated the findings by interpreting one response in one manner, while treating another similar response differently.

FIGURE 15-4 Contrasting Views of Satisfaction-Dissatisfaction

Traditional View

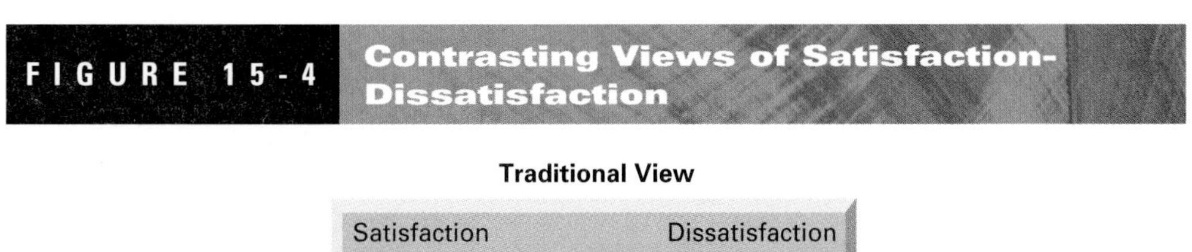

Herzberg's View

3. No overall measure of satisfaction was used. A person may dislike part of his or her job yet still think the job is acceptable.
4. The theory is inconsistent with previous research in that it ignores situational variables.
5. Herzberg assumed that there's a relationship between satisfaction and productivity, but the research methodology he used looked only at satisfaction, not at productivity. To make such research relevant, you must assume a close relationship between satisfaction and productivity.[8]

Even with these criticisms, Herzberg's theory has been widely popularized, and few managers are unfamiliar with his recommendations. Much of the enthusiasm for job enrichment, discussed later in this chapter, can be attributed to Herzberg's findings and recommendations.

CONTEMPORARY APPROACHES TO MOTIVATION

While the previous theories are well known, unfortunately they haven't held up well under close empirical examination. However, all isn't lost! A number of contemporary theories have one thing in common: each has a reasonable degree of valid supporting documentation. The following theories represent the current "state-of-the-art" explanations of employee motivation.

Three-Needs Theory

three-needs theory
The needs for achievement, power, and affiliation are major motives in work.

need for achievement (nAch)
The drive to excel, to achieve in relation to a set of standards, to strive to succeed.

need for power (nPow)
The need to make others behave in a way that they wouldn't have behaved otherwise.

need for affiliation (nAff)
The desire for friendly and close interpersonal relationships.

David McClelland and others have proposed the **three-needs theory**—the theory that there are three major motives or needs in work situations:

1. **Need for achievement (nAch):** the drive to excel, to achieve in relation to a set of standards, to strive to succeed
2. **Need for power (nPow):** the need to make others behave in a way that they wouldn't have behaved otherwise
3. **Need for affiliation (nAff):** the desire for friendly and close interpersonal relationships[9]

Some people have a compelling drive to succeed, but they're striving for personal achievement rather than for the trappings and rewards of success. They have a desire to do something in a better way, or more efficiently than it's been done before. This drive is the need for achievement *(nAch)*. From research concerning the achievement need, McClelland found that high achievers differentiate themselves from others by their desire to do things better.[10] They seek situations in which they can take personal responsibility for finding solutions to problems, in which they can receive rapid and unambiguous feedback on their performance in order to tell whether or not they're improving, and in which they can set moderately challenging goals. (See Figure 15-5.) High achievers aren't gamblers; they dislike succeeding by chance. They prefer the challenge of working at a problem and accepting the personal responsibility for success or failure, rather than leaving the outcome to chance or the actions of others. An important point is that they avoid what they perceive to be very easy or very difficult tasks.

High achievers perform best when they perceive their probability of success as fifty-fifty. They dislike gambling when the odds are high because they get no achievement satisfaction from accidental success. Similarly, they dislike low odds (high probability of success) because then there's no challenge to their skills. They like to set goals that require stretching themselves a bit. When there's an approximately equal chance of success or failure, then there's the optimum opportunity to experience feelings of successful accomplishment and satisfaction from their efforts.

1 What is motivation and how is Maslow's hierarchy of needs theory a theory of motivation?

2 What are McGregor's Theory X and Theory Y assumptions?

3 Describe Herzberg's motivation-hygiene theory.

FIGURE 15-5 Matching Achievers and Jobs

The need for power is the desire to have impact and to be influential. Individuals high in *nPow* enjoy being "in charge", strive for influence over others, and prefer to be in competitive and status-oriented situations.

The third need isolated by McClelland is affiliation, which is the desire to be liked and accepted by others. This need has received the least attention from researchers. Individuals with high *nAff* strive for friendships, prefer co-operative situations rather than competitive ones, and desire relationships involving a high degree of mutual understanding.

How do you find out your levels of each of these three needs? All three motives are typically measured by a projective test in which respondents react to a set of pictures. Each picture is briefly shown to a subject, who then writes a story based on the picture. Trained interpreters then determine an individual's levels of nAch, nPow and nAff, from the stories written.

Based on an extensive amount of research, some reasonably well-supported predictions can be made between the relationship of the achievement need and job performance. Although less research has been done on power and affiliation needs, there are consistent findings here too. First, individuals with a high need to achieve prefer job situations with personal responsibility, feedback, and an intermediate degree of risk. When these characteristics are prevalent, high achievers are strongly motivated. The evidence consistently demonstrates, for instance, that high achievers are successful in entrepreneurial activities like running their own business, managing a self-contained division or unit within a large organization, and many sales positions.[11] Second, a high need to achieve doesn't necessarily lead to being a good manager, especially in large organizations. A high nAch salesperson at Pfizer doesn't necessarily make a good sales manager, and good managers in large organizations like PetroCanada, Nova Scotia Power, or Canadian Natural Resources, don't necessarily have a high need to achieve.[12] Third, the needs for affiliation and power are closely related to managerial success.[13] The best managers are high in the need for power and low in the need for affiliation. Last, employees can be trained successfully to stimulate their achievement need.[14] If a job calls for a high achiever, management can select a person with high nAch, or develop its own candidate through achievement training.

PetroCanada
www.petro-canada.ca

Nova Scotia Power Inc.
www.nspower.com

Goal-Setting Theory

In Chapter 7 in our discussion of MBO, we stated that there was substantial support for the proposition that specific goals increase performance and that difficult goals, when accepted, result in higher performance than easy goals. This proposition has been labelled **goal-setting theory**. It's not necessary to review the evidence again, but the results are important, so let's summarize what we know about goals as motivators.

goal-setting theory
Specific goals increase performance and difficult goals, when accepted, result in higher performance than easy goals.

Intention to work towards a goal is a major source of job motivation. Studies on goal setting have demonstrated the superiority of specific and challenging goals as motivating forces.[15] While we can't say that having employees participate in the goal-setting process is *always* desirable, participation is probably preferable to assigning goals when you expect resistance to accepting more difficult challenges.[16]

You may have noticed what appears to be a contradiction between the research findings on achievement motivation and goal setting. Is it a contradiction that achievement motivation is stimulated by moderately challenging goals, whereas goal-setting theory says that motivation is maximized by difficult goals? No, and our explanation is twofold.[17] First, goal-setting theory deals with people in general. The conclusions on achievement motivation are based only on people who have a high nAch. Given the probability that no more than 10 to 20 per-

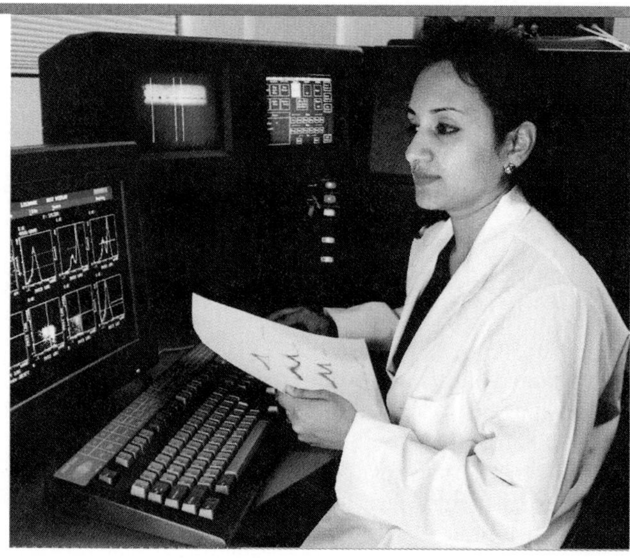

Motivating creative employees such as this scientist at Connaught Laboratories calls for new approaches, since scientists and inventors don't usually respond to traditional incentives. Companies that employ these types of individuals are devising motivational incentives such as patent royalty compensation, recognition programs, and opportunities to challenge their technical abilities.

cent of North Americans are naturally high achievers—and that proportion is undoubtedly far lower in underdeveloped countries—difficult goals are still recommended for the majority of employees. Second, the conclusions of goal-setting theory apply to those who accept, and are committed to, the goals. Difficult goals will lead to higher performance only if they're accepted.

Reinforcement Theory

reinforcement theory
Behaviour is a function of its consequences.

reinforcer
Any consequence immediately following a response that increases the probability that the behaviour will be repeated.

A counterpoint to goal-setting theory is **reinforcement theory**. Goal-setting theory proposes that an individual's purpose directs his or her actions. Reinforcement theory argues that behaviour is externally caused. What controls behaviour are **reinforcers**—consequences that, when immediately following a response, increase the probability that the behaviour will be repeated. Hence, reinforcement theorists argue that behaviour is a function of its consequences.

The key to reinforcement theory is that it ignores factors such as goals, expectations and needs. Instead, it focuses solely on what happens to a person when he or she takes some action. This helps to explain why publishers such as Simon & Schuster provide incentive clauses in their authors' contracts. If every time an author submits a completed chapter, the company sends an advance cheque against future royalties, the person is motivated to keep working and submitting chapters.

In Chapter 13 we showed how reinforcers shape behaviour and help people to learn. But the concept of reinforcement is also widely believed to explain motivation. According to B F Skinner, reinforcement theory can be explained as follows: People will most likely engage in desired behaviour if they're rewarded for doing so; these rewards are most effective if they immediately follow a desired response; and behaviour that isn't rewarded, or is punished, is less likely to be repeated.[18]

Following reinforcement theory, managers can influence employees' behaviour by reinforcing acts they deem favourable. However, because the emphasis is on positive reinforcement, not punishment, managers should ignore, not punish, unfavourable behaviour. Even though punishment eliminates undesired behaviour faster than non-reinforcement does, its effect is often only temporary and may later have unpleasant side effects, including dysfunctional behaviour such as workplace conflicts, absenteeism, and turnover.

TESTING... TESTING...

4 What are the three basic motivational needs McClelland identified in work situations?

5 Describe how goal-setting theory and reinforcement theory explain employee motivation.

Companies have traditional and not so traditional ways to reward employees. At Hewlett-Packard, an employee came to his manager with the solution to a problem that a group had struggled with for weeks. The manager fumbled around in his desk for something to give as a "reward" and finally handed him a banana from his lunch, exclaiming, "Well done!" Now the Golden Banana Award has become one of the company's most prestigious honours for inventiveness. At Lionel Trains Inc., a marching band came into the plant and led the way to a party for exceptional employees. Mobil, Toyota and Nabisco send outstanding employees on a "shopping spree" in which they have two minutes to fill a warehouse cart. IBM, Monsanto and Nikon give outstanding employees Star Certificates which declare their ownership of an actual star, with a sky chart and verification record.

The evidence indicates that reinforcement is undoubtedly an important influence on work behaviour. But reinforcement isn't the *only* explanation for differences in employee motivation.[19] Goals also affect motivation, as do levels of achievement needs, job design, inequities in rewards, and expectations.

Designing Motivating Jobs

Since managers are primarily interested in how to motivate individuals on the job, we need to look at ways in which to design motivating jobs. If you look closely at what an organization is and how it works, you'd find that it's composed of thousands, maybe even millions, of tasks. These tasks, in turn, are aggregated into jobs.[20] We use the term **job design** to refer to the way in which tasks are combined to form complete jobs. The jobs that people perform in organizations shouldn't evolve by chance. Management should design jobs deliberately and thoughtfully to reflect the demands of the changing environment, as well as the organization's technology and the skills, abilities, and preferences of its employees.[21] When this is done, employees are motivated to reach their full productive capabilities. Let's take a closer look at how managers can design motivating jobs.

job design
The way tasks are combined to form complete jobs.

Job Enlargement. As we saw earlier in Chapters 2 and 10, job design historically has concentrated on making jobs smaller and more specialized. Yet when jobs are narrow in focus and highly specialized, it's a real challenge to motivate employees. Thus, many organizations have looked at other job design options. One of the earliest efforts at overcoming the drawbacks of specialization involved the horizontal expansion of a job through increasing **job scope**—the number of different tasks required in a job and the frequency with which these tasks are

job scope
The number of different tasks required in a job and the frequency with which these tasks are repeated.

job enlargement
The horizontal expansion of a job; an increase in job scope.

job enrichment
Vertical expansion of a job by adding planning and evaluating responsibilities.

job depth
The degree of control employees have over their work.

job characteristics model (JCM)
A framework for analyzing and designing jobs; identifies five primary job characteristics, their interrelationships, and impact on outcome variables.

repeated. For instance, a mail sorter's job could be enlarged to include physically delivering the mail to the various departments, or running outgoing letters through the postage meter, as well as sorting the mail. This type of job design option is called **job enlargement**.

Efforts at job enlargement that focused solely on task enlargement have had less-than-exciting results. As one employee who experienced such a redesign said, "Before, I had one lousy job. Now, thanks to job enlargement, I have three lousy jobs!" However, a recent study that looked at how knowledge enlargement activities (expanding the scope of knowledge used in a job) affected workers found benefits such as more satisfaction, enhanced customer service, and fewer errors.[22] Even so, most job enlargement efforts provided few challenges and little meaning to a worker's activities, although they addressed the lack of diversity in overspecialized jobs.

Job Enrichment. Another approach to designing motivating jobs is through the vertical expansion of a job by adding planning and evaluating responsibilities—**job enrichment**. Job enrichment increases **job depth**, which is the degree of control employees have over their work. In other words, employees are empowered to assume some of the tasks typically done by their supervisors. Thus, the tasks in an enriched job should allow workers to do a complete activity with increased freedom, independence, and responsibility. And these tasks should also provide feedback so individuals can assess and correct their own performance. Although job enrichment can improve the quality of work output, employee motivation, and satisfaction, the research evidence on the use of job enrichment programs has been inconclusive.[23]

Job Characteristics Model. Even though many organizations have implemented job enlargement and job enrichment programs and have experienced mixed results, neither of these job design approaches provided a conceptual framework for analyzing jobs or for guiding managers in designing motivating jobs. However, the **job characteristics model (JCM)** offers such a framework.[24] It identifies five primary job characteristics, their interrelationships, and their effect on employee productivity, motivation and satisfaction.

MANAGERS WHO MAKE A DIFFERENCE

Frank Delfino, Chief Operating Officer (COO), Teknion Furniture Systems, Downsview, Ontario

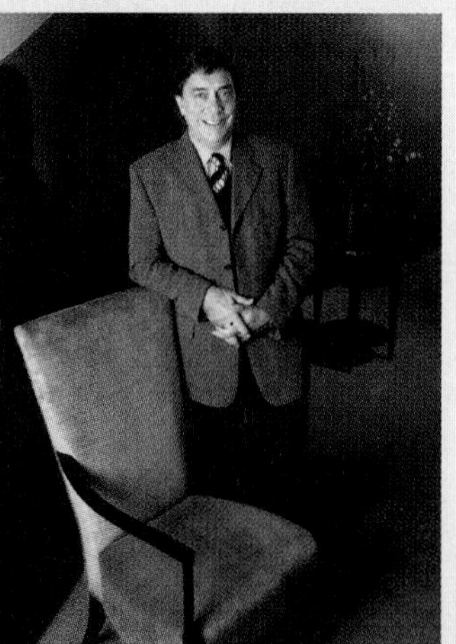

The furniture manufacturing business is a cyclical one, fluctuating between boom times and drought. For instance, during the recession of the early 1990s, more than 500 companies in the industry went out of business. Teknion, however, looked to global markets to compensate, and even managed to add to its workforce during the recession. No matter what the market conditions, COO Frank Delfino knows that his workforce is an essential asset, and acts accordingly. When orders have disappeared and production is slowed down, Teknion will put its employees to work in different areas (like cleaning and painting machinery), rather than lay them off. "People are not an expendable resource. When you lay off, you lose skill sets, morale, and most important, trust," says Delfino. This attitude has instilled high employee loyalty and trust in the company. When employees know that their employer appreciates their work, wants to retain their skills, and would lay them off only as a last resort, their work will reflect their contentment. Teknion's growth from 1997 to 1998 was a whopping 45.3 percent (with revenues of $260 million).[25]

Teknion Furniture Systems
www.teknion.com

According to the JCM, any job can be described in terms of five core dimensions, defined as follows:

- **Skill variety;** the degree to which a job requires a variety of activities so that an employee can use a number of different skills and talents
- **Task identity;** the degree to which a job requires completion of a whole and identifiable piece of work
- **Task significance;** the degree to which a job has a substantial impact on the lives or work of other people
- **Autonomy;** the degree to which a job provides substantial freedom, independence, and discretion to the individual in scheduling the work and determining the procedures to be used in carrying it out
- **Feedback;** the degree to which carrying out the work activities required by a job results in the individual's obtaining direct and clear information about the effectiveness of his or her performance.

Figure 15-6 presents the model. Notice how the first three dimensions—skill variety, task identity, and task significance—combine to create meaningful work. What we mean is that if these three characteristics exist in a job, we can predict that the person will view his or her job as being important, valuable and worthwhile. Notice, too, that jobs that possess autonomy give the job incumbent a feeling of personal responsibility for the results and that, if a job provides feedback, the employee will know how effectively he or she is performing.

From a motivational standpoint, the JCM suggests that intrinsic (internal) rewards are obtained when an employee *learns* (knowledge of results through feedback) that he or she *personally* (experienced responsibility through autonomy of work) has performed well on a task that he or she *cares about* (experienced meaningfulness through skill variety, task identity, and/or task significance).[26] The more these three conditions characterize a job, the greater the employee's motivation, performance and satisfaction, and the lower his or her absenteeism and likelihood of resigning. As the model shows, the links between the job dimensions and the outcomes are moderated by the strength of the individual's growth need (his or her desire for self-esteem and self-actualization). This means that individuals with a high growth need are more likely to experience the psychological states and respond positively when their jobs include the core dimensions than are low-growth-need individuals.

skill variety
The degree to which a job requires a variety of activities so that an employee can use a number of different skills and talents.

task identity
The degree to which a job requires completion of a whole and identifiable piece of work.

task significance
The degree to which a job has a substantial impact on the lives or work of other people.

autonomy
The degree to which a job provides substantial freedom, independence, and discretion to a person in scheduling and carrying out his or her work.

feedback
The degree to which carrying out the work activities required by a job results in a person's obtaining direct and clear information about the effectiveness of his or her performance.

FIGURE 15-6 Job Characteristics Model

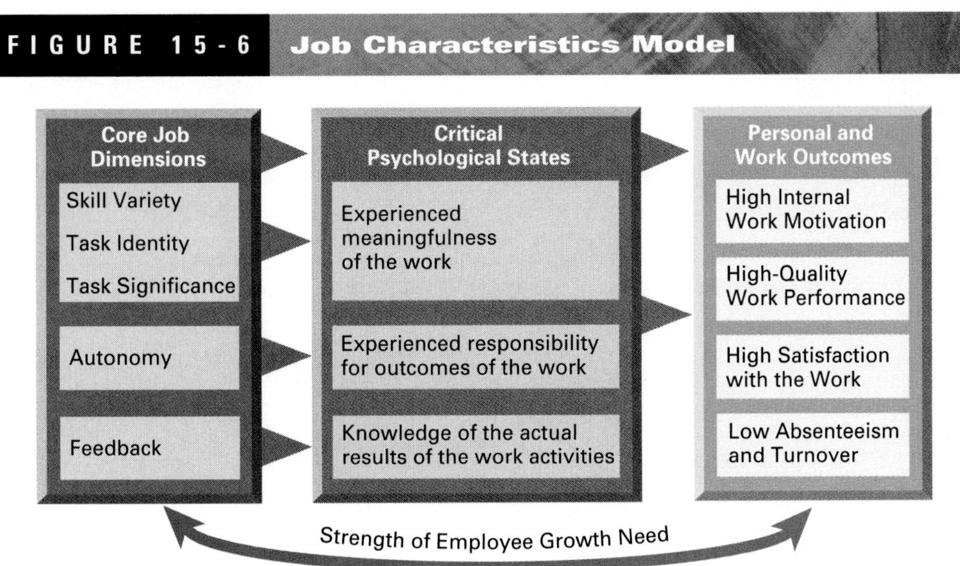

Source: J Richard Hackman and Lloyd Shuttle, eds., *Improving Life at Work* (Glenview, IL: Scott, Foresman and Co., 1977). With permission of the authors.

FIGURE 15-7 Computing Motivating Potential Score

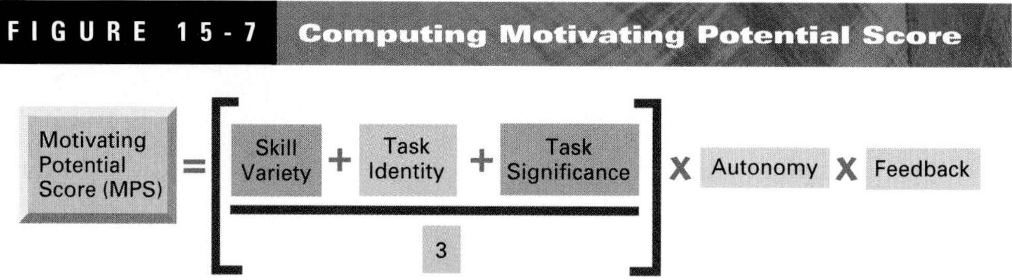

Source: J Richard Hackman and Lloyd Shuttle, eds., *Improving Life at Work* (Glenview, IL: Scott, Foresman and Co., 1977). With permission of the authors.

The core dimensions can be combined into a single index, as shown in Figure 15-7. To score high on motivating potential, jobs must be high on at least one of the three factors that lead to experiencing meaningfulness; they must also score high on both autonomy and feedback. If jobs score high on motivating potential, the model predicts that motivation, performance, and satisfaction will be positively affected, while the likelihood of absence and turnover will be diminished.[27]

The JCM provides specific guidance to managers for job design. (See Figure 15-8.) The following suggestions, which are based on the JCM, specify the types of changes in jobs that are most likely to lead to improvement in each of the five core job dimensions. You'll notice that two of these suggestions from the JCM incorporate the earlier job design concepts we discussed (job enlargement and job enrichment), although the other suggestions also involve more than vertically and horizontally expanding jobs.

1. *Combine tasks.* Managers should put existing fragmented tasks back together to form a new, larger module of work (job enlargement). This increases skill variety and task identity.

2. *Create natural work units.* Managers should design tasks that form an identifiable and meaningful whole. This increases employee "ownership" of the work, and encourages employees to view their work as meaningful and important, rather than as irrelevant and boring.

3. *Establish client relationships.* The client is the user of the product or service that the employee works on, and the client could be an internal organizational unit or person, as well as an external customer. Wherever possible, managers should establish direct relationships between workers and their clients. This increases skill variety, autonomy, and feedback for the employee.

FIGURE 15-8 Guidelines for Job Redesign

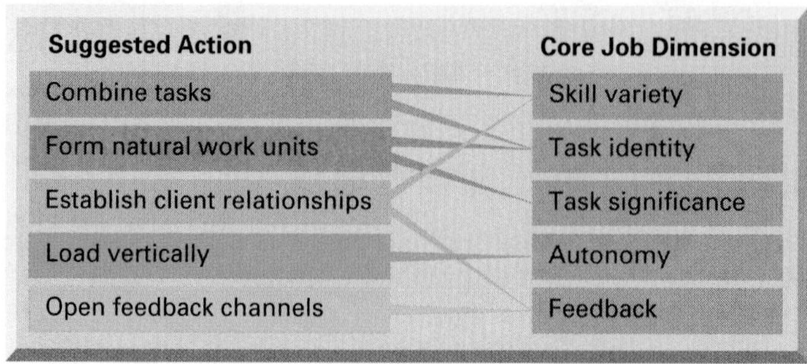

Source: J Richard Hackman and Lloyd Shuttle, eds., *Improving Life at Work* (Glenview, IL: Scott, Foresman and Co., 1977). With permission of the authors.

Ernie Garcia, an employee at Cadet Uniform of Toronto, has an enriched job—with a significant amount of freedom, independence and responsibility. He drives a delivery truck, as well as performing duties that would normally be done by supervisors, such as handling customer requests and complaints.

4. *Expand jobs vertically.* Vertical expansion (job enrichment) gives employees responsibilities and controls that were formerly reserved for management. It partially closes the gap between the "doing" and the "controlling" aspects of the job and increases employee autonomy.

5. *Open feedback channels.* By increasing feedback, employees not only learn how well they're performing at their jobs, but also whether their performances are improving, deteriorating, or remaining at a constant level. Ideally, employees should receive performance feedback directly while they do their jobs, rather than from management on an occasional basis.[28]

Equity Theory

Have you ever been curious about what kind of grade the person sitting next to you in class makes on a test or on a major class project? Most of us have been! Being the humans that we are, we tend to compare ourselves to others. If someone offered you $40 000 a year on your first job after graduating from college, you'd probably jump at the offer and report to work enthusiastic, ready to tackle whatever needed to be done, and certainly satisfied with your pay. How would you react, though, if you found out a month or so into the job that a co-worker—another recent graduate, your age, with comparable grades from a comparable school, and with comparable work experience—was getting $45 000 a year? You'd probably be pretty upset! Even though, in absolute terms, $40 000 is a lot of money for a new graduate to make (and you *know* it!), but that suddenly isn't the issue. You see the issue now as relative rewards and what you believe is fair—what's equitable. The term *equity* relates to the concept of fairness and equal treatment compared to others who behave in similar ways. There's considerable evidence that employees make comparisons of their job inputs and outcomes relative to others, and that inequities influence the degree of effort that employees exert.[29]

TABLE 15-2 Equity Theory

Perceived Ratio Comparison[a]	Employee's Assessment
$\frac{\text{Outcomes A}}{\text{Inputs A}} < \frac{\text{Outcomes B}}{\text{Inputs B}}$	Inequity (underrewarded)
$\frac{\text{Outcomes A}}{\text{Inputs A}} = \frac{\text{Outcomes B}}{\text{Inputs B}}$	Equity
$\frac{\text{Outcomes A}}{\text{Inputs A}} > \frac{\text{Outcomes B}}{\text{Inputs B}}$	Inequity (overrewarded)

[a] Person A is the employee, and person B is a relevant other or referent.

equity theory
The theory that an employee compares his or her job's inputs–outcomes ratio to that of relevant others and then corrects any inequity.

Equity theory, developed by J. Stacey Adams, proposes that employees perceive what they get from a job situation (outcomes) in relation to what they put into it (inputs), and then compare their inputs–outcomes ratio with the inputs–outcomes ratio of relevant others. (See Table 15-2.) If employees perceive their ratio to be equal to those of relevant others, a state of equity exists. In other words, they perceive that their situation is fair—that justice prevails. However, if the ratio is unequal, inequity exists and they view themselves as under- or overrewarded. When inequities occur, employees attempt to do something about it. And what will employees do when they perceive that an inequity exists? Let's look closer at their probable behavioural responses.

Equity theory proposes that employees might (1) distort either their own or others' inputs or outcomes, (2) behave in some way to induce others to change their inputs or outcomes, (3) behave in some way to change their own inputs or outcomes, (4) choose a different comparison person, and/or (5) quit their jobs. Also, when pay is specifically perceived to be inequitable, the theory suggests that employees who are either underrewarded or overrewarded will react in certain ways depending on whether their wages are based on time factors or quantity of output (see Figure 15-9). These types of employee reactions have generally proven to be correct.[30] And a review of the research consistently confirms the equity thesis:

FIGURE 15-9 Reactions to Perceptions of Inequitable Pay

1. **Given payment by time, overrewarded employees will produce more than equitably paid employees.** Hourly and salaried employees will generate a high quantity or quality of production in order to increase the input side of the ratio and bring it above equity.

2. **Given payment by quantity of production, overrewarded employees will produce fewer but higher-quality units than equitably paid employees.** Individuals paid on a piece-rate basis will increase their effort to achieve equity, which can result in greater quality or quantity. However, increases in quantity will only increase inequity, because every unit produced results in further overpayment. Therefore, effort is directed toward increasing quality rather than quantity.

3. **Given payment by time, underrewarded employees will produce less or poorer-quality output.** Effort will be decreased, which will bring about lower productivity or poorer-quality output than is produced by equitably paid employees.

4. **Given payment by quantity of production, underrewarded employees will produce a large number of low-quality units in comparison with equitably paid employees.** Employees on piece-rate pay plans can bring about equity because trading off quality of output for quantity will result in an increase in rewards with little or no increase in contributions.

Employee motivation is influenced significantly by relative rewards as well as absolute rewards. Whenever employees perceive inequity, they'll act to correct the situation.[31] The result might be lower or higher productivity, improved or reduced quality of output, increased absenteeism, or voluntary resignation.

The other question we need to ask in equity theory is: Who are these "others" against whom people compare themselves? The **referent** is an important variable in equity theory.[32] Three referent categories have been defined: other, system, and self. The "other" category includes other people with similar jobs in the same organization, and also includes friends, neighbours or professional associates. On the basis of what they hear at work or read about in newspapers or trade journals, employees compare their pay with that of others. The "system" category includes organizational pay policies and procedures, and the administration of the system. Whatever precedents have been established by the organization regarding pay allocation are major elements of this category. The "self" category refers to inputs–outcomes ratios that are unique to the individual. It reflects past personal experiences and contacts, and is influenced by criteria such as past jobs or family commitments. The choice of a particular set of referents is related to the information available about the referents as well as to their perceived relevance.

referents
The people, systems, or selves against which a person compares him- or herself to assess equity.

However applicable it might be to understanding employee motivation, we shouldn't conclude that equity theory is flawless. The theory leaves some key issues still unclear.[33] For instance, how do employees define inputs and outcomes? How do they combine and weigh their inputs and outcomes to arrive at totals? When and how do the factors change over time? In spite of these problems, equity theory does have an impressive amount of research support and offers us some important insights into employee motivation.

Expectancy Theory

The most comprehensive explanation of motivation to date is Victor Vroom's **expectancy theory**.[34] Although the theory has critics,[35] most research evidence supports it.[36]

expectancy theory
The theory that an individual tends to act in a certain way based on the expectation that the act will be followed by a given outcome, and on the attractiveness of that outcome to the individual.

Expectancy theory states that an individual tends to act in a certain way, based on the expectation that the act will be followed by a given outcome and on the attractiveness of that outcome to the individual. It includes three variables or relationships (see Figure 15-10):

1. *Expectancy* or *effort–performance linkage*, which is the probability perceived by the individual that exerting a given amount of effort will lead to a certain level of performance.
2. *Instrumentality* or *performance–reward linkage*, which is the degree to which the individual believes that performing at a particular level is instrumental in leading to the attainment of a desired outcome.

FIGURE 15-10 Simplified Expectancy Model

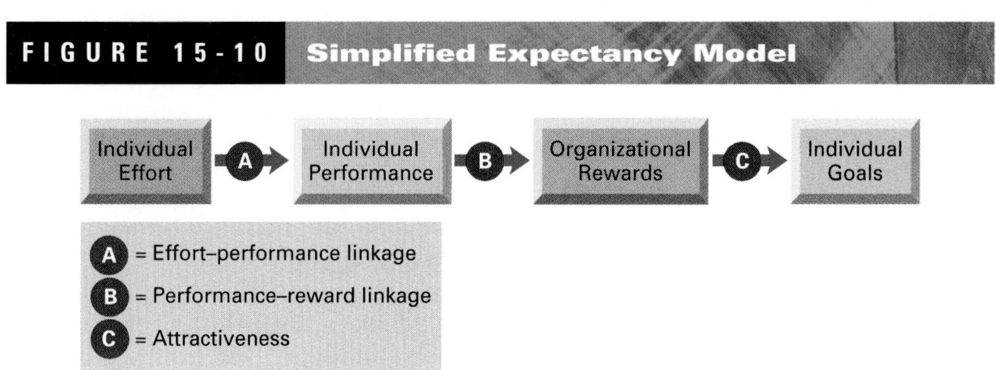

6 **Define job enlargement and job enrichment.**

7 **Describe the job characteristics model as a way to design motivating jobs.**

8 **What are the motivation implications of equity theory?**

3. *Valence* or *attractiveness of reward*, which is the importance that the individual places on the potential outcome or reward that can be achieved on the job. Valence considers both the goals and needs of the individual.

While this explanation of motivation might sound complex, it really isn't that difficult to visualize. It can be summed up in the questions: How hard do I have to work to achieve a certain level of performance, and can I actually achieve that level? What reward will performing at that level of performance get me? How attractive is the reward to me and does it help me achieve my goals? Whether you're motivated to exert effort (i.e., produce) at any given time, depends on your particular goals and your perception of whether or not a certain level of performance is necessary to attain those goals. Let's look at the features inherent in the theory and attempt to apply it.

First, what perceived outcomes does the job offer the employee? Outcomes (rewards) may be positive—things such as pay, security, companionship, trust, fringe benefits, a chance to use talents or skills, or congenial relationships. Or the employee may view the outcomes as negative—fatigue, boredom, frustration, anxiety, harsh supervision, or threat of dismissal. And keep in mind that reality isn't relevant here. The crucial issue is what the person *perceives* the outcome to be, regardless of whether the perceptions are accurate.

Second, how attractive are these outcomes or rewards to employees? Are they valued positively, negatively, or neutrally? This obviously is a personal and internal issue that depends on the individual's attitudes, personality and needs. A person who finds a particular reward attractive—that is, he or she values it positively—would rather attain it than not attain it. Others may find it negative and therefore prefer not to attain it. And others may be neutral about the outcome.

Third, what kind of behaviour must the employee exhibit in order to achieve these rewards? The rewards aren't likely to have any effect on any individual employee's performance unless he or she knows, clearly and unambiguously, what must be done to achieve them. For example, what is "doing well" in terms of performance appraisal? What criteria will be used to judge the employee's performance?

Finally, how does the employee view his or her chances of doing what is asked? After an employee has considered his or her own skills and ability to control those variables that lead to success, what's the likelihood that he or she can successfully perform at the necessary level?[37]

Let's look at the classroom organization for an example of how you can use the expectancy theory of motivation.

Most students prefer their instructor to tell them what the course expectations are. They want to know what the assignments and exams will be like, when they're going to be due or taken, and how much weight each carries in the final determination of the grade. They also like to think that the amount of effort exerted in attending classes, taking notes, and studying outside class will be reasonably related to the grade they'll make in the course. Let's assume that you feel this way. Consider that five weeks into a class you're really enjoying (we'll call it MGT 301), a test is given back to you. You studied hard for this examination and put in several hours of reading the chapters and going over your notes. And, in the past, you've consistently made *A*s and *B*s on tests in other courses where you've expended this kind of effort. The reason you work so hard is to make top grades, which you believe are important for getting a good job after graduation. Also, you're not sure, but you might want to go on to graduate school. Again, you think good grades are important for getting into a good graduate program.

Well, the results of the test are in. The class median was 72. Ten percent of the class scored an 85 or higher and got an *A*. Your grade was 46; the minimum passing mark was 50. You're mad. You're frustrated. Even more, you can't understand it! How could you possibly have done so poorly on the test when you usually score in the top range in other classes by preparing as you did for this one?

Several interesting things might happen to your behaviour now. Suddenly, you're no longer interested in attending MGT 301 regularly. You find that you don't study for the course either. When you do attend class, you daydream a lot—the result is an empty notebook instead of several pages of notes. "Lacking in motivation" would probably be an apt description at this point. Why did your motivation level change? You know and we know. But let's explain it by using expectancy theory.

If we use Figure 15-10 to understand this situation, we might say the following: You study and prepare for MGT 301 (exert effort) in order to correctly answer the questions on the test (performance), which will produce a high grade (reward), and which will lead, in turn, to the security, prestige, and other benefits that come from obtaining a good job (individual goal). The attractiveness of the outcome, which in this case is a good grade, is high. But what about the performance–reward linkage? Do you feel that the grade you received truly reflects your knowledge of the material? In other words, did the test fairly measure what you knew? If the answer is yes, then this linkage is strong. If the answer is no, then at least part of the reason for your reduced motivational level is your belief that the test wasn't a fair measure of your performance.

Another possible demotivating force may be the effort–performance relationship. If, after you took the test, you believe that you couldn't have passed it even with the amount of preparation you'd done, then your motivation to study will drop. Placing a low value on all your hard work and study efforts that you thought would lead you to answer the test questions correctly makes your motivational level and level of effort decrease.

The key to the expectancy theory is understanding an individual's goal—and the linkages between effort and performance, between performance and rewards and, finally, between rewards and individual goal satisfaction. As a contingency model, expectancy theory recognizes that there is no *universal* principle for explaining each person's motivation. In addition, knowing what needs a person seeks to satisfy doesn't ensure that the individual will perceive that high performance will necessarily lead to satisfying those needs.

Let's summarize some of the issues surrounding expectancy theory. First, it emphasizes payoffs, or rewards. As a result, we have to believe that the rewards an organization is offering align with what the individual wants. It's a theory based on self-interest, since each individual seeks to maximize his or her expected satisfaction of needs. Second, expectancy theory stresses that managers understand why employees view certain outcomes as attractive or unattractive. We want to reward individuals with those things they value positively. Third, expectancy theory emphasizes expected behaviours. Do employees know what's expected of them and how they'll be evaluated? Finally, the theory is concerned with perceptions. Reality is irrelevant. An individual's own perceptions of performance, reward, and goal satisfaction outcomes —not the objective outcomes themselves— will determine his or her level of effort.

Integrating Contemporary Theories of Motivation

We've presented a number of motivation theories in this chapter. You might be tempted, at this point, to view them independently. However, this is a mistake. The fact is that many of the ideas underlying the theories are complementary, and your understanding of how to motivate people is maximized when you see how the theories fit together.[38]

Figure 15-11 presents a model that integrates much of what we know about motivation. Its basic foundation is the simplified expectancy model shown in Figure 15-10. Let's work through this model, beginning at the left.

The individual effort box has an arrow leading into it. This arrow flows from the individual's goals. Consistent with goal-setting theory, this goals–effort link is meant to illustrate that goals direct behaviour.

Expectancy theory predicts that an employee will exert a high level of effort if he or she perceives that there's a strong relationship between effort and performance, performance and rewards, and rewards and satisfaction of personal goals. Each of these relationships, in turn, is influenced by certain factors. You can see from the model that the level of individual performance is determined not only by the level of individual effort, but also by the individual's ability to perform, and whether or not the organization has a fair and objective performance evaluation system. The performance–reward relationship will be strong if the individual perceives that it's performance—rather than seniority, personal favourites, or some other criteria—that's rewarded. The final link in expectancy theory is the rewards–goal relationship. Need theories come into play at this point. Motivation would be high to the degree that the rewards an individual achieved for his or her high performance satisfied the dominant needs consistent with his or her individual goals.

A closer look at the model also shows that it considers the achievement need, reinforcement, equity, and JCM theories. The high achiever isn't motivated by the organization's assess-

FIGURE 15-11 Integrating Contemporary Theories of Motivation

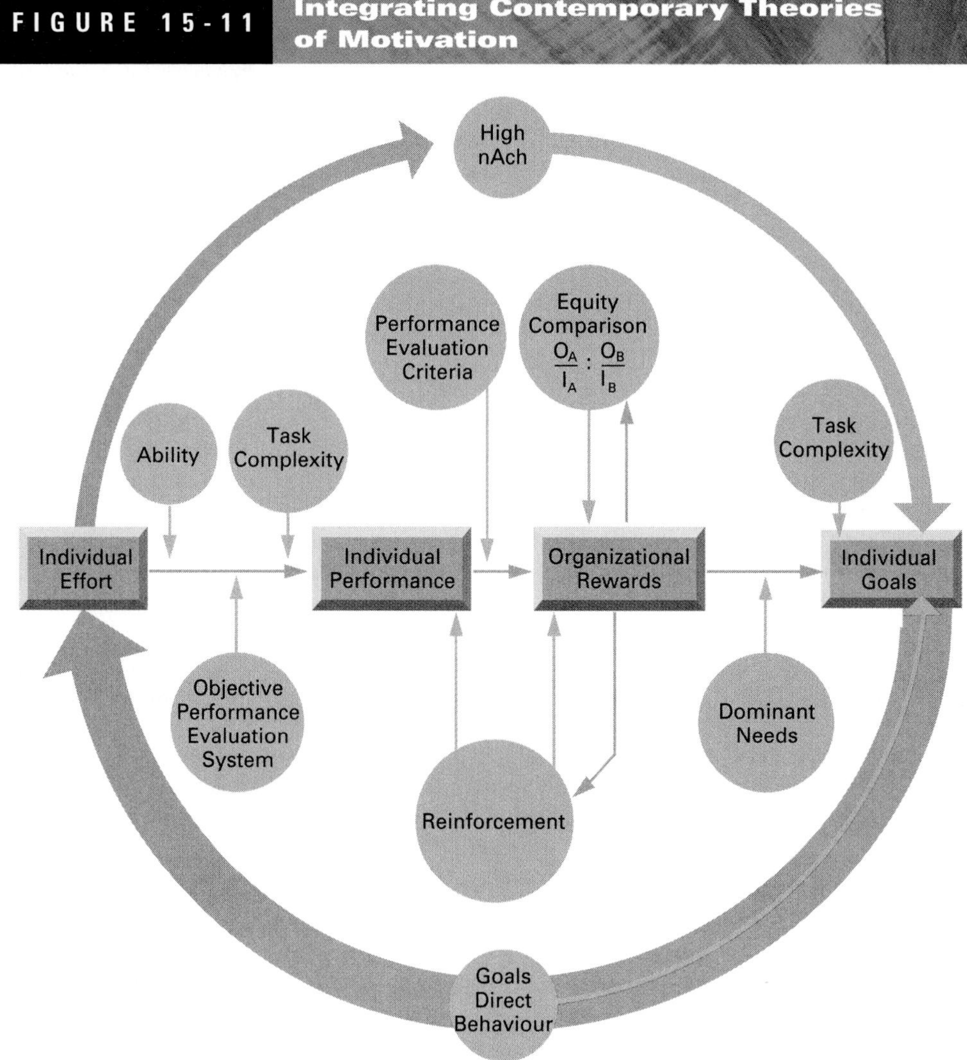

ment of his or her performance or organizational rewards; hence the jump from effort to individual goals for those with a high nAch. Remember that high achievers are internally driven, as long as the jobs they're doing provide them with personal responsibility, feedback, and moderate risks. They're not concerned with the effort–performance, performance–rewards, or rewards–goal linkages.

Reinforcement theory is seen in the model by recognizing that the organization's rewards reinforce the individual's performance. If management has designed a reward system that's seen by employees as "paying off" for good performance, the rewards will reinforce and encourage continued good performance. Rewards also play a key part in equity theory. Individuals will compare the rewards (outcomes) they've received from the inputs or efforts they made, with the inputs–outcomes ratio of relevant others. If inequities exist, the effort expended may be influenced.

9 Describe the three key linkages in expectancy theory.

10 What role does perception play in expectancy theory?

11 How might the contemporary motivation theories be integrated to explain employee motivation?

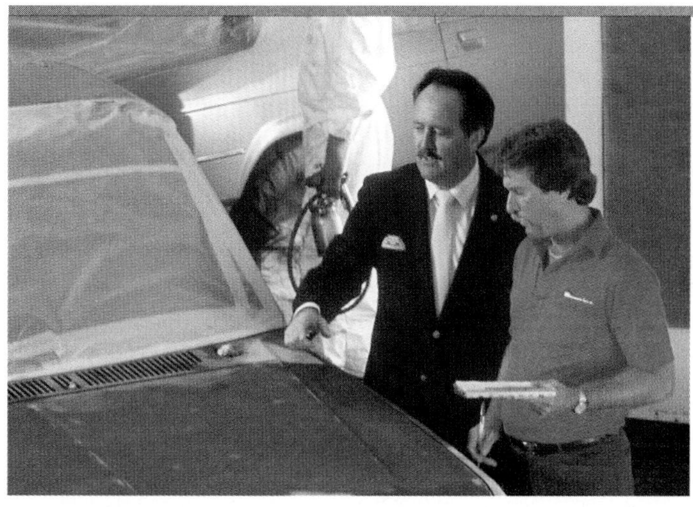

Managers at GM Canada, motivate factory workers by reinforcing desired workplace behaviours.

Finally, we can see the JCM in this integrative model. Task characteristics (job design) influence job motivation at two different places. First, jobs that score high in motivating potential are likely to lead to higher actual job performance, since the individual's motivation is stimulated by the job itself. So jobs that are high in complexity (motivating potential) increase the linkage between effort and performance. Second, jobs that score high in motivating potential also increase an employee's control over key elements in his or her work. Therefore, jobs that offer autonomy, feedback, and similar complex task characteristics help to satisfy the individual goals of those employees who desire greater control over their work.

CONTEMPORARY ISSUES IN MOTIVATION

Up to this point, we've covered a lot of the theoretical bases of employee motivation. Understanding and predicting employee motivation continues to be one of the most popular areas in management research. However, even current studies of employee motivation are influenced by several significant workplace issues—issues such as motivating a diverse workforce, pay-for-performance programs, ESOPs, and motivating minimum-wage employees. Let's take a closer look at each of these issues.

Motivating a Diverse Workforce

To maximize motivation in today's diverse workforce, managers need to think in terms of *flexibility*. For instance, studies tell us that men place more importance on having autonomy in their jobs than women. In contrast, the opportunity to learn, convenient work hours, and good interpersonal relations are more important to women.[39] Managers need to recognize that what motivates a single mother with two dependent children who's working full time to support her family may be very different from the needs of a young, single, part-time employee, or the older employee who's working only to supplement his or her retirement income. Employees have different personal needs and goals that they're hoping to satisfy through their job. Offering various types of rewards to meet these diverse needs can be highly motivating for employees.

Many of the so-called family-friendly programs (as we discussed in Chapter 11) and flexible working schedules that organizations have developed are a response to the varied needs of a diverse workforce. For instance, a job for most people in North America means leaving home and going to a place of work, arriving at 8 or 9 in the morning, putting in a fixed set of hours, and doing this routine five days a week. Yet it doesn't have to be this way. Depending on labour market conditions, the type of work that has to be done, and employee preferences, managers might consider implementing a compressed workweek, flexible work hours, job sharing, or telecommuting.

A **compressed workweek** consists of four ten-hour days. Proponents claim that these "4-40" programs have a favourable effect on employee absenteeism, job satisfaction, and productivity.[40] However, studies of organizations using compressed workweeks have shown that

compressed workweek
A workweek consisting of four ten-hour days.

there are also drawbacks, such as a decrease in workers' productivity near the end of the longer workday, a decrease in service to customers or clients, unwillingness to work longer days if a deadline needs to be met, and underutilization of equipment.[41] Because the compressed workweek does have its problems for employees *and* managers, many organizations have tried a different approach to giving workers increased freedom—flexible work hours.

flexible work hours (flextime)
A scheduling system in which employees are required to work a number of hours a week, but are free, within limits, to vary the hours of work.

In **flexible work hours** (also popularly known as **flextime**) scheduling, employees are required to work a specific number of hours a week, but are free to vary those hours within certain limits. In a flextime schedule, there are certain common core hours when all employees are required to be on the job, but starting, ending, and lunch-hour times are flexible. How widespread is flextime? In the early 1970s, few companies offered this scheduling option. By the mid 1990s, however, about 85 percent of major companies offered some type of flextime option.[42] And how well does flextime work? Most of the evidence shows that it tends to reduce absenteeism, improve morale, and improve worker productivity.[43] Since flextime allows employees to schedule their work hours to better align with personal demands, it can have a motivating effect. However, flextime does have its drawbacks, particularly for managers. Some of these problems are that it creates difficulties in directing subordinates outside the common core times, causes confusion in shift work, increases difficulties when someone with a particular skill or knowledge isn't available; and it makes planning and controlling more cumbersome and costly. And there are some jobs where flextime just isn't possible because of the interdependence of tasks—jobs such as assembly-line operator, salesperson in a department store, and office receptionist, where the jobholder depends on others inside or outside the organization.

job sharing
The practice of having two or more people split a 40-hour-a-week job.

Another job-scheduling option that can be effective in motivating a diverse workforce is job sharing. **Job sharing** is the practice of having two or more people split a 40-hour-a-week job. This type of job schedule might be attractive, for example, to retirees or people with school-aged children, who want to work but don't want the demands and hassles of a full-time position. The individual benefits by having a job that meets his or her needs and the organization benefits by having the talents of more than one individual in a given job, as well as acquiring skilled workers who might not want to work on a full-time basis. In addition, job sharing can enhance productivity. Job sharers typically have better attendance records than regular, full-time employees.[44]

telecommuting
The linking, by computer and modem, of workers at home with co-workers and management at an office.

Computer technology has opened still another alternative for managers in the way in which they design motivating jobs for a diverse workforce. This alternative is to allow employees to perform their work at home by **telecommuting.**[45] Many white-collar occupations can now be carried out at home—at least technically. Modems and computers allow employees who work at home to be linked electronically to their co-workers and managers at the office.

For employees, the two big advantages of telecommuting are the decrease in the time and stress of commuting in urban areas, and the increase in flexibility in coping with family demands. But it may have some potential drawbacks as well. For example, will telecommuters miss the regular social contact that a formal office provides? Will they be less likely to be considered for salary increases and promotions? Is being out of sight equivalent to being out of

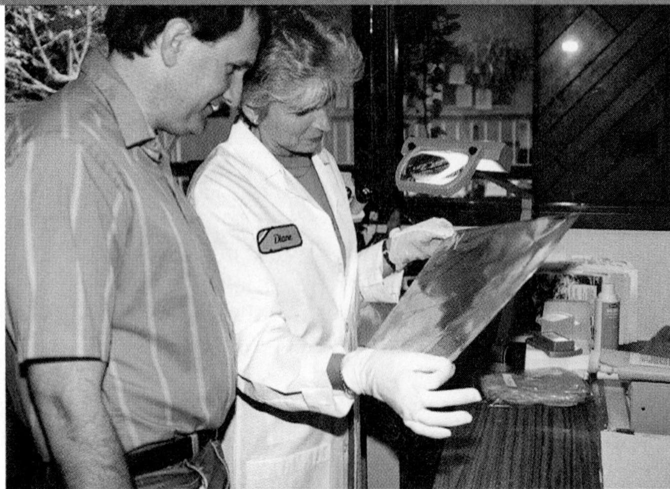

Cray Research Inc. has devised several family-friendly arrangements for its highly educated, creative and innovative workforce. Arrangements such as flexible work hours, sick-child care, and family leave, in addition to several reward and recognition programs, encourage superior performance from its employees.

mind? Will they be able to separate their work and home roles? Answers to such questions are central in determining whether telecommuting will continue to expand in the future.

Managing a diverse workforce also means that managers need to be flexible by being aware of *cultural* differences. The theories of motivation we've been studying were developed largely by North American psychologists and validated with North American workers. These theories may need to be modified for different cultures.[46]

For instance, the self-interest concept is consistent with capitalism and the extremely high value placed on individualism in Canada. Because almost all the motivation theories presented in this chapter are based on the self-interest motive, they should be applicable to organizations in such countries as Great Britain and Australia, where capitalism and individualism are also highly valued. However, in more collectivist countries—such as Venezuela, Singapore, Japan and Mexico—the link to the organization is the individual's *loyalty* to the organization or society, rather than his or her self-interest. Employees in collectivist cultures should be more receptive to team-based job design, group goals, and group performance evaluations. Reliance on the fear of being fired in such cultures is also likely to be less effective—even if laws allow managers to do so—because of the belief that the fired person will be "taken care of" by their extended family, friends or community.

The need achievement concept provides another example of a motivation theory with a North American bias. The view that a high need for achievement acts as an internal motivator presupposes the existence of two cultural characteristics: a willingness to accept a moderate degree of risk and a concern with performance. These characteristics would exclude countries with high uncertainty avoidance scores and high quality-of-life ratings. The remaining countries are mostly Anglophone countries such as New Zealand, Ireland, the United States, and Canada.

Yet the results of some recent studies of managers in countries outside North America indicate that some aspects of motivation theory are transferable.[47] For instance, the various reinforcement techniques were shown to be effective in changing performance-related behaviours of Russian textile mill workers. However, we shouldn't automatically assume that what works with North American workers will have the same results with workers from different cultures.

Also, keep in mind that changing motivational techniques to fit a culture works both ways. Motivation techniques that work well in China, for example, may be inappropriate in North America. A large department store in Xian, China, selects its 40 *worst* sales clerks each year.[48] These clerks write self-criticisms and analyze their own shortcomings. Management then hangs a plaque over their workstations, complete with picture, proclaiming them as members of the "40 Worst". This approach was a response to the generally poor service that management felt its clerks were giving customers and the fact that lifetime employment is guaranteed for Chinese employees. The store's management has found that those employees selected for the "40 Worst" awards are strongly motivated to improve their performances and to get the plaques removed from their work areas. However, motivation through humiliation might be acceptable and effective in China, but it isn't likely to work in Canada.

Pay for Performance

Why do most people work? Although there may be many reasons why people work, most of us work because it pays us an amount of money that allows us to satisfy our needs and wants. Because pay is an important variable in motivation as one type of reward, we need to look at how we can use pay to motivate high levels of employee performance. And this explains the intent and logic behind pay-for-performance programs.

Pay-for-performance programs are compensation plans that pay employees on the basis of some performance measure.[49] Piece-rate pay plans, wage incentive plans, profit sharing, and lump sum bonuses are examples. What differentiates these forms of pay from more traditional compensation plans is that, instead of paying a person for *time* on the job, pay is adjusted to reflect some performance measure. These performance measures might include such things as individual productivity, team or work group productivity, departmental productivity, or the overall organization's profit performance.

pay-for-performance programs
Compensation plans that pay employees on the basis of some performance measure.

Performance-based compensation is probably most compatible with expectancy theory. Specifically, individuals should perceive a strong relationship between their performance and the rewards they receive, if motivation is to be maximized. If rewards are allocated only on

THINKING CRITICALLY ABOUT ETHICS

You have been hired as a telephone sales representative at a travel agency. You book vacation plans for customers. Most car rental firms and hotels run contests for the sales representatives who book the most car rentals or hotel rooms. The incentives are very attractive, enough to encourage you to "steer" customers towards one of those companies, even though it might not be the cheapest or most convenient for them. Your supervisor doesn't discourage participation in these programs. Do you see anything wrong with this situation? Explain. What ethical issues do you see for (a) the employees, (b) the organization, and (c) the customer? How could an organization design performance incentive programs that encourage high levels of performance without compromising ethics? ■

non-performance factors—such as seniority, job title, or across-the-board pay raises—then employees are likely to reduce their efforts.

Needless to say, pay-for-performance programs are gaining in popularity. One survey of 2000 companies found that 68 percent of the respondents were practising some form of pay-for-performance for salaried employees.[50] The growing popularity can be explained in terms of both motivation and cost control. From a motivation perspective, making some or all of a worker's pay conditional on some performance measure focuses his or her attention and effort towards that measure, then reinforces the continuation of the effort with a reward. If the employee, team, or organization's performance declines, so does the reward. Thus, there's an incentive to keep efforts and motivation strong. Also, performance-based bonuses and other incentive rewards avoid the fixed expense of permanent salary increases and so save money.

Open-Book Management

Many organizations of various sizes are involving their employees in workplace decisions by opening up the financial statements (the "books"). They share that information so that employees will be motivated to make better decisions about their work and will be better able to understand the implications of what they do, how they do it, and the ultimate impact they have on the bottom line. This approach is called **open book management**. The goal is to get employees to think like an owner by seeing the impact their decisions and actions have on financial results. Of course, most employees will not have had the training to understand the finance, so they have to be taught how to read the statements. Some organizations take open-book management a step further and, along with sharing financial statements, give employees bonuses and incentive pay based on profit improvements.

open book management
A motivational approach in which an organization's financial statements are opened to all employees.

Employee Share Ownership Plans (ESOPs)

Many companies are using ESOPs as an incentive for improving and motivating employee performance. An **employee share ownership plan (ESOP)** is a compensation program in which employees become part owners of the organization by receiving shares as a performance incentive. Also, many ESOPs allow employees to purchase additional shares at attractive, below-market prices. Under an ESOP, employees are often motivated to work harder because it makes them owners who will share in any gains and losses. The fruits of their labours are no longer just going into the pockets of some unknown owner—the employees *are* the owners!

employee share ownership plan (ESOP)
A compensation program in which employees become part owners of the organization by receiving shares as a performance incentive.

Do ESOPs affect productivity and employee satisfaction? Yes, they do! The research on ESOPs indicate that they increase employee satisfaction and frequently result in higher performance. For instance, one study compared 45 ESOP companies with 238 conventional companies. The ESOP firms outperformed the conventional ones, both in terms of employment and sales growth.[51] However, other studies showed that, although productivity in organizations with ESOPs does increase, the impact is greater the longer the ESOP has been in existence.[52] So organizations shouldn't expect immediate increases in employee motivation and productiv-

TESTING... TESTING...

12 **What are some options for motivating a diverse workforce?**

13 **How is performance-based compensation compatible with expectancy theory?**

This team of young managers at Yoplait, a division of General Mills Inc., collects big rewards for meeting performance objectives. Top performers get bonus cheques of up to $50 000!

ity if an ESOP is implemented. But in the long run, employee productivity and satisfaction should go up.

Although ESOPs have the potential to increase employee satisfaction and work motivation, employees need to psychologically experience ownership in order to realize this potential.[53] What we mean is that, in addition to merely having a financial stake in the organization, employees need to be regularly informed on the status of the business and have the opportunity to exercise influence over the business. When these conditions are met, "employees will be more satisfied with their jobs, more satisfied with their organizational identification, motivated to come to work, and motivated to perform well while at work".[54]

Motivating the "New Workforce"

Special groups present unique challenges in terms of motivation. In this section, we look at some of the unique problems faced in trying to motivate professional employees, contingent workers, and low-skilled minimum-wage employees.

Motivating Professionals. Highly trained professionals have a strong, long-term commitment to their field of expertise. Their loyalty is more often to their profession than to their employer. To keep current in their field they need to regularly update their knowledge and, because of their commitment to their profession, their workweek is rarely defined by the tra-

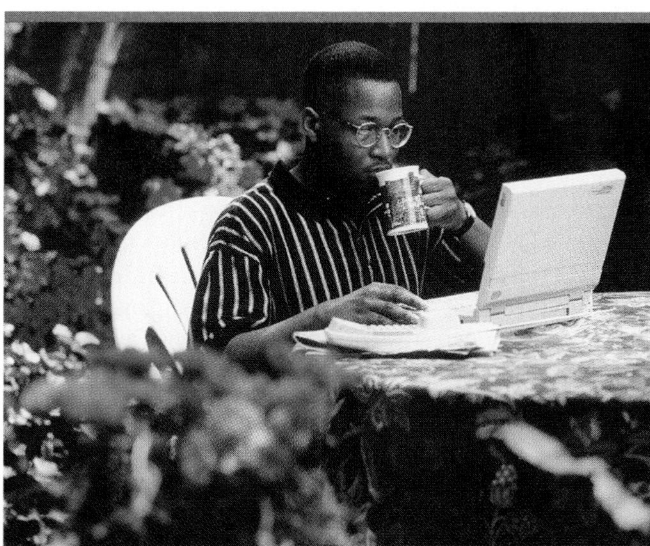

Professionals who derive intrinsic satisfaction from their work are driven by loyalty to their profession. Motivating them often means simply giving them the means and opportunity to do what they do best. This Price Waterhouse employee is using a laptop to work at home.

ditional 40-hour, Monday-to-Friday workweek. What motivates professionals? Money and promotions are typical motivators for most people but, for professionals, job challenges generally far outweigh these considerations. They like to tackle problems and find solutions. Their chief reward in the job is the work itself. Professionals also value support. They want others to think that what they are doing is important. This may be true to some degree for all employees, but professionals tend to be focused on their work as their central life interest, whereas non-professionals typically have other interests outside of work that can compensate for needs not met in the job. Guidelines for motivating professionals therefore should include providing autonomy to follow their interests; allowing them to structure their work in ways they find productive; rewarding them with educational opportunities—training, workshops, attending conferences—that allow them to keep current in their field; and rewarding them with recognition of their work.

Motivating Contingent Workers. As we mentioned in Chapter 2, there is an increase in the number of temporary or contingent workers in the workforce. The elimination of many jobs through downsizing has increased the number of openings for part-time, contract, and other forms of temporary workers. Contingent workers don't have the security or stability that permanent employees have, and they don't identify with the organization or display the commitment that other employees do. Temporary workers are also typically provided with no health care, pensions, or other benefits.

There is no simple solution for motivating contingent employees. For that small set of temps who prefer the freedom of their temporary status—some students, working mothers, seniors—the lack of stability may not be an issue. In addition, temporariness might be preferred by highly compensated physicians, engineers, accountants, or financial planners who don't want the demands of a stable job. But these are exceptions. For the most part, temporary employees are not temporary by choice.

What will motivate involuntary temporary employees? An obvious answer is the opportunity for permanent status. In cases in which permanent employees are selected from a pool of temporaries, temps will often work hard in the hope of becoming permanent. A less obvious answer is the opportunity for training. The ability of a temporary employee to find a new job is largely dependent on his or her skills. If the employee sees that the job he or she is doing can help to develop marketable skills, then motivation is increased. From an equity standpoint, you should also consider the repercussions of mixing permanent and temporary workers when pay differentials are significant. When temps work alongside permanent employees who earn more—and get benefits too—for doing the same job, the performance of temps is likely to suffer. Separating such employees, or perhaps converting all employees to a variable-pay or skill-based pay plan, might help minimize the problem.

Motivating Minimum-Wage Employees

Let's pretend that, in your first managerial position after graduating, you're responsible for managing a work group composed of minimum-wage employees. Offering more pay to these employees for high levels of performance is out of the question; the company just can't afford it. What are your motivational options at this point?[55] One of the toughest motivation challenges a manager faces is how to achieve and keep high performance levels among minimum-wage workers.

One trap we often fall into is thinking that people are only motivated by money. And although money is important as a motivator, it's not the only "reward" that people seek and that managers can use. In motivating minimum-wage employees, managers often look at other types of rewards that serve the function of helping motivate employee performance. What are some other types of rewards that managers can use? Many companies use employee recognition programs such as employee of the month, quarterly employee performance awards ceremonies, or other celebrations of employees' accomplishments. For instance, at many fast-food restaurants or retail stores, you'll often see plaques hanging in prominent places that feature the "Employee of the Month". These types of programs serve the purpose of highlighting employees whose work performance has been of the type and level the organization wants to encourage in all its employees. Many managers also recognize the power of praise. However, you need to be sure that these "pats on the back" are sincere and done for the right reasons. Otherwise, employees may see right through them, thus discounting their motivational power.

Managers at Raleigh Cycle Company are out on the floor, the same as their employees. They expect every employee to make suggestions and run quality checks on their own production. In return, they make themselves available to solve problems and provide positive feedback.

But we know from the motivation theories presented earlier that rewards are only part of the motivation picture. What else can managers do to motivate high levels of performance from minimum-wage employees?

Again, we can look to job design and expectancy theories for some answers. In service industries such as travel and hospitality, retail sales, child care, and maintenance, where pay for front-line employees generally doesn't get above the minimum-wage level, successful companies are empowering these front-line employees with more authority to address customers' problems. If we use the JCM to examine this change, we can see that this type of job redesign provides enhanced motivating potential, because employees now experience increased skill variety, task identity, task significance, autonomy and feedback. For instance, at Marriott International, almost every job in its hotels is being redesigned to place more workers in contact with more guests more of the time.[56] These employees are now able to take care of customer complaints and requests that formerly were referred to a supervisor or another department.

So, even though motivating minimum-wage workers may be more of a challenge, we can still use what we know about employee motivation to help us to come up with some answers.

FROM THEORY TO PRACTICE: SUGGESTIONS FOR MOTIVATING EMPLOYEES

In this chapter, we've covered a lot of information about motivation. But if you're a manager concerned with motivating your employees, what specific recommendations can you draw from the theories and issues presented in this chapter? While there's no simple, all-encompassing set of guidelines, the suggestions outlined in Table 15-3 draw on the essence of what we know about motivating employees. Let's look at these more closely.

TABLE 15-3 Suggestions for Motivating Employees

- Recognize individual differences.
- Match people to jobs.
- Use goals.
- Ensure that goals are perceived as being attainable.
- Individualize rewards.
- Link rewards to performance.
- Check the system for equity.
- Don't ignore money.

Recognize Individual Differences. Almost every contemporary motivation theory recognizes that employees aren't homogeneous. They have different needs. They also differ in terms of attitudes, personality, and other important individual variables. For instance, expectancy predictions are more accurate with individuals who have an internal rather than external locus of control.[57] Why? The former believe that events in their lives are largely under their own control, which is consistent with the expectancy theory's self-interest assumptions.

Match People to Jobs. There's a great deal of evidence showing the motivational benefits of carefully matching people to jobs. For example, high achievers should be sought for a job of running a small business, or an autonomous unit within a larger business. However, if the job to be filled is a managerial slot in a large bureaucratic organization, a candidate high in nPow and low in nAff should be selected. Along these same lines, don't put a high achiever into a job that's inconsistent with his or her needs. Achievers will do best in jobs that provide opportunities to participate in setting moderately challenging goals and in which there's autonomy and feedback. Keep in mind that not everybody is motivated by jobs that are high in autonomy, variety, and responsibility. Such jobs are most attractive and motivating to employees with a high growth need.

Use Goals. The literature on goal-setting theory suggests that managers should ensure that employees have hard, specific goals, and feedback on how well they're doing in pursuit of those goals. For those with high achievement needs, typically a minority in any organization, the existence of external goals is less important because high achievers are already internally motivated.

Should the goals be assigned by a manager, or should employees participate in setting goals? The answer depends on your perception of goal acceptance and the organization's culture. If you expect resistance to goals, the use of participation should increase acceptance. If participation is inconsistent with the culture, use assigned goals. When participation and the culture are incongruous, employees are likely to perceive the participative process as manipulative and be turned off by it.

Ensure That Goals Are Perceived as Being Attainable. Regardless of whether goals are actually attainable, employees who see these goals as unattainable will reduce their effort—their feeling being "why bother". Managers must be sure, therefore, that employees feel confident that increased efforts *can* lead to performance goals. For managers, this means that employees must be capable of doing the job and must perceive the performance appraisal process as both reliable and valid.

Individualize Rewards. Because employees have different needs, what acts as a reinforcer for one may not for another. Managers should use their knowledge of employee differences to individualize the rewards over which they have control. Some of the more obvious rewards that managers allocate include pay, promotions, autonomy, and the opportunity to participate in goal setting and decision making.

Link Rewards to Performance. Managers need to make rewards contingent on performance. Rewarding factors other than performance will only reinforce those other factors. Key rewards such as pay increases and promotions should be given for the attainment of the employee's specific goals. Managers should also look for ways in which to increase the visibility of rewards. Eliminating the secrecy surrounding pay by openly communicating everyone's compensation, publicizing performance bonuses, and allocating annual salary increases in a lump sum rather than spreading them out over the entire year are examples of actions that will make rewards more visible and, potentially, more motivating.

Check the System for Equity. Employees should perceive that rewards or outcomes are equal to the inputs given. On a simplistic level, experience, ability, effort, and other obvious inputs should explain differences in pay, responsibility, and other obvious outcomes. The problem, however, is complicated by the existence of dozens of both inputs and outcomes, and by the fact that employee groups place different degrees of importance on them. For instance, a study comparing clerical and production workers identified nearly 20 inputs and outcomes.[58]

The clerical workers considered factors such as quality of work performed and job knowledge near the top of their input list, but these factors were at the bottom of the production workers' list. Similarly, production workers thought the most important inputs were intelligence and personal involvement with the task to be accomplished, two factors that were quite low in the clerks' importance ratings. There were also important, though less dramatic, differences on the outcome side. For example, production workers rated advancement very high, whereas clerical workers rated advancement in the lower third on their list. Such findings suggest that one person's equity is another's inequity, so an ideal reward system should probably weigh inputs differently in arriving at the proper rewards for each job.

Don't Ignore Money. It's easy to get so caught up in setting goals, creating interesting jobs, and providing opportunities for participation, that one forgets that money is a major reason why most people work. Thus, the allocation of performance-based wage increases, piecework bonuses, and other pay incentives is important in determining employee motivation. A review of 80 studies evaluating motivational methods and their impact on employee productivity, supports this point.[59] Goal setting alone produced, on average, a 16 percent increase in productivity; redesign efforts to enrich jobs yielded 8 to 16 percent increases; employee participation in decision making produced a median increase of less than 1 percent; and monetary incentives led to an average increase of 30 percent. We're not saying that management should focus solely on money. Rather, we're simply stating the obvious—that is, if money is removed as an incentive, people aren't going to show up for work. The same can't be said for removing goals, enriched work, or participation.

14 **How can ESOPs be used to motivate employees?**

15 **What are some of the challenges in motivating (a) professionals; (b) contingent workers; and (c) low-skilled, minimum-wage workers?**

16 **List some practical suggestions for motivating employees.**

SUMMARY

This summary is organized by the learning objectives found at the beginning of the chapter.

1. Motivation is the willingness to exert high levels of effort towards organizational goals, conditioned by the effort's ability to satisfy some individual need. The motivation process begins with an unsatisfied need, which creates tension and drives an individual to search for goals that, if attained, will satisfy the need and reduce the tension.
2. The hierarchy of needs theory states that there are five needs—physiological, safety, social, esteem, and self-actualization—that people attempt to satisfy in a steplike progression. A substantially satisfied need no longer motivates.
3. Theory X is basically a negative view of human nature, assuming that employees dislike work, are lazy, seek to avoid responsibility, and must be coerced to perform. Theory Y is basically positive, assuming that employees are creative, seek responsibility, and can exercise self-direction.
4. The motivation–hygiene theory states that not all job factors can motivate employees. The presence or absence of certain job characteristics—or hygiene factors—can only placate employees and not lead to satisfaction or motivation. Factors that people find intrinsically rewarding, such as achievement, recognition, responsibility, and growth, act as motivators and produce job satisfaction.
5. High achievers prefer jobs that offer personal responsibility, feedback, and moderate risks.
6. Goals motivate employees by providing specific and challenging benchmarks to guide and stimulate performance.
7. Reinforcement theory emphasizes the pattern in which rewards are administered. It suggests that only positive, not negative reinforcement be used, and then only to reward desired behaviour. The theory assumes that behaviour is environmentally caused. Goal-setting theory views motivation as coming from an individual's internal statements of purpose.
8. Organizations have attempted to design motivating jobs by using job enlargement, job enrichment, and the job characteristics model (JCM). Job enlargement is the horizontal expansion of a job that increases job scope, the number of different tasks required in a job and the frequency with which these tasks are repeated. Job enrichment is the vertical expansion of a job that increases job depth, which is the degree of control employees have over their work. The JCM proposes that jobs have five core job dimensions—skill variety, task identity, task significance, autonomy, and feedback—that can be combined to create more motivating jobs.
9. In equity theory, individuals compare their job's inputs–outcomes ratio to those of relevant others. If they perceive that they're underrewarded, their work motivation declines. When people perceive that they're overrewarded, they often are motivated to work harder in order to justify their pay.
10. The expectancy theory states that an individual tends to act in a certain way, based on the expectation that the act will be followed by a given outcome and on the attractiveness of that outcome to the individual. Its prime components are the relationships between effort and performance, performance and rewards, and rewards and individual goals.
11. Management practices that are likely to lead to more motivated employees include recognizing individual differences, matching people to jobs, using goals, ensuring that employees perceive goals as attainable, individualizing rewards, linking rewards to performance, checking the reward system for equity, and realizing that money is an important incentive.

THINKING ABOUT MANAGEMENT ISSUES

1. Would an individual with a high nAch be a good candidate for a management position? Explain.
2. Most of us have to work for a living (i.e., hold down a paying job) and work is a central part of our lives. So why do managers have to worry so much about employee motivation issues?
3. What motivates you to perform really well at some task? Explain by using any of the motivation theories.
4. If you had to develop an incentive system for a small manufacturing company, which elements from which motivation theories would you use? Why? Would your choice of incentive systems be the same if it were a medical research lab? Explain.
5. List five criteria (for example, pay, recognition, challenging work, friendships) that are most important to you in a job. Rank them according to their importance. Break into small groups and compare your responses. What patterns, if any, did you find?

SELF-ASSESSMENT EXERCISE

WHAT MOTIVATES YOU?

Circle the number that most closely agrees with how you feel (1 = strongly disagree; 5 = strongly agree). Consider your answers in the context of your current job or past work experience.

1. I try very hard to improve on my past performance at work.	1	2	3	4	5
2. I enjoy competition and winning.	1	2	3	4	5
3. I often find myself talking to those around me about nonwork matters.	1	2	3	4	5
4. I enjoy a difficult challenge.	1	2	3	4	5
5. I enjoy being in charge.	1	2	3	4	5
6. I want to be liked by others.	1	2	3	4	5
7. I want to know how I am progressing as I complete tasks.	1	2	3	4	5
8. I confront people who do things I disagree with.	1	2	3	4	5
9. I tend to build close relationships with co-workers.	1	2	3	4	5
10. I enjoy setting and achieving realistic goals.	1	2	3	4	5
11. I enjoy influencing other people to get my way.	1	2	3	4	5
12. I enjoy belonging to groups and organizations.	1	2	3	4	5
13. I enjoy the satisfaction of completing a difficult task.	1	2	3	4	5
14. I often work to gain more control over the events around me.	1	2	3	4	5
15. I enjoy working with others more than working alone.	1	2	3	4	5

See scoring key on page SK–4.

Source: Based on R Steers and D Braunstein, "A Behaviorally Based Measure of Manifest Needs in Work Settings," *Journal of Vocational Behavior*, October 1976, p. 254; and R N Lussier, *Human Relations in Organizations: A Skill Building Approach* (Homewood, IL: Richard D. Irwin, 1990), p. 120.

for your IMMEDIATE action

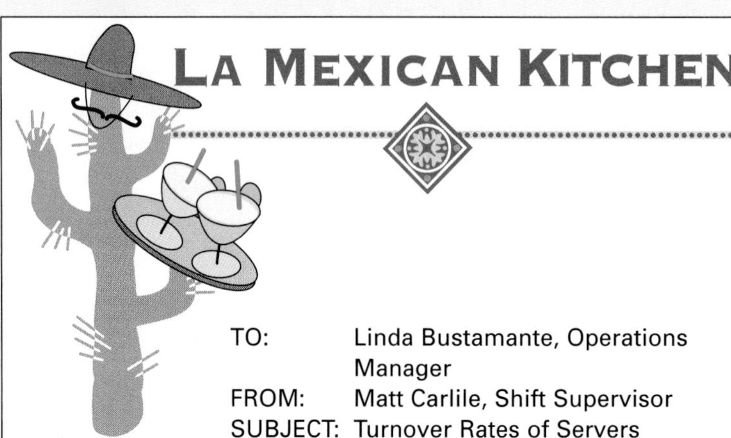

TO: Linda Bustamante, Operations Manager
FROM: Matt Carlile, Shift Supervisor
SUBJECT: Turnover Rates of Servers

Linda, I need your help. As you know, we're having a difficult time keeping food servers for any period of time. It seems like I just get them trained and then they leave. I know we both agree that our servers are a key element in our company's commitment to excellent customer service. We can have the best food in town, yet if our servers aren't motivated to provide excellent service, we won't have any customers.

Although these positions pay minimum wage, you and I both know a motivated server can make additional money from customer tips. But it seems that even this isn't enough to motivate them. So what would you recommend I do? Do you have any ideas about how I can better motivate our food servers? I'd appreciate your jotting down some ideas (keep them under two pages, please) and getting them to me as soon as possible. Thanks for your input!

This is a fictionalized account of a potentially real problem. It was written for academic purposes only and is not meant to reflect either positively or negatively on actual management practices at La Mexican Kitchen.

TAKE IT TO THE NET

We invite you to visit the Robbins/Coulter/Stuart-Kotze Companion Website at www.prenticehall.ca/robbins for this chapter's Internet resources.

CASE APPLICATION

Barrick Gold Corp. Toronto

Shamee Samad and Jamie Sokalsky have struck gold. They work for Barrick Gold Corporation, but they aren't miners. As members of the world's most profitable and third-largest gold-mining operation, all Barrick employees enjoy generous benefits from the company's stock-option program.

Barrick introduced the idea of supplementing regular paycheques with stock in 1984. At the time, the company was strapped for cash, so management decided to use stock options as a way to motivate its employees. In contrast to most stock-option plans, Barrick's plan covers *all* the company's employees (5000 of them), not just upper-level management. So far, the program seems to be a winner for both employees and the company.

Samad, for example, has been an accounts payable clerk with the company for 10 years. She joined Barrick as a 19-year-old, fresh out of high school. In her first year with the company, she earned stock options worth $11 000. That was in addition to her $24 000 salary. In the decade that she has been with Barrick, Samad has cashed in $51 000 from options she's been granted and still holds another $64 000 worth of stock. Sokalsky, meanwhile, has been with the company for two years. As corporate treasurer, however, he has already accumulated $320 000 worth of stock options. Not bad, considering his annual salary is just over $100 000.

Do stock options motivate? Samad says, "If I have to come in early or stay late, I do it. No questions asked". And the company has come a long way from the days when it was strapped for money. A share of Barrick bought in 1983 for $1.75 is now worth more than $42.

QUESTIONS

1. How are stock options at Barrick motivating employees? (Use Figure 15-10 for your answer).
2. What might be some drawbacks of a stock option incentive program for (a) the individual and (b) the organization?
3. Would stock options be effective motivators for employees at a gold producer in Peru? Defend your position.

Source: P Simao, "Eureka!", *Canadian Business*, June 1996, pp. 66–69.

LEARNING OBJECTIVES

After Reading This Chapter, You Should Be Able To:

1 Explain the difference between managers and leaders
2 Identify the two underlying leadership behaviours and the five key leadership styles in the managerial grid
3 Describe the Fiedler contingency model
4 Summarize the path–goal model
5 Explain the attribution theory of leadership
6 Describe the key characteristics of charismatic leaders
7 Contrast transactional and transformational leadership
8 Identify the various sources of power a leader might possess
9 Explain gender and cultural differences in leadership
10 Explain when leaders might not be that important
11 Identify the main skills of visionary leaders

A MANAGER'S CHALLENGE

John Roth, CEO, Northern Telecom, Brampton, Ontario

John Roth is leading Canada's fourth-biggest company, the telecommunications giant Northern Telecom, through a major change in focus. Roth wants to move the company into the rapidly growing market for data communications. Roth aims to make Nortel networks as much of a global force in Internet products as it is in telephone equipment; or to put it another way, he wants to do through the Internet what his predecessor, Jean Monty, did through the wireless communications industry.[1]

Jean Monty came to Nortel networks in its darkest hour, with the company posting losses of roughly $1 billion. The previous CEO had been consumed by the idea of cost-cutting and,

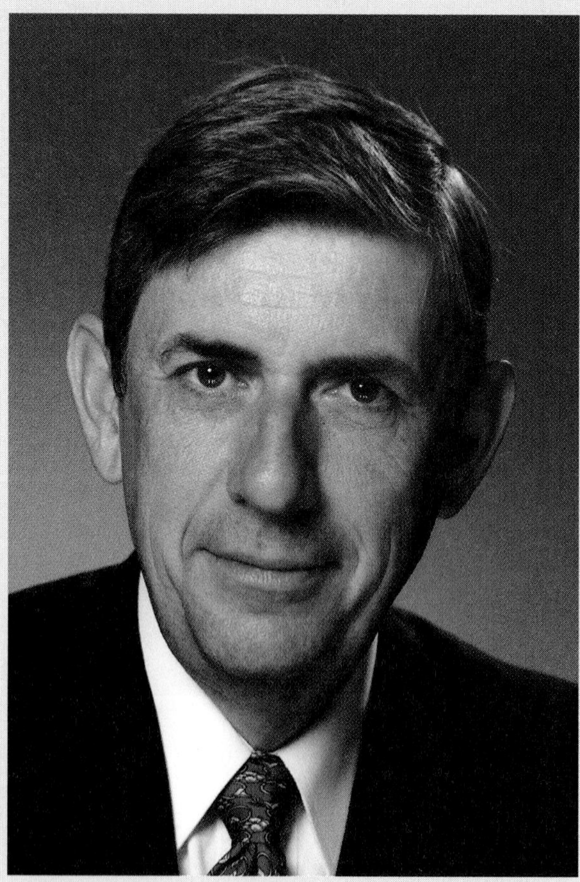

while the policy showed positive effects at first, the cuts included research and development. It wasn't long before the company started to lag behind its competitors in innovation. Monty changed all this: "We invested massively, particularly in R&D, and we didn't try to shrink ourselves to greatness". By the time Monty left in 1997 to take over as CEO of parent company BCE, Nortel networks was a major player (third in the world) in the burgeoning wireless communications industry; had solidified its position as the world's sixth-largest telecommunications equipment manufacturer; and ranked seventh in the country in terms of corporate profits.

Now John Roth—CEO under Monty's tenure—plans to continue the legacy of innovation at Nortel networks, while taking the company into uncharted territory. Roth's first major move as CEO came in the beginning of 1998 when he set up a new data communications division. Since then, Nortel networks has been acquiring Internet-related companies, while focusing its innovation (Nortel networks is Canada's top R&D spender) on data communications technology, rather than the traditional fibre-optic systems that were developed pri- marily for voice communications. The Internet will require new networks that are designed specifically for data transmission, and Roth wants Nortel networks to be at the forefront of technological development in this area. But as he has said, "The Web's not a stationary tar- get. Trying to anticipate where it's going is very difficult".

The challenges of a changing industry, such as Nortel networks faces, necessitate excellent leadership. But if leadership is so important, it's only natural to ask: Are leaders born or made? What differentiates leaders from non-leaders? What is the most appropriate style of leadership? And what can *you* do if you want to be seen as a leader? In this chapter, we'll try to answer these and other questions about leaders.

CHAPTER 16

Leadership

MANAGERS VERSUS LEADERS

Let's begin by clarifying the distinction between managers and leaders. Authors and practitioners often confuse the two, although they're not necessarily the same.

Managers are appointed. Their ability to influence is based on the formal authority inherent in their positions. In contrast, leaders may either be appointed or may emerge from within a group. Leaders can influence others to perform beyond the actions dictated by formal authority.

Should all managers be leaders? Conversely, should all leaders be managers? Because no one has yet been able to demonstrate—either through research or logical argument—that leadership ability is a handicap to a manager, we can state that all managers should *ideally* be leaders. However, not all leaders necessarily have the capabilities or skills in other managerial functions, and thus, not all should hold managerial positions. The fact that an individual can influence others doesn't indicate whether or not he or she can also plan, organize and control. Given (even if only ideally) that all managers should be leaders, we'll pursue the subject from a managerial perspective. Therefore the definition of **leaders** in this chapter refers to those who are able to influence others *and* who possess managerial authority.

leaders
Those who are able to influence others and who possess managerial authority.

Leadership, just like motivation, is another organizational behaviour topic that's been heavily researched, and practically all the research has been aimed at answering the question: "What is an effective leader?" We can clearly see an evolution in our understanding of the leadership process in the various theories proposed to understand and explain it. Let's take a closer look at the major theories that provide us with a basic understanding of leadership.

TRAIT THEORIES

Ask the average person on the street what comes to mind when he or she thinks of leadership. You're likely to get a list of qualities such as intelligence, charisma, decisiveness, enthusiasm, strength, bravery, integrity and self-confidence. These responses represent, in essence, **trait theories** of leadership. The search for specific traits or characteristics that differentiate leaders from non-leaders, though done in a more sophisticated manner than our on-the-street survey, dominated the early research efforts in the study of leadership.

trait theories
Theories isolating characteristics that differentiate leaders from non-leaders.

Is it possible to isolate one or more traits in people who are generally acknowledged to be leaders—for instance, Martin Luther King, Jr., Aung San Suu Kyi, Paul Desmarais, Nelson Mandela, Pierre Trudeau, Mo Mowlam, Mahatma Gandhi—that non-leaders don't possess? We may agree that these people meet our definition of a leader, but they are individuals with completely different characteristics. If the concept of traits is valid, there should be specific characteristics that *all* leaders possess.

Research efforts that attempted to isolate these traits resulted in a number of dead ends. Researchers failed to identify a set of traits that would *always* differentiate leaders from followers and effective leaders from ineffective leaders. Perhaps it was a bit optimistic to believe that a set of consistent and unique personality traits could apply across the board to all effective leaders, whether they were in charge of the Vancouver Grizzlies, PanCanadian Petroleum, the Anglican Church of Canada, Quebecor Printing, the Canadian Cancer Society, or Newfoundland Capital Corp.

PanCanadian Petroleum
www.pcp.ca/

Anglican Church of Canada
www.anglican.ca

Quebecor Printing
www.quebecorusa.com/

Canadian Cancer Society
www.bc.cancer.ca/ccs/

However, attempts to identify traits consistently *associated* with leadership have been more successful. Six traits on which leaders are seen to differ from non-leaders include drive, the desire to lead, honesty and integrity, self-confidence, intelligence, and job-relevant knowledge.[2] These traits are briefly described in Table 16-1.

Yet traits alone aren't sufficient for explaining leadership. Explanations based solely on traits ignore the interactions of the leader and his or her subordinates, as well as ignoring situational factors. Possessing the appropriate traits only makes it *more likely* that an individual will be an effective leader. He or she still has to take the right actions. And what's right in one situation isn't necessarily right for a different situation. So while there has been some resurgent interest in traits during the past decade, a major movement away from trait theories began as early as the 1940s. Leadership research from the late 1940s through the mid-1960s concentrated on the preferred behavioural styles that leaders demonstrated. Researchers wondered whether there was something unique in what effective leaders did—in other words, in their *behaviour*.

TABLE 16-1	Six Traits That Differentiate Leaders from Non-leaders

1. *Drive.* Leaders exhibit a high effort level. They have a relatively high desire for achievement, they're ambitious, they have a lot of energy, they're tirelessly persistent in their activities, and they show initiative.
2. *Desire to lead.* Leaders have a strong desire to influence and lead others. They demonstrate the willingness to take responsibility.
3. *Honesty and integrity.* Leaders build trusting relationships between themselves and followers by being truthful or non-deceitful, and by showing high consistency between word and deed.
4. *Self-confidence.* Followers look to leaders for an absence of self-doubt. Leaders, therefore, need to show self-confidence in order to convince followers of the rightness of goals and decisions.
5. *Intelligence.* Leaders need to be intelligent enough to gather, synthesize, and interpret large amounts of information; and to be able to create visions, solve problems, and make correct decisions.
6. *Job-relevant knowledge.* Effective leaders have a high degree of knowledge about the company, industry, and technical matters. In-depth knowledge allows leaders to make well-informed decisions and to understand the implications of those decisions.

Source: Shelly A Kirkpatrick and Edwin A Locke, "Leadership: Do Traits Really Matter?" *Academy of Management Executive,* May 1991, pp. 48–60.

BEHAVIOURAL THEORIES

Researchers hoped that the **behavioural theories** approach would not only provide increasingly definitive answers about the nature of leadership but, if successful, would also have practical implications quite different from those of the trait approach. If trait research had been successful, it would have provided a basis for *selecting* the "right" people to assume formal leadership positions in organizations. In contrast, if behavioural studies turned up critical behavioural determinants of leadership, people could be *trained* to be leaders. There are four main behaviour studies we need to look at (see Table 16-2 for a summary of the major leader behaviour dimensions and the conclusions of each of these studies).

behavioural theories
Theories identifying behaviours that differentiate effective from ineffective leaders.

autocratic style
Describes a leader who typically tends to centralize authority, dictate work methods, make unilateral decisions, and limit subordinate participation.

democratic style
Describes a leader who tends to involve subordinates in decision making, delegate authority, encourage participation in deciding work methods and goals, and use feedback as an opportunity for coaching.

laissez-faire style
Describes a leader who generally gives the group complete freedom to make decisions and complete the work in whatever way it sees fit.

The University of Iowa Studies

The University of Iowa studies (conducted by Kurt Lewin and his associates) explored three leadership styles, or ways of behaving.[3] The **autocratic** style described a leader who typically tended to centralize authority, dictate work methods, make unilateral decisions, and limit subordinate participation. The **democratic** style of leadership described a leader who tended to involve subordinates in decision making, delegate authority, encourage participation in deciding on work methods and goals, and use feedback as an opportunity for coaching subordinates. Finally, the **laissez-faire** style leader generally gave the group complete freedom to make decisions and complete the work in whatever way it saw fit. Lewin and his associates wondered which was the most effective. Their results seemed to indicate that the democratic style contributed to both good quantity and good quality of work. Had the answer to the question of most effective leadership behaviour been found? Unfortunately, it wasn't that simple. Later studies of the autocratic and democratic styles of leadership showed mixed results. For instance, the democratic leadership style sometimes produced higher performance levels than the autocratic style, but at other times it produced group performance that was lower than, or just equal to, the performance produced by the autocratic leadership style. More consistent results were found, however, when a measure of subordinate satisfaction was used. Group

TABLE 16-2 Behavioural Theories of Leadership

	Behavioural Dimension	Conclusion
University of Iowa	*Democratic style:* involving subordinates, delegating authority, and encouraging participation *Autocratic style:* dictating work methods, centralizing decision making, and limiting participation *Laissez-faire style:* giving group freedom to make decisions and complete work	Democratic style of leadership was most effective, although later studies showed mixed results.
Ohio State	*Consideration:* being considerate of followers' ideas and feelings *Initiating structure:* structuring work and work relationship to meet job goals	High-high leader (high in consideration and high in initiating structure) achieved high subordinate performance and satisfaction, but not in all situations.
University of Michigan	*Employee oriented:* emphasized interpersonal relationships and taking care of employees' needs *Production oriented:* emphasized technical or task aspects of job	Employee-oriented leaders were associated with high group productivity and higher job satisfaction.
Managerial Grid	*Concern for people:* measured leader's concern for subordinates on a scale of 1 to 9 (low to high) *Concern for production:* measured leader's concern for getting job done on a scale of 1 to 9 (low to high)	Managers performed best with a 9,9 style (high concern for production and high concern for people).

members' satisfaction levels were generally higher under a democratic leader than under an autocratic one.[4]

Now leaders had a dilemma! Should they focus on achieving higher performance levels or on achieving higher subordinate satisfaction? This recognition of the dual nature of a leader's behaviour—that is, focusing on the work to be done (the task) and focusing on the people within the group—was also a key characteristic of the other important early behavioural studies.

The Ohio State Studies

initiating structure
The extent to which a leader defines and structures his or her role and those of subordinates to attain goals.

consideration
The extent to which a person has job relationships characterized by mutual trust, respect for subordinates' ideas, and regard for their feelings.

The most comprehensive and replicated of the behavioural theories resulted from research that began at Ohio State University in the 1940s.[5] These studies sought to identify independent dimensions of leader behaviour. Beginning with over 1000 dimensions, they eventually narrowed the list down to just two categories that accounted for most of the leadership behaviour described by subordinates. They called these two dimensions *initiating structure* and *consideration*.

The term **initiating structure** refers to the extent to which a leader is likely to define and structure his or her role and those of subordinates in the search for goal attainment. It includes behaviour that attempts to organize work, work relationships, and goals. For example, the leader who's characterized as high in initiating structure assigns group members to particular tasks, expects workers to maintain definite standards of performance, and emphasizes meeting deadlines.

The term **consideration** is defined as the extent to which a person has job relationships characterized by mutual trust and respect for subordinates' ideas and feelings. A leader who

Lisa Conte left her former career as a venture capitalist to collect a "dream team of scientists" and found Shaman Pharmaceuticals. Now, she manages to maintain a vision of where she needs her highly successful business to go, while retaining the trust and loyalty of the scientists, physicians and ethnobotanists she sends worldwide to collect data and review findings.

is high in consideration helps subordinates with personal problems, is friendly and approachable, and treats all subordinates as equals. He or she shows concern for (is considerate of) his or her followers' comfort, well-being, status, and satisfaction.

Extensive research based on these definitions found that a leader who is high in initiating structure *and* consideration (a **high–high leader**), achieved high subordinate performance and satisfaction more frequently than one who rated low on either consideration, initiating structure, or both. However, the high–high style did not *always* yield positive results. For example, leader behaviour characterized as high on initiating structure led to greater rates of grievances, absenteeism and turnover, and lower levels of job satisfaction for workers performing routine tasks. Other studies found that high consideration was negatively related to performance ratings of the leader by his or her superior. In conclusion, the Ohio State studies suggested that the high–high style generally produced positive outcomes, but enough exceptions were found to indicate that situational factors needed to be integrated into the theory.

high–high leader
A leader high in both initiating structure and consideration.

The University of Michigan Studies

Leadership studies completed at the University of Michigan's Survey Research Center, at about the same time as those being done at Ohio State, had similar research objectives: to identify behavioural characteristics of leaders that were related to performance effectiveness.

The Michigan group also came up with two dimensions of leadership behaviour that they labelled *employee oriented* and *production oriented*.[6] Leaders who were *employee oriented* were described as people emphasizing interpersonal relations; they took a personal interest in the needs of their subordinates and accepted individual differences among members. The *production-oriented* leaders, in contrast, tended to emphasize the technical or task aspects of the job, were concerned mainly with accomplishing their group's tasks, and regarded group members as a means to that end.

The conclusions of the Michigan researchers strongly favoured leaders who were employee oriented. Employee-oriented leaders were associated with high group productivity and higher job satisfaction. Production-oriented leaders were associated with low group productivity and lower worker satisfaction.

The concepts that each of these three studies developed provided the basis for the development of a grid for looking at, and appraising, leadership styles. Let's take a look at it.

The Managerial Grid

A two-dimensional view of leadership style was developed by Blake and Mouton.[7] They proposed a **managerial grid** based on the styles of "concern for people" and "concern for production", which essentially reflect the Ohio State dimensions of consideration and initiating structure, and the Michigan dimensions of employee orientation and production orientation.

The grid, shown in Figure 16-1, has 9 possible positions along each axis, creating 81 different categories into which a leader's style may fall. The grid doesn't show the results produced, but rather the dominating factors in a leader's approach to getting results.

managerial grid
A two-dimensional portrayal of leadership based on concerns for people and for production.

FIGURE 16-1 The Managerial Grid

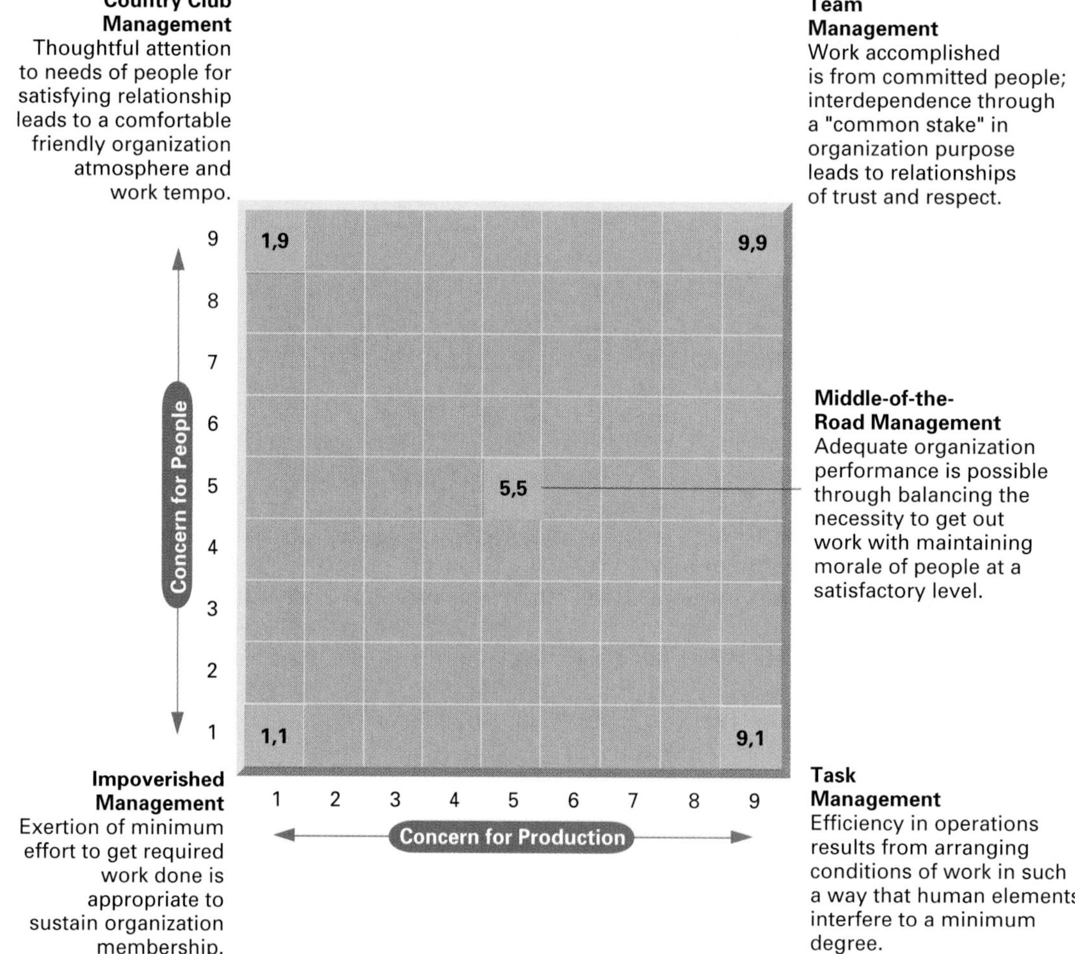
Country Club Management
Thoughtful attention to needs of people for satisfying relationship leads to a comfortable friendly organization atmosphere and work tempo.
Team Management
Work accomplished is from committed people; interdependence through a "common stake" in organization purpose leads to relationships of trust and respect.
1,9
9,9
Middle-of-the-Road Management
Adequate organization performance is possible through balancing the necessity to get out work with maintaining morale of people at a satisfactory level.
5,5
Concern for People
9
8
7
6
5
4
3
2
1
1,1
9,1
1 2 3 4 5 6 7 8 9
Concern for Production
Impoverished Management
Exertion of minimum effort to get required work done is appropriate to sustain organization membership.
Task Management
Efficiency in operations results from arranging conditions of work in such a way that human elements interfere to a minimum degree.

Source: Reprinted by permission of *Harvard Business Review.* An Exhibit from "Breakthrough in Organization Development" by Robert R Blake, Jane S Mouton, Louis B Barnes, and Larry E Greiner, November–December 1964, p. 136.

Although there are 81 positions on the grid, the 5 key positions identified by Blake and Mouton are as follows:

1,1. *Impoverished*: The leader exerts a minimum of effort to accomplish the work.

9,1. *Task:* The leader concentrates on task efficiency but shows little concern for the development and morale of subordinates.

1,9. *Country club:* The leader focuses on being supportive and considerate of subordinates to the exclusion of concern for task efficiency.

5,5. *Middle of the road*: The leader maintains adequate task efficiency and satisfactory morale.

9,9. *Team*: The leader facilitates task efficiency and high morale by co-ordinating and integrating work-related activities.

From these findings, Blake and Mouton concluded that managers perform best using a 9,9 style. Unfortunately, the grid offers no answers to the question of what makes a manager an effective leader, but only a framework for conceptualizing leadership style. In fact, there's little substantive evidence to support the conclusion that a 9,9 style is most effective in all situations.[8]

Summary of Behavioural Theories

We've described the most popular and important attempts to explain leadership in terms of behaviour. There have been other efforts,[9] but they faced the same problem that confronted the Iowa, Ohio State, and Michigan researchers. They had very little success in identifying consistent relationships between patterns of leadership behaviour and successful group performance. General statements couldn't be made because results would vary over different ranges of circumstances. What was missing from these theories was a recognition of the situational factors that influence success or failure. For example, would Mother Teresa have been able to accomplish all that she has for the poor and unfortunate at the turn of the century? Would Ralph Nader have risen to lead a consumer activist group had he been born in 1834 rather than in 1934, or in Costa Rica rather than in Connecticut? It seems quite unlikely, yet the behavioural approaches we've described couldn't clarify such situational factors. Would a high–high leadership style work equally well for a shirt factory in Pakistan and a computer-assisted design studio in Toronto? What about a 9,9 approach? These types of uncertainties about applying certain leadership styles in *all* situations led researchers to try to better understand the effect of the situation on effective leadership style.

CONTINGENCY THEORIES

It became increasingly clear to those studying leadership that predicting leadership success involved something more complex than isolating a few leader traits or preferable behaviours. The failure to attain consistent results led to a new focus on situational influences. The relationship between leadership style and effectiveness suggested that under condition *a*, leadership style *x* would be appropriate, whereas style *y* would be more suitable for condition *b*, and style *z* for condition *c*. But what were the conditions *a, b, c,* and so forth? It was one thing to say that leadership effectiveness depended on the situation and another to be able to isolate those situational conditions.

There has been no shortage of studies attempting to isolate crucial situational factors that affect leadership effectiveness. One author, in reviewing the literature on the topic, found that the task being performed (that is, the complexity, type, technology, and size of the project) was a significant moderating variable; but he also uncovered studies that isolated situational factors such as style of the leader's immediate supervisor, group norms, span of control, external threats and stress, and organizational culture.[10]

Several approaches to isolating key situational variables have proven more successful than others and, as a result, have gained wider recognition. We'll consider three of these: the Fiedler model, path–goal theory, and the leader participation model.

Fiedler contingency model
The theory that effective groups depend on a proper match between a leader's style of interacting with subordinates, and the degree to which the situation gives control and influence to the leader.

The Fiedler Model

The first comprehensive contingency model for leadership was developed by Fred Fiedler.[11] The **Fiedler contingency model** proposes that effective group performance depends on the proper match between the leader's style of interacting with his or her subordinates, and the degree to which the situation allows the leader to control and influence others, or situations. The model is based on the premise that a certain leadership style would be most effective in different situations. The key is to define those leadership styles and the different situations, and then to identify the appropriate combinations of style and situation. In order to understand Fiedler's model, let's look at the first of these variables—leadership style.

least-preferred co-worker (LPC) questionnaire
A questionnaire that measures whether a person is task or relationship oriented.

Fiedler proposed that a key factor in leadership success was an individual's basic leadership style. He further suggested that a person's style was one of two types, much like the dual behaviours isolated by the behavioural theorists; that is, either the leader was task oriented or relationship oriented. To measure a leader's style, Fiedler developed the **least-preferred co-**

TESTING... TESTING...

1 What are leadership traits, and what has leadership research shown about traits?

2 Compare and contrast the findings of (a) the University of Iowa studies; (b) the Ohio State studies; (c) the University of Michigan studies; and (d) the managerial grid.

worker (LPC) questionnaire. As shown in Figure 16-2, it contains 16 pairs of contrasting adjectives. Respondents are asked to think of all the co-workers they've ever had and to describe the one person they *least enjoyed* working with, by rating him or her on a scale of 1 to 8 for each of the 16 sets of adjectives. Based on the responses to the LPC questionnaire, Fiedler believed that you could determine a person's basic leadership style. What was his description of each of these styles?

Fiedler believed that if the least-preferred co-worker was described in relatively positive terms (in other words, a "high" LPC score), then the respondent is primarily interested in good personal relations with this co-worker. That is, if you describe the person that you're least able to work with in favourable terms, you'd be labelled *relationship oriented*. In contrast, if you see the least-preferred co-worker in relatively unfavourable terms (a low LPC score), you're primarily interested in productivity and getting the job done; thus you'd be labelled *task oriented*. Fiedler did acknowledge that there's a small group of people who fall in between these two extremes and don't have a cut-and-dried personality sketch. One other point we need to make about leadership style is that Fiedler assumed that a person's leadership style is innate

FIGURE 16-2 Fiedler's LPC Scale

Pleasant	8	7	6	5	4	3	2	1	Unpleasant
Friendly	8	7	6	5	4	3	2	1	Unfriendly
Rejecting	1	2	3	4	5	6	7	8	Accepting
Helpful	8	7	6	5	4	3	2	1	Frustrating
Unenthusiastic	1	2	3	4	5	6	7	8	Enthusiastic
Tense	1	2	3	4	5	6	7	8	Relaxed
Distant	1	2	3	4	5	6	7	8	Close
Cold	1	2	3	4	5	6	7	8	Warm
Co-operative	8	7	6	5	4	3	2	1	Unco-operative
Supportive	8	7	6	5	4	3	2	1	Hostile
Boring	1	2	3	4	5	6	7	8	Interesting
Quarrelsome	1	2	3	4	5	6	7	8	Harmonious
Self-Assured	8	7	6	5	4	3	2	1	Hesitant
Efficient	8	7	6	5	4	3	2	1	Inefficient
Gloomy	1	2	3	4	5	6	7	8	Cheerful
Open	8	7	6	5	4	3	2	1	Guarded

Source: From Fred E Fiedler and Martin M Chemers, *Leadership and Effective Management* (Scott, Foresman & Co., 1974). Reprinted by permission of the authors.

and thus fixed. In other words, if you're a relationship-oriented leader, you'll always be one. And the same for a task-oriented leader.

After an individual's basic leadership style has been assessed through the LPC, it's necessary to evaluate the situation in order to match the leader with the situation. Fiedler identified three contingency dimensions that, he argued, define the key situational factors for determining leader effectiveness. These are as follows:

1. **Leader–member relations:** The degree of confidence, trust, and respect subordinates have for their leader; rated as either good or poor
2. **Task structure:** The degree to which the job assignments are formalized and procedure-based; rated as either high or low
3. **Position power:** The degree of influence a leader has over power-based activities such as hiring, firing, discipline, promotions, and salary increases; rated as either strong or weak

leader–member relations
The degree of confidence, trust, and respect subordinates have in their leader.

task structure
The degree to which the job assignments are procedure-based.

position power
The degree of influence a leader has over power variables such as hiring, firing, discipline, promotions, and salary increases.

Each leadership situation must be evaluated in terms of these three contingency variables. Altogether, by mixing the three contingency variables, there are eight possible different situations in which a leader could find him- or herself. (See bottom chart in Figure 16-3.) He further classified these eight situations as being *very favourable, moderately favourable,* or *very unfavourable* for the leader. As shown in Figure 16-3, Situations I, II and III were classified as being very favourable. Situations IV, V, and VI were moderately favourable, and Situations VII and VIII were described as being very unfavourable.

In order to define the specific contingencies for leadership effectiveness, Fiedler studied 1200 groups in which he compared relationship- versus task-oriented leadership styles in each of the eight situational categories. He concluded that task-oriented leaders tended to perform better in situations that were very favourable to them and in situations that were very unfavourable. In contrast, relationship-oriented leaders seemed to perform better in moderately favourable situations.

Remember that, according to Fiedler, an individual's leadership style is fixed. Therefore, there are really only two ways to improve leader effectiveness. First, you can bring in a new leader who better fits the situation. For instance, if the group situation currently rates as

FIGURE 16-3 Findings of the Fiedler Model

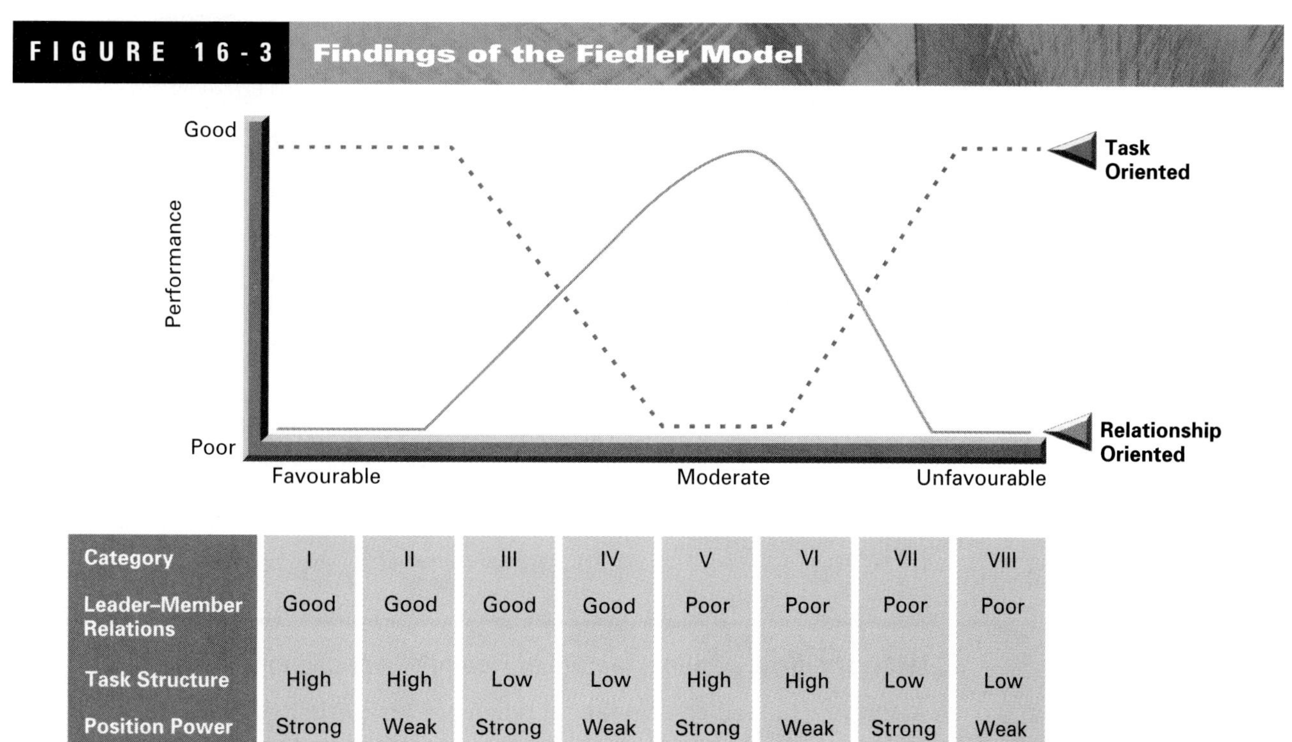

Category	I	II	III	IV	V	VI	VII	VIII
Leader–Member Relations	Good	Good	Good	Good	Poor	Poor	Poor	Poor
Task Structure	High	High	Low	Low	High	High	Low	Low
Position Power	Strong	Weak	Strong	Weak	Strong	Weak	Strong	Weak

Beth Randolph, manager at Choice Hotels, calls herself "the 911 car". After perceiving problems among her supervisors, she put a self-constructed cardboard highway on her office wall and designated a vehicle for each supervisor and a "911" car for herself. After their three-hour, one-on-one discussions, Beth made it clear to everyone that their unstinting co-operation was expected. Her style of leadership combines the participative and directive approaches.

highly unfavourable but is led by a relationship-oriented leader, the group's performance could be improved by replacing that person with a task-oriented leader. The second alternative is to change the situation to fit the leader. This can be done by restructuring tasks, or by increasing or decreasing the power that the leader has over factors such as salary increases, promotions, and disciplinary actions.

As a whole, reviews of the major studies undertaken to test the overall validity of the Fiedler model lead to a generally positive conclusion. That is, there's considerable evidence to support the model.[12] But additional variables are probably needed to fill in some gaps in the model. Moreover, there are problems with the LPC, and the practicality of it needs to be addressed. For instance, the logic underlying the LPC isn't well understood, and studies have shown that respondents' LPC scores aren't stable.[13] In addition, it's probably unrealistic to assume that a person can't change his or her leadership style to fit the situation. Often, effective leaders can, and do, change their styles to meet the needs of a particular situation. Finally, the contingency variables are complex and difficult for practitioners to assess. It's often difficult in practice to determine how good the leader–member relations are, how structured the task is, and how much position power the leader has.[14]

Despite its shortcomings, the Fiedler model provides us with evidence that we can differentiate effective leadership style and situation. Let's look at the other contingency models of leadership.

Path-Goal Theory

path–goal theory
A theory that the most effective leadership style is one that compensates for shortcomings in either the employees or the work setting

Currently, one of the most respected approaches to understanding leadership is **path–goal theory**. Developed by Robert House, path–goal theory is a contingency model of leadership that extracts key elements from the Ohio State leadership research and the expectancy theory of motivation.[15]

The essence of the theory is that it's the leader's job to assist his or her followers in attaining their goals, and to provide the necessary direction and/or support to ensure that their goals are compatible with the overall objectives of the group or organization. The term "path–goal" is derived from the belief that effective leaders clarify the path to help their followers get from

TESTING... TESTING...

3 What are the situational factors in Fiedler's contingency model?

4 According to Fiedler's model, (a) when are task-oriented leaders more effective, and (b) when are relationship-oriented leaders more effective?

where they are to the achievement of their work goals, and make the journey along the path easier by reducing roadblocks and pitfalls.

According to path–goal theory, a leader's behaviour is *acceptable* to subordinates to the degree that they view it as an immediate source of satisfaction or as a means of future satisfaction. A leader's behaviour is *motivational* to the extent that it (1) makes subordinate need–satisfaction contingent on effective performance, and (2) provides the coaching, guidance, support and rewards that are necessary for effective performance. To test these statements, House identified four leadership behaviours:

- *Directive leader:* Lets subordinates know what's expected of them, schedules work to be done, and gives specific guidance as to how to accomplish tasks—similar to *initiating structure* from the Ohio State studies
- *Supportive leader:* Is friendly and shows concern for the needs of subordinates—essentially synonymous with the Ohio State dimension *consideration*
- *Participative leader:* Consults with subordinates and uses their suggestions before making a decision
- *Achievement-oriented leader:* Sets challenging goals and expects subordinates to perform at their highest level

In contrast to Fiedler's view of a leader's behaviour, House assumes that leaders are flexible. Path–goal theory implies that the same leader can display any or all of these leadership styles, depending on the situation.

As Figure 16-4 illustrates, path–goal theory proposes two classes of situational or contingency variables that moderate the leadership behaviour–outcome relationship—those in the *environment* that are outside the control of the subordinate (factors including task structure, the formal authority system, and the work group) and those that are part of the personal characteristics of the *subordinate* (locus of control, experience, and perceived ability). Environmental factors determine the type of leader behaviour required if subordinate outcomes are to be maximized, while personal characteristics of the subordinate determine how the environment and leader behaviour are interpreted. The theory proposes that leader behaviour will be ineffective when it is not in line with the environment or with the characteristics of subordinates.

FIGURE 16-4 Path-Goal Theory

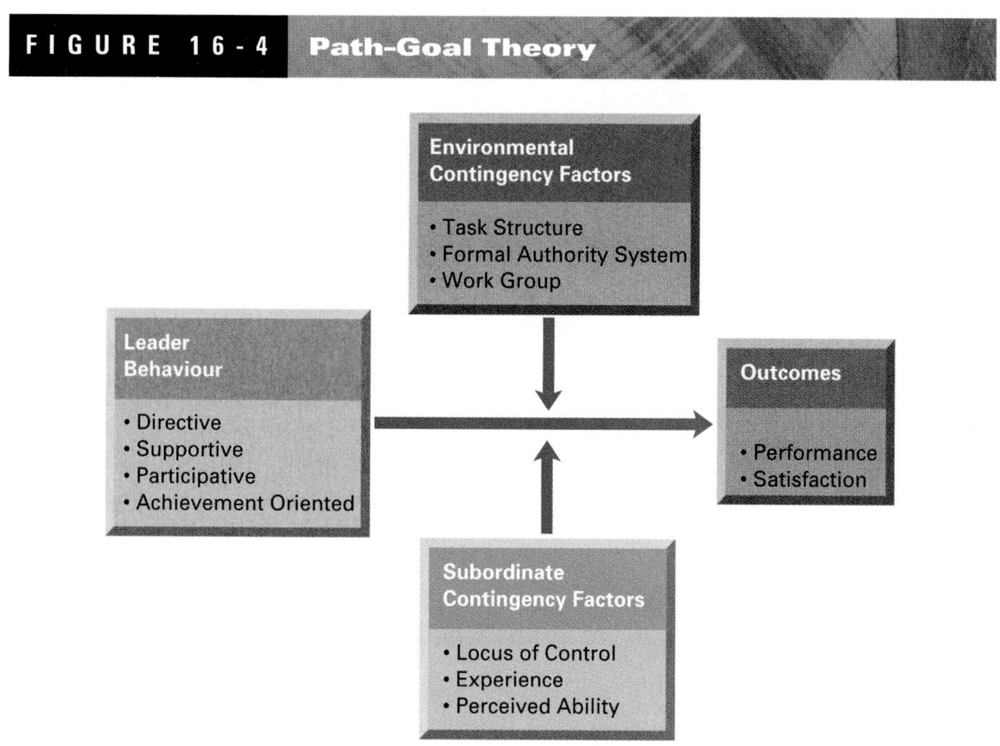

The following are some examples of hypotheses that have evolved out of path–goal theory:

- Directive leadership leads to greater satisfaction when tasks are ambiguous or stressful than when they're highly structured and well laid out.
- Supportive leadership results in high employee performance and satisfaction when subordinates are performing structured tasks.
- Directive leadership is likely to be perceived as redundant among subordinates with high perceived ability or with considerable experience.
- The more clear and bureaucratic the formal authority relationships, the more leaders should exhibit supportive behaviour and de-emphasize directive behaviour.
- Directive leadership will lead to higher employee satisfaction when there's substantive conflict within a work group.
- Subordinates with an internal locus of control (those who believe they control their own destiny) will be more satisfied with a participative style.
- Subordinates with an external locus of control will be more satisfied with a directive style.
- Achievement-oriented leadership will increase subordinates' expectancies that effort will lead to high performance when tasks are ambiguously structured.

Research to validate hypotheses such as these is generally encouraging, although not every study has found positive support.[16] However, the majority of the evidence supports the logic underlying the theory. That is, employee performance and satisfaction are likely to be positively influenced when the leader compensates for shortcomings in either the employee or the work setting. However, if the leader spends time explaining tasks when those tasks are already clear, or the employee has the ability and experience to handle them without interference, the employee is likely to see such directive behaviour as redundant or even insulting.

Leader Participation Model

leader participation model
A leadership theory that provides a set of rules to determine the form and amount of participative decision making in different situations.

Back in 1973, Victor Vroom and Phillip Yetton developed a **leader participation model** that related leadership behaviour and participation to decision making.[17] These researchers argued that leader behaviour must adjust to reflect the task structure—whether it is routine, non-routine, or anywhere in between. Vroom and Yetton's model is what we call a *normative* one, since it provided a sequential set of rules (norms) that the leader should follow in determining the form and amount of participation in decision making, as determined by the different types of situations. The model was set up as a decision tree, incorporating seven contingencies about task structure (whose relevance could be identified by making yes-or-no choices) and five alternative leadership styles. These leadership styles are described in Table 16-3.

More recent work by Vroom and Arthur Jago has resulted in a revision of this model.[18] The new model retains the same five alternative leadership styles but expands the contingency variables to twelve, including factors such as the importance of technical quality of the decision, importance of subordinate commitment to the decision, level of leader information about the decision, and likelihood of subordinate conflict over preferred solutions. Vroom and Jago have developed a computer program that cuts through all the complexity of the new model. But managers can still use decision trees to select their leadership style, assuming that there are no "shades of grey" (i.e., that the status of a variable is a clear-cut yes or no), that there are no critically severe time constraints, and that subordinates aren't geographically dispersed. Figure 16-5 illustrates one of these decision trees.

Research testing the original leader participation model was very encouraging.[19] But the new model, which is a direct extension of the 1973 version, is also consistent with our current

TESTING... TESTING...

5 How does path–goal theory explain leadership?

6 Describe the leader participation model.

TABLE 16-3 Possible Leadership Styles in Vroom-Yetton Leader Participation Model

Autocratic I (AI):	You solve the problem or make a decision yourself using information available to you at that time.
Autocratic II (AII):	You obtain the necessary information from subordinates and then decide on the solution to the problem yourself. You may or may not tell subordinates what the problem is in getting information from them. The role of your subordinates in making the decision is clearly one of providing the necessary information to you rather than generating or evaluating alternative solutions.
Consultative I (CI):	You share the problem with relevant subordinates individually, getting their ideas and suggestions without bringing them together as a group. Then you make the decision that may or may not reflect your subordinates' influence.
Consultative II (CII):	You share the problem with your subordinates as a group, collectively obtaining their ideas and suggestions. Then you make the decision that may or may not reflect your subordinates' influence.
Group II (GII):	You share the problem with your subordinates as a group. Together you generate and evaluate alternatives and attempt to reach an agreement (consensus) on a solution.

Source: V H Vroom and P W Yetton, *Leadership and Decision-Making* (Pittsburgh: University of Pittsburgh Press, 1973).

knowledge on the benefits and costs of participation. So, at this time, we have every reason to believe that the revised model provides an excellent guide to help managers choose the most appropriate leadership style in different situations.

EMERGING APPROACHES TO LEADERSHIP

We conclude our review of leadership theories by presenting three emerging approaches to the subject: an attribution theory of leadership, charismatic leadership, and transactional versus transformational leadership. If there's one theme that characterizes the approaches in this section, it's that they take a more practical view of leadership than previous theories have, with the exception of trait theories. The following approaches to leadership tend to look at the subject more like the way the average "person on the street" does.

Attribution Theory of Leadership

In Chapter 13, we discussed attribution theory in relation to perception. Attribution theory has also been used to help explain the perception of leadership.

Attribution theory, as you remember, deals with trying to make sense out of cause–effect relationships. When an event happens, people want to attribute it to a certain cause. The **attribution theory of leadership** says that leadership is merely an attribution that people make about other individuals.[20] Using the attribution framework, researchers have found that people tend to characterize leaders as having traits such as intelligence, outgoing personality, strong verbal skills, aggressiveness, understanding, and industriousness.[21] Similarly, the model of the high–high leader of the Ohio State study has been found to be consistent with people's attributions of what makes a good leader.[22] That is, regardless of the situation, a high–high leadership style tends to be perceived as the best one. At the organizational level, the attribution framework explains why people are prone to attribute either the extremely negative or the extremely positive performance of an organization to its leadership.[23] It also helps to

attribution theory of leadership
Proposes that leadership is merely an attribution that people make about other individuals.

FIGURE 16-5 The Revised Leader-Participation Model

(time-driven decision tree—group problems)

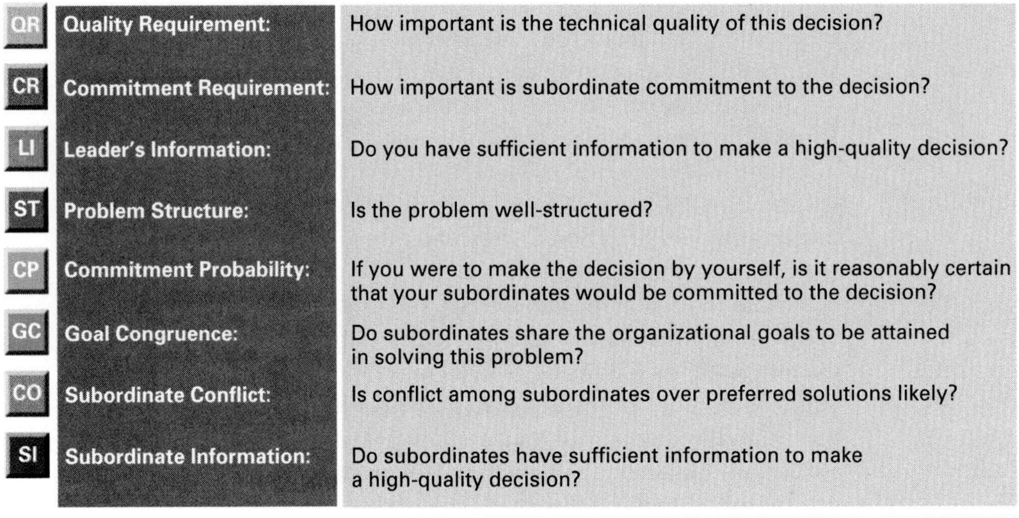

QR	Quality Requirement:	How important is the technical quality of this decision?
CR	Commitment Requirement:	How important is subordinate commitment to the decision?
LI	Leader's Information:	Do you have sufficient information to make a high-quality decision?
ST	Problem Structure:	Is the problem well-structured?
CP	Commitment Probability:	If you were to make the decision by yourself, is it reasonably certain that your subordinates would be committed to the decision?
GC	Goal Congruence:	Do subordinates share the organizational goals to be attained in solving this problem?
CO	Subordinate Conflict:	Is conflict among subordinates over preferred solutions likely?
SI	Subordinate Information:	Do subordinates have sufficient information to make a high-quality decision?

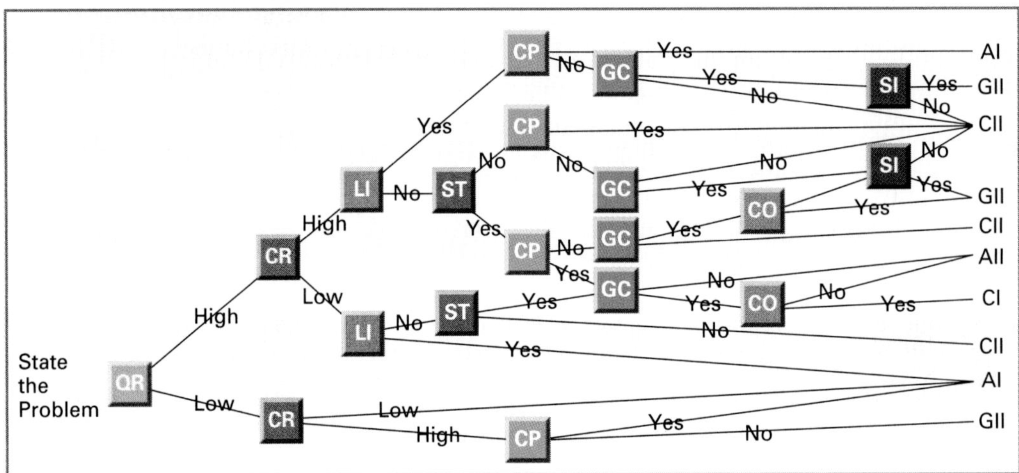

Source: V H Vroom and A G Jago, *The New Leadership: Managing Participation in Organizations* (Englewood Cliffs, NJ: Prentice-Hall, 1988), p. 184. With permission.

explain the vulnerability of CEOs when their organizations suffer major financial setbacks, regardless of whether or not they had anything to do with it. It also clarifies why these CEOs tend to be given credit for extremely positive financial results, again regardless of how much or how little they contributed.

One of the more interesting themes in the attribution theory of leadership literature is the perception that effective leaders are generally considered consistent or unwavering in their decisions. One of the explanations for why Edgar Bronfman Sr. and René Levesque were perceived as leaders was that both were fully committed, steadfast, and consistent in the decisions they made and in the goals they set. Evidence indicates that a "heroic" leader is perceived as being someone who takes up a difficult or unpopular cause but, through determination and persistence, ultimately succeeds.[24]

charismatic leadership Followers make attributions of heroic or extraordinary leadership abilities when they observe certain behaviours.

Charismatic Leadership Theory

Charismatic leadership theory is an extension of attribution theory. It says that followers make attributions of heroic or extraordinary leadership abilities when they observe certain behaviours.[25] Studies on charismatic leadership have, for the most part, been directed at identifying those behaviours that differentiate charismatic leaders from their non-charismatic counterparts.

Several authors have attempted to identify personal characteristics of the charismatic leader. Robert House (of path–goal theory fame) has identified three: extremely high confidence, dominance, and strong convictions in his or her beliefs.[26] Warren Bennis, after studying 90 of the most effective and successful leaders in the United States, found that they had four common competencies: they had a compelling vision or sense of purpose; they could communicate that vision in clear terms with which their followers could readily identify; they demonstrated consistency and focus in the pursuit of their vision; and they knew their own strengths and capitalized on them.[27] The most recent and comprehensive analysis, however, has been completed by Jay Conger and Rabindra Kanungo at McGill University in Montreal.[28] Among their conclusions, they propose that charismatic leaders have an idealized goal that they want to achieve, and a strong personal commitment to that goal; are perceived as unconventional; are assertive and self-confident; and are perceived as agents of radical change rather than as managers of the status quo. Table 16-4 summarizes the key characteristics that appear to differentiate charismatic leaders from non-charismatic ones.

What can we say about the charismatic leader's effect on his or her followers? An increasing body of research shows impressive correlations between charismatic leadership, and high performance and satisfaction among followers.[29] People working for charismatic leaders are motivated to exert extra work effort and, because they like their leaders, express greater satisfaction.

If charisma is desirable, can people learn to be charismatic leaders? Or are charismatic leaders born with their qualities? While a small majority still think that charisma can't be learned, most experts believe that individuals can be trained to exhibit charismatic behaviours.[30] For example, researchers have succeeded in actually scripting undergraduate business students to "play charismatic".[31] The students were taught to articulate an overarching goal, communicate high performance expectations, exhibit confidence in the ability of subordinates to meet these expectations, and empathize with the needs of their subordinates. They learned to project a powerful, confident, and dynamic presence, and they practised using a captivating and engaging voice tone. To further capture the dynamics and energy of charisma, the leaders were trained to evoke charismatic non-verbal characteristics. They alternated between pacing

TABLE 16-4 Key Characteristics of Charismatic Leaders

1. *Self-confidence.* Charismatic leaders have complete confidence in their judgment and ability.
2. *Vision.* They have an idealized goal that proposes a future better than the status quo. The greater the disparity between this idealized goal and the status quo, the more likely that followers will attribute extraordinary vision to the leader.
3. *Ability to articulate the vision.* They are able to clarify and state the vision in terms that are understandable to others. This articulation demonstrates an understanding of the followers' needs and, hence, acts as a motivating force.
4. *Strong convictions about the vision.* Charismatic leaders are perceived as being strongly committed, and willing to take on high personal risk, incur high costs, and engage in self-sacrifice to achieve their vision.
5. *Behaviour that is out of the ordinary.* They engage in behaviour that is perceived as being novel, unconventional, and counter to norms. When successful, these behaviours evoke surprise and admiration in followers.
6. *Appearance as a change agent.* Charismatic leaders are perceived as agents of radical change rather than as caretakers of the status quo.
7. *Environment sensitivity.* They are able to make realistic assessments of the environmental constraints and resources needed to bring about change.

Source: Based on Jay A Conger and R N Kanungo, "Behavioral Dimensions of Charismatic Leadership," in Jay A Conger and R N Kanungo, *Charismatic Leadership* (San Francisco: Jossey-Bass, 1988), p. 91.

and sitting on the edges of their desks, leaned towards the subordinate, maintained direct eye contact, and had a relaxed posture and animated facial expressions. The researchers found that these students could *learn* how to project charisma. Moreover, subordinates of these leaders had higher task performance, task adjustment, and adjustment to the leader and to the group, than subordinates who worked in groups led by non-charismatic leaders.

One last point on this topic—charismatic leadership may not always be needed to achieve high levels of employee performance. It may be most appropriate when the follower's task has an ideological component.[32] This may explain why, when charismatic leaders surface, it's more likely to be in politics, religion, or a business firm that's introducing a radically new product or facing a life-threatening crisis. Premier Ralph Klein offered a vision to lead Alberta out of its deficit. Daniel Green was unyielding in his fight to keep the federal government from raising the PCB-laden sunken barge, the Irving Whale, from the bottom of the Gulf of St. Lawrence. CEO Elliott Wahle of Toronto's Dylex Ltd. shaped the turnaround of his company from the emergence from bankruptcy protection in 1995, to post record earnings in 1998. Charismatic leaders, in fact, may become a liability to an organization once a crisis and need for dramatic change subsides.[33] Why? Because the charismatic leader's overwhelming self-confidence often becomes problematic. He or she is unable to listen to others, becomes uncomfortable when challenged by aggressive subordinates, and begins to hold an unjustifiable belief in his or her "rightness" on issues.

Visionary Leadership

visionary leadership The ability to create and articulate a realistic, credible, attractive vision of the future for an organization or organizational unit that grows out of, and improves upon, the present.

Although the term *vision* is often linked with charismatic leadership, **visionary leadership** goes beyond charisma, since it is the ability to create and articulate a realistic, credible, and attractive vision of the future for an organization or organizational unit that grows out of, and improves upon, the present situation.[34] This vision, if properly selected and implemented, is so energizing that it "in effect jump-starts the future by calling forth the skills, talents, and resources to make it happen".[35]

A review of various definitions finds that *a vision* differs from other forms of organizational direction (such as *mission* or *purpose*) in several ways. "A vision has clear and compelling imagery that offers an innovative way to improve, which recognizes and draws on traditions, and connects to actions that people can take to realize change. Vision taps people's emotions and energy. Properly articulated, a vision creates the enthusiasm that people have for sporting events and other leisure time activities, bringing the energy and commitment to the workplace."[36]

The key properties of a vision seem to be inspirational possibilities that are value-centred, are realizable, have superior imagery, and are well articulated. Visions should be able to generate possibilities that are inspirational and unique and that offer a new way of doing things—leading to organizational distinction. A vision is likely to fail if it does not offer a view of the future that is clearly and demonstrably better for the organization and its members. Desirable visions fit the times and circumstances and reflect the uniqueness of the organization. People in the organization must also believe that the vision is attainable. The vision should be seen as being challenging, but within reach. Visions that are clearly articulated and have powerful imagery are easily grasped and accepted.

What skills do visionary leaders exhibit? Once the vision is identified, these leaders appear to have three qualities that are related to effectiveness in their visionary roles: firstly, *the ability to explain the vision to others;* secondly, *the ability to express the vision not just verbally but through behaviour*; and thirdly, *the ability to extend or apply the vision to different leadership contexts.*

Team Leadership

As the use of teams in organizations continues to grow, managers face the challenge of becoming effective team leaders. They have to learn skills such as having the patience to share infor-

7 What is the attribution theory of leadership?

8 How is visionary leadership different from charismatic leadership?

mation, being able to trust others and to give up authority, and understanding when to intervene. Effective leaders perform the difficult balancing act of knowing when to leave their teams alone and when to get involved. New team leaders may try to retain too much control at a time when team members need more autonomy, or they may abandon their teams at times when the teams need support and help.[37]

One study of organizations that had reorganized themselves around employee teams found certain common responsibilities that all leaders had to assume. These included coaching, facilitating, handling disciplinary problems, reviewing team and individual performance, training, and communication.[38] You would probably agree that many of these responsibilities apply to managers' jobs in general. However, a more meaningful way to describe the team leader's job is to focus on two priorities: (1) managing the team's external boundary, and (2) facilitating the team process.[39] These priorities can be broken down into four specific leadership roles.

First, team leaders are *liaisons with external constituencies*. These may include upper management, other internal teams, customers or suppliers. The leader represents the team to other constituencies, secures needed resources, clarifies others' expectations of the team, gathers information from the outside, and shares that information with team members.

Second, team leaders are *troubleshooters*. When the team has problems and asks for assistance, team leaders sit in on meetings and try to help resolve the problems. Troubleshooting rarely involves technical or operational issues, because the team members typically know more about the tasks being done than the team leader does. The leader is most likely to contribute by asking penetrating questions, helping the team to talk through problems, and getting needed resources from external constituencies.

Third, team leaders are *conflict managers*. When disagreements arise, they help to process the conflict. Team leaders help to identify issues such as the source of conflict, who's involved, the issues, the resolution options available, and the advantages and disadvantages of each. By getting team members to address questions such as these, the leader minimizes the disruptive aspects of conflicts within the team.

Fourth, team leaders are *coaches*. They clarify expectations and roles, teach, offer support, and do whatever else is necessary in order to help team members keep their work performance levels high.

Transactional Versus Transformational Leadership

The final branch of research we'll touch on is the recent interest in differentiating transformational leaders from transactional leaders.[40] As you'll see, because transformational leaders are also charismatic, there's some overlap between this topic and our previous discussion of charismatic leadership.

Most of the leadership theories presented in this chapter—for instance, the Ohio State studies, Fiedler's model, path–goal theory, and the leader participation model—have been addressing **transactional leaders**. These leaders guide or motivate their followers in the direction of established goals by clarifying role and task requirements. But there's another type of leader who inspires followers to transcend his or her own self-interests for the good of the organization and who is capable of having a profound and extraordinary effect on his or her followers. These are **transformational leaders**, and include Claude Masse of Famili-Prix Inc. in Québec, Ross Fitzpatrick of Viceroy Resource Corp. in Vancouver, and Brian Craig of Merak Projects Ltd., in Calgary. They pay attention to the concerns and developmental needs of individual followers; they change followers' awareness of issues by helping those followers to look at old problems in new ways; and they're able to excite, arouse, and inspire followers to put out extra effort to achieve group goals.

transactional leaders Leaders who guide or motivate their followers in the direction of established goals by clarifying role and task requirements.

transformational leaders Leaders who provide individualized consideration and intellectual stimulation, and possess charisma.

Transactional and transformational leadership shouldn't be viewed as opposing approaches to getting things done.[41] Transformational leadership is built on top of transactional leadership. Transformational leadership produces levels of subordinate effort and performance that go beyond what would occur with a transactional approach alone. Moreover, transformational leadership is more than charisma. "The purely charismatic (leader) may want followers to adopt the charismatic's worldview and go no further; the transformational leader will attempt to instill in followers the ability to question not only established views but, eventually, those established by the leader."[42]

Famili-Prix
www.famili-prix.com

Viceroy Resource Corp.
www.viceroyresource.com

The evidence supporting the superiority of transformational leadership over the transactional variety is overwhelmingly impressive. For instance, a number of studies with US,

Vic Young, CEO of Newfoundland's Fisheries Products International, is a good example of a charismatic leader. When the moratorium on cod was imposed, Young had to undertake a massive restructuring of his company in order for FPI to survive.

Canadian, and German military officers found, at every level, that transformational leaders were evaluated as being more effective than their transactional counterparts.[43] Managers at Federal Express who were rated by their followers as exhibiting more transformational leadership, were evaluated by their immediate supervisors as being higher performers and as being more promotable.[44] In summary, the overall evidence indicates that transformational, as compared with transactional, leadership is more strongly correlated with lower turnover rates, higher productivity, and higher employee satisfaction.[45]

CONTEMPORARY ISSUES IN LEADERSHIP

As you can tell from the preceding discussion on the various theories and models of leadership, the concept of "effective leadership" is continually being refined, as researchers continue to study leadership in organizations and discover more about it. Let's take a closer look at some of the contemporary issues in leadership.

legitimate power
The power a person has as a result of his or her position in the formal organizational hierarchy; also called *authority.*

coercive power
Power that rests on the application, or the threat of application, of physical sanctions such as the infliction of pain; the arousal of frustration through restriction of movement; or the controlling by force of basic physiological or safety needs.

Leaders and Power

We first introduced the concept of power in Chapter 10 when we discussed authority relationships in the organizational structure. Remember that power is the capacity to influence decisions. Since leadership is about the process of influence, we need to look at how leaders acquire power. John French and Bertram Raven have identified five sources or bases of power: legitimate, reward, coercive, expert, and referent.[46]

Legitimate power and authority are one and the same. Legitimate power represents the power a person has as a result of his or her position in the formal organizational hierarchy. Positions of authority also have reward and coercive power, but legitimate power is broader than the power to coerce and reward. Specifically, it includes acceptance of the authority of a position by members of an organization. When school principals, bank presidents, or army captains speak (assuming that their directives are viewed to be within the authority of their positions), teachers, tellers, and first lieutenants listen and usually comply.

The **coercive power** base is defined by French and Raven as being dependent on fear. One reacts to this power out of fear of the negative results that might occur if you don't comply. It rests on the application, or the threat of application, of physical sanctions such as the

TESTING... TESTING...

9 **How is the role of team leader different from the traditional leadership role performed by first-line supervisors?**

10 **Describe the four specific leadership roles that team leaders play.**

11 **What are the differences between transactional and transformational leaders?**

infliction of pain; the arousal of frustration through restriction of movement; or the controlling by force of basic physiological or safety needs. If you're a manager, typically you have some coercive power. You may be able to suspend or demote employees. You may be able to assign them work activities that they find unpleasant. You may even have the option of dismissing employees. These all represent coercive actions. But you don't have to be a manager to hold coercive power. For instance, a subordinate who is in a position to embarrass his or her boss in public and who successfully uses this power to gain advantage is using coercion.

The opposite of coercive power is **reward power**. People comply with the wishes or directives of another because it produces positive benefits; therefore, one who can distribute rewards that others view as valuable will have power over them. These rewards can be anything that another person values. In an organizational context, we think of money, favourable performance appraisals, promotions, interesting work assignments, friendly colleagues, and preferred work shifts or sales territories.

reward power
Power that produces positive benefits or rewards.

Coercive and reward power are actually counterparts of each other. If you can remove something of positive value from someone or inflict something of negative value on him or her, you have coercive power over that person. If you can give someone something of positive value or remove something of negative value, you have reward power over that person. Again, as with coercive power, you don't need to be a manager to be able to exert influence through rewards. Rewards such as friendliness, acceptance and praise are available to everyone in the organization. To the degree that an individual seeks such rewards, your ability to give to, or withhold from, them gives you power over that individual.

Expert power is influence wielded as a result of expertise, special skill, or knowledge. In recent years, as a result of the explosion in technical knowledge, expert power has become an increasingly potent power source in organizations. As jobs have become more specialized, management has increasingly become dependent on staff "experts" to achieve the organization's goals. As an employee increases his or her knowledge of information that's crucial to the operation of a work group, and to the degree that this knowledge isn't possessed by others, expert power is enhanced. To illustrate the point: if a computer system is crucial to a unit's work, and if one employee, say Chris, knows how to repair it and no one else within 100 kilometres does, then the unit is dependent on Chris. If the system breaks down, Chris can use her expertise to obtain ends that she could never achieve by her position's authority alone. In such a situation, you should expect the unit's manager to try to have others trained in the workings of the computer system, or to hire someone with this knowledge in order to reduce Chris's power. As others become capable of duplicating Chris's specialized activities, her expert power diminishes.

expert power
Influence that results from expertise, special skill, or knowledge.

The last category of influence that French and Raven identified was **referent power**. Its base is identification with a person who has desirable resources or personal traits. If I admire and identify with you, you can exercise power over me because I want to please you. Referent power develops out of admiration for someone and a desire to be like that person. You might consider the person you identify with as having what we discussed earlier—*charisma*. If you admire someone to the point of modelling your behaviour and attitudes on him or her, this person possesses referent power over you. In organizations, the charismatic individual—manager or otherwise—can influence superiors, peers and subordinates.

referent power
Power that arises from identification with a person who has desirable resources or personal traits.

As we mentioned at the beginning of this section, leadership is about the power—or process of influence—that leaders have over their followers, and how they use this power to affect the behaviour and performance of followers. Most effective leaders rely on several dif-

THINKING CRITICALLY ABOUT ETHICS

Your boss is not satisfied with the way one of your colleagues is handling a project and she reassigns the project to you. She tells you to work with this person to find out what he has done already, and to discuss any other necessary information that he might have. She wants your project report by the end of the month. This person is pretty upset and angry over the reassignment and won't give you the information you need to even start, much less complete, the project. You won't be able to meet your deadline unless you get this information.

What type of power does your colleague appear to be using? What type of influence could you possibly use to gain his co-operation? If you were involved in this situation, what could you do to resolve it successfully, yet ethically? ■

Fishery Products International Ltd.
www.fpil.com

ferent bases of power. For instance, a manager may find that he or she needs to use legitimate power and referent power to influence subordinates to accept a planned organizational change. When the fish stocks off Newfoundland's coast disappeared, the results were devastating to the fishing industry. A blow of this magnitude could easily signal the collapse of a fish products company, but Fishery Products International Ltd. of St. John's, Newfoundland, managed to survive this catastrophe and even thrive during it. The collapse of the fish stocks and the resulting uncertainty could easily have undermined efforts to reorganize. But CEO Vic Young managed to use both his authority and charisma to lead his company through this trying time. Young led a reorganization of FPI as the company lost 90 percent of its fish stock. FPI now buys 15 times the amount of fish it used to from outside Canada, and is North America's biggest frozen fish company.[47]

Leading Through Empowerment

As we've described in different sections throughout the text, managers are increasingly leading by empowering their employees. Millions of individual employees and teams of employees are making the key operating decisions that directly affect their work. They're developing budgets, scheduling workloads, controlling inventories, solving quality problems, and engaging in similar activities that, until very recently, were viewed exclusively as part of management's job.

The increased use of empowerment is being driven by two forces. First is the need for quick decisions by those people who are most knowledgeable about the issues. This requires moving decisions to lower levels. If organizations are to successfully compete in a dynamic global economy, they have to be able to make decisions and implement changes quickly. Second is the reality that the downsizing of organizations during the late 1980s and early 1990s left many managers with considerably larger spans of control than they had earlier. In order to cope with the demands of an increased load, managers had to empower their people.

Is the empowerment movement inconsistent with the contingency perspective on leadership? Yes and no! It's being sold, in some circles, as a universal panacea. That is, it's claimed that empowerment will work anywhere. This universal perspective is an anticontingency approach to leadership. In contrast, where a workforce has the knowledge, skills, and experience to do jobs competently, and where employees seek autonomy and possess an internal locus of control, empowering people through delegation and participation would be consistent with contingency theories such as situational leadership and path–goal theories. For instance, it's not a coincidence that empowerment efforts are almost always coupled with extensive training. By giving employees enhanced skills, abilities and confidence, management increases the likelihood that empowerment will succeed.

Gender and Leadership

There was a time when the question "Do males and females lead differently?" could be accurately characterized as a purely academic issue—interesting but not very relevant. That's certainly not true today! Millions of women are now in management positions. Millions more will join the management ranks in the next few years. Gender myths about leadership can

John Martino, Industrial-Engineering Manager of the IV Systems Division of Baxter Healthcare Corporation, has empowered employees as part of the company's QLP (Quality Leadership Process) program.

adversely affect hiring, performance evaluation, promotion, and other human resource decisions for both men and women. So this timely topic needs to be addressed.

First, however, a warning: This topic is controversial.[48] If male and female styles differ, does this imply that one is inferior? Moreover, if there is a difference, does labelling leadership styles by gender encourage stereotyping? These aren't easily dismissed questions, and they should be considered. We'll come back to them later in this section.

The Evidence. A number of studies that have focused on gender and leadership style have been conducted in recent years.[49] Their general conclusion is that males and females *do* use different styles. Specifically, women tend to adopt a more democratic or participative style, and a less autocratic or directive style than men. Women are more likely to encourage participation, share power and information, and attempt to enhance followers' self-worth, than men. They lead through inclusion and rely on their charisma, expertise, contacts, and interpersonal skills to influence others. Women tend to use transformational leadership, motivating others by transforming their self-interest into the goals of the organization.[50]

Men are more likely to use a directive, command-and-control style. They rely on the formal authority of their position for their influence base. Men tend to use transactional leadership, handing out rewards for good work and punishment for bad.[51]

There's an interesting qualifier to these findings. This tendency for female leaders to be more democratic than males declines when women are in male-dominated jobs. Apparently group norms and stereotypes of male roles override personal preferences, so that women abandon their natural styles in such jobs and act more autocratically.

Is Different Better? Given that males have historically held the majority of leadership positions in organizations, it may be tempting to assume that the existence of differences between males and females would automatically favour males. Not necessarily! In today's organizations, flexibility, teamwork, trust, and information sharing are rapidly replacing rigid structures, competitive individualism, control and secrecy. The best managers listen, motivate, and provide support to their people. They inspire and influence rather than control. And, generally speaking, women seem to do these things better than men. As a specific example, the expanded use of cross-functional teams in organizations means that effective managers must become skillful negotiators. Women's leadership styles makes them better at negotiating. They don't focus on wins, losses, and competition the way men do. Women treat negotiations in the context of a continuing relationship—trying hard to make the other party a winner in its own and others' eyes.[52]

A Few Concluding Thoughts. The research evidence we've presented suggests a general relationship between gender and leadership style. But certainly gender doesn't imply destiny. Not all female leaders prefer a democratic style. And many men use transformational leadership. Thus, we need to show caution in labelling leadership styles by gender. To refer to a "feminine style of leadership", for example, may create more confusion than clarity. In addition, the research we've reviewed has looked at leadership *styles*, not leadership *effectiveness*. Which style is effective will depend on the situation. So even if men and women differ in their leadership styles, we should be careful not to assume that one is always preferable to the other. There are, for instance, organizations with inexperienced and unmotivated workers performing ambiguous tasks in which directive leadership is likely to be most effective. In addition, both genders should be looking for a leadership style that synergistically combines the best of both masculine and feminine approaches.[53]

One last point. Some people are more flexible in adjusting their leadership behaviours to different situations than others.[54] That said, it's probably best to think of gender as providing a behavioural *tendency* in leadership. A person may, for instance, tend towards a participative style, but use an autocratic one because the situation requires the latter.

Leadership Styles and Different Cultures

One general conclusion that surfaces from the leadership literature is that effective leaders don't use any single style. They adjust their style to the situation. Although not mentioned explicitly, national culture is certainly an important situational variable in determining which leadership style will be most effective. For instance, one study of Asian leadership styles revealed that Asian managers preferred leaders who were competent decision makers, effective communicators, and who were supportive of employees.[55]

National culture of subordinates *can* affect leadership style. A leader can't choose his or her style at will. "What is feasible depends to a large extent on the cultural conditioning of a leader's subordinates."[56] For example, a manipulative or autocratic style is compatible with high power distance, and we find high power-distance scores in Arab, Far Eastern, and Latin countries. Power distance rankings should also be good indicators of employee willingness to accept participative leadership. Participation is likely to be most effective in low power-distance cultures such as those in Norway, Finland, Denmark and Sweden.

Sometimes Leadership Is Irrelevant!

The belief that some leadership style will always be effective regardless of the situation may not be true. Leadership may not always be important! Data from numerous studies demonstrate that, in many situations, any behaviours a leader exhibits are irrelevant. In other words, certain individual, job, and organizational variables can act as "substitutes for leadership", negating the influence of the leader.[57]

For instance, characteristics of subordinates such as experience, training, "professional" orientation, or need for independence can neutralize the effect of leadership. These characteristics can replace the subordinate's need for a leader's support or ability to create structure and reduce task ambiguity. Similarly, jobs that are inherently unambiguous and routine or that are intrinsically satisfying may place fewer demands on the leadership variable. Finally, such organizational characteristics as explicit formalized goals, rigid rules and procedures, or cohesive work groups can act in the place of formal leadership.

12 What are the various sources of power that a leader might use?

13 How is empowerment related to leadership?

14 Describe the relationship between gender and leadership style.

SUMMARY

This summary is organized by the learning objectives found at the beginning of the chapter.

1. Managers are appointed. Their ability to influence others is based on the formal authority inherent in their positions. In contrast, leaders may either be appointed or may emerge from within a group. Leaders can influence others to perform beyond the actions dictated by formal authority.
2. According to the studies done by Lewin and his associates at the University of Iowa, leaders will use one of three behavioural styles: autocratic, democratic, or laissez-faire. Research completed at Ohio State University identified two independent dimensions of leader behaviour: initiating structure and consideration. Another study of leadership behaviours completed by researchers at the University of Michigan also found two dimensions of leader behaviour which they labelled *employee oriented* and *production oriented*.
3. The two leader behaviours used in the managerial grid are concern for people and concern for production. The five key leadership styles identified in the grid are 1,1 (impoverished); 9,1 (task); 1,9 (country club); 5,5 (middle of the road); and 9,9 (team).
4. Fiedler's contingency model identifies three situational variables: leader–member relations, task structure, and position power. In situations that are highly favourable or highly unfavourable, task-oriented leaders tend to perform best. In moderately favourable or unfavourable situations, relationship-oriented leaders are preferred.
5. The path–goal theory proposes two classes of contingency variables—those in the environment and those that are part of the personal characteristics of the subordinate. Leaders select a specific behaviour—directive, supportive, participative, or achievement oriented—that's congruent with the demands of the environment and the characteristics of the subordinate.
6. The attribution theory of leadership proposes that leadership is merely an attribution that people make about other individuals. Using the attribution framework, researchers have found that people tend to characterize leaders as having traits such as intelligence, outgoing personality, strong verbal skills, aggressiveness, understanding, and industriousness.
7. Charismatic leaders are self-confident, possess a vision of a better future, have a strong belief in that vision, engage in unconventional behaviour, and are perceived as being agents of radical change.
8. Transactional leaders guide their followers in the direction of established goals by clarifying role and task requirements. Transformational leaders inspire followers to transcend their own self-interests for the good of the organization and are capable of having a profound and extraordinary effect on their followers.
9. French and Raven identified five sources or bases of power that a leader might have: legitimate, coercive, reward, expert, and referent.
10. Research finds that women tend to adopt a more democratic or participative style of leadership, while men are more likely to use a directive, command-and-control style. National culture of subordinates will also affect choice of effective leadership style. For instance, a manipulative or autocratic style would be best suited for cultures with high power distance, such as Arab, Far Eastern, and Latin countries. Along these same lines, participation is likely to be most effective in low power-distance cultures such as those in Norway, Sweden, Finland and Denmark.
11. Leaders might not be important when individual variables replace the need for a leader's support or ability to create structure and reduce task ambiguity; when jobs are unambiguous, routine, or intrinsically satisfying; or when such organizational characteristics as explicit goals, rigid rules and procedures, or cohesive work groups act as substitutes for formal leadership.

THINKING ABOUT MANAGEMENT ISSUES

1. What kinds of campus activities could a full-time university student do that might lead to the perception that he or she is a charismatic leader? In pursuing these activities, what might the student do to enhance this perception of being charismatic?
2. Do you think that successful leaders of both genders in specific organizations tend to have similar leadership styles? Discuss.
3. What types of power are available to you? Which ones do you use most? Why?
4. Do you think that most managers in real life use a contingency approach to increase their leadership effectiveness? Discuss.
5. When average people on the street are asked to explain why a given individual is a leader, they tend to describe the person in terms such as competent, consistent, self-assured, inspiring a shared vision, invoking enthusiasm for goal attainment, and being supportive of his or her followers. Can you reconcile this description with leadership concepts presented in this chapter?

SELF-ASSESSMENT EXERCISE

ARE YOU A CHARISMATIC LEADER?

You know from reading the chapter that a charismatic leader has certain characteristics, including self-confidence, vision, the ability to articulate the vision, strong convictions about the vision, behaviour that's out of the ordinary, appearance as a change agent, and environment sensitivity. This Self-Assessment Exercise measures your charismatic potential.

Instructions: The following statements refer to the possible ways in which you might behave towards others when you are in a leadership role. Please read each statement carefully and decide to what extent it applies to you. Then circle the appropriate number.

1 = To a very great extent
2 = To a considerable extent
3 = To a moderate extent
4 = To a slight extent
5 = To little or no extent

You:

1. Pay close attention to what others say when they are talking	1	2	3	4	5
2. Communicate clearly	1	2	3	4	5
3. Are trustworthy	1	2	3	4	5
4. Care about other people	1	2	3	4	5
5. Do not put excessive energy into avoiding failure	1	2	3	4	5
6. Make the work of others more meaningful	1	2	3	4	5
7. Seem to focus on the key issues in a situation	1	2	3	4	5
8. Get across your meaning effectively, often in unusual ways	1	2	3	4	5
9. Can be relied on to follow through on commitments	1	2	3	4	5
10. Have a great deal of self-respect	1	2	3	4	5
11. Enjoy taking carefully calculated risks	1	2	3	4	5
12. Help others to feel more competent in what they do	1	2	3	4	5
13. Have a clear set of priorities	1	2	3	4	5
14. Are in touch with how others feel	1	2	3	4	5
15. Rarely change once you have taken a clear position	1	2	3	4	5
16. Focus on strengths, of yourself and of others	1	2	3	4	5
17. Seem most alive when deeply involved in some project	1	2	3	4	5
18. Show others that they are all part of the same group	1	2	3	4	5
19. Get others to focus on the issues which you see as important	1	2	3	4	5

20. Communicate feelings as well as ideas	1	2	3	4	5
21. Let others know where you stand	1	2	3	4	5
22. Seem to know just how you "fit" into a group	1	2	3	4	5
23. Learn from mistakes; do not treat errors as disasters, but as learning	1	2	3	4	5
24. Are fun to be around	1	2	3	4	5

See scoring key on page SK-5.

Source: Marshall Sashkin and William C Morris, *Experiencing Management,* © 1987 by Addison-Wesley Publishing Company, Inc. Reprinted with permission of the publisher.

for your IMMEDIATE action

TO: Patrick Muenks, Vice President of Employee Relations
FROM: Ray Plemmons, Director of Customer Service Operations
RE: Leadership Training Program for Customer Service Team Leaders

I agree completely with your recommendation that we need a leadership training program for our customer service team leaders. I think these individuals could benefit from such a program. Our team leaders continually struggle with keeping our customer service representatives focused on our departmental goal of providing timely, accurate, and friendly service to our bank card holders who call in with questions or complaints. I'd like you to put together a two-page proposal that describes what leadership topics you think should be covered. Plan on the program being 10 hours long. Also, develop some suggestions for presenting the information in a way that would be appealing to the participants. If we plan on implementing this program later this year, we'll need to get started immediately. Therefore, could you have your report to me by the end of next week?

This is a fictionalized account of a potentially real problem. It was written for academic purposes and is not meant to reflect either positively or negatively on actual management practices at Preferred Bank Card, Inc.

TAKE IT TO THE NET

We invite you to visit the Robbins/Coulter/Stuart-Kotze Companion Website at www.prenticehall.ca/robbins for this chapter's Internet resources.

CASE APPLICATION

Corel Corp., Ottawa

You would be hard-pressed to find a more charismatic leader in the Canadian business world than Michael Cowpland, CEO of Corel Corp. His flamboyant lifestyle matches his image as a take-no-prisoners leader. Cowpland founded Corel back in 1985, with 30 employees—today it has more than 1500, with revenues of $370 million. The company made its fortune with its CorelDraw graphic design programs, which captured more than 80 percent of the worldwide market. But Cowpland realized that to sit on his heels and allow Corel to become complacent with its success would be a major mistake in such an ever-changing industry. In order to end its dependence on its graphic design programs, Corel moved into office software with the purchase of WordPerfect in 1996. Buying WordPerfect for the bargain price of $185 million (US) from Novell, who had paid $1 billion for it two years earlier, put Corel in direct competition with the giant of giants—Microsoft. The comparisons of David and Goliath emerged immediately throughout the Canadian media. And Cowpland himself relished the idea of Corel versus Microsoft, head-on. But taking on a competitor 100 times your size is not such an easy task.

After all the hype, Corel's WordPerfect has failed to deliver and, after a decade of solid profitability and growth, 1998 found the company being besieged on many sides. Corel began posting losses in 1997, and its share price fell from $9 to $3 between 1997 and 1998. Shareholders began calling for Cowpland's resignation if disappointing results continued. Market analysts were almost unanimously pessimistic about Corel's future. To make matters worse, the cornerstone of Corel's business came under serious threat in 1998. Adobe Systems Inc., which had long ruled the graphics software market for Macintosh computer users, began to move heavily into Windows-based software, threatening to take over Corel's long-established reign.

Forays into new areas had been met with failure before at Corel, but were viewed by the public as being insignificant in the face of the company's continued profitability. In 1996, Corel abandoned attempts to develop a hand-held computer and, in early 1997, the company sold its CD-ROM division. But these were minor aberrations, and didn't affect Cowpland's aura of infallibility. However, later in the year, some chinks began to appear in Cowpland's armour, and these could not be shrugged off so easily. Corel had been touting development of Java-based software (functional on any operating system) as the weapon Corel would use to battle Microsoft. But again, Corel's bark appeared worse than its bite, and the company's Java-based programs did not develop as had been hoped. Cowpland himself came under heavy fire from stockholders when he sold $20.5 million worth of Corel shares, a month before the share price nose-dived in the midst of more losses. "Patience is going to be rewarded," Cowpland told his detractors in 1998, but he has shown that even he can be wrong—and shareholders and analysts are no longer so confident of his leadership.

QUESTIONS

1. What characteristics of a charismatic leader do you think Michael Cowpland exhibits? How could these characteristics be beneficial to Corel? How might they be liabilities?
2. Would you characterize Cowpland as a visionary leader? Why or why not?
3. How might transactional and transformational approaches to leadership work at a company like Corel?

Source: Patrick Brethour, "Corel at the Crossroads", *Globe and Mail,* February 4, 1998, p. B27; Patrick Brethour, "Cowpland Vows Corel Will Turn Profit This Year", *Globe and Mail,* April 3, 1998, p. B1; Patrick Brethour, "Adobe Targets Corel's Last Stronghold", *Globe and Mail,* February 5, 1998, p. B1; Patrick Brethour, "Corel Posts Fifth Quarterly Loss", *Globe and Mail,* March 27, 1998, p. B1; Patrick Brethour, "Shareholders Put Corel CEO on Hot Seat", *Globe and Mail,* April 16, 1998, p. B1; Tamsen Tillson, "Corel Inside Out", *Canadian Business Technology,* Spring 1997, pp. 58–62; and Jill Vardy, "Corel Fights for Time and a Jittery Market", *Financial Post,* March 8–10, 1997, p.1.

VIDEO CASE APPLICATION

Canadian Banks

When the Royal Bank and the Bank of Montreal announced the proposal of their merger, what do you imagine there collective 92 000 employees were thinking? The banking industry has never been renowned for its good treatment of employees and, in these years of rapid technological change, job security is constantly eroded. With regard to the workforce, the writing has been on the wall for some time. When, at one staff meeting, management tells the tellers that their jobs are not threatened, then at the next meeting, instructs them to stress the benefits of automatic telling to customers, employees probably get the gist of what's really happening.

The Royal Bank is not only Canada's biggest bank, as of 1999 it is also the country's most profitable company. When the big banks began disclosing record profits—a few of them topping the $1 billion mark—in the late-1990s, the public was not amused. Alexa McDonough's comment in the video that "banks are insensitive to the needs of communities and customers and employees", is an opinion that is shared by most Canadians. There are few places in Canada filled with more silent seething than a bank line. And, of course, workers—especially the front-line workers—bare the brunt of public dissatisfaction.

When the bank of Montreal used Bob Dylan's old tune, "The Times They Are A-Changin'" in a television ad, the majority of the public found it either laughable or disgusting. For the Bank of Montreal's workforce, the ad was filled with a distinct irony. Indeed the times are changing, but as far as employees are concerned, it is definitely not for the better.

When this mega-merger was announced, initial reports mentioned that the banks did not anticipate job losses and branch closings. But it doesn't take a genius to realize that having two branches of the same bank across the street from each other in towns across Canada is more than a little unnecessary. Employees understand that they have to think about their futures, and that their futures at the banks might be limited. How much loyalty do you think employees have to the banks in this environment? One of the greatest challenges facing John Cleghorn and Matthew Barrett will be to try to keep their workforces loyal and motivated during these rapidly changing times.

QUESTIONS

1. Matthew Barrett says that "what [we] are worried most about is how you preserve and grow jobs because that means you're preserving and growing sales". What do you think about this comment? Is it simply political in nature? Is there any validity to it? What do you think Barrett's employees would think of it?
2. Is it inevitable that many jobs will be lost in the new banking industry? If so, how should upper management handle the situation? If not, how will jobs be preserved?
3. What do you think management could do to motivate employees and increase their loyalty?

Video Source: "Banks" and "Panel," *The National* (January 23, 1998).

VIDEO CASE APPLICATION

ACE Clear Defence

Peter Fabian of ACE Clear Defence may not be a John Roth or a Michael Cowpland, but he faces some similar leadership challenges—albeit on a much smaller scale. But then, Cowpland began Corel with only 30 employees just 14 years ago, and now it is Ottawa's biggest success story. Peter Fabian would doubtless like to emulate this success for his own Ottawa-based company. And, just as Corel had a single product that took its global marketplace by storm, ACE Clear is counting on global opportunities for its product—security film for windows.

When US embassies were bombed in Dar es Salaam and Nairobi, in the summer of 1998, Ossama Bin Laden became the new face of America's enemy. Now that the US—the world's biggest economic and military power—has declared a "war on terrorism", the global market for Fabian's product is enormous.

ACE Clear presently has only a small staff, but they are going after large contracts. The company has an opportunity to become a global concern and it is up to Peter Fabian to lead it there.

QUESTIONS

1. Compare Peter Fabian with John Roth (from this chapter's Manager's Challenge). What sorts of leadership traits could Fabian pick up from observing Roth?
2. Describe Peter Fabian and ACE Clear Defence in terms of path–goal theory.
3. Using the leader participation model, describe which style would be most effective for Peter Fabian to adopt. Explain your reasons.

Video Source: "Bulletproof Business," *Venture* #666 (October 28, 1997).

P A R T   S I X

Controlling

LEARNING OBJECTIVES

After Reading This Chapter, You Should Be Able To:

1 Define control
2 Describe the three approaches to control
3 Explain why control is important
4 Describe the control process
5 Distinguish between the three types of control
6 Describe the qualities of an effective control system
7 Explain how controls can become dysfunctional
8 Identify three current ethical issues in control

A MANAGER'S CHALLENGE

Pam Burdi, Director of Human Resources, Western Digital Corporation

Picture yourself as a manager walking around the offices at your workplace, watching people at their desks. You wonder to yourself: "What are these people really doing on those computers all day? Cyber-slacking? Surfing around in mildly amusing but irrelevant websites for hours?"

As more and more organizations try to provide employees with the latest in technology, they are simultaneously providing both the opportunity and temptation for those employees to be distracted by this technology for non-work-related activities. Giving many adults Internet access is somewhat like sitting a child in front of a television—they can drift off in a mild reverie for hours. The potential for workplace abuse of the Internet is significantly large and is growing. A diversion such as the Internet can obviously take away from the time workers commit to their jobs, creating new opportunities for "loafing off" at work. From a loafer's point of view, the Internet provides the perfect cover, as an employee can appear to be

hard at work when they are in fact trying to download a graphic of Mr. Bean's head.

Although not every log-on for using e-mail or visiting a Website involves an employee slacking off, organizations are becoming increasingly aware of the threat. Organizations are beginning to recognize that they must establish some controls for new technologies. At Western Digital Corporation, managers weighed the pros and cons of providing Internet access to its 10 000 employees worldwide. A global company's operations can of course benefit tremendously from the use of a tool such as the Internet—it could greatly improve communications systems and customer service. There is, however, the downside. Western Digital's upper management were aware of the need to create some guidelines to govern the use of the Internet at work. They put the responsibility for developing these guidelines in the hands of Pam Burdi, Director of Human Resources.

Burdi had to determine which employees could benefit the most from use of the Web; develop guidelines for Internet use among these employees; determine how to measure any misuse of Web access; create a system of penalties to discourage abuse; and provide employees some type of training in the use and abuse of Internet access in their jobs. Try to put yourself in Pam Burdi's position. How would you go about dealing with this situation? What sort of policy guidelines do you think should be instituted?

Human resources and costs are only two aspects of what managers try to control. If an organization has inadequate controls, it may face skyrocketing costs or it may find that it's not achieving its goals. Regardless of the thoroughness of the planning, an idea may still be poorly or improperly implemented without a satisfactory control system. Effective management, therefore, needs to consider the benefits of a well-designed organizational control system.

Foundations of Control

WHAT IS CONTROL?

control
The process of monitoring activities to ensure they're being accomplished as planned and of correcting any significant deviations.

Control can be defined as the process of monitoring activities to ensure that they're being accomplished as planned, and of correcting any significant deviations. All managers should be involved in the control function, even if their units are performing as planned. Managers can't really know whether their units are performing properly until they've evaluated what activities have been done, and until they've compared the actual performance with the desired standard.[1] An effective control system ensures that activities are completed in ways that lead to the attainment of the organization's goals. The criterion that determines the effectiveness of a control system is how well it facilitates goal achievement. The more it helps managers to achieve their organization's goals, the better the control system.[2]

Trans Canada Pipelines
http://transcanada.com

Canadian Wheat Board
www.cwb.ca

Ideally, every organization would like to efficiently and effectively reach its goals. Does this mean, however, that the control systems organizations use are identical? In other words, would TransCanada Pipelines, The Canadian Wheat Board, Sun Ice Ltd., and Maple Leaf Gardens all have the same types of control systems? Probably not. William G Ouchi suggests that there are three different approaches to designing control systems: market, bureaucratic, and clan.[3] (See Figure 17-1.)

market control
An approach to designing control systems that emphasizes the use of external market mechanisms to establish the standards used in the control system.

Market control is an approach to control that emphasizes the use of external market mechanisms, such as price competition and relative market share, to establish the standards used in the control system. This approach is typically used by organizations where the firm's products or services are clearly specified and distinct, and where there's considerable marketplace competition. Under such conditions, the divisions of a company are often turned into profit centres, each being evaluated by the percentage of total corporate profits it generates. For instance, at Matsushita, the various divisions (such as video, audio, home appliances, and information or industrial equipment) are evaluated according to the profits each contributes to the company's total profits. Using these measures, corporate managers make decisions about future resource allocation, strategic changes, and other work activities that may need attention.

FIGURE 17-1 Characteristics of Three Approaches to Control Systems

Type of Control	Characteristics
Market	Uses external market mechanisms, such as price competition and relative market share, to establish standards used in system. Typically used by organizations whose products or services are clearly specified and distinct and who face considerable marketplace competition.
Bureaucratic	Emphasizes organizational authority. Relies on administrative and hierarchical mechanisms, such as rules, regulations, procedures, policies, standardization of activities, well-defined job descriptions, and budgets, to ensure that employees exhibit appropriate behaviours and meet performance standards.
Clan	Regulates employee behaviour by the shared values, norms, traditions, rituals, beliefs, and other aspects of the organization's culture. Often used by organizations in which teams are common and technology is changing rapidly.

Another approach to a control system is **bureaucratic control**, which emphasizes organizational authority and relies on administrative rules, regulations, procedures, and policies. This type of control depends on standardization of activities, well-defined job descriptions, and other administrative mechanisms such as budgets to ensure that employees exhibit appropriate behaviour and meet performance standards. British Petroleum provides a good example of bureaucratic control. Although managers at BP's various divisions are allowed considerable autonomy and freedom to run their units as they see fit, they're expected to stick closely to their budgets and stay within corporate guidelines.

bureaucratic control
An approach to designing control systems that emphasizes organizational authority and relies on administrative rules, regulations, procedures, policies, standardization of activities, and other administrative mechanisms to ensure that employees exhibit appropriate behaviours and meet performance standards.

Under **clan control**, employee behaviours are regulated by the shared values, norms, traditions, rituals, beliefs, and other aspects of the organization's culture. For instance, corporate rituals, such as annual employee performance award dinners or holiday bonuses, play a significant part in establishing control. Whereas bureaucratic control is based on strict organizational hierarchical mechanisms, clan control depends on the individual and the group (or clan) to identify appropriate and expected behaviours and performance measures. Because clan controls arise from the shared values and norms of the group, we tend to find this type of control system in organizations where teams are commonly used for work activities and where technologies are changing often. For instance, at Microsoft, individuals are well aware of the expectations regarding appropriate work behaviour and performance standards. The organizational culture—through the shared values, norms, and stories about the company's legendary founder, Bill Gates—conveys to individual employees "what's important around here" and "what's not important". Rather than relying on prescribed administrative controls, Microsoft's employees are guided and controlled by the clan's culture.

clan control
An approach to designing control systems in which employee behaviours are regulated by the shared values, norms, traditions, rituals, beliefs, and other aspects of the organization's culture.

Most organizations don't rely totally on just one of these approaches to designing an appropriate control system. Instead, the organization chooses to emphasize either bureaucratic or clan control, in addition to using some market control measures. The key is designing an appropriate control system that helps the organization to reach its goals effectively and efficiently.

THE IMPORTANCE OF CONTROL

Why is control so important? Planning can be done, an organizational structure can be created to facilitate the achievement of objectives efficiently, and employees can be directed and moti-

Just as control is essential in many situations in everyday life, it is also essential in organizations. In an organization, control is important because it allows management to see whether or not goals are being met.

vated. Still, there's no assurance that activities are going as planned and that the goals which managers are seeking are, in fact, being attained. Control is important, therefore, because it's the final link in the functional chain of management activities. It's the only way managers know whether or not organizational goals are being met, and why or why not. The specific value of the control function, however, lies in its relation to planning and delegating activities.

In Chapter 7, we described objectives as the foundation of planning. Objectives give specific direction to managers. However, just stating objectives or having subordinates accept your objectives is no guarantee that the necessary actions to accomplish these objectives have been taken. The effective manager needs to follow up to ensure that the actions others are supposed to take, and the objectives they are supposed to achieve, are, in fact, being done. Because, in reality, management is an ongoing process, controlling activities provide the crucial link back to planning. (See Figure 17-2.) If managers didn't control, they'd have no way of knowing whether or not their objectives and plans were on target and what future actions to take.

The other area where controlling is important is in delegation. In our discussion of interpersonal skills, we noted that many managers find it difficult to delegate. A major reason given was the fear that subordinates would do something wrong for which the manager would be held responsible. Thus, many managers are tempted to do things themselves to avoid delegating. This reluctance to delegate, however, can be reduced if managers develop an effective control system. Such a control system can provide information and feedback on the perfor-

FIGURE 17-2 The Planning-Controlling Link

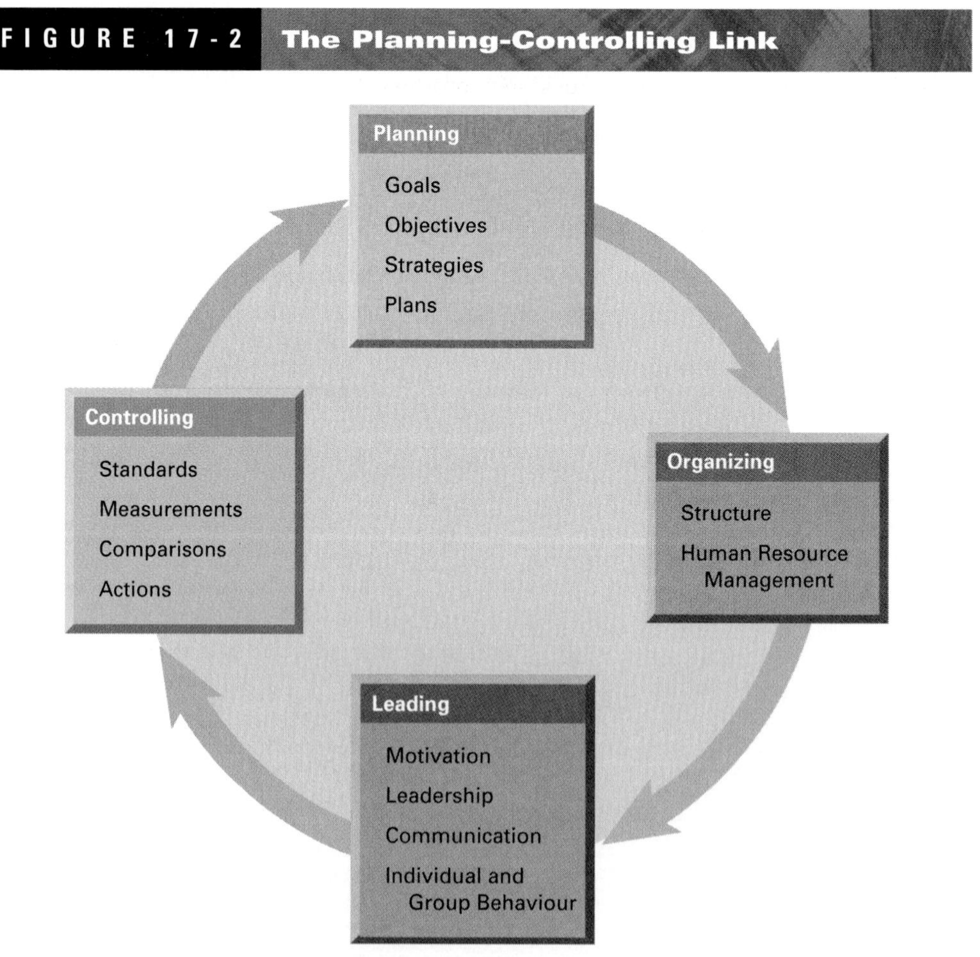

1 What is the role of control in management?

2 Contrast market, bureaucratic, and clan control.

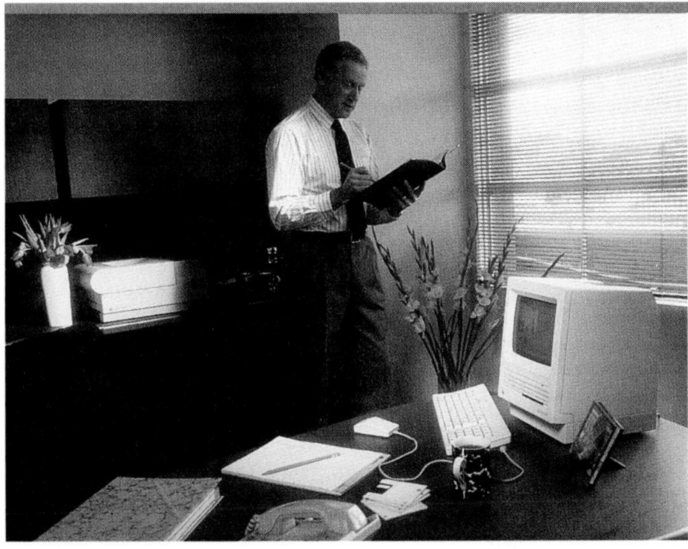

Statistical software, as well as written and oral reports, provide much needed information for managers to use in controlling.

mance of subordinates to whom they've delegated authority. An effective control system is important, therefore, because managers need to delegate authority. But because they're ultimately held responsible for the decisions that their subordinates make, managers also need a feedback mechanism, which the control system provides.

THE CONTROL PROCESS

The **control process** consists of three separate and distinct steps: (1) *measuring* actual performance; (2) *comparing* actual performance against a standard, and (3) taking *managerial action* to correct deviations or inadequate standards. Before we consider each step in detail, you should be aware that the control process assumes that standards of performance *already exist*. These standards, which are created during the planning process, are the specific objectives against which progress can be measured. If managers use MBO, then objectives are, by definition, tangible, verifiable, and measurable. In such instances, these objectives are the standards against which performance is measured and compared. If MBO isn't practised, then standards are the specific performance indicators that management uses. Our point is that these standards are developed in the planning process; planning must *precede* control.

control process
The process of measuring actual performance, comparing it against a standard, and taking managerial action to correct deviations or inadequate standards.

Measuring

To determine what actual performance is, a manager must acquire information about it. The first step in control, then, is measuring. Let's consider *how* we measure and *what* we measure.

How We Measure. Four common sources of information, frequently used by managers to measure actual performance, are personal observation, statistical reports, oral reports, and written reports. Each has particular strengths and weaknesses; however, a combination of information sources increases both the number of input sources, and the probability of receiving reliable information.

Personal observation provides firsthand, intimate knowledge of the actual activity—information that isn't filtered through others. It permits intensive coverage because minor, as well as major, performance activities can be observed, and it provides opportunities for a manager to "read between the lines". Management, by walking around, can pick up omissions, facial expressions, and tones of voice that may be missed by other sources. Unfortunately, in a time when quantitative information suggests objectivity, personal observation is often considered an inferior information source. It's subject to personal biases—what one manager sees, another might not. Personal observation also consumes a good deal of time. As corporations continue to re-engineer and managers' spans of control increase, this can be a significant drawback. Finally, this method suffers from obtrusiveness. Employees might interpret a manager's overt observation as a sign of a lack of confidence in them, or of mistrust.

The current wide use of computers in organizations has led managers to rely increasingly on *statistical reports* for measuring actual performance. This measuring device, however, isn't limited to computer outputs. It also includes graphs, bar charts, and numerical displays of any form that managers may use for assessing performance. Although statistical data are easy to visualize and effective for showing relationships, they provide limited information about an activity. Statistics report on only a few key areas that can be measured numerically and often ignore other important, often subjective, factors.

Information can also be acquired through *oral reports*—that is, through conferences, meetings, one-to-one conversations, or telephone calls. The advantages and disadvantages of this method of measuring performance are similar to those of personal observation. Although the information is filtered, it's fast, allows for feedback, and permits language expression and tone of voice, as well as words themselves, to convey meaning. Historically, one of the major drawbacks of oral reports was the problem of documenting information for later references. However, technological capabilities have progressed to the point where oral reports can be recorded efficiently and become as permanent as if they were written.

Actual performance may also be measured by *written reports*. As with statistical reports they are slower, yet more formal, than firsthand or secondhand reports. This formality also often means greater comprehensiveness and conciseness than is found in oral reports. In addition, written reports are usually easy to file and reference.

Given the varied advantages and disadvantages of each of these four measurement techniques, comprehensive control efforts by managers should use all four.

What We Measure. *What* we measure is probably more critical to the control process than *how* we measure. The selection of the wrong criteria can result in serious dysfunctional consequences. Besides, what we measure determines, to a great extent, what people in the organization will attempt to excel at.[4]

Some control criteria are applicable to any management situation. For instance, because all managers, by definition, direct the activities of others, criteria such as employee satisfaction, turnover and absenteeism rates can be measured. Most managers also have budgets for their area of responsibility, set in dollar costs. Keeping costs within budget is therefore a fairly common control measure. However, any comprehensive control system needs to recognize the diversity of activities among managers. For instance, a production manager in a manufacturing plant might use measures of the quantity of units produced per day, units produced per labour hour, scrap per unit of output, or percentage of rejects returned by customers. In contrast, the manager of an administrative unit in a government agency might use number of document pages typed per day, number of orders processed per hour, or average time required to process paperwork. Marketing managers often use measures such as percentage of market held, average dollar value per sale, or number of customer visits per salesperson.

As you might imagine, the performance of some activities is difficult to measure in quantifiable terms. It's more difficult, for instance, for an administrator to measure the performance of a research chemist or an elementary school counsellor, than of a person who sells life insurance. But most activities can be grouped into some objective segments that allow for measurement. The manager needs to determine what value a person, department, or unit contributes to the organization, and then has to convert the contribution into measurable standards.

Most jobs and activities can be expressed in tangible and measurable terms. When a performance indicator can't be stated in quantifiable terms, managers should look for and use subjective measures. Certainly, subjective measures have significant limitations. Still, they're better than having no standards at all and ignoring the control function. If an activity is important, the excuse that it's difficult to measure is unacceptable. In such cases, managers should use subjective performance criteria. Of course, any analysis or decision based on subjective criteria should recognize the limitations of such information.

Comparing

range of variation
The acceptable parameters of variance between actual performance and the standard.

The comparing step determines the degree of variation between actual performance and the standard. Some variation in performance can be expected in all activities. It's crucial, therefore, to determine the acceptable **range of variation**. (See Figure 17-3.) Deviations that exceed this range become significant and need the manager's attention. In the comparison stage, managers are particularly concerned with the size and direction of the variation.

FIGURE 17-3 Defining the Acceptable Range of Variation

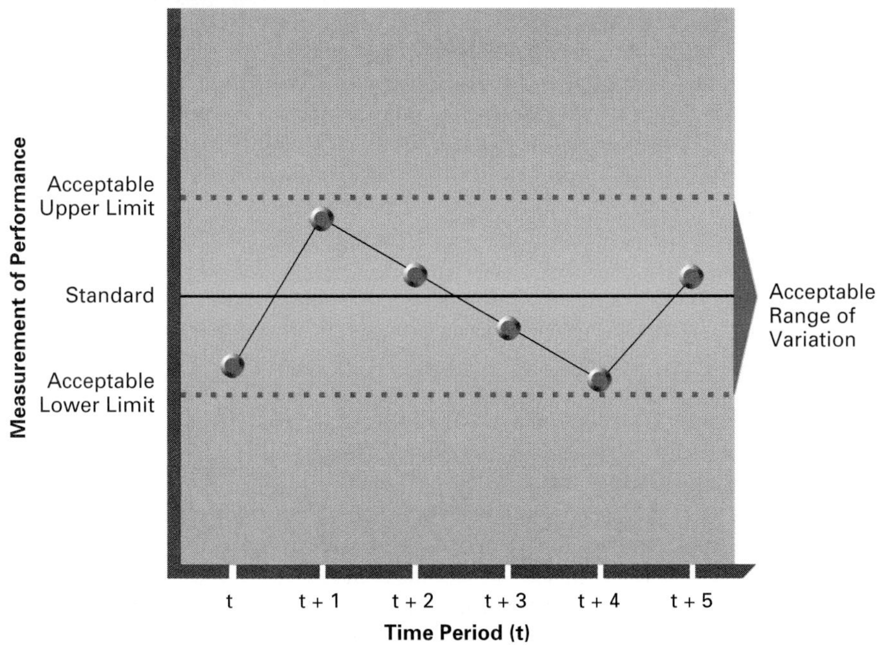

An example should make this concept clearer. Chris Tanner is sales manager for CanuckBrew, a distribution company that supplies bars in Ontario with beer from the rest of the country. Chris prepares a report during the first week of each month that describes sales for the previous month, classified by brand name. Table 17-1 displays both the standard and actual figures for the month of July.

Should Chris be concerned about the July performance? Sales were a bit higher than originally targeted, but does that mean that there were no significant deviations? Even though overall performance was generally quite favourable, several brands might need to be examined more closely by the sales manager. However, the number of brands that deserve attention depends on what Chris believes to be *significant*. How much variation should Chris allow before corrective action is taken?

TABLE 17-1 CanuckBrew's Sales Performance for July (in Cases)

Brand	Standard	Actual	Over (Under)
Alexander Keith's I.P.A.	1075	913	(162)
Big Rock Warthog Ale	630	634	4
Okanagan Spring Pale Ale	800	912	112
Moosehead Export	620	622	2
Olands Export Ale	540	672	132
McAuslan's St. Ambroise	160	140	(20)
Granville Island Lager	225	220	(5)
Unibroue's La Maudite	80	65	(15)
Nelson After Dark	170	286	116
TOTAL CASES	4300	4464	164

Moosehead Beer
www.moosehead.ca

Labatt Brewing Company
www.labatt.com

The deviation on several brands (such as Big Rock, Moosehead, and Granville Island) is very small, and undoubtedly not worthy of special attention. On the other hand, are the shortages for McAuslan's and Unibroue brands significant? That's a judgment that Chris must make. Alexander Keith's sales were 15 percent below Chris's goal. This is a significant deviation and needs attention. Chris should look for a cause.

In this instance, Chris attributes the loss to aggressive advertising and promotion programs by the big domestic producers, Labatt and Molson. Because Alexander Keith's is the number one seller for CanuckBrew, it's most vulnerable to the promotional clout of the big domestic producers. If the decline in Keith's is more than a temporary slump (that is, if it happens again next month), then Chris will need to reduce sales orders with the brewery and lower inventory stock.

An error in understating sales can be as troublesome as an overstatement. For instance, is the surprising popularity of Nelson After Dark a one-month aberration, or is this brand increasing its market share? If the brand is increasing its market share, Chris will want to order more of this product from the brewery to meet consumer demands, so that he will not run short and risk losing customers. Again, Chris will have to interpret the information and make a decision. Our CanuckBrew example illustrates that both overvariance and undervariance in any comparisons of measures require managerial attention.

Taking Managerial Action

The third and final step in the control process is taking managerial action. Managers can choose among three possible courses of action: They can do nothing; they can correct the actual performance; or they can revise the standards. Because "doing nothing" is fairly self-explanatory, let's look more closely at the other two.

Correct Actual Performance. If the source of the variation in actual performance has been deficient work activities or actions, the manager will want to take corrective action. Examples of such corrective action might include changes in strategy, structure, compensation practices, or training programs; job redesign; or the replacement of personnel.

immediate corrective action
Correcting an activity at once in order to get performance back on track.

basic corrective action
Determining how and why performance has deviated and correcting the source of deviation.

A manager who decides to correct actual performance has to make another decision: Should immediate or basic corrective action be taken? **Immediate corrective action** corrects problems at once and gets performance back on track. **Basic corrective action** asks how and why performance has deviated and then proceeds to correct the source of deviation. It's not unusual for managers to rationalize that they don't have time to take basic corrective action, and therefore must be content to perpetually "put out fires" with immediate corrective action. Effective managers, however, analyze deviations and, when the benefits justify it, take the time to permanently correct significant variances between standard and actual performance.

To return to our example of CanuckBrew, Chris Tanner might take basic corrective action on the negative variance for Keith's by increasing promotion efforts, increasing the advertising budget for this brand, or reducing future orders with the manufacturer. The action Chris takes will depend on the assessment of each brand's potential effectiveness.

Revise the Standard. It's possible that the variance was a result of an unrealistic standard—that is, the goal may have been too high or too low. In such cases, it's the standard that needs corrective attention, not the performance. In our example, Chris might need to raise the standard for Nelson to reflect its growing popularity. This type of upwards adjustment of standard frequently happens in sports when athletes adjust their performance goals upwards during a season, if they achieve their season goal early.

The more troublesome problem is the revision of a performance standard downwards. If an employee or unit falls significantly short of reaching its target, the natural response is to shift the blame for the variance to the standard. For instance, students who make a low grade on a test often attack the grade cutoff points as being too high. Rather than accept the fact that their performance was inadequate, students argue that the standards are unreasonable. Similarly, salespeople who fail to meet their monthly quota may attribute the failure to an unrealistic quota. Maybe standards *are* too high, resulting in a significant variance, and acting to demotivate those employees being measured against it. But keep in mind that, if employees or managers don't meet the standard, the first thing they're likely to attack is the standard itself. If you believe the standard is realistic, hold your ground. Explain your position, reaffirm to the employee or manager that you expect future performance to improve, and then take the necessary corrective action to turn that expectation into reality.

Summary

Figure 17-4 summarizes the control process. Standards evolve out of objectives, but because objectives are developed during planning, they're tangential to the control process. The process is essentially a continuous flow between measuring, comparing, and managerial action. Depending on the results of the comparing stage, management's course of action is to do nothing, revise the standard, or correct the performance.

At this point, we'd also like to reiterate the importance of information to the whole control process. Without some organized system for collecting and disseminating information, it would be impossible for a manager to control work activities and performance. We'll cover aspects of information and its relationship to control in more detail in Chapter 19.

FIGURE 17-4 The Control Process

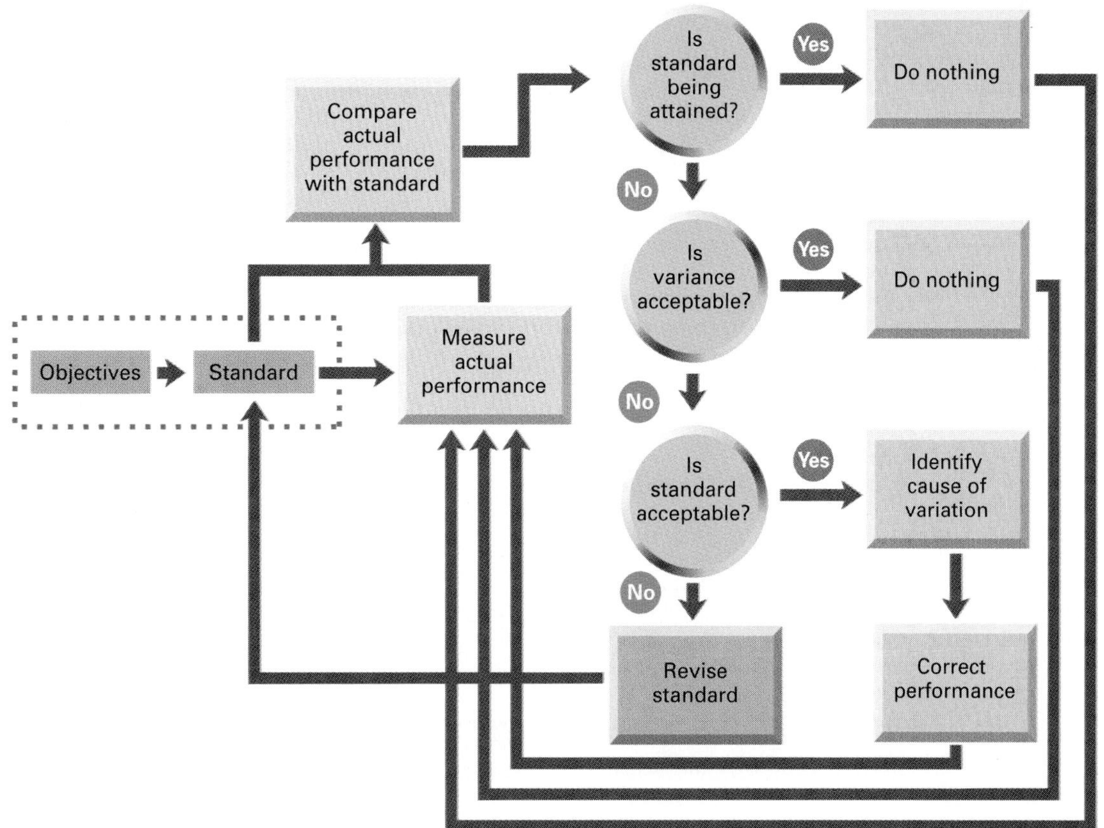

3 **What are the three steps in the control process?**

4 **Name four methods managers can use to acquire information about actual performance.**

5 **Contrast the managerial actions of correcting actual performance and revising standards.**

TYPES OF CONTROL

Management can implement controls before an activity commences, while the activity is going on, or after the activity has been completed. The first type is called *feedforward control,* the second is *concurrent control,* and the last is *feedback control.* (See Figure 17-5.)

Feedforward Control

feedforward control
Control that prevents anticipated problems.

The most desirable type of control—**feedforward control**—prevents anticipated problems. It's called *feedforward control* because it takes place in advance of the actual activity. It's future directed.[5] For instance, managers at OCS Technologies in Richmond, BC, may hire additional personnel as soon as the provincial government announces that it will be making major purchases of OCS's court and prison management software. The hiring of personnel ahead of time prevents potential delays. Likewise, scheduled preventive maintenance programs for aircraft that major airlines are required to institute are a form of feedforward control. They're designed to detect and prevent structural damage that might lead to a tragic crash. The key to feedforward controls, therefore, is to take managerial action before a problem occurs.

Feedforward controls are desirable because they allow management to prevent problems, rather than having to cure them later. Unfortunately, these controls require timely and accu rate information that's often difficult to develop. As a result, managers frequently have to rely on the other two types of controls.

Concurrent Control

concurrent control
Control that occurs while an activity is in progress.

Concurrent control, as its name implies, takes place while an activity is in progress. When control is enacted while the work is being performed, management can correct problems before they become too costly.

The best-known form of concurrent control is direct supervision. When a manager directly oversees the actions of a subordinate, the manager can concurrently monitor the employee's actions and correct problems as they occur. Although there's obviously some delay between the activity and the manager's corrective response, the delay is minimal. Technical equipment can be designed to include concurrent controls. Most computers, for instance, are programmed to provide operators with immediate response if an error is made. If you input the wrong command, the program's concurrent controls reject your command and may even tell you why it's wrong. Also, many organizational quality programs rely on concurrent controls to inform workers if their performance output and levels are of sufficient quality, and to ensure that quality standards are being met.

Feedback Control

feedback control
Control imposed after an action has occurred.

The most popular type of control relies on feedback. The control takes place after the activity is done. The control report that Chris Tanner used for assessing beer sales is an example of a **feedback control**.

The major drawback of this type of control is that by the time the manager has the information, the damage is already done. It's analogous to the proverbial closing the barn door after

FIGURE 17-5 Types of Control

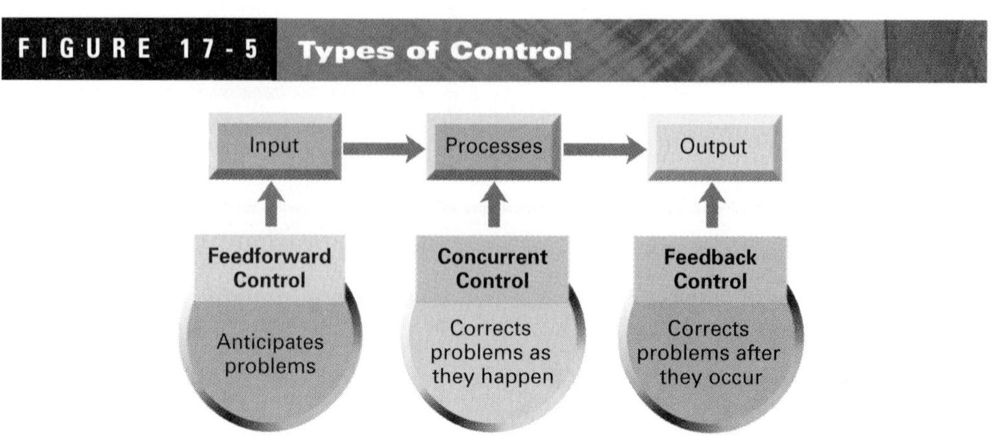

the horse has already gone. But, for many activities, feedback is the only viable type of control available. For instance, financial statements are an example of feedback controls. If, for example, the income statement shows that sales revenues are declining, the decline has already occurred. So, at this point, the manager's only option is to try and determine why sales fell, and to try to correct the situation.

We should note that feedback has two advantages over feedforward and concurrent control.[6] First, feedback provides managers with meaningful information on how effective its planning effort was. If feedback indicates little variance between standard and actual performance, this is evidence that planning was generally on target. If the deviation is great, a manager can use this information when formulating new plans, in order to make them more effective. Second, feedback control can enhance employee motivation. People want information on how well they've performed. Feedback control provides that information.

QUALITIES OF AN EFFECTIVE CONTROL SYSTEM

Effective control systems tend to have certain characteristics in common.[7] The importance of these qualities varies with the situation, but we can generalize that the following characteristics should make a control system more effective. (See Figure 17-6.)

1. *Accuracy*. A control system that generates inaccurate information can result in management neglecting to take action when it should, or responding to a problem that doesn't exist. An accurate control system is reliable and produces valid data.
2. *Timeliness*. Controls should call management's attention to variations in time to prevent serious effects on a unit's performance. The best information has little value if it's dated. Therefore, an effective control system must provide timely information.
3. *Economy*. A control system must be economical to operate. Any system of control should justify the benefits it gives in relation to the costs it incurs. To minimize costs, management should try to impose the least amount of control that's necessary to produce the desired results.
4. *Flexibility*. Effective controls must be flexible enough to adjust to adverse change or to take advantage of new opportunities. Few organizations face environments that are so stable that there's no need for flexibility. Even highly mechanistic structures require controls that can be adjusted as times and conditions change.
5. *Understandability*. Controls that can't be understood by users have no value. It's sometimes necessary, therefore, to substitute less complex controls for sophisticated devices.

FIGURE 17-6 Qualities of an Effective Control System

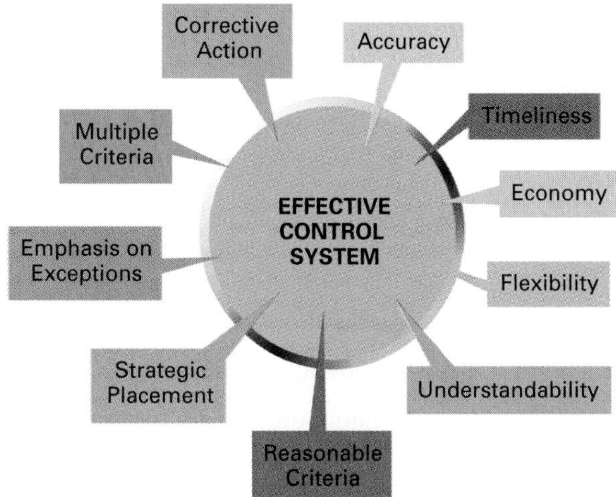

A control system that's difficult to understand can cause unnecessary mistakes, frustrate employees, and eventually be ignored.

6. *Reasonable criteria*. Control standards must be reasonable and attainable. If they're too high or unreasonable, they no longer motivate. Because most employees don't want to risk being labelled incompetent by accusing superiors of asking too much, employees may resort to unethical or illegal shortcuts just to meet the standards. Controls should enforce standards high enough to challenge and "stretch" people to reach higher performance levels, but not so high as to demotivate or encourage deception.

7. *Strategic placement*. Management can't control everything that goes on in an organization. Even if it could, the benefits couldn't justify the costs. As a result, managers should place controls on those factors that are strategic to the organization's performance. Controls should cover the crucial activities, operations, and events within the organization. They should focus on places where variations from standards are most likely to occur, or where a variation would do the greatest harm. For instance, in a department where labour costs are $20 000 a month and postage costs are $50 a month, a 5 percent cost overrun in the former is more critical than a 20 percent overrun in the latter. Hence, management should establish controls for labour but not necessarily for postage.

8. *Emphasis on the exception*. Because managers can't control all activities, they should place their strategic control devices where those devices can call attention only to the exceptions. This type of "exception system" ensures that a manager isn't overwhelmed by information on variations from standard. For example, an organization might have a policy that gives supervisors the authority to give annual employee raises up to $200 a month, approve individual expenses up to $500, and make capital expenditures up to $5000. Then, only deviations above these amounts require approval from higher levels of management. These checkpoints become controls that are part of the structural authority constraints and that free management from reviewing routine expenditures.

9. *Multiple criteria*. Managers and employees alike will seek to "look good" on the criteria that are controlled. If management controls by using a single measure such as unit profit, work efforts will be focused only on looking good on this standard. Multiple measures of performance broaden the focus.

   Multiple criteria have a dual positive effect. Because they're more difficult to manipulate than a single measure, they can discourage efforts to merely "look good". Also, because performance can rarely be objectively evaluated from a single indicator, multiple criteria make possible more accurate work performance assessments.

10. *Corrective action*. An effective control system not only indicates when a significant deviation from standard occurs, but also suggests what action should be taken to correct it. That is, it ought to both point out the problem and specify a solution. This is frequently done by establishing *if-then guidelines*. For instance, *if* unit revenues drop more than 5 percent, *then* unit costs should be reduced by a similar amount.

THE DYSFUNCTIONAL SIDE OF CONTROLS

Have you ever had to deal with a university registrar's or records office where the staff didn't seem to care very much about a student's problem? Perhaps they had become so fixated on making sure that every rule was followed to the letter that they lost sight of the fact that their job is to *serve* students, not hassle them!

At United Parcel Services—long a model of corporate efficiency—managers have been pushing employees to get even more productive.[8] The company recently rolled out several new

6 Why is feedforward control the most desirable type of control?

7 Contrast the advantages and disadvantages of concurrent and feedback control.

8 What qualities will an effective control system have?

Management by Walking Around

Entrepreneurs often fall into the trap of thinking that just because their business is small, they don't really need a comprehensive system of organizational controls. They may rationalize that designing an effective organizational control system is beyond their capabilities, because of their limited knowledge about possible methods of effective control; that it's too expensive; and that they really don't have the time to implement and monitor the controls, even if they did have such a system. However, entrepreneurs have at their disposal one of the most effective and inexpensive controlling techniques—something called "management by walking around".[9]

And just what is **management by walking around (MBWA)**? It's a controlling technique that consists of an entrepreneur or manager being out in the work area, interacting directly with employees, and exchanging information about what's going on. By practising MBWA, entrepreneurs can find out what's happening in their workplace by talking directly and informally with their employees. The entrepreneur is out of his or her office, "wandering around", and seeing for himself or herself what's happening with employees. There's no need for formal, lengthy reports. In fact, the informality of the process often reveals a richness of information that employees might not be willing to explain in a formal, written report. Take for instance Frank Hasenfratz, CEO of Linamar Corp., a producer of auto parts and agricultural equipment. He finds management by walking around to be an extremely easy and useful way to find out what employees are thinking and what problems they're facing. Based on their informal information exchange, Hasenfratz then finds that he can take whatever action is necessary to deal with employees' concerns, or act on ideas that they've expressed to him during his wanderings. And simply by walking around his Guelph, Ontario plant, Hasenfratz can keep direct control over much of the operation.

An organizational control system doesn't have to be complex or cumbersome to be effective. A simple technique like MBWA can be quite useful to an entrepreneur, or even to a manager of a single department within a large, hierarchical organization. ■

management by walking around (MBWA)
A controlling technique in which the manager is out in the work area, interacting directly with employees, and exchanging information about what's going on.

products and services, including computerized tracking systems, bulk discounts on large shipments, higher limits on package weights, and earlier and earlier "guaranteed arrival" times. These new services require employees to haul more packages, move heavier loads, spend more time on complicated deliveries, *and* do all of this without sacrificing their productivity. Although customers love the changes, the company's highly unionized workers have been rebelling.

These examples illustrate what can happen when controls are inflexible or control standards are unreasonable. People lose sight of the organization's overall goals.[10] Instead of the organization running the controls, sometimes the controls run the organization.

How much control is too much? The Japanese firm that controls 7-Eleven uses automated cash registers not only to record sales and monitor inventory but also to schedule tasks for store managers and to track their use of the built-in analytical graphs and forecasts. If they don't use them enough, managers are told to increase their activities.

Because any control system has imperfections, problems occur when individuals or organizational units attempt to look good exclusively in terms of the control devices. The result is dysfunctional in terms of the organization's goals. More often than not, this dysfunctionality is caused by incomplete measures of performance. If the control system evaluates only the quantity of output, people will ignore quality. Similarly, if the system measures activities rather than results, people will spend their time attempting to look good on the activity measures.

To avoid being reprimanded by managers because of the control system, people can engage in behaviours that are designed solely to influence the information system's data output during a given control period. Rather than actually performing well, employees can manipulate measures to give the appearance that they're performing well. The manipulation of control isn't a random phenomenon. It depends on the importance of the activity. Organizationally, important activities are more likely to make a difference in a person's rewards; therefore, there's a greater incentive to look good on these particular measures.[11] When rewards are at stake, individuals tend to manipulate data to appear in a favourable light by, for instance, distorting actual figures, emphasizing successes, and suppressing evidence of failures. In contrast, only random errors occur when the distribution of rewards isn't affected.[12]

So what's our conclusion? It's important to recognize that controls have both an up side and a down side. Failure to design flexibility into an organizational controls system can create problems more severe than those the controls were designed to prevent.

ADJUSTING CONTROLS FOR NATIONAL DIFFERENCES

The concepts of control we've been discussing to this point are appropriate for an organization whose various units aren't geographically distant or culturally distinct. But what about organizations that operate in a few or many locations worldwide? Would control systems be different, and what should managers know about adjusting controls for national differences?

Methods of controlling people and operations can be quite different in foreign countries. In fact, the differences we see in organizational control systems of multinational organizations are primarily in the measurement and corrective action steps of the control process.

For the multinational corporation, managers of foreign operations tend to be less closely controlled by the home office, if for no other reason than that distance keeps them from having direct controls. The home office of a multinational must rely on extensive formal reports in order to maintain control. But collecting data that are comparable between countries can also create problems. For instance, a company's factory in Mexico might produce the same products as its factory in Canada. However, the Mexican factory might be much more labour intensive than its Canadian counterpart (by taking strategic advantage of lower labour costs in Mexico). If headquarters executives were to control costs by, for example, calculating labour costs per unit or output per worker, the figures wouldn't be comparable. Therefore, distance creates a tendency to formalize controls, and technological differences can make control data uncomparable.

Technology's impact on control is most evident when comparing technologically advanced nations with less technologically advanced countries. Organizations in technologically advanced nations such as Canada, Japan, Great Britain, Germany, the United States and Australia use indirect control devices—particularly computer-related reports and analyses—in addition to standardized rules and direct supervision to ensure that activities are going as planned. In less technologically advanced countries, managers tend to rely more on direct supervision and highly centralized decision making as the basic means of control. Constraints on managerial corrective action may also affect managers in foreign countries because laws in some countries don't allow management the option of closing plants, laying off employees, taking money out of the country, or bringing in a new management team from outside the country.

ETHICAL ISSUES IN CONTROL

Even though we know how important control is in organizations and the significant role it plays in the management process, ethical issues can and do arise as managers design efficient and effective control systems. Technological advances in computer hardware and software, for example, have made the process of controlling much easier, but these advances have brought with them difficult questions regarding what managers have the right to know about employees, and how far they can go in controlling employee behaviour, both on and off the job. In this section we look at three ethical issues in employee control: employee workplace privacy, computer monitoring of employees' work, and control of employees' off-the-job behaviour.

Employee Workplace Privacy

If you work, do you think you have a right to privacy at your workplace? What *can* your employer find out about you and your work? You might be surprised by the answers! Employers can, among other things, read your e-mail (even those marked "personal or confidential"), tap your telephone, monitor your work by computer, and monitor you in the employee bathroom or dressing room. A recent poll found employees' concerns about workplace privacy to be at an all-time high, as more than half of the respondents said they were "very concerned" about threats to their privacy at the workplace.[13]

One area that's been a hot topic of debate over employee workplace privacy is e-mail communications. The use of e-mail is flourishing throughout Canadian organizations and employees are concerned about whether they can be fired or disciplined for things they've written and sent. Many companies can, and do, monitor these electronic transmissions. For instance, an extensive survey of over 300 organizations showed that 22 percent of these organizations' corporate managers had reviewed employees' electronic files and mail.[14]

Ethical questions arise over the use and misuse of the information that's communicated through electronic mail networks. For instance, is the e-mail system strictly for business use? What about an employee who e-mails work information to a co-worker but also throws in some personal chitchat? Is that OK or not? What's the appropriate use of the system? Who owns the information that flows along the network? These are tough questions to which there are no easy answers. To minimize employee concerns, it's important for managers to develop policies regarding e-mail usage and communicate these to all system users. But e-mail communications is just one aspect of the concern over the ethics of employee workplace privacy. Computer monitoring is another area in controlling workplace behaviour where ethical questions arise.

Computer Monitoring

Closely related to the issue of employee privacy at the workplace is the practice of computer monitoring of employee work performance and behaviour on the job. Computer monitoring can be an excellent control mechanism.[15] Computer monitoring systems can be used to collect, process, and provide performance feedback information about employees' work that can help managers with performance improvement suggestions and with employee development.[16] And it's also been used to help managers identify employee work practices that might be potentially unethical or costly. For instance, many hospitals and other health care organizations use computer monitoring to control costs of medical procedures and access to controlled medications. Likewise, many business organizations use computer monitoring systems for controlling costs, employee work behaviour, and any number of other areas of organizational activities. Telemarketing organizations often monitor telephone calls of their service operators. They do it to help employees improve at their jobs and to identify skills areas where employees may need more training.[17] Other organizations monitor employees who deal with customer complaints to make sure they're being handled appropriately. Unfortunately, computer monitoring has a questionable reputation because of instances of overuse and abuse.

Many people perceive computer monitoring as nothing more than a technologically sophisticated form of "eavesdropping" or a surveillance technique to "catch" people being bad or slacking off on the job. Critics also claim that these techniques lead to an increase in stress-related complaints from employees who feel the pressure of being under constant surveillance.[18] Supporters argue, however, that computer monitoring can be an effective employee training device and a way to improve work performance levels.

How can organizations benefit from the control information provided by a computer monitoring system and yet minimize the potential behavioural and legal drawbacks? Experts suggest that organizations do the following: (1) Tell employees, both current and new, that they may be monitored. (2) Have a written company policy on monitoring that's posted where employees will see it and distributed to each and every employee, and have them acknowledge in writing that they've received a copy of the policy and that they understand it. (3) Monitor only those situations where a legitimate business purpose is at stake—such as training or evaluating workers or controlling costs.[19] When used in this manner, computer monitoring can be an effective—and ethical—managerial control tool.

Computer monitoring techniques are so sophisticated they have created an issue of workplace privacy. To what extent should managers be able to electronically eavesdrop? When does performance appraisal become an invasion of privacy?

Off-the-Job Behaviour

The last area we want to look at in terms of the ethical issues associated with control is that concerning employees' off-the-job behaviour. Just how much control should a company have over the private lives of its employees off the job? Where should an employer's rules and controls end? Does the boss have the right to dictate what you do in your own free time and in your own home?

While drug testing is not very common in Canada, in the US, employees will go to great lengths to evade being caught out (for example, drinking gallons of water before testing, taking B2 pills, sneaking bags of drug-free urine into testing booths). Traditionally, Canadian courts have upheld individual rights over the control attempts of organizations, even with regard to on-the-job behaviour. A recent case in Ontario is an extreme example. A sales executive met a client for lunch, the two drank heavily, and proceeded to get into a physical fight. The sales exec, drunk, then drove his company vehicle back to work. He was fired and he sued for wrongful dismissal. The courts found in his favour, citing his 27 years of good service to the company. With precedents like this relating to on-the-job behaviour, the monitoring of off-the-job behaviour in Canada is obviously almost impossible.[20]

To control health care costs, many organizations are beginning to use proactive measures such as providing financial incentives to those who have a healthy lifestyle (e.g., wearing safety belts, not smoking, not participating in dangerous recreational activities, drinking moderately or not at all, and controlling weight and blood pressure). At Husky Injection Molding Systems, employees are encouraged to adhere to a healthy lifestyle. Vegetarian dishes are subsidized in the workplace cafeteria to promote them over meat dishes. Herbal tea is free, whereas coffee costs 85 cents. The company also employs a doctor, a fitness consultant, and a naturopath to aid employees. These efforts to instill a devotion to personal health among employees saves Husky roughly $350 per worker in insurance costs, compared with other Canadian manufacturing firms. Husky is a good example of how a company may strive to influence employees' off-the job behaviour by promoting personal health.

TESTING... TESTING...

9 **What can managers do to reduce the dysfunctionality of controls?**

10 **Describe what ethical issues can arise in the controlling process.**

11 **What can organizations do to ensure that their control systems are ethical as well as effective?**

Many American companies go so far as to prohibit certain off-the-job behaviours—such as skydiving, motorcycle racing, and mountain climbing—in attempts to keep insurance costs down. Some even forbid smoking at home. While these types of controls are virtually non-existent here, Canadian managers must be aware of American trends.

Do you think it's ethical for companies to tell employees that they can't ride a motorcycle for recreation or smoke in their own homes? Even where the law does not bar an employer from making such rules, do you feel they are justified in doing so?

SUMMARY

This summary is organized by the learning objectives found at the beginning of the chapter.

1. Control is the process of monitoring activities to ensure that they're being accomplished as planned, and of correcting any significant deviations.
2. The three approaches to control include market control, bureaucratic control, and clan control. Market control is an approach that emphasizes the use of external market mechanisms, such as price competition and relative market share, to establish the standards used in the control system. Bureaucratic control emphasizes organizational authority and relies on administrative rules, regulations, procedures and policies. Under clan control systems, employee behaviours are regulated by the shared values, norms, traditions, rituals, beliefs, and other aspects of the organizational culture.
3. Control is important because it monitors whether objectives are being accomplished as planned and whether delegated authority is being abused.
4. In the control process, management must first have standards of performance, which arise from the objectives formed in the planning stage. Then management must measure actual performance and compare that performance to the standards. If a variance exists between standards and actual performance, management must either adjust performance, adjust the standards, or do nothing, according to the situation.
5. The three types of control are as follows: Feedback control is future directed and prevents anticipated problems. Concurrent control takes place while an activity is in progress. Feedback control takes place after the activity.
6. An effective control system is accurate, timely, economical, flexible, and understandable. It uses reasonable criteria, has strategic placement, emphasizes the exception, uses multiple criteria, and suggests corrective action.
7. Controls can become dysfunctional when they redirect behaviour away from an organization's goals. This can occur as a result of inflexibility or unreasonable standards. In addition, when rewards are at stake, individuals are more likely to manipulate data so that their performance will be perceived positively.
8. Current ethical issues in control include employee workplace privacy, computer monitoring of employees' work, and control of employees' off-the-job behaviour. These ethical issues are interrelated and concern the rights of employees versus the rights of employers. Employees are concerned about protecting their workplace privacy, the stress of being under constant computer surveillance, and their employer's intrusion into their personal lives. Employers are primarily concerned with employee work practices that might be potentially unethical or costly.

THINKING ABOUT MANAGEMENT ISSUES

1. What would an organization have to do to change its dominant control approach from bureaucratic to clan? How about from clan to bureaucratic?
2. In Chapter 12 we discussed the "white-water rapids" view of change. Do you think it's possible to establish and maintain effective standards and controls in this type of atmosphere? Explain.
3. How could you use the concepts of control in your own personal life? Be specific. (Think in terms of feedforward, concurrent, and feedback controls, as well as controls for the different areas of your life.)
4. Do you think effective control systems for organizations in today's environment will have to be more future oriented and continuous in nature? Why or why not?
5. "Every individual employee in the organization plays a role in controlling work activities." Do you agree, or do you think control is just something that managers are responsible for? Explain.

SELF-ASSESSMENT EXERCISE

WHO CONTROLS YOUR LIFE?

Instructions: Read the following statement and indicate whether you agree more with choice A or choice B.

A	B	
1. Making a lot of money is largely a matter of getting the right breaks.	**1.** Promotions are earned through hard work and persistence.	____
2. I have noticed that there is usually a direct connection between how hard I study and the grades I get.	**2.** Many times the reactions of teachers seem haphazard to me.	____
3. The number of divorces indicates that more and more people are not trying to make their marriages work.	**3.** Marriage is largely a gamble.	____
4. It is silly to think that one can really change another person's basic attitudes.	**4.** When I am right, I can convince others.	____
5. Getting promoted is really a matter of being a little luckier than the next person.	**5.** In our society a person's future earning power depends on his or her ability.	____
6. If one knows how to deal with people, they are really quite easily led.	**6.** I have little influence over the way other people behave.	____
7. The grades I make are the result of my own efforts; luck has little or nothing to do with it.	**7.** Sometimes I feel that I have little to do with the grades I get.	____
8. People like me can change the course of world affairs if we make ourselves heard.	**8.** It is only wishful thinking to believe that one can really influence what happens in our society at large.	____
9. A great deal that happens to me is probably a matter of chance.	**9.** I control my own destiny.	____
10. Getting along with people is a skill that must be practised.	**10.** It is almost impossible to figure out how to please some people.	____

Turn to page SK-5 for scoring directions and key.

Source: Adapted from Julian B Rotter, "External Control and Internal Control," *Psychology Today,* June 1971, p. 42.

for your IMMEDIATE action

Northern College
SCHOOL OF ACCOUNTANCY

TO: Dr. Rita Novakovich, Chair of Committee on Student Ethics
FROM: Dr. Corinne Karuppan, Director
SUBJECT: Minimizing Student Cheating

As you may have heard, several faculty members have expressed an interest in developing some specific controls to minimize opportunities for our students to engage in incidents of cheating on homework assignments and exams. Since this topic falls under your committee's area of responsibility, I'd like you to get together with them and develop some suggestions.

As you look at this topic, I'd like you to address your suggestions from the perspective of controlling possible student cheating (1) before it happens, (2) while in-class exams or assignments are being completed, and (3) after it's happened.

Please keep your committee's report brief (no more than two pages). I'd also like to have it by the end of the month so I have an opportunity to look at it before presenting it to the entire faculty at our next scheduled meeting.

This is a fictionalized account of a potentially real problem. It is not intended to reflect either positively or negatively on management practices at any college.

TAKE IT TO THE NET

We invite you to visit the Robbins/Coulter/Stuart-Kotze Companion Website at www.prenticehall.ca/robbins for this chapter's Internet resources.

CASE APPLICATION

Swain, Adney and Brigg (SAB), England

SAB has been producing upscale leather goods since the 1750s. During the 1980s, managers decided to expand their facilities. They built new factories and consolidated all manufacturing operations under one roof. These same executives decided to significantly expand their firm's retail space, even opening a site in San Francisco to process mail orders coming from the US. With the expansion came increased costs— including a move of its famous Piccadilly Street location in London to a new facility a few blocks away, at 100 times the cost. But the 1980s ended with significant changes in SAB's business. The British pound weakened against the dollar, virtually halving SAB's mail-order business. Furthermore, consumers were beginning to change their taste and preferences. Luxury items—which make up a significant portion of SAB's production—were no longer in such demand. These events led SAB to the brink of financial disaster, as annual losses soon exceeded £3 million. In 1990, the Adney family, which had controlled the company for 240 years, sold its interest to other investors, leaving the company to be run by an impersonal corporation. For the next four years, SAB languished. Then John de Bruyne came along and bought the company.

What de Bruyne found when he took over the company in 1994 was nothing short of chaos. Few, if any, control measures were in place. No one really knew what was going on or how well plans were being met. He concluded that it was doubtful that standards were being set at all. De Bruyne knew he had to make some major changes. One of the first things he did was to focus on the firm's core business—making upscale leather goods—to recapture the firm's competitive advantage. He also reduced costs by eliminating jobs and moving the main production facility to one that had much lower rent. He implemented production controls to help increase output, while simultaneously increasing the quality of each item produced. De Bruyne also implemented procedures to address customer concerns. And he established plans and monitoring systems for capturing new business in such locations as Paris, New York, Moscow and Hamburg.

What John de Bruyne did for SAB was remarkable. In just over a year, he turned the firm completely around. In 1995, the company earned more than £2 million, up from a £3 million loss a year earlier. Today, the company continues its phenomenal success.

QUESTIONS

1. How could John de Bruyne have used the steps in the control process to help him address the problems plaguing SAB?
2. What types of feedforward, concurrent, and feedback controls might de Bruyne have used? Be as specific as possible.
3. Describe the three major approaches to control systems and how SAB might use each.
4. Given the fact that SAB operates in different global locations, would the company's control systems have to be different as well? Explain.

Source: G Lesser, "A Hard Rain's Gonna Fall", *Sky,* August 1996, pp. 22–27.

A MANAGER'S CHALLENGE

MDS Laboratory Services, Toronto

MDS operates medical testing laboratories across Canada, and its Toronto lab is the largest in the country but, up until a few years ago, all of these labs were being run very inefficiently. Thousands of medical samples were being analyzed, moving through different departments for testing. The problem was that highly skilled technicians would find their time taken up by menial tasks such as loading, unloading, and moving around trays of specimens. Up to three-quarters of technicians' time was being spent on unskilled tasks.[1]

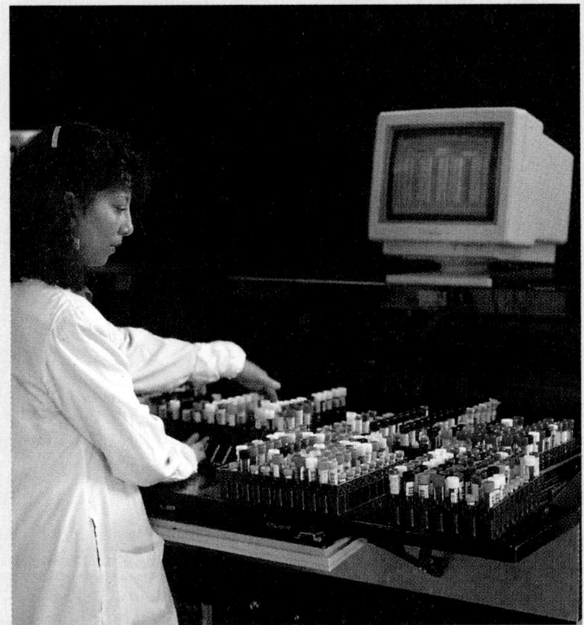

LEARNING OBJECTIVES

After Reading This Chapter, You Should Be Able To:

1 Describe the role of the transformation process in operations management

2 Explain what factors determine organizational productivity

3 Discuss what re-engineering of work processes involves

4 Describe how adding a "manufacturing focus" to organizational strategy affects an organization

5 Identify the four key decisions that provide the long-term strategic direction for operations planning

6 Describe the three decisions that make up tactical operations planning

7 Identify the three approaches to maintenance control

8 Explain the contingency factors that affect the implementation of TQM

9 Discuss the advantages and potential problems of just-in-time (JIT) inventory systems

10 Explain how flexible manufacturing systems could give an organization a competitive advantage

11 Describe how speed can be a competitive advantage

A completely new system was instituted, beginning with the Toronto lab. A bar-code system was put in place, whereby samples moved through the entire facility on a conveyer belt (all walls were taken out). A software system was developed whereby information—that had previously been gathered on worksheets—was now collected by computers scanning bar codes. And a control centre now kept track of where each specimen had been sent and where the results of various tests were done.

Within two-and-a-half years, efficiency at the lab had improved to the extent that three times the number of samples were being completed. Increases in productivity quickly paid for the $25 million investment in developing the new system. MDS has continued to record increasing revenues, growing by 42.5 percent between 1995 and 1998. And now, MDS wants to market the control system it has developed to laboratories all over the globe. The company's Autolab Systems division is marketing the technology internationally.

This chapter focuses on the importance of efficiency, productivity, and controls in the operations side of the organization. As our opening Manager's Challenge showed, it's important for managers to have well-thought-out and well-designed operating systems and tight controls in order to survive in the increasingly competitive global economy. If managers like those at MDS can do this, they'll be able to produce higher-quality products and services at prices that meet or beat those of their rivals.

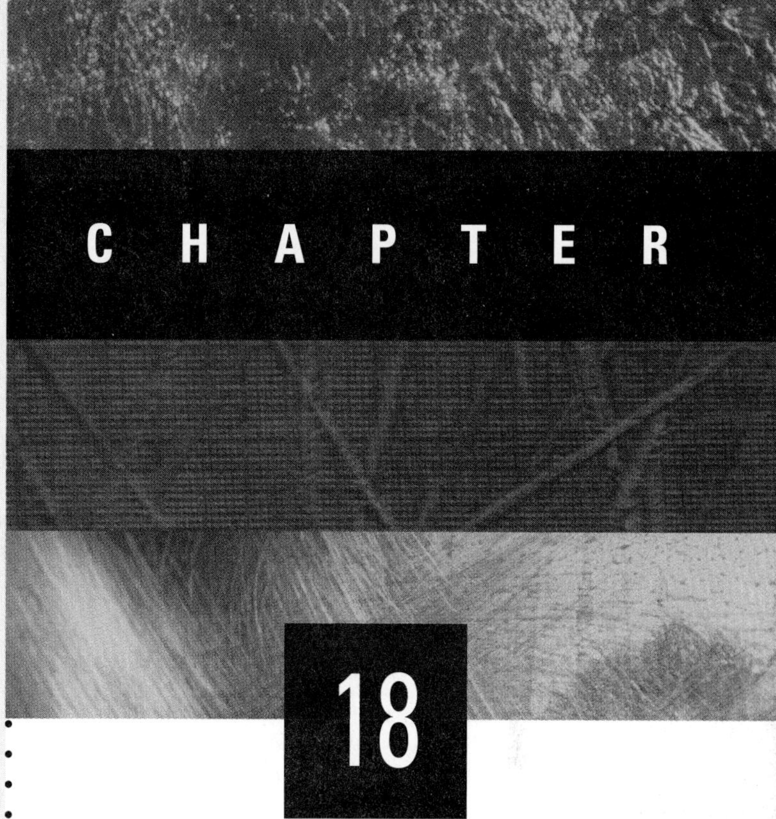

CHAPTER 18

Operations Management

OPERATIONS MANAGEMENT AND THE TRANSFORMATION PROCESS

operations management
The design, operation, and control of the transformation process that converts resources into finished goods and services.

The term **operations management** refers to the design, operation, and control of the transformation process that converts such resources as labour and raw materials into finished goods and services. Remember that every organization produces something. Unfortunately, however, this is often overlooked, except in obvious cases such as in the manufacturing of automobiles, tractors, or telephones. But hospitals produce medical services, airlines produce transportation services that move people from one location to another, the military forces produce defence capabilities, and so on. Take a university as a specific example. University administrators bring together professors, books, academic journals, audiovisual materials, classrooms, and similar resources to transform "unenlightened" students into educated and skilled individuals.

Figure 18-1 portrays, in a very simplified fashion, the fact that every organization has an operations system that creates value by transforming inputs into outputs. The system takes inputs—people, capital, equipment, materials—and transforms them, with an operations system, into desired finished goods and services. Thus, the transformation process is just as relevant to service organizations as it is to those in manufacturing.

Just as every organization produces "something", every unit in an organization also produces something. Marketing, finance, research and development, human resources, and accounting convert inputs into outputs such as sales, increased market share, high rates of return on capital, new and innovative products, productive and satisfied employees, and accounting reports. As a manager, you need to be familiar with operations management concepts, regardless of the area in which you manage, in order to achieve your objectives more efficiently.

MANAGING PRODUCTIVITY

productivity
The overall output of goods and services produced, divided by the inputs needed to generate that output.

Improving productivity has become a major goal in virtually every organization. By **productivity**, we mean the overall output of goods or services produced, divided by the inputs needed to generate that output. For countries, higher productivity generates "costless growth".[2] Employees can receive higher wages and company profits can increase without causing inflation. For individual organizations, increased productivity means a more competitive cost structure and the ability to offer more competitive prices.

Increasing productivity is the key to global competitiveness. For instance, a great deal of Japan's prosperity in the 1980s can be explained in terms of its growth in manufacturing productivity. Between 1979 and 1986, Japan's productivity increased at an annual rate of 5.5 percent, much higher than productivity gains in Canada and the US.[3] But Canadian firms have responded over the last decade by making dramatic improvements to increase their efficiency. An example is Inglis Ltd. in Cambridge, Ontario, which has replaced its assembly lines with a cell-based manufacturing system. Productivity enhancement of both workforce and technology make Canadian companies more competitive in the global marketplace.

FIGURE 18-1 The Operations System

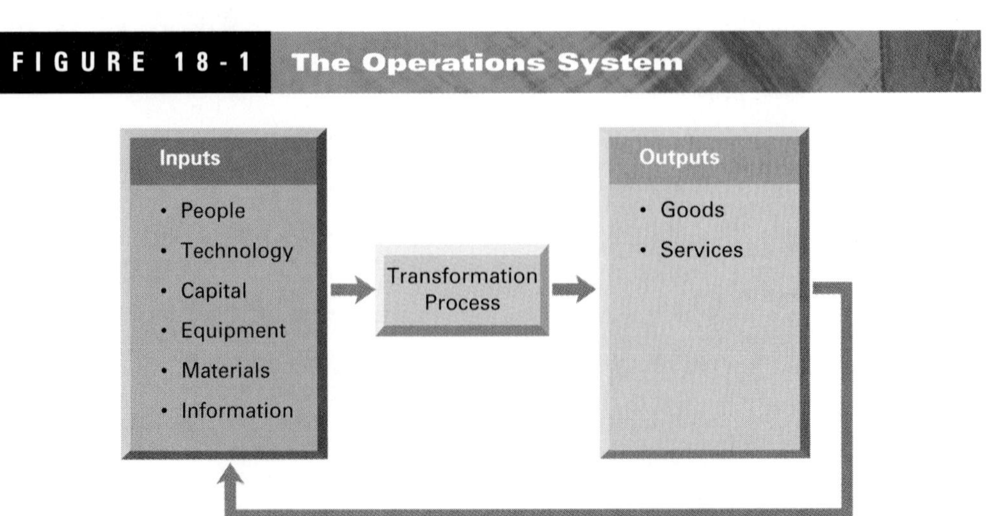

Sometimes very simple changes can be effective. Chrysler Corporation, in the US, found that a number of small changes—such as having assembly-line workers take coffee breaks in shifts rather than all at once—boosted worker productivity by 10 to 12 percent in just two years.[4] Another company that approached productivity improvement from a simplicity point of view was Toyota Motor Corporation. Mikio Kitano, the company's top production whiz, has instituted subtle, incremental changes to improve manufacturing efficiency. He says, "The key to productivity is simplicity. Men control machines, not the other way around".[5] Dr. Michael Black, a pediatric surgeon at Toronto's Hospital for Sick Children, has developed a small, innovative change in operation technique for heart surgery. Rather than making an incision from the navel to just below the neck, he makes a five-centimetre long cut. Healing time is much faster. The procedure shortens the stay of patients by an entire day (saving $1440 in costs), not to mention the benefits of a scar that will disappear rather than remain for life, as they used to.[6]

Hospital for Sick Children
www.sickkids.on.ca

Managers in all countries are striving to improve the productivity of their employees and organizations. In this competitive climate, organizations have no choice but to look for ways to significantly improve productivity.

How can organizations improve their productivity? Productivity is a composite of people *and* operations variables. To improve productivity, management needs to focus on both.

On the people side, techniques discussed in previous chapters should be considered. Participative decision making, management by objectives, team-based work groups, and equitable pay systems are examples of people-oriented approaches towards productivity improvement. A survey conducted by Steelcase Canada in 1997 determined that 26 percent of office workers find working conditions frustrating due to poor use of space and lack of privacy, and one-third of them believe that productivity is negatively affected as a result.[7] Northern Telecom spared no expense in creating its new corporate headquarters in Brampton, Ontario, in order to establish "a unique work environment where employee innovation and creativity can flourish".[8]

The late W Edwards Deming, a management consultant and quality expert, believed that managers, not workers, were the primary source of increased productivity. He outlined 14 points for improving management's productivity, which are listed in Table 18-1.

A close look at this table reveals Deming's understanding of the interplay between people and operations. High productivity can't come solely from good "people management". The truly effective organization will maximize productivity by successfully integrating people into the overall operations system. For instance, field engineers on service calls for General Electric Medical Systems used to haul around a trunkful of service and repair manuals that weighed about 200 pounds to repair the company's huge imaging machines that were installed at hospitals and clinics around the world. If the technician didn't have the right manual on hand while working on the equipment, a trip to the car trunk was necessary to get the right one. The engineers estimated that they wasted as much as 15 percent of their time during a service call going back and forth to their cars. The company solved the problem by equipping its field engineers (2500 in the United States alone) with laptop computers that held all the information the technician might ever need. Although this outlay of funds was a major capital expenditure, the company found that its field engineers' productivity rose by 9 percent. The company recognized the important interplay between people and the operations system.[9] Increased capital investment will make facilities more modern and efficient. But it also explains why so many organizations have downsized employees in recent years. These organizations hope to get more output per labour hour—that is, to increase their productivity.

In this chapter, we'll show that factors such as size and layout of operating facilities, capacity utilization, inventory usage, and maintenance controls are important determinants of an organization's overall productivity performance.

1 Define operations management.

2 Explain what the operations system is.

3 Why is productivity important for operations management?

TABLE 18-1 Deming's 14 Points for Improving Management's Productivity

1. Plan for the long-term future, not for next month or next year.
2. Never be complacent concerning the quality of your product.
3. Establish statistical control over your production processes and require your suppliers to do so as well.
4. Deal with the fewest number of suppliers—the best ones, of course.
5. Find out whether your problems are confined to particular parts of the production process, or stem from the overall process itself.
6. Train workers for the job that you are asking them to perform.
7. Raise the quality of your line supervisors.
8. Drive out fear.
9. Encourage departments to work closely together rather than to concentrate on departmental or divisional distinctions.
10. Do not be sucked into adopting strictly numerical goals, including the widely popular formula of "zero defect".
11. Require your workers to do quality work, not just to be at their stations from 9 to 5.
12. Train your employees to understand statistical methods.
13. Train your employees in new skills as the need arises.
14. Make top managers responsible for implementing these principles.

Source: W Edwards Deming, "Improvement of Quality and Productivity Through Action by Management," *National Productivity Review*, Winter 1981–1982, pp. 12–22. With permission.

manufacturing organizations Organizations that produce physical goods such as steel, automobiles, textiles and farm machinery.

service organizations Organizations that produce non-physical outputs such as educational, medical, and transportation services that are intangible, can't be stored in inventory, and incorporate the customer or client in the actual production process.

de-industrialization The conversion of an economy from dominance by manufacturing to dominance by service-oriented businesses.

customer-driven operations system An operations system that is designed around meeting and exceeding customers' needs.

OPERATIONS MANAGEMENT INCLUDES BOTH MANUFACTURING AND SERVICES

For the first half of this century, **manufacturing organizations**—that is, organizations that produce physical goods such as steel, automobiles, textiles and farm machinery—dominated most advanced industrialized nations. Today, in Canada, Australia, the United States and western Europe, **service organizations** dominate. Service organizations produce non-physical outputs such as educational, medical, retail, food, and transportation services. Figure 18-2 lists the characteristics of services.

In more advanced global economies, a process called **de-industrialization** is taking place. Blue-collar jobs in manufacturing are being replaced by jobs in the service sector. The manufacturing firms that survive are becoming smaller and leaner. The bulk of new jobs are being created in services—from janitors to fast-food cooks and servers, to computer technicians and programmers, to accountants and health care technicians.

A major challenge for management in a de-industrialized society will be increasing productivity in the service sectors. Many managers and administrators in colleges, hospitals, airlines, government agencies, and similar service-sector organizations are responding to the challenge by transferring concepts and techniques that worked in manufacturing to services.

CUSTOMER-DRIVEN OPERATIONS

Organizations—for-profit and non-profit—exist to meet the needs of customers. The revenues earned from customers whose needs are thoroughly satisfied are the lifeblood of any organization.[10] However, it is only through *absolute* satisfaction of their needs that customers keep coming back. This type of customer loyalty can reap big rewards for an organization. A **customer-driven operations system** is an operations system designed around meeting and exceeding customers' needs. Successful organizations in the twenty-first century will need to (1) think constantly about who their customers are; (2) maintain close and frequent contact

FIGURE 18-2 Characteristics of Services

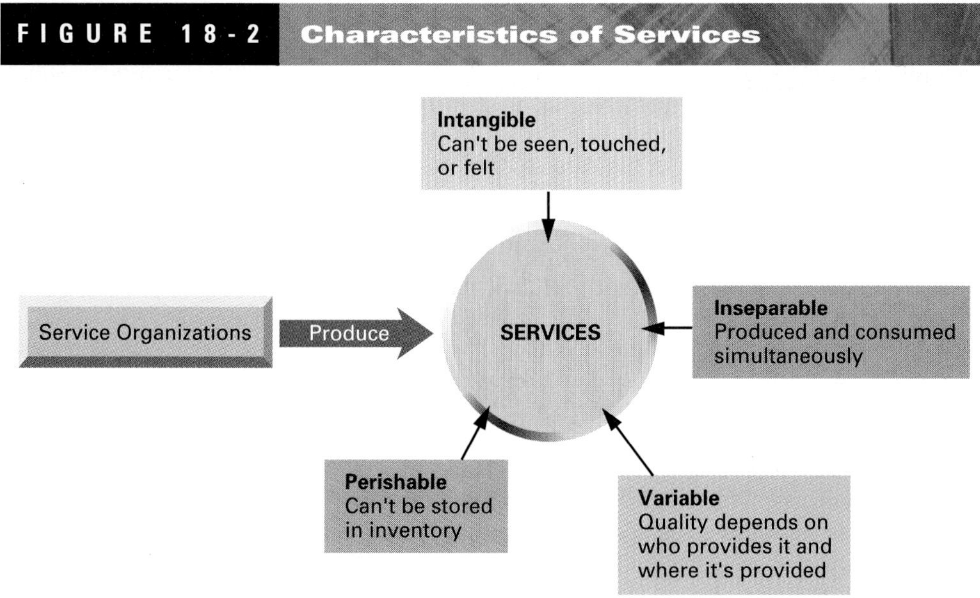

with their customers; (3) determine how to provide products in a way that competitors cannot imitate; and (4) determine how to satisfy customers' current, anticipated, and even unanticipated needs.[11] In addition, their operations systems must support the people and work processes in order to meet those needs. Managers at Canadian Pacific Hotels looked for ways to make good on the company's promise of personalized service to customers. They found that they had excellent systems in place for serving groups of customers, but the systems were not adequate or appropriate for providing personalized individual service. So the hotel's operations systems had to change. The managers appointed a "champion" at each hotel, and gave that person broad cross-functional authority to see that the products and services provided to individual customers were personalized to each customer's desire. Changing to customer-driven operations wasn't easy, but it worked. The company's share of Canadian business travel jumped by 16 percent in one year, even though the market as a whole increased by only 3 percent.[12]

RE-ENGINEERING WORK PROCESSES

We discussed the concept of re-engineering earlier in the text and pointed out the dramatic improvements in work efficiency and effectiveness that are possible when a company radically

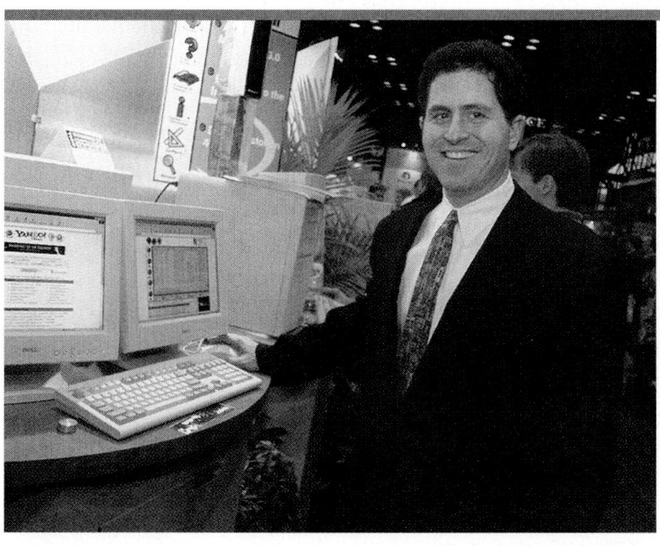

Michael Dell, CEO of Dell Computer, has built an empire selling computers by mail, by telephone, and now through the Internet. Dell has eliminated the middleperson, and handles all aspects of sales and services itself—always dealing directly with the customer. Dell prides itself on fast response to customer problems, and is a good example of a customer-driven operation.

changes and redesigns its work processes. For instance, when Union Carbide re-engineered, it eliminated $400 million of fixed costs.[13] But just what does re-engineering involve? How *are* work processes changed and redesigned?

Re-engineering is about totally redesigning a company's operations—whether it's a manufacturing or a service organization. And, believe it or not, re-engineering's primary tool is a clean sheet of paper. It truly does involve starting from scratch in rethinking and re-arranging the way in which work is done—that is, the work processes. In effect, managers who guide re-engineering efforts should ask, "If this were a new company or department, how would we do things?" The longstanding, familiar ways of approaching work are completely axed, as the organization's old operations system is totally revamped. Referring back to our illustration of the operations system in Figure 18-1, the transformation process is completely erased, as those in charge of the re-engineering effort start anew in designing the way the organization's product or service will be produced and delivered. Work processes and crucial operations processes are boldly attacked with no regard to "that's the way it's always been done". In fact, the "way it's always been done" won't, and shouldn't, even provide a starting point for the re-engineering effort. As we described in Chapter 12 on managing change, re-engineering is radical, quantum change that will shake the very foundations of the organization. And yet, for all the enormously stressful uncertainty placed on employees, the payoffs from re-engineering can be powerful. For instance, at GTE, the giant communications company with over $20 billion in annual revenues, several operations inefficiencies were identified and eliminated in its re-engineering efforts. The radical changes in work processes resulted in almost a 30 percent increase in employee productivity.[14] At Clearly Canadian Beverage Corp., the manufacturing and distribution systems were completely revolutionized. A central control system was implemented, and the order cycle was cut down from 30 days to just 2.

As you might guess from the preceding description, re-engineering isn't easy. And any organization that's made a commitment to re-engineering its work operations should recognize the extensive and intensive nature of the path it's pursuing. However, as the global environment becomes more dynamic and competitive, a complete overhaul of organizational operations may be the only feasible route to surviving and prospering.

STRATEGIC OPERATIONS MANAGEMENT

The era of modern manufacturing originated over 80 years ago in North America. The success that American and Canadian manufacturers experienced during World War II led executives of manufacturing firms to believe that the troublesome problems of production had been conquered. These executives focused their attention on other functional areas such as finance and marketing. From the late 1940s through the mid 1970s, manufacturing activities were taken for granted and were, to some extent, slighted. With only the occasional exception (such as the aerospace industry), top management gave manufacturing little attention, managers "on the way up the corporate ladder" avoided it, and market leadership dwindled.

Meanwhile, with North American executives neglecting the production side of their businesses, managers in Japan, Germany, and other countries took the opportunity to develop mod-

Toyota led the auto industry in efficiency and productivity in the 1970s and 1980s, and despite being overtaken by Detroit in the 1990s it may easily return to the forefront with its trademark strategic operations management.

ern, computer-assisted facilities that fully integrated manufacturing operations into strategic planning decisions. The competition's success at this realigned world manufacturing leadership. For example, Canadian and US manufacturers soon discovered that foreign goods were being made not only less expensively, but also better. By the late 1970s, North American manufacturers were facing a true crisis, and a good percentage of them responded.[15] They invested heavily in improving manufacturing technology, increased the authority of manufacturing executives, and began incorporating existing and future production requirements into the organization's overall strategic plan. Today, successful manufacturers are taking a top-down approach to operations and implementing comprehensive manufacturing planning systems.[16]

Harvard University professor Wickham Skinner has been urging a "manufacturing focus" to strategy for more than a quarter of a century.[17] He argues that too many important production decisions have been relegated to lower-level managers. Production needs to be managed from the top down, rather than from the bottom up. According to Skinner, the organization's overall strategy should directly reflect its manufacturing capabilities and limitations, and should include operations objectives and strategies. He points out, for example, that each organization's operations strategy needs to be unique and reflect the inherent tradeoffs in any production process. Cost reduction and quality enhancement often work against each other. So, too, do short delivery times and limited inventory levels. Because there's no single "most efficient way" to produce things, top management needs to identify and emphasize its competitive advantage in operations. Some organizations are competing on the more traditional basis of low prices achieved through cost reduction. Others are competing on the basis of quality, reliable delivery, warranties, short lead times, customer service, rapid product introduction, or flexible capacity.

As we noted, Skinner's appeals have been heeded. The manufacturing organizations that expect to compete successfully in global markets are incorporating operations decisions in their strategic plans, and returning manufacturing executives to a place of prominence in the organization's power structure.[18]

PROJECT MANAGEMENT REVISITED

We discussed the concept of project management in Chapter 9. We are revisiting it briefly in this chapter, because an organization's operations system needs to support the project organizational structure.

In a project organization, the operations system should provide an effective and efficient means of pooling the people and physical resources needed, in order to complete the specific project or goal within the specified time period. In the illustration of the operations system shown in Figure 18-1, the inputs now encompass the project teams and the resources needed by those teams. The transformation process includes the various activities involved with project planning, project scheduling, and project controlling used by the project teams to produce the specific outputs of the project.

Operations management is just as important to project organizations as it is to those that do not use projects. As an organization makes the move to projects, its operations system must adapt to reflect the changed inputs and transformation processes. Why? To make sure that projects are completed effectively and efficiently within the time frame allotted. In fact, many of the operations planning and controlling tools and techniques that we are going to discuss next are appropriate for project teams as well as for other types of organizations.

PLANNING OPERATIONS

As we've noted in several places throughout this book, planning must precede control. Therefore, before we can introduce operations management control techniques, we need to review a few of the more important decisions related to *planning* operations.

4 How is re-engineering related to the operations system?

5 What role should operations management play in an organization's strategy?

6 How does an organization's use of projects affect its operations system?

Four key decisions—capacity, location, process, and layout—provide the long-term strategic direction for operations planning. They determine the proper size of an operating system, where the physical facilities should be located, the best methods for transforming inputs into outputs, and the most efficient layout of equipment and workstations. Once these decisions have been made, three short-term decisions—the aggregate plan, the master schedule, and a material requirements plan—need to be established. These provide the tactical plans for the operating system. In this section, we'll review these seven types of planning decisions. (See Figure 18-3.)

Capacity Planning

Assume that you've decided to go into the boat-building business. On the basis of your analysis of the market and other environmental factors (see Chapter 8), you believe there's a market for a premium-quality 28-foot sailboat. You know *what* you want to produce. What's your next step? You need to determine *how many* boats you expect to build. This, in turn, will determine the proper size of your plant and other facility-planning issues. When managers assess their operating system's capabilities for producing a desired number of output units for each type of product anticipated during a given time period, they're engaged in **capacity planning**.

capacity planning
Assessing an operating system's ability to produce a desired number of output units for each type of product during a given time period.

Capacity planning begins by taking the sales demand forecasts (see Chapter 9) and converting them into capacity requirements. If you produce only one type of boat, plan to sell the boats for an average of \$50 000 each, and anticipate generating sales of \$2.5 million during the first year, your physical capacity requirements mean that you need to be able to handle fifty boats (\$50 000 × 50 = \$2 500 000). This calculation is obviously much more complex if you're producing dozens of different products.

If your organization is already established, you compare this forecast against your production capacity. Then you can determine whether you'll need to add to, or subtract from, your existing capacity. Keep in mind that you don't have to be in a manufacturing business to

FIGURE 18-3 Decisions Made in Planning Operations

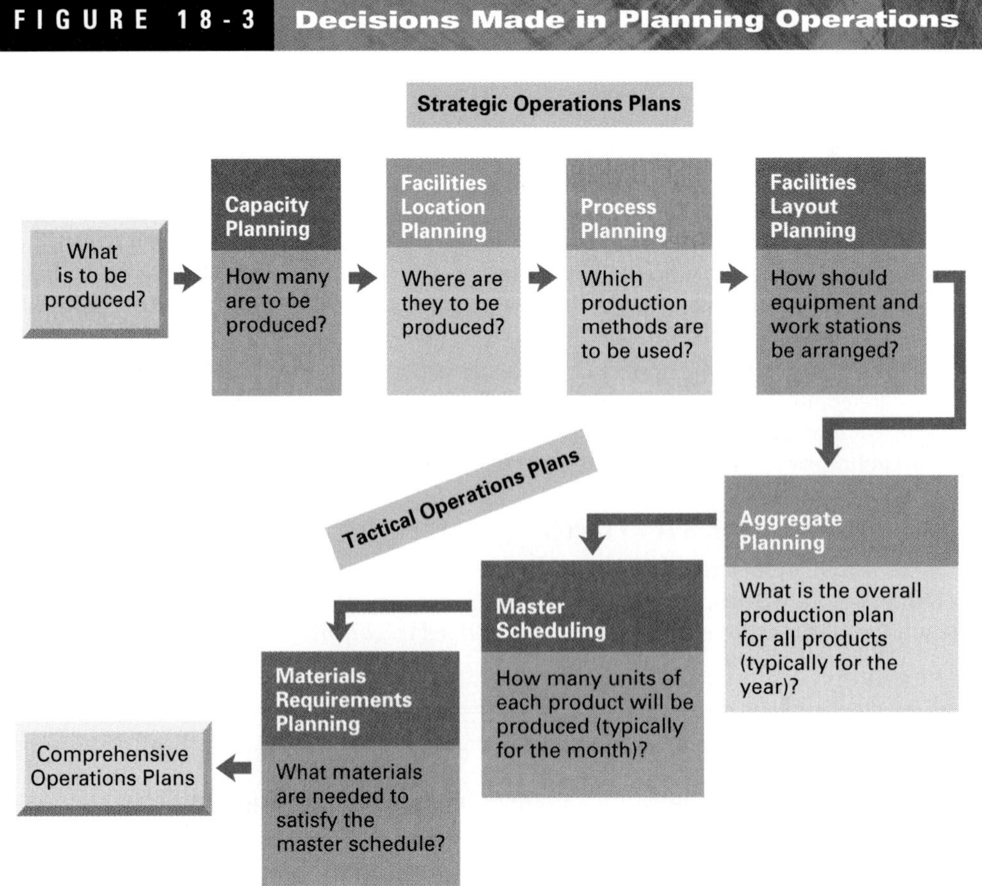
Strategic Operations Plans
What is to be produced?
Capacity Planning
How many are to be produced?
Facilities Location Planning
Where are they to be produced?
Process Planning
Which production methods are to be used?
Facilities Layout Planning
How should equipment and work stations be arranged?
Tactical Operations Plans
Aggregate Planning
What is the overall production plan for all products (typically for the year)?
Master Scheduling
How many units of each product will be produced (typically for the month)?
Materials Requirements Planning
What materials are needed to satisfy the master schedule?
Comprehensive Operations Plans

use capacity planning. The following steps are just as relevant for determining the number of beds needed in a hospital as they are for determining the maximum number of sandwiches that a Wendy's can serve during rush hour.

Once you've converted the forecast into physical capacity requirements, you'll be able to develop a set of alternative capacity plans that will meet the requirements. You'll often have to make some modifications—that is, you'll have to expand or reduce capacity. In the long term, you can alter the size of your operation significantly and permanently by buying new equipment or selling off existing facilities. In the short term, however, you're forced to make more temporary modifications. You can add an extra work shift, increase overtime, or reduce employee work hours; temporarily shut down operations; or subcontract work out to other organizations. If you manufacture a product that can be stored (such as sailboats), you can build inventories during slack periods, to be used when demand exceeds capacity.

Facilities Location Planning

When you determine the need for additional capacity, you must design and choose a facility. This process is called **facilities location planning**. Where you choose to locate will depend on which factors have the greatest impact on total production and distribution costs. These include availability of needed labour skills, labour costs, energy costs, proximity to suppliers or customers, and the like. Rarely are all these factors of equal importance. The kind of business you're in dictates your critical contingencies, which then dictate—to a large degree—the optimum location.

facilities location planning The design and location of an operations facility.

For example, the need for skilled technical specialists has led an increasing number of high-tech firms to locate in the Toronto area. The area's high concentration of colleges and universities makes it easier for firms who require employees with computer, engineering, and research skills to find and hold onto such people. Similarly, it's not by chance that many manufacturers whose transformation processes are labour intensive have moved their manufacturing facilities overseas to places such as South Korea and Malaysia. When labour costs are a critical contingency, organizations will locate their facilities where labour wage rates are low. For instance, the US women's shoemaker, Nine West Group Inc., does all its production in the region of Val do Sinos, Brazil, because of the low labour costs.[19] Many companies have moved their call centre facilities to Moncton, New Brunswick, due to the combined benefits of a state-of-the-art provincial fibre optics system, a bilingual population, and very low wages. When customer convenience is critical, as it is for many retail stores, the location decision is often dictated by concerns such as proximity to a highway or pedestrian traffic.

What contingencies are going to be critical in your sailboat business? Obviously, you'll need employees with boat-building skills, and they're most likely to be plentiful in coastal areas such as Nova Scotia, Newfoundland and the Vancouver area. Shipping costs of the final product are likely to be a major expenditure. So, to keep your prices competitive, you might want to locate close to your customers. That might suggest Nova Scotia (for access to American markets), Vancouver, or the Great Lakes region. Weather might be an additional factor. It might be less expensive to build boats outside in the relatively warm climate of the West Coast, rather than inside, during the long maritime winter. If labour availability, shipping costs, and weather are your critical contingencies, you still have a great deal of latitude in your location decision. After you choose a region, you still must select a community and a specific site.

Process Planning

In **process planning,** management determines how a product or service will be produced. Process planning encompasses evaluating the available production methods, and selecting those that will best achieve the operating objectives.

process planning Determining how a product or service will be produced.

For any given production process, whether in manufacturing or the service sector, there are always alternative conversion methods. Designing a restaurant, for instance, allows for a number of process choices: Should we use inventoried fast food (as served at McDonald's); should we have limited-option fast food (as served at Wendy's); should we have cafeteria-style delivery, drive-in, take-out, a no-option fixed menu, or complex meals prepared to order? Key questions that ultimately determine how an organization's products or services will be produced include the following: Will the technology be routine or non-routine? What degree of automation will be used? Should the system be developed to maximize efficiency or flexibility? How should the product or service flow through the operations systems?[20]

In our sailboat-manufacturing example, the boats could be made by an assembly-line process. If you decide to keep them highly standardized, you might find a routine transformation process to be the most cost efficient. But if you want each boat to be made to a customer's order, you'll require a different technology and a different set of production methods.

Process planning is complex. Deciding on the best combinations of processes in terms of costs, quality, labour efficiency, and similar considerations is difficult, because the decisions are interrelated. A change in one element of the production process often has spillover effects on a number of other elements. As a result, the detailed planning is usually left to production and industrial engineers, under the overall guidance of top management.

Facilities Layout Planning

The final strategic decision in operations planning is to assess and select among alternative layout options for equipment and workstations. This is called **facilities layout planning.** The objective of layout planning is to find a physical arrangement that will best facilitate production efficiency and will also appeal to employees or customers.

facilities layout planning
Assessing and selecting among alternative layout options for equipment and workstations.

Layout planning begins by assessing space needs. Space has to be provided for work areas, tools and equipment, storage, maintenance facilities, rest rooms, offices, lunch areas and cafeterias, waiting rooms, and even parking lots. Then, based on the previously decided process plans, various layout configurations can be evaluated to determine how efficient each is for handling the work flow. To help make these decisions, a number of layout-planning devices are available, ranging from simple, scaled-to-size paper cutouts, to sophisticated computer software programs that can manipulate hundreds of variables and print out alternative layout designs.[21]

process layout
Arranging manufacturing components together according to similarity of function.

product layout
Arranging manufacturing components according to the progressive steps by which a product is made.

fixed-position layout
A manufacturing layout in which the product stays in place while tools, equipment and people skills are brought to it.

There are basically three work flow layouts.[22] The **process layout** arranges components (such as work centres, equipment, or departments) together, according to similarity of function. Figure 18-4 illustrates the process layout at a medical clinic. In **product layout**, the components are arranged according to the progressive steps by which the product is made. Figure 18-5 illustrates a product layout in a plant that manufactures aluminum tubing. The third approach, the **fixed-position layout**, is used when, because of its size or bulk, the product remains at one location. The product stays in place, and tools, equipment, and people skills are brought to it. Movie lot sound stages, or the manufacturing of airplanes or cruise ships, illus-

Layout planning must account for the physical positioning of equipment, the movement of workers between pieces of equipment, and the availability of prime parts.

TESTING... TESTING...

7 Why is capacity planning important in operations management?

8 What contingencies affect facilities location planning?

9 What role does process planning play in operations management?

FIGURE 18-4 A Process Layout at a Medical Clinic

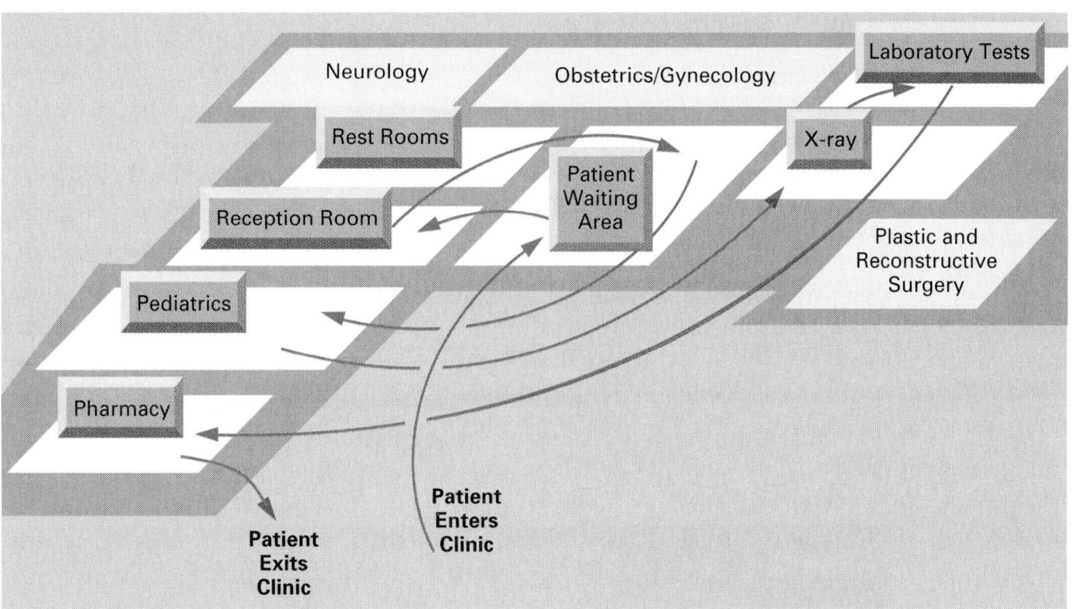

Source: From Everett E Adam, Jr. and Ronald J Ebert, *Production and Operations Management: Concepts, Models, and Behavior,* 5th ed. (Englewood Cliffs, NJ: Prentice Hall, 1992), p. 254. With permission.

trate the fixed-position layout. The building of your 28-foot sailboats is likely to use either a product or fixed-position layout.

Aggregate Planning

Once the strategic decisions have been made, we move to the tactical operations decisions. The first of these deals with planning the overall production activities and the operating resources needed to do them. This is called **aggregate planning** and often deals with a time frame of up to a year.

aggregate planning Planning overall production activities and their associated operating resources.

The aggregate plan provides a "big picture". On the basis of the sales demand forecast and capacity plan, the aggregate plan establishes inventory levels and production rates, and estimates the size of the total operation's labour force on a monthly basis, for approximately the next 12 months. The focus is on *generalities*, not specifics. Categories of products are considered, not individual items. A paint company's aggregate plan would look at the total number of litres of house paint to be manufactured, but would avoid decisions about colour or size of container. As such, the aggregate plan is particularly valuable to large operations that have

FIGURE 18-5 A Product Layout in an Aluminum Tubing Plant

Raw Aluminum Ingot	Receiving Dept.	Casting Dept.	Press Dept.	Tube Dept.	Finishing Dept.	Inspection Dept.	Packing Dept.	Shipping Dept.
Shipped to plant	Ingot accepted	Ingot melted	Metal pressed into large tubes	Large tubes stretched into various dimensions	Finished tubing cleaned	Finished tubes inspected	Finished tubes packed	Finished tubes shipped to customers

a varied product line. As you'll see in the next section, for the small, one-product firm—such as our sailboat-manufacturing operation—the aggregate plan will look like the master schedule, only it covers a longer time frame.

When completed, the aggregate plan often points out two basic decisions: the best overall production rate to adopt, and the overall number of workers to be employed during each period in the planning time frame.[23]

Master Scheduling

master schedule
A schedule that specifies quantity and type of items to be produced; how, when, and where they should be produced; labour force levels; and inventory.

The **master schedule** is derived from the aggregate plan. It specifies the following: quantity and type of each item to be produced; how, when, and where they should be produced for the next day, week, or month; labour force levels; and inventory.

The first requirement of master scheduling is *disaggregation*—that is, breaking the aggregate plan down into detailed operational plans for each of the products or services the organization produces.[24] After that, these plans need to be scheduled against one another in a master schedule.

Figure 18-6 shows a master schedule for a manufacturer of automobile transmissions. The top portion of the figure informs lower-level managers (through the aggregate plan) that top management has authorized the capacity, inventory, and people to produce 100 heavy-duty

FIGURE 18-6 Developing a Master Schedule from an Aggregate Plan

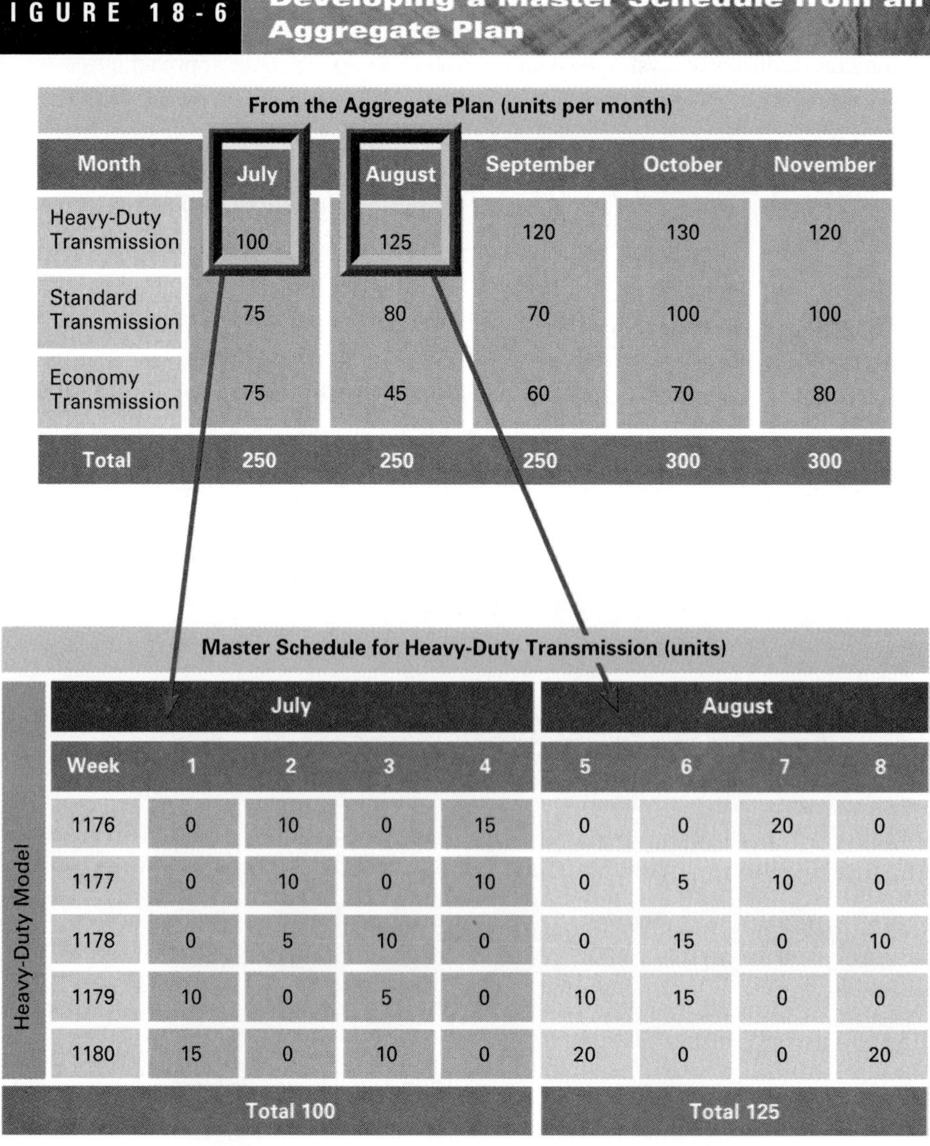

From the Aggregate Plan (units per month)

Month	July	August	September	October	November
Heavy-Duty Transmission	100	125	120	130	120
Standard Transmission	75	80	70	100	100
Economy Transmission	75	45	60	70	80
Total	250	250	250	300	300

Master Schedule for Heavy-Duty Transmission (units)

Heavy-Duty Model	July				August			
Week	1	2	3	4	5	6	7	8
1176	0	10	0	15	0	0	20	0
1177	0	10	0	10	0	5	10	0
1178	0	5	10	0	0	15	0	10
1179	10	0	5	0	10	15	0	0
1180	15	0	10	0	20	0	0	20
	Total 100				Total 125			

transmissions in July, 125 in August, and so forth. The lower part of the figure illustrates a master schedule. For example, it shows how lower-level managers consider the July production for 100 heavy-duty transmissions and determine which models to make. Not only do they determine what specific models to make each week, they also state how many. During the first week of July, for instance, 10 units of Model 1179 and 15 units of Model 1180 will be assembled.

Material Requirements Planning

After the specific products have been determined, each should be analyzed to determine the precise materials and parts that it requires. **Material requirements planning (MRP)** is a system that uses these data for purchasing, inventorying, and priority-planning purposes.

material requirements planning (MRP)
A system that dissects products into the materials and parts necessary for purchasing, inventorying, and priority-planning purposes.

Using a computer, product design specifications can pinpoint all the materials and parts necessary to produce the product. By merging this information with computerized inventory records, management will know the quantities of each part in inventory, and when each is likely to be used up. When lead times and safety stock requirements are established and entered into the computer, MRP ensures that the right materials are available when needed.

CONTROLLING OPERATIONS

Once the operating system has been designed and implemented, its key elements must be monitored. In the following sections, we discuss ways in which to control costs, purchasing, maintenance and quality.

Cost Control

An automobile industry analyst once compared the US and Japanese approaches to cost control: "The Japanese regard cost control as something you wake up every morning and do. Americans have always thought of it as a project. You cut costs 20 percent and say, 'Whew! That's over.' We can't afford to think that way anymore."[25]

Canadian managers, too, have often treated cost control as an occasional corporate crusade that's initiated and controlled by the accounting staff. Accountants establish cost standards per unit, and if deviations occur, management looks for the cause. Have material costs increased? Is labour being used efficiently? Do employees need additional training to cut waste and scrap? As the previous quotation implies, cost control needs to play a central part in the design of an operations system, and it needs to be a continuing concern of every manager.

Many organizations have adopted the cost centre approach to controlling costs. Work areas, departments, or entire manufacturing plants are identified as distinct **cost centres,** and their managers are held responsible for the cost performance of these units. Any unit's total costs are made up of two types of costs: direct and indirect. **Direct costs** are costs incurred in proportion to the output of a particular product or service. Labour and materials typically fall into this category. In contrast, **indirect costs** are largely unaffected by changes in output. Even if output is zero, these costs are still incurred. Insurance expenses and the salaries of staff employees are examples of typical indirect costs. This direct–indirect distinction is important. While cost centre managers are held responsible for all direct costs in their units, indirect costs aren't necessarily within their control. However, because all costs are controllable at some level in the organization, top managers should identify where the control lies, and hold lower-level managers accountable for costs under their control.[26]

cost centre
A unit in which managers are held responsible for all associated costs.

direct costs
Costs incurred in proportion to the output of a particular good or service.

indirect costs
Costs that are largely unaffected by changes in output.

Purchasing Control

It's been said that humans *are* what they eat. Metaphorically, the same applies to organizations. Their processes and outputs depend on the inputs they "eat". It's difficult to make quality products out of inferior inputs. Highly skilled leather workers need quality cowhides if they're going to produce high-quality wallets. Gas station operators depend on a regular and

10 Contrast process, product, and fixed-position layouts.
11 How are the aggregate plan and the master schedule related?
12 What role does MRP play in operations management?

dependable inflow of certain octane-rated gasolines from their suppliers in order to meet their customers' demands. If the gas isn't there, they can't sell it. If the gasoline is below the specified octane rating, customers may become dissatisfied and take their business elsewhere. Management must therefore monitor the delivery, performance, quality, quantity and price of inputs from suppliers. Purchasing control seeks to ensure availability, acceptable quality, continued reliable sources and, at the same time, reduced costs.

What can managers do to facilitate control of inputs? They need to gather information on the dates and conditions of arriving supplies. They need to gather data about the quality of supplies and the compatibility of those supplies with operations processes. Finally, they need to obtain data on supplier price performance. Are the prices of delivered goods the same as those quoted when the order was placed?

This information can be used to rate suppliers, identify problem suppliers, and guide management in choosing future suppliers. Trends can be detected. Suppliers can be evaluated, for instance, on responsiveness, service, reliability and competitiveness.

Building Close Links with Suppliers. A growing trend in manufacturing is turning suppliers into partners.[27] Instead of using 10 or 12 vendors and forcing them to compete against each other to gain the company's business, manufacturers are using only 2 or 3 vendors, and working closely with them to improve efficiency and quality.

For instance, Motorola sends its design-and-manufacturing engineers to suppliers to help with any problems.[28] Other companies now routinely send inspection teams to rate suppliers' operations. They're assessing suppliers' manufacturing and delivery techniques, statistical process controls used to identify causes of defects, and ability to handle data electronically. Companies in Canada and around the world are doing what has long been a corporate tradition in Japan—developing long-term relationships with suppliers. As collaborators and partners, rather than adversaries, companies are finding that they can achieve better quality of inputs, fewer defects, and lower costs. Furthermore, when problems arise with suppliers, open communication channels facilitate quick resolutions.

Inventory Ordering Systems. In many personal chequebooks, you'll find a re-order form inserted in among the remaining cheques, after you've used about 95 percent of them. It reminds you that it's time to re-order. This is an example of a **fixed-point re-ordering system.** At some pre-established point in the operations process, the system is designed to "flag" or alert users to the fact that the inventory needs to be replenished. The flag is triggered when the inventory reaches a certain point or level.

fixed-point re-ordering system
A system that "flags" the fact that inventory needs to be replenished when it reaches a certain level.

The goal of a fixed-point re-ordering system is to minimize inventory carrying costs and to ensure a reasonable level of customer service (limiting the probability of an item running out—a *stockout.*) Therefore, the re-order point should be established to equate the time remaining before a stockout, and the lead time to receive delivery of the re-ordered quantity. Ideally, in such cases, the newly ordered items would arrive at the same time as the last item in inventory was used up. More realistically, management doesn't usually allow the inventory to fall below some safety stock level. (See Figure 18-7.) By using certain statistical procedures, decision makers can set a re-order point at a level that gives an organization enough inventory to get through the lead-time period and some reasonable insurance against a stockout. This buffer, or safety stock, gives protection against greater usage than expected during the lead time or an unexpected delay in receiving new stock.

As a simple example, to determine a personal cheque re-order point, let's assume that the order lead time averages 3 weeks and that we write about 20 cheques a week. We would need 60 cheques to get us through a "normal" re-ordering lead time. If we feel, on the basis of past history of use, that a 1-week safety stock would be sufficient to get us through most lead-time periods, the order should be placed when there are 80 (60 + 20) cheques left in the chequebook. This is the re-order point. Another word of caution: The more safety stock, the less the risk of stockout. But the additional inventory will add to the carrying costs. Thus, we again face a cost–benefit decision. At times, it may be more prudent (cost-wise) to run out of stock.

One of the most primitive, but certainly effective, manual uses of the fixed-point re-ordering system is to keep the item—for example, pens and copy paper in an office or boxes of shoes in a retail shoe store—in two separate containers. Inventory is drawn from one until it's empty. At that point, a re-order is placed, and items are drawn from the second container. If

FIGURE 18-7 Inventory Cycle with Safety Stock

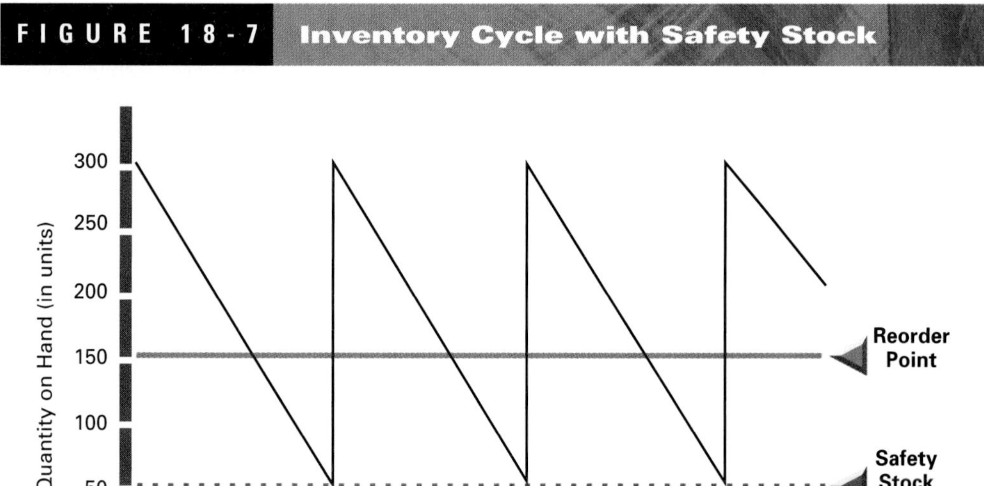

demand for an item has been estimated properly, the replacement order to replenish the stock should arrive before the second container is used up.

Another, more recent version of the fixed-point re-order system relies on computer control. Sales are automatically recorded by a central computer that's been programmed to initiate a purchase order for an item when its inventory reaches some crucial fixed point. Many retail stores now use such systems. The cash registers are actually computers, and when each product's bar code is scanned at the time a customer checks out, the store's inventory record is automatically adjusted. When the inventory of an item hits the critical point, the computer tells management to re-order or, in some systems, actually prints out the purchase order requisition.

Another common inventory system is the **fixed-interval re-ordering system.** The fixed-interval system uses *time* as the determining factor for inventory control. At a predeter-

fixed-interval re-ordering system
A system that uses time as the determining factor for reviewing and re-ordering inventory items.

Clearly Canadian has instituted control systems to improve productivity.

mined time—say once a week or every 90 days—the inventory is counted, and an order is placed for the number of items necessary to bring the inventory back to the desired level. The desired level is established so that if demand and ordering lead time are average, consumption will draw the inventory down to zero (or some safety lead time can be added) just as the next order arrives. This system may have some transportation economies and quantity discount economies over the fixed-point system. For example, it might allow the organization to consolidate orders from one supplier if all the items purchased from this source are reviewed at the same time. This isn't possible with the fixed-point system.

In the 1800s, economist Vilfredo Pareto found that 80 percent of the wealth was controlled by only 20 percent of the population. Professors typically find that a few students cause most of their problems, and students have probably similarly found that a few professors cause most of *their* problems. This concept—the vital few and the trivial many—can be applied to inventory control.

It's not unusual for a company to have thousands of items in inventory. However, evidence indicates that roughly 10 percent of the items in most organizations' inventory account for 50 percent of the annual dollar inventory value. Another 20 percent of the items account for 30 percent of the value. The remaining 70 percent of the items appear to account for only 20 percent of the value. These have been labelled as A, B, and C categories, respectively. Thus we have the name **ABC system.** (See Figure 18-8.)

ABC system
A priority system for monitoring inventory items.

Cost-benefit analysis would suggest that A items receive the tightest control, B items moderate control, and C items, the least control. This can be done because there are so few A items and they represent a large dollar investment. Similarly, there are so many C items but so little dollar investment, that tight control wouldn't be justified. The A items, for example, might be monitored weekly, B items monthly, and C items quarterly because they account for so little dollar value. Or C items might be controlled by using a simple form of order point.

One other popular mathematical technique for determining appropriate levels of inventory is the economic order quantity model. We'll discuss this widely used model more fully in the next chapter, as we look at different controlling tools and techniques that managers can use.

Maintenance Control

Delivering goods or services in an efficient and effective manner requires operating systems with high equipment use and a minimum amount of downtime. Therefore, managers need to

FIGURE 18-8 Example of an ABC Inventory System

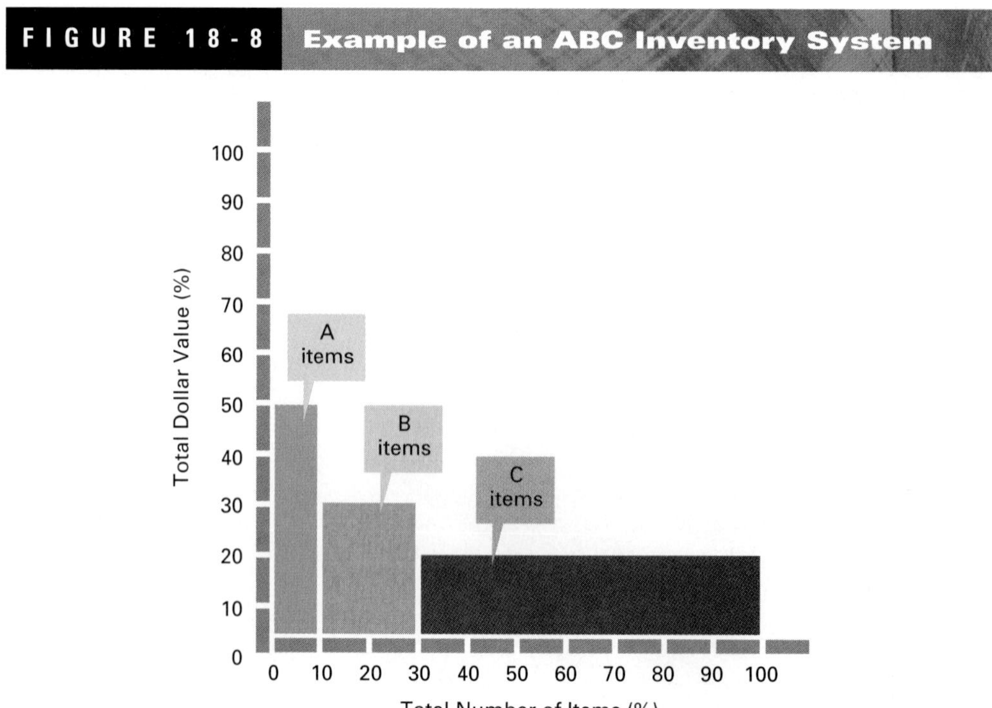

be concerned with maintenance control. The importance of maintenance control, however, depends on the process technology used. For example, if a standardized assembly-line process breaks down, it can affect hundreds of employees. On an automobile or refrigerator assembly line, it's not unusual for a serious breakdown on one machine to bring an entire manufacturing plant to a halt. In contrast, most systems using more general-purpose and redundant processes have less interdependency between activities, therefore a machine breakdown is likely to have less impact. Nevertheless, an equipment breakdown—like an inventory stockout—may mean higher costs, delayed deliveries or lost sales.

There are three approaches to maintenance control.[29] **Preventive maintenance** is performed before a breakdown occurs. **Remedial maintenance** is a complete overhaul, replacement, or repair of the equipment when it breaks down. **Conditional maintenance** refers to overhaul or repair in response to an inspection and measurement of the equipment's state. For instance, when Air Canada tears down its jet engines every 1000 hours, it's engaging in preventive maintenance. When it inspects the plane's tires every 24 hours and changes them when conditions warrant, it's performing conditional maintenance. Finally, if Air Canada's operations policy is to repair window shades or seat pockets on its planes only after the equipment breaks, then it's using remedial maintenance practices.

preventive maintenance Maintenance performed before a breakdown occurs.

remedial maintenance Maintenance that calls for the overhaul, replacement, or repair of equipment when it breaks down.

conditional maintenance Maintenance that calls for an overhaul or repair in response to an inspection.

The Air Canada example points out that the type of maintenance control depends on the costs of a breakdown. The greater the cost in terms of money, time, liability and customer goodwill, the greater the benefits from preventive maintenance. That is, the benefits can easily justify the costs.

Maintenance control should also be considered in the design of equipment. If downtime is highly inconvenient or costly, reliability can be increased by designing redundancy into the equipment. Nuclear power plants, for example, have elaborate backup systems built in. Similarly, equipment can be designed to facilitate fast or low-cost maintenance. Equipment that has fewer parts has fewer things to go wrong. High-failure items can also be placed in locations that are easily accessible, or in independent modular units that can quickly be removed and replaced. Cable television operators follow these guidelines. Breakdowns infuriate customers so, when they occur, management wants to be able to correct them quickly. Speed is facilitated by centralizing equipment in easy-access locations and making extensive use of modular units. If a piece of equipment fails, the whole module of which it's a part can be pulled or replaced in just a few minutes. Television service is resumed rapidly, and the pulled modular unit can be repaired without time pressures.

Dofasco is a steel producer based in Hamilton, Ontario. To ensure efficiency of production, which relates directly to the company's profit, equipment must be kept running. Dofasco has developed a maintenance management system that keeps tabs on each individual piece of machinery. Information about the production computers running the equipment gets fed into a database, which can then be accessed by maintenance workers from desktop PCs.

Quality Control

We've discussed the concept of total quality management throughout this book. We've described it as a comprehensive, customer-focused program to continuously improve the quality of the organization's processes, products and services. In this section, we present the more limited and traditional approach to quality by focusing on its control. While TQM emphasizes actions to prevent mistakes, quality control emphasizes identifying mistakes that may have already occurred.

THINKING CRITICALLY ABOUT ETHICS

You work in the office of a company that distributes repair parts for heavy machinery throughout British Columbia. When someone calls (sometimes desperately) for a part, you look up its stock number, price and inventory level on the computer. Your supervisor has instructed you to *always* say that the part is in stock, even if the computer indicates that it is not. His rationale is that the part can be obtained in a day or two from the supplier, and a short delay isn't going to hurt anyone. Then, if the customer calls back wanting to know where the part is, the delivery service or mail can be blamed. This situation happens at least once a day, and you're uncomfortable with it. What can you do? How could this situation hurt (a) your customer, and (b) your company? What types of ethical guidelines might you suggest for a company that wanted an effective, efficient, and ethical inventory system? ■

So what do we mean by *quality control?* It refers to monitoring quality—weight, strength, consistency, colour, taste, reliability, finish, or any one of a myriad characteristics—to ensure that the product or service meets some pre-established standard. Quality control will probably be needed at one or more points, beginning with the receipt of inputs. It will continue with work in process and steps up to the final product. Assessments at intermediate stages of the transformation process are typically part of quality control. Early detection of a defective part or process can save the cost of further work on the item.

Before implementing any quality control measures, managers need to ask whether they expect to examine 100 percent of the items produced or whether a sample can be used. The inspection of each and every item makes sense if the cost of continuous evaluation is very low or if the consequences of a statistical error are very high (as in the manufacturing of a drug used in open-heart surgery). Statistical samples are usually less costly, and sometimes they're the only viable option. For example, if the quality test destroys the product—as happens with flash bulbs or fireworks or home pregnancy test kits—then sampling has to be used.

acceptance sampling
A quality control procedure in which a sample is taken and a decision to accept or reject a complete lot is based on a calculation of sample risk error.

process control
A quality control procedure in which sampling is done during the transformation process to determine whether the process itself is under control.

There are two categories of statistical quality control procedures: acceptance sampling and process control. The term **acceptance sampling** refers to the evaluation of purchased or manufactured materials or products that already exist—a form of feedforward and feedback control. A sample is taken; then the decision to accept or reject the whole lot is based on a statistical calculation of sample risk error, and whether or not the sample meets acceptable quality levels. The term **process control** refers to statistically sampling items during the transformation process—a form of concurrent control—to see whether the transformation process itself is under control. For example, a process control procedure at Cott Corp. of Toronto would be able to detect if a bottling machine was out of adjustment because it was filling 2-litre bottles with only 1750 ml of ginger ale. Managers could then stop the process and readjust the machine. Statistical tests would also be used in process control to determine if the variations were outside the range of acceptable quality level. Since most production processes aren't perfectly adjusted and have some innate variations, these tests would indicate serious problems within the production process itself—quality problems that should be addressed immediately.

attribute sampling
A quality control technique that classifies items as acceptable or unacceptable on the basis of a comparison to a standard.

variable sampling
A quality control technique in which a measurement is taken to determine how much an item varies from the standard.

A final consideration in quality control relates to whether the test is done by examining attributes or variables. The inspection and classification of items as acceptable or unacceptable is called **attribute sampling.** This is the way that products such as paint colour, fabric used to make boxer shorts, or potato chips are evaluated. An inspector compares the items against some standard and rates their quality as acceptable or not acceptable. In contrast, **variable sampling** involves taking a measurement to determine how much an item varies from the standard. It involves a range rather than a dichotomy. Management typically identifies the standard and an acceptable deviation. Any sample that measures within the range is accepted, and those outside are rejected. For instance, Alcan might test some steel bar to see whether the average breaking strength is between 9 kg and 11 kg per square centimetre. If it's not, the cause is investigated and corrective action is initiated.

CURRENT ISSUES IN OPERATIONS MANAGEMENT

Capitalizing on new technology! Successfully implementing TQM! Reducing inventories! Developing even closer manufacturer–supplier partnerships! Using flexibility and speed as competitive advantages! These issues currently head up management's list for improving operations productivity. Because managers consider them to be essential for making products and services competitive in world markets, we'll review each of them in this section.

TESTING... TESTING...

13 Why are cost controls and purchasing controls important parts of operations management?

14 What types of maintenance controls might a manager implement?

15 How could quality control be designed into an organization's operations system?

Technology and Product Development

Today's competitive marketplace has put tremendous pressure on manufacturers to deliver products with high quality and low cost, and to significantly reduce time to market. Even if you've built the proverbial "better mousetrap", customers won't be beating a path to your door if your competitor develops a mousetrap that's almost as good, but is in stores a year or two ahead of yours. Two key ingredients to successfully accelerating the product development process are organizational commitment to improving the development cycle, and investment in the technology to make it happen.

One of the most effective tools that manufacturers have in meeting the time-to-market challenge is **computer-integrated manufacturing (CIM).** This brings together the organization's strategic business plan and manufacturing plan with state-of-the-art computer applications.[30] The technologies of computer-aided design (CAD) and computer-aided manufacturing (CAM) are typically the basis for CIM.

computer-integrated manufacturing (CIM) Combines the organization's strategic business plan and manufacturing plan with state-of-the-art computer applications.

CAD essentially has made manual drafting obsolete. Using computers to visually display graphics, CAD enables engineers to develop new product designs in about half the time required for manual drafting. Eagle Engine Manufacturing, for instance, used its CAD system to design a new racing car engine in nine months instead of the traditional two-plus years.[31]

CAM relies on computers to guide and control the manufacturing process. Numerically controlled programs can direct machines to cut patterns, shape parts, assemble units, and perform other complicated tasks.

As technology continues to improve, CIM will soon permit the entire manufacturing process to be viewed as a continuum. Every step—from order entry to order shipping—will be expressed as data and computerized. This will let management respond rapidly to changing markets. It will give companies the ability to test hundreds of design changes in hours, rather than months, and then provide the flexibility to produce multiple variations of products efficiently in lot sizes as small as one or two items. When manufacturing is computer integrated, it's no longer necessary to stop the assembly line and spend valuable time changing dies or equipment in order to produce a new standard or non-standard product. A single change in the computer program—which can be done in seconds—immediately re-aligns the manufacturing process.

Implementing TQM Successfully

Surveys done by Bain & Co. Canada Inc. of Toronto, have shown that TQM has remained popular among North American companies in the 1990s, with more than half using it. The list of companies that have implemented TQM programs is long and impressive. It includes such notable firms as Motorola, Xerox and IBM. But total quality improvement is important to service firms and small businesses as well. Total quality management has had a huge effect on Standard Aero Ltd., a Winnipeg-based aircraft-engine repair company. Launched by Standard Aero in early 1990, the TQM makeover has already cost the company in excess of $13 million,

Standard Aero of Winnipeg has been extremely successful in implementing a TQM program. A large investment in employee training has helped the company to achieve goals such as making operations faster and less costly.

but it has brought impressive results. A year after the TQM program was begun, Standard undercut its competitors by 50 percent on a $10 million (US) contract with the American military. And Standard promised to do the job in a far shorter time than any of the other bidding companies. Pentagon officials had to fly to Winnipeg to see for themselves how this could be possible. Today, Standard Aero spends $1.5 million each year to provide 120 hours of training per employee, a small price to pay in order to see production rise by the 30 percent that Standard Aero has achieved.[32] TQM has also proved effective in Circo Craft Co. Inc., a producer of printed circuit boards based in Kirkland, Quebec. The TQM measures implemented in this company have led to reduced breakage of the circuit boards, less paperwork for employees (saving time and money), and reduced production times.[33]

Unfortunately, not all TQM efforts are equally successful. A study of 584 companies in Canada, Germany, the United States and Japan provides some important insights into factors that may hinder TQM effectiveness.[34] Consistent with the contingency approach to management, the survey found that the successful application of certain TQM concepts—including teams, benchmarking, training efforts, and empowering employees—depends on the company's current performance. The following suggestions highlight the study's recommendations for lower-, medium-, and higher-performing organizations.[35]

For Lower-Performing Firms. Increase training of all types. Emphasize teams across and within departments. The formation of teams to help identify and solve small problems can help lower-performing companies as they begin their quality improvement efforts. But teams lose their value and can distract from broader strategic issues once corporate performance improves. Don't use benchmarking, because it tends to create unreasonable goals and can thus frustrate quality efforts. And don't empower employees yet, because they usually don't have the training to make empowerment work.

For Medium-Performing Firms. Simplify corporate processes such as design, and focus employee training on problem-solving skills.

For Higher-Performing Firms. Use benchmarking to identify new processes, products, and services. Encourage company-wide quality meetings. Actively disperse decision-making power by empowering employees. Don't increase departmental teams, because this tends to inhibit co-operation across functions.

While the preceding contingency suggestions provide important limitations for the implementation of TQM, the survey also found some practices that tended to be universally effective. These included explaining the organization's strategy to all employees, customers, and suppliers; improving and simplifying operations and development processes; and reducing the amount of time it takes from the design to the delivery of a product.

ISO 9000

ISO 9000
Quality management standards established by the International Organization for Standardization, adhered to by companies around the world.

To publicly demonstrate their quality commitment, many organizations have pursued quality certification, such as **ISO 9000**. This is a series of quality management standards being embraced by organizations around the world.[36] These standards cover everything from contract review to product design, to product delivery. The ISO 9000 standards were established by the International Organization for Standardization and are becoming the internationally recognized standard for evaluating and comparing firms in the global marketplace. Gaining ISO 9000 certification provides proof that a quality operations system is in place. It provides a competitive advantage in the marketplace, it assures customers, and it can reduce production costs. In fact, this type of certification is rapidly becoming a prerequisite for doing business globally.

The number of ISO 9000-registered sites presently exceeds 100 000. Certification is sought by large manufacturers, distribution services, consulting services, software developers, public utilities, and a host of organizations in other industries—even some financial and educational institutions. It is important for managers to recognize, however, that although many positive benefits can accrue from obtaining ISO 9000 certification, the key benefit to organizations comes from the quality improvement journey itself. In other words, the goal of ISO 9000 certification should be to create work processes and an operations system that enables employees throughout the organization to perform their jobs in a consistently high-quality way.

The first IT firm in North America to receive ISO certification was Montreal-based CGI Group, Inc., whose CEO, Serge Godin, calls ISO "the company's best-kept secret". CGI is, in fact, certified ISO 9001, which is a step up from ISO 9000. Along with establishing a framework for quality production, ISO has helped CGI digest its recent acquisitions: "ISO has allowed us to integrate professionals into our company, because there is a methodology to be learned which ensures that everybody operates in the same ISO-certified manner," says CGI's VP of corporate affairs.[37]

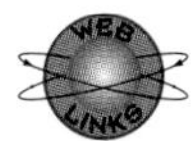

CGI Group, Inc.
www.cgi.ca

Reducing Inventories

A major portion of many companies' assets is tied up in inventories. For instance, Dow Chemical recently reported its inventory assets at $2.5 billion; Hewlett-Packard's were $3.7 billion; and Boeing's inventory exceeded $10.5 billion.[38] Firms that can significantly cut their inventories of raw materials and of in-process and finished goods can reduce costs and improve their efficiency.

This fact hasn't been lost on management. In recent years, managers have been seeking ways to manage inventories better. On the output side, managers have been improving the information link between internal manufacturing schedules and forecast customer demand. Marketing managers are increasingly being relied upon to provide accurate, up-to-date information on future sales. This is then being co-ordinated with operating systems data, to get a better match between what's produced and what the customers want. Manufacturing resource planning systems are particularly well suited to this function. On the input side, marketing managers have been experimenting with another technique widely used in Japan: **just-in-time (JIT) inventory systems.**[39] This is a system in which inventory items arrive when they're needed in the production process, instead of being stored in stock.

just-in-time (JIT) inventory system
A system in which inventory items arrive when they're needed in the production process instead of being stored in stock.

In Japan, JIT systems are called ***kanban***. The derivation of the word gets to the essence of the just-in-time concept. *Kanban* is Japanese for "card" or "sign". Japanese suppliers ship parts to manufacturers in containers. Each container has a card, or *kanban*, slipped into a side pocket. When a production worker opens a container, he or she takes out the card and sends it back to the supplier. This initiates the shipping of a second container of parts that, ideally, reaches the production worker just as the last part in the first container is being used up. The ultimate goal of a JIT inventory system is to eliminate raw material inventories by co-ordinating production and supply deliveries precisely. When the system works as designed, it results in a number of benefits for a manufacturer: reduced inventories, reduced setup time, better work flow, shorter manufacturing time, less space usage, and even higher quality. Of course, suppliers must be found who can be depended on to deliver quality materials on time. Because there are no inventories, there's no slack in the system to absorb defective materials or delays in shipment.

kanban
The Japanese name for a just-in-time inventory system.

An illustration of JIT's benefits can be seen at Fred Deeley Imports in Toronto. Fred Deeley is the Canadian distributor for Harley Davidson Inc. Instead of investing in more warehouse space to keep up inventories, Fred Deeley decided to employ a system of just-in-time delivery. Deeley uses a process called crossdocking, in which inventory comes in one end of the warehouse and is rearranged, without shelving, to be sent out at the other end of the warehouse to retailers. Deeley uses electronic data interchange to link his operations to his supplier in the US and to the outlets with which he deals in Canada. This system not only saves money in less warehouse space, it also saves the time and labour required to shelve goods before shipping them, and it allows Deeley to achieve a 95 percent on-time delivery level, which keeps both his retailers and their customers happy.[40]

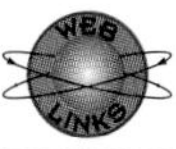

Harley Davidson
www.gainesville.fl.us/harley/

The final stage of just-in-time delivery would be to do away completely with warehouse space and have inventory constantly moving in trucks, planes or ships. Xerox Canada is presently in the process of doing away with its warehouses, having closed roughly half of its

16 What role has computer-integrated manufacturing played in operations management?

17 How can TQM be implemented successfully?

18 Why might managers want to pursue ISO 9000 certification?

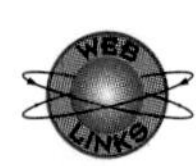

Alliance of Manufacturers and Exporters Canada
www.the-alliance.org

Canadian warehouse space in the past three years. According to Bob Savage, Xerox Canada's director of logistics, the goal of the company is to completely do away with warehouses. Savage says of the future of Xerox: "We believe totally in having our warehouses on the road." This attitude towards JIT is growing among Canadian companies. According to Jayson Myers, the chief economist at the Alliance of Manufacturers and Exporters Canada, the average Canadian manufacturer presently has stocks to supply their customers for one and a quarter months. But Myers believes that this is changing as companies attempt to make delivery more efficient and cut inventory costs.[41]

A JIT system isn't for every manufacturer.[42] It requires that suppliers be located in close proximity to the manufacturer's production facility, and that suppliers be capable of providing consistently defect-free materials. Such a system also requires reliable transportation links between suppliers and manufacturer; efficient receiving, handling and distribution of materials; and precisely tuned production planning. Where these conditions can be met, JIT can help management to reduce inventory costs.

Manufacturer–Supplier Partnerships

One of the biggest changes in operations management today is the steady evolution towards even stronger partnerships between manufacturers and suppliers.[43] These newly forged relationships are more than just the outsourcing of production, where manufacturers lowered their high labour costs by shifting production to suppliers with lower costs. No—these new relationships between manufacturer and supplier are much more than that.

What we see happening today with many manufacturers and suppliers is a closer-knit association between them. Suppliers are becoming more heavily involved with a manufacturer's *total* production process. Many of the tasks that were once performed only by the manufacturer are now being shared with key suppliers. The manufacturer's role is becoming more of an orchestrator and co-ordinator of various suppliers' work. For instance, Whirlpool Corporation's newest model of gas range was developed without hiring its own design engineers. Rather, the design work was performed by Eaton Corporation, one of the company's suppliers that already made gas valves and regulators for other appliance manufacturers. Whirlpool capitalized on this supplier's expertise and thus got its new product to market much sooner.[44] And McDonnell–Douglas Corporation trimmed about $300 million off the $500 million development costs of its new 100-seat jet, by having its suppliers provide the up-front tooling and development costs and by subcontracting the plane's assembly.[45] Markham, Ontario's auto parts giant, Magna International Inc., has recorded heavy growth as a result of the trend for worldwide automobile manufacturers to rely increasingly on outsourcing. These strong and close-knit manufacturer–supplier partnerships are likely to continue as manufacturers look for ways in which to develop and sustain competitive advantages in the global marketplace.

Flexibility as a Competitive Advantage

In today's changing world of business, companies that can't adjust rapidly won't survive. This reality puts a premium on being able to develop manufacturing flexibility.[46] As a result, many organizations are developing flexible manufacturing systems.[47]

Celestica Inc.
www.celestica.com

IBM Canada
www.can.ibm.com

The "factories of tomorrow" look like something out of a science fiction movie in which remote-controlled carts deliver a basic casting to a computerized machining centre. With robots positioning and repositioning the casting, the machining centre calls on its hundreds of tools to perform varying operations that turn the casting into a finished part. Completed parts, each a bit different from the others, are finished at a rate of one every 90 seconds. Neither skilled machinists nor conventional machine tools are used. Nor are there any costly delays for changing dies or tools in this factory. A single machine can make dozens or even hundreds of different parts in any order management wants. For instance, at Celestica Inc.'s factory in Toronto, the production line can be, and often is, changed in less than 48 hours to produce a different product. Celestica produces electronic components, an industry where products change between two and four times a year. Celestica is a newly formed spin-off of IBM Canada. It was formerly the manufacturing division of IBM Canada, but became a wholly owned subsidiary in January of 1994. Nine months later Celestica's 1994 revenues equalled its total revenue in 1993. By 1998, revenue had hit $2.8 billion. Making Celestica more flexible has led to great increases in production, and nearly all of the increased revenue has come from new business.[48]

Production lines at Toronto's Celestica Inc. can be changed in less than 48 hours. Manufacturing flexibility is a key factor in Celestica's success, allowing it to constantly keep up with customer demands for different products.

The unique characteristic of **flexible manufacturing systems** is that by integrating computer-aided design, engineering, and manufacturing, they can produce low-volume, custom products at a cost comparable to that of mass production. Flexible manufacturing systems are replacing the laws of economies of scale with the laws of economies of scope. Management no longer has to mass produce thousands of identical products to achieve low per-unit production costs. With a flexible manufacturing system, when management wants to produce a new part, it doesn't change machines—it just changes the computer program.

flexible manufacturing systems
Systems in which custom-made products can be inexpensively produced by means of computer-aided design, engineering and manufacturing.

Some automated plants can build a wide variety of flawless products, and can switch from one product to another on cue from a central computer. Clearly Canadian's factories in Toronto, St. Louis, California, and Vancouver are all equipped to change production processes quickly, in response to varying demand for its wide range of products. And John Deere has a $1.5 billion automated factory that can turn out 10 basic tractor models with as many as 3000 options, without plant shutdowns for retooling. In one corner of a mammoth IBM plant in Charlotte, North Carolina, 40 workers on an assembly line are building 12 different products at once, ranging from hand-held bar-code scanners to portable medical computers to satellite communications devices for truckers. And the assembly line was designed to simultaneously make as many as 27 different products.[49] National Bicycle Industrial Company, which sells its bikes under the Panasonic brand, uses flexible manufacturing to produce any of 11 231 862 possible variations on 18 models of racing, road, and mountain bikes, in 199 colour patterns and an almost unlimited number of sizes.[50]

Speed as a Competitive Advantage

For years we've heard that on the highway, speed kills. Managers are now learning that the same principle applies in business: Speed kills, only this time it's your competitors' speed.[51] By quickly developing, making, and distributing products and services, organizations can gain a powerful competitive advantage. Just as customers may select one organization over another because its products or services are less expensive, uniquely designed, or of superior quality, customers also choose organizations because they can get the product or service they want *fast*. In essence, Domino's Pizza created a billion-dollar business using speed as a competitive advantage by stressing quick delivery of its pizzas.

A number of other companies have also made incredible improvements in the time it takes them to design and produce their products. Laura Ashley—the British fabrics company—completely overhauled its information systems and consolidated its warehouses, and found that it

19 **How is JIT a dynamic inventory system?**

20 **What benefits and drawbacks might outsourcing have for a manufacturer?**

21 **Why are flexibility and speed important competitive advantages today?**

was able to move its inventory five times faster than it could in the early 1990s.[52] At the plant where Motorola makes pagers, orders flow in from retailers and Motorola sales representatives. The order data are digitized and sent to the assembly line where robots and humans complete the order, often within 80 minutes after being received. Depending on where the customer lives, the pagers can be delivered that same day or the day after.[53] And at Hewlett-Packard, managers have recognized the importance of speed. Many of their products are brought to market nine to twelve months after work on them started.[54]

These organizations and many others worldwide are cutting red tape; flattening their organizational structures; adding cross-functional teams; redesigning their distribution chains; and using JIT, CIM, and flexible manufacturing systems to speed up their operations and put increased pressure on their competitors.

SUMMARY

This summary is organized by the learning objectives found at the beginning of the chapter.

1. The transformation process is the essence of operations management. Operations management takes inputs, including people and materials, and then acts on them by transforming them into finished goods and services. This applies in service organizations, as well as in manufacturing companies.
2. Canadian managers and managers around the globe are increasingly concerned with improving productivity. How people are integrated into the overall operations system determines how productive an organization will be. Factors such as the size and layout of operating facilities, capacity utilization, inventory usage, and maintenance controls are operations management concepts that have a crucial bearing on overall productivity.
3. Customer-driven operations are important because organizations exist to meet the needs of their customers. The operations system should be designed around meeting and exceeding customers' expectations.
4. Re-engineering of work processes involves totally redesigning a company's operations. It means starting from scratch in rethinking and rearranging the way in which work is done in the organization. In the operations system, the inputs and transformation process are completely redesigned as managers redefine the organization's work processes.
5. A manufacturing focus added to strategy pushes important production decisions to the top of the organization. It recognizes that an organization's overall strategy should directly reflect its manufacturing capabilities and limitations, and should include operations objectives and strategies.
6. Four key decisions—capacity, location, process, and layout—provide the long-term strategic direction for operations planning. They determine the proper size of an operating system, the location of physical facilities, the best methods for transforming inputs into outputs, and the most efficient layout of equipment and workstations.
7. The three decisions that make up the tactical operations plan are the aggregate plan, the master schedule, and the materials requirement plan. The aggregate plan determines the overall production plan, the master schedule determines how many units of each product will be produced, and the material requirements plan determines what materials are needed to satisfy the master schedule.
8. The three types of maintenance control are preventive, remedial and conditional. Preventive maintenance is performed before a breakdown occurs. Remedial maintenance is performed when the equipment breaks down. Conditional maintenance is a response to an inspection.
9. Evidence demonstrates that the application of certain TQM concepts should reflect whether the organization is a low, medium, or high performer. Low-performing companies, for instance, should emphasize team creation and downplay benchmarking and empowerment. High-performing companies, in contrast, should encourage benchmarking and empowerment, and de-emphasize departmental teams.
10. Just-in-time (JIT) inventory systems seek to reduce inventories, reduce setup time, improve work flow, cut manufacturing time, reduce space consumption, and raise the quality of production by co-ordinating the arrival of inventory items to their demand in the production process. However, they require precise co-ordination; if this is lacking, they can threaten the smooth, continuous operation of a production system.
11. A flexible manufacturing system can give an organization a competitive advantage by allowing it to produce a wider variety of products, at a lower cost, and in considerably less time than the competition.
12. For an organization that's in a highly complex and dynamic environment, speed can be a strong competitive advantage. By reducing the amount of time it takes to design and produce products, organizations can get a lead on their competitors in the marketplace.

THINKING ABOUT MANAGEMENT ISSUES

1. How might operations management apply to other managerial functions besides control? Discuss.
2. How could you use operations management concepts in your everyday life? Describe.
3. Would you see any potential problems with implementing both CIM and TQM in the same organization? Discuss.
4. Could service organizations apply the concepts of flexible manufacturing technology? Explain.
5. Choose some large organization that you're interested in studying (based in Canada or some other country). Do some library research on this company to find out what types of operations management techniques it's using. Is it doing anything in the area of operations management that's unusual or effective, or both? Describe.

SELF-ASSESSMENT EXERCISE

HOW CUSTOMER-FOCUSED ARE YOU?

Instructions: Read through the statements and circle the answer that best describes your situation.

1 = Strongly disagree
2 = Disagree
3 = Uncertain
4 = Agree
5 = Strongly agree

1. I know who our organization's customers are.	1	2	3	4	5
2. I know how my work affects our customers' results.	1	2	3	4	5
3. My work creates value for our customers.	1	2	3	4	5
4. I'm rewarded for delivering superior results to our customers.	1	2	3	4	5
5. I use measures of customer satisfaction in my job.	1	2	3	4	5
6. I act as the customers' advocate in my job.	1	2	3	4	5
7. I know what our customers want.	1	2	3	4	5
8. I regularly ask my customers about their future plans.	1	2	3	4	5

See scoring key on page SK–5.

Source: Based on M. Treacy and F. Wiersema, *The Discipline of Market Leaders* (Reading, MA: Addison-Wesley, 1995); and Wiersema, *Customer Intimacy* (Santa Monica, CA: Knowledge Exchange, 1996).

for your IMMEDIATE action

TO: Ebben Crawford, Director of Operations
FROM: Anne Mendales, President
SUBJECT: Applying TQM to our travel business

I've been doing a lot of reading on TQM and it's made me realize that TQM principles should be applicable to service businesses like ours.

As you know, we've grown from one small agency to five offices and nearly forty employees by responding to the needs of the business traveller. However, in the last six months we've lost several valuable clients to more aggressive competitors. Our competitors, especially Chapman Travel and the American Express travel agency, seem to be doing a better job of meeting customers' needs.

Maybe TQM could help us. I'd like you to think about how we might implement TQM in our travel agencies. Please prepare an analysis describing how we could apply the concepts of continuous process improvement, customer focus, benchmarking, training, teamwork, and empowerment to our travel business to make us more competitive.

S

This is a fictionalized account of a potentially real problem. It is not intended to reflect either positively or negatively on management practices at any travel service.

TAKE IT TO THE NET

We invite you to visit the Robbins/Coulter/Stuart-Kotze Companion Website at www.prenticehall.ca/robbins for this chapter's Internet resources.

CASE APPLICATION

St Michael's Hospital, Toronto

In 1991, St. Michael's Hospital was operating with the largest debt of any hospital in the country—a debt of $63 million. As of 1999, it has become one of Canada's most efficient hospitals. The CEO of St. Michael's, Jeff Lozon, boasts: "We have successfully re-engineered. We changed every job in the hospital, collapsed job classifications, and streamlined admissions". The hospital was put through a rigorous re-engineering program that has touched on every aspect of the organization's operations. Simple policies, such as buying only one type of surgical gloves from one supplier (as opposed to the fifteen St. Mike's used to order from), have saved significant amounts of money—around $60 000 for surgical gloves. More dramatic changes have resulted in greater cost savings. Apart from doctors, nurses and administrators, every job title in the hospital was made redundant, and every employee then had to re-apply for new, streamlined positions. Many employees were offered early retirement or buyouts; others were simply laid off. St. Michael's estimates an annual saving of $22 million from this restructuring. A just-in-time delivery system for supplies has accounted for a $700 000 saving in inventory.

But change of this magnitude does not come without some unpleasant side-effects. One major area of concern is among staff. Greater demands placed upon nurses, for instance, have led to a sharp increase in workplace stress. One nurse has said: "There's a lot of pressure in working in an operation that's running so tightly". Indeed, although recent studies have found St. Michael's to be highly efficient compared with other Ontario hospitals, one report has made mention of certain areas that have suffered. Negative changes mentioned include: "less nursing time per patient, less palatable food, lower levels of cleanliness in facilities, high employee stress, slow recording of patient data, and reduced patient supervision". Also, the inventory system seems far from efficient, and is derided by nurses who say that, "just in time is a day late". Running out of necessary supplies during busy times is frustrating for staff and, as one nurse points out, "It's time away from the patient, trying to find [an item] elsewhere in the hospital".

Management at St. Michael's recognizes that in a hospital, re-engineering for cost-control and efficiency can be taken too far. Michael Heilbronn, chief financial officer, explained the situation succinctly, if somewhat understatedly, when he commented that: "You've got to be sensitive that the core business is patient care. In the private sector, if you make a lousy product you get an unsatisfied customer. At a hospital, your patient is dead. So you've got to be sensitive and balance it out". Heilbronn has instituted highly effective cost controls at St Michael's, but understands that the bottom line is not the only essential component in operation. "Maybe we have to back up a bit on efficiency and spend more time per patient," he has said.

QUESTIONS

1. In what ways and to what degrees do you think productivity is important at St. Michael's and in hospitals in general?
2. Use Deming's 14 Points as a guide, and discuss how each could be effective with regard to managing St. Michael's.
3. Discuss the roles that cost controls, purchasing controls, maintenance controls and quality controls could play in operations at St. Michael's.

Source: Peter Kuitenbrouwer, "St. Efficiency's Caring Ways", *Financial Post,* February 7, 1998, page 8.

LEARNING OBJECTIVES

After Reading This Chapter, You Should Be Able To:

1. Explain the purpose of a management information system (MIS)
2. Differentiate between data and information
3. Outline the key elements in designing an MIS
4. Explain how MIS is changing the manager's job and communications in organizations
5. Describe how budgets are used as control tools
6. Explain what the various financial ratios measure
7. Describe TQM control charts
8. Explain how to determine the most economic order quantity
9. Identify six performance appraisal methods
10. Describe the organizational factors that serve as indirect behavioural controls

A MANAGER'S CHALLENGE

Playdium Entertainment Corp., Toronto

Perhaps you've been to one of Playdium's indoor "game parks" across Canada. Playdium's giant game complexes (ranging from 30 000 to 60 000 square feet) provide a fantasy world of entertaining video and virtual-reality games, geared more towards an adult market than the typical teenage-oriented arcade. The biggest contingent in Playdium's customer-base is 18-34-year-olds, but a significant force among the company's market is corporate clients. At present, a third of Playdium's business comes from companies who hire out the sites for their employees, to help foster team spirit in an entertaining setting. This is a sector upon which Playdium increasingly hopes to capitalize in the future.[1]

At the Playdium game parks, customers use Playcards, which they insert into any game they want to try. These Playcards provide the convenience of not having to use coins, but they also serve a far more important purpose. Playdium compiles detailed demographic information on its ever-growing "Virtua Citizens" (150 000 at last count). Every game is linked to

a central computer, and every time a Playcard is inserted into a game, more data is added. Combining the demographic information of its clients (age, marital status, household income, etc.) with specific game usage, Playdium compiles detailed knowledge on its customers. Says Playdium's director of games and attractions: "We know who's using what, at what times of the day, how often, and how much they're spending—which is very powerful from a marketing standpoint". This sort of information control is a powerful weapon for a company like Playdium, allowing them to make adjustments to cater specifically to different customers' needs. "We can create a different social environment on Saturday mornings when we're doing family business, than on Friday nights when it's more of a nightclub atmosphere".

As for Playdium's corporate clients, who pay up to $60 000 to rent sites out for their employees, Playdium can sit down with them and devise specific atmospheres and events conducive to their goals. If a company wants to heavily challenge its employees to boost their confidence as individuals, or create a greater sense of team cohesion through group activities, Playdium can provide the appropriate environment. As the company grows, Playdium's information systems will make it more and more effective in targeting its operations to specific client desires.

Playdium is trying to utilize its information controls to better understand and serve its customers' desires. In the process of controlling the different areas of the organization, managers have various tools and techniques to help them. In this chapter, we'll be looking at the wide range of tools and techniques which managers can use in controlling four distinct organizational areas: information, finances, operations, and employee behaviour.

CHAPTER 19

Control Tools and Techniques

INFORMATION CONTROLS

Controlling information can be vital to an organization's success. Managers use information in every activity they perform, and in every decision they make. To be effective and efficient, managers need the right information, at the right time, and in the right amount. Inaccurate, incomplete, excessive, or delayed information will seriously impede their performance. How can managers use information for control, and how can information be controlled through management information systems? In the upcoming pages we will describe what a Management Information System (MIS) is, and how it can be used for controlling. Then we will look at how an MIS is designed and implemented.

What Is a Management Information System?

management information system (MIS)
A system that provides management with needed information on a regular basis.

Although there's no universally agreed-upon definition of **management information system (MIS)**, we'll define it as a system used to provide management with needed information on a regular basis.[2] In theory, this system can be manual- or computer-based, although all current discussions—including ours—focus on computer-supported applications.

The term *system* in MIS implies order, arrangement and purpose. Further, an MIS focuses specifically on providing management with *information*, not merely *data*. These two points are important and require elaboration.

data
Raw, unanalyzed facts.

information
Analyzed and processed data.

A library provides a good analogy. Although it can contain millions of volumes, a library doesn't do users much good if they can't *find* what they want *quickly*. That's why libraries spend a great deal of time cataloguing their collections and ensuring that volumes are returned to their proper locations. Organizations today are like well-stocked libraries. There's no lack of data. Many organizations, however, lack the ability to process those data so that the right information is available to the right person when he or she needs it.[3] They are like a library that has the book that you need immediately, but either you can't find it or the library takes a week to retrieve it from storage. An MIS, in contrast, has data organized in some meaningful way and can access the information in a reasonable time. **Data** are raw, unanalyzed facts, such as numbers, names or quantities. But as data, these facts are relatively useless to managers.[4] When data are analyzed and processed, they become **information**. A 1997 survey of 150 Canadian companies found that 58 percent of them had a customer database.[5] However, only 48 percent of those companies with databases had a structure in place to respond to different customer needs. Without the ability to capitalize on it, the information is simply ineffectual. An MIS collects data and turns them into relevant information for managers to use. Figure 19-1 summarizes these observations.

How Are Information Systems Used in Controlling?

Managers need information in order to control the various organizational areas efficiently and effectively. Without information, they'd find it difficult to perform the activities that we discussed in Chapter 18 as part of the controlling process. For instance, in measuring actual performance, managers need information about what is, in fact, happening within their area of responsibility. Also, they need information about what the standards are to be able to compare actual performance with the standard. In addition, managers need information to help them

FIGURE 19-1 MIS Makes Data Usable

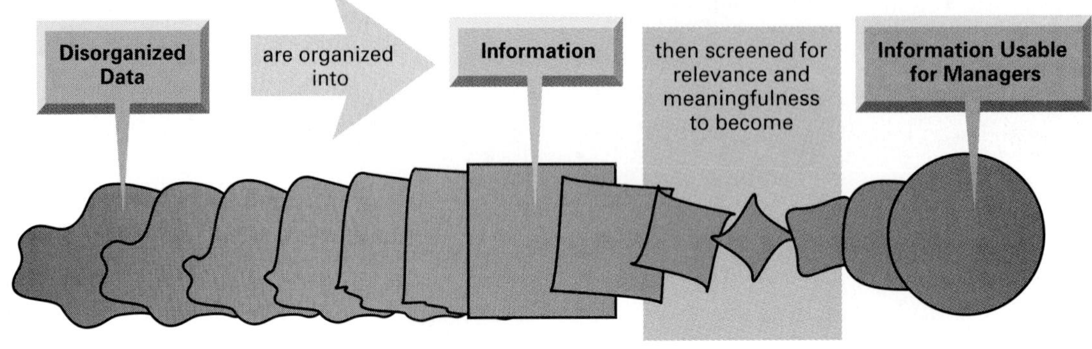

This is EDS's command post—its MIS centre. From here, the information services company manages its global communications in more than 42 countries. This is MIS on a very grand scale.

determine acceptable ranges of variation within these comparisons. Finally, they rely on information to help them develop appropriate courses of action, if there are or aren't significant deviations from standard. As you can see, information plays a vital role in the controlling process. But how does a manager get the information he or she needs?

Designing the MIS

Just as there's no universal definition of an MIS, there's also no universally agreed-upon approach to designing a management information system. However, the following steps represent the key elements in putting an MIS together. (See Figure 19-2.)

1. *Analyze the decision system.* The decisions that managers make should drive the design of any MIS. Therefore, the first step is to identify all the management decisions for which information is needed. This should encompass all the functions within the organization, and every management level from first-level supervisor to the chief executive officer.

   This step should also consider whether each decision is being made by the right person. Is it being made at the right level? By the right department? Failure to ask these questions can misdirect the design of the entire MIS. If the wrong people are making the decision and this problem isn't corrected before a sophisticated information system is put in place, these people will continue to make the decision erroneously, only faster.

2. *Analyze information requirements.* Once the decisions are isolated, we need to know the exact information required to effectively make these decisions.

   Information needs differ according to managerial functions in the organization. The information that a marketing manager needs differs from that required by a financial manager. Thus, the MIS has to be tailored to meet the varying needs of different functional managers.

   As Figure 19-3 illustrates, a manager's information needs also vary according to organizational level. Top-level managers are looking for environmental data and summary reports. At the other extreme, lower-level supervisors want detailed reports of

FIGURE 19-2 Steps in Designing an MIS

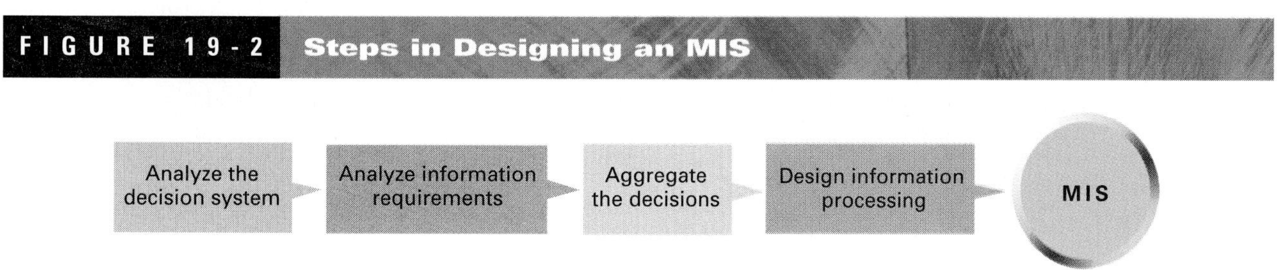

FIGURE 19-3 **Matching Information Requirements with Managerial Level**

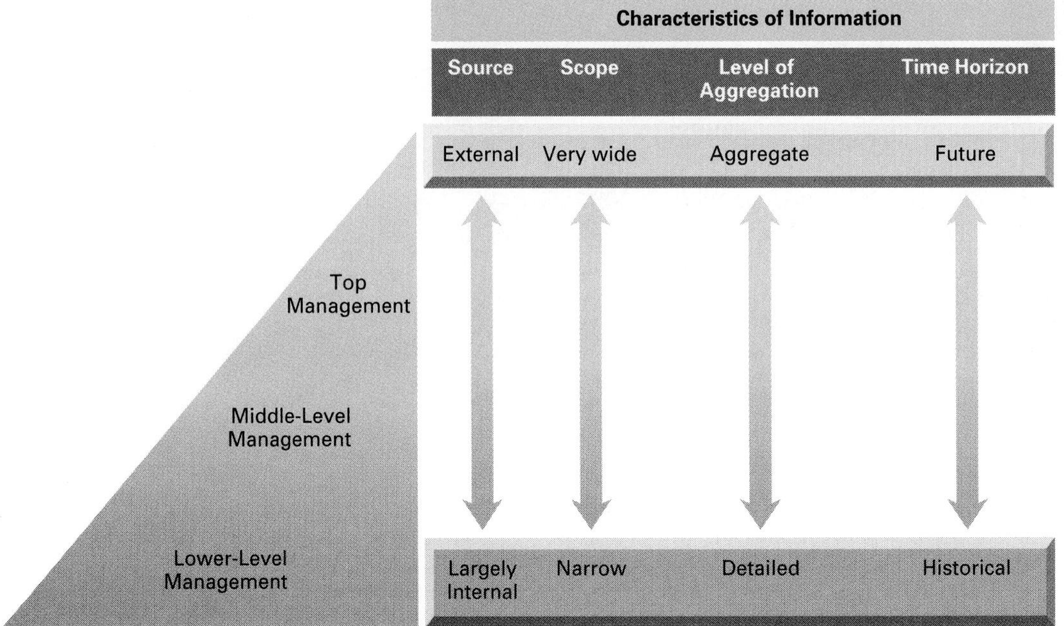

operating problems. The well-designed MIS must consider these diverse requirements if it's to satisfy the varied needs of managers.

3. *Aggregate the decisions.* After each functional area and manager's needs have been identified, those that have the same or largely overlapping information requirements should be located. Even though needs vary up, down and across the organization, redundancies often occur. Both sales and production executives, for example, may want feedback data on a given product's quality level. One executive, however, wants the feedback to ensure customer satisfaction, while the other wants it to control for variances in the production processes. By identifying these redundancies, management can create systems that contain the least amount of duplication, and that group together similar decisions under a single manager.

4. *Design information processing.* In this step, internal technical specialists or outside consultants develop the actual system for collecting, storing, transmitting and retrieving information. A detailed flowchart of the desired system will be drawn up. It will include, among other things, sources and types of data, locations of users, and storage requirements. The precise hardware and software requirements will also be determined.

Before the system is implemented, it is carefully evaluated to ensure that it will do what management wants it to do. That is, the bottom-line test of the system's effectiveness is its ability to meet each manager's information needs. A design that meets all of most managers' needs or most of all managers' needs won't provide the optimum quantity or quality of information for the organization as a whole.

Implementing the MIS

Once the MIS design has been resolved, the system needs to be implemented. The implementation phase should begin with pretesting the system, and should conclude with building in regular evaluations in the system. The following points highlight concerns that need to be addressed during the implementation phase.

1. *Pretest the system before installation.* Flaws found before an information system is installed are much easier and less costly to fix than those found when the system is in place and people are depending on it. If a full pretest isn't feasible, then management should con-

sider introducing the new system in parallel with the old. Running the two systems side by side for a short period of time can make it easier to identify and correct bugs or omissions in the new system, with minimal disturbances to the organization's operations.

2. *Prepare users with proper training.* No matter how well a system is designed, if users aren't aware of its full capabilities and don't know how to obtain those capabilities, it will never achieve its full potential. Therefore, the budget of any new MIS installation must cover time and money for training users. Even the brightest and most competent managers will require some training if they're going to be able to make full use of a new information system.

3. *Prepare for resistance.* As we discussed in the chapter on change, people tend to resist changes that appear threatening to them. A sizeable body of research indicates that the introduction of computer-based information systems can be highly threatening.[6] Some people have difficulty adapting to the introduction of any new technology. Some also fear being unable to learn the new system. Others may be threatened by the new system's potential for reducing their power and status in the organization, changing interpersonal relationships, or reducing their job security.

4. *Get users involved.* One of the most effective ways of neutralizing resistance to an MIS is to have those who will be affected by the system participate fully in its design and implementation.[7] Participation will familiarize users with the system before they *have* to use it, increase their commitment to it because they were involved in its creation, and lessen the likelihood that their needs will be overlooked.

5. *Check for security.* As information systems become decentralized, there's a crucial need to ensure that unauthorized people don't gain access to valuable or privileged information. When information was centralized at a single source, only a few people could tap into important data bases such as production schedules, customer records, inventory accounts, credit data, and employee files. Today, however, such data bases are much more vulnerable to unauthorized access. The solution is to ensure that adequate security measures are included in the system. For instance, access to the place where hardware is located should be controlled. Software should be locked up when not in use. A system should also use impossible-to-guess passwords or codes for gaining access, should change them frequently, require users to identify themselves once into the system, and impose strict controls over telephone access.

6. *Build in regular reviews.* The information that a manager needed last year isn't necessarily the same as he or she needs today. As customers, suppliers, government regulations, and other environmental factors change, so, too, will the information needs of managers. Implementation should be viewed as the beginning of an ongoing process. If an information system is to be valuable to managers over time, it must be regularly evaluated and modified to adapt to the changing needs of its users.

How MISs Are Changing the Manager's Job

No discussion of management information systems would be complete without assessing their impact on the manager's job. In this section, we'll touch on several key areas that are changing as a result of computer-based MISs.

Hands-on Involvement. A few years ago, managers could avoid computers by claiming, "I don't have to know how to use computers. I can hire people to do that for me." Those days are long gone.[8]

Today's younger managers—exposed to computers in college, or even elementary and high school—feel at home in front of a keyboard. If anything, they've swung to the other extreme—they've become dependent on their computers and feel threatened when access to them is limited. By the late 1990s, the "Nintendo generation" will be filling many lower- and middle-level managerial positions in organizations. Managers who fail to fully learn their systems and take advantage of their MIS capabilities will find it increasingly difficult to perform as effectively as their peers.

How will hands-on use change what managers do? Among other things, managers will spend less time on the phone, travelling to conferences, and waiting for subordinates to provide progress reports. They'll be using networks for electronic mail, videoconferencing, and closely monitoring organizational activities.

Decision-Making Capability. Because managers rely on information to make decisions and because a sophisticated MIS significantly alters the quantity and quality of information, as well as the speed with which it can be obtained, we can naturally conclude that an effective MIS will improve management's decision-making capability.[9]

The effect will be seen in ascertaining the need for a decision, in the development and evaluation of alternatives, and in the final selection of the best alternative. On-line, real-time systems allow managers to identify problems almost as they occur. Gone are the long delays between the appearance of a serious discrepancy and a manager's ability to find out about it. At Clearly Canadian Beverages Corp., a central control software system keeps tabs on every facet of the business—from orders to suppliers, to production at all the plants, to distribution, to accounting. This system has allowed Clearly Canadian to cut its order cycle down from 30 days to just 2.[10]

Clearly Canadian Beverage Corp.
www.clearly.ca

Taco Bell Corp.
www.tacobell.com

Database management programs allow managers to look things up or get to the facts without either going to other people, or digging through piles of paper. This reduces a manager's dependence on others for data and makes fact gathering far more efficient. Today's manager can identify alternatives quickly, evaluate those alternatives by using a spreadsheet program and posing a series of what-if questions based on financial data, and, finally, select the best alternative on the basis of answers to those questions. For instance, Taco Bell's CEO, John Martin, is a fanatic about collecting customer information. His company's management information system allows him to pull up real-time sales updates from any of Taco Bell's 3000 company stores in just 15 minutes. With this information, Martin can make decisions about product mix, marketing, employee training, or whatever else might be crucial at that moment.[11]

Organizational Design. Sophisticated information systems are reshaping organizations. For instance, traditional departmental boundaries will be less confining as networks cut across departments, divisions, geographic locations, and levels in the organization. But the most evident change is probably that MISs are making organizations flatter and more organic.[12]

Managers can now handle more subordinates. Why? Because computer control substitutes for personal supervision. As a result, there are wider spans of control and fewer levels in the organization. The need for staff support is also reduced with an MIS. As was noted previously, hands-on involvement allows managers to tap information directly, thus making large staff support groups—which traditionally compiled, tabulated and analyzed data—redundant.[13] Both forces—wider spans and reduced staff—lead to flatter organizations.

One of the more interesting phenomena created by sophisticated information systems is that they've allowed management to make organizations more organic without any loss in control.[14] Management tends to prefer bureaucracy because bureaucracy facilitates control.[15] But there's more than one way to maintain control. Management can lessen formalization and become more decentralized—thus making its structure more organic—without giving up control. In this case, an MIS substitutes computer control for rules and limited decision discretion. Because of computer technology, managers can be rapidly apprised of the consequences of any decision, and can take corrective action if the decision isn't to their liking. This gives the appearance of decentralization, without any commensurate loss of control.

Power. Information is power. Anything that changes the access to scarce and important information is going to change power relationships within an organization.[16]

An MIS changes the status hierarchy in an organization. Middle managers have less status because they carry less clout. They no longer serve as the vital link between operations and the executive suite. Similarly, staff units have less prestige because senior managers no longer depend on them for evaluation and advice.

THINKING CRITICALLY ABOUT ETHICS

Duplicating software for friends and co-workers is a widespread practice, but software is legally protected by copyright law. Is reproducing copyrighted software ever an acceptable practice? Is it wrong for employees of a corporation to pirate software, but permissible for struggling university students who can't afford to buy it? As a manager, what types of ethical guidelines could you establish for software use? ■

Centralized computer departments, which were extremely influential units in organizations during the 1970s, have had their role modified and their power reduced.[17] Now organized as information support centres, they no longer have exclusive control over access to databases.

In total, probably the most important effect that computer-based control systems have had on the power structure has been to tighten the reins of top management. In earlier years, top management regularly depended on lower-level managers to feed information upward. Because information was filtered and "enhanced", managers knew only what their subordinates wanted them to know. Now these top managers have the power of information at their fingertips because they have direct access to data.

FINANCIAL CONTROLS

One of the primary purposes of every business firm is to earn a profit. In pursuit of this objective, managers need financial controls. Managers might, for instance, carefully analyze quarterly income statements for excessive expenses. They might also perform several financial ratio tests to ensure that sufficient cash is available to pay ongoing expenses, that debt hasn't become too large and burdensome, or that assets are being used productively. In addition, they might look at budgets to see if cash, employees, or units of production are going according to plan. These are examples of how financial controls can be used to reduce costs and make the best use of an organization's financial resources. Two specific financial control tools that a wide range of managers need to understand are budgets and ratio analysis.

Budgets Revisited

In Chapter 9, we discussed budgets as a planning tool. When the budget is formulated, it's a planning tool because it gives direction. It indicates which activities are important, and how many resources should be allocated to each activity. As we noted, however, budgets are used for both planning *and* control.

Budgets also provide managers with quantitative standards against which to measure and compare resource consumption. By pointing out deviations between standard and actual consumption, they become control tools. If the deviations are judged to be significant enough that something must be done, the manager wants to examine what's happened and try to uncover the reasons behind the deviations. With this information, he or she can take whatever action is necessary at that point. For example, if you use a personal budget for controlling your monthly expenses, you might find that, one month, your miscellaneous expenses were higher than you'd budgeted for. At that point, your options might include the following: cut back spending in another area, work extra hours to try to get more income, or call home for additional money.

Ratio Analysis

Table 19-1 summarizes some of the most popular financial ratios used in organizations. Taken from the organization's primary financial statements (the balance sheet and income statement), they compare two significant figures and express them as a percentage, or ratio. Because you've undoubtedly encountered these ratios in introductory accounting and finance courses, or you will in the near future, we aren't going to elaborate on how they're calculated.

What do these ratios mean? The liquidity ratios measure an organization's ability to meet its current debt obligations. Leverage ratios examine the organization's use of debt to finance its assets, and indicate whether it's able to meet the interest payments on the debt. The operations ratios measure how efficiently the firm is using its assets. Finally, the profitability ratios measure how efficiently and effectively the firm is using its assets to generate profits. We mention these ratios only briefly here to remind you that managers use such ratios as internal con-

1 **How can an MIS assist a manager in the control function?**

2 **What are the steps in implementing an MIS?**

3 **How are MISs changing the manager's job?**

TABLE 19-1 Popular Financial Ratios

Objective	Ratio	Calculation	Meaning
Liquidity test	Current ratio	Current assets / Current liabilities	Tests the organization's ability to meet short-term obligations
	Acid test	Current assets less inventories	Tests liquidity more accurately when inventories turn over slowly or are difficult to sell
Leverage test	Debt-to-assets	Total debt	The higher the ratio, the more leveraged the organization
	Times-interest-earned	Profits before interest and taxes	Measures how far profits can decline before the organization is unable to meet its interest expenses
Operations test	Inventory turnover	Sales	The higher the ratio, the more efficiently inventory assets are being used
	Total asset turnover	Sales	The fewer assets used to achieve a given level of sales, the more efficiently management is using the organization's total assets
Profitability	Profit margin on sales	Net profit after taxes	Identifies the profits that various products are generating
	Return on investment	Net profit after taxes	Measures the efficiency of assets to generate profits

trol devices for monitoring how efficiently and profitably the organization uses its assets, debt inventories, and the like.

OPERATIONS CONTROLS

The success of an organization depends to a large extent on its ability to produce goods and services effectively and efficiently. Operations control techniques are designed to assess how effectively and efficiently an organization's transformation processes are working.

Operations control typically encompasses monitoring production activities to ensure that they're on schedule; assessing purchasing's ability to provide the proper quantity and quality of supplies needed at the lowest possible cost; monitoring the quality of the organization's products or services to ensure that they meet pre-established standards; and making sure equipment is well maintained. We covered many of these operations activities in the previous chapter on operations management. However, two important operations control tools deserve elaboration: TQM control charts and the EOQ model.

TQM Control Charts

We discussed the general concept of quality control in the previous chapter on operations management. But effective quality control involves more than just expressing a desire to produce quality products. Managers must control all the various aspects of the operations system in order to achieve total quality in both products and processes. One tool they use in doing this is TQM control charts.

TQM control charts allow managers to detect unwanted fluctuations in their operations. This is another aspect of quality control.

Control charts are a management control tool that shows results of measurements over a period of time, with statistically determined upper and lower limits. They provide a visual means of determining whether a specific process is staying within predefined limits. For instance, employees at Ralston Purina sample the weight of dry dog food bags after they're filled to determine their exact quantity, and then plot the data on a control chart. This alerts management to whether or not the filling equipment needs adjustment. As long as the process variables fall within the acceptable range, the system is said to be "in control". (See Figure 19-4.) When a measurement falls outside the set limits, then the variation is unacceptable. Improvements in quality should, over time, result in a narrowing of the range between the upper and lower limits through elimination of common causes of variation. But just what do managers have to do to construct a control chart?

control charts
A management control tool that shows results of measurements over a period of time, with statistically determined upper and lower limits.

First of all, in developing a control chart, managers must recognize that there are two possible sources of process variability. One is chance, which includes variations caused by

FIGURE 19-4 Sample Control Chart

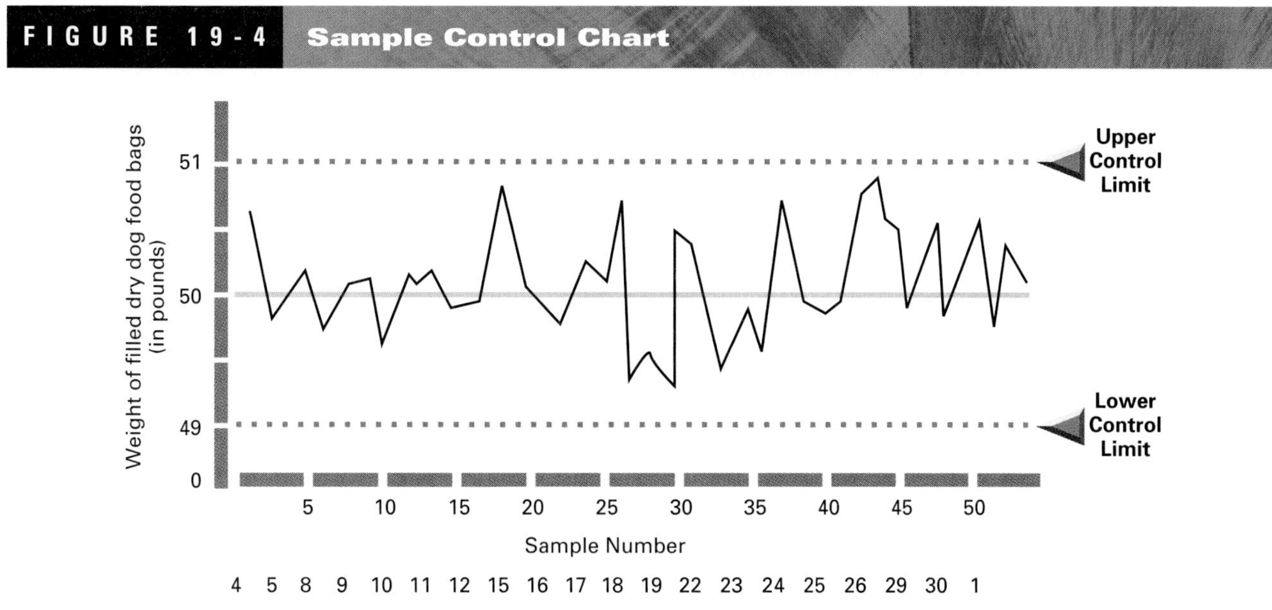

Source: Marshall Sashkin and Kenneth J Kiser, *Putting Total Quality Management to Work* (San Francisco: Berrett-Koehler, 1993), p. 170.

randomness in the process. These variations are found in every process and are impossible to control unless the process is fundamentally changed. The other source of variation is due to assignable causes, or non-chance variations. These variations *can* be identified and controlled. Control charts are used to identify these assignable causes of variation.

Control charts are put together with the help of some basic statistical concepts. In an introductory statistics class, you probably previously covered the idea of a normal distribution (the concept that variations are assumed to follow a bell-shaped distribution curve) and a standard deviation (a measure of variability in a group of numerical values). In developing a control chart, the upper and lower limits are defined by the degree of deviation you're willing to accept. In a normal distribution (which we know a sampling distribution becomes more like, as the size of the sample increases), approximately 68 percent of a set of values will fall between a +1 and –1 standard deviation from the mean. Ninety-five percent will fall in the range of +2 and –2 standard deviations. In a typical operations setting, the limits are set at 3 standard deviations, which means that 99.7 percent of the mean (or average) values should lie between the control limits. (See Figure 19-5.) What happens when variations occur? What should a manager do at that point? When a sample average falls outside these limits—that is, above the upper control limit or below the lower limit—the process is very likely out of control. The manager should then initiate a search for the cause of the problem.

EOQ Model

As we pointed out in the last chapter, controlling inventory is one of the important managerial tasks associated with operations control. Since the organization typically has a large dollar investment in inventory, managers want to know the appropriate amount of inventory to order and how often to order. That's what the EOQ model does.

economic order quantity (EOQ) model
A technique for balancing purchase, ordering, carrying, and stockout costs to derive the optimum quantity for a purchase order.

One of the best-known techniques for mathematically deriving the optimum quantity for a purchase order is the **economic order quantity model (EOQ).** The EOQ model seeks to balance four costs associated with ordering and carrying inventory: the *purchase costs* (purchase price plus delivery charges minus any discounts); the *ordering costs* (paperwork, follow-up, inspection on arrival, and other processing costs); *carrying costs* (money tied up in inventory, storage, insurance, taxes, and so forth); and *stockout costs* (profits forgone from orders lost because the product wasn't available, the cost of re-establishing goodwill, and additional expenses incurred to expedite late shipments).

The objective of the EOQ model, as shown in Figure 19-6, is to minimize the total costs of two of these four costs—carrying costs and ordering costs. As the amount ordered gets larger and larger, average inventory increases and so do carrying costs. But placing larger orders

FIGURE 19-5 Control Chart Using Three Standard Deviations as Limits

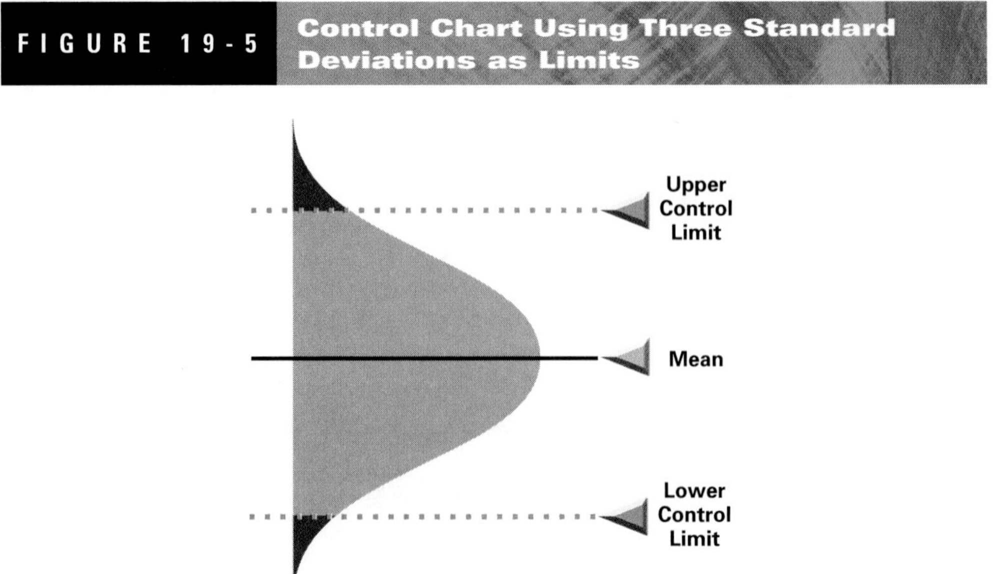

Source: Stephen P Robbins, *Supervision Today!* (Englewood Cliffs, NJ: Prentice-Hall, 1995), p. 152.

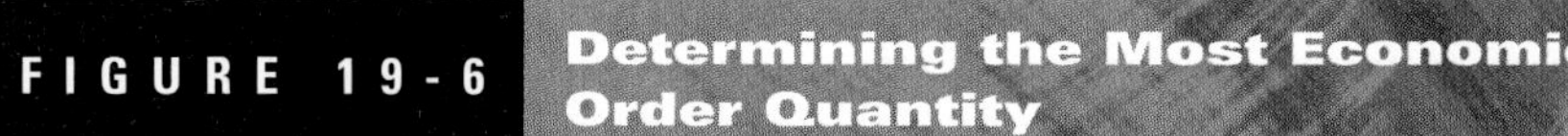

FIGURE 19-6 Determining the Most Economic Order Quantity

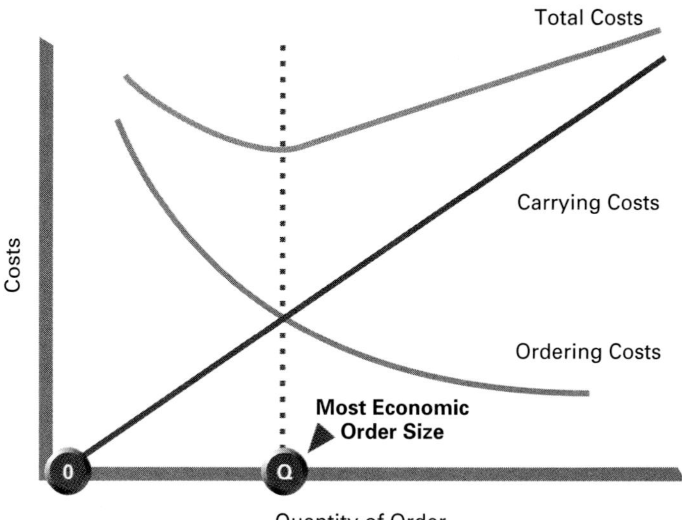

means placing fewer orders, thus reducing ordering costs. For example, if annual demand for an inventory item is 26 000 units, and we order 500 each time, we'll place 52 (26 000/500) orders per year. This gives us an average inventory of 250 (500/2) units. However, if the order quantity is increased to 2 000 units, there'll be fewer orders placed—only 13 (26 000/2 000)—but the average inventory on hand will increase to 1000 (2000/2) units. Thus, as holding costs go up, ordering costs go down, and vice versa. As shown in Figure 19-6, the lowest total cost—and thus the most economic order quantity—is reached at the lowest point on the total cost curve. That's the point at which ordering costs equal carrying costs—the *economic order quantity*.

To compute this optimal order quantity, you need the following data: forecast demand for the item during the period (*D*), the cost of placing each order (*OC*), the value or purchase price of the item (*V*), and the carrying cost of maintaining the total inventory expressed as a percentage (*CC*). We can now present the standard EOQ formula and demonstrate its use:

$$\text{EOQ} = \sqrt{\frac{2 \times D \times OC}{V \times CC}}$$

Take, for example, Playback Electronics—a retailer of high-quality sound and video equipment—which is trying to determine its economic order quantities. The item in question is a Yamaha compact sound system. The company forecasts sales of 4000 units a year. The purchasing manager believes that the cost of each system will be \$500. The accountants estimate the cost of placing an order for the sound system at \$75 per order and annual insurance, taxes, and other carrying costs at 20 percent of the system's value. Using the EOQ formula and the preceding information, we find:

$$\text{EOQ} = \sqrt{\frac{2 \times 4000 \times 75}{500 \times 0.20}}$$

$$\text{EOQ} = \sqrt{6000}$$

$$\text{EOQ} = 77.45 \text{ units} \cong @\ 78 \text{ units}$$

The inventory model suggests to Playback's management that it's most economic to order in quantities or lots of approximately 78 units. Stated differently, Playback should order about 52 (4000/78) times a year.

However, what would happen if the supplier Yamaha offered Playback a 5 percent discount on purchases, if Playback buys in minimum quantities of 120 units? Should Playback's management now purchase in quantities of 78 or 120? Without the discount, and therefore ordering 78 each time, Playback's annual costs for this sound system would be as follows:

Purchase cost:	$500 × 4 000 =	$2 000 000
Carrying cost (average inventory units × value of item × percentage):	78/2 × $500 × 0.20 =	3 900
Ordering cost (number of orders × cost to place order):	52 × 75 =	3 900
Total cost:	=	$2 007 800

With the 5 percent discount for ordering 120 units, the item cost would be $475. The annual inventory costs would be as follows:

Purchase cost:	$475 × 4 000 =	$1 900 000
Carrying cost:	120/2 × 475 × .20 =	5 700
Ordering cost:	4 000/120 × 75 =	2 500
Total cost:	=	$1 908 200

These computations suggest to Playback's management that it should take the 5 percent discount. Even though it now has to stock larger quantities, the annual savings amount to almost $100 000.

A word of caution should be added. The EOQ model assumes that demand and lead time are known and constant. If these conditions can't be met, the model shouldn't be used. For example, it generally shouldn't be used for manufactured component inventory because the components are taken out of stock all at once, or in lumps or odd lots rather than at a constant rate. Does this mean that the EOQ model is useless when demand is variable? No. The model can still be of some use in demonstrating tradeoffs in costs and the need to control lot sizes. However, there are more sophisticated lot-sizing models for handling bulky demand and special situations.

BEHAVIOURAL CONTROLS

Managers accomplish goals by working with other people. To achieve their unit goals, managers need and depend on their employees. It's important, therefore, for managers to ensure that employees are performing as they're supposed to. Table 19-2 lists several behavioural control devices that managers have at their disposal. However, the most explicit ways in which managers control employee behaviour are by direct supervision, performance appraisals and discipline. Let's look closer at each of these behavioural control techniques.

Direct Supervision

On a day-to-day basis, managers oversee employees' work and correct problems as they occur. For instance, the supervisor who spots an employee taking an unnecessary risk when operating his or her equipment may point out the correct way to perform the task and tell the employee to do it the correct way in future.

We introduced the concept of MBWA (management by walking around) in Chapter 17 as a simple control technique that entrepreneurs could use. However, managers at every level of any organization can engage in MBWA to detect problems that employees might have, or to monitor employee work activities. Many practising managers admit that they learn a lot more by getting out of their offices and into the workplace than by sitting and reading subordinates'

4 Why are financial controls important?

5 How can managers use TQM control charts?

6 Describe the important variables in EOQ and how it is calculated.

TABLE 19-2 Behavioural Control Techniques

Selection. Appropriate behaviour is more likely when management identifies and hires people whose values, attitudes, and personality fit with what management desires.

Goals. When employees accept specific goals, the goals then direct and limit behaviour.

Job design. The way jobs are designed determines, to a large degree, the tasks that a person does, the pace of the work, the people with whom he or she interacts, and similar activities.

Orientation. New-employee orientation defines which behaviours are acceptable and which aren't.

Direct supervision. The physical presence of supervisors acts to constrain employee behaviour and allows for rapid detection of deviant behaviour.

Training. Formal training programs teach employees desired work practices.

Mentoring. Informal and formal mentoring activities by senior employees convey to junior employees "the ropes to skip and the ropes to know".

Formalization. Formal rules, policies, job descriptions and other regulations define acceptable practices and constrain behaviour.

Performance appraisals. Employees will behave in such a way as to look good on the criteria by which they will be appraised.

Organizational rewards. Rewards act as reinforcers to encourage desired behaviours and to extinguish undesirable ones.

Organizational culture. Through stories, rituals, and top management practices, culture conveys what constitutes proper behaviour.

Discipline. Actions taken by managers that enforce the organization's standards and regulations.

reports or by having formal meetings. The close and direct contact between supervisor and subordinates that's possible with MBWA, can prevent many minor behavioural problems from becoming serious.

performance appraisal
The evaluation of an individual's work performance in order to arrive at objective human resource decisions.

Performance Appraisal

However, managers also assess their employees' work in a more formal way by means of systematic performance appraisals. A **performance appraisal** is a process of evaluating individuals in order to arrive at objective human resource decisions. Although organizations use formal employee performance appraisals for a number of reasons, one of their most important functions is to control employee behaviour. Since performance appraisals play such a significant role in behaviour control, we need to look at the different methods that managers can use. The following discussion reviews the major performance appraisal methods and looks at how feedback should be provided in the appraisal review.[18]

written essay
A performance appraisal technique in which an evaluator writes out a description of an employee's strengths, weaknesses, past performance and potential, and then makes suggestions for improvement.

Written Essays. Probably the simplest method of appraisal is to write a narrative describing an employee's strengths, weaknesses, past performance and potential, and then to provide suggestions for improvement. The **written essay** requires no complex forms or extensive training to complete. However, a "good" or "bad" appraisal may be determined as much by the evaluator's writing skill as by the employee's actual level of performance.

critical incidents
A performance appraisal technique in which an evaluator lists key behaviours that separate effective from ineffective job performance.

Critical Incidents. The use of **critical incidents** focuses the evaluator's attention on those critical or key behaviours that separate effective from ineffective job performance. The appraiser writes down little anecdotes that describe what the employee did that was especially effective or ineffective. The key here is that only specific behaviours are cited, not vaguely defined personality traits. A list of critical incidents for a given employee provides a rich set of examples that the manager can use to point out desirable and undesirable behaviours to the employee.

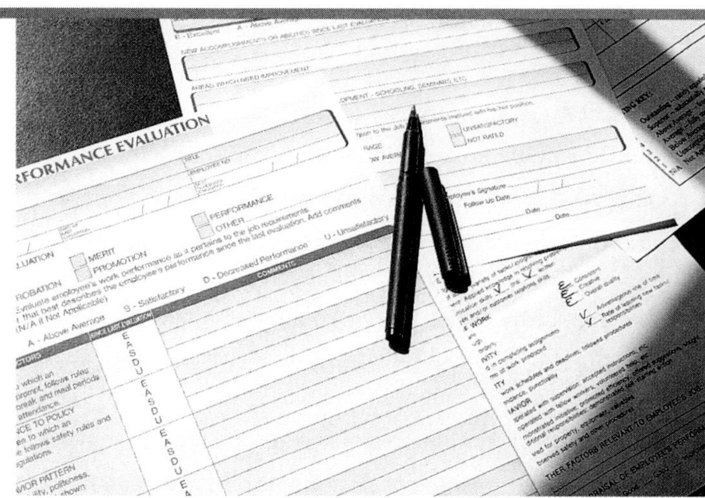

Performance evaluation forms question many different work habits, from consistency and co-operation to creativity.

graphic rating scales
A performance appraisal technique in which an evaluator rates a set of performance factors on an incremental scale.

Graphic Rating Scales. One of the oldest and most popular methods of appraisal is **graphic rating scales**. This method lists a set of performance factors such as quantity and quality of work, job knowledge, co-operation, loyalty, attendance, honesty and initiative. The evaluator then goes down the list and rates each on an incremental scale. The scales typically specify five points—for instance, a factor such as job knowledge might be rated from 1 ("poorly informed about work duties") to 5 ("has complete control of all phases of the job").

Why are graphic rating scales so popular? Although they don't provide the depth of information that essays or critical incidents do, they're less time consuming to develop and administer. They also allow for quantitative analysis and comparison.

behaviourally anchored rating scales (BARS)
A performance appraisal technique in which an evaluator rates employees on specific job behaviours derived from performance dimensions.

Behaviourally Anchored Rating Scales. An approach that's received a great deal of attention in recent years involves **behaviourally anchored rating scales (BARS)**.[19] These scales combine major elements from the critical incident and graphic rating scale approaches. The appraiser rates an employee according to items along a numerical scale, but the items are examples of actual behaviour on a given job, rather than general descriptions or traits.

Behaviourally anchored rating scales focus on specific and measurable job *behaviours*. Key elements of jobs are broken down into performance dimensions, and then specific illustrations of effective and ineffective behaviours are identified for each performance dimension. The result is behavioural descriptions such as "anticipates", "plans", "executes", "solves immediate problems", "carries out orders" and "handles emergency situations". So, for example, a manager might rate one of her subordinate supervisors on a 5-point scale of 0 (almost never) to 4 (almost always), for statements such as "Distributes overtime equally taking seniority into account" or "Tells workers if they have questions or problems to feel free to come and talk to him or her".

multiperson comparisons
A performance appraisal technique in which individuals are compared to one another.

Multiperson Comparison. **Multiperson comparisons** compare one individual's performance to those of one or more others. It's a relative, not an absolute, measuring device. The three most popular uses of this method are group order rankings, individual rankings, and paired comparisons.

group order ranking
A performance appraisal approach that groups employees into ordered classifications.

The **group order ranking** requires the evaluator to place employees into a particular classification such as "top one-fifth" or "second one-fifth". This method is often used in recommending a student for graduate school admission. Evaluators are asked to rank the student in the top 5 percent, the next 5 percent, the next 15 percent, and so on. When this method is used to appraise employees, managers rank all their subordinates. If a rater has 20 subordinates, only 4 can be in the top fifth and, of course, this means that 4 must be assigned to the bottom fifth.

individual ranking
A performance appraisal approach that ranks employees in order from highest to lowest.

The **individual ranking** approach requires the evaluator merely to list the employees in order from highest to lowest. Only one can be "best" or "number one". In an appraisal of 30 employees, the difference between the first and second employee is assumed to be the same as that between the twenty-first and twenty-second. Even though some employees may be closely grouped with respect to their performance levels, there can be no ties.

In the **paired comparison** approach, each employee is compared to every other employee in the comparison group, and rated as either the superior or weaker member of the pair. After all paired comparisons are made, each employee is assigned a summary ranking based on the number of superior scores he or she received. While this approach ensures that each employee is compared against every other, it can become cumbersome when large numbers of employees are being assessed.

paired comparison
A performance appraisal approach in which each employee is compared to every other employee, and rated as either the superior or weaker member of the pair.

Multiperson comparisons can be combined with other methods to yield a blend of the best from both absolute and relative standards. For example, a college could use the graphic rating scale and the individual ranking methods to provide more accurate information about its students' performance levels. An absolute grade (*A, B, C, D* or *F*) could be assigned, and a student's relative rank in a class ascertained. A prospective employer or graduate school admissions committee could then look at two students who each got a *B* in financial accounting and draw considerably different conclusions about each when, next to one grade, it says, "ranked fourth out of twenty-six" and, next to the other, it says, "ranked seventeenth out of thirty".

Objectives. We previously introduced management by objectives (MBO) in our discussion on planning. MBO, however, is also a mechanism for appraising performance. In fact, it's the preferred method for assessing managers and professional employees.[20]

With MBO, employees are evaluated by how well they accomplish a specific set of objectives that have been determined to be crucial in the successful completion of their jobs. As you'll remember from our discussion in Chapter 7, these objectives need to be tangible, verifiable, and measurable.

MBO's popularity for assessing managers is probably due to its focus on end goals. Managers tend to emphasize such results-oriented outcomes as profit, sales, and costs. This emphasis aligns with MBO's concern with quantitative measures of performance. Because MBO emphasizes ends rather than means, this appraisal method allows managers the discretion to choose the best ways in which to achieve their goals.

New Approaches to Performance Appraisal. Some companies are experimenting with different approaches to appraising employees' performance.[21] For instance, at Hoffmann-La Roche Inc., the Swiss pharmaceutical maker, all the managers and subordinates sit down in January and negotiate a performance plan that's tied to the company's strategic priorities. Then managers are required to hold a formal performance review with their subordinates twice a year, and hold informal "coaching" sessions every quarter. Other companies, like Ceridian Corporation and Wisconsin Power & Light Company, are dropping routine performance appraisals for everyone except poor performers.

The most rapidly growing innovation in performance appraisal is something called **360 degree feedback**, which is a performance appraisal review that uses feedback from supervisors, subordinates and co-workers. In other words, this type of review uses information from the full circle of people with whom the manager interacts. Companies like Alcoa, Pitney Bowes, Nestlé's Perrier division, Du Pont, Levi Strauss, and UPS are using this innovative approach. But users of this approach caution that, while it's effective for career coaching and helping a manager to recognize his or her strengths and weaknesses, it's not appropriate for determining pay, promotions or terminations.

360 degree feedback
A performance appraisal review that uses feedback from supervisors, subordinates and co-workers—the full circle of people with whom the manager interacts.

What are the benefits and drawbacks to these full-circle reviews?[22] One advantage is that it provides a more comprehensive perspective of an employee's performance. By soliciting information from all the individuals a person interacts with in his or her normal work activities, a broader and more complete picture of that person's performance can be obtained. This in turn, increases the credibility of an employee's performance appraisal, since it's less likely to be overly biased either positively or negatively, which is another benefit. Lastly, an advantage of 360 degree appraisal is that the feedback provided can enhance an employee's individual self-development. It permits an employee to compare his or her own perceptions with the perceptions that others have of his or her skills, styles, and performance.

Du Pont Canada Inc.
www.dupont.ca

But there are also drawbacks to the process. It's very time consuming and complex to administer. Collecting and compiling information from a number of sources takes more time than when only one person does the evaluation. Also, some employees aren't comfortable providing feedback on their supervisors. Overcoming some of these fears and reluctance to change may require extensive employee training and change efforts within those organizations that are changing to 360 degree feedback techniques.

Providing Feedback in the Appraisal Review. Many managers are reluctant to give a formal performance appraisal review for each employee. Why? Probably the two main reasons are that (1) they lack complete confidence in the appraisal method used, and (2) they fear a confrontation with the employee, or an unpleasant reaction from him or her if the results aren't overwhelmingly positive. Nevertheless, managers should conduct such reviews because they're the primary means by which employees get feedback on their performance, and from which they can then make adjustments to their work methods or habits.

An effective review—in which the employee perceives the appraisal as fair, the manager as sincere, and the climate as constructive—is likely to result in the employee leaving the interview in an enthusiastic mood, informed about the performance areas in which he or she needs to improve, and determined to correct the deficiencies. Unfortunately, this isn't the way it usually happens.

The problem is that performance appraisal reviews have a built-in barrier. Statistically speaking, half of all employees must be below-average performers. But evidence shows us that the *average* employee's estimate of his or her own performance level generally falls around the seventy-fifth percentile.[23] In other words, employees tend to have inflated assessments of their own performances. Any good news that the manager does convey may be perceived as not being good enough. Here are six specific suggestions on providing effective feedback: focus on specific behaviours, keep the feedback impersonal, keep the feedback goal oriented, make the feedback well timed, ensure understanding, and direct negative feedback towards behaviour that the recipient can control.

Performance Appraisal in Other Countries. Formal performance appraisals, particularly of managers, are quite common around the globe.[24] But, there are some exceptions. For instance, in Sweden and China, formal performance appraisal systems aren't commonly used. In countries where performance appraisal *is* an accepted practice, a wide variety of techniques are used. In Germany, for example, organizations prefer to use quantitative instruments. In countries such as Japan, China and South Korea, where saving face is an important cultural value, more informal or indirect ways are used to provide feedback. Israeli companies, like Canadian ones, use a number of different techniques, including trait, behavioural, and MBO systems. However, in countries like Poland and the Commonwealth of Independent States, where organizations are adapting to a free-market philosophy, performance appraisal still tends to be tied to personal traits and bureaucratic measures.

Discipline

discipline
Actions taken by a manager to enforce the organization's standards and regulations.

"hot stove" rule
Discipline should immediately follow an infraction, provide ample warning, be consistent, and be impersonal.

When an employee's performance regularly isn't up to par or when an employee consistently ignores the organization's standards and regulations, the manager may have to use discipline as a way to control behaviour. What specifically do we mean when we use the term **discipline**? The term refers to actions taken by a manager to enforce the organization's standards and regulations. Table 19-3 lists the most common types of behavioural problems for which discipline is used as a controlling and corrective measure. But knowing *what* managers discipline isn't enough. We also need to look at *how* managers can discipline employees effectively.

The "Hot Stove" Rule of Discipline. The **"hot stove" rule** is a frequently cited set of principles that can guide you in effectively disciplining an employee.[25] The name comes from the similarities between touching a hot stove and receiving discipline. Both are painful, but the

7 What behavioural controls can a manager use?

8 How could a manager use direct supervision as a way to control behaviour?

9 Contrast the advantages and disadvantages of the following performance appraisal techniques: written essays; critical incidents; graphic rating scales; BARS; multiperson comparisons; MBO; and 360 degree feedback.

TABLE 19-3 Types of Discipline Problems and Examples of Each

Attendance	Absenteeism, tardiness, abuse of sick leave
On-the-Job Behaviours	Insubordination, abuse of alcohol, drug abuse, or failure to use safety devices
Dishonesty	Theft, lying to superiors, falsifying information on employment applications
Outside Activities	Working for a competing organization, criminal activities, unauthorized strike activities

analogy goes further. When you touch a hot stove, you get an *immediate* response. The burn you receive is instantaneous, leaving no doubt in your mind about the relation between cause and effect. You have ample *warning*. You know what happens if you touch a hot stove. Furthermore, the result is *consistent*. Every time you touch a hot stove, you get the same result—you get burned. Finally, the result is *impersonal*. Regardless of who you are, if you touch a hot stove, you will get burned.

The analogy with discipline should be apparent, but let's briefly expand on each of these four points, since they're central ideas in developing your disciplining skills.

1. *Immediacy.* The effectiveness of a disciplinary action will be reduced as the time between the infraction and the penalty lengthens. The more quickly the discipline follows the offence, the more likely it is that the employee will associate the discipline with the offence, rather than with you as the dispenser of the discipline. Therefore, it's best to begin the disciplinary process as soon as possible after you notice a violation. Of course, the immediacy requirement shouldn't result in undue haste. Fair and objective treatment shouldn't be compromised for expediency.

2. *Advance warning.* As a manager, you have an obligation to give advance warning before initiating disciplinary action. This means that the employee *must* be aware of the organization's rules and accept its standards of behaviour. Disciplinary action is more likely to be interpreted by employees as fair when they've received clear warning that a given violation will lead to discipline, and when they know what that discipline will be.

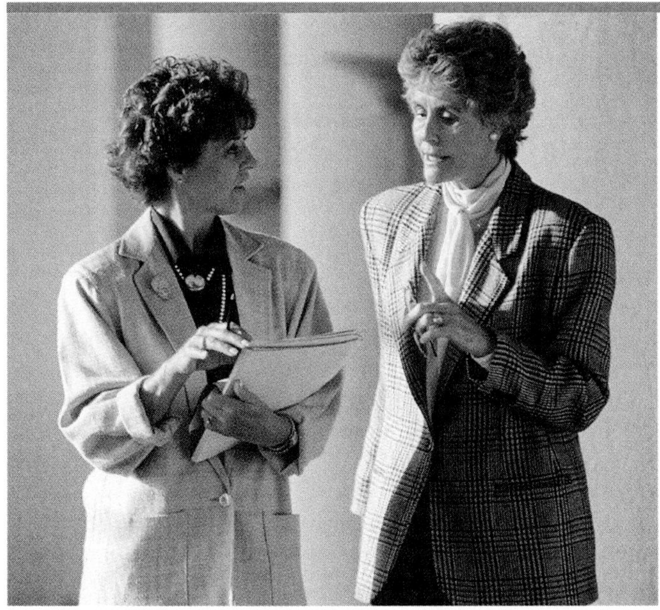

Effective discipline punishes the violation, not the employee, and skilled managers are able to administer appropriate discipline and move on, without allowing uncomfortable feelings to linger in the work relationship.

3. *Consistency.* Fair treatment of employees demands that disciplinary action be consistent. If you enforce rule violations in an inconsistent manner, the rules will lose their impact, morale will decline, and employees will question your competence. Productivity will suffer as a result of employee insecurity and anxiety. Your employees will want to know the limits of permissible behaviour, and they'll look to your actions for guidance. Consistency, by the way, need not result in treating everyone exactly alike, because that ignores mitigating circumstances. It does, however, put the responsibility on you to clearly justify disciplinary actions that might appear inconsistent to employees.

4. *Impersonal nature.* The last guideline that flows from the "hot stove" rule is to keep the discipline impersonal. Penalties should be connected with a given violation, not with the personality of the individual violator. That is, discipline should be directed at what the employee has done, not at the employee. You're penalizing the rule violation, not the individual. Once the penalty has been imposed, you must make every effort to forget the incident and attempt to treat the employee just as you did before the problem occurred.

More Serious Employee Behaviour Problems. As a manager, you may find, at some point in your career, that you have to deal with more serious employee behavioural problems, such as alcohol and drug abuse. Employee substance abuse problems can have significant negative consequences for both the organization and the individuals involved. For instance, one survey found that US businesses lose around \$60 billion to \$90 billion annually, due to employee substance abuse.[26] So what are companies doing to minimize the workplace disruptions and job performance problems that result when employees abuse alcohol or drugs?

One tactic that many companies are using is drug tests of both current employees and job candidates. For instance, one US study found that close to 90 percent of the workplaces surveyed tested their workers for drug use.[27] Practice is more divided in Canada, where drug testing is still controversial. As Burlington Northern Railroad managers discovered, a drug testing program by itself isn't enough to reduce problems of employee drug abuse.[28] BN's comprehensive substance abuse program includes—in addition to a drug testing program—supervisory training, an employee assistance program, and community safety awareness programs. An employee drug testing program can't be implemented indiscriminately, however. Legal experts caution organizations that use employee drug testing to plan the program carefully, implement it consistently, and enforce it uniformly.[29] Otherwise, the organization could be a target for employee lawsuits, such as the one Imperial Oil recently faced.

Another approach to dealing with serious employee behavioural problems that's becoming quite popular is the use of **employee assistance programs (EAPs)**. These are company-sponsored programs whose goal is to help employees adjust to, and overcome, personal problems that are adversely affecting their workplace performance.[30] Usually, these programs are designed so that supervisors can refer workers to company EAP counsellors or outside counsellors, who help employees pinpoint problems and arrange for help. In most EAPs, employees can also contact the counsellors themselves. Although alcohol and drug abuse are the major problems that EAP counsellors deal with, many also provide assistance for a broad range of employee problems such as stress management, weight control, financial counselling, legal counselling, smoking cessation, or any other personal issues that create difficulties for employees. These programs are one more way in which organizations are investing in their most important resource—their employees.

employee assistance programs (EAPs)
Company-sponsored programs whose goal is to help employees adjust to, and overcome, personal problems that are adversely affecting their workplace performance.

Substitutes for Direct Control

Although managers can, and do, use the direct forms of behavioural control that we've just described (direct supervision, performance appraisal and discipline) to ensure that their employees' actual work performance meets some performance standard, there are other organizational factors that act as substitutes for these direct controls. These subtle but powerful indirect organizational control mechanisms include the selection process, organizational culture, degree of formalization, and employee training.[31]

Selection Process. As we discussed in Chapter 11, managers don't choose employees at random. Job applicants are processed through a series of selection devices in order to differentiate those individuals who are likely to be successful job performers from those who aren't likely to be successful. An effective selection process should be designed to determine whether job candidates "fit" into the organization. The term *fit* in this situation implies not only the ability to do the job, but also the personality, values, work habits, and attitudes that the organization desires. The selection process, therefore, screens out people who don't have the ability to do the job and prevents the employment of "misfits". As such, selection is one of the most widely used techniques by which management can indirectly control employee behaviour.

Organizational Culture. The more that employees accept and are committed to the values and norms of the organization's culture, the greater the likelihood that their behaviour will conform to what management desires. Organizational culture, to the degree it's accepted by employees, acts to constrain and control their behaviour. Since employees who don't accept the organization's culture aren't likely to stay employed there long, culture plays a significant role in controlling and influencing the behaviour of all continuing employees. Thus, management can indirectly control employee behaviour through the culture it creates and supports.

Degree of Formalization. Management provides most employees with a job description to clarify what their job encompasses, to whom they're responsible, and what is and isn't within their authority. This document formalizes behaviour and, of course, also controls behaviour. Since employees modify their behaviour to align with their job description, it acts as a control device. Furthermore, since management develops and defines each individual job description, they can assert indirect behavioural control through it.

But the job description isn't the only dimension of formalization that acts as a constraint on employee behaviour. An organization's rules, procedures and policies are other formalized controls. Each serves to guide, direct and control an employee's work activities.

Employee Training. When management trains employees, the intention is to instill preferred work behaviours and attitudes. This is probably most obvious during new employee orientation, which is a type of training. During orientation, employees are often exposed to the organization's history, objectives, philosophy and rules. In many cases, this is then followed by specific job training. Although this training helps the employee to adjust more readily to his or her new job, it also serves to mould and indirectly control the employee's behaviour.

10 Describe the "hot stove" rule of discipline.

11 Why might an organization need employee assistance programs?

12 How do managers use indirect behavioural controls?

SUMMARY

This summary is organized by the learning objectives at the beginning of the chapter.

1. The purpose of a management information system is to provide managers with accurate and current information for decision making and control.
2. Data are raw, unanalyzed facts. Information is data that have been organized into a usable form.
3. The key elements in designing an MIS include analyzing the decision system, analyzing information requirements, aggregating the decisions, and developing the actual information-processing capability.
4. An MIS changes the manager's job in the following ways: managers have more hands-on involvement, their decision-making capability is improved, organizational structures are becoming flatter and more organic, and the power that's inherent in having access to information is shifting.
5. Budgets provide managers with quantitative standards against which to measure and compare resource consumption. By pointing out deviations between standard and actual consumption, they serve as control tools.
6. The liquidity ratios measure an organization's ability to meet its current debt obligations. Leverage ratios examine the organization's use of debt to finance its assets, and whether it's able to meet its interest payments on debt. The operations ratios measure how efficiently the firm is using its assets. Finally, the profitability ratios measure how efficiently and effectively the firm is using its assets to generate profits.
7. TQM control charts are a management control tool designed to show results of measurements over a period of time, with statistically determined upper and lower limits. They provide a visual means of determining whether a specific process is staying within predefined limits.
8. The economic order quantity model balances the costs of ordering and carrying inventory. To calculate the optimal order quantity, you need to know the forecast demand for an item during a specific period, the cost of placing each order, the value or purchase price of the item, and the carrying cost of maintaining the total inventory.
9. Six performance appraisal methods are (a) written essays (written descriptions of an employee's strengths, weaknesses, past performance, potential, and areas in need of improvement); (b) critical incidents (lists of key behaviours that separate effective from ineffective job performance); (c) graphic rating scales (ratings of performance factors on an incremental scale); (d) BARS (rating employees on specific job behaviours derived from performance dimensions of the job); (e) multiperson comparisons (comparing individual employees against one another); and (f) objectives (evaluating employees against tangible, verifiable, and measurable objectives).
10. The four organizational factors that serve as indirect behavioural controls are the employee selection process, organizational culture, degree of organizational formalization, and employee training.

THINKING ABOUT MANAGEMENT ISSUES

1. In what ways might the functional area in which a manager works (for example, production, sales, or accounting) affect the emphasis he or she places on information, operations, financial, and behavioural controls?
2. Describe how you might design a performance evaluation system that would minimize the dysfunctional aspects of the behavioural control devices.
3. In what ways is information a unique resource for organizations? Give examples.
4. Does the use of an MIS empower all employees, all managers, or only top managers? Discuss.
5. Which do you think is more important for success in organizations—quality control or total quality management? Support your position.

SELF-ASSESSMENT EXERCISE

HOW INTERNET LITERATE ARE YOU?

The increasing use of the Internet by businesses and by individuals has spawned a whole new terminology. For instance, in 'Net lingo, "flame" has nothing to do with fire and a "server" is not someone who brings you food in a restaurant. Just how Internet literate are you? This self-assessment exercise tests your knowledge of Internet terminology. Match the terms with their correct definitions.

Internet Terms:

a. Browser
b. Bookmark
c. Domain
d. Dot
e. Download
f. Emoticon
g. FAQ
h. Flame
i. Home page
j. HTTP
k. Netiquette
l. Newsgroup
m. ROTFL
n. Spam
o. WWW

_____ **1.** Specific ways to act with people over the Internet; common-sense guidelines people follow in order not to disrupt or annoy other users.
_____ **2.** Often referred to as a period, this is what separates parts of an Internet address.
_____ **3.** Ranting and raving at someone who said something offensive.
_____ **4.** Messages sent out over the Internet to try and sell products or to get people's attention; also known as electronic junk mail.
_____ **5.** Stands for hypertext transfer protocol; the way Web pages are passed to the browser.
_____ **6.** Otherwise known as the World Wide Web.
_____ **7.** The last part of an address, such as .com or .edu.
_____ **8.** The first page of a Website and a starting point for Web users.
_____ **9.** An abbreviation often used in e-mail messages and chat rooms when someone says something humorous.
_____ **10.** A way to show your feelings about something someone wrote. For instance, :-).
_____ **11.** A Usenet conference or discussion forum.
_____ **12.** Many server providers have these files posted for beginners to answer commonly asked questions.
_____ **13.** A browser function that allows a user to save frequently used Web sites so they are easier to locate at a later time.
_____ **14.** Copying a host file to a personal computer to view it.
_____ **15.** A program used to view the World Wide Web.

For scoring information, turn to page SK–5.

for your IMMEDIATE action

COMPTON HILLS CLASSICS
Specializing in Quality Historical and Classical Literature
HARTFORD NEW JERSEY

To: Jack Manganella,
Director of Human Resources
From: Daniel Tran,
Vice President of Administration

As we've discussed several times previously, the rapid growth of our company has brought positive benefits as well as some areas of concern. One of the things that I'm most concerned about is whether or not we're doing all we can, as a socially responsible employer, to assist our employees with personal problems that might be negatively affecting their work performance.

While I was catching up on my reading last night at home, I ran across a reference to something called "employee assistance programs" (EAPs). Maybe there's something in this topic that we can develop for our employees. I'd like you to do some research on EAPs and write up a report that you can present at our next executive council meeting. Keep your report short—under two typed pages. Focus on the most current references you can find and address these points: (1) What are employee assistance programs? (2) What are the advantages and disadvantages of these types of programs? and (3) What do we need to know to implement one successfully?

This is a fictionalized account of a potentially real management problem. It is meant for academic purposes and is not meant to reflect either positively or negatively on management practices at Compton Hill Classics.

TAKE IT TO THE NET

We invite you to visit the Robbins/Coulter/Stuart-Kotze Companion Website at www.prenticehall.ca/robbins for this chapter's Internet resources.

CASE APPLICATION

Discovery Zone

Discovery Zone is a North-America-wide company operating indoor playgrounds. The original idea behind Discovery Zone was that stressed-out parents would gladly pay to take their energetic kids to a clean, safe, indoor play area filled with games, climbing areas and mazes—particularly on rainy days (perfect for a market like Vancouver). The original idea was developed by a gymnastics coach named Ronald Matsch, who sold the company to an owner of several Blockbuster video store franchises, as well as a minority stake to Blockbuster itself. The new owners' growth strategy was simple: apply the Blockbuster approach to indoor playgrounds. This involved rapidly opening new units, which cost about $600 000 apiece to equip while, at the same time, purchasing competitors to become the biggest player in the industry. The original franchises were bought back by Discovery Zone, in order to tighten control. Within 3 years, more than 300 Discovery Zone locations had been set up.

However, the owners soon found that managing Discovery Zones was a lot tougher than running a video store. Indoor playgrounds—filled with energetic, sweaty, and very active kids—get a lot dirtier, a lot faster, than video stores. They require significantly more maintenance and service. In location after location, other problems cropped up. Broken games stayed broken for days, frustrating the kids. Many locations stopped selling candy because most of it wound up being stolen, due to lax controls. Poor supervision by employees resulted in some kids wandering away by themselves off of the premises. The Discovery Zone had so many basic operational problems that it was losing $21 million on revenues of $163 million. Mounting losses led to the company's default on $100 million in bank debt. Eventually, the company filed for Chapter 11 bankruptcy in the US.

At that time, Donna Moore, who had launched and managed Walt Disney Company's chain of retail stores during the 1980s, was brought in as CEO. She immediately recognized that the company's basic operations had to be fixed in order to rectify the financial problems. She says, "When you're dealing with children, you learn that the experience can never be fixed afterwards. We cannot redo a birthday party. You can refund it, but the parents will never forgive you, nor will the child. This is about getting it right the first time."

QUESTIONS

1. What types of information might the following managers at Discovery Zone need: (a) the CEO, Donna Moore; (b) the manager of a local Discovery Zone; and (c) the company's vice president of marketing?
2. What would a company-wide management information system for Discovery Zone need to include? What are the implications for designing an appropriate MIS?
3. What types of behavioural controls would be needed at a local Discovery Zone? Support your choices.
4. Overly rapid growth has caused many companies to stumble. What types of controls would be important for a company that is growing rapidly? Explain.

Source: L Gubernick, "Disaster Zone", *Forbes,* June 17, 1996, pp. 66–75; and company information obtained from Compustat.

VIDEO CASE APPLICATION

Canadian Manufacturing

There is no doubt that the retail industry in Canada has been undergoing vast and rapid change during the past decade. Spearheaded by the super-efficient operating techniques of Wal-Mart—who first devoured the retail industry in the US and who has now moved into Canada—the changes have led to the demise of several Canadian retailers. When Eatons filed for bankruptcy protection in 1997, it was frighteningly apparent that even such a giant of the Canadian retail world could fall prey to the revolution that had destroyed Consumers Distributing and Woolco. Being such a major purchaser, Wal-Mart can, and does, make strict demands on its suppliers. In the new Canadian retail environment, the rest of the big stores have followed this lead.

For manufacturers (as Diane Brisebois of the Retail Council of Canada suggests), this means "adapt or die". Customer satisfaction is essential when you only have a handful of possible organizations to sell to. The major retailers are taking full advantage of the fact that there are only half-a-dozen of them. For their own efficiency, the big retailers obviously gain by placing strict controls on their suppliers. Having manufacturers use the retailer's ordering software forges a strong link between retailers and their suppliers. The penalty system that was described in the video is a good example of how much power retailers have over manufacturers today.

For many manufacturers, this new way of doing business has bankrupted them. Others have managed to improve their operating efficiency to comply with the new demands. As Gerry Smith says in the video, "It has forced us to become efficient and to remove redundancies from our business". Manufacturers can no longer afford to be complacent in managing their operations.

QUESTIONS

1. In this "Venture" program, the reporter states that, "Orders come in demanding fast delivery, meaning manufacturers must keep huge stores of pricey inventory, ready to be shipped at a moment's notice". Do you think this is true? How could manufacturers avoid such a scenario?
2. How could TQM be an effective tool for manufacturers doing business with the major retailers?
3. Discuss how cost controls, purchasing controls, maintenance controls and quality controls could help manufacturers to remain profitable in this new environment.

Video source: "Manufacturers Squeezed," *Venture* #666 (October 28, 1997).

VIDEO CASE APPLICATION

Via Rail

Even a crown corporation has to strive for profitability, especially when they are providing what could be classified as a non-essential service. Since a large part of the passenger-rail industry in Canada has disappeared over the past few decades without much of a public protest, it could be said that if Via disappeared, many of us would not miss it. There are, of course, many arguments in favour of preserving a passenger rail service in this country, but when service is poor, availability is limited, *and* it is costing us large sums of our tax money to fund it, it is difficult to defend Via's existence. Herein lies the challenge facing Terry Ivany. With the federal government making cutbacks in spending virtually everywhere, Via is a prime target. Providing remote areas with access to the rest of the country is bound to be costly, but it is in the country's interests to support it. Is it in the country's interests to support Ivany's plans to move Via into the tourism business? Ivany must find ways to significantly reduce Via's burden on the government coffers, but obviously he faces many obstacles in turning Via into a viable business. Ivany wants a long-term commitment from the government, but this is somewhat unlikely considering Via's continual losses. The potential profitability of business in the Montreal-to-Toronto corridor is hampered by Via's subjugation by CN and CP. While these two companies control the tracks, Via are allowed only one trip per day in this lucrative corridor. As mentioned in the video, Via's trains are also often held up, because CN and CP trains take precedence. Estimates of $10 million-per-year losses in revenue from dissatisfied customers do not bode well for the company. Since customers' main concern is with trains being on time, Via is fighting a difficult battle for customer satisfaction.

Ivany wants new and faster trains in order to revitalize the company. As he says, "Eventually, because of the older equipment, reliability will deteriorate and customers will abandon us and we will wither on the vine". While Bombardier refuses to lease new trains without a long-term financing commitment from the government, and the government is hesitant to provide this commitment while Via's operations are so unprofitable, it seems that Via is caught in a catch-22 situation. The constraints imposed by CN and CP exacerbate the situation. Meanwhile, customers continue to give up on Via in the face of worsening service. The idea to create a "high end" tourism operation will undoubtedly meet with severe protest from the public sector, as Via will be seen to have an unfair advantage with its government funding. The future of Via is very uncertain. Ivany will have his work cut out for him in his attempts to create a sustainable business out of this crown corporation.

QUESTIONS

1. How might an MIS be used at Via? Explain your answer.
2. How useful would a TQM control chart be for Via? Explain.

Video source: "Staying on the Rails," *Venture* #685 (April 14, 1998).

Photo Credits

Chapter 1

p.xxx, Canapress/Frank Gunn; p.2, Canapress/Andre Forget; p.3, Courtesy Great Adventure People; p.8, Andrew Badia, Iris Hosiery Inc.; p.11, Courtesy Envirolutions Inc.

Chapter 2

p.22, Greg Pacek Photographer; p.24, Geoffrey Clifford/Woodfin Camp & Associates; p.26, The Bettmann Archive; p.28, The Bettmann Archive; p.31, W. Michael Brown, The Thomson Corporation; p.32, The Evening Telegram, St. John's Newfoundland; p.33, AT&T Archives (top), The Bettmann Archive (bottom); p.40, Courtesy of Elvie Paryano, Head Nurse, Day Surgery Centre, Montreal Children's Hospital

Chapter 3

p.50, Canapress/Toronto Star/Keith Beaty; p.53, Gulf Canada Resources Ltd.; p.57, Courtesy of Hollinger; p.58, Action Press/SABA Press Photos Inc.; p.66, Courtesy of PCI Construction; p.67, Al Harvey/The Slide Farm; p.68, Stewart Cohen/Tony Stone Images

Chapter 4

p.76, Paul Lawrence Photography; p.79, Canadian Press/Toronto Star/Andrew Stawicki; p.80, Courtesy of Maple Leaf Foods; p.85, Mitsuhiro Wasa/Gamma-Liaison, Inc.; p.87, Courtesy of Aloro Foods; p.89, Jim Brown/Offshoot Stock

Chapter 5

p.100, The Montreal Gazette/John Mahoney; p.104, Michael Abramson; p.110, Tom's of Maine; p.111, Image Network/Owen Broad; p.114, Courtesy of Nortel Networks; p.117, Marc Tamolty

Chapter 6

p.128, Spyros Bouroulis; p.132, Churchill & Klehr Photography; p.137, Graham Jones; p.140, Courtesy Antoine Paquin/Andre Balfour, Photographer; p.144, Greg Girard/Contact-Woodfin Camp & Associates; p.147, Berkeley Systems Inc.; p.149, Bill Horsman/Stock Boston Inc.; p.150, Sepp Seitz/Woodfin Camp & Associates

Chapter 7

p.158, Wescam Inc.; p.160, Wescana Energy; p.164, Geoff Gilpin; p.165, Courtesy of George Weston Ltd., photo by V. Tony Hauser © 1992; p.166, Mark Duncan/AP/Wide World Photos; p.169, PBJ Pictures/Gamma-Liaison, Inc.

Chapter 8

p.176, Furnald/Gray Photography; p.180, Bombardier Motor Company (top left), Canapress/AP Photo/Hans Edinger (top right), Canapress/AP Photo/Ou Neakiry (bottom right); p.182, Algonquin Productions; p.183, Jeff McIntosh/Canadian Press; p.189, CanadaWide (top), Canapress/AP Photo/Chris Martinez (bottom); p.191, Hewlett-Packard; p.195, Ed Quinn/SABA Press Photos, Inc. (top), Jeff Sciortino Photography (bottom); p.196, David Fields/Onyx

Chapter 9

p.202, Indigo Books, Music & Cafe; p.204, Courtesy of Poco Petroleum Ltd.; p.205, Bonnie Kamin; p.209; Robert Brenner/PhotoEdit; p.218, Willie Hill Jr./Stock Boston Inc.; p.219, Levere Photography

Chapter 10

p.228, Canapress/Paul Chiasson; p.231, James Schnepf Photography, Inc.; p.236, Holland Productions; p.238, Marko Shark; p.240, Courtesy of Merck Frost Canada Inc.; p.248, Tony Stone Images/Steven Peters

Chapter 11

p.256, Courtesy Husky Injection Mouldings Ltd.; p.262, Hewlett-Packard Corp.; p.266, Bonnie Kamin; p.268, Elena Dorfman/Offshoot Stock; p.271, Canapress/Maclean's Photo/Phill Snel; p.272 Ed Lallo/Gamma-Liaison, Inc.; p.276, Jim Cummins/FPG International; p.277, David Jolliffe

Chapter 12

p.284, Spyros Bouroulis Photographer; p.288, Acadian Seaplants Limited; p.290, Lara Del Pino/Federal Express; p.294, Canapress/Frank Gunn; p.298, Ko Ho Park/Kistone; p.299, Courtesy of Imperial Oil Limited; p. 302, Husky Wellness Centre; p.305, John Abbott Photography

Chapter 13

p.314, Canapress/Edmonton Sun/Brendon Dlouhy; p.317, Dick Hemingway; p.320, Stacy Pick/Stock Boston; p.322, Tony Stone Images/Ed Pritchards; p.329, Digital Renaissance; p.332, Tony Stone Images/J.P. Williams

Chapter 14

p.338, Tony Stone Images/Bruce Ando; p.342, Donald Stampfli/AP/Wide World Photos; p.345, Louis Psihoyos/Matrix International; p.352, Avcorp Industries Inc.; p.354, Robbie McClaren; p.356, George Lange/Outline Press Syndicate Inc.

Chapter 15

p.364, Teranet Land Information Services; p.372, Connaught Laboratories Limited; p.373, John Curtis/Offshoot Stock (top), Service Master (bottom); p.374, Teknion Furniture Systems; p.377, Kenneth Jarecke/Contact Press Images (all); p.383, Tony Stone Images/Tom Tracy; p.384, Cray Research Inc.; p.387, James Schnepf/Liaison (top), Price Waterhouse LLP (bottom); p.389, Raleigh Cycle Company

Chapter 16

p.396, Courtesy of Nortel Networks; p.401, Andy Freeberg; p.406, Robb Kendrick; p.414, Fisheries Products International Limited of St. John's Newfoundland; p.416, Nancy Pierce/Black Star

Chapter 17

p.426, Western Digital Corporation; p.429, RCMP-GRC/74-30A; p.431, Apple Computer Inc.; p.439, Dick Hemingway; p.442, Ed Lallo/Gamma-Liaison, Inc.

Chapter 18

p.448, Courtesy of MDS Laboratories; p.453, Richard Drew/AP/Wide World Photos; p.454, Torin Boyd; p.458, Courtesy LTV Corp.; p.463, Clearly Canadian Beverage Corporation; p.467, Courtesy of Standard Aero; p.471, Celestica Inc. 1996

Chapter 19

p.478, Canapress/Toronto Star/Keith Beaty; p.481, EDS Corporation; p.487, Apple Computer Inc.; p.495, Bruce Ayres/Tony Stone Images

Scoring Key

Chapter 1: Self-Perception Rating Scale

Complete Your Feedback Chart

This chart is easier to complete if you draw a horizontal line across it at the neutral value (4). Then plot your individual values. The chart is for your own information and will not be given to the instructor.

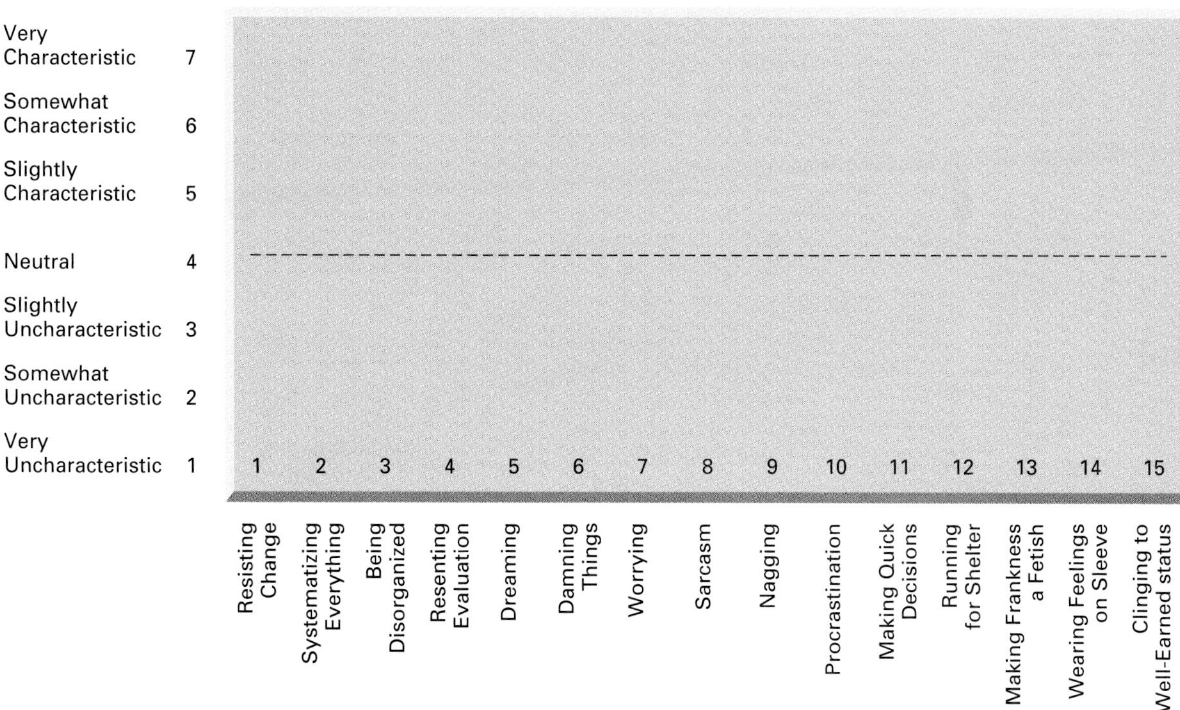

Chapter 2: Is a Bureaucracy for You?

Give yourself one point for each statement for which you responded in the bureaucratic direction:

1. Mostly agree
2. Mostly agree
3. Mostly disagree
4. Mostly agree
5. Mostly disagree
6. Mostly disagree
7. Mostly agree
8. Mostly agree
9. Mostly disagree
10. Mostly agree
11. Mostly agree
12. Mostly disagree
13. Mostly disagree
14. Mostly agree
15. Mostly disagree
16. Mostly agree
17. Mostly agree
18. Mostly agree
19. Mostly agree
20. Mostly disagree

A very high score (15 or over) suggests that you would enjoy working in a bureaucracy. A very low score (5 or lower) suggests that you would be frustrated by working in a bureaucracy, especially a large one.

Do you think your score is representative of most college students in your major? Discuss.

Chapter 3: What Kind of Organizational Culture Fits You Best?

For items 5, 6, 7, and 9, score as follows:

Strongly agree = +2
Agree = +1
Uncertain = 0
Disagree = –1
Strongly disagree = –2

For items 1, 2, 3, 4, 8, and 10, reverse the score (Strongly agree = –2, and so on). Add up your total. Your score will fall somewhere between +20 and –20.

What does your score mean? The higher your score (positive), the more comfortable you'll be in a formal, stable, rule-oriented, and structured culture. This is synonymous with large corporations in stable environments and government agencies. Negative scores indicate a preference for small, innovative, flexible, team-oriented cultures that are more likely to be found in research units or small businesses.

Chapter 4: What Are Your Cultural Attitudes?

Instructions:

Sum up items 1 through 5 and divide by 5. This is your mean *uncertainty avoidance* score.
Sum up items 6 through 10 and divide by 5. This is your mean *individualism-collectivism* score.
Sum up items 11 through 16 and divide by 6. This is your mean *power distance* score.
Sum up items 17 through 25 and divide by 9. This is your mean *masculinity-femininity* score.

The exercise should be interpreted on the basis of the mean scores, as follows:

1. *Uncertainty avoidance*—Defines the extent to which people in a culture feel threatened by uncertainty and ambiguous situations and try to avoid such situations. The higher the mean score (5 is the maximum mean score), the more likely the manager is to feel threatened in new cultures.
2. *Individualism-collectivism*—Individualism implies a loosely knit social framework in which people are supposed to take care of themselves (as opposed to collectivist cultures, characterized by "individual groups" that are expected to take care of their members). The higher the mean score, the more likely it is that a manager will be productive in a team or group environment.
3. *Power distance*—Defines the extent to which the less powerful person in a society accepts inequality in power and considers it normal. The higher the mean score, the more likely it is that a person will be power oriented and may have difficulty working in an environment where power is distributed among many individuals or groups. This type of person may even be manipulative and may overemphasize control.
4. *Quantity of life/Quality of life*—Defines the extent to which the dominant values of society emphasize materialism and competition or relationships and concern for the welfare of others. The higher the mean score, the more likely that "quantity of life" traits are dominant. In a country such as present-day Japan, a "quality of life" type may have trouble coping.

You can compare your scores with a sample of US and Mexican students to see how well you would embrace their cultures. The closer your mean score is to their mean scores, the greater the likelihood that you would mesh with their culture.

Dimension	US Students	Mexican Students
Uncertainty avoidance	3.41	4.15
Individualism-collectivism	2.19	3.33
Power distance	1.86	2.22
Quantity of life/Quality of life	2.78	2.75

Chapter 5: Attitudes Towards Business Ethics

Scoring Key and a Summary of the Differences Between Management and Liberal Arts Students

Item	Liberal Arts Students (*N* = 286) Mean	Management Students (*N* = 243) Mean
1	2.90	3.09
2	1.76	1.88
3	2.50	2.60
4	2.62	2.54
5	3.18	3.41
6	3.75	3.88
7	2.42	2.53
8	2.67	2.88
9	3.41	3.62
10	3.58	3.79
11	3.06	3.44
12	1.50	1.33
13	1.66	1.58
14	2.29	2.31
15	3.15	3.36
16	2.61	2.78
17	3.69	3.79
18	3.52	3.38

Scoring Directions

Compare your scores on each statement against the mean score (average) scores of both liberal arts and management students. Which group were you closest to on the statements? Five of the 18 statements (5, 8, 11, 12, and 18) were the most significant in terms of showing differences between the two groups of students. Why do you think the two groups of students differed significantly on these five statements?

Chapter 6: What Is Your Decision-Making Style?

Scoring the decision-style inventory:

1. Add the points in each of the four columns—I, II, III, IV.
2. The sum of the four columns should be 300 points. If your sum does not equal 300 points, check your addition and your answers.
3. Place your score for each column—I, II, III, IV—into the box of the corresponding number.

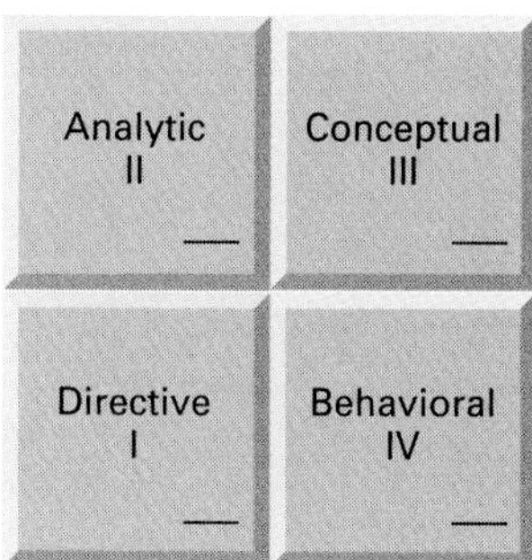

4. The box with the highest score reflects your dominant style. The closer the distribution is to a score of 75 in each category, the greater flexibility you show.

Chapter 7: How Well Do I Set Goals?

The goal-setting assessment helps you to focus on basic aspects of goal-setting processes in your personal and professional or school life. The intent of this brief assessment is to get you to think about goal setting as it relates to your school, personal life, and/or work.

In the first part of the assessment, we focus on whether your personal goal setting is *passive* or *active*. Question 1 examines your general tendency around "action", and questions 4 and 5 show a specific example of proaction versus reaction (having a plan for completing your major). Questions 2 and 3 concern the *allocation of resources*. Finally, Question 6 focuses on a cornerstone of effective goal setting—creating goals that are *challenging yet attainable*. If your score on any of these questions is 3 or less, you need to gain a better understanding of the importance of goal setting and what is involved in setting goals.

In the second part of the assessment, we focus on the goal-setting processes of an organizational unit that you may work in or have knowledge about. Questions 1, 6, and 12 focus on the extent to which goal setting is an *integral part* of a work unit's operation (planning is proactive, is completed at all organizational levels, is predictable, and is done at periodic intervals). Questions 2, 3, and 13 examine the extent to which goal-setting processes are *supported by other organizational factors*. The *comprehensiveness* of organizational goal setting is addressed in Questions 4, 5, 7, 8, and 9. Finally, questions 10, 11, and 14 address the *appropriateness* of goals. If the organizational unit you assessed scored low in any of these areas, you may want to examine more closely the planning processes being used and try to identify ways in which they could be improved.

Chapter 8: Are You a Risk Taker?

Give yourself one point for each true answer for items 1, 3, 4, 7, 9, 11, 13, 14, 16, and 18; and one point for each false answer for items 2, 5, 6, 8, 10, 12, 15, 17, and 19.

The more points you have, the more willing you are to take risks with your money and career.

Chapter 9: Am I a Good Planner?

According to the author of this questionnaire, the perfect planner would have answered:

1. Yes;	2. No;	3. Yes;	4. Yes;
5. Yes;	6. Yes;	7. Yes;	8. No

Chapter 10: How Willing Are You to Delegate?

Scoring: To determine your scores, add up the points you assigned as follows:

Sum of a, d, e, g, j, l, m, o, r, and s = (X)
Sum of b, c, f, h, i, k, n, p, q, and t = (Y)

Interpretation: The higher one's X scores, the less inclined one is to delegate tasks. Theory X assumes that people are not motivated to take responsibility unless pressured. Theory Y assumes that people seek additional responsibility and the delegated tasks will be accepted.

Chapter 11: Diversity Questionnaire

The lower your score, the better you communicate and improve the climate in your diverse organization and the community at large.

Chapter 12: How Innovative Are You?

Scoring: Give yourself the following points for each circled response:

SA = 5 points
A = 4 points
? = 3 points
D = 2 points
SD = 1 point

Total your points to get your score.

Interpretation: The higher the score, the more willing you are to be innovative. Your attitude towards innovation is more positive than that of people who score low. A score of 72 or greater is high, while a score of 45 or less is low. People who are not innovators have a tendency to maintain the status quo. Innovative people are entrepreneurs and ones who like to create changes in their organizations.

Chapter 13: What's Your Personality Type?

Mark each of your responses on the following scales. Then use the point value column to arrive at your score. For example, if you answered *a* to the first question, you would check *1a* in the feeling column. This response receives zero points when you add up the point value column. Instructions for classifying your scores are indicated below the scales.

Sensation	Point Value	Intuition	Point Value	Thinking	Point Value	Feeling	Point Value
2b ______	1	2a ______	2	1b ______	1	1a ______	0
4a ______	1	4b ______	1	3b ______	2	3a ______	1
5a ______	1	5b ______	1	7b ______	1	7a ______	1
6b ______	1	6a ______	0	8a ______	0	8b ______	1
9b ______	2	9a ______	2	10b ______	2	10a ______	1
12a ______	1	12b ______	0	11a ______	2	11b ______	1
15a ______	1	15b ______	1	13b ______	1	13a ______	1
16b ______	2	16a ______	0	14b ______	0	14a ______	1
(Maximum) Point Value	(10)		(7)		(9)		(7)

Classifying Total Scores

- Write *intuition* if your intuition score is equal to or greater than your sensation score.
- Write *sensation* if your sensation score is greater than your intuition score.
- Write *feeling* if your feeling score is greater than your thinking score.
- Write *thinking* if your thinking score is greater than your feeling score.

Chapter 14: Are You a Team Player?

If you answered more than half the questions with "Very like me" or "Somewhat like me", you are likely be a good team member. However, you might also want to ask yourself the following questions to explore further your feelings about being a team player.

1. Do these self-assessment items agree with your concept of team membership? Why or why not?
2. On the basis of your responses, what do you think your strengths are as far as working in a team? What are your weaknesses?
3. On the basis of your responses, how would you evaluate yourself as a team member?

Chapter 15: What Motivates You?

To determine your dominant needs—and what motivates you—place the number 1 through 5 that you circled for each statement next to the number for that statement.

	Achievement	Power	Affiliation
	1. ______	2. ______	3. ______
	4. ______	5. ______	6. ______
	7. ______	8. ______	9. ______
	10. ______	11. ______	12. ______
	13. ______	14. ______	15. ______
Total:	______	______	______

Total each column. The sum in each column will be between 5 and 25 points. The column with the highest score tells you your dominant need.

Chapter 16: Are You a Charismatic Leader?

The questionnaire measures each of the six basic behaviour leader patterns, as well as a set of emotional responses. Your score can range from 4 to 20. Each question is stated as a measure of the extent to which you engage in the behaviour or elicit the feelings. The higher your score, the more you demonstrate charismatic leader behaviours.

Index 1: Management of Attention (1, 7, 13, 19). Your score ______. You pay especially close attention to people with whom you are communicating. You are also "focused in" on the key issues under discussion and help others to see these key points clearly. You have clear ideas about the relative importance or priorities of different issues under discussion.

Index 2: Management of Meaning (2, 8, 14, 20). Your score ______. This set of items centres on your communication skills, specifically your ability to get the meaning of a message across, even if this means devising some innovative approach.

Index 3: Management of Trust (3, 9, 15, 21). Your score ______. The key factor is your perceived trustworthiness as shown by your willingness to follow through on promises, avoidance of "flip-flop" shifts in position, and willingness to take clear positions.

Index 4: Management of Self (4, 10, 16, 22). Your score ______. This index concerns your general attitudes towards yourself and others; that is, your overall concern for others and their feelings, as well as for "taking care of" feelings about yourself in a positive sense (e.g., self-regard).

Index 5: Management of Risk (5, 11, 17, 23). Your score ______. Effective charismatic leaders are deeply involved in what they do and do not spend excessive amounts of time or energy on plans to "protect" themselves against failure. These leaders are willing to take risks, not on a hit-or-miss basis, but after careful estimation of the odds of success or failure.

Index 6: Management of Feelings (6, 12, 18, 24). Your score ______. Charismatic leaders seem to consistently generate a set of feelings in others. Others feel that their work becomes more meaningful and that they control their own behaviour; that is, they feel competent. They feel a sense of community, a "we-ness" with their colleagues and co-workers.

Chapter 17: Who Controls Your Life?

This exercise is designed to measure your locus of control. Give yourself 1 point for each of the following selections: 1B, 2A, 3A, 4B, 5B, 6A, 7A, 8A, 9B, and 10A. Scores can be interpreted as follows:

8–10 = High internal locus of control
6–7 = Moderate internal locus of control
5 = Mixed
3–4 = Moderate external locus of control
1–2 = High external locus of control

The higher your internal score, the more you believe that you control your own destiny. The higher your external score, the more you believe that what happens to you in your life is due to luck or chance.

Chapter 18: How Customer Focused Are You?

Add your points and refer to the following scoring key.

32–40	You are highly customer focused.
24–31	You have good knowledge of the customer but could become more focused.
Less than 24	You need to become more customer focused.

Chapter 19: How Internet Literate Are You?

Scoring: (1) k; (2) d; (3) h; (4) n; (5) j; (6) o; (7) c; (8) i; (9) m; (10) f; (11) l; (12) g; (13) b; (14) e; (15) a

14–15 correct	You're a real Web wizard!
10–13 correct	You know a lot about the Web but aren't quite qualified as a Web expert yet!
7–9 correct	You qualify as a Web novice!
Under 7 correct:	You need to get out of your Model T and get on the Information Superhighway! :-)

Notes

Introduction

1. John W. Redston, "The Canadian Business Context: Conclusions from a Survey of Canadian General Business Texts 1960–1987," Working Paper, Red River Community College, September 1988.
2. Peter C. Newman, *Sometimes a Great Nation* (Toronto: McClelland and Stewart, 1988).
3. Ibid.
4. Shona McKay, "Make Room, Madison Ave.," *Canadian Business,* January 1993.
5. "Canada Inc.," *Report on Business Magazine,* June 1993.
6. *Canadian Business,* June 1995.
7. Peter Foster, "The New Meddlers," *Canadian Business,* January 1993.
8. Walter Stewart, *Uneasy Lies the Head: The Truth About Canada's Crown Corporations* (Don Mills, Ontario: Collins, 1987).
9. Peter Newman, 1988.
10. Michael Porter, "Canada at the Crossroads: The Reality of a New Competitive Environment." Study prepared for the Business Council on National Issues and the Government of Canada, October 1991.
11. Marie Josée Drouin, "The Outlook is Rosy... Maybe," *The Financial Post Report on the Nation,* Winter 1988–89.
12. *Canadian Business,* June 1993.

Chapter 1

1. John Greenwood, "Job One", *Financial Post Magazine,* June 1997, pp. 18–23; John Lorinc, "Now the Customer is Job One", *Canadian Business,* July 1997, pp. 22–28.
2. Kenneth Kidd, "Cracks in the Glass Ceiling", *Report on Business Magazine,* May 1997, p. 9; Jennifer Wells, "Stuck on the Ladder", *Maclean's,* October 20, 1997, pp. 60–64.
3. Henri Fayol, *Industrial and General Administration* (Paris: Dunod, 1916).
4. Harold Koontz and Cyril O'Donnell, *Principles of Management: An Analysis of Managerial Functions* (New York: McGraw-Hill, 1955).
5. Henry Mintzberg, *The Nature of Managerial Work* (New York: Harper & Row, 1973).
6. See, for example, Larry D. Alexander, "The Effect Level in the Hierarchy and Functional Area Have on the Extent Mintzberg's Roles Are Required by Managerial Jobs," *Academy of Management Proceedings* (San Francisco, 1979), pp. 186–89; Alan W. Lau and Cynthia M. Pavett, "The Nature of Managerial Work: A Comparison of Public and Private Sector Managers," *Group and Organization Studies,* December 1980, pp. 453–66; Morgan W. McCall, Jr., and C. A. Segrist, *In Pursuit of the Manager's Job: Building on Mintzberg,* Technical Report No. 14 (Greensboro, NC: Center for Creative Leadership, 1980); Cynthia M. Pavett and Alan W. Lau, "Managerial Work: The Influence of Hierarchical Level and Functional Specialty," *Academy of Management Journal,* March 1983, pp. 170–77; Hales; Allen I. Kraut, Patricia R. Pedigo, D. Douglas McKenna, and Marvin D. Dunnette, "The Role of the Manager: What's Really Important in Different Management Jobs," *Academy of Management Executive,* November 1989, pp. 286–93; and Mark J. Martinko and William L. Gardner, "Structured Observation of Managerial Work: A Replication and Synthesis," *Journal of Management Studies,* May 1990, pp. 330–57.
7. Pavett and Lau, "Managerial Work."
8. Stephen J. Carroll and Dennis A. Gillen, "Are the Classical Management Functions Useful in Describing Managerial Work?" *Academy of Management Review,* January 1987, p. 48.
9. See, for example, Harold Koontz, "Commentary on the Management Theory Jungle—Nearly Two Decades Later," in Harold Koontz, Cyril O'Donnell, and Heintz Weihrich (eds.), *Management: A Book of Readings,* 6th ed. (New York: McGraw-Hill, 1984), pp. 10–14; and Carroll and Gillen, pp. 38–51.
10. Ibid.; and Peter Allan, "Managers at Work: A Large-Scale Study of the Managerial Job in New York City Government," *Academy of Management Journal,* September 1981, pp. 613–19.
11. Robert L. Katz, "Skills of an Effective Administrator," *Harvard Business Review,* September–October 1974, pp. 90–102.
12. Katrina Onstad, "If You Have a Lemon, Make Lemonade", *Canadian Business,* September, 1996, pp. 48–54.
13. D.A. Whetten and K.S. Cameron, *Developing Management Skills,* 4th ed. (New York: Harper Collins, 1998); D.B. Curtis, J.L. Winsor, and R.D. Stephens, "National Preferences in Business and Communication Education", Communication Education 38, 1989, pp. 6–15; K. Cameron and M. Tschirhart, Managerial Competencies and Organizational Effectiveness, Working Paper, School of Business Administration, University of Michigan, 1988; F. Luthans, S.A. Rosenkrantz, and H.W. Hennessey, "What Do Successful Managers Really Do? An Observation Study of Managerial Activities", *Journal of Applied Behavioural Science,* Vol. 21, 1985, pp. 255–270.
14. See, for example, James W. Driscoll, Gary Cowger, and Robert Egan, "Private Managers and Public Myths—Public Managers and Private Myths," *Sloan Management Review,* Fall 1979, pp. 53–57; David Rogers, "Managing in the Public and Private Sectors: Similarities and Differences," *Management Review,* May 1981, pp. 48–54; Graham Allison, "Public and Private Management: Are They Fundamentally Alike in All Unimportant Respects?" in F. S. Lane (ed.), *Current Issues in Public Administration,* 2d ed. (New York: St. Martin's Press, 1982); Douglas Yates, Jr., *The Politics of Management* (San Francisco: Jossey-Bass, 1985), pp. 12–39; J. Norman Baldwin, "Public vs. Private: Not That Different, Not That Consequential," *Public Personnel Management,* Summer 1987, pp. 181–91; and Hal G. Rainey, "Public Management: Recent Research on the Political Context and Managerial Roles, Structures, and Behaviors," *Journal of Management,* June 1989, pp. 229–50.
15. See, for example, William A. Nowlin, "Factors That Motivate Public And Private Sector Managers: A Comparison," *Public Personnel Management Journal,* Fall 1982, pp. 224–27.
16. This box is based on the following: Thomas M. Begley and David P. Boyd, "A Comparison of Entrepreneurs and Managers of Small Business Firms," *Journal of Management,* Spring 1987, pp. 99–108; Howard H. Stevenson, M.J. Roberts, and H.I. Grousbeck, *New Business Ventures and the Entrepreneur* (Homewood, IL: Irwin, 1989); Robert D. Hisrich, "Entrepreneurship/Intrapreneurship," *American Psychologist,* February 1990, p. 218; Michael Warshaw, "The Entrepreneurial Mind," *Success,* April 1994, pp. 48–51; and Andrew E. Serwer, "Lessons from America's Fastest-Growing Companies," *Fortune,* August 8, 1994, pp. 42–60.
17. Jennifer Wells, "We Can Get It For You Wholesale," *Report on Business Magazine,* March 1995, pp. 52–61.
18. G. Koretz, "Startups: Still a Job Engine", *Business Week,* March 24, 1997, p. 26; F. Katayama, "Small Business Fuels Economic Growth", *CNNfn World Wide Web Page,* March 25, 1996; and J. Chun and C.E. Griffin, "The Mouse That Roared: The True State of Small Business", *Entrepreneur,* September, 1996, pp. 118–122.
19. W. Sengenberger, G. Loveman, and M. J. Piore (eds.), The Re-Emergence of Small Enterprises: Industrial Restructuring in Industrial Countries (Geneva: International Institute for Labour Studies, 1990); and "Entrepreneurs Pop Up in

China," *Wall Street Journal,* April 7, 1994, p. A10.

20. Joseph G. P. Paolillo, "The Manager's Self-Assessments of Managerial Roles: Small vs. Large Firms," *American Journal of Small Business,* January–March 1984, pp. 58–64.
21. See, for example, Gerald d'Amboise and Marie Muldowney, "Management Theory for Small Business: Attempts and Requirements," *Academy of Management Review,* April 1988, pp. 226–40.
22. See, for example, Dianne H. B. Welsh, Fred Luthans, and Steven M. Sommer, "Managing Russian Factory Workers: The Impact of U.S.-based Behavioral and Participative Techniques," *Academy of Management Journal,* February 1993, pp. 58–79; Geert Hofstede, "Cultural Constraints in Management Theories," *Academy of Management Executive,* February 1993, pp. 81–94; Avraham Shama, "Management Under Fire: The Transformation of Managers in the Soviet Union and Eastern Europe," *Academy of Management Executive,* February 1993, pp. 22–35; Olukemi O. Sawyerr, "Environmental Uncertainty and Environmental Scanning Activities of Nigerian Manufacturing Executives: A Comparative Analysis," *Strategic Management Journal,* May 1993, pp. 287–99; Richard G. Linowes, "The Japanese Manager's Traumatic Entry into the United States: Understanding the American–Japanese Cultural Divide," *Academy of Management Executive,* November 1993, pp. 21–40; Michael Cakrt, "Management Education in Eastern Europe: Toward Mutual Understanding," *Academy of Management Executive,* November 1993, pp. 63–68; Mariah E. de Forest, "Thinking of a Plant in Mexico," *Academy of Management Executive,* February 1994, pp. 33–40; and Sheila M. Puffer, "Understanding the Bear: A Portrait of Russian Business Leaders," *Academy of Management Executive,* February 1994, pp. 41–61.
23. Bureau of Labour Statistics, January, 1996, Bulletin 2471.

Chapter 2

1. Katrina Onstad, "Can the Digital Diva Deliver?", *Canadian Business,* March 13, 1998, pp. 80-85; and Patricia D'Souza, "Bill and Me", *Profit,* June, 1998, p. 100.
2. Claude S. George, Jr., *The History of Management Thought,* 2d ed. (Englewood Cliffs, NJ: Prentice Hall, 1972), p. 4.
3. Frederick W. Taylor, *Principles of Scientific Management* (New York: Harper, 1911), p. 44.
4. See for example, Frank B. Gilbreth, *Motion Study* (New York: Van Nostrand, 1911); and Frank B. Gilbreth and Lillian M. Gilbreth, *Fatigue Study* (New York: Sturgis and Walton, 1916).
5. Max Weber, *The Theory of Social and Economic Organizations,* ed. Talcott Parsons, trans. A. M. Henderson and Talcott Parsons (New York: Free Press, 1947).
6. Robert A. Owen, *A New View of Society* (New York: Bliss and White, 1825).
7. W. Jack Duncan, *Great Ideas in Management* (San Francisco: Jossey-Bass, 1989), p. 137.
8. Hugo Munsterberg, *Psychology and Industrial Efficiency,* 6th ed. (Boston: Houghton Mifflin, 1913).
9. Mary Parker Follett, *The New State: Group Organization the Solution of Popular Government* (London: Longmans, Green, 1918); Dana Wechsler Linden, "The Mother of Them All," *Forbes,* January 16, 1995, pp. 75–76.
10. Chester Barnard, *The Functions of the Executive* (Cambridge, MA: Harvard University Press, 1938).
11. Elton Mayo, *The Human Problems of an Industrial Civilization* (New York: Macmillan, 1933); and Fritz J. Roethlisberger and William J. Dickson, *Management and the Worker* (Cambridge, MA: Harvard University Press, 1939).
12. See for example, Alex Carey, "The Hawthorne Studies: A Radical Criticism," *American Sociological Review,* June 1967, pp. 403–16; Richard H. Franke and James Kaul, "The Hawthorne Experiments: First Statistical Interpretations," *American Sociological Review,* October 1978, pp. 623–43; Berkeley Rice, "The Hawthorne Defect: Persistence of a Flawed Theory," *Psychology Today,* February 1982, pp. 70–74; Jeffrey A. Sonnenfeld, "Shedding Light on the Hawthorne Studies," *Journal of Occupational Behavior,* April 1985, pp. 111–30; and Stephen R.G. Jones, "Worker Interdependence and Output: The Hawthorne Studies Reevaluated," *American Sociological Review,* April 1990, pp. 176–90; Stephen R. Jones, "Was There a Hawthorne Effect?" *American Sociological Review,* November 1992, pp. 451–68; and Gary W. Yunker, "An Explanation of Positive and Negative Hawthorne Effects: Evidence From the Relay Assembly Test Room and Bank Wiring Observation Room Studies," paper presented, at Academy of Management Annual Meeting, August 1993, Atlanta, Georgia.
13. Dale Carnegie, *How to Win Friends and Influence People* (New York: Simon & Schuster, 1936).
14. Daniel A. Wren, *The Evolution of Management Thought,* 3d ed. (New York: Wiley, 1987), p. 422.
15. Abraham Maslow, *Motivation and Personality* (New York: Harper & Row, 1954).
16. Douglas McGregor, *The Human Side of Enterprise* (New York: McGraw-Hill, 1960).
17. Lyndall Urwick, *The Elements of Administration* (New York: Harper & Row, 1944).
18. Harold Koontz, "The Management Theory Jungle," *Journal of the Academy of Management,* December 1961, pp. 174–88.
19. Harold Koontz, ed., *Toward a Unified Theory of Management* (New York: McGraw-Hill, 1964).
20. Kenyon B. DeGreene, *Sociotechnical Systems: Factors in Analysis, Design and Management* (Englewood Cliffs, NJ: Prentice Hall, 1973), p. 13.
21. See for example, Louis W. Fry and Deborah A. Smith, "Congruence, Contingency, and Theory Building," *Academy of Management Review,* January 1987, pp. 117–32.
22. See, for instance, R.R. Thomas Jr., "From Affirmative Action to Affirming Diversity," *Harvard Business Review,* March–April 1990, pp.107–17; B. Mandrell and S. Kohler-Gray, "Management Development That Values Diversity," *Personnel,* March 1990, pp.41–47; and Joel Dreyfuss, "Get Ready For The New Work Force," *Fortune,* April 23, 1990, pp.165–81.
23. E.W. Morrison and S.L. Robinson, "When Employees Feel Betrayed: A Model of How Psychological Contract Violation Develops", *Academy of Management Review,* January, 1997, pp. 226–256; M.V. Roehling, "The Origins and Early Development of the Psychological Contract Construct", *Academy of Management Proceedings on Disk,* August, 1996, pp. 1–5; and D.M. Rousseau, "Changing the Deal While Keeping the People", *Academy of Management Executive,* February 1996, pp. 50–61.
24. L. Grant, "Can Fisher Focus Kodak?", *Fortune,* January 13, 1997, pp. 76–79.
25. Rick Tetzeli, "Business Students Cheat Most," *Fortune,* July 1, 1991, p. 14.
26. See for example, Bob Krone, "Total Quality Management: An American Odyssey," *The Bureaucrat,* Fall 1990, pp. 35–38; Andrea Gabor, *The Man Who Discovered Quality* (New York: Random House, 1990); Jim Clemmer, "How Total Is Your Quality Management?" *Canadian Business Review,* Spring 1991, pp. 38–41; Marshall Sashkin and Kenneth J. Kiser, *Total Quality Management* (Seabrook, MD: Ducochon Press, 1991); James W. Dean, Jr. and David E. Bowen, "Management Theory and Total Quality: Improving Research and Practice Through Theory Development," *Academy of Management Review,* July 1994, pp. 392–418; Carol A. Reeves and David A. Bednar, "Defining Quality: Alternatives and Implications," *Academy of Management Review,* July 1994, pp. 419–45; and Rhonda K. Reger, Loren T. Gustafson, Samuel M. Demarie, and John V. Mullane, "Reframing the Organization: Why Implementing Total Quality Is Easier Said Than Done," *Academy of Management Review,* July 1994, pp. 565–84.
27. Albert C. Hyde, "Rescuing Quality Management from TQM," *The Bureaucrat,* Winter 1990–1991, p. 16.
28. See Kenneth W. Thomas and Betty A. Velthouse, "Cognitive Elements of Empowerment: An 'Interpretive' Model of Intrinsic Task Motivation," *Academy of*

Management Review, October 1990, pp. 66–81.

29. G. Koretz, "Big Payoffs From Layoffs", *Business Week,* February 24, 1997, p. 30.
30. G. Koretz, "The Downside of Downsizing", *Business Week,* April 28, 1997, p. 26.

Chapter 3

1. David Olive, "Tire On a Roll", *Report on Business Magazine,* July 1997, pp. 17–25; Stephen E. Bachand, "There's a Lot More to Canadian Tire", *Business Quarterly,* Spring 1995, pp. 31–39.
2. For insights into the symbolic view, see Jeffrey Pfeffer, "Management as Symbolic Action: The Creation and Maintenance of Organizational Paradigms," in L. L. Cummings and B. M. Staw (eds.), *Research in Organizational Behavior,* vol. 3 (Greenwich, CT: JAI Press, 1981), pp. 1–52; Donald C. Hambrick and Sidney Finkelstein, "Managerial Discretion: A Bridge Between Polar Views of Organizational Outcomes," in L. L. Cummings and B. M. Staw (eds.), *Research in Organizational Behavior,* vol. 9 (Greenwich, CT: JAI Press, 1987), pp. 369–406; John A. Byrne, "The Limits of Power," *Business Week,* October 23, 1987, pp. 33–35; James R. Meindl and Sanford B. Ehrlich, "The Romance of Leadership and the Evaluation of Organizational Performance," *Academy of Management Journal,* March 1987, pp. 91–109; Charles R. Schwenk, "Illusions of Management Control? Effects of Self-Serving Attributions on Resource Commitments and Confidence in Management," *Human Relations,* April 1990, pp. 333–47; and Sheila M. Puffer and Joseph B. Weintrop, "Corporate Performance and CEO Turnover: The Role of Performance Expectations," *Administrative Science Quarterly,* March 1991, pp. 1–19.
3. Monica Andreef, "A Load of Grief", *Canadian Business,* March 27, 1998, pp. 15–16; Brent Jang, "Bryan Leaves Gulf Canada", *Globe and Mail,* February 10, 1998, page B1; Brent Jang, "Gulf CEO Engineers Debt Strategy", *Globe and Mail,* March 20, 1998; and Toni Mack, "Bryan's Way", *Forbes,* August 28, 1995, p. 49.
4. Pfeffer.
5. Linda Smircich, "Concepts of Culture and Organizational Analysis," *Administrative Science Quarterly,* September 1983, p. 339; Daniel R. Denison, "What Is the Difference Between Organizational Culture and Organizational Climate? A Native's Point of View on a Decade of Paradigm Wars," paper presented at Academy of Management Annual Meeting, August 1993, Atlanta, Georgia; and Mary Jo Hatch, "The Dynamics of Organizational Culture, *Academy of Management Review,* October 1993, pp. 657–93.
6. Alice M. Sapienza, "Believing Is Seeing: How Culture Influences the Decisions Top Managers Make," in Ralph H. Kilmann and others (eds.), *Gaining Control of the Corporate Culture* (San Francisco: Jossey-Bass, 1985), p. 68.
7. J. A. Chatman and K. A. Jehn, "Assessing the Relationship Between Industry Characteristics and Organizational Culture: How Different Can You Be?", *Academy of Management Journal,* June 1994, pp. 522–523; and C. A. O'Reilly III, J. Chatman, and D. F. Caldwell, "People And Organizational Culture: A Profile Comparison Approach to Assessing Person-Organization Fit", *Academy of Management Journal,* September, 1991, pp. 487–516.
8. Christopher Orpen, "The Effect of Organizational Cultural Norms on the Relationships Between Personnel Practices and Employee Commitment," *Journal of Psychology,* September 1993, pp. 577–79.
9. J. C. Collins and J. I. Porras, *Built to Last* (New York: Harper Business, 1994); Collins and Porras, "Building Your Company's Vision", *Harvard Business Review,* September–October 1996, pp. 65–77; and R. Goffee and G. Jones, "What Holds the Modern Company Together?" *Harvard Business Review,* November–December 1996, pp. 133–148.
10. Sean Silcoff, "Move Over Timothy Eaton", *Canadian Business,* June 26/ July 10, 1998, pp. 58–64.
11. Marlene Cartash, "Tucows Interactive Ltd.", *Profit,* June 1998, p. 140.
12. Tema Frank, "Kinder, Gentler, Smarter", *Profit,* April–May 1998, pp. 50–52.
13. Ijeoma Ross, "Cyberpunks know how to operate", *Globe and Mail,* February 6, 1998, p. B25.
14. Jean Benoit Nadeau, "Priorities in Paper", *The Financial Post 500,* 1998, pp. 58–62.
15. Robert H. Miles, *Macro Organizational Behavior* (Santa Monica, CA: Goodyear Publishing, 1980), p. 195.
16. This box is based on Taylor H. Cox, Jr., "The Multicultural Organization," *Academy of Management Executive,* April 1991, pp. 34–47; Taylor H. Cox and Stacy Blake, "Managing Cultural Diversity: Implications for Organizational Competitiveness," *Academy of Management Executive,* August 1991, pp. 45–46; "The Challenge of Managing Diversity in the Workplace," *Black Enterprise,* July 1993, pp. 79–90; and John Huey, "The New Post-Heroic Leadership," *Fortune,* February 21, 1994, pp. 42–50.
17. Gord McLaughlin, "Selling Equity," *Financial Post Magazine,* September, 1994, pp. 20–25.
18. Nomi Morris, "Cooling on Cuba", *Maclean's,* March 9, 1998, pp. 40–41.
19. "Technology 100—Top 5", *Canadian Business,* June 12, 1998, p. 83.
20. Jean Benoit Nadeau and Julie Barlow, "The Miracle of St. Pie," *Profit,* October 1994, pp. 20–27.
21. Don Sutton, "CAE Takes the Long View," *Globe and Mail,* August 1, 1995, p.B19.
22. This box is based on Zenas Block and Ian C. MacMillan, "Size 'Em Up: How to Evaluate New Business Opportunities," *Success,* March 1994, p. 80; Amir Bhide, "How Entrepreneurs Craft Strategies That Work," *Harvard Business Review,* March–April 1994, pp. 150–61; Ingrid Abramovitch, "Revenge of the Wimp," *Success,* April 1994, p. 21; Zoltan J. Acs, "Where New Things Come from," *Inc.,* May 1994, p. 29; and Ingrid Abramovitch, "Seize the Moment," *Success,* June 1994, p. 23.
23. John Heinzl, "College Kids Win High Marks in Real World", *Globa and Mail,* March 30, 1998, p. B11.
24. Allan Lynch, "Reinventing the Family Tree", *Profit,* April-May, 1998, p. 14.
25. Donna Green, "Versent Corp.", *Profit,* June 1998, p. 120.
26. Brian Hutchinson, "Mooooooo-La!," *Canadian Business,* August 1995, pp. 62–64.
27. Timothy S. Mescon and George S. Vozikis, "Federal Regulation—What Are the Costs?" *Business,* January–March 1982, pp. 33–39.
28. See, for instance, Arthur S. Hayes, "Layoffs Take Careful Planning to Avoid Losing the Suits That Are Apt to Follow," *Wall Street Journal,* November 2, 1990, p. B1.
29. Margot Gibb-Clark and Elizabeth Church, "Pot Policing Fails the Workplace Test", *Globe and Mail,* February 12, 1998, p. B16.
30. Edward Allen, "MacMillan Bloedel bows to pressure from Greenpeace", *The Financial Times (U.K.),* June 19, 1998, p. 28.
31. Harvey Schacter, "Power Shift," *Canadian Business,* August 1995, pp. 20–30.
32. Thomas A. Stewart, "Welcome to the Revolution," *Fortune,* December 13, 1993, pp. 66– 78.
33. Brent Jang, "Syncrude's Success Entices Texas Oil Man," *Globe and Mail,* August 1, 1995, p. B5; and Edward Kay, "Sultan of Stink," *Canadian Business,* August 1995, p.88.
34. "Business Week/Harris Executive Poll," *Business Week,* September 20, 1993, p. 44.

Chapter 4

1. David Menzies, "Meeting the Challenge", *Profit,* June, 1998, pp. 148-154.
2. Nancy Adler, *International Dimensions of Organizational Behavior,* 2d ed. (Boston: PWS-Kent, 1991), p. 11.
3. Ann Walmsley, "The Deal That Almost Got Away," *Report on Business Magazine,* August, 1995, pp. 26–36.
4. John A. Byrne and others, "Borderless Management," *Business Week,* May 23, 1994, pp. 24–26.
5. See, for instance, Mark Maremont and Richard A. Melcher, "Tearing Down Even More Fences in Europe," *Business Week,* November 4, 1991, pp. 50–52; Sara Hammes, "Europe's Growing Market," *Fortune,* December 2, 1991, pp. 144–45; Mark M. Nelson, "EC

Is Swamped by Would-Be Members," *Wall Street Journal,* May 13, 1992, p. A12; Desmond Dinan, "The European Community," *The Annals of the American Academy of Political and Social Science,* January 1994, p. 10–24; Amy Bernstein, "Nordic Eyes on Europe's Big Trading Bloc," *U.S. News & World Report,* June 27, 1994, p. 12; and John S. McClenahen (ed.), "15, Not 16," *Industry Week,* January 9, 1995, p. 57.

6. Wolfgang Munchau, "The Euro Versus The Dollar", *Financial Times,* July, 1998, p. 22.
7. "The Language of Trade," *Business America,* July 1994, p. 5.
8. Amy Borrus, "A Free-Trade Milestone, with Many More Miles to Go," *Business Week,* August 24, 1992, pp. 30–31; Polly LaBarre, "Pace Varies, But Direction Is Right," *Industry Week,* June 6, 1994, pp. 36–38; Bob Davis, "Growth of Trade Binds Nations, But It Also Can Spur Separatism," *Wall Street Journal,* June 20, 1994, pp. A1+; Neela Banerjee, "Canada's Recovery Is Expected to Cross Border and Boost Business in the United States," *Wall Street Journal,* June 20, 1994, p. A2; Neal Templin, "Mexican Industrial Belt Is Beginning to Form as Car Makers Expand," *Wall Street Journal,* June 29, 1994, pp. A1+; and Geri Smith, "NAFTA: A Green Light for Red Tape," *Business Week,* July 25, 1994.
9. Bernard Wysocki, Jr., "Blocking Trade," *Wall Street Journal,* September 21, 1990, p. R31.
10. James Brooke, "In Latin America, A Free Trade Rush," *New York Times,* June 13, 1994, pp. C1+.
11. Alex Gillis, "Grease", *Report on Business Magazine*, March 1998, pp. 58–68.
12. Gordon Pitts, "Hold the Pepperoni," *Globe and Mail,* January 16, 1995, p. B6.
13. See, for example, Geert Hofstede, *Culture's Consequences: International Differences in Work-Related Values* (Beverly Hills, CA: Sage Publications, 1980), pp. 25–26.
14. Geert Hofstede, *Culture's Consequences: International Differences in Work-Related Values;* and Geert Hofstede, "The Cultural Relativity of Organizational Practices and Theories," *Journal of International Business Studies,* Fall 1983, pp. 75–89.
15. Hofstede called this last dimension "masculinity–femininity" but we've changed it because of the strong sexist connotation in his choice of terms.
16. Rosalie L. Tung, "Human Resources Planning in Japanese Multinationals: A Model for U.S. Firms?" *Journal of International Business Studies,* Fall 1984, p. 146.
17. J. T. Gullahorn and J. E. Gullahorn, "An Extension of the U-Curve Hypothesis," *Journal of Social Sciences,* January 1963, pp. 34–47.

Chapter 5

1. Rob Roberts, "Commensal's Comeback", *Montreal Gazette,* May 25, 1998, p. C1.
2. Archie B. Carroll, "A Three-Dimensional Conceptual Model of Corporate Performance," *Academy of Management Review,* October 1979, p. 499.
3. Milton Friedman, *Capitalism and Freedom* (Chicago: University of Chicago Press, 1962); and "The Social Responsibility of Business Is to Increase Profits," *New York Times Magazine,* September 13, 1970, p. 33.
4. Saul W. Gellerman, "Why 'Good' Managers Make Bad Ethical Choices," *Harvard Business Review,* July–August 1986, p. 89.
5. Steven L. Wartick and Philip L. Cochran, "The Evolution of the Corporate Social Performance Model," *Academy of Management Review,* October 1985, p. 760.
6. Christopher Caggiano, "Is Social Responsibility a Crock?" *Inc.,* May 1993, p. 15.
7. This section is based on R. Joseph Monsen, Jr., "The Social Attitudes of Management," in Joseph M. McGuire (ed.), *Contemporary Management: Issues and Views* (Englewood Cliffs, NJ: Prentice Hall, 1974), p. 616; and Keith Davis and William C. Frederick, *Business and Society: Management, Public Policy, Ethics,* 5th ed. (New York: McGraw-Hill, 1984), pp. 28–41.
8. See, for example, Rogene A. Buchholz, *Essentials of Public Policy for Management,* 2d ed. (Englewood Cliffs, NJ: Prentice Hall, 1990).
9. See S. Prakash Sethi, "A Conceptual Framework for Environmental Analysis of Social Issues and Evaluation of Business Response Patterns," *Academy of Management Review,* January 1979, pp. 68–74.
10. See, for example, Donna J. Wood, "Corporate Social Performance Revisited," *Academy of Management Review,* October 1991, pp. 703–08.
11. Wartick and Cochran, p. 763.
12. Dennis Slocum, "TD Gives Gay Couples Benefits," *Globe and Mail,* December 20, 1994, p. B3.
13. Wartick and Cochran, p. 762.
14. Alanna Mitchell, "Calgary Board Plans to Take School to Work," *Globe and Mail,* January 6, 1995, p. A5.
15. See, for instance, Philip Cochran and Robert A. Wood, "Corporate Social Responsibility and Financial Performance," *Academy of Management Journal,* March 1984, pp. 42–56; Kenneth Aupperle, Archie B. Carroll, and John D. Hatfield, "An Empirical Examination of the Relationship Between Corporate Social Responsibility and Profitability," *Academy of Management Journal,* June 1985, pp. 446–63; Jean B. McGuire, Alison Sundgren, and Thomas Schneeweis, "Corporate Social Responsibility and Firm Financial Performance," *Academy of Management Journal,* December 1988, pp. 854–72; David M. Georgoff and Joel Ross, "Corporate Social Responsibility and Management Performance," paper presented at the National Academy of Management Conference, Miami, August 1991; Shaker A. Zahra, Benjamin M. Oviatt, and Karen Minyard, "Effects of Corporate Ownership and Board Structure on Corporate Social Responsibility and Financial Performance," paper presented at the National Academy of Management Conference, Atlanta, August 1993; "Social Responsibility and the Bottom Line," *Business Ethics,* July–August, 1994, p. 11.
16. See Arieh A. Ullmann, "Data in Search of a Theory: A Critical Examination of the Relationships Among Social Performance, Social Disclosure, and Economic Performance of U.S. Firms," *Academy of Management Review,* July 1985, pp. 540–57; and Richard E. Wokutch and Barbara A. Spencer, "Corporate Saints and Sinners: The Effects of Philanthropic and Illegal Activity on Organizational Performance," *California Management Review,* Winter 1987, pp. 62–77.
17. McGuire, Sungren, and Schneeweis.
18. Cochran and Wood.
19. Jack Egan, "Investing in an Activist Agenda," *U.S. News & World Report,* November 15, 1993, p. 85.
20. Georgoff and Ross.
21. George P. Alexander, "Establishing Shared Values Through Management Training Programs," *Training and Development Journal,* February 1987, pp. 45–47.
22. George P. Alexander, "Establishing Shared Values Through Management Training Programs"; and Joseph L. Badaracco, Jr. and Richard R. Ellsworth, *Leadership and the Quest for Integrity* (Boston: Harvard Business School Press, 1989).
23. Ibid.
24. Robert Howard, "Values Make the Company: An Interview with Robert Haas," *Harvard Business Review,* September–October 1990, pp. 133–44; Jim Impoco, "Working for Mr. Clean Jeans," *U.S. News & World Report,* August 2, 1993, pp. 49–50; and Russell Mitchell and Michael Oneal, "Managing by Values," *Business Week,* August 1, 1994, pp. 46–52.
25. Alan Farnham, "State Your Values, Hold the Hot Air," *Fortune,* April 19, 1993, pp. 117–24; Anne Murphy, "Too Good to Be True?" *Inc.,* July 1994, pp. 34–43; and Interview with Gun Denhart, CEO of Hanna Andersson, *Business Ethics,* July–August 1994, pp. 18–21.
26. Robin Kamen, "Values: For Show or For Real?" *Working Woman,* August, 1993, p. 10.
27. Badaracco and Ellsworth.
28. Janet Bamford, "Changing Business as Usual," *Working Woman,* November 1993, pp. 62+.
29. This section has been influenced by Kimberly B. Boal and Newman Peery, "The Cognitive Structure of Social Responsibility," *Journal of Management,* Fall–Winter 1985, pp. 71–82.
30. Archie B. Carroll, Social Responsibility of Management (Chicago: Science Research Associates, 1984), p. 13.

31. Davis and Frederick, p. 76.
32. Frederick D. Sturdivant, *Business and Society: A Managerial Approach,* 3d ed. (Homewood, IL: Irwin, 1985), p. 128.
33. Gerald F. Cavanagh, Dennis J. Moberg, and Manuel Valasquez, "The Ethics of Organizational Politics," *Academy of Management Journal,* June 1981, pp. 363–74. See F. Neil Brady, "Rules for Making Exceptions to Rules," *Academy of Management Review,* July 1987, pp. 436–44 for an argument that the theory of justice is redundant with the prior two theories. See Thomas Donaldson and Thomas W. Dunfee, "Toward a Unified Conception of Business Ethics: Integrative Social Contracts Theory," *Academy of Management Review,* April 1994, pp. 252–84, for a discussion of integrative social contracts theory.
34. David J. Fritzsche and Helmut Becker, "Linking Management Behavior to Ethical Philosophy—An Empirical Investigation," *Academy of Management Journal,* March 1984, pp. 166–75.
35. Lawrence Surtees, "The VP in Charge of Clean Business", *Globe and Mail,* March 18, 1997, p. B12.
36. Brian Dumaine, "Exporting Jobs and Ethics," *Fortune,* October 5, 1992, p. 10.
37. Lawrence Kohlberg, *Essays in Moral Development: The Philosophy of Moral Development,* vol. 1 (New York: Harper & Row, 1981); and Lawrence Kohlberg, *Essays in Moral Development: The Psychology of Moral Development,* vol. 2 (New York: Harper & Row, 1984).
38. See, for example, James Weber, "Managers' Moral Reasoning: Assessing Their Responses to Three Moral Dilemmas," *Human Relations,* July 1990, pp. 687–702.
39. John H. Barnett and Marvin J. Karson, "Personal Values and Business Decisions: An Exploratory Investigation," *Journal of Business Ethics,* July 1987, pp. 371–82; and William C. Frederick and James Weber, "The Value of Corporate Managers and Their Critics: An Empirical Description and Normative Implications," in William C. Frederick and Lee E. Preston (eds.), *Business Ethics: Research Issues and Empirical Studies* (Greenwich, CT: JAI Press, 1990), pp. 123–44.
40. Linda Klebe Trevino and Stuart A. Youngblood, "Bad Apples in Bad Barrels: A Causal Analysis of Ethical Decision-Making Behavior," *Journal of Applied Psychology,* August 1990, pp. 378–85; and Melany E. Baehr, John W. Jones, and Alan J. Nerad, "Psychological Correlates of Business Ethics Orientation in Executives," *Journal of Business and Psychology,* Spring 1993, pp. 291–308.
41. Barry Z. Posner and William H. Schmidt, "Values and the American Manager: An Update," *California Management Review,* Spring 1984, pp. 202–16; and Ronald B. Morgan, "Self- and Co-Worker Perceptions of Ethics and Their Relationships to Leadership and Salary," *Academy of Management Journal,* February 1993, pp. 200–14.
42. Bart Victor and John B. Cullen, "The Organizational Bases of Ethical Work Climates," *Administrative Science Quarterly,* March 1988, pp. 101–25; John B. Cullen, Bart Victor, and Carroll Stephens, "An Ethical Weather Report: Assessing the Organization's Ethical Climate," *Organizational Dynamics,* Autumn 1989, pp. 50–62; Bart Victor and John B. Cullen, "A Theory and Measure of Ethical Climate in Organizations," in William C. Frederick and Lee E. Preston (eds.), *Business Ethics: Research Issues and Empirical Studies* (Greenwich, CT: JAI Press, 1990), pp. 77–97; and Ronald R. Sims, "The Challenge of Ethical Behavior in Organizations," *Journal of Business Ethics,* July 1992, pp. 505–13.
43. Thomas M. Jones, "Ethical Decision Making by Individuals in Organizations: An Issue-Contingent Model," *Academy of Management Review,* April 1991, pp. 366–95.
44. Ibid., pp. 374–78.
45. Alex Gillis, "Grease", *Report on Business Magazine*, March, 1998, pp. 58-68.
46. John A. Byrne, "The Best-Laid Ethics Programs ..." *Business Week,* March 9, 1992, pp. 67–68.
47. Trevino and Youngblood, p. 384.
48. See, for example, M. Cash Matthews, "Codes of Ethics: Organizational Behavior and Misbehavior," in William C. Frederick and Lee E. Preston (eds.), *Business Ethics,* pp. 99–122.
49. Paul Richter, "Big Business Puts Ethics in Spotlight," *Los Angeles Times,* June 19, 1986, p. 29.
50. Fred R. David, "An Empirical Study of Codes of Business Ethics: A Strategic Perspective," paper presented at the 48th Annual Academy of Management Conference; Anaheim, California, August 1988.
51. Rick Wartzman, "Nature or Nurture? Study Blames Ethical Lapses on Corporate Goals," *Wall Street Journal,* October 9, 1987, p. 27.
52. Ibid.
53. D. R. Cressey and C. A. Moore, "Managerial Values and Corporate Codes of Ethics," *California Management Review,* Summer 1983, p. 71.
54. Laura Nash, "Ethics Without the Sermon," *Harvard Business Review,* November–December 1981, p. 81.
55. John Heinzl, "Survey Finds Few Firms Act on Code of Ethics", *Globe and Mail,* February 21, 1997, p. B11; and Alan Toulin, "Canadian Firms Sign on to New Code of Ethics", *Financial Post.*
56. Rebecca Goodell, "Ethics in American Business: Policies, Programs and Perceptions," *Ethics Resource Center,* 1994, p. 5; and Don L. Boroughs, "Can Business Ethics Be Taught?" *U.S. News & World Report,* March 20, 1985, p. 66.
57. Thomas A. Gavin, "Ethics Education," *Internal Auditor,* April 1989, pp. 54–57.
58. Ibid.
59. Ibid.
60. William Penn and Boyd D. Collier, "Current Research in Moral Development as a Decision Support System," *Journal of Business Ethics,* January 1985, pp. 131–36.
61. James Weber, "Measuring the Impact of Teaching Ethics to Future Managers: A Review, Assessment, and Recommendations," *Journal of Business Ethics,* April 1990, pp. 182–90.
62. "Ethics: Part of the Game at Citicorp," *Fortune,* October 26, 1987, p. 12.
63. See, for instance, Susan J. Harrington, "What Corporate America Is Teaching About Ethics"; and Peter F. Miller and William T. Coady, "Teaching Work Ethics," *Education Digest,* February 1990, pp. 54–55.
64. See, for example, Andrew Stark, "What's the Matter with Business Ethics?" *Harvard Business Review,* May–June 1993, pp. 38–48; "More Big Businesses Set Up Ethics Offices," *Wall Street Journal,* May 10, 1993, p. B1; William D. Hall, *Making the Right Decision: Ethics for Managers* (New York: Wiley, 1993); Susan Gaines, "Handing Out Halos," *Business Ethics,* March–April 1994, pp. 20–24; and Lynn Sharp Paine, "Managing for Organizational Integrity," *Harvard Business Review,* March–April 1994, pp. 106–17.
65. John Dalla Costa, "Getting It", *Report on Business Magazine,* April 1998, pp. 102–106.

Chapter 6

1. Jean Benoit Nadeau, "The Making of a Super Grocer", *The Financial Post Magazine,* May 1998, pp. 14-20.
2. William Pounds, "The Process of Problem Finding," *Industrial Management Review,* Fall 1969, pp. 1–19.
3. Roger J. Volkema, "Problem Formulation: Its Portrayal in the Texts," *Organizational Behavior Teaching Review,* vol. 11, no. 3, 1986–87, pp. 113–26.
4. Morgan W. McCall, Jr., and Robert E. Kaplan, *Whatever It Takes: Decision Makers at Work* (Englewood Cliffs, NJ: Prentice Hall, 1985), pp. 36–38.
5. Herbert A. Simon, *The New Science of Management Decision* (New York: Harper & Row, 1960), p. 1.
6. See Herbert A. Simon, "Rationality in Psychology and Economics," *Journal of Business,* October 1986, pp. 209–24; and Ann Langley, "In Search of Rationality: The Purposes Behind the Use of Formal Analysis in Organizations," *Administrative Science Quarterly,* December 1989, pp. 598–631.
7. See Neil McK. Agnew and John L. Brown, "Bounded Rationality: Fallible Decisions in Unbounded Decision Space," *Behavioral Science,* July 1986, pp. 148–61; Bruce E. Kaufman, "A New Theory of Satisficing," *Journal of Behavioral Economics,* Spring 1990, pp. 35–51; and David R. A. Skidd, "Revisiting Bounded Rationality," *Journal of Management Inquiry,* December 1992, pp. 343–47.
8. V. Pospisil, "Gut Feeling or Skilled Reasoning?", *IW,* March 3, 1997, p. 12.

9. John R. Schermerhorn, Jr., *Management for Productivity,* 4th ed. (New York: Wiley, 1993), p. 150.
10. Alan J. Rowe, James D. Boulgarides, and Michael R. McGrath, *Managerial Decision Making,* Modules in Management Series (Chicago: SRA, 1984), pp. 18–22.
11. This box is based on Ellen F. Jackofsky, John W. Slocum, Jr., and Sara J. McQuaid, "Cultural Values and the CEO: Alluring Companions?" *Academy of Management Executive,* February 1988, pp. 39–49; Stephen P. Robbins, *Organizational Behavior: Concepts, Controversies, and Applications,* 6th ed. (Englewood Cliffs, NJ: Prentice Hall, 1993), p. 158; Noriya Sumihara, "A Case Study of Cross-Cultural Interaction in a Japanese Multinational Corporation Operating in the United States: Decision-Making Processes and Practices," in Ronald R. Sims and Robert F. Dennehy (eds.), *Diversity and Differences in Organizations: An Agenda for Answers and Questions* (Westport, CT: Quorum Books, 1993), pp. 135–47; Scott J. Vitell, Saviour L. Nwachukwu, and James H. Barnes, "The Effects of Culture on Ethical Decision-Making: An Application of Hofstede's Typology," *Journal of Business Ethics,* October 1993, pp. 753–60; and Richard M. Hodgetts and Fred Luthans, *International Management,* 2nd ed. (New York: McGraw-Hill, 1994), pp. 214–15.
12. "Meaningful Meetings," *Inc.,* September 1994, p. 122.
13. Irving L. Janis, *Victims of Groupthink* (Boston: Houghton Mifflin, 1972); Ramon J. Aldag and Sally Riggs Fuller, "Beyond Fiasco: A Reappraisal of the Groupthink Phenomenon and a New Model of Group Decision Processes," *Psychological Bulletin,* May 1993, pp. 533–52; and Tatsuya Kameda and Shinkichi Sugimori, "Psychological Entrapment in Group Decision Making: An Assigned Decision Rule and a Groupthink Phenomenon," *Journal of Personality and Social Psychology,* August 1993, pp. 282–92.
14. See, for example, L. K. Michaelson, W. E. Watson, and R. H. Black, "A Realistic Test of Individual vs. Group Consensus Decision Making," *Journal of Applied Psychology,* vol. 74, no. 5, 1989, pp. 834–39; Rebecca A. Henry, "Group Judgment Accuracy: Reliability and Validity of Postdiscussion Confidence Judgments," *Organizational Behavior and Human Decision Processes,* October 1993, pp. 11–27; Paul W. Paese, Mary Bieser, and Mark E. Tubbs, "Framing Effects and Choice Shifts in Group Decision Making," *Organizational Behavior and Human Decision Processes,* October 1993, pp. 149–65; N. John Castellan, Jr. (ed.), *Individual and Group Decision Making* (Hillsdale, NJ: Erlbaum, 1993); Daniel Gigone and Reid Hastie, "The Common Knowledge Effect: Information Sharing and Group Judgment," *Journal of Personality and Social Psychology,* November 1993, pp. 959–74; Jan B. Baurdoux, "Caesars and Committees," *Challenge,* January–February 1994, pp. 51–53; and Susan G. Straus and Joseph E. McGrath, "Does the Medium Matter? The Interaction of Task Type and Technology on Group Performance and Member Reactions," *Journal of Applied Psychology,* February 1994, pp. 87–97.
15. André L. Delbecq, Andrew H. Van de Ven, and David H. Gustafson, *Group Techniques for Program Planning* (Glenview, IL: Scott, Foresman, 1975).
16. Shull, Delbecq, and Cummings, p. 151.

Chapter 7

1. Robert Hercz, "Shooting for Profits", *Canadian Business,* June 12, 1998, pp. 71–73.
2. See, for example, John A. Pearce II, K. Keith Robbins, and Richard B. Robinson, Jr., "The Impact of Grand Strategy and Planning Formality on Financial Performance," *Strategic Management Journal,* March–April 1987, pp. 125–34; Lawrence C. Rhyne, "Contrasting Planning Systems in High, Medium, and Low Performance Companies," *Journal of Management Studies,* July 1987, pp. 363–85; Richard Brahm and Charles B. Brahm, "Formal Planning and Organizational Performance: Assessing Emerging Empirical Research Trends," paper presented at the National Academy of Management Conference, New Orleans, August 1987; John A. Pearce II, Elizabeth B. Freeman, and Richard B. Robinson, Jr., "The Tenuous Link Between Formal Stategic Planning and Financial Performance," *Academy of Management Review,* October 1987, pp. 658–75; Deepak K. Sinha, "The Contribution of Formal Planning to Decisions," *Strategic Management Journal,* October 1990, pp. 479–92; and Noel Capon, John U. Farley, and James M. Hulbert, "Strategic Planning and Financial Performance: More Evidence," *Journal of Management Studies,* January 1994, pp. 22–38.
3. Russell Ackoff, "A Concept of Corporate Planning," *Long Range Planning,* September 1970, p. 3.
4. Michael B. McCaskey, "A Contingency Approach to Planning: Planning with Goals and Planning Without Goals," *Academy of Management Journal,* June 1974, pp. 281–91.
5. Several of these factors were suggested by J. Scott Armstrong, "The Value of Formal Planning for Strategic Decisions: Review of Empirical Research," *Strategic Management Journal,* July–September 1982, pp. 197–211; and Rudi K. Bresser and Ronald C. Bishop, "Dysfunctional Effects of Formal Planning: Two Theoretical Explanations," *Academy of Management Review,* October 1983, pp. 588–99.
6. Richard F. Vancil, "The Accuracy of Long-Range Planning," *Harvard Business Review,* September–October 1970, p. 99.
7. Based on Ronald Henkoff, "How to Plan for 1995," *Fortune,* December 31, 1990, pp. 70– 77.
8. Rick Molz, "'How Leaders Use Goals," *Long Range Planning,* October 1987, p. 91.
9. Arthur A. Thompson, Jr. and A. J. Strickland III, *Strategic Management* (Homewood, IL: Irwin, 1992), p. 28.
10. This box based on Ellyn E. Spragins, "The Diverse Work Force," *Inc.,* January 1993, p. 33; "The Challenge of Managing Diversity in the Workplace," *Black Enterprise,* July 1993, pp. 79+; Dean Elmuti, "Managing Diversity in the Workplace: An Immense Challenge for Both Managers and Workers," *Industrial Management,* July–August 1993, pp. 19–22; Barbara Jorgensen, "Diversity: Managing a Multicultural Work Force," *Electronic Business Buyer,* September 1993, pp. 70–76; Lisa Harrington, "Why Managing Diversity Is so Important," *Distribution,* November 1993, pp. 88–92; Stephen P. Robbins, *Organizational Behavior: Concepts, Controversies, and Applications* (Englewood Cliffs, NJ: Prentice Hall, 1993), p. 144; Bob Smith, "Recruitment Insights for Strategic Workforce Diversity," *HR Focus,* January 1994, p. 7; and Faye Rice, "How to Make Diversity Pay," *Fortune,* August 8, 1994, pp. 78–86.
11. "The Challenge of Managing Diversity in the Workplace," p. 84.
12. Ibid.
13. See, for instance, Charles K. Warriner, "The Problem of Organizational Purpose," *Sociological Quarterly,* Spring 1965, pp. 139–46; and Jeffrey Pfeffer, *Organizational Design* (Arlington Heights, IL: AHM Publishing, 1978), pp. 5–12.
14. Francis D. Tuggle, *Organizational Processes* (Arlington Heights, IL: AHM Publishing, 1978), p. 108.
15. A.W. Schrader and G.T. Seward, "MBO Makes Dollar Sense", *Personnel Journal,* July, 1989, pp. 32-37.
16. R. Rodgers and J.E. Hunter, "Impact of Management by Objectives on Organizational Productivity", *Journal of Applied Psychology,* April, 1991, pp. 322-326.

Chapter 8

1. Rick Spence, "Fast Learners", *Profit,* June 1998, pp. 77-82
2. See, for example, Larry J. Rosenberg and Charles D. Schewe, "Strategic Planning: Fulfilling the Promise," *Business Horizons,* July–August 1985, pp. 54–62; Walter Kiechel III, "Corporate Strategy for the 1990s," *Fortune,* February 29, 1988, pp. 34–42; Alan D. Meyer, "What Is Strategy's Distinctive Competence?" *Journal of Management,* 1991, vol. 17, no. 4, pp. 821–33; Alexander Hiam, "Strategic Planning Unbound," *Journal of Business Strategy,* March–April 1993, pp. 46–52; Marjorie A. Lyles, Inga S. Baird, Burdeane Orris, and Donald F. Kuratko, "Formalized Planning in Small Business: In-

creasing Strategic Choices," *Journal of Small Business Management,* April 1993, pp. 38–50; Nandini Rajagopalan, Abdul M. A. Rasheed, and Deepak K. Datta, "Strategic Decision Processes: Critical Review and Future Directions," *Journal of Management,* Summer 1993, pp. 349–84; Jaime A. Roquebert, Catherine A. Duran, and Robert L. Phillips, "How Much Does Strategic Management Matter?" paper presented at the 1993 Academy of Management Meeting, Atlanta, Georgia; and Stuart Hart and Catherine Banbury, "How Strategy Making Processes Can Make a Difference," *Strategic Management Journal,* May 1994, pp. 251–69.

3. "A Solid Strategy Helps Companies' Growth," *Nation's Business,* October 1990, p. 10.
4. Laurence C. Rhyne, "The Relationship of Strategic Planning to Financial Performance," *Strategic Management Journal,* 1986, pp. 423–36; Elaine Mosakowski, "A Resource-Based Perspective on The Dynamic Strategy-Performance Relationship: An Empirical Examination of the Focus and Differentiation Strategies in Entrepreneurial Firms," *Journal of Management,* Winter 1993, pp. 819–39; and Noel Capon, John U. Farley, and James M. Hulbert, "Strategic Planning and Financial Performance: More Evidence," *Journal of Management Studies,* January 1994, pp. 22–38.
5. "Colleges Undergo Reassessment," *Time,* April 14, 1992, p. 81.
6. William K. Hall, "SBUs: Hot, New Topic in Management of Diversification," *Business Horizons,* February 1978, p. 17.
7. Stephen E. Bachand, "There's A Lot More To Canadian Tire," *Business Quarterly,* Spring 1995, pp. 31–39.
8. Gary Samuels, "Covering the Bases," *Forbes,* May 9, 1994, pp. 44–45.
9. Jens Ohlin, "Graduating into the Work Force," *Montreal Gazette,* August 29, 1995, p.D1.
10. N. Venkatraman and John E. Prescott, "Environment–Strategy Co-alignment: An Empirical Test of Its Performance Implications," *Strategic Management Journal,* January 1990, pp. 1–23; Peter S. Davis and Patrick L. Schul, "Addressing the Contingent Effects of Business Unit Strategic Orientation on Relationships Between Organizational Context and Business Unit Performance," *Journal of Business Research,* July 1993, pp. 183–200; Mingfang Li and Robert J. Litschert, "Linking Strategy-Making Process and Environment: A Theory," paper presented at the 1993 Academy of Management Meeting, Atlanta, Georgia; and Dan Marline, Bruce T. Lamont, and James J. Hoffman, "Choice Situation, Strategy, and Performance: A Reexamination," *Strategic Management Journal,* March 1994, pp. 229–39.
11. Ian Austen, "Supplier to the Stars", *Canadian Business,* May 29, 1998, pp. 81-85.
12. See Susan E. Jackson and Jane E. Dutton, "Discerning Threats and Opportunities," *Administrative Science Quarterly,* September 1988, pp. 370–87.
13. Alan D. Gray, "Arrow Takes Aim," *Montreal Gazette,* September 5, 1995, pp. C3–C4.
14. See, for example, Jay B. Barney, "Organizational Culture: Can It Be a Source of Sustained Competitive Advantage?" *Academy of Management Review,* July 1986, pp. 656–65; Christian Scholz, "Corporate Culture and Strategy—The Problem of Strategic Fit," *Long Range Planning,* August 1987, pp. 78–87; Sebastian Green, "Understanding Corporate Culture and Its Relation to Strategy," *International Studies of Management and Organization,* Summer 1988, pp. 6–28; Toyohiro Kono, "Corporate Culture and Long-Range Planning," *Long Range Planning,* August 1990, pp. 9–19; and C. Marlene Fiol, "Managing Culture as a Competitive Resource: An Identity-Based View of Sustainable Competitive Advantage," *Journal of Management,* March 1991, pp. 191–211.
15. J. P. Kotter and J. L. Heskett, *Corporate Culture and Performance* (New York: Free Press, 1992).
16. Casey Mahood, "Family Owned Grocer Serves Fresh Ideas", *Globe and Mail,* June 15, 1998, p. B13.
17. This box is based on Roy J. Lewicki, Donald D. Bowen, Douglas T. Hall, and Francine S. Hall, *Experiences in Management and Organizational Behavior,* 3d ed. (New York: Wiley, 1988), pp. 261–67; Armstrong Williams, "Career Planning: Build on Strengths, Strengthen Weaknesses," *The Black Collegian,* September–October 1993, pp. 78–86; C.C. Campbell-Rock, "Career Planning Strategies That Really Work," *The Black Collegian,* September–October 1993, pp. 88–93; Beverly Kaye, "Career Development—Anytime, Anyplace," *Training and Development,* December 1993, pp. 46–49; William Wooten, "Using Knowledge, Skill, and Ability (KSA) Data to Identify Career Pathing Opportunities," *Public Personnel Management,* Winter 1993, pp. 551–63; Catherine Mossop, "Values Assessment: Key to Managing Careers," *CMA—The Management Accounting Magazine,* March 1994, p. 33; and Andrea Davis Pinkney, "Winning in the Workplace," *Essence,* March 1994, pp. 79–80.
18. This box is based on Arnold C. Cooper and others, *New Business in America: The Firms and Their Owners* (Washington, DC: The NFIB Foundation, 1990), p. 1; Jeffrey A. Timmons, *New Venture Creation: Entrepreneurship in the 1990s* (Homewood, IL: Irwin, 1990), p. 9; Robert H. Brockhaus, Sr., "The Psychology of the Entrepreneur," in Calvin A. Kent, Donald L. Sexton, and Karl H. Vesper (eds.), *Encyclopedia of Entrepreneurship* (Englewood Cliffs, NJ: Prentice Hall, 1982), pp. 41–49; Howard H. Stevenson and David E. Gumpert, "The Heart of Entrepreneurship," *Harvard Business Review,* March–April 1985, pp. 85–94; Richard L. Osborne, "Second Phase Entrepreneurship: Breaking Through the Growth Wall," *Business Horizons,* January–February 1994, pp. 80–86; and Brian O'Reilly, "The New Face of Small Business," *Fortune,* May 2, 1994, pp. 82–88.
19. See William F. Glueck, *Business Policy: Strategy Formulation and Management Action,* 2d ed. (New York: McGraw-Hill, 1976), pp. 120–47; John A. Pearce II, "Selecting Among Alternative Grand Strategies," *California Management Review,* Spring 1982, pp. 23–31; and Theodore T. Herbert and Helen Deresky, "Generic Strategies: An Empirical Investigation of Typology Validity and Strategy Content," *Strategic Management Journal,* March–April 1987, pp. 135–47.
20. See, for example, Kathryn Rudie Harrigan, *Strategies for Declining Businesses* (Lexington, MA: Lexington, 1980); Kim S. Cameron, Myung U. Kim, and David A. Whetten, "Organizational Effects of Decline and Turbulence," *Administrative Science Quarterly,* June 1987, pp. 222–40; "Downsizing Record Set by Firms in Year: 56% Report Job Cuts," *Wall Street Journal,* August 12, 1991, p. A2; and Kim S. Cameron, Sarah J. Freeman, and Aneil K. Mishra, "Best Practices in White-Collar Downsizing: Managing Contradictions," *Academy of Management Executive,* August 1991, pp. 57–73; Catherine M. Daily, "CEO and Director Turnover in Failing Firms: The Illusion of Change," paper presented at the 1993 Academy of Management Annual Meeting, Atlanta, Georgia; and J. L. Morrow Jr. and Lowell Busenitz, "Turnaround and Retrenchment in Mature and Growth Industries," paper presented at the 1993 Academy of Management Annual Meeting, Atlanta, Georgia.
21. Phillipe Haspeslagh, "Portfolio Planning: Uses and Limits," *Harvard Business Review,* January–February 1982, pp. 58–73.
22. *Perspective on Experience* (Boston: Boston Consulting Group, 1970).
23. See, for example, Donald C. Hambrick, Ian C. Macmillan, and Diana L. Day, "Strategic Attributes and Performance in the BCG Matrix: A PIMS-Based Analysis of Industrial Product Businesses," *Academy of Management Journal,* September 1982, pp. 510–31; H. Kurt Christensen, Arnold C. Cooper, and Cornelis A. DeKluyver, "The Dog Business: A Re-Examination," *Business Horizons,* November–December 1982, pp. 12–18; William Baldwin, "The Market Share Myth," *Forbes,* March 14, 1983, pp. 109–15; Richard A. Bettis and William K. Hall, "The Business Portfolio Approach—Where It Falls Down in Practice," *Long Range Planning,* April 1983, pp. 95–104; and Jaclyn Fierman, "How to Make Money in Mature Markets," *Fortune,* November 25, 1985, pp. 47–53.
24. See, for example, Michael E. Porter, *Competitive Strategy: Techniques for*

Analyzing Industries and Competitors (New York: Free Press, 1980); Michael E. Porter, *Competitive Advantage: Creating and Sustaining Superior Performance* (New York: Free Press, 1985); Gregory G. Dess and Peter S. Davis, "Porter's (1980) Generic Strategies as Determinants of Strategic Group Membership and Organizational Performance," *Academy of Management Journal,* September 1984, pp. 467–88; Gregory S. Dess and Peter S. Davis, "Porter's (1980) Generic Strategies and Performance: An Empirical Examination with American Data—Part I: Testing Porter," *Organization Studies,* no. 1, 1986, pp. 37–55; Gregory G. Dess and Peter S. Davis, "Porter's (1980) Generic Strategies and Performance: An Empirical Examination with American Data—Part II: Performance Implications," *Organization Studies,* no. 3, 1986, pp. 255–61; Michael E. Porter, "From Competitive Advantage to Corporate Strategy," *Harvard Business Review,* May–June 1987, pp. 43–59; Alan I. Murray, "A Contingency View of Porter's 'Generic Strategies,'" *Academy of Management Review,* July 1988, pp. 390–400; Charles W. L. Hill, "Differentiation Versus Low Cost or Differentiation and Low Cost: A Contingency Framework," *Academy of Management Review,* July 1988, pp. 401–12; Ingolf Bamberger, "Developing Competitive Advantage in Small and Medium-Sized Firms," *Long Range Planning,* October 1989, pp. 80–88; Michael E. Porter, "Know Your Place," *Inc.,* September 1991, pp. 90–93; and Daniel F. Jennings and James R. Lumpkin, "Insights Between Environmental Scanning Activities and Porter's Generic Strategies: An Empirical Analysis," *Strategic Management Journal,* 1992, vol. 18, no. 4, pp. 791–803.

25. Danny Miller and Jean-Marie Toulouse, "Strategy, Structure, CEO Personality, and Performance in Small Firms," *American Journal of Small Business,* Winter 1986, pp. 47–62.
26. Peter Wright, Charles D. Pringle, and Mark J. Kroll, *Strategic Management* (Boston: Allyn and Bacon, 1994), p. 135.
27. Dean M. Schroeder and Alan G. Robinson, "America's Most Successful Export to Japan: Continuous Improvement Programs," *Sloan Management Review,* Spring 1991, pp. 67–81; Richard J. Schonenberger, "Is Strategy Strategic? Impact of Total Quality Management on Strategy," *Academy of Management Executive,* August 1992, pp. 80–87; Charles A. Barclay, "Quality Strategy and TQM Policies: Empirical Evidence," *Management International Review,* Special Issue 1993, pp. 87–98; David W. Waldman, "A Theoretical Consideration of Leadership and Total Quality Management," *Leadership Quarterly,* 1993, vol. 4, no. 1, pp. 65–79; Tracy E. Benson, "A Business Strategy Comes of Age," *Industry Week,* May 3, 1993, pp. 40–44; Rahul Jacob, "TQM: More Than a Dying Fad?" *Fortune,* October 18, 1993, pp. 66–72; R. Krishnan, A. B. (Rami) Shani, R. M. Grant, and R. Baer, "In Search of Quality Improvement Problems of Design and Implementation," *Academy of Management Executive,* November 1993, pp. 7–20; Bristol Voss, "Quality's Second Coming," *Journal of Business Strategy,* March–April 1994, pp. 42–46; Michael Barrier, "Raising TQM Consciousness," *Nation's Business,* April 1994, pp. 62–64; and special issue of *Academy of Management Review* devoted to TQM, July 1994, pp. 390–584.
28. Celine Bak, "Lessons Learned from the Veterans of TQM", *Canadian Business Review,* Winter 1992.

Chapter 9

1. Sean Silcoff, "Secrets of a Best Seller", *Canadian Business,* June 26/July 10, 1998, pp. 89–93; Brian Hutchinson, "Merchants of Boom", *Canadian Business,* May 1997, pp. 30–48; Gina Mallet, "Book Store Wars", *Financial Post Magazine,* May, 1997, pp. 42–49; Ann Gibbon, "Bollums Books Grows Up Too Fast", *Globe and Mail,* April 10, 1997, p. B17; Sean Eckford, "Ottawa's Independent Bookstores Join Forces", *Marketing Magazine,* January 27, 1997, p. 2; John Heinzl, "Books, Bach, and Beer", *Globe and Mail,* September 4, 1997, p. B1.
2. John Diffenbach, "Corporate Environmental Analysis in Large U.S. Corporations," *Long Range Planning,* June 1983, pp. 107–16; Subhash C. Jain, "Environmental Scanning in U.S. Corporations," *Long Range Planning,* April 1984, pp. 117–28; Leonard M. Fuld, *Monitoring the Competition* (New York: Wiley, 1988); Elmer H. Burack and Nicholas J. Mathys, "Environmental Scanning Improves Strategic Planning," *Personnel Administrator,* April 1989, pp. 82–87; James B. Thomas, Shawn M. Clark, and Dennis A. Gioia, "Strategic Sensemaking and Organizational Performance: Linkages Among Scanning, Interpretation, Action, and Outcomes," *Academy of Management Journal,* April 1993, pp. 239–70; Olukemi O. Sawyerr, "Environmental Uncertainty and Environmental Scanning Activities of Nigerian Manufacturing Executives: A Comparative Analysis," *Strategic Management Journal,* May 1993, pp. 194–203; Ethel Auster and Chun Wei Choo, "Environmental Scanning by CEOs in Two Canadian Industries," *Journal of the American Society for Information Science,* May 1993, pp. 194–203; and Ram Subramanian, Nirmala Fernandes, and Earl Harper, "Environmental Scanning in U.S. Companies: Their Nature and Their Relationship to Performance," *Management International Review,* July 1993, pp. 271–86.
3. Benjamin Gilad, "The Role of Organized Competitive Intelligence in Corporate Strategy," *Columbia Journal of World Business,* Winter 1989, pp. 29–35; Betsy D. Gelb, Mary Jane Saxton, George M. Zinkhan, and Nancy D. Albers, "Competitive Intelligence Insights from Executives," *Business Horizons,* January–February 1991, pp. 43–47; Leonard Fuld, "A Recipe for Business Intelligence," *Journal of Business Strategy,* January–February 1991, pp. 12–17; Gary B. Roush, "A Program for Sharing Corporate Intelligence," *Journal of Business Strategy,* January–February 1991, pp. 4–7; and Richard S. Teitelbaum, "The New Role for Intelligence," *Fortune,* November 2, 1992, pp. 104–07.
4. Mark Robichaux, "Competitor Intelligence: A Grapevine to Rivals' Secrets," *Wall Street Journal,* April 12, 1989, p. B2.
5. William H. Davidson, "The Role of Global Scanning in Business Planning," *Organizational Dynamics,* Winter 1991, pp. 5–16.
6. Manuel Werner, "Planning for Uncertain Futures: Building Commitment Through Scenario Planning," *Business Horizons,* May–June 1990, pp. 55–58.
7. See James K. Glassman, "The Year of Gazing Dangerously," *Business Month,* March 1990, pp. 13–14; Anne B. Fisher, "Is Long-Range Planning Worth It?" *Fortune,* April 23, 1990, pp. 281–84; Jill Andresky Fraser, "On Target," *Inc.,* April 1991, pp. 113–14; Peter Schwartz, *The Art of the Long View* (New York: Doubleday/Currency, 1991); Stan Davis, "Twenty Tips for Developing 20/20 Vision for Business," *Journal of Management Development,* September 1993, pp. 15–20; and Gary Hamel and C. K. Prahalad, "Competing for the Future," *Harvard Business Review,* July–August 1994, pp. 122–28.
8. P. Narayan Pant and William H. Starbuck, "Innocents in the Forest: Forecasting and Research Methods," *Journal of Management,* June 1990, pp. 433–60.
9. This section is based on Bruce Brocka and M. Suzanne Brocka, *Quality Management* (Homewood, IL: Business One Irwin, 1992), pp. 231–36; George A. Weimer, "Benchmarking Maps the Route to Quality," *Industry Week,* July 20, 1992, pp. 54–55; Jeremy Main, "How to Steal the Best Ideas Around," *Fortune,* October 19, 1992, pp. 102–106; Howard Rothman, "You Need Not Be Big to Benchmark," *Nation's Business,* December 1992, pp. 64–65; Y. K. Shetty, "Benchmarking for Superior Performance," *Long Range Planning,* 1993, vol. 1, pp. 39–44; Gregory H. Watson, "How Process Benchmarking Supports Corporate Strategy," *Planning Review,* January–February 1993, pp. 12–15; Michael Cavallon and Scott Winslow, "Strategic Benchmarking Helps Make Quality Progams Work," *American Banker's Management Strategies,* March 29, 1993, p. 9A; Neela Banerjee, "Firms Analyze Rivals to Help Fix Themselves," *Wall Street Journal,* May 3, 1994, p. B1+; Karen Caplan and Christopher Bogan, "Benchmarking Basics," *Business Ethics,* May–June

1994, p. 30; and Stephen George and Arnold Weimerskirch, *Total Quality Management: Strategies and Techniques Proven at Today's Most Successful Companies* (New York: Wiley, 1994), pp. 207–21.

10. See Harold E. Fearon, William A. Ruch, Vincent G. Reuter, C. David Wieters, and Ross R. Reck, *Fundamentals of Production/Operations Management,* 3d ed. (St. Paul, MN: West, 1986), p. 97.
11. Earl Hazen, "Project Management Ensures On-Time Completion," *Transmission and Distribution,* April 1989, pp. 24–27.
12. For a discussion of software and application to a project for restructuring a large retail chain, see Paul A. Strassman, "The Best-Laid Plans," *Inc.,* October 1988, pp. 135–88. Also, see D. L. Kimbler, "Operational Planning: Going Beyond PERT With TQM Tools," *Industrial Management,* September–October 1993, pp. 26–29.
13. See, for example, Sarah Stiansen, "Breaking Even," *Success,* November 1988, p. 16.
14. Stephen E. Barndt and Davis W. Carvey, *Essentials of Operations Management* (Englewood Cliffs, NJ: Prentice Hall, 1982), p. 134.

Chapter 10

1. John Partridge, "Abitibi Dares to Digest Another Deal", *Globe and Mail,* February 27, 1998, p. B27; and Jean Benoit Nadeau, "Priorities in Paper", *The Financial Post 500,* pp. 58–62.
2. R. L. Daft, *Organization Theory and Design,* 6th ed. (St. Paul, Minnesota: West Publishing, 1998)
3. L. Urwick, *The Elements of Administration* (New York: Harper & Row, 1944), pp. 52–53.
4. D. Van Fleet, "Span of Management Research and Issues", *Acadaemy of Management Journal,* September, 1983, pp. 546–552.
5. A Ross, "BMO's Big Bang", *Canadian Business*, January 1994, pp. 58–63.
6. Tom Burns and G. M. Stalker, *The Management of Innovation* (London: Tavistock, 1961).
7. Alfred D. Chandler, Jr., *Strategy and Structure: Chapters in the History of the Industrial Enterprise* (Cambridge, MA: MIT Press, 1962).
8. See, for instance, Raymond E. Miles and Charles C. Snow, *Organizational Strategy, Structure, and Process* (New York: McGraw-Hill, 1978); Herman L. Boschken, "Strategy and Structure: Reconceiving the Relationship," *Journal of Management,* March 1990, pp. 135–50; and Herbert A. Simon, "Strategy and Organizational Evolution," *Strategic Management Journal,* January 1993, pp. 131–42.
9. See, for instance, Peter M. Blau and Richard A. Schoenherr, *The Structure of Organizations* (New York: Basic Books, 1971); D. S. Pugh, "The Aston Program of Research: Retrospect and Prospect," in A. H. Van de Ven and W. F. Joyce (eds.), *Perspectives on Organization Design and Behavior* (New York: Wiley, 1981), pp. 135–66; and R. Z. Gooding and J. A. Wagner III, "A Meta-Analytic Review of the Relationship Between Size and Performance: The Productivity and Efficiency of Organizations and Their Subunits," *Administrative Science Quarterly,* December 1985, pp. 462–81.
10. J. Woodward, *Industrial Organization: Theory and Practice* (London: Oxford University Press, 1965).
11. C. C. Miller, W. H. Glick, Y.-D. Wang, and G. Huber, "Understanding Technology-Structure Relationships: Theory Development and Meta-Analytic Theory Testing", *Academy of Management Journal,* June 1991, pp. 370–399.
12. See, for instance: C. Perrow, "A Framework for the Comparative Analysis of Organizations", *American Sociological Review,* April 1967, pp. 194–208; J.D. Thompson, *Organizations in Action* (New York: McGraw Hill, 1967); and J. Hage and M. Aiken, "Routine Technology, Social Structure, and Organizational Goals", *Administrative Science Quarterly,* September 1969, pp. 366–377.
13. D. Gerwin, "Relationships between Structure and Technology", in P. C. Nystrom and W. H. Starbuck (eds.), *Handbook of Organizational Design,* vol. 2 (New York: Oxford University Press, 1981), pp. 3–38; and D.M. Rousseau and R. A. Cooke, "Technology and Structure: The Concrete, Abstract, and Activity Systems of Organizations", *Journal of Management,* Fall–Winter 1984, pp. 345–361.
14. See Stephen P. Robbins, *Organization Theory: Structure, Design, and Applications,* pp. 210–32.
15. Henry Mintzberg, *Structure in Fives: Designing Effective Organizations* (Englewood Cliffs, NJ: Prentice Hall, 1983), p. 157.
16. This box is based on Fred L. Fry, *Entrepreneurship: A Planning Approach* (Minneapolis/St. Paul: West, 1993), pp. 319–40; Richard L. Osborne, "Second Phase Entrepreneurship: Breaking Through the Growth Wall," *Business Horizons,* January–February 1994, pp. 80–86; Roy Cammarano, "The Four Stages of Growth," *Nation's Business,* June 1994, pp. 64–65; and Justin G. Longenecker, Carlos W. Moore, and J. William Petty, *Small Business Management* (Cincinnati: South Western Publishing, 1994), pp. 421–25.
17. See, for example, Leslie Brokaw, "Thinking Flat," *Inc.,* October 1993, pp. 86–88; Robert E. Hoskisson, Charles W. L. Hill, and Hicheon Kim, "The Multidivisional Structure: Organizational Fossil or Source of Value?" *Journal of Management,* 1993, vol. 19, no. 2, pp. 269–98; Ian I. Mitroff, Richard O. Mason, and Christine M. Pearson, "Radical Surgery: What Will Tomorrow's Organizations Look Like?" *Academy of Management Executive,* February 1994, pp. 11–21; Tony Clancy, "Radical Surgery: A View from the Operating Theater," *Academy of Management Executive,* February 1994, pp. 73–78; Tom Peters, "Organization Models Point to Dire Need for Change," *Springfield Business Journal,* March 14, 1994, p. 15; Gifford and Elizabeth Pinchot, "Beyond Bureaucracy," *Business Ethics,* March–April 1994, pp. 26–29; Elizabeth and Gifford Pinchot, *The End of Bureaucracy and the Rise of the Intelligent Organization* (San Francisco: Berrett-Koehler Publishers, 1994); William Spindle and others, "Toyota Retooled," *Business Week,* April 4, 1994, pp. 54–57; U.S. Department of Labor, "The New American Workplace—Union Style," *American Workplace Newsletter,* May 1994, pp. 1–4; Tom Peters, "Crazy Times Call for Crazy Organizations," *Success,* July–August 1994, pp. 24A+; and Thomas H. Davenport and June E. K. Delano, "On Tomorrow's Organizations: Moving Forward, or a Step Backwards?" *Academy of Management Executive,* August 1994, pp. 93–98.
18. See, for example, Howard Rothman, "The Power of Empowerment," *Nation's Business,* June 1993, pp. 49–52; Briane Dumaine, "Payoff from the New Management"; John A. Byrne, "The Horizontal Corporation"; Jon R. Katzenback and Douglas K. Smith, *The Wisdom of Teams* (Boston: Harvard Business School Press, 1993); and Linda Grant, "New Jewel in the Crown," *U.S. News & World Report,* February 28, 1994, pp. 55–57.
19. This box based on Jill Andresky Fraser, "Women, Power, and the New GE," *Working Woman,* December 1992, pp. 58+; Stephen P. Robbins, *Organizational Behavior: Concepts, Controversies, and Applications,* 6th ed. (Englewood Cliffs, NJ: Prentice Hall, 1993), p. 537; and "Mother Nurture," *Wall Street Journal,* August 23, 1994, p. A1.
20. Cited in *At Work,* May–June 1993, p. 3.
21. See, for example, Charles C. Snow, Raymond E. Miles, and Henry J. Coleman, Jr., "Managing 21st Century Network Organizations," *Organizational Dynamics,* Winter 1992, pp. 5–20; William H. Davidow and Michael S. Malone, *The Virtual Corporation: Customization and Instantaneous Response in Manufacturing and Service: Lessons from the World's Most Advanced Companies* (New York: Harper Business, 1992); John A. Byrne, Richard Brandt, and Otis Port, "The Virtual Corporation," *Business Week,* February 8, 1993, pp. 98–102; Shawn Tully, "The Modular Corporation," *Fortune,* February 8, 1993, pp. 22–26; John R. Wilke, "Computer Links Erode Hierarchical Nature of Workplace Culture," *Wall Street Journal,* December 9, 1993, pp. A1+; David Kirkpatrick, "Groupware Goes Boom," *Fortune,* December 27, 1993, pp. 99–106; James C. Hyatt, "GE Chairman's Annual Letter Notes Strides by 'Stretch' of the Imagination," *Wall Street Journal,* March 8, 1994, p. B6;

Jessica Lipnack and Jeffrey Stamps, "The Best of Both Worlds," *Inc.*, March 1994, p. 33; Robert W. Keidel, "Rethinking Organizational Design," *Academy of Management Executive,* November 1994, pp. 12–27.

22. Tom Peters, "Successful Electronic Changeovers Depend on Daring," *Springfield Business Journal,* August 8, 1994, p. 15.
23. P. M. Senge, *The Fifth Discipline: The Art and Practice of Learning Organizations* (New York: Doubleday, 1990).
24. J. M. Liedtka, "Collaborating Across Lines of Business for Competitive Advantage", *Academy of Management Executive*, April 1996, pp. 20-37; and G. Szulanski, "Exploring Internal Stickiness: Impediments to the Transfer of Best Practice Within the Firm", *Strategic Management Journal*, Winter Special Issue, 1996, pp. 27–43.
25. See, for example, R. Hotch, "Communications Revolution", *Nation's Business*, May 1993, pp. 20–28; and L. Rout (ed.), "The Corporate Connection", *Wall Street Journal Special Reports*, November 18, 1996, pp. R1–R34.

Chapter 11

1 Bruce Livesey, "Provide and Conquer", *Report on Business Magazine*, March 1997, pp. 32–42; Greg Keenan, "Husky and Healthy", *Globe and Mail*, August 1, 1995, p. B8; and David Menzies, "What Do You Mean There Are No More Donuts?", *Financial Post Magazine*, December, 1996, p. 10.

2. B. Downie and M. C. Cotes, *The Changing Face of Industrial Relations and Human Resources Management* (Kingston: Industrial Relations Centre, Queen's University
3. P. M. Wright and G. C. McMahan, "Theoretical Perspectives for Strategic Human Resource Management", *Journal of Managment* 18, No.1 (1992), pp. 295–320; A. A. Lado, and M. C. Wilson, "Human Resource Systems and Sustained Competitive Advantage", *Academy of Management Review*, October, 1994, pp. 699–727; and J. Pfeffer, *Competitive Advantage Through People* (Boston: Harvard Business School Press, 1994).
4. See, for example, Michael A. Verespej, "Partnership in the Trenches," *Industry Week,* October 17, 1988, pp. 56–64; "Unions and Management Are in a Family Way," *U.S. News & World Report,* June 12, 1989, p. 24; Thomas A. Kochan, "Toward a Mutual Gains Paradigm for Labor–Management Relations," *Labor Law Journal,* August 1993, pp. 454–464; and Aaron Bernstein, "Why America Needs Unions, But Not the Kind It Has Now," *Business Week,* May 23, 1994, pp. 70–82.
5. Elmer H. Burack, "Corporate Business and Human Resource Planning Practices: Strategic Issues and Concerns," *Organizational Dynamics,* Summer 1986, pp. 73–87; and David E. Ripley, "How to Determine Future Workforce Needs," *Personnel Journal,* January 1995, pp. 83–89.
6. Thomas J. Bergmann and M.S. Taylor, "College Recruitment: What Attracts Students to Organizations?" *Personnel,* May–June 1984, pp. 34–46.
7. Judith R. Gordon, *Human Resource Management: A Practical Approach* (Boston: Allyn and Bacon, 1986), p. 170.
8. See, for example, Jean Powell Kirnan, John E. Farley, and Kurt F. Geisinger, "The Relationship Between Recruiting Source, Applicant Quality, and Hire Performance: An Analysis by Sex, Ethnicity, and Age," *Personnel Psychology,* Summer 1989, pp. 293–308.
9. See, for example, Leonard Greenhalgh, Anne T. Lawrence, and Robert I. Sutton, "Determinants of Work Force Reduction Strategies in Declining Organizations," *Academy of Management Review,* April 1988, pp. 241–54.
10. This story was directly influenced by a similar example in Arthur Sloane, *Personnel: Managing Human Resources* (Englewood Cliffs, NJ: Prentice Hall, 1983), p. 127.
11. James J. Asher, "The Biographical Item: Can It Be Improved?" *Personnel Psychology,* Summer 1972, p. 266.
12. George W. England, *Development and Use of Weighted Application Blanks,* rev. ed. (Minneapolis: Industrial Relations Center, University of Minnesota, 1971).
13. John Aberth, "Pre-Employment Testing Is Losing Favor," *Personnel Journal,* September 1986, pp. 96–104.
14. Chris Lee, "Testing Makes a Comeback," *Training,* December 1988, pp. 49–59.
15. Ibid., p. 50.
16. Edwin E. Ghiselli, "The Validity of Aptitude Tests in Personnel Selection," *Personnel Psychology,* Winter 1973, p. 475.
17. G. Grimsley and H. F. Jarrett, "The Relation of Managerial Achievement to Test Measures Obtained in the Employment Situation: Methodology and Results," *Personnel Psychology,* Spring 1973, pp. 31–48; and Abraham K. Korman, "The Prediction of Managerial Performance: A Review," *Personnel Psychology,* Summer 1986, pp. 295–322.
18. I. T. Robertson and R. S. Kandola, "Work Sample Tests: Validity, Adverse Impact, and Applicant Reaction," *Journal of Occupational Psychology,* vol. 55, no. 3, 1982, p. 171–83.
19. G. C. Thornton, Assessment Centers in Human Resource Management (Reading, MA: Addison Wesley, 1992).
20. Robert L. Dipboye, *Selection Interviews: Process Perspectives* (Cincinnati, OH: South-Western Publishing, 1992), p. 6.
21. See, for instance, Richard D. Arveny and James E. Campion, "The Employment Interview: A Summary and Review of Recent Research," *Personnel Psychology,* Summer 1982, pp. 281–322; and Michael M. Harris, "Reconsidering the Employment Interview: A Review of Recent Literature and Suggestions for Future Research," *Personnel Psychology,* Winter 1989, pp. 691–726.
22. Dipboye, p. 180.
23. See, for instance, Eugene C . Mayfield and Neal Schmitt, "Social and Situational Determinants of Interview Decisions: Implications for Employment Interview," *Personnel Psychology,* Spring 1976, p. 81; Richard D. Arvey and James E. Campion, "The Employment Interview: A Summary and Review of Recent Research," Milton D. Hakel, "Employment Interview," in K. M. Rowland and G. R. Ferris (eds.), *Personnel Management: New Perspectives* (Boston: Allyn and Bacon, 1982), pp. 192–55; Edward C. Webster, *The Employment Interview: A Social Judgment Process* (Schomberg, Ontario: S.I.P. Publications, 1982); Michael M. Harris, "Reconsidering the Employment Interview," Amanda Peek Phillips and Robert L. Dipboye, "Correlational Tests of Predictions from a Process Model of the Interview," *Journal of Applied Psychology,* February 1989, pp. 41–52; and Robert C. Liden, Christopher L. Martin, and Charles K. Parsons, "Interviewer and Applicant Behavior in Employment Interviews," *Academy of Management Journal,* April 1993, pp. 372–86.
24. See Irwin L. Goldstein, "The Application Blank: How Honest Are the Responses?" *Journal of Applied Psychology,* October 1971, pp. 491–92; and Winifred Yu, "Firms Tighten Résumé Checks of Applicants," *Wall Street Journal,* August 20, 1985, p. 27.
25. Monica Belcourt, Arthur W. Sherman, Jr., George W. Bohlander, and Scott H. Snell, *Managing Human Resources,* Canadian ed. (Scarborough, ON: Nelson Canada, 1996), p. 224.
26. P. Wright, "Protect Yourself, Be Professional When Checking References," *Interim Report,* Chartered Accountants of New Brunswick, 6(2), 1994, pp. 18–19.
27. Eugene C. Mayfield in Neal Schmitt, "Social and Situational Determinants of Interview Decisions: Implications for Employment Interviews."
28. Sandra L. Robinson, Matthew S. Kraatz, and Denise M. Rousseau, "Changing Obligations and the Psychological Contract: A Longitudinal Study," *Academy of Management Journal,* February 1994, pp. 137–52.
29. Cited in "The Five Factors That Make for Airline Accidents," *Fortune,* May 22, 1989, p. 80.
30. Nicholas Jennings, "Front and Centre Stage", *Maclean's*, July 28, 1997, pp. 48–51; and Peter Waal, "The New Kid's Nettwerk", *B.C. Business*, March, 1997, pp. 28–31.
31. 13th Annual Survey, *Training,* October 1994, p. 36.
32. See, for example, Joan C. Szabo, "Boosting Workers' Basic Skills," *Nation's Business,* January 1992, pp. 38–40; and Ronald Henkoff, "Companies That Train Best," *Fortune,* March 22, 1993, pp. 20–25.

33. Bruce Little, "A Factory Learns to Survive," *Globe and Mail,* May 18, 1993, p. B22.
34. This box is based on Victoria A. Parker and Kathy E. Kram, "Women Mentoring Women: Creating Conditions for Connection," *Business Horizons,* March–April 1993, pp. 42–51; Howard Rothman, "The Boss as Mentor," *Nation's Business,* April 1993, pp. 66–67; J. Barton Cunningham and Ted Eberle, "Characteristics of the Mentoring Experience: A Qualitative Study," *Personnel Review,* June 1993, pp. 54–66; William T. Whitely and Pol Coetsier, "The Relationship of Career Mentoring to Early Career Outcomes," *Organization Studies,* Summer 1993, pp. 419–41; Susan Crandell, "The Joys of Mentoring," *Executive Female,* March–April 1994, pp. 38–42; and William Heery, "Corporate Mentoring Can Break the Glass Ceiling," *HR Focus,* May 1994, pp. 17–18.
35. This section based on Richard I. Henderson, *Compensation Management,* 6th ed. (Englewood Cliffs, NJ: Prentice Hall, 1994), pp. 3–24.
36. M. Rowland, "It's What You Can Do That Counts", *New York Times,* June 6, 1993, p. F17.
37. Alan Murray, "Mom, Apple Pie, and Small Business," *Wall Street Journal,* August 15, 1994, p. A1.
38.. Interview with Bill Gates, "Bill Gates on Rewiring the Power Structure," *Working Woman,* April 1994, p. 62.
39. Schwind, Das, et al., pp. 113–114
40. Arjun P. Aggarwal, *Sexual Harrassment in the Workplace,* 2nd ed. (Unionville, ON: Butterworths Canada, 1992).
41. Belcourt, Sherman, Bohlander, and Snell, p. 105.
42. See Alan Deutschman, "Dealing With Sexual Harassment," *Fortune,* November 4, 1991, pp. 145–48; Robert T. Gray, "How to Deal with Sexual Harassment," *Nation's Business,* December 1991, pp. 28–31; Troy Segal, "Getting Serious About Sexual Harassment," *Business Week,* November 9, 1992, pp. 78–82; Orin M. Kurland, "Dealing with Workplace Sexual Harassment," *Risk Management,* April 1993, pp. 22–24; Cheryl R. Saban, "Sexual Harassment: Does It Exist in Your Workplace?" *Chain Store Age Executive,* May 1993, p. 282; Samuel J. Bresler and Rebecca Thacker, "Four-Point Plan Helps Solve Harassment Problems," *HR Magazine,* May 1993, pp. 117–21; Jan Bohren, "Six Myths of Sexual Harassment," *Management Review,* May 1993, pp. 61–63; "Sexual Harassment in the Workplace: It's Against the Law," Pamphlet from Justice Management Division of Equal Employment Opportunity Commission, June 29, 1993; Rick Van Warner, "Harassment Won't Stop Without Aggressive Action from the Top," *Nation's Restaurant News,* August 30, 1993, p. 19; Jonathan A. Segal, "Proceed Carefully, Objectively to Investigate Sexual Harassment Claims," *HR Magazine,* October 1993, pp. 91–94; Susan Fry Bovet, "Sexual Harassment: What's Happening and How to Deal with It," *Public Relations Journal,* November 1993, pp. 26–29; Roger L. Anderson and James W. Robinson, "The Rest of the Story in Sexual Harassment Cases," *Review of Business,* Winter 1993, pp. 13–16; "Beyond Sexual Harassment," *Supervisory Management,* January 1994, p. 10; Rebecca A. Thacker, "Innovative Steps to Take in Sexual Harassment Prevention," *Business Horizons,* January–February 1994, pp. 29–32; Thomas R. Haggard and Mason G. Alexander, Jr., "Tips on Drafting and Enforcing a Policy Against Sexual Harassment," *Industrial Management,* January–February 1994, pp. 2–5; Jennifer J. Loabs, "HR Puts its Questions on the Line—Sexual Harassment," February 1995, pp. 36–45; and Sharon Nelton, "Sexual Harassment: Reducing the Risks," *Nation's Business,* March 1995, pp. 24–26.
43. Anne B. Fisher, "Sexual Harassment: What to Do," p. 85.
44. *Wall Street Journal,* January 11, 1994, p. A1.
45. Kenneth E. Newgren, C.E. Kellogg, and William Gardner, "Corporate Responses to Dual-Career Couples: A Decade of Transformation," *Akron Business and Economic Review,* Summer 1988, p. 85.
46. Ibid., pp. 85–96.
47. Mary L. Holton, *AIDS and the Employment Relationship* (Kingston: Industrial Relations Centre, Queen's University, 1989).
48. Schwind, Das, et al, p. 468; and Wright, Mondy, and Noe, p. 168.
49. Belcourt, Sherman, Bohlander, and Snell, p. 240.
50. Wright, Mondy, and Noe.

Chapter 12

1. Jean Benoit Nadeau, "Well-tempered Ideas", *Financial Post 500,* 1998, pp. 66-68.
2. The idea for these metaphors came from Peter B. Vaill, *Managing as a Performing Art: New Ideas for a World of Chaotic Change* (San Francisco: Jossey-Bass, 1989).
3. Kurt Lewin, *Field Theory in Social Science* (New York: Harper & Row, 1951).
4. See, for instance, Tom Peters, *Thriving on Chaos* (New York: Knopf, 1987); Tom Peters, "Thriving in Chaos," *Working Woman,* September 1993, pp. 42+; and John P. Kotter, "Why Transformation Efforts Fail," *Harvard Business Review,* March–April 1995, pp. 59–67.
5. Peters, p. 3.
6. Ibid.
7. See, for example, Barry M. Staw, "Counterforces to Change," in Paul S. Goodman and Associates (eds.), *Change in Organizations* (San Francisco: Jossey-Bass, 1982), pp. 87–121.
8. John P. Kotter and Leonard A. Schlesinger, "Choosing Strategies for Change," *Harvard Business Review,* March–April 1979, pp. 107–09.
9. John P. Kotter and Leonard A. Schlesinger, "Choosing Strategies for Change," pp. 106–11; Deanne Rosenberg, "Eliminating Resistance to Change," *Security Management,* January 1993, pp. 20–21; Ken Matejka and Ramona Julian, "Resistance to Change Is Natural," *Supervisory Management,* October 1993, p. 10; Carol O'Connor, "Resistance: The Repercussions of Change," *Leadership & Organization Development Journal,* October 1993, pp. 30–36; Jennifer Landau, "Organizational Change and Barriers to Innovation: A Case Study in the Italian Public Sector," *Human Relations,* December 1993, pp. 1411–29; Abraham Sagie and Meni Koslowsky, "Organizational Attitudes and Behaviors as a Function of Participation in Strategic and Tactical Change Decisions: An Application of Path–Goal Theory," *Journal of Organizational Behavior,* January 1994, pp. 37–47; and Veron D. Miller, John R. Johnson, and Jennifer Grau, "Antecedents to Willingness to Participate in a Planned Organizational Change," *Journal of Applied Communication Research,* February 1994, pp. 59–80.
10. See, for example, Wendell L. French and Cecil H. Bell, Jr., *Organization Development: Behavioral Science Interventions for Organization Improvement,* 4th ed. (Englewood Cliffs, NJ: Prentice Hall, 1990); Christa L. Walck, "Organization Development in the USSR: An Overview and a Case Sample," *Journal of Managerial Psychology,* March 1993, pp. 10–17; Thomas C. Head and Peter F. Sorensen, "Cultural Values and Organizational Development: A Seven-Country Study," *Leadership & Organization Development Journal,* March 1993, pp. 3–7; Michael P. O'Driscoll and James L. Eubanks, "Behavioral Competencies, Goal Setting, and OD Practitioner Effectiveness," *Group & Organization Management,* September 1993, pp. 308–26; and Allan H. Church, W. Warner Burke, and Donald F. Van Eynde, "Values, Motives, and Interventions of Organization Development Practitioners," *Group & Organization Management,* March 1994, pp. 5–50.
11. P. B. Smith, "Controlled Studies of the Outcome of Sensitivity Training," *Psychological Bulletin,* July 1975, pp. 597–622.
12. John P. Campbell and Marvin D. Dunnette, "Effectiveness of T-Group Experience in Managerial Training and Development," *Psychological Bulletin,* August 1968, pp. 73–104.
13. Morton A. Lieberman, Irvin D. Yalom, and Matthew B. Miles, *Encounter Groups: First Facts* (New York: Basic Books, 1973); and Carl A. Bramlette and Jeffrey H. Tucker, "Encounter Groups: Positive Change or Deterioration? More Data and a Partial Replication," *Human Relations,* April 1981, pp. 303–14.
14. Edgar H. Schein, *Process Consultation: Its Role in Organizational Development* (Reading, MA: Addison-Wesley, 1969), p. 9.

15. See Thomas H. Fitzgerald, "Can Change in Organizational Culture Really Be Managed?" *Organizational Dynamics,* Autumn 1988, pp. 5–15; Brian Dumaine, "Creating a New Company Culture," *Fortune,* January 15, 1990, pp. 127–31; Peter F. Drucker, "Don't Change Corporate Culture—Use It!" *Wall Street Journal,* March 28, 1991, p. A14; Joanne Martin, *Cultures in Organizations: Three Perspectives* (New York: Oxford University Press, 1992); Diana C. Pheysey, *Organizational Cultures: Types and Transformations* (London: Routledge, 1993); Clayton G. Smith and Robert P. Vecchio, "Organizational Culture and Strategic Management: Issues in the Strategic Management of Change," *Journal of Managerial Issues,* Spring 1993, pp. 53–70; Paul Bate, *Strategies for Cultural Change* (Boston: Butterworth-Heinemann, 1994); and Peter Anthony, *Managing Culture* (Philadelphia: Open University Press, 1994).
16. See, for example, Ralph H. Kilmann, Mary J. Saxton, and Roy Serpa, eds., *Gaining Control of the Corporate Culture* (San Francisco: Jossey-Bass, 1985); and Donald C. Hambrick and Sidney Finkelstein, "Managerial Discretion: A Bridge Between Polar Views of Organizational Outcomes," in L. L. Cummings and B. M. Staw (eds.), *Research in Organizational Behavior,* vol. 9 (Greenwich, CT: JAI Press, 1987), p. 384.
17. Michael Albert, "Assessing Cultural Change Needs," *Training and Development Journal,* May 1985, pp. 94–98; Achilles A. Armenakis, Stanley G. Harris, and Kevin W. Mossholder, "Creating Readiness for Organizational Change," *Human Relations,* June 1993, pp. 681–703; and David Nicoll, "Corporate Change Programmes: A False Panacea?" *Management Decision,* September 1993, pp. 4–9.
18. This box is based on Beverly Kaye, "Career Development—Anytime, Anyplace," *Training & Development,* December 1993, pp. 46–49; Andrea Davis Pinkney, "Winning in the Workplace," *Essence,* March 1994, pp. 79–80; Chris B. Bardwell, "Career Planning & Job Search Guide 1994," *The Black Collegian,* March–April 1994, pp. 59–64; and Walter Kiechel III, "A Manager's Career in the New Economy," *Fortune,* April 4, 1994, pp. 68–72.
19. Kyle Pope, "Nokia Sheds Some Old Businesses for a New Calling," *Wall Street Journal,* August 19, 1994, p. B3.
20. This box is based on C. Lindsay, "Paradoxes of Organizational Diversity: Living Within the Paradoxes," in L. R. Jauch and J. L. Wall (eds.), *Proceedings of the 50th Academy of Management Conference* (San Francisco, 1990), pp. 374–78.
21. Dan Ciampa, *Total Quality: A User's Guide for Implementation* (Reading, MA: Addison-Wesley, 1992), pp. 100–04; Michael K. Allio, "3M's Sophisticated Formula for Teamwork," *Planning Review,* November–December 1993, pp. 19–21; Jim Clemmer, "Making Change Work: Integrating Focus, Effort, and Direction," *Canadian Business Review,* Winter 1993, pp. 29–31; and Michael Shandler and Michael Egan, "Leadership for Quality," *Journal for Quality and Participation,* March 1994, pp. 66–71.
22. Keith H. Hammonds, "Where Did We Go Wrong?" *Business Week,* Quality 1991 Special Issue, p. 38; Raymond J. Jeszenka, "Breaking Through the Resistance: Achieving TQM in Maintenance," *Plant Engineering,* January 14, 1993, pp. 132–33; Alex McLeod, "Make It Happen," *The Quill,* April 1993, pp. 27–28; Keith A. Smith, "Total Quality Management in the Public Sector: The Nuts and Bolts of a TQM Effort," *Quality Progress,* July 1993, pp. 57–62; Shari Caudron, "How HR Drives TQM," *Personnel Journal,* August 1993, pp. 48A–59A; Shari Caudron, "Change Keeps TQM Programs Thriving," *Personnel Journal,* October 1993, pp. 104–09; Kevin Bright and Carl L. Cooper, "Organizational Culture and the Management of Quality: Towards a New Framework," *Journal of Managerial Psychology,* November 1993, pp. 21–27; and Michael Rigg, "Organization Change and Individual Behavior," *Industrial Engineering,* December 1993, pp. 12–13.
23. Dawn Anfuso, "At L. L. Bean, Quality Starts with People," *Personnel Journal,* January 1994, p. 60.
24. Dan Ciampa, *Total Quality,* pp. 113–52; David A. Waldman, "A Theoretical Consideration of Leadership and Total Quality Management," *Leadership Quarterly,* vol. 4, no. 1, 1993, pp. 65–79; Jonathan P. West, Evan M. Berman, and Michael E. Milakovich, "Implementing TQM in Local Government: The Leadership Challenge," *Public Productivity and Management Review,* Winter 1993, pp. 175–89; Robert G. McGrath, "Regaining Competitive Advantage Through Leadership," *Quality Progress,* December 1993, pp. 109–10; M. J. Whalen and M. A. Rahim, "Common Barriers to Implementation and Development of a TQM Program," *Industrial Management,* March–April 1994, pp. 19–21; and Cyndee Miller, "TQM Out: 'Continuous Process Improvement' In," *Marketing News,* May 9, 1994, pp. 5–6.
25. John Huey, "Nothing Is Impossible," *Fortune,* September 23, 1991, pp. 134–40; Jerome H. Want, "Managing Radical Change," *Journal of Business Strategy,* May–June 1993, pp. 20–28; W. Harvey Hegarty, "Organizational Survival Means Embracing Change," *Business Horizons,* November–December 1993, pp. 1–4; Tracy Goss, Richard Pascale, and Anthony Athos, "The Reinvention Roller Coaster: Risking the Present for a Powerful Future," *Harvard Business Review,* November–December 1993, pp. 97–108; Bristol Voss, Jill Vitiello, Clelland Johnson, and Charles D. Winslow, "Setting a Course for Radical Change," *Journal of Business Strategy,* November–December 1993, pp. 52–57; Stratford Sherman, "A Master Class in Radical Change," *Fortune,* December 13, 1993, pp. 82–90; Richard M. Hodgetts, Fred Luthans, and Sang M. Lee, "New Paradigm Organizations: From Total Quality to Learning to World-Class," *Organizational Dynamics,* Winter 1994, pp. 4–19; Bruce T. Lamont, Robert J. Williams, and James J. Hoffman, "Performance During 'M-Form' Reorganization and Recovery Time: The Effects of Prior Strategy and Implementation Speed," *Academy of Management Journal,* February 1994, pp. 153–66; Margaret J. Wheatley, "Can the U. S. Army Become a Learning Organization?" *The Journal for Quality and Participation,* March 1994, pp. 50–55; and Sheila Rothwell, "Culture and Change," *Journal of General Management,* Spring 1994, pp. M22–M35.
26. Patrick Brethour, "Wary CEO Gambles on New Market", *Globe and Mail,* February 18, 1998, p. B29.
27. This section is based on Michael Hammer and James Champy, *Reengineering the Corporation: A Manifesto for Business Revolution* (New York: HarperBusiness, 1993); Howard Gleckman and others, "The Technology Payoff," *Business Week,* June 14, 1993, pp. 56–68; Thomas A. Stewart, "Reengineering: The Hot New Managing Tool," *Fortune,* August 23, 1993, pp. 40–48; Gilbert Fuchsberg, "Small Firms Struggle with Latest Management Trends," *Wall Street Journal,* August 26, 1993, p. B2; Michael Barrier, "Re-engineering Your Company," *Nation's Business,* February 1994, pp. 16–22; and James P. Womack and Daniel T. Jones, "From Lean Production to the Lean Enterprise," *Harvard Business Review,* March–April 1994, pp. 93–103.
28. "Workplace Stress Is Rampant, Especially with the Recession," *Wall Street Journal,* May 5, 1992, p. A1; Virginia M. Gibson, "Stress in the Workplace: A Hidden Cost Factor," *HR Focus,* January 1993, p. 15; John Iacovini, "The Human Side of Organization Change," *Training and Development,* January 1993, pp. 65–68; Robert Waxler and Thomas Higginson, "Discovering Methods to Reduce Workplace Stress," *Industrial Engineering,* June 1993, pp. 19–21; and Cynthia L. Cordes and Thomas W. Dougherty, "A Review and an Integration of Research on Job Burnout," *Academy of Management Review,* October 1993, pp. 621–56.
29. Adapted from Randall S. Schuler, "Definition and Conceptualization of Stress in Organizations," *Organizational Behavior and Human Performance,* April 1980, p. 189.
30. Ibid., p. 191.
31. "Stress and Boredom," *Behavior Today,* August 1975, pp. 22–25.
32. Robert L. Kahn, B. N. Wolfe, R. P. Quinn, and J. D. Snock, *Organizational Stress: Studies in Role Conflict and Ambiguity* (New York: Wiley, 1964); and

Carlla S. Smith and John Tisak, "Discrepancy Measures of Role Stress Revisited: New Perspectives on Old Issues," *Organizational Behavior & Human Decision Processes,* November 1993, pp. 285–307.

33. Thomas H. Holmes and Minoru Masuda, "Life Change and Illness Susceptibility," in J. P. Scott and E. C. Senay (eds.), *Separation and Depression,* publication no. 94 (Washington, DC: American Association for the Advancement of Science, 1973), pp. 176–79.
34. Arthur P. Brief, Randall S. Schuler, and Mary Van Sell, *Managing Job Stress* (Boston: Little, Brown, 1981), pp. 94–98.
35. See, for instance, Meyer Friedman and Ray H. Rosenman, *Type A Behavior and Your Heart* (New York: Knopf, 1974); and Muhammed Jamal, "Type A Behavior and Job Performance: Some Suggestive Findings," *Journal of Human Stress,* Summer 1985, pp. 60–68.
36. Schuler, pp. 200–205.
37. Terry A. Beehr and John E. Newman, "Job Stress, Employee Health, and Organizational Effectiveness: A Facet Analysis, Model, and Literature Review," *Personnel Psychology,* Winter 1978, pp. 665–99.
38. Ibid, p. 687.
39. Susan E. Jackson, "Participation in Decision Making as a Strategy for Reducing Job-Related Strain," *Journal of Applied Psychology,* February 1983, pp. 3–19; Cynthia D. Fisher, "Boredom at Work: A Neglected Concept," *Human Relations,* March 1993, pp. 395–417; Catherine A. Heaney and others, "Industrial Relations, Worksite Stress Reduction and Employee Well-Being: A Participatory Action Research Investigation," *Journal of Organizational Behavior,* September 1993, pp. 495–510; Paul Froiland, "What Cures Job Stress?" Training, December 1993, pp. 32–36; C. L. Cooper and S. Cartwright, "Healthy Mind; Healthy Organization—A Proactive Approach to Occupational Stress," *Human Relations,* April 1994, pp. 455–71; Armin A. Brott, "New Approaches to Job Stress," *Nation's Business,* May 1994, pp. 81–82; and Christopher J. Bachler, "Workers Take Leave of Job Stress," *Personnel Journal,* January 1995, pp. 38-48.
40. Tamsen Tillson, "War In The Work Zone," *Canadian Business,* September 1995, pp. 40–42.
41. See Randall S. Schuler, "Time Management: A Stress Management Technique," *Personnel Journal,* December 1979, pp. 851–55; and M. E. Haynes, *Practical Time Management: How to Make the Most of Your Most Perishable Resource* (Tulsa, OK: Penn Well Books, 1985).
42. Nealia S. Bruning and David R. Frew, "Effects of Exercise, Relaxation, and Management Skills Training on Physiological Stress Indicators: A Field Experiment," *Journal of Applied Psychology,* November 1987, pp. 515–21; and Patricia Buhler, "Stress Management," *Supervision,* May 1993, pp. 17–19.
43. Michael Salter, "Full Throttle," *Report on Business Magazine,* May 1995, pp. 48–65.
44. These definitions are based on Teresa M. Amabile, "A Model of Creativity and Innovation in Organizations," in B. M. Staw and L. L. Cummings (eds.), *Research in Organizational Behavior,* vol. 10 (Greenwich, CT: JAI Press, 1988), p. 126.
45. Richard W. Woodman, John E. Sawyer, and Ricky A. Griffin, "Toward a Theory of Organizational Creativity," *Academy of Management Review,* April 1993, pp. 293–321.
46. Fariborz Damanpour, "Organizational Innovation: A Meta-Analysis of Effects of Determinants and Moderators," *Academy of Management Journal,* September 1991, pp. 555–90; Shoukry D. Saleh and Clement K. Wang, "The Management of Innovation: Strategy, Structure, and Organizational Climate," *IEEE Transactions on Engineering Management,* February 1993, pp. 14–22; Joseph F. Coates and Jennifer Jarratt, "Workplace Creativity," *Employment Relations Today,* Spring 1994, pp. 11–22.
47. Peter R. Monge, Michael D. Cozzens, and Noshir S. Contractor, "Communication and Motivational Predictors of the Dynamics of Organizational Innovations," *Organization Science,* May 1992, pp. 250–74.
48. Christopher Farrell and Michael Mandel, "Why Are We So Afraid of Growth?" *Business Week,* May 16, 1994, p. 68.
49. Robert Bott, "True Grit," *Report on Business Magazine,* May, 1995, pp. 46–53.
50. See, for instance, Teresa M. Amabile, "A Model of Creativity and Innovation in Organizations," p. 147; Michael Tushman and David Nadler, "Organizing for Innovation," *California Management Review,* Spring 1986, pp. 74–92; Rosabeth Moss Kanter, "When a Thousand Flowers Bloom: Structural, Collective, and Social Conditions for Innovation in Organization," in B. M. Staw and L. L. Cummings (eds.), *Research in Organizational Behavior,* Vol. 10, pp. 169–211; Gareth Morgan, "Endangered Species: New Ideas," *Business Month,* April 1989, pp. 75–77; Susanne G. Scott and Reginald A. Bruce, "Determinants of Innovative People: A Path Model of Individual Innovation in the Workplace," *Academy of Management Journal,* June 1994, pp. 580–607; Marshall Loeb, "Ten Commandments for Managing Creative People," *Fortune,* January 16, 1995, pp. 135–36; and Tim Stevens, "Creativity Killers," *Industry Week,* January 23, 1995, p. 63.

Chapter 13

1. Andrew Nikiforuk, "Why Safeway Struck Out", *Canadian Business,* September, 1997, p. 27.
2. S. J. Breckler, "Empirical Validation of Affect, Behavior, and Cognition as Distinct Components of Attitude," *Journal of Personality and Social Psychology,* May 1984, pp. 1191–1205; and James M. Olson and Mark P. Zanna, "Attitudes and Attitude Change," *Annual Review of Psychology,* vol. 44, 1993, pp. 117–54.
3. Paul P. Brooke, Jr., Daniel W. Russell, and James L. Price, "Discriminant Validation of Measures of Job Satisfaction, Job Involvement, and Organizational Commitment," *Journal of Applied Psychology,* May 1988, pp. 139–45.
4. In the area of job satisfaction, see, for example, Augustine O. Agho, Charles W. Mueller, and James L. Price, "Determinants of Employee Job Satisfaction: An Empirical Test of a Causal Model," *Human Relations,* August 1993, pp. 1007–27; and John E. Mathieu, David A. Hofmann, and James L. Farr, "Job Perception–Job Satisfaction Relations: An Empirical Comparison of Three Competing Theories," *Organizational Behavior and Human Decision Processes,* December 1993, pp. 370–87. In the area of job involvement, see for example, Irina M. Paullay, George M. Alliger, and Eugene F. Stone-Romero, "Construct Validation of Two Instruments Designed to Measure Job Involvement and Work Centrality," *Journal of Applied Psychology,* April 1994, pp. 224–28. In the area of organization commitment, see, for example, Donna M. Randall, "Cross-Cultural Research on Organizational Commitment: A Review and Application of Hofstede's Value Survey Module," *Journal of Business Research,* January 1993, pp. 91–110; Robert J. Vandenberg and Robin M. Self, "Assessing Newcomers' Changing Commitments to the Organization During the First 6 Months of Work," *Journal of Applied Psychology,* August 1993, pp. 557–68; and Aaron Cohen, "Organizational Commitment and Turnover: A Meta-Analysis," *Academy of Management Journal,* October 1993, pp. 1140–57.
5. Icek Ajzen and Martin Fishbein, *Understanding Attitudes and Predicting Behavior* (Englewood Cliffs, NJ: Prentice Hall, 1980).
6. Leon Festinger, *A Theory of Cognitive Dissonance* (Stanford, CA: Stanford University Press, 1957).
7. Victor H. Vroom, Work and Motivation (New York: Wiley, 1964); M. T. Iaffaldano and P. M. Muchinsky, "Job Satisfaction and Job Performance: A Meta-Analysis," *Psychological Bulletin,* March 1985, pp. 251–73; and Cheri Ostroff, "The Relationship Between Satisfaction, Attitudes, and Performance: An Organizational Level Analysis," *Journal of Applied Psychology,* December 1992, pp. 963–74.
8. See, for example, Jean B. Herman, "Are Situational Contingencies Limiting Job Attitude–Job Performance Relationship?" *Organizational Behavior and Human Performance,* October 1973, pp. 208–24; and M. M. Petty, Gail W. McGee, and Jerry W. Cavender, "A

Meta-Analysis of the Relationship Between Individual Job Satisfaction and Individual Performance," *Academy of Management Review,* October 1984, pp. 712–21.

9. Charles N. Greene, "The Satisfaction–Performance Controversy," *Business Horizons,* February 1972, pp. 31–41; Edward E. Lawler III, *Motivation and Organizations* (Monterey, CA: Brooks/Cole, 1973); Petty, McGee, and Cavender; Barry M. Staw, Sigal G. Barsade, "Affect and Managerial Performance: A Test of the Sadder-but-Wiser vs. Happier-and-Smarter Hypotheses," *Administrative Science Quarterly,* June 1993, pp. 304–28; Stephen P. Brown and Robert A. Peterson, "The Effect of Effort on Sales Performance and Job Satisfaction," *Journal of Marketing,* April 1994, pp. 70–80.
10. See, for example, Edwin A. Locke, "The Nature and Causes of Job Satisfaction," in Marvin D. Dunnette (ed.), *Handbook of Industrial and Organizational Psychology* (Chicago: Rand McNally, 1976), pp. 1297–1350; Peter W. Hom, Ralph Katerberg, Jr., and Charles L. Hulin, "Comparative Examination of Three Approaches to the Prediction of Turnover," *Journal of Applied Psychology,* June 1979, pp. 280–90; Robert P. Tett and John P. Meyer, "Job Satisfaction, Organizational Commitment, Turn-over Intention, and Turnover: Path Analyses Based on Meta-Analytic Findings," *Personnel Psychology,* Summer 1993, pp. 259–93; Timothy A. Judge, "Does Affective Disposition Moderate the Relationship Between Job Satisfaction and Voluntary Turnover?" *Journal of Applied Psychology,* June 1993, pp. 395–401; and Stacey S. Kohler and John E. Mathieu, "Individual Characteristics, Work Perceptions, and Affective Reactions Influences on Differentiated Absence Criteria," *Journal of Organizational Behavior,* November 1993, pp. 515–30.
11. Julian B. Rotter, "Generalized Expectancies for Internal Versus External Control of Reinforcement," *Psychological Monographs,* vol. 80, no. 609 (1966).
12. See, for instance, Dennis W. Organ and Charles N. Greene, "Role Ambiguity, Locus of Control, and Work Satisfaction," *Journal of Applied Psychology,* February 1974, pp. 101–02; and Terence R. Mitchell, Charles M. Smyser, and Stan E. Weed, "Locus of Control: Supervision and Work Satisfaction," *Academy of Management Journal,* September 1975, pp. 623–31.
13. T. Adorno and others, *The Authoritarian Personality* (New York: Harper & Brothers, 1950).
14. Harrison Gough, "Personality and Personality Assessment," in Marvin Dunnette (ed.), *Handbook of Industrial and Organizational Psychology* (Skokie, IL: Rand McNally, 1976), p. 579.
15. R. G. Vleeming, "Machiavellianism: A Preliminary Review," *Psychological Reports,* February 1979, pp. 295–310.
16. Based on Joel Brockner, *Self-Esteem at Work* (Lexington, MA: Lexington Books, 1988), chap. 1–4.
17. See M. Snyder, *Public Appearances/Private Realities: The Psychology of Self-Monitoring* (New York: W. H. Freeman, 1987).
18. M. Snyder, *Public Appearances/Private Realities: The Psychology of Self-Monitoring,* 1987; and J. Michael Jenkins, "Self-Monitoring and Turnover: The Impact of Personality on Intent to Leave," *Journal of Organizational Behavior,* January 1993, pp. 83–90.
19. R. N. Taylor and M. D. Dunnette, "Influence of Dogmatism, Risk-Taking Propensity, and Intelligence on Decision-Making Strategies for a Sample of Industrial Managers," *Journal of Applied Psychology,* August 1974, pp. 420–23.
20. N. Kogan and M. A. Wallach, "Group Risk Taking as a Function of Members' Anxiety and Defensiveness," *Journal of Personality,* March 1967, pp. 50–63; and Jane M. Howell and Christopher A. Higgins, "Champions of Technological Innovation," *Administrative Science Quarterly,* June 1990, pp. 317–41.
21. Isabel Briggs Myers, *Introduction to Type* (Palo Alto, CA: Consulting Psychologists Press, 1980); Charles K. Coe, "The MBTI: Potential Uses and Misuses in Personnel Administration," *Public Personnel Management,* Winter 1992, pp. 511–22; and J. Austin Davey, Bernadette H. Schell, and Kim Morrison, "The Myers-Briggs Personality Indicator and Its Usefulness for Problem Solving by Mining Industry Personnel," *Group & Organization Management,* March 1993, pp. 50–65.
22. John L. Holland, *Making Vocational Choices: A Theory of Vocational Personalities and Work Environments,* 2d ed. (Englewood Cliffs, NJ: Prentice Hall, 1985).
23. See, for example, A. R. Spokane, "A Review of Research on Person–Environment Congruence in Holland's Theory of Careers," *Journal of Vocational Behavior,* June 1985, pp. 306–43; D. Brown, "The Status of Holland's Theory of Career Choice," *Career Development Journal,* September 1987, pp. 13–23; and T. J. Tracey and J. Rounds, "Evaluating Holland's and Gati's Vocational-Interest Models: A Structural Meta-Analysis," *Psychological Bulletin,* March 1993, pp. 229–46.
24. This box is based on Robert H. Brockhaus, Sr., "The Psychology of the Entrepreneur," in Calvin A. Kent, Donald L. Sexton, and Karl H. Vesper (eds.), *Encyclopedia of Entrepreneurship* (Englewood Cliffs, NJ: Prentice Hall, 1982), pp. 41–49; John A. Hornaday, "Research About Living Entrepreneurs," in Calvin A. Kent, Donald L. Sexton, and Karl H. Vesper (eds.), *Encyclopedia of Entrepreneurship,* p. 28; Michael Warshaw, "The Entrepreneurial Mind," *Success,* April 1994, pp. 48–51; Brian O'Reilly, "The New Face of Small Business," *Fortune,* May 2, 1994, pp. 82–88; and Ronald E. Merrill and Henry D. Sedgwick, "To Thine Own Self Be True," *Inc.,* August 1994, pp. 50–56.
25. H. H. Kelley, "Attribution in Social Interaction," in E. Jones and others (eds.), *Attribution: Perceiving the Causes of Behavior* (Morristown, NJ: General Learning Press, 1972).
26. See A. G. Miller and T. Lawson, "The Effect of an Informational Option on the Fundamental Attribution Error," *Personality and Social Psychology Bulletin,* June 1989, pp. 194–204.
27. See, for example, Susan T. Fiske, "Social Cognition and Social Perception," *Annual Review of Psychology,* 1993, pp. 155–94; and Gary N. Powell and Yasuaki Kido, "Managerial Stereotypes in a Global Economy: A Comparative Study of Japanese and American Business Students' Perspectives," *Psychological Reports,* February 1994, pp. 219–26.
28. B. F. Skinner, *Contingencies of Reinforcement* (East Norwalk, CT: Appleton-Century-Crofts, 1971).
29. This box is based on Forrest F. Aven, Jr., Barbara Parker, and Glenn M. McEvoy, "Gender and Attitudinal Commitment to Organizations: A Meta-Analysis," *Journal of Business Research,* January 1993, pp. 63–73; Kong Beng Ang, Chye Tee Goh, and Hian Chye Koh, "The Impact of Age on the Job Satisfaction of Accountants," *Personnel Review,* January 1993, pp. 31–39; Bilha Mannheim, "Gender and the Effects of Demographics, Status and Work Values on Work Centrality," *Work and Occupations,* February 1993, pp. 3–22; Peter V. Marsden, Arne L. Kalleberg, and Cynthia R. Cook, "Gender Differences in Organizational Commitment: Influences of Work Positions and Family Roles," *Work and Occupations,* August 1993, pp. 368–90; Esther R. Greenglass, "Structural and Social-Psychological Factors Associated with Job Functioning by Women Managers," *Psychological Reports,* December 1993, pp. 979–86; and Joel Lefkowitz, "Sex-Related Differences in Job Attitudes and Dispositional Variables: Now You See Them ...," *Academy of Management Journal,* April 1994, pp. 323–49.

Chapter 14

1. Mick Lowe, "Steel Resolve", *Financial Post Magazine*, April, 1995, pp. 20-29; and *Canadian Business*, "Performance 2000", June 26/July 10, 1998.
2. Bruce W. Tuckman and Mary Ann C. Jensen, "Stages of Small-Group Development Revisited," *Group and Organizational Studies,* vol. 2, no. 3, 1977, pp. 419–27; and Patricia Buhler, "Group Membership," *Supervision,* May 1994, pp. 8–10.
3. Linda N. Jewell and H. J. Reitz, *Group Effectiveness in Organizations* (Glenview, IL: Scott, Foresman, 1981); and

Margaret Kaeter, "Repotting Mature Work Teams," *Training,* April 1994, pp. 54–56.

4. Solomon E. Asch, "Effects of Group Pressure Upon the Modification and Distortion of Judgments," in Harold Guetzkow (ed.), *Groups, Leadership and Men* (Pittsburgh: Carnegie Press, 1951), pp. 177–90.
5. See, for instance, E. J. Thomas and C. F. Fink, "Effects of Group Size," *Psychological Bulletin,* July 1963, pp. 371–84; and Marvin E. Shaw, *Group Dynamics: The Psychology of Small Group Behavior,* 3d ed. (New York: McGraw-Hill, 1981).
6. See Robert Albanese and David D. Van Fleet, "Rational Behavior in Groups: The Free-Riding Tendency," *Academy of Management Review,* April 1985, pp. 244–55.
7. See, for example, L. Berkowitz, "Group Standards, Cohesiveness, and Productivity," *Human Relations,* November 1954, pp. 509–19; and Brian Mullen and Carolyn Copper, "The Relation Between Group Cohesiveness and Performance: An Integration," *Psychological Bulletin,* March 1994, pp. 210–27.
8. Stanley E. Seashore, *Group Cohesiveness in the Industrial Work Group* (Ann Arbor: Survey Research Center, University of Michigan, 1954).
9. K. M. Eisenhardt, J. L. Kahwajy, and L. J. Bourgeois III, "How Management Teams Can Have a Good Fight", *Harvard Business Review*, July-August 1997, pp. 77–85.
10. K. W. Thomas, "Conflict and Negotiation Processes in Organizations", in M. D. Dunnette and L. M. Hough (eds.), *Handbook of Industrial and Organizational Psychology*, 2d ed., Vol. 3, (Palo Alto, California: Consulting Psychologists Press, 1992), pp. 651-717.
11. This model is substantially based on the work of Paul S. Goodman, E. Ravlin, and M. Schminke, "Understanding Groups in Organizations," in L. L. Cummings and B. M. Staw (eds.), *Research in Organizational Behavior,* vol. 9 (Greenwich, CT: JAI Press, 1987), pp. 124–28; and J. Richard Hackman, "The Design of Work Teams," in J. W. Lorsch (ed.), *Handbook of Organizational Behavior* (Englewood Cliffs, NJ: Prentice Hall, 1987), pp. 315–42.
12. Fred Friedlander, "The Ecology of Work Groups," in J. W. Lorsch (ed.), *Handbook of Organizational Behavior,* pp. 301–14.
13. Marvin E. Shaw, *Contemporary Topics in Social Psychology* (Morristown, NJ: General Learning Press, 1976), pp. 350–51.
14. See, for example, J. Richard Hackman and C. G. Morris, "Group Tasks, Group Interaction Process and Group Performance Effectiveness: A Review and Proposed Integration," in L. Berkowitz (ed.), *Advances in Experimental Social Psychology* (New York: Academic Press, 1975), pp. 45–99.
15. Brian Dumaine, "The Trouble with Teams," *Fortune,* September 5, 1994, p. 86.
16. Based on Eric Sundstrom, Kenneth P. DeMeuse, and David Futrell, "Work Teams," *American Psychologist,* February 1990, p. 120; and Carl E. Larson and Frank M. J. LaFasto, *TeamWork* (Newbury Park, CA: Sage Publications).
17. Glenn M. Parker, *Cross-Functional Teams* (San Francisco: Jossey-Bass, 1994), p. 34.
18. Ibid, pp. 9–10.
19. Glenn M. Parker, *Cross-Functional Teams,* pp. 35–39.
20. Howard Rothman, "The Power of Empowerment," *Nation's Business,* June 1993, pp. 49–51.
21. Ibid.
22. Linda Grant, "New Jewel in the Crown," *U.S. News & World Report,* February 28, 1994, p. 56.
23. John A. Byrne, "The Horizontal Corporation," *Business Week,* December 20, 1993, p. 80.
24. This box based on Lennie Copeland, "Making the Most of Cultural Differences at the Workplace," *Personnel,* June 1988, pp. 52–60; Charles R. Bantz, "Cultural Diversity and Group Cross-Cultural Team Research," *Journal of Applied Communication Research,* February 1993, pp. 1–19; Lauren Strach and Linda Wicander, "Fitting In: Issues of Tokenism and Conformity for Minority Women," *SAM Advanced Management Journal,* Summer 1993, pp. 22–25; Terry K. Gilliam, "Managing the Power of Creativity," *Bank Marketing,* December 1993, pp. 14–17; Martha L. Maznevski, "Understanding Our Differences: Performance in Decision-Making Groups with Diverse Members," *Human Relations,* May 1994, pp. 531–52; and Faye Rice, "How to Make Diversity Pay," *Fortune,* August 8, 1994, pp. 78–86.
25. Jon R. Katzenbach and Douglas K. Smith, "The Discipline of Teams," *Harvard Business Review,* March–April 1993, pp. 111–20.
26. See Sundstrom, DeMeuse, and Futrell; Larson and LaFasto; J. Richard Hackman (ed.), *Groups That Work (and Those That Don't)* (San Francisco: Jossey-Bass, 1990); and Dean W. Tjosvold and Mary M. Tjosvold, *Leading the Team Organization* (New York: Lexington Books, 1991).
27. Larson and LaFasto, p. 75.
28. Paul E. Brauchle and David W. Wright, "Fourteen Team Building Tips," *Training & Development,* January 1992, pp. 32–34; Richard S. Wellins, "Building a Self-Directed Work Team," *Training & Development,* December 1992, pp. 24–28; Sam T. Johnson, "Work Teams: What's Ahead in Work Design and Rewards Management," *Compensation and Benefits Review,* March–April 1993, pp. 35–41; Victoria A. Hoevemeyer, "How Effective Is Your Team?" *Training & Development,* September 1993, pp. 67–71; Susan G. Cohen and Gerald E. Ledford, Jr., "The Effectiveness of Self-Managing Teams: A Quasi-Experiment," *Human Relations,* January 1994, pp. 13–43; Joe Panepinto, "Maximize Teamwork," *Computerworld,* March 21, 1994, p. 119; and Susan Caminiti, "What Team Leaders Need to Know," *Fortune,* February 20, 1995, pp. 93–100.
29. David M. Enlen, "Team Goals: Aligning Groups and Management," *Canadian Manager,* Winter 1993, pp. 17–18; Anne M. O'Leary, Joseph J. Martocchio, and Dwight D. Frink, "A Review of the Influence of Group Goals on Group Performance," *Academy of Management Journal,* October 1994, pp. 1285–1301; and Verlin B. Hinsz, "Group and Individual Decision Making for Task Performance Goals: Processes in the Establishment of Goals in Groups," *Journal of Applied Social Psychology,* 1995, vol. 25, no. 4, pp. 353-370.
30. Christopher Meyer, "How the Right Measures Help Teams Excel," *Harvard Business Review,* May–June 1994, pp. 95–103.
31. Glenn M. Parker, *Cross-Functional Teams,* pp. 107–08.
32. Ibid., p. 127.
33. Bob Krone, "Total Quality Management: An American Odyssey," *The Bureaucrat,* Fall 1990, p. 37.
34. Everett E. Adam, Jr., "Quality Circle Performance," *Journal of Management,* March 1991, pp. 25–39; George R. Gray, "Quality Circles: An Update," *SAM Advanced Management Journal,* Spring 1993, pp. 41–47; John Malone, "Creating an Atmosphere of Complete Employee Involvement in TQM," *Healthcare Financial Management,* June 1993, pp. 126–27; Nonaka Izumi, "The History of the Quality Circle," *Quality Progress,* September 1993, pp. 81–83; and Thomas Li-Ping Tang, Peggy Smith Tollison, and Harold D. Whiteside, "Differences Between Active and Inactive Quality Circles in Attendance and Performance," *Public Personnel Management,* Winter 1993, pp. 579–90.
35. *Profiles in Quality: Blueprints for Action from 50 Leading Companies* (Boston: Allyn and Bacon, 1991), pp. 71–72 and 76–77.

Chapter 15

1. Branham 200, "A Sector For All Seasons", *The Financial Post Magazine*, March 1998, pp. 56–70; Bruce Livesey, "Making Nice", *Report on Business Magazine*, March 1998, pp. 96–104; and Tema Frank, "Kinder, Gentler, Smarter", *Profit*, April–May, 1998, pp. 50–52.
2. See Kenneth A. Kovach, "What Motivates Employees? Workers and Supervisors Give Different Answers," *Business Horizons,* September–October 1987, pp. 58–65.
3. Ralph Katerberg and Gary J. Blau, "An Examination of Level and Direction of

Effort and Job Performance," *Academy of Management Journal,* June 1983, pp. 249–57.

4. Abraham Maslow, *Motivation and Personality* (New York: Harper & Row, 1954).
5. See, for example, Douglas T. Hall and Khalil E. Nongaim, "An Examination of Maslow's Need Hierarchy in an Organizational Setting," *Organizational Behavior and Human Performance,* February 1968, pp. 12–35; and Edward E. Lawler III, and J. Lloyd Suttle, "A Causal Correlational Test of the Need Hierarchy Concept," *Organizational Behavior and Human Performance,* April 1972, pp. 265–87.
6. Douglas McGregor, *The Human Side of Enterprise* (New York: McGraw-Hill, 1960).
7. Frederick Herzberg, Bernard Mausner, and Barbara Snyderman, *The Motivation to Work* (New York: Wiley, 1959); and Frederick Herzberg, *The Managerial Choice: To Be Effective or to Be Human,* rev. ed. (Salt Lake City: Olympus, 1982).
8. See, for instance, Michael E. Gordon, Norman M. Pryor, and Bob V. Harris, "An Examination of Scaling Bias in Herzberg's Theory of Job Satisfaction," *Organizational Behavior and Human Performance,* February 1974, pp. 106–21; Edwin A. Locke and Roman J. Whiting, "Sources of Satisfaction and Dissatisfaction Among Solid Waste Management Employees," *Journal of Applied Psychology,* April 1974, pp. 145–56; and John B. Miner, *Theories of Organizational Behavior* (Hinsdale, IL: Dryden Press, 1980), pp. 76–105.
9. David C. McClelland, *The Achieving Society* (New York: Van Nostrand Reinhold, 1961); John W. Atkinson and Joel O. Raynor, *Motivation and Achievement* (Washington, DC: Winston, 1974); and David C. McClelland, *Power: The Inner Experience* (New York: Irvington, 1975).
10. McClelland, *The Achieving Society.*
11. David C. McClelland and David G. Winter, *Motivating Economic Achievement* (New York: Free Press, 1969).
12. McClelland, Power: The Inner Experience; David C. McClelland and David H. Burnham, "Power Is the Great Motivator," *Harvard Business Review,* March–April 1976, pp. 100–10.
13. "McClelland: An Advocate of Power," *International Management,* July 1975, pp. 27–29.
14. David Miron and David C. McClelland, "The Impact of Achievement Motivation Training on Small Businesses," *California Management Review,* Summer 1979, pp. 13–28.
15. James C. Naylor and Daniel R. Ilgen, "Goal Setting: A Theoretical Analysis of a Motivational Technique," in B. M. Staw and L. L. Cummings (eds.), *Research in Organizational Behavior,* vol. 6 (Greenwich, CT: JAI Press, 1984), pp. 95–140; Arthur R. Pell, "Energize Your People," *Managers Magazine,* December 1992, pp. 28–29; Edwin A. Locke, "Facts and Fallacies About Goal Theory: Reply to Deci," *Psychological Science,* January 1993, pp. 63–64; Mark E. Tubbs, "Commitment as a Moderator of the Goal–Performance Relation: A Case for Clearer Construct Definition," *Journal of Applied Psychology,* February 1993, pp. 86–97; Margaret P. Collingwood, "Why Don't You Use the Research?" *Management Decision,* May 1993, pp. 48–54; and Mark E. Tubbs, Donna M. Boehne, and James S. Dahl, "Expectancy, Valence, and Motivational Force Functions in Goal-Setting Research: An Empirical Test," *Journal of Applied Psychology,* June 1993, pp. 361–73.
16. John A. Wagner III, "Participation's Effects on Performance and Satisfaction: A Reconsideration of Research and Evidence," *Academy of Management Review,* April 1994, pp. 312–30; and Beth Ann Martin and Donald J. Manning, Jr., "Combined Effects of Normative Information and Task Difficulty on the Goal Commitment–Performance Relationship," *Journal of Management,* Spring 1995, pp. 65–80.
17. Miner, p. 65.
18. B. F. Skinner, *Science and Human Behavior* (New York: Free Press, 1953); and B. F. Skinner, *Beyond Freedom and Dignity* (New York: Knopf, 1972).
19. The same data, for instance, can be interpreted in either goal-setting or reinforcement terms, as shown in Edwin A. Locke, "Latham vs. Komaki: A Tale of Two Paradigms," *Journal of Applied Psychology,* February 1980, pp. 16–23.
20. See, for example, Ricky W. Griffin, "Toward An Integrated Theory of Task Design," in L. L. Cummings and Barry M. Staw (eds.), *Research in Organizational Behavior,* vol. 9 (Greenwich, CT: JAI Press, 1987), pp. 79–120; and Michael Campion, "Interdisciplinary Approaches to Job Design: A Constructive Replication with Extensions," *Journal of Applied Psychology,* August 1988, pp. 467–81.
21. Shari Caudron, "The De-Jobbing of America," *Industry Week,* September 5, 1994, pp. 31–36; William Bridges, "The End of the Job," *Fortune,* September 19, 1994, pp. 62–74; and Keith H. Hammonds, Kevin Kelly, and Karen Thurston, "Rethinking Work," *Business Week,* October 12, 1994, pp. 75–87.
22. Michael A. Campion and Carol L. McClelland, "Follow-Up and Extension of the Interdisciplinary Costs and Benefits of Enlarged Jobs," *Journal of Applied Psychology,* June 1993, pp. 339–51.
23. See, for example, J. R. Hackman and G. R. Oldham, *Work Redesign* (Reading, MA: Addison-Wesley, 1980); and Miner, pp. 231-66.
24. J. Richard Hackman and Greg R. Oldham, "Development of the Job Diagnostic Survey," *Journal of Applied Psychology,* April 1975, pp. 159–70.
25. Shona McKay, "Betting on a Full House", *Report on Business Magazine,* December, 1996, pp. 59-60.
26. J. Richard Hackman, "Work Design," in J. Richard Hackman and J. Lloyd Suttle (eds.), *Improving Life at Work* (Glenview, IL: Scott, Foresman, 1977), p. 129.
27. General support for the JCM is reported in Yitzhak Fried and Gerald R. Ferris, "The Validity of the Job Characteristics Model: A Review and Meta-Analysis," *Personnel Psychology,* Summer 1987, pp. 287–322.
28. Hackman, pp. 136–40.
29. J. Stacey Adams, "Inequity in Social Exchanges", in L. Berkowitz (ed.), *Advances in Experimental Social Psychology,* vol. 2 (New York: Academic Press, 1965), pp. 267–300.
30. Paul S. Goodman and A. Friedman, "An Examination of Adams' Theory of Inequity," *Administrative Science Quarterly,* September 1971, pp. 271–88.
31. See, for example, Michael R. Carrell, "A Longitudinal Field Assessment of Employee Perceptions of Equitable Treatment," *Organizational Behavior and Human Performance,* February 1978, pp. 108–18; Robert G. Lord and Jeffrey A. Hohenfeld, "Longitudinal Field Assessment of Equity Effects on the Performance of Major League Baseball Players," *Journal of Applied Psychology,* February 1979, pp. 19–26; and John E. Dittrich and Michael R. Carrell, "Organizational Equity Perceptions, Employee Job Satisfaction, and Departmental Absence and Turnover Rates," *Organizational Behavior and Human Performance,* August 1979, pp. 29–40.
32. Paul S. Goodman, "An Examination of Referents Used in the Evaluation of Pay," *Organizational Behavior and Human Performance,* October 1974, pp. 170–95; Simcha Ronen, "Equity Perception in Multiple Comparisons: A Field Study," *Human Relations,* April 1986, pp. 333–46; R. W. Scholl, E. A. Cooper, and J. F. McKenna, "Referent Selection in Determining Equity Perception: Differential Effects on Behavioral and Attitudinal Outcomes," *Personnel Psychology,* Spring 1987, pp. 113–27; and Carol T. Kulik and Maureen L. Ambrose, "Personal and Situational Determinants of Referent Choice," *Academy of Management Review,* April 1992, pp. 212–37.
33. Paul S. Goodman, "Social Comparison Process in Organizations," in B. M. Staw and G. R. Salancik (eds.), *New Directions in Organizational Behavior* (Chicago: St. Clair, 1977), pp. 97–132.
34. Victor H. Vroom, *Work and Motivation* (New York: Wiley, 1964).
35. See, for example, Herbert G. Heneman III, and Donald P. Schwab, "Evaluation of Research on Expectancy Theory Prediction of Employee Performance," *Psychological Bulletin,* July 1972, pp. 1–9; and Leon Reinharth and Mahmoud Wahba, "Expectancy Theory as a Predictor of Work Motivation, Effort Expenditure, and Job Performance," *Academy of Management Journal,* September 1975, pp. 502–37.
36. See, for example, Victor H. Vroom, "Organizational Choice: A Study of Pre- and

Postdecision Processes," *Organizational Behavior and Human Performance,* April 1966, pp. 212–25; and Lyman W. Porter and Edward E. Lawler III, *Managerial Attitudes and Performance* (Homewood, IL: Irwin, 1968).
37. This four-step discussion was adapted from K. F. Taylor, "A Valence-Expectancy Approach to Work Motivation," *Personnel Practice Bulletin,* June 1974, pp. 142–48.
38. See, for instance, Marc Siegall, "The Simplistic Five: An Integrative Framework for Teaching Motivation," *The Organizational Behavior Teaching Review,* vol. 12, no. 4 (1987–88), pp. 141–43.
39. Itzhak Harpaz, "The Importance of Work Goals: An International Perspective," *Journal of International Business Studies,* First Quarter 1990, pp. 75–93.
40. See, for instance, Randall B. Dunham, Jon L. Pierce, and Maria B. Castaneda, "Alternative Work Schedules: Two Field Quasi-Experiments," *Personnel Psychology,* Summer 1987, pp. 215–42.
41. Dan Olson and Arthur P. Brief, "The Impact of Alternative Workweeks," *Personnel,* January–February 1978, p. 73.
42. Nancy K. Austin, "How Managers Manage Flexibility," *Working Woman,* July 1994, pp. 19–20.
43. See, for example, Jay S. Kim and A. F. Campagna, "Effects of Flextime on Employee Attendance and Performance: A Field Experiment," *Academy of Management Journal,* December 1981, pp. 729–41; and David R. Ralston, William P. Anthony, and David J. Gustafson, "Employees May Love Flextime, But What Does It Do to the Organization's Productivity?" *Journal of Applied Psychology,* May 1985, pp. 272–79.
44. Ellen Graham, "Flexible Formulas," *Wall Street Journal,* June 4, 1990, p. R34.
45. See, for example, Steve Shirley, "A Company Without Offices," *Harvard Business Review,* January–February 1986, pp. 127–36; C. A. Hamilton, "Telecommuting," *Personnel Journal,* April 1987, pp. 91–101; Donald C. Bacon, "Look Who's Working at Home," *Nation's Business,* October 1989, pp. 20–31; Michael Alexander, "Travel-Free Commuting," *Nation's Business,* December 1990, pp. 33–37; Leah Beth Ward, "The Mixed Blessings of Telecommuting," *New York Times,* September 20, 1992, p. F23; and David C. Churbuck and Jeffrey S. Young, "The Virtual Workplace," *Forbes,* November 23, 1992, pp. 184–90.
46. Geert Hofstede, "Motivation, Leadership, and Organizations: Do American Theories Apply Abroad?" *Organizational Dynamics,* Summer 1980, p. 55.
47. Diane H. B. Walsh, Fred Luthans, and Steven M. Sommer, "Organizational Behavior Modification Goes to Russia: Replicating an Experimental Analysis Across Cultures and Tasks," *Journal of Organizational Behavior Management,* Fall 1993, pp. 15–35; and J. Robert Baum and others, "Nationality and Work Role Interactions: A Cultural Contrast of Israeli and US Entrepreneurs' Versus Managers' Needs," *Journal of Business Venturing,* November 1993, pp. 499–512.
48. Adi Ignatius, "Now If Ms. Wong Insults a Customer, She Gets an Award," *Wall Street Journal,* January 24, 1989, p. 1.
49. Randall K. Abbott, "Performance-Based Flex: A Tool for Managing Total Compensation Costs," *Compensation and Benefits Review,* March–April 1993, pp. 18–21; Jay R. Schuster, and Patricia K. Zingheim, "The New Variable Pay: Key Design Issues," *Compensation and Benefits Review,* March–April 1993, pp. 27–34; Charles R. Williams and Linda Parrack Livingstone, "Another Look at the Relationship Between Performance and Voluntary Turnover," *Academy of Management Journal,* April 1994, pp. 269–98; and Alyce M. Dickinson and Kirk L. Gillette, "A Comparison of the Effects of Two Individual Monetary Incentive Systems on Productivity: Piece Rate Pay Versus Base Pay Plus Incentives," *Journal of Organizational Behavior Management,* Spring 1994, pp. 3–82.
50. Shawn Tully, "Your Paycheck Gets Exciting," *Fortune,* November 1, 1993, p. 83.
51. C. M. Rosen and M. Quarrey, "How Well Is Employee Ownership Working?" *Harvard Business Review,* September–October 1987, pp. 126–32.
52. Subal C. Kumbhakar and Amy E. Dunbar, "The Elusive ESOP–Productivity Link: Evidence from U.S. Firm-Level Data," *Journal of Public Economics,* September 1993, pp. 273–83; and Shelley A. Lee, "ESOP Is a Powerful Tool to Align Employees with Corporate Goals," *Pension World,* April 1994, pp. 40–42.
53. J. L. Pierce and C. A. Furo, "Employee Ownership: Implications for Management," *Organizational Dynamics,* Winter 1990, pp. 32–43.
54. Ibid., p. 38.
55. Scott W. Kelley, "Discretion and the Service Employee," *Journal of Retailing,* Spring 1993, pp. 104–26; Susan Sonnesyn Brooks, "Noncash Ways to Compensate Employees," *HR Magazine,* April 1994, pp. 38–43; and Samuel Greengard, "Leveraging a Low-Wage Work Force," *Personnel Journal,* January 1995, pp. 90–102.
56. Ronald Henkoff, "Finding, Training, and Keeping the Best Service Workers," *Fortune,* October 3, 1994, pp. 110–22.
57. Laurie A. Broedling, "Relationship of Internal–External Control to Work Motivation and Performance in Expectancy Model," *Journal of Applied Psychology,* February 1975, pp. 65–70; and Terry L. Lied and Robert D. Pritchard, "Relationships Between Personality Variables and Components of the Expectancy–Valence Model," *Journal of Applied Psychology,* August 1976, pp. 463–67.
58. David W. Belcher and Thomas J. Atchison, "Equity Theory and Compensation Policy," Personnel Administration, vol. 33, no. 3 (1970), pp. 22–33; and Thomas J. Atchison and David W. Belcher, "Equity Rewards and Compensation Administration," *Personnel Administration,* vol. 34, no. 2 (1971), pp. 32–36.
59. Edwin A. Locke, D. B. Feren, V. M. McCaleb, K. N. Shaw, and A. T. Denny, "The Relative Effectiveness of Four Methods of Motivating Employee Performance," in K. D. Duncan, M. M. Gruneberg, and D. Wallis (eds.), *Changes in Working Life* (London: Wiley, 1980), pp. 363–383.

Chapter 16

1. Philip DeMont, "The CEO in the Fast Lane", *Financial Post,* October 11, 1997, p. 6; Bruce Livesey, "Tag Team", *Report on Business Magazine,* July, 1997, pp. 39–48; Susan Bourette, "NorTel Wins German Deal", *Globe and Mail,* August 7, 1997, p. B1; Ian Austen, "Hooked on the Net", *Canadian Business,* June 26/July 10, 1998, pp. 95–103; and Lawrence Surtees, "Nortel's New Vision Calls on the Web", *Globe and Mail,* February 25, 1998, p. B29.
2. See Shelly A. Kirkpatrick and Edwin A. Locke, "Leadership: Do Traits Matter?" *Academy of Management Executive,* May 1991, pp. 48–60.
3. K. Lewin and R. Lippitt, "An Experimental Approach to the Study of Democracy and Autocracy: A Preliminary Note", *Sociometry* 1 (1938), pp. 292–300; Lewin, "Field Theory and Experiment in Social Psychology: Concepts and Methods", *American Journal of Sociology* 44 (1939), pp. 868–896; Lewin, Lippitt, and R. K. White, "Patterns of Agressive Behavior in Experimentally Created Social Climates", *Journal of Social Psychology* 10 (1939), pp. 271–301; and Lippitt, "An Experimental Study of the Effect of Democratic and Authoritarian Group Atmospheres", *University of Iowa Studies in Child Welfare* 16 (1940), pp. 43–95.
4. B. M. Bass, *Stogdill's Handbook of Leadership* (New York: Free Press, 1981), pp. 289–299.
5. Ralph M. Stogdill and Alvin E. Coons, eds., *Leader Behavior: Its Description and Measurement,* Research Monograph no. 88 (Columbus: Ohio State University, Bureau of Business Research, 1951). For an updated literature review of Ohio State research, see Steven Kerr, Chester A. Schriesheim, Charles J. Murphy, and Ralph M. Stogdill, "Toward A Contingency Theory of Leadership Based upon the Consideration and Initiating Structure Literature," *Organizational Behavior and Human Performance,* August 1974, pp. 62–82; and Bruce M. Fisher, "Consideration and Initiating Structure and Their Relationships With Leader Effectiveness: A Meta-Analysis," in F. Hoy (ed.), *Proceedings of the 48th Annual Academy of Management Conference,* Anaheim, California, 1988, pp. 201–05.
6. R. Kahn and D. Katz, "Leadership Practices in Relation to Productivity and

Morale," in D. Cartwright and A. Zander (eds.), *Group Dynamics: Research and Theory,* 2d ed. (Elmsford, NY: Row, Peterson, 1960).

7. Robert R. Blake and Jane S. Mouton, *The Managerial Grid III* (Houston: Gulf Publishing, 1984).
8. L. L. Larson, J. G. Hunt, and R. N. Osborn, "The Great Hi-Hi Leader Behavior Myth: A Lesson from Occam's Razor," *Academy of Management Journal,* December 1976, pp. 628–41; and Paul C. Nystrom, "Managers and the Hi-Hi Leader Myth," *Academy of Management Journal,* June 1978, pp. 325–31.
9. See, for example, the 3-D theory proposed by William J. Reddin, *Managerial Effectiveness* (New York: McGraw-Hill, 1970).
10. Jeffrey C. Barrow, "The Variables of Leadership: A Review and Conceptual Framework," *Academy of Management Review,* April 1977, pp. 231–51.
11. Fred E. Fiedler, *A Theory of Leadership Effectiveness* (New York: McGraw-Hill, 1967).
12. Lawrence H. Peters, D. D. Hartke, and J. T. Pholmann, "Fiedler's Contingency Theory of Leadership: An Application of the Meta-Analysis Procedures of Schmidt and Hunter," *Psychological Bulletin,* March 1985, pp. 274–85.
13. See, for instance, Robert W. Rice, "Psychometric Properties of the Esteem for the Least Preferred Co-Worker (LPC) Scale," *Academy of Management Review,* January 1978, pp. 106–18; and Chester A. Schriesheim, B. D. Bannister, and W. H. Money, "Psychometric Properties of the LPC Scale: An Extension of Rice's Review," *Academy of Management Review,* April 1979, pp. 287–90.
14. See Edgar H. Schein, *Organizational Psychology,* 3d ed. (Englewood Cliffs, N J: Prentice Hall, 1980), pp. 116–17; and Boris Kabanoff, "A Critique of Leader Match and Its Implications for Leadership Research," *Personnel Psychology,* Winter 1981, pp. 749–64.
15. Robert J. House, "A Path–Goal Theory of Leader Effectiveness," *Administrative Science Quarterly,* September 1971, pp. 321–38; Robert J. House and Terence R. Mitchell, "Path–Goal Theory of Leadership," *Journal of Contemporary Business,* Autumn 1974, p. 86; and Robert J. House, "Retrospective Comment," in Louis E. Boone and Donald D. Bowen (eds.), *The Great Writings in Management and Organizational Behavior,* 2d ed. (New York: Random House, 1987), pp. 354–64.
16. Julie Indrik, "Path–Goal Theory of Leadership: A Meta-Analysis," paper presented at the National Academy of Management Conference, Chicago, August 1986; Robert T. Keller, "A Test of the Path–Goal Theory of Leadership with Need for Clarity as a Moderator in Research and Development Organizations," *Journal of Applied Psychology,* April 1989, pp. 208–12; J. C. Wofford and Laurie Z. Liska, "Path–Goal Theories of Leadership: A Meta-Analysis," *Journal of Management,* Winter 1993, pp. 857–76; and Abraham Sagie and Meni Koslowsky, "Organizational Attitudes and Behaviors as a Function of Participation in Strategic and Tactical Change Decisions: An Application of Path–Goal Theory," *Journal of Organizational Behavior,* January 1994, pp. 37–47.
17. Victor H. Vroom and Phillip W. Yetton, *Leadership and Decision-Making* (Pittsburgh: University of Pittsburgh Press, 1973).
18. Victor H. Vroom and Arthur G. Jago, *The New Leadership: Managing Participation in Organizations* (Englewood Cliffs, NJ: Prentice Hall, 1988). See especially chapter 8.
19. See, for example, R. H. George Field, "A Test of the Vroom-Yetton Normative Model of Leadership," *Journal of Applied Psychology,* October 1982, pp. 523–32; Carrie R. Leana, "Power Relinquishment Versus Power Sharing: Theoretical Clarification and Empirical Comparison of Delegation and Participation," *Journal of Applied Psychology,* May 1987, pp. 228–33; Jennifer T. Ettling and Arthur G. Jago, "Participation Under Conditions of Conflict: More on the Validity of the Vroom-Yetton Model," *Journal of Management Studies,* January 1988, pp. 73–83; and R. H. George Field and Robert J. House, "A Test of the Vroom-Yetton Model Using Manager and Subordinate Reports," *Journal of Applied Psychology,* June 1990, pp. 362–66.
20. See, for instance, James C. McElroy, "A Typology of Attribution Leadership Research," *Academy of Management Review,* July 1982, pp. 413–417; James R. Meindl and Sanford B. Ehrlich, "The Romance of Leadership and the Evaluation of Organizational Performance," *Academy of Management Journal,* March 1987, pp. 91–109; James C. McElroy and J. David Hunger, "Leadership Theory as Causal Attribution of Performance," in James G. Hunt, B. Ran Baliga, H. P. Dachler, and Chester A. Schriesheim (eds.), *Emerging Leadership Vistas* (Lexington, MA: Lexington Books, 1988); and Boas Shami, "Attribution of Influence and Charisma to the Leader: The Romance of Leadership Revisited," *Journal of Applied Social Psychology,* March 1992, pp. 1–15.
21. Robert G. Lord, C. L. DeVader, and G. M. Alliger, "A Meta-Analysis of the Relation Between Personality Traits and Leadership Perceptions: An Application of Validity Generalization Procedures," *Journal of Applied Psychology,* August 1986, pp. 402–10.
22. Gary N. Powell and D. Anthony Butterfield, "The 'High–High' Leader Rides Again!" *Group and Organization Studies,* December 1984, pp. 437–50.
23. James R. Meindl, Sanford B. Ehrlich, and Janet M. Dukerich, "The Romance of Leadership," *Administrative Science Quarterly,* March 1985, pp. 78–102.
24. Barry M. Staw and Jerry Ross, "Commitment in an Experimenting Society: A Study of the Attribution of Leadership from Administrative Scenarios," *Journal of Applied Psychology,* June 1980, pp. 249–60.
25. Jay C. Conger and R. N. Kanungo, "Behavioral Dimensions of Charismatic Leadership," in J. A. Conger, R. N. Kanungo, and Associates, *Charismatic Leadership* (San Francisco: Jossey-Bass, 1988), p. 79.
26. Robert J. House, "A 1976 Theory of Charismatic Leadership," in J. G. Hunt and L. L. Larson (eds.), *Leadership: The Cutting Edge* (Carbondale: Southern Illinois University Press, 1977), pp. 189–207.
27. Warren Bennis, "The 4 Competencies of Leadership," *Training and Development Journal,* August 1984, pp. 15–19.
28. Conger and Kanungo, "Behavioral Dimensions of Charismatic Leadership," pp. 78–97.
29. Robert J. House, J. Woycke, and E. M. Fodor, "Charismatic and Noncharismatic Leaders: Differences in Behavior and Effectiveness," in J. A. Conger and R. N. Kanungo, *Charismatic Leadership,* pp. 103–04.
30. Jay C. Conger and R. N. Kanungo, "Training Charismatic Leadership: A Risky and Critical Task," in J. A. Conger and R. N. Kanungo, *Charismatic Leadership,* pp. 309–23.
31. Jane M. Howell and Peter J. Frost, "A Laboratory Study of Charismatic Leadership," *Organizational Behavior and Human Decision Processes,* April 1989, pp. 243–69.
32. House.
33. D. Machan, "The Charisma Merchants," *Forbes,* January 23, 1989, pp. 100–01.
34. This definition is based on M. Sashkin, "The Visionary Leader", in Conger and Kanungo et al., *Charismatic Leadership,* pp. 124–125; B. Nanus, *Visionary Leadership* (New York: Free Press, 1992), p. 8; and N. H. Snyder and M. Graves, "Leadership and Vision", *Business Horizons,* January–February 1994, p. 1.
35. B. Nanus, *Visionary Leadership* (New York: Free Press, 1992), pp. 178–179.
36. P. C. Nutt and R. W. Backoff, "Crafting Vision", Working paper, College of Business, Ohio State University, July 1995, p. 4.
37. N. Steckler and N. Fondas, "Building Team Leader Effectiveness: A Diagnostic Tool", *Organizational Dynamics,* Winter 1995, p. 20.
38. R. S. Wellins, W. C. Byham, and G. R. Dixon, *Inside Teams* (San Francisco: Jossey-Bass, 1994), p. 318.
39. Steckler and Fondas, "Building Team Leader Effectiveness", p. 21.
40. See James M. Burns, *Leadership* (New York: Harper & Row, 1978); B. M. Bass, Leadership and Performance Beyond Expectations (New York: Free Press, 1985); B. M. Bass, "From Transactional to Transformational Leadership: Learning to Share the Vision," *Organizational Dynamics,* Winter 1990, pp. 19–31; and

David A. Nadler and Michael L. Tushman, "Beyond the Charismatic Leader: Leadership and Organizational Change," *California Management Review,* Winter 1990, pp. 77–97.

41. B. M. Bass, "Leadership: Good, Better, Best," *Organizational Dynamics,* Winter 1985, pp. 26–40; and J. Seltzer and B. M. Bass, "Transformational Leadership: Beyond Initiation and Consideration," *Journal of Management,* December 1990, pp. 693–703.
42. B. J. Avolio and B. M. Bass, "Transformational Leadership, Charisma, and Beyond," Working paper, School of Management, State University of New York, Binghamton, 1985, p. 14.
43. Cited in B. M. Bass and B. J. Avolio, "Developing Transformational Leadership: 1992 and Beyond," *Journal of European Industrial Training,* January 1990, p. 23.
44. J. J. Hater and B. M. Bass, "Supervisors' Evaluation and Subordinates' Perceptions of Transformational and Transactional Leadership," *Journal of Applied Psychology,* November 1988, pp. 695–702.
45. B. M. Bass and B. J. Avolio, "Developing Transformational Leadership"; Robert T. Keller, "Transformational Leadership and the Performance of Research and Development Project Groups," *Journal of Management,* September 1992, pp. 489–01; Jane M. Howell and Bruce J. Avolio, "Transformational Leadership, Transactional Leadership, Locus of Control, and Support for Innovation: Key Predictors of Consolidated-Business-Unit Performance," *Journal of Applied Psychology,* December 1993, pp. 891–911; and John P. Schuster, "Transforming Your Leadership Style," *Association Management,* January 1994, pp. 39–43.
46. See John R. P. French, Jr. and Bertram Raven, "The Bases of Social Power," in Dorwin Cartwright and A. F. Zander (eds.), *Group Dynamics: Research and Theory* (New York: Harper & Row, 1960), pp. 607–23; Philip M. Podsakoff and Chester A. Schriesheim, "Field Studies of French and Raven's Bases of Power: Critique, Reanalysis, and Suggestions for Future Research," *Psychological Bulletin,* May 1985, pp. 387–411; Ramesh K. Shukla, "Influence of Power Bases in Organizational Decision Making: A Contingency Model," *Decision Sciences,* July 1982, pp. 450–70; Dean E. Frost and Anthony J. Stahelski, "The Systematic Measurement of French and Raven's Bases of Social Power in Workgroups," *Journal of Applied Social Psychology,* April 1988, pp. 375–89; and Timothy R. Hinkin and Chester A. Schriesheim, "Development and Application of New Scales to Measure the French and Raven (1959) Bases of Social Power," *Journal of Applied Psychology,* August 1989, pp. 561–67.
47. Deborah Jones, "Global Harvest," *Report on Business Magazine,* October 1994, pp. 29–36.
48. See, for instance, Mary Billard, "Do Women Make Better Managers?" *Working Woman,* March 1992, pp. 68–71, 106–07; and Stephen H. Applebaum and Barbara T. Shapiro, "Why Can't Men Lead Like Women?" *Leadership & Organization Development Journal,* December 1993, pp. 28–34.
49. See J. Grant, "Women as Managers: What They Can Offer to Organizations," *Organizational Dynamics,* Winter 1988, pp. 56–63; Sally Helgesen, *The Female Advantage: Women's Ways of Leadership* (New York: Doubleday, 1990); Alice H. Eagly and Blair T. Johnson, "Gender and Leadership Style: A Meta-Analysis," *Psychological Bulletin,* September 1990, pp. 233–56; Judith B. Rosener, "Ways Women Lead," *Harvard Business Review,* November–December 1990, pp. 119–25; "Debate: Ways Men and Women Lead," *Harvard Business Review,* January–February 1991, pp. 150–60; and Alice H. Eagly, Steven J. Karau, and Blair T. Johnson, "Gender and Leadership Style Among School Principals: A Meta-Analysis," *Educational Administration Quarterly,* February 1992, pp. 76–102.
50. Ibid.
51. Ibid.
52. Helgesen.
53. Patricia L. Smith and Stanley J. Smits, "The Feminization of Leadership?" *Training and Development,* February 1994, pp. 43–46.
54. Gregory H. Dobbins, William S. Long, Esther J. Dedrick, and Tanya Cheer Clemons, "The Role of Self-Monitoring and Gender on Leader Emergence: A Laboratory and Field Study," *Journal of Management,* September 1990, pp. 609–18.
55. Fredric William Swierczek, "Leadership and Culture: Comparing Asian Managers," *Leadership & Organization Development Journal,* December 1991, pp. 3–10.
56. Geert Hofstede, "Motivation, Leadership, and Organization: Do American Theories Apply Abroad?" *Organizational Dynamics,* Summer 1980, p. 57; and Andrew Ede, "Leadership and Decision Making: Management Styles and Culture," *Journal of Managerial Psychology,* July 1992, pp. 28–31.
57. Steven Kerr and John M. Jermier, "Substitutes for Leadership: Their Meaning and Measurement," *Organizational Behavior and Human Performance,* December 1978, pp. 375–403; Jon P. Howell and Peter W. Dorfman,"Substitutes for Leadership: A Statistical Refinement," paper presented at the 42nd Annual Academy of Management Conference, New York, August 1982; Jon P. Howell, Peter W. Dorfman, and Steven Kerr, "Leadership and Substitutes for Leadership," *Journal of Applied Behavioral Science,* vol. 22, no.1, 1986, pp. 29–46; Jon P. Howell, D. E. Bowen, Peter W. Dorfman, Steven Kerr, and Philip M. Podsakoff, "Substitutes for Leadership: Effective Alternatives to Ineffective Leadership," *Organizational Dynamics,* Summer 1990, pp. 21–38; and Philip M. Podsakoff, Brian P. Niehoff, Scott B. MacKenzie, and Margaret L. Williams, "Do Substitutes for Leadership Really Substitute for Leadership? An Empirical Examination of Kerr and Jermier's Situational Leadership Model," *Organizational Behavior and Human Decision Processes,* February 1993, pp. 1–44.

Chapter 17

1. Kenneth A. Merchant, "The Control Function of Management," *Sloan Management Review,* Summer 1982, pp. 43–55.
2. Eric Flamholtz, "Organizational Control Systems as a Managerial Tool," *California Management Review,* Winter 1979, p. 55.
3. William G. Ouchi, "A Conceptual Framework for the Design of Organizational Control Mechanisms," *Management Science,* August 1979, pp. 833–38; and William G. Ouchi, "Markets, Bureaucracies, and Clans," *Administrative Science Quarterly,* March 1980, pp. 129–41.
4. Steven Kerr, "On the Folly of Rewarding A, While Hoping for B," *Academy of Management Journal,* December 1975, pp. 769–83.
5. Harold Koontz and Robert W. Bradspies, "Managing Through Feedforward Control," *Business Horizons,* June 1972, pp. 25–36.
6. William H. Newman, *Constructive Control: Design and Use of Control Systems* (Englewood Cliffs, NJ: Prentice Hall, 1975), p. 33.
7. See, for instance, Newman.
8. Robert Frank, "As UPS Tries to Deliver More to Its Customers, Labor Problems Grow," *Wall Street Journal,* May 23, 1994, p. A1+.
9. This box is based on Thomas J. Peters and Robert H. Waterman, *In Search of Excellence* (New York: Harper & Row, 1982); Tom Peters and Nancy Austin, *A Passion for Excellence: The Leadership Difference* (New York: Random House, 1985); Peter R. Monge, Lynda White Rothman, Eric M. Eisenberg, Katherine I. Miller, and Kenneth K. Kirste, "The Dynamics of Organizational Proximity," *Management Science,* vol. 31, 1985, pp. 1129–41; and Andrew E. Serwer, "Lessons from America's Fastest-Growing Companies," *Fortune,* August 8, 1994, pp. 59–60.
10. See, for instance, Bernard J. Jaworski and S. Mark Young, "Dysfunctional Behavior and Management Control: An Empirical Study of Marketing Managers," *Accounting, Organizations and Society,* January 1992, pp. 17–35.
11. Edward E. Lawler III and John Grant Rhode, *Information and Control in Organizations* (Santa Monica, CA: Goodyear, 1976), p. 108.
12. James D. Thompson, *Organizations in Action* (New York: McGraw-Hill, 1967), p. 124.

13. Frank Jossi, "Eavesdropping in Cyberspace," *Business Ethics,* May–June 1994, pp. 22–25.
14. Frances A. McMorris, "Is Office Voice Mail Private? Don't Bet on It," *Wall Street Journal,* February 28, 1995, p. B1.
15. Terri L. Griffith, "Teaching Big Brother to Be a Team Player: Computer Monitoring and Quality," *Academy of Management Executive,* February 1993, pp. 73–80.
16. Ibid.
17. David Warner, "The Move to Curb Worker Monitoring," *Nation's Business,* December 1993, p. 37.
18. Jeffrey Rothfeder, Michele Galen, and Lisa Driscoll, "Is Your Boss Spying on You?" *Business Week,* January 15, 1990, pp. 74–75; and Gene Bylinsky, "How Companies Spy on Employees," *Fortune,* November 4, 1991, pp. 131–40.
19. Warner, p. 38.
20. Malcolm MacKillop, "How To Cope With Substance Abuse", *Globe and Mail,* March 18, 1997, p. B12.

Chapter 18

1. John Southerst, "How MDS Cut Lab Costs", *Globe and Mail,* March 10, 1997, p. B6.
2. "The Productivity Paradox," *Business Week,* June 6, 1988, p. 101.
3. Ibid., p. 102.
4. "Price Discipline," *U.S. News & World Report,* April 25, 1994, p. 17.
5. Karen Lowry Miller, "The Factory Guru Tinkering with Toyota," *Business Week,* May 17, 1993, pp. 95–97.
6. Lila Sarick, "Surgeon Shortens Scars, Hospital Stays", *Globe and Mail,* January 3, 1998, p. A16.
7. Michael G. Crawford, "Health Matters", *Profit,* April-May 1998, p. 22.
8. Chris Howard, "It's The Same Job, After All", *Canadian Business,* June 26/July 10, 1998, pp. 125–127.
9. Terence P. Pare, "A New Tool for Managing Costs," *Fortune,* June 14, 1993, p. 129.
10. A. W. H. Grant and L. A. Schlesinger, "Realize Your Customers' Full Profit Potential", *Harvard Business Review,* September–October 1995, pp. 59–72.
11. G. Hamel and C. K. Prahalad, *Competing For The Future* (Boston: Harvard Business School Press, 1994); R. McKenna, "Real Time Marketing", *Harvard BusinessReview,* July–August, 1995, pp. 87–95; S.F. Wiggins, "New Ways To Create Lifetime Bonds With Your Customers", *Fortune,* October 30, 1995, p. 115; S. E. Prokesch, "Competing on Customer Service: An Interview With British Airways' Sir Colin Marshall", *Harvard Business Review,* November–December 1995, pp. 101–112; and A. J. Slywotzky, *Value Migration* (Boston: Harvard Business School Press, 1996).
12. T. A. Stewart, "A Satisfied Customer Isn't Enough", *Fortune,* July 21, 1997, pp. 112–113.
13. Thomas A. Stewart, "Reengineering—The Hot New Managing Tool," *Fortune,* August 23, 1993, p. 41.
14. Ibid., p. 42.
15. "Manufacturing Is in Flower," *Time,* March 26, 1984, pp. 50–52.
16. See, for example, Norman Gaither, Production and Operations Management, 5th ed. (Orlando, FLA: Dryden Press, 1992), chap. 2.
17. See Wickham Skinner, "Manufacturing—Missing Link in Corporate Strategy," *Harvard Business Review,* May–June 1969, pp. 136–45.
18. See, for instance, Tamara J. Erickson, John F. Magee, Philip A. Roussel, and Kamal N. Saad, "Managing Technology as a Business Strategy," *Sloan Management Review,* Spring 1990, pp. 73–78; and George Stalk, Jr., and Thomas M. Hout, *Competing Against Time: How Time-Based Competition Is Reshaping Global Markets* (New York: Free Press, 1990).
19. Nancy Rotenier, "Quick Wits, Low Costs," *Forbes,* January 2, 1995, p. 150.
20. Richard B. Chase and Nicholas J. Aquilano, *Production and Operations Management: A Life-Cycle Approach,* 3d ed. (Homewood, IL: Irwin, 1981), pp. 34–41.
21. Everett E. Adam, Jr., and Ronald J. Ebert, *Production and Operations Management: Concepts, Models, and Behavior,* 5th ed. (Englewood Cliffs, NJ: Prentice Hall, 1992), pp. 53–60.
22. Ibid., pp. 231–33.
23. Ibid., pp. 341–44.
24. Adam and Ebert, p. 340; and Neng-Pai Lin, Lee Krajewski, G. Keong Leong, and W. C. Benton, "The Effects of Environmental Factors on the Design of Master Production Scheduling Systems," *Journal of Operations Management,* March 1994, pp. 367–74.
25. Cited in *Fortune,* October 28, 1985, p. 47.
26. Stephen E. Barndt and Davis W. Carvey, *Essentials of Operations Management* (Englewood Cliffs, NJ: Prentice Hall, 1982), p. 112.
27. Joel Dreyfuss, "Shaping Up Your Suppliers," *Fortune,* April 10, 1989, pp. 116–22; and Thomas M. Rohan, "Supplier–Customer Links Multiplying," *Industry Week,* April 17, 1989, p. 20.
28. Rohan.
29. Richard B. Chase and Nicholas J. Aquilano, *Production and Operations Management: A Life-Cycle Approach,* pp. 551–52.
30. John H. Sheridan, "The CIM Evolution," *Industry Week,* April 20, 1992, pp. 29–51.
31. John Teresko, "Speeding the Product Development Cycle," *Industry Week,* July 18, 1988, p. 41.
32. Ted Wakefield, "No Pain, No Gain," *Canadian Business,* January, 1993, pp. 50–54.
33. Ann Gibbon, "Quality Circo," *Globe and Mail,* January 3, 1995, p. B10.
34. See Gilbert Fuchsberg, "Quality Programs Show Shoddy Results," *Wall Street Journal,* May 14, 1992, p. B1; Gilbert Fuchsberg, "'Total Quality' Is Termed Only Partial Success," *Wall Street Journal,* October 1, 1992, p. B1; and "Customer-Driven Strategies: Moving From Talk to Action," *Planning Review,* September–October 1993, pp. 25–29.
35. Fuchsberg, "Quality Programs Show Shoddy Results"; and Fuchsberg, "'Total Quality' Is Termed Only Partial Success."
36. This discussion of ISO 9000 is based on D. R. Arter, "Demystifying the ISO 9000/Q90 Series Standards", *Quality Progress,* November 1992, pp. 65–67; A. Marash, "The Future of ISO 9000", *The Corporate Board,* May–June 1994, pp. 20–24; J. Staines, "ISO 9000 Explained", *American Paint and Coatings Journal,* June 6, 1994, pp. 55–59; A. Zuckerman, "The Basics of ISO 9000", *Industrial Engineering,* June 1994, pp. 13–15; T. H. Landelles-Gordon, "ISO 9000: A New Opportunity for CPA Firms", *The CPA Journal,* June 1995, pp. 68–69; and P. Dolack, "ISO 9000 Comes of Age", *CMR Special Report,* April 8, 1996, pp. SR7-SR8.
37. Luis Milan, "Northern Lite", *Canadian Business,* April 10, 1998, pp. 79–87; and "Safe in The Arms of Ma Bell", *Financial Post,* January 10, 1998, p. 11.
38. Reported in the 1993 annual reports of Dow Chemical, Hewlett-Packard, and the Boeing Company.
39. See, for instance, Arjan T. Sadhwani and Mostafa H. Sarhan, "Putting JIT Manufacturing Systems to Work," *Business,* April–June 1987, pp. 30–37; Lad Kuzela, "Efficiency—Just in Time," *Industry Week,* May 2, 1988, p. 63; Ernest H. Hall, Jr., "Just-in-Time Management: A Critical Assessment," *Academy of Management Executive,* November 1989, pp. 315–18; and Eugene Richman and William B. Zachary, "Creating Strategies for Successful Materials Management," *Industrial Management,* March–April 1994, pp. 24–27.
40. Gordon Arnaut, "High on the Hog," *Globe and Mail,* April 11, 1995, p.B14.
41. Leonard Zehr, "Keep Your Warehouse on the Road,"*Globe and Mail,* June 6, 1995, p.B12.
42. Dexter Hutchins, "Having a Hard Time with Just-in-Time," *Fortune,* June 9, 1986, pp. 64–66; and Amal Kumar Naj, "Some Manufacturers Drop Efforts to Adopt Japanese Techniques," *Wall Street Journal,* May 7, 1993, pp. A1+.
43. See for example, Shawn Tully, "You'll Never Guess Who Really Makes ...," *Fortune,* October 3, 1994, pp. 124–28; and Neal Templin and Jeff Cole, "Manufacturers Use Suppliers to Help Them Develop New Products," *Wall Street Journal,* December 19, 1994, pp. A1+.
44. Neal Templin and Jeff Cole, "Manufacturers Use Suppliers to Help Them Develop New Products."
45. Ibid.
46. Patricia L. Nemetz and Louis W. Fry, "Flexible Manufacturing Organizations: Implications for Strategy Formulation

and Organization Design," *Academy of Management Review,* October 1988, pp. 627–38; and Arnaud De Meyer and others, "Flexibility: The Next Competitive Battle the Manufacturing Futures Survey," *Strategic Management Journal,* March–April 1989, pp. 135–44.

47. See, for example, Thomas A. Stewart, "Brace for Japan's Hot New Strategy," *Fortune,* September 21, 1992, pp. 62–74; and Otis Port, "Moving Past the Assembly Line," *Business Week/Reinventing America Special Issue,* November 1992, pp. 177–80.
48. Barbara Hawkins, "Divide and Conquer," *Canadian Business,* December, 1994, pp. 113–16.
49. Bylinsky, p. 93.
50. Susan Moffat, "Japan's New Personalized Production," *Fortune,* October 22, 1990, pp. 132–35.
51. George Stalk, Jr., "Time—The Next Source of Competitive Advantage," *Harvard Business Review,* July–August 1988, pp. 41–51; Joseph T. Vesey, "The New Competitors: They Think in Terms of 'Speed-to-Market,'" *Academy of Management Executive,* May 1991, pp. 23–33; Donna E. Vinton, "A New Look at Time, Speed, and the Manager," *Academy of Management Executive,* November 1992, pp. 7–16; and John W. Jones, *High-Speed Management* (San Francisco: Jossey-Bass, 1993).
52. Ronald Henkoff, "Delivering the Goods," *Fortune,* November 28, 1994, p. 64–66.
53. Bylinsky, pp. 93–94.
54. John H. Sheridan, "Lew Platt: Creating a Culture for Innovation," *Industry Week,* December 19, 1994, p. 30.

Chapter 19

1. Geoffrey Rowan and Gayle MacDonald, "Playdium Has Fun and Games in Mind for Edmonton", *Globe and Mail,* March 18, 1998, p. B3; and Shawna Steinberg, "Playing for Keeps", *Canadian Business,* June 12, 1998, pp. 74–78.
2. John T. Small and William B. Lee, "In Search of an MIS," *MSU Business Topics,* Autumn 1975, pp. 47–55.
3. Herbert A. Simon, *Administrative Behavior,* 3d ed. (New York: Free Press, 1976), p. 294.
4. John C. Carter and Fred N. Silverman, "Establishing an MIS," *Journal of Systems Management,* January 1980, p. 15.
5. "Elizabeth Church, "How To Keep Customers", *Globe and Mail,* February 27, 1997, p. 14.
6. See, for example, G. W. Dickson and John K. Simmons, "The Behavioral Side of MIS," *Business Horizons,* August 1970, pp. 59–71; Craig Brod, "Managing Technostress: Optimizing the Use of Computer Technology," *Personnel Journal,* October 1981, p. 754; and Sara Kiesler, Jane Siegel, and Timothy W. McGuire, "Social Psychological Aspects of Computer-Mediated Communication," *American Psychologist,* January 1985, pp. 14–19.
7. Blake Ives and Margrethe H. Olson, "User Involvement and MIS Success: A Review of Research," *Management Science,* May 1984, pp. 586–603.
8. See, for instance, Gene Bylinsky, "Saving Time with New Technology," *Fortune,* December 30, 1991, pp. 98–104; and Peter F. Drucker, "The Information Executives Truly Need," *Harvard Business Review,* January–February 1995, pp. 54–62.
9. See, for instance, Stephen W. Quickel, "Management Joins the Computer Age," *Business Month,* May 1989, pp. 42–46; George P. Huber, "A Theory of the Effects of Advanced Information Technology on Organizational Design, Intelligence, and Decision Making," *Academy of Management Review,* January 1990, pp. 47–71; and Uma G. Gupta, "An Empirical Investigation of the Contribution of Information Systems to Productivity," *Industrial Management,* March–April 1994, pp. 15–18.
10. This information came from an advertising supplement.
11. Rich Karlgaard, "ASAP Interview with Susan Cramm and John Martin," *Forbes ASAP,* Summer 1994, pp. 67–70.
12. Lynda M. Applegate, James I. Cash, Jr., and D. Quinn Mills, "Information Technology and Tomorrow's Manager," *Harvard Business Review,* November–December 1988, pp. 128–36.
13. Joseph H. Boyett and Henry P. Conn, *Workplace 2000* (New York: Dutton, 1991), p. 25.
14. Ibid.
15. Stephen P. Robbins, *Organization Theory: Structure, Design, and Applications,* 3d ed. (Englewood Cliffs, NJ: Prentice Hall, 1990), pp. 267–68.
16. Jeffrey Pfeffer, *Managing with Power* (Boston: Harvard Business School Press, 1992), pp. 247–65.
17. Michael Newman and David Rosenberg, "Systems Analysts and the Politics of Organizational Control," *Omega,* vol. 13, no. 5 (1985), pp. 393–406.
18. See, for example, David A. DeCenzo and Stephen P. Robbins, *Human Resource Management,* 4th ed. (New York: Wiley, 1994), pp. 385–93.
19. BARS have not been without critics. See, for example, Luis R. Gomez-Mejia, "Evaluating Employee Performance: Does the Appraisal Instrument Make a Difference?" *Journal of Organizational Behavior Management,* Winter 1988, pp. 155–71.
20. Robert D. Bretz, Jr., George T. Milkovich, and Walter Read, "The Current State of Performance Appraisal Research and Practice: Concerns, Directions, and Implications," *Journal of Management,* June 1992, p. 331.
21. See, for example, Marcie Schorr Hirsch, "360 Degrees of Evaluation," *Working Woman,* August 1994, pp. 20–21; Joann S. Lublin, "It's Shape-Up Time for Performance Reviews," Wall Street Journal, October 3, 1994, pp. B1+; Joann S. Lublin, "Turning the Tables: Underlings Evaluate Bosses," *Wall Street Journal,* October 4, 1994, pp. B1+; Sue Shellenbarger, "Reviews from Peers Instruct—and Sting," *Wall Street Journal,* October 4, 1994, pp. B1+; and Brian O'Reilly, "360 Feedback Can Change Your Life," *Fortune,* October 17, 1994, pp. 93–100.
22. John F. Milliman, Robert A. Zawacki, Carol Norman, Lynda Powell, and Jay Kirksey, "Companies Evaluate Employees from All Perspectives," *Personnel Journal,* November 1994, pp. 99–103.
23. Ronald J. Burke, "Why Performance Appraisal Systems Fail," *Personnel Administration,* June 1972, pp. 32–40.
24. Richard B. Peterson, ed., *Managers and National Culture: A Global Perspective* (Westport, CT: Quorum Books, 1993), pp. 405–29.
25. Alan N. Schoonmaker, *Executive Career Strategy* (New York: American Management Association, 1971); Andrew J. DuBrin, *Fundamentals of Organizational Behavior: An Applied Perspective,* 2d ed. (Elmsford, NY: Pergamon Press, 1978), chap. 5; and Eugene E. Jennings, "Success Chess," *Management of Personnel Quarterly,* Fall 1980, pp. 2–8.
26. Gerald Grinstein and William D. Oliver, "Winning the War Against Substance Abuse," *Chief Executive,* January–February 1994, pp. 32–37.
27. "Testing ... Testing," *Business Week,* May 2, 1994, p. 6.
28. Gerald and Oliver, p. 32.
29. Dean Elmuti, "Effects of Drug-Testing Programs on Employee Attitudes, Productivity, and Attendance Behaviors," *International Journal of Manpower,* June 1993, pp. 58–69; Bill Oliver, "Fight Drugs with Knowledge," *Training and Development,* May 1994, pp. 105–08; Erica Gordon Sorohan, "Making Decisions About Drug Testing," *Training and Development,* May 1994, pp. 111–16; Helen LaVan, Marsha Katz, and Jodi Suttor, "Litigation of Employer Drug Testing," *Labor Law Journal,* June 1994, pp. 346–51; and Richard F. Lisko, "A Manager's Guide to Drug Testing," *Security Management,* August 1994, pp. 92–95.
30. See, for example, Bernice Caldwell, "EAPs Broaden Their Focus, Evolve from Substance Abuse Genesis," *Employee Benefit Plan Review,* November 1993, pp. 26–28; Sharon A. Haskins and Brian H. Kleiner, "Employee Assistance Programs Take New Directions," *HR Focus,* January 1994, p. 16; and Irena St. John-Brooks, "Workplace Counselling to Support Change," *Benefits and Compensation International,* March 1994, p. 32.
31. It has been argued that indirect control mechanisms are most appropriate in organic structures. See Steven Kerr and John W. Slocum, Jr., "Controlling the Performance of People in Organizations," in Paul C. Nystrom and William H. Starbuck, eds., *Handbook of Organizational Design,* vol. 2 (New York: Oxford University Press, 1981), pp. 128–30.

Name Index

The pages on which Weblinks appear are printed in boldface.

Organization Index

The pages on which Weblinks appear are printed in boldface.

Subject Index

The pages on which key terms appear are printed in boldface.

READ THIS LICENSE CAREFULLY BEFORE OPENING THIS PACKAGE. BY OPENING THIS PACKAGE, YOU ARE AGREEING TO THE TERMS AND CONDITIONS OF THIS LICENSE. IF YOU DO NOT AGREE, DO NOT OPEN THE PACKAGE. PROMPTLY RETURN THE UNOPENED PACKAGE AND ALL ACCOMPANYING ITEMS TO THE PLACE YOU OBTAINED THEM. ***THESE TERMS APPLY TO ALL LICENSED SOFTWARE ON THE DISK EXCEPT THAT THE TERMS FOR USE OF ANY SHAREWARE OR FREEWARE ON THE DISKETTES ARE AS SET FORTH IN THE ELECTRONIC LICENSE LOCATED ON THE DISK:***

1. **GRANT OF LICENSE and OWNERSHIP:** The enclosed computer programs <<and any data>> ("Software") are licensed, not sold, to you by Prentice-Hall Canada Inc. ("We" or the "Company") in consideration of your adoption of the accompanying Company textbooks and/or other materials,and your agreement to these terms. You own only the disk(s) but we and/or our licensors own the Software itself. This license allows instructors and students enrolled in the course using the Company textbook that accompanies this Software (the "Course") to use and display the enclosed copy of the Software for academic use only, so long as you comply with the terms of this Agreement. You may make one copy for back up only. We reserve any rights not granted to you.

2. **USE RESTRICTIONS:** You may not sell or license copies of the Software or the Documentation to others. You may not transfer, distribute or make available the Software or the Documentation, except to instructors and students in your school who are users of the adopted Company textbook that accompanies this Software in connection with the course for which the textbook was adopted. You may not reverse engineer, disassemble, decompile, modify, adapt, translate or create derivative works based on the Software or the Documentation. You may be held legally responsible for any copying or copyright infringement which is caused by your failure to abide by the terms of these restrictions.

3. **TERMINATION:** This license is effective until terminated. This license will terminate automatically without notice from the Company if you fail to comply with any provisions or limitations of this license. Upon termination, you shall destroy the Documentation and all copies of the Software. All provisions of this Agreement as to limitation and disclaimer of warranties, limitation of liability, remedies or damages, and our ownership rights shall survive termination.

4. **DISCLAIMER OF WARRANTY: THE COMPANY AND ITS LICENSORS MAKE NO WARRANTIES ABOUT THE SOFTWARE, WHICH IS PROVIDED "AS-IS." IF THE DISK IS DEFECTIVE IN MATERIALS OR WORKMANSHIP, YOUR ONLY REMEDY IS TO RETURN IT TO THE COMPANY WITHIN 30 DAYS FOR REPLACEMENT UNLESS THE COMPANY DETERMINES IN GOOD FAITH THAT THE DISK HAS BEEN MISUSED OR IMPROPERLY INSTALLED, REPAIRED, ALTERED OR DAMAGED. THE COMPANY DISCLAIMS ALL WARRANTIES, EXPRESS OR IMPLIED, INCLUDING WITHOUT LIMITATION, THE IMPLIED WARRANTIES OF MERCHANTABILITY AND FITNESS FOR A PARTICULAR PURPOSE. THE COMPANY DOES NOT WARRANT, GUARANTEE OR MAKE ANY REPRESENTATION REGARDING THE ACCURACY, RELIABILITY, CURRENTNESS, USE, OR RESULTS OF USE, OF THE SOFTWARE.**

5. **LIMITATION OF REMEDIES AND DAMAGES: IN NO EVENT, SHALL THE COMPANY OR ITS EMPLOYEES, AGENTS, LICENSORS OR CONTRACTORS BE LIABLE FOR ANY INCIDENTAL, INDIRECT, SPECIAL OR CONSEQUENTIAL DAMAGES ARISING OUT OF OR IN CONNECTION WITH THIS LICENSE OR THE SOFTWARE, INCLUDING, WITHOUT LIMITATION, LOSS OF USE, LOSS OF DATA, LOSS OF INCOME OR PROFIT, OR OTHER LOSSES SUSTAINED AS A RESULT OF INJURY TO ANY PERSON, OR LOSS OF OR DAMAGE TO PROPERTY, OR CLAIMS OF THIRD PARTIES, EVEN IF THE COMPANY OR AN AUTHORIZED REPRESENTATIVE OF THE COMPANY HAS BEEN ADVISED OF THE POSSIBILITY OF SUCH DAMAGES.** SOME JURISDICTIONS DO NOT ALLOW THE LIMITATION OF DAMAGES IN CERTAIN CIRCUMSTANCES, SO THE ABOVE LIMITATIONS MAY NOT ALWAYS APPLY.

6. **GENERAL:** THIS AGREEMENT SHALL BE CONSTRUED AND INTERPRETED ACCORDING TO THE LAWS OF THE PROVINCE OF ONTARIO. This Agreement is the complete and exclusive statement of the agreement between you and the Company and supersedes all proposals, prior agreements, oral or written, and any other communications between you and the company or any of its representatives relating to the subject matter.

Should you have any questions concerning this agreement or if you wish to contact the Company for any reason, please contact in writing: Customer Service, Prentice Hall Canada, 1870 Birchmount Road, Scarborough, Ontario M1P 2J7.